Tierck Clafsen DeWitt

and Descendants of his son Luycas DeWitt

To my best friend, Doreen Todhunter

Vona (DeWitt) Smith

Vona E. Smith

© Copyright 2004 Vona Smith. All rights reserved.

No part of this publication may be reproduced, stored in a retrieval system, or transmitted, in any form or by any means, electronic, mechanical, photocopying, recording, or otherwise, without the written prior permission of the author.

Printed in Victoria, Canada

Note for Librarians: a cataloguing record for this book that includes Dewey Classification and US Library of Congress numbers is available from the National Library of Canada. The complete cataloguing record can be obtained from the National Library's online database at: www.nlc-bnc.ca/amicus/index-e.html

ISBN 1-4120-1956-7

This book was published *on-demand* in cooperation with Trafford Publishing.
On-demand publishing is a unique process and service of making a book available for retail sale to the public taking advantage of on-demand manufacturing and Internet marketing. **On-demand publishing** includes promotions, retail sales, manufacturing, order fulfilment, accounting and collecting royalties on behalf of the author.

Suite 6E, 2333 Government St., Victoria, B.C. V8T 4P4, CANADA
Phone   250-383-6864   Toll-free   1-888-232-4444 (Canada & US)
Fax   250-383-6804   E-mail   sales@trafford.com
Web site www.trafford.com   TRAFFORD PUBLISHING IS A DIVISION OF TRAFFORD HOLDINGS LTD.
Trafford Catalogue #03-2434   www.trafford.com/robots/03-2434.html

10   9   8   7   6   5   4   3   2

Statue of Johan & Cornelis DeWitt, Dordrecht, Holland

Disclaimer

Although I gratefully acknowledge the help of all those who made this "work in progress" possible, none are in any way responsible for transcription errors or omissions which may be found. I believe, to the best of my knowledge, records to be accurate, but in advance apologize if in any instance records contain errors and or omissions. I accept responsibility for these. In spite of our best attempts, errors will undoubtedly arise and when these become evident, they will be corrected. And finally, permission to cite others' works has been diligently sought, and if any have been left out, I assure you it was not intentional. Again I apologize in advance for these omissions.

Any errors found within this book should be noted and mailed to the compiler at 2288 Gale Avenue, Coquitlam, B.C. V3K 2Y8. All will gratefully be accepted.

© Vona (DeWitt) Smith

VONA & GILBERT SMITH

PREFACE

Since this volume is the culmination of the work of many researchers past and present and varied recording styles over the years, it is felt a clear explanation of the author's methodology is required.

Dutch names and English equivalents are included. "Alias" meant nicknames or Dutch version of English names (Jan Macklin for John McLean). Reduced punctuation and abbreviations saves space. It mainly depended on the education of the scribe as to how facts were recorded. Please refer to the original texts cited if they are available to you. Abbreviations used are those of recurring words such as born, died etc. and Provinces or States. Codes for the names of De Witt descendant contributors are used throughout family records. Also Codes for book titles in the Bibliography are used citing book or document used, volume, number and page. Sources used are many and varied: baptisms, marriages, cemetery, land, census, bible and state records, documentary, county, family and other histories, court, probate, military records, ship's lists, personal family records. Oral history, especially some material collected for or after the 1934, 1939 De Witt family picnics, is included as theory when proof may be lacking.

Since no German vital statistics exist for the early 1600's, Ambassador Lester De Witt Mallory's overseas research gives us what information is available on Tierck Claefsen De Witt's ancestry. Brief notes on Tjerck, wife Barbara Andriessen, their parents, siblings and children are presented..

Doing the genealogy of any family line over a long period is a monumental task and to consider the thirteen children of Tjerck who began life over three centuries ago, would give pause. Three died without issue and three are traced in genealogies of other families. For Geertruy, see seven volumes by R Heidgerd, et al. The Schoonmaker Family. Tjerck' son Tjerck does not after appear after 1687 in records searched. William Bogardus' very extensive research of Anneke Jans and the Kierstede and Bogardus descendants includes Rachel and Jan. This leaves seven:: Andries, Taatje, Jacob, Leucas/Luykas, Peek, Marrietje and Aagie DeWitt. The authors' line is Leucas and as most material has been collected on his descendants, this work deals with them.

A simple numbering system is used assigning a number to only each De Witt descendant. Generations are divided by periods. Each number represents one generation and that digit also is a person's place in that family.

For example: 1. NICHLAES de WITT
        1.1 TIERCK CLAFSEN De WITT
        1.1.9 LEUCAS de WITT
        1.1.9.1 JANNETJE de WITT
        1.1.9.2 BARBARA de WITT dy.
        1.1.9.3 JAN de WITT
        1.1.9.4 LUCAS de WITT

Author Vona (DeWitt) Smith

TABLE OF CONTENTS

Dedication to the Mallorys and G.D. Smith
Preface
Acknowledgements: Codes and names of DeWitt Contributors.
Acknowledgement of major contributors, my nephew Murray Hugill and his wife Marlene (Ackles) Hugill
Author and picture.
List of abbreviations used throughout the book.
Family notes, short stories, Cemetery Records, Wills, Land Records, pictures etc. throughout the text.
Some English equivalents of Dutch names.
Introduction: Early notes on Tierck Claefsen De Witt and his father Nicholaas De Witt.

Generation 1 - Nicholaas de Witt married Taatje Cornelis daughter of Cornelis Pieterz of Oosterbeus of Westeraccum, East Friesland, Germany. They had seven children.
　　Dordrcht DeWitts Coat of Arms.

　　Mercator, Gerardus 1512-1594. Maps of "Atlas Minor" Published in 1610.

Generation 2 - Tjerck DeWitt married Barbara Andriessen. They had thirteen or fourteen children.
　　A picture of Tierck Clafen De Witt's stone house

　　Andries Luycaszen born 1519 Fredrickstad, Denmark, married Jannetje Sebyns.

Generation 3 - Ships Captain Luykas de Wit married Annetje Delva. This book traces their descendants.

Generation 4 - 12 #1 Jannetje de Witt married Cornelis Langendyk.

Generation 4 - 13 #2 Jan de Wit married Arriantje Osterhoud. Some descendents moved at an early time from New York to Pennsylvania, Ohio, Maryland, West Virginia and eventually Washington State.

Generation 4 - 12 #4 Luycas de Wit married Catherina Roosa. Luycas was a posthumous child.

FAMILY STORIES

Stockton, Margaret. "Moving from New Brunswick [Canada] to Ontario".
DeWitt, Katherine Lorena Alexander. John [King] DeWitt
Phillips, Miriam L. Excerpts from '1932 Tales of Ancestors' Lives'.
Wooden, Alexander. A love letter to Mary Ann Smith..
DeWitt, Katherine Lorena Alexander. Henry DeWitt of Sunpoke.
Dodge, Mildred. Notes on Napinka, Manitoba DeWitts from "Bridging Brenda" Published in1990.
Telegraph Journal, Saint John, New Brunswick, Canada. Brief notes from an article on Colby DeWitt.
De Witt, Ernest B. Stories of his family's adventures in New Brunswick, Cuba and Alberta, Canada.
Mallory, Lester DeWitt. Excerpt from "Enrique Mallory 1878 – 1965".
A letter from Mrs. Eleanor (Stuck) Mallory informed the Diplomatic Corp, friends and family of the death of Ambassador Lester DeWitt Mallory 1904 – 1994.
Obituary of Mrs. Eleanor (Struck) Mallory 1913 – 1936.
Obituary of Mrs. June Lavona (McAllister) Mallory 1918 – 1997 widow of Donald Mallory.
Nielson, Wendy. Diva at the Metropolitan Opera for many years.
Mallory, Lester W. Recollections of his grandmother May DeWitt Mallory 1882 - 1976 and Images of his uncle Lester De Witt Mallory.
Mallory (McAllister) June. Family stories of life with Enrique Mallory and his wife May (DeWitt) Mallory.
Autobiography of American Ambassador Lester DeWitt Mallory PhD written in Guadalajara, Mexico1984.
DeWitt, Charles Clifford. 1915 -1998. Excerpts from "One Fruit Farm"

EARLY DeWITTS IN HOLLAND

　　Balen, Mattys, Jans Zoon. "Beschryvinge Der Stad Dotdrecht" Published 1677. Ambassador Mallory obtained a copy copy of the die Witte family pages 1293 – 1333 from the Royal Library at the Hague Holland.

Bibliography with Codes are just before the Selected Index

ACKNOWLEDGEMENTS: LIST OF CODES for DeWITT CONTRIBUTORS.

This book is the collective work of many DeWitt descendants both living and dead whose diverse research survived. Some do not cite their sources. This researcher can only suggest it as a guide to further exploration. Time, money, distance and language have prohibited the author rechecking some of the material so conclusions reached depended on the reliability of published English interpretation of handwriting and translation. Corrections and additions will be gratefully accepted. To recheck all the material here is beyond the resources or time left to this compiler. The author is indebted to all of the people who shared family records and traditions (MY GRATEFUL THANKS! from Vona Edna (DeWitt) Smith).

(fr ACB)	Mr Allen C Boone, Oromotco NB	
(fr ACCH)	Mrs Ava Cecelia (Christiansen) Harris, Minnedosa, MB	
(fr AFR)	Alexander Family Records	
(fr AMF)	Mrs Annie (Mulholland) Foxley	
(fr AMS)	Mrs Arletta M Sullivan, Gorham ME	
(fr AWSM)	Mrs Anna Wilhelmina (Stuart) Molestien, Bridgeville DL	
(fr BBVK)	Mrs Barbara Brown (Vaughn) Haskell, correction for BEH & ABEH	
(fr BDP)	Mrs Barbara (DeWitt) Phillips	
(fr BGD)	Mrs Beryl (Green) DeWitt	
(fr BHD)	Mrs Barbara (Hudson) DeWitt, Trail, BC	
(fr BMN)	Mrs Bertha (McCracken) Nielsen	
(fr CAB)	Mrs C A Baines	
(fr CB1)	Mrs Cleadie Barnet	
(fr CB2)	Mr George Bell, NB	
(fr CFD)	Mr Carroll Fleming DeWitt, Sarasota FL	
(fr CCD1)	Mr Charles Clifford DeWitt, Stoney Creek ON, dec	
(fr CCD2)	Mr Clifford Carleton DeWitt, Oakland MD	
(fr CEN)	Mrs Cora E Nelson, Tumwater WA	
(fr DBN)	Mrs Doris (Buyers) Nason	
(fr DMBN)	Mrs Dorthey Minnie (Bell) Nason	
(fr DDD)	Mr Daniel Darwin DeWitt, Sequim WA	
(fr DM)	Ms Della Mason	
(fr DMBN)	Mrs Dorthory Minnie (Bell) Nason	
(fr DN)	Ms Donna Nason	
(fr DPP)	Mrs Dorothy (Pride) Pheasant	
(fr EAW)	Mrs Elizabeth (Allen) Whittaker	
(fr EBSD)	Mrs Ethel Blanche (Shortt) Donaldson, Saugerties NY	
(fr EDS)	Mrs Effie (DeWitt) Smith, New Westminster BC (5th cousin of Effie DeWitt, Vancouver BC	
(fr EJDL)	Mrs Elinor Jane/Ella (DeWitt) Livesley, Winnipeg MB, dec	
(fr EM)	Ms Elsie Mulholland	
(fr EMB)	Miss Eva Madeline Boone, Lincoln ME	
(fr FCC)	Mr Ford Crombie	
(fr FDSS)	Mrs Florence (Dedrick) Smithson Stevens, Kingston ON	
(fr FVD)	Mr Francis Vernon Dedrick, Simcoe ON	
(fr GB)	Mr George Bell, New Brunswick	
(fr GDS)	Mr Gordon D Smithson	
(fr GJN)	Mr Grant John Norton, Burlington ON	
(fr GMAW)	Mrs Gladys May (Alexander) Webb	
(fr GMD)	Mr George McLeod DeWitt, Airdrie AB	
(fr GRAH)	Mrs Gladys R (Armstrong) Hyland also as GRH	
(fr HBS)	Mr Howard Blake Smith, Vineland On, dec	
(fr HERF)	Mrs Helen Eva (Randall) Foxley	
(fr HKPSM)	Mrs Honor Kathleen (Pettit) Saligmam Mikesell, Fresno CA, dec	
(fr ICSP)	Dr Ida Carolyn (Smith) Pellettier, Guelph ON started our DeWitt family research.	
(fr IMS)	Mrs Ida (Mersereau) Smith	
(fr IMWH)	Mrs Irma Mavis (Webb) Hartt	
(fr IGD)	Mr Ira George DeWitt, Stoney Mountain MB and Chillawack BC, dec	
(fr ISD)	Mr Ira Smith DeWitt, Sandy Lake MB, dec	
(fr JD)	Mr James DeWitt, Chippewa ON	
(fr JDW)	Mrs Jean (DeWitt) Wilkins	
(fr JJ)	Mrs Joyce Jewitt, Hamburg NY	
(fr JS)	Ms Janice Seely, Fredericton NB	

(fr KBG)	Ms Kathryn Goodwin
(fr KDMSC)	Mrs Kathleen Donna (McFaddin) St Amand Candlemire, Sicamous BC
(fr KLAD)	Mrs Katharine Lorena (Alexander) DeWitt, Hoyt NB
(fr LCB)	Mrs Lucinda (Charlton) Bell
(fr LDM)	Mr Lester (DeWitt) Mallory PhD, dec, Lake Forest CA bur Washington DC
(fr LKRKS)	Mrs Louise Katherine Ray (Kenyon) Stuart
(fr LLM)	Mr Lewis Lorain Miller
(fr LMB)	Mrs Louise (Miler) Beery, West Lake Village, CA
(fr LOH)	Mrs Lois (O'Leary) Harris
(fr LN)	Mr Lemual Nason
(fr LPD)	Mrs Lois (DeWitt) Pfister, Minneapolis MN
(fr LWB)	Mrs Lewis W Beam, Abbington IL
(fr MA)	Ms Margaret Armstrong, compiled "Samuel Armstrong History"
(fr MAH)	Mrs Margaret/Dolly (Anderson) Hannay, Vancouver BC
(fr MAYS)	Mrs Myrtle Alice (York) Short
(fr MCB)	Mrs Margaret Elizabeth (Coleman) Baines. Note sometimes as MECB.
(fr MDG)	Mrs Mildred (DeWitt) Golden
(fr MEJLS)	Mrs Mildred Eunice Jane (Livesley) Smeddon
(fr MELD)	Mrs Margaret Evelyn (Lane) DeWitt, Sequim WA
(fr MIML)	Mrs Marlene Isabel (McFaddin) Lindsay, Duncan BC
(fr MJPSM)	Mrs Margaret Jane Penelope (Smith) Moyer
(fr MKW)	Mrs Marilyn K Walker, Saugerties NY
(fr MLMB)	Mrs Mary Louise (Miller) Beery, Westlake Village CA
(fr MLS)	Mrs Marilyn Lang Smith
(fr MS)	Miss Margaret Stockton, Woodstock ON
(fr MTD)	Mrs Mildred (Tufts) Dodds, Melita MB
(fr MWD)	Miss Martha Wooden DeWitt, Fredericton NB; dec
(fr MWM)	Mrs Mabel (Wathen) Miller
(fr NG)	Mrs Nadine Gooding
(fr OLD)	Mr Omar LeRoy DeWitt, Grand Ledge IL
(fr PJDS)	Mrs Phoebe Jane (DeWitt) Smith
(fr RADE)	Mrs Ruth A (DeWit) Esty,
(fr RDB)	Mrs Ruby Lillian (DeWitt) Butcher, Saint John NB, dec. Note sometimes as RLDB.
(fr RFHJB)	Mrs Rae Frances (Harpham) Johnson Benedict, Surrey BC
(fr RGD)	Mrs Regina (Gallison) DeWitt
(fr RGHM)	Mrs Rhea Grace Eleanor (Hugill) Mayes, Oakville ON
(fr RMB)	Mr Robert N Bahl, Binghampton, NY
(fr ROPR)	Mrs Ruth Olive (Pettit) Ryder
(fr RPR)	Mr Robert Percy Rickard, Kingwood TX
(fr SCBG)	Mrs Shirley Claire (Bailey) Goatcher, Naniamo BC
(fr SCC)	Six Canadian Compilers: New Brunswick Canada DeWitt Family History by George DeWitt, Mrs Sweet, Norman DeWitt, John Tracy, James DeWitt, William Murphy, 1933
(fr SDM)	Mrs Sandra (DeWitt) Michel
(fr SP-APB)	Sylvester Pettit - Abigail Pettit Bible
(fr VDC)	Mrs Virginia (DeWitt) McCambridge
(fr VEDS)	Mrs Vona Edna (DeWitt) Smith, Coquitlam BC
(fr VSK)	Mrs Viola (Smith) Kirkpatrick
(fr WBB)	Mr William B Bogardus, Wilmington, OH
(fr WD)	Mrs William DeWitt of Maryland

Marilyn K Walker wrote "LONGENDYKE HISTORY AND GENEALOGY" [26 pp] quoted here was compiled by Ethel S Donaldson in 1985. "I have drawn from research done by my mother, Myrtle A Short, Miriam Longendyke MacDonald and Allen Longendyke as well as my own research. It is my hope that anyone who can, will fill in the blank areas and share with the rest of the family, also share new additions. If you find errors please let us know".

In 1933 in response to ads appearing in North American newspapers, a group in the Province of New Brunswick, Canada, descendants of Loyalist Evert DeWitt, compiled a family history. They were George DeWitt, Mrs Sweet, Norman DeWitt, John Tracy, James DeWitt, William Murphy and others.

ABOUT THE AUTHOR VONA DeWITT SMITH, UE

Vona Edna (DeWitt) Smith UE was born in Sandy Lake Manitoba, Canada in 1923 to Ira Smith DeWitt and Edna Belle Barker, the youngest of seven. She graduated with a scholarship from high school and enrolled in Brandon MB Normal School [Teachers College] and taught in rural schools in the Province. In 1942 she married Gilbert Doran Smith who served in the Royal Canadian Air Force. They moved to Vancouver BC in 1948. They have 4 children – Corrine, Gilbert who has a daughter Kasia, Aida, and Julia who married Howard Webb whose children are Brennan and Jenna. The author has 5 certificates and her husband has 7 granted by the United Empire Loyalists' Association of Canada. The children and grandchildren all have their certificates.

She has a lifetime interest in family history. Her mother was an American, a descendant of Ebenezer Judd who fought against the British 1776-1783. She visited his grave near Syracuse, NY as well as the graves of her grandmother Lovina Gertrude (Judd) Barker and great grandparents Philo and Mary (Adams) Barker in Brookfield MO. They had previously lived in North East, Erie County PA. Her grandfather Wilbur Jay Barker served in the Union Army in the American War between the North and South and moved with his parents and sisters to Missouri after the end of the war. With his second wife and children he moved to Manitoba in 1898. He is buried near Newdale, MB. Vona's mother was born in 1883, Grandfather Wilbur in 1843 and great grandfather Philo in 1803.

Vona DeWitt Smith is a skilled lecturer, journalist, researcher and mentor. Vona has lectured in Canada and the United States, has served as both Loyalist Librarian and Genealogist for more than 15 years and is the past President of the Vancouver Branch of the UEL Association of Canada. Vona has been a major part in keeping the Association alive in BC working with others to help establish two new Branches in BC (the total now being four). It is Vona's dedication to research that has enabled so many British Columbians to affix UE (Unity of the Empire) after their names. This is the only hereditary title given by the Crown outside of Britain.

Vona is an expert in many areas of genealogical research: Atlantic Canada, Ontario, the United States, Palatines, and Loyalists etc. Vona's personal library is a treasure of Canadian and American.histories. She has travelled extensively across Canada and the US in order to do major research on her family, as well as writing her own book on Tierck Claeszen deWitt b. 1620 (son of Nicholaas deWit) and his descendants).

Vona is also a master seamstress and has made innumerable ladies and men's period costumes complete with mob caps and tricorn hats. Many workshops, conventions and luncheons have been graced by Vona's Loyalist costumes. The costumes were also featured on TV in the series 'Genealogy and Basic Genealogy' (Rogers Community Channel) and in particular were worn at the 1994 BC Convention of the UEL Association of Canada, held for the first time outside of Ontario.

"N.B. Those Loyalists who have adhered to the Unity of the Empire; and joined the Royal Standard before the Treaty of Separation in the year 1783, and all their Children; and their Descendants, by either sex, are to be distinguished by the following Capitals affixed to their names

U.E.

Alluding to their great principle The Unity of the Empire."

LIST OF ABBREVIATIONS USED THROUGHOUT THE BOOK

A	acre	to	
abb	abbreviation	info	information
Adm	Administration	Inst	Institute
adm	admitted	inv	inventory
ae	age(d)	Jct	Junction
agst	against	jd	(Dutch) young woman
&	and	jm	(Dutch) young man
App	appendix	Jr, jr	Junior, junior
@	at	j/o	jurisdiction of
b	born	JP	Justice of the Peace
b/r/o	born & resident of	L&A	Lennox & Addington
bro	brother	lib	library
bp	baptized	£	English Pound
Brn	Breuklen, Brooklyn	Lt	Lieutenant
bur	buried	m	married
ca	circa	{m}	m & both De Witt desc
Can, Cdn	Canada, Canadian	ma	mother
Capt	Captain	M.D.	Medical Doctor
CEF	Canadian Expeditionary Force	Meth	Methodist
Cem	Cemetery	mo	month
cert	certificate	Mt	Mount
ch, chn	child, children	NC Meth	New Connexion Methodist
CH	Church	NYC	New York City
COY	Company	OC	Order-in-Council
Co	County	pp	page(s)
Coll	College	pa	father
Com	Community	pall	shroud
Coms	Commissioner	Par	Parish
conf	confession	Presby	Presbyterian
Cpl	Corporal	Pr Ed	Prince Edward County
cult	cultivate	Pro	Probate, Proven
d, dec	died, deceased	Prop	Proprietor
DD	Doctor of Divinity	pt	part
dau(s) d/o	daughter(s) of	prt	parent(s)
deft	defendant	Pub	Published
dis	dismissed	Reg't	Regiment
dist	district	res	reside(nt), reside(d)
div	divorced	Rev	Reverend
dy	died young	Revo	Revolution
DRC, RDC	Dutch Reformed Church	Scot	Scotland
E	Episcopalian	(sic)	exactly as written
EM	Episcopalian Methodist	sis	sister
Ed	Editor	Sgt	Sergeant
et al	and others	s/o	son/of
Ex:	executors	So	Society
fmr	farmer	sp	sponsor(s)
fathom	six feet	Stn	Station
F	Frontenac Co, ON	T, Twp	Town, township
gggf	great, great, grand father	tbstn	tombstone
Gen	Genealogy, Genealogical	U	University
gov't	government	W	Wesleyan
Grd	burying ground	WM	Wesleyan Methodist
grpa	grandfather	wd/o	widow of, widower of
grma	grandmother	wf, w/o	wife, wife/of
grpt	grandparents	wit:	witness(es)
hus	husband	WWI, WWII	World War I, II

Abbreviations for Canadian Provinces and Territories

YT - Yukon, NT - Northwest Territories, NU - Nunavut, BC - British Columbia, AB - Alberta, SK - Saskatchewan, MB - Manitoba, ON - Ontario, QC - Quebec, NB - New Brunswick, NS - Nova Scotia, PE - Prince Edward Island, NL - New Foundland and Labrador

Some States of the USA - United States of America
NY - New York, NJ - New Jersey, PA - Pennsylvania, OH - Ohio, ME - Maine, MD - Maryland, MA – Massachusetts, WV - West Virginia, FL - Florida, TX - Texas, DE - Delaware, WA - Washington, CA - California, MN - Minnesota, IL - Illinois

There was a Family Picnic in 1934 at Hurley, New York with a visit to Tjerck De Witt's home place and a second gathering in 1939 near Pieter Jansen De Witt, Bushwick, New York location. Cora E. Nelson collected 225 pages of descendant's genealogy. She placed a copy in the Seattle, Washington Library on the 30th August 1967, Call Number q P29.2, D517P stamped with the Latter Day Saints' Library number # 2,356,280. Kevin De Witt of Perryville, Ohio wrote the Collection reached a thousand pages and he had a copy. In the summer of 1998 the author learned that the Latter Day Saints' Church had filmed in 1985 "De Witt Family Notes, a Lifetime of Research" by Helen Hayes Perry, #2,056,030 with 1500 pages of any progenitors with the De Witt name. Researchers can order either film on loan from Salt Lake, Utah to their local LDS Church Library.

If both parents have De Witt ancestry, numbering used is the one listed first chronologically. In such cases marriage, m, is indicated as {m}. Both parents numbers are given and the one used in succeeding generations is underlined. Full citation is listed when facts appear for the first time. Names are copied as shown in the source used. Where variant spellings of names occur, the first listing is the usage in that entry. Where there is not a preponderance of proof it is indicated by * or an alphabetical letter or both.

Phoebe Jane (De Witt) Smith 1845 - 1929, Wentworth County, Ontario, Canada was the daughter of John De Witt 1808 - 1879 and Phoebe Nevers 1809 - 1803, granddaughter of Jacob De Witt 1766 - 1826, and wife Abigail (Cram) Kinney De Witt Pearson 1777 - 1861, who moved to Ontario in 1824. Phobe was told that in New Brunswick, Canada in early days they had only three choices for marriage: 'Hinjins, Hinglishmen or Relatives', so they chose Relatives.

Phoebe Jane (DeWitt) Smith b 1845 d 1929

DUTCH NAMES AND SOME ENGLISH EQUIVALENTS (Olde Ulster 1:231 and others)

DUTCH	ENGLISH
Aaltje	Alice
Aaghje, Aagje, Aagt, Agt	Agatha
Adriaantje,	Adrian (female)
Aefje, Eefje, Ifje, Aagje, Ephia, Aetje	Eva
Aeltje	Alida
Aldert	
Annatje, Annetje, Antje, Annaaten, Annatien	Ann, Anna, Annie
Andreas, Andries, Arie, Dries, Androus	Andrew
Arendt, Arent	Aaron
Ariaantje, Arriantje	Harriet
Barent	Bernard
Betje, Baetje, Elisabet, Lisabet, Eliza	Elizabeth
Catrina, Catharina, Kaatje, Katryne, Catrijn	
Tryntje	Catherine
Christeintje, Styntie, Tyne	Christina
Clafsen, Claes, Klaas; Claessen, Claezen, Claetz, Nikolaas	Nicholaes, Claes
Claesje	Claudia
Elsje	Alice
Evert	Everard
Emmerentjen, Amerentje, Emeretje	Emma, little Emma
Faelde	not listed (? German)
Femmetje	Phoebe
Frederik, Frederic, Friko, Frits	Frederick
Geertje, Geertie, Gerretje, Gerretie	Charity
Geertruy, Gerthroy, Gertruda, Gierrje, Geertje	
Gertroud, Truytje, Gertruai, Geertrui, Geesje	Gertrude
Gysbert	Gilbert
Henricus, Henrik, Hein	Henry
Heyltje	Helena
Hillitje, Hilletje	Maria
Jacobus, 'Cobus, Jafobus, Kobus, Jacob	James
Jacomina, Jacomeyntie, Jakomyntje, Jacoba	Jemima
Jan, Hans, Johannes, Janty, Joannes	John, Johnny
Jannetje, Jantje, Jannetjen, Natte, Jenneken	Jane
Joris, Jury, Jurian, Ury	George
Leucas, Luykas, Lukas, Lysje, Luytje	Lucas, Luke
Lodewyck, Lodewijk	Lewis
Louw	Lawrence
Margritje, Margaretha, Margaretta, Greitje	Margaret
Mariken, Maritje, Maartje, Maaike, Marritje,	
Marytje, Marytjen, Mariah, Mietje, Marrietje	Mary, Maria
Martinus, Maarten,	Martin
Morrendy	not listed (? Miranda)
Nelly, Neeltje, Beeltje, Keetje, Pietje	Cornelia
Peek, Peiter, Pieter, Petrus	Peter
Polly, Pallie, Molly	Mary
Ritchart, Rutsjert, Rykaard, Derrik, Dirk	Richard
Saartje, Sary, Sellie, Tialie, Tjaatje	Sally, Sarah
Sefeya, Saphia, Sephia	Sophia
Teunis	Anthony
Tialie, Taatje, Tjaetje, Tjaatje, (?Aechtje)	Charity, Sarah
Tierck, Tjerck, Tjark, Shark, Cherck, Dierck	Theodorick (as Richard)
Theodoric, Rykaard, Shark, Derrick, Dirk	Richard
Van Tassel	from Texel
Wilhelm, Willem, Wilhelmus, Wim	William
Wyntje	Lavinia

INTRODUCTION
TIERCK CLAFEN DeWITT
Son of Nicolaes/Claes de Witt and Tjaetje Cornelisz

Tierck, Tjerck, Tjarck is a Friesian name. It is pronounced Charick, German for Theodorus or Theodorick. Theodoric, which in turn, is translated as Richard (OU 1:231). Most records show the name as Tjerck or Tierck. Later generations recorded the name as Charck, Chark, Chercke, Direch, Jerck, Shark, Tharck, Tserck, Tirck, their phonetic transcription.

The early DeWitt researchers knew our people were a related branch of the famous DeWitts of Holland. Kornelis DeWitt, born in Dordrecht in 1545, prospered in the timber business and was Mayor of his home city. An article by Louis Hasbrouck Von Sahler in 1898 states Tjerck's wax seal showing two dogs chasing a hare, the same arms as the branches of the Dordrecht Dutch family, was used as a wax seal imprint in the old records of the Ulster County Clerk's Office (NYGBR 29:243/4). The Clerk said by letter 20 Nov 1987 she checked this page and does not find the aforementioned seal, but she would have examined a clerk's copy of the page.

May 1990 SALVATORE GRECO, Ulster County New York Records Manager very kindly obtained copies of Tjerck's signature for the author. He said the Old Dutch Records are in the Rosedale, New York Archive Repository and microfilm was also at Queen's University, New York City.

There is an explanation of the origin of many New Netherland Emigrants. "Included are also settlers from Holstein-East Friesland, bordering on the Dutch Province of Gronigen, many of whom were without a doubt originally of Dutch origin and were refugees who fled across the border when, following the treason of Count Renneberg, Gronigen joined the Spanish side and adhered to the Catholic faith. There were many settlers [in America] from Norden, Emsden, ESENS, Flenburg, and other towns situated in the general district" (LNYNJ 11:94). Our ancestors, as refugees from Catholicism, would give rise to the belief they were Huguenots. It is certain our DeWitts were originally of Dutch extraction and Lutheran.

Tjerck Claeszen deWith's marriage record states he was "of Groothelde Zunderland." Theories say the latter place is probably Saterland or Embertland. A New York lawyer, George DeWitt, in the late 1800's, made five trips overseas trying to pin down this clue, but found several "Great Forests" (Groothelde). On a Modern German map Emden, Oosterbeus, then GroBheide between Norden and Esens and shows GrootCelte further inland. Tjerck's early documented records in the New Netherlands show he was in the timber business. He built sloops later. A reasonable explanation of the marriage record may be Tjerck was born in Groothelde, a forest logging camp, and later _may_ have lived in Zuiderland, which is a tiny hamlet on Texel Island shown in a current German Atlas [one version]. As a sailor this could be a logical base. One reads that all Dutch ships departed from Texel in this time period. The 1610 Map shows the towns mentioned.

Proof of Tjerck's date of arrival in the New Netherlands has not been found. One likely character who might have been Tjerck is a fiery tempered sailor called Dirck Claessen Boot [boat i.e. sailor] of Munnikedam mentioned several times in Court Records, sued at Rensselaerswyck by a tavern keeper 17 Oct 1646 for 284 Carolus guilders for consumed liquor & victuals; second suit by Sander Leendertsen Glen for 130 guilders 24 Oct 1646 (NYHMD 1:347/8 3:117). Stoffel Elswaert (Theophilus Ellsworth) from Bristol made an agreement on 25 Apr 1652 before Notary J. de Winter at Amsterdam with Dirck Claesz Boot, Skipper of `de Romeyn', to sail to New Netherland "for adventure and half the profit." He acknowledged having received from the latter 154 gl. in advance (Settlers of Dutch Descent: 82). Later New Amsterdam records show this sailor bringing in a prize vessel from the West Indies. Research is difficult because of the use of patronymics [your surname is your father's first name with a suffix added e.g. Claes, Claesen] even after the British took over the New Netherlands in 1665/70. Various aliases (nicknames) were used in baptisms and in official records, with variable spelling depending on pronunciation or understanding, and the nationality and education of the recorder.

First definite record found by the author of Tierck Klasen was in The Dutch Settlers Society. A F J Van Laer, "Deacon's Account Book 1652-64 Albany" (DSS 39:2/3)
- p2 24 Apr 1655 To T(i)erk, the carman, for carting clapboards & other boards-   15
- p2 23 May 1655 To same for carting posts and rails   70
- p3 19 May 1657 To Tierck Klasen for posts for the barn   25

Minutes of the Court of Fort Orange and Beverwyck 1652-1656 1.

"Tuesday 01 Feb 1656 John de Deckere, ex officio plaintiff, against Tierk Claesen, defendant. He demands that the defendant be fined sixteen guilders for having fought last Sunday with William Teller and killed a goat of Sander Leendertsz [an alias of Alexander Lindsay of the Glen], brother-in-law of William Teller. The Court having heard the defendant's confession condemns (sic) him to pay a fine of two and a half beavers [Evidently a sword fight!].

Idem, plaintiff against the same defendant for having been found last Sunday in the company of the Lutherans performing divine service, contrary to the ordinance against it. Demands therefore he be fined 6 fl [florin]. The court, having heard the confession of the defendant, condemns (sic) him to pay the fine demanded" (MCFOB 1:247).

10 Oct 1657 Claes deWitt signed a petition at New Amsterdam asking for a Lutheran minister (SINY:39). Tjerck, if born in 1620 and may have been thirty-six when he married Barbara Andriessen in New Amsterdam in 1656. Her last child was born in 1684 so Barbara may have been under twenty when she married in 1656. Four children were baptized in the Dutch Reformed Church until the British took over. From 1668 the next six children were not baptized in the Dutch Reformed Church until the last child in 1684. The Lutheran Records are not extant. Lendert Dirckzen DeWitt also lived in Wildwyck in 1663 which leads to speculation as to whether he may have been a son of Tjerck from an earlier marriage. He arrived on the same ship in 1662 as did Tjerck's sister Ida, her husband Jan Albertson Van Steenwyck and their daughter, Emmerentine deWitt and one Jan Classen. Tjerck and Barbara's children do not conform to the naming pattern of the period supporting the idea he may have had an earlier family. Usually they named the first male for the paternal grandfather, second son for the maternal grandfather, first daughter for the paternal grandmother, the second one for the maternal grandmother and following the same pattern with uncles and aunts. One Andries De Witt was Governor of West Friesland at the right time but the Dutch Genealogy does not list Nicholaes among his children.

<u>Minutes of the Court of Fort Orange and Beverwyck 1657-1660 Vols 1 & 2.</u>
"Fort Orange 08 Feb 1658 Abraham Pietersen Vosburch, plaintiff, against Tierck Claessen and Cobus Teunissen, defendants. The plaintiff complains the defendant had a tree hauled out of the woods, which he cut down for lumber. The defendant admits that he did so, saying that the log had lain there in the woods for three years. The court dismisses the plaintiff's complaint against the defendant, on the ground that the plaintiff did not have his log hauled out of the woods within the space of three years (MCFOB 2:98).
Fort Orange 14 May 1658 Cornelis Wyncoop, plaintiff, against Tjerck Classen and his <u>servants,</u> defendants. Default (MCFOB 2:112).
Fort Orange 01 Oct 1658 Eldert Gerbertsen, plaintiff, against T'Jerck Claessen [copied as found] defendant. The plaintiff demands of the defendant two hundred logs, the least to be one fathom in circumference, according to the oral contract made with each other, and says that it is a matter of great importance to him and therefore claims compensation for loss and damage sustained by him. The defendant admits the oral contract made with the plaintiff and promises to haul them out within the space of fourteen days and not to do any other work until the plaintiff is satisfied. The court having heard the parties, ordered the defendant, according to his promise, to deliver within the space of fourteen days the two hundred logs the thinnest to be one fathom in circumference and to pay the costs of the suit. Under penalty of the loss and damage the plaintiff has already suffered or may still suffer" (MCFOB 2:160/1). This indicates Tjerck DeWitt had a considerable logging/sawmill operation in the Albany area.

In 1661 Tjerck gave power of attorney to his brother-in-law, Ida Claeszen DeWitt's husband, Jan Albertsen Van Steenwyck. He was to collect rental money owed Tjerck from his father's estate while overseas from Pieter Jansen Van Hoorn, widower of Tjerck's sister Faelde. The money was to be applied to Tjerck's debts. So Ida and Jan can be presumed to have visited Esens and Oosterbeus, East Friesland, Germany. On 31 Aug 1662 Ida, and Jan, their young daughter and Ida's sister Emmerentine/Ammerens de Witt arrived back in the New Netherlands in <u>The Fox.</u> Lendert Dirckzen DeWitt of Venloo and Roermond, French towns on the border of the Netherlands, was also on the same ship. Ida and family, Lendert and wife died in the Indian massacre 07 Jun 1663 at Wildwyck. Tjerck's four-year-old daughter Taatje was among the thirty-five people taken hostage. It was the litigation and settlement of Ida deWitt's estate that provided proof of siblings and residence in America. In 1982 before any of our research group was aware another Ida was part of the family, genealogist Klas Vander Barren, Morrisburgh Ontario, Canada brought back from the Aurich, East Friesland Archive, Wyt's church records and the baptism near Esens of a child named Ida deWitt in the 1670's. There, at that time, they were still using patronymics.

Penny Smith Stabler, living in Switzerland, sister of Dr I Carolyn Smith Pellettier, one of our group, corresponded with DeWitts living near Esens, East Friesland, Germany. Andries DeWitt and his son Peter are fishermen. They were told it is virtually impossible to trace their ancestry.

Tjerck had a volatile temper as shown by extensive court records. His descendants, known to this researcher, in Andries and Leucas lines seven to ten generations removed have inherited this notable temper. <u>New York Historical Manuscripts: Dutch Kingston Papers</u> p103 20 Nov 1663. The Schout (chief magistrate), Roelof Swartwout, presents this complaint against Tjerck Claesen deWit, according to his understanding as follows: "Whereas Aeltje Wygers and Albert Gysbertsen have complained to me that on November 13, Tjerck Claesen, armed with a drawn knife, openly quarreled in his house, acting as if he wished to kill every man, woman and child, I therefore, on this complaint inform the Court of the matter, and also decide to exclude him for the present from the Bench, until he shall have cleared himself of the charge, and shall have been declared cleared by the Honorable Court. The advice of the Commissaries is requested herein. The Honorable Court orders that, whereas, Tjerck Claesen deWit has already amicably settled the above matter with his accuser, Albert Gysbertsen, and they have come to an agreement regarding it, he shall remain away from the Bench until he shall have adjusted this matter with the Schout" (NYHMD 1:103).

The Early History of Saugerties says Tjerck Claesen DeWitt and William Montania petitioned Governor Lovelace, April 1670, for a grant of seventy five acres upon which to set up a sawmill for the public benefit, it's location to be a place called "Dead Man's Bones" (EHS:90). Tjerck's son Leucas, who captained a sloop owned in partnership with his father, died a young man in 1703. His children, Jannetje (deWit) Langendyke and Lucas deWit, located in Saugerties Town [Township] Ulster County. Lucas was at what is now Mount Marion four miles north of the village of Saugerties, which is at the junction of Esopus Creek and the Hudson River. Son Jan deWit was in the Catskill Town area. Most of Leucas descendants remained in this area or north into Greene County for the next hundred years.

Tjerck exchanged his house in Beverwyck for a house and property in Wildwyck in 1660, possession given 01 May 1661. In January 1669/70 Governor Lovelace issued a permit to "erect a house and barne with convenient outhouses for his cattle upon his own land at Esopus lying betwixt Hurley and Kingston" (DHHV: 193/4). Andries returned from Marbletown after his father's death living in Tjerck's house at the time of his own death in 12 Nov 1710 (note Tjerck's will). The oldest portion, about 30' by 39' is one end of the present structure. [Three English feet make one Dutch foot.] The filled in door opening and restructured windows show the front was changed from its original design. These filled in areas, the second story and the additions are different coloured stone. The two extensions with full basement, and adding a second storey and dormers, certainly changed the character of the building. Records state Andries was killed by a falling beam possibly during one stage of remodeling (DHHV:194/5).

Tierck Claeszen deWith b 1620 (d 17 Feb 1700) in his will gave his wife Barbara his whole estate to be divided after her demise. After the death of Captain Andries DeWitt 22 July 1710 his eldest son Tjerck (b 1683 d 1762) probated Andries' will on 28 Sep 1710. After Barbara's death grandson Tjerck handled the probate of his grandfather's will 28 Feb 1716/7. He seemed to receive "the land and buildings in Kingston corporation devised by his grandfather to his father" DHHV:194). Grandson Tjerck apparently did the next addition according to an iron fireback photographed by the author, reading "Tjerck Claessen DeWitt 1749". In the earliest segment the axe work squaring the floor joists is remarkable in it's precision. The ceiling beams were sawn lumber. It's to be noted the door openings and ceilings were much higher than other dwellings of the period, bearing out the tradition they were very tall men. The house now is about 39' by 81', full basement, and two stories. Can carbon dating of wood from a basement joist authenticate the building's date?

Calendar of British Historical Manuscripts in the Office of the New York Secretary of State 1664-1776. O'Callaghan. The Gregg Press. Ridgeway NJ. p240 1694 May 14. Petition. Dierck Claes DeWitt of Esopus, for an order for a survey of 280 acres of land purchased by him of the Indians at Coxinke, in Ulster County. [There are other items.]

Minutes of the Supreme Court of Judicature Oct 1696 p101. "John Ward ver Tyreche Claese: The Sheriffe of Ulster Returning A writt of Habere facias Possessionem Complaining that in the Execution thereof he was resisted by Direch Claese Dewitt & his Daughter & many others whereupon he applyd himself to Coll Henry Beeckman one of his Majts Justices of ye peace of ye sd County who did also Refuse to give Any Aid - - - ". Tjerck owned much property, farmed, logged, had a sawmill, built sailing vessels, and owned a sloop in partnership with his son Leucas. He served as a Schepen (chief Magistrate). Names of Dutch Settlers at Esopus provides this list: DeWitt, Tierck Claesen, 1661 Schepen; 1662 was one of four who were said to have a "double" farm; was Sergeant of the local Militia in 1665; examiner of fences 1665; Schepen 1668; nominated for Schepen 1671. (NYGBR: 2:121). After the English takeover of the New Netherlands in the Naturalization of the Oath of Allegiance in 1689 under the category "Did not appear" is Dewitt, Terrick Claes -- Duitcher (German [DHSNY1:282]).

One story says Nicholaes DeWitt was the doctor on Henry Hudson's ship in 1611. Remember a ship's barber was also the doctor. Several sources name the English sailors but no Dutch names. References to this doctor state he had a terrible disposition and on shore, the mate, in a fistfight "beat him in English and Dutch". Nicholaes is not recorded in this occupation in the New World. One Jan DeWitt sailed as first mate of the Little Fox to the Hudson River in 1613 and when the Indians killed the Captain, he assumed command. Jan returned the next year trading in furs. Boudewyn DeWitt was a doctor at Kingston, New York (Wildwyck) who died in 1702 but there's no indication of relationship, if any, found so far. Pieter Jansen De Witt arrived about 1660, settled at Bushwick. Bastiaan DeWitt of Long Island (possibly Pieter's son) married 05 Mar 1704 Margariet Peersen of Kingston NY. One Peter DeWitt was in New Jersey records around 1665. There's a record of the arrival in 1662 of Skipper Peter Jansen DeWitt of Emden, East Friesland. Perhaps a misreading of all of this or the repeating of oral history attributed the stories to Nicholaes. His children were known as "Claeszen" or a variant spelling. Theory at the time of the Picnics suggests Captain Jan DeWitt, the early sailor, was Nicholaes' father. Ancestry overseas of Nicholaes deWitt is difficult to prove. There was no indexing of land records and church baptisms and marriage records begin too late for our needs. The lawsuit and land records we do have provide a few clues to his wife's identity. Nicholas patronymic has not been positively identified. If his father was "Witt" logically he would have been called Claes Wits, Wittzen, Wittsen or Wittse. Only more prominent people had family names in that era. Interestingly there was a Nicholaes deWitt in London belonging to the Dutch Reformed Church at Austin Friars in 1595.

Pomissory note of Richard Brudnil to Nicholaes White.
    I the undersigned Retsert Brudnil acknowledge that I am well and truly indebted to Nicholaes Whith in the some (sic) of forty pound sterling arising from certain surety bond which the above Nicholaes Whith has paid for me. I promise to pay the aforesaid money into the hands aforesaid free of costs and charges without any gainsay in two installments to wit the first £20 sterling in this year 1639 and the last payment in 1640. For all of which the undersigned bind my person and property, moveable and immovable, present and future, without any exception, under submission to all lords, courts, judges and justices. All in good faith, I have signed together with the witnesses. Done this 22nd of July 1639 in Fort Amsterdam in the New Netherlands.
    Richard Brudnil
    C.V. Eslant
    J. Van Culer Witnesses (NYHMD 1:197).

Author's note: The translator seems to have decided 'Whith' was White but we often note it is a form of De Witt. Retsert is also changed to Richard. One wonders what the exact reading of the original Dutch document was.

Of three men found there is a _slight_ possibility that one could be our Nicholas DeWitt.
1   Correspondence of Jeremias Van Rensselaer 1651-1674, Translated and edited by A. J. F. Van Laer (Archivist, Archives and History Division) Albany, State University NY 1932 p. 235. Amsterdam, September 7, 1660 Addressed:
Mr Jeremias van Rensselaer Director of the colony of Renselaerswyck on the North River in New Netherland
    By the ship DeLiefde
    Skipper Claes Jansz deWit
Some notes (no proof offered) say this Jansz deWit is Tjerck's grandfather. If this is correct Tjerck brother Jan could be the oldest son according to naming patterns. Tjerck's birth year is given as 1620, not proven. By 1660 Claes Jansz might be 60 years old, not very likely on sailing ships of that era.

One Jansz deWit was the first mate on the second voyage to American in 1613. His captain was killed by the Indians and Jan's returned to America next time as Captain in 1614 trading for furs with the Indians. Tjerck's father Claes might [no proof] be a son of Jan DeWitt of the 1613/4 trips to America. Most Captains employed by the Dutch were from the North Sea coast of Germany as was Jan DeWitt. In 1657 Claes deWitt signed a Lutheran petition in New Amsterdam (fr SINY) so he lived there. By 1661 Tjerck was trying to collect overdue rent on property inherited from his father, Claes deWitt in Oosterbeus, East Friesland, Germany from his brother-in-law Pieter Jansen Van Hoorn.

2   Nicholaas deWitt's wife Tjaetje Cornelisz was the daughter of Cornelis Pieterz of Oosterbeus, Westeraccum, East Friesland, Germany, who is identified as Nicholaes' father-in-law in the 1684 thirty-one page German lawsuit, copy obtained by Ambassador Lester DeWitt Mallory from the Aurich Archive in Germany. There is no indexing of archival material. One _possibility_ in New Amsterdam is Claes Jansen Kust (ie Coast [note Esens on the coast]) also called Claes Jansen de Backer (Baker) widower of Aechtje Cornelisz [could this possibly have been Tjaetje?]. He married second time 21 Jul 1647 Geertje Nannicks (Nonnicks) widow of Tjerck Hendricksy and also of Abel Reddenhasen. Since our Tjerck's marriage record said he was born in Groothelde (Great Forest) Claes' occupation then may have been in the timber business and his livelihood during his later years, if this is the same man, was as a baker. The evidence presented here supports one possible theory, _not proof_. Emmertine of Esens East Friesland married Martin Hoffman. Martin, Tjerck and Nickolaas DeWitt were Lutheran. They were literate and signed their names.

3   Nicolaes Coorn, an official at Renselaerswyck for several years, who on 25 Jul 1647 gives his power of attorney to a man going to the Netherlands to collect for him money owed by Susanna Franse at Dordrecht; also money from his inheritance from his mother's estate (Janneken Kassers, matron of the hospital at Steenbergen near Dordrecht [NYHMD 2:442/3]). Nicolaus Koorn, sergeant or wachtmeester succeeded Adriaen Van der Donck as Sheriff in 1642 (fr Settlers of Rensselaerwyck:75. If this was our Nicholaes could his father's name have been Kornelis? With the naming system used at that time the first son would be named for his grandfather.

When Tjerck first appears in New Netherland records he seems to be struggling and concentrating on paying his debts. By his own effort he became very prosperous by the end of his life.

Three other items, when viewed together, seem to parallel in an interesting way our DeWitt line. Settlers of Rensselaerwyck states Barent Janz, from Esens . . . does not appear in that colony after 1634 (SR:6).
Jan Van Tassel [name evolved from Van Texel meaning from Texel] one of the earliest settlers in the New Netherlands, whose wife Cateronas was the daughter of Wyandance, an Indian Chief and Sachem of Long Island. These are the names along with Peter and Lucas DeWitt that appear in early New Jersey Records.

Vona (DeWitt) Smith

<u>Van Tassel and Allied Lines</u> lists:
1. Jan Van Texel was b circa 1600. His son was Cornelius Jansen Van Texel.
2. Dirck Theodorus Van Texel 1605 -1652 whose son Reverend Pieter Van Texel married Ida DeWith. Pieter Van Der Werff's oil painting dated 1710 of Reverend Peter Van Texel is said to be in the museum at Rotterdam. This must have been a portrait of him as an old man.

Barent DeWitt, Van Coln [Cologne] had a son Jacob Barentsen DeWitt who came to New Amsterdam prior to 1649 . . returned to Holland and married 03 Feb 1660 Tryntje Dutcher. Their son Barent was said to have been born at Grootholdt en Zunderlandt, District of Westphalia, ? Germany [no proven source named] 18 Jan 1666. . . settling in Tarrytown, Westchester County NY . . . married Sarah Van Tassel, granddaughter of Jan Van Tassel. Barent and Sarah's children were Andreas, Petrus, Paulus, Barent, Catherine, Sara, and Titus (VTAL:3)

New York Genealogical and Biographical Record #29 1898 pages 243/4
"The DeWitts of Dordrecht and New York. When my esteemed friend and kinsman, Thomas Grier Evans, Esq., of New York, wrote the genealogy of the earlier generations of our ancestor, Tjerck Claessen DeWitt, of Ulster County, he was unable, after the most careful researching, to find what he considered positive proof that said DeWitt was connected with the distinguished DeWitt family of Dordrecht, although he supposed such was the case. The DeWitt family in this country has also been distinguished by such members as DeWitt Clinton, Governor of New York State, Simeon DeWitt, chief of the topographical staff of General Washington and Surveyor-General of New York and Rev Thomas DeWitt, D.D., pastor of the Collegiate Dutch Church of New York, and others; but one naturally appreciates a proved connection with an honorable family in the mother country. The coat of arms of the DeWitts of Dordrecht is described thus: De sinople un lievre, un levier, et un braque est tout d'argent 2 et 1. Cr. le lievre est entre un vol de sinople d'argent. Of course genealogists are often obligated to accept proof derived from seals and other heraldically ornamented things. Recently I found when researching the old records of the Ulster County Clerk's Office the wax impression of a seal, which undoubtedly would be accepted as proof by any authority. It is on page 307 of book A.A., the first volume of the so-called English records, to distinguish them from the earliest set of records, which are entirely in Dutch. Unfortunately several of the preceding pages are missing, evidently torn out through carelessness, but fortunately enough remains to show that the record was connected with the settlement of Tjerck Claessen DeWitt's estate after the death of his widow, Barbara [Andriessen van Amsterdam] DeWitt, and is dated February 30 1716/17. The wax seal, attached to the signature of Major Johannis Hardenbergh, one of the gentlemen who assisted at the final settlement of the estate, was stamped with a seal, engraved with the coat of arms borne by Jan DeWitt, the Grand Pensionary of Holland, and his family, the DeWitts of Dordrecht. It is in good preservation considering that it has [may have] been generally handled for nearly two centuries and shows that the seal was round, and engraved with a hare and a dog at the top and a dog at the bottom, and there were initials at the top, which are now quite illegible, with the exception of the first, which looks like a C. The absence of the lines to denote the tincture of the field is accounted for by the fact that before Silvestre di Petrasancta, an Italian, introduced the present system denoting tinctures about 1630, such means were no doubt not much in use, and probably the adoption of Petrasancta's system was slow. Undoubtedly Tjerck Claessen DeWitt brought the seal over with him, and it may have belonged to some forefather. I have studied much of European and British heraldry, and researched very extensively among the early records of this country, but I do not remember ever to have seen a coat of arms similar to that of the DeWitts, which is truly an unusual one, so that there is not the possibility of confusion. The absence of the crest is of no consequence, as often simply the shield has been used, especially when it was the charge, or one of the charges, of the shield. I do not think the descendants of Tjerck Claessen DeWitt should not hesitate considering the proof, to use the said coat of arms, and I shall quarter it with the other coats of arms to which I am entitled. Of course I do not believe in carrying the use of coats of arms too far in a Republic, but I think it is our duty to the memory of our forefathers to make proper use of them. Forefathers should never be expected to carry us through our earthly pilgrimage, but to make a foundation on which to build.
    LOUIS HASBROUCK VON SALER
    Van Deusen Lodge, Van Duesen.
    Old Records are now in a repository at Rosedale, N.Y.

University of British Columbia, Mercator, Gerardus. 1512 – 1594.
Atlas Minor . Special Collections: G1007/M42. 1610
Emden, Norden, Ooserbeus, Jever, Saderlant, GrootCelte

Two wonderful people, my nephew Murray Hugill and his wife Marlene (Ackles) Hugill of Burlington Ontario, Canada contributed a great deal to the production of this book. Over a period of yearly visits for 25 years they drove me around Ontario to New Brunswick, Canada, New York State, Pennsylvania, Vermont, Maryland and New Jersey helping in the research. They have given four weeks of their time to indexing, adding pictures, proof reading, editing and setup with the publishers. Only with their contribution was this production possible. My most grateful thanks.   Vona E Smith.

GENERATION I

1 NICHOLAAS/CLAES deWITT it is known to have res in Grootholt, Oosterbeus & Esens, East Friesland, Germany before going to the New Netherlands. In New Amsterdam Claes deWitt signed a petition asking the authorities to allow them a Lutheran Minister 10 Oct 1657 (SlNY:39). He seems to have died between 1657 & 1660. His wife was TJAETJE CORNELISZ, daughter of Cornelis Pieterz. New York Old Dutch Records name family members in Holland & America who inherit Ida Claessen deWitt's estate in 1663 (NYHMD:591/2, 600). Dates & order of some births are unknown. In the Dordrecht Genealogy the Dutch spelling is Nikolaas.

1. TIERCK CLAESZEN deWITH b *1620 Oosterbeus, East Friesland (P-DS1) source not noted (Will 04 Mar 1687, d 17 Feb 1700 Registered 06 Mar 1700/1 [UCPR 1:56]) at New Amsterdam m 24 Apr 1656 Barbara Andrieszen of Amsterdam (MRDNA:20). Barbara inherited Tjerck's estate to be divided after her death according to his will. Note information previous page indicated Pro was Feb 30 1716/17 - Gustave Anjou's translation of the probate records. Included in this genealogy are places of bp & names of witnesses. The spelling used is copied & you see who was present in that place at that time. You recognize grandparents, assorted relatives or sometimes neighbors & friends. The Dutch used "i" and "j", also "g" & "f" interchangeably but most records use Tjerck; his signature is as Tierck. <u>OSTERIESISCHEN FAMILIEN – UND WAPPEN – KUNDE.</u> Herausgegeben von der Ostfricsischen Landschaft, Arbeitsgruppe Familienkunde und Heraldik, Aurich. 1969. (lists) #5 ? DeWitt, Tjark Klassen, aus Esens, Vorfahr der deWitt-Sippe [Sippe is family, from German book]. When an English Proclamation for Naturalization was ordered, Ulster County oath of allegiance was taken 01 Sep 1687. DeWitt, Terrick Claes, Duitcher ["the German"] was present but did not swear allegiance. Thomas Evans' early DeWitt genealogy is in NYGBR 5:161/8, 17:251/9, 18:13/21, 21:185/190, 22:2/6, 34:200/6.J

2. JAN CLAETZ deWITT Will 31 Mar 1699 Pro 26 Jun 1699 states "of Amsterdam in Hollandt." (UCPR 1:54) Pro was within three months which states "All I have here in America" indicating he died in America.

3. TIALIE CLAESSEN deWITT in Jan's will (as TJAETJE in Ida's estate papers) or as Tjaetje m ? Heerkeus living in "Hollandt" in 1699; had issue and was willed Jan Claetz de Witt's property in Holland.

4. FAELDE CLAESSEN deWITT predeceased Ida. Her unnamed children were to receive her share. Her husband was Pieter Jansen Van Hoorn. Pieter who owed Tjerck rental money for what had been Nicholaes' property in Oosterbeus, East Friesland in 1661 but on 10 Apr 1665 his 2nd wife Divertje Volkerts was applying to the court in Kingston (Wildewyck) for money they said was owed from Jan Albertsen Van Steenwyck's estate (NYHMD:225).

5. IDA CLAESSEN deWITT m Jan Albertze Van Steenwyck. The Indian massacre at Wildwyck 07 Jun 1663 "List of killed at Wildwyck, Men . . Jan Alberts, murdered in his house . . Women. . Jan Albertsen's wife, big with child, killed in front of her house. . Children . . Jan Alberts little girl murdered with her mother" (p31 DHSNY 4:30-62). Jan Albertse Van Steenwyck requested a site for a tannery in 1662. (NYGBR 2:118)
On 26 Nov 1663 Tjerck Classen DeWitt deposited with the court an inventory taken 14 Nov 1663 of the estate of his brother-in-law, Jan Albertse Van Steenwyck, requesting that a curator be appointed and a guardian over the minor children (NYHMD 1:592). Had minor children survived Ida & Jan they would have inherited. In the settlement of the estate the only minor children on record belong to her sister Faelde. Proof that Ida was in the New World at an earlier time is as follows: "13 Aug 1658 Ida Classen against Dirck Cartensen for calling her a thief. Evidence in the case, then he was fined 50 guilders and costs" at Albany (MCFOB:148).

6. GRIETJE CLASSEN DeWitt received an equal share of Ida's Estate (NYHMD:600). [NOTE spelling in the record (DRCK:30) 13 Nov 1687 of Ghiertruy de Witthe in the bp of Matthys Mattyssen & Thiatje deWitthe's son Klaes] *One alternate spelling of GRIETJE is likely same person as GHIERTRUY deWITTHE from New Amsterdam m 26 Feb 1655 to Hendrick Folkers/Volkertz (Bries) of Jever, Oldenburghlandt which was near Esens Germany (MRDNA:19). On 18 Apr 1657 in New Amsterdam Hendrick Volkertsen had the small burgher right. Their descendants res on Staten Island & New Jersey. Her chn found were:
   <u>Volkert Hendricksen Bries</u> m1 at Flatland, NY 31 Oct 1690 Neltje Jans wd/o Gerret Dirckse Croejier; m2 Elizabeth Poulis; sold his farm at Brooklyn 20 Oct 1701 (ESKC:47). Six chn & wives are identified.
   <u>Gerrit Hendrickse Bries</u> "of Flacklands"
   <u>Jeurian Hendrickse Bries</u> bp 05 Dec 1660 d 15 Dec 1660
   <u>Jeurian Hendrickse Bries</u> bp 06 Nov 1661 parents from the Ferry. Albany Church Records state p22, 01 Oct 1686 1st banns Juriaan Hendricksz Bries jm/o Long Island & Agnietje Barents jd/o New Amsterdam.

7. EMMERENTJEN/AMMERENS/EMMERENTINE CLAESSEN deWITT b Esens, East Friesland. In New Amsterdam Emmerentje de With m 16 May 1664 Marten Hofman as his 2nd wife (GHF:96). He m1 31 Mar 1663 Lysbeth Hermans; **no chn**. "Death 1712, in summer, in 'Sopos, Marten Hoffman, a very aged man" (NYGBR 86:4). They were progenitors of the Theodore Roosevelt family. Martin Hermanzen Hofman was born in 1645 in Revel on the Gulf of Finland. He came to America in 1657, settled at Esopus, then moved to New Amsterdam. According to the City Directory in 1661 he lived on De Heere Straat (now Broadway). He moved to Albany then Kingston. Quote: "he probably lived prior to emigration to

America at Ezen, Ostenbenzie, and Holland [Germany]" - - authorized by his brother-in-law Terrick Classen de Witt to recover some property for him from Ezen." (no date given; GHF:96,100).

Annetje Hofman bp 01 Mar 1665 MRDNA New York 01 Mar 1665 sp Jerck Claeszen de Witt (her ma's bro) & Annetje Croesvelt. She m 04 Jan. 1702 Hendrik Pruyn b 13 Jun 1670; (GHF:101) **no ch**.

Marritje Hofman bp 12 Dec 1666 (RDCNY) wit Bay Cruysvert & Marritie Elsenhuysen.

Zecharias Hofman jm[young man] b 167? Fort Orange Albany [d 1744]) res in Kingstowne 1st banns 24 Mar 1706 m Hester Bruyn bp 11 Feb 1683 (GHF:102).

Nicholaes Hofman b circa 1680 Kingstowne, Ulster County NY 1st banns 05 Nov 1607 m 30 Dec 1704 Jannetje Crispell b Hurley (GHF:109\10).

Taatje Hofman b168? m Everardus Bogardus.

Jan Claetz DeWitt willed his property in America to niece Taatje Hofman & hus Evard Bogardus & pieces of eight to nephew Nicholas Hofman.

Tuesday 29 Jan 1664 Jacomyntie Janz against Emmerentine Claaz, defendant. Briefly Jacomytie sold a pair of bracelets to Emmerentie, claimed they were pawned & wanted to recover them. She had received yard goods & cash but we don't learn the results of the case (CMNA:10/11).

8 * CORNELIS/CORNELIA [typo?] CLAESSEN WITS is another **possible** family member & may well be the reason the deWitts migrated. She married William Kieft.

On 14 Aug 1647 "Power of Attorney (to Jacob Stofflesen and Johannes Reiger) by Cornelis (sic) [Cornelia] Claessen Wits and wife to William Kieft (Director-General of the New Netherlands) to receive money due them in Holland" (CHDSS 2:40). "Relieved from the personal supervision of the general officers of the Company, and with extensive powers conferred upon them over the new settlers, they became veritable Sancho Panzas in the colonies. Of these, perhaps the worst specimen was Willem Kieft, Director-General at New Amsterdam from 1638 to 1647. It is somewhat difficult to describe the character of this man, or to decide which was his leading trait, his hypocrisy, his self-importance, his administrative incapacity, or the rancorous venom of his disposition toward his opponents." But what he did accomplish was "very exact maps and accounts of New Netherland" which would now be of priceless value.

The Dutch West Indies Company was unfortunate in the Administrative Officers of its Colonies. These men, usually advanced through various gradations from Clerk's desks, were often entirely lacking in the qualities essential to a successful magistracy. Kieft embroiled in endless squabbles, attempts to eradicate the Indians and blame others, then had a most notable quarrel with Dominie Evarardus Bogardus. Recalled to Holland to settle the matters, Kieft, Melyn & Kuyster together with Dominie Bogardus and several other prominent characters of New Amsterdam sailed on <u>The Princess</u> 17 August 1647. They were shipwrecked during a violent storm upon the rocks near Swansea, Wales. Of about a hundred persons on board, eighty perished, among them Bogardus and Kieft. No mention is made of Kieft's wife, though one would expect she accompanied him. The two volumes make interesting reading on the people and times (NAP 1:21/2/3/9,101/13/15).

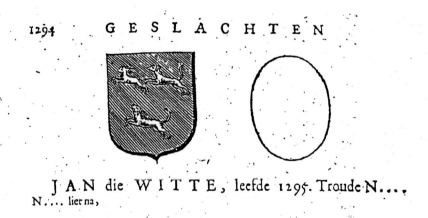

De WITT AMORIAL BEARING

GENERATION 2

THE NEW NETHERLAND'S AGE OF MAJORITY WAS TWENTY FIVE (LNYNJ:103)

1.1 TIERCK CLAESZEN DeWITT m 24 Apr 1656 Barbara Andriessen

They had 13 chn. Included in this book are places of bp & names of witnesses. The spelling used is copied & you see who was present in that place at that time. You recognize grprts, assorted relatives, & sometimes neighbors & friends. Tjerck was said to have been b 1620, Will 04 Mar 1687, d 17 Feb 1700, Pro 30 Feb 1716/17, (NYGBR #29 1898 p 243/4). Thomas Evans early DeWitt genealogy is in NYGBR 34:200-206 17:251-259 18:13-21 21:185-190 22:3-6 5:161-168.

1   ANDRIES deWITH b New Amsterdam early 1657 (NYGBR 17:254) & (d 22 Jul 1714 struck by 2 falling sleepers [beams]) of Esopus m banns 04 Mar 1682 Jannetje Egbertsen (DRCK:506) d/o Egbert Meindertse & Jaepe Jans, 12 chn (UCPRI:58).

2   TAATJE/THIATJE deWITH/DeWITTHE b 1659 Albany (d before 1724). "Taken Prisoners . . children. . . Tjerck Claessen deWitt's oldest girl (ae 4, among 8 women, 26 chn taken hostages by the Indians [DHSNY 4:31]) m in 1677 Mattys/Mattyssen Van Keuren, 13 chn (NYGBR 17:254). He was a Capt in 1685 & later served against the French on the northern frontier (UCPR 1:34).

3   JANNETJEN deWITH bp 12 Feb 1662 sp (uncle & grma) Jan Jansen, Jannetje Sebyns, Elsie Jans (DRCK:2) & (d 1744) m Cornelis Swits **no chn** (UCPR 1:20).

4   KLAES/CLAES deWITH bp 17 Feb 1664 sp Luycas Andriessen residing in the Manhathans, Jan Claessen, Geertruy Andriessen from Fort Orange, Tryntje Tysen (DRCK:3). Claas deWit & Maritie Egbertz were sp for Andies' son Jacob bp 28 Sep 1684. The inventory of Estate of Class deWith 30 Nov 1686 in NYC, was a small amount (NYHSC 26:445, p 14) presumed single.

5   JAN deWITH bp 14 Feb 1666 sp (aunt & hus, uncle) Martin Hoffman, Jan Andriesse, Amerens Claessen (DRCK:5) & (pro 12 Apr 1715) m Wyntie Kiersted; (UCPR 1:118) she m2 Dirrick Roosekrans, 5 DeWitt chn.

6   GEERTRUYD deWITH bp 15 Oct 1668 sp (uncles & aunt) Jan Andriesen, Luykas Andries, Martie Andriesen (DRCK:6) m 24 Mar 1688 Hendrick Hendrickse Shoonmaker/Schoumaecker (DRCK:510; UCPR 1:81) 14 chn. They are grdpr/o Geertruy Person who m Evert DeWitt.

7   JACOB deWIT m 01 Mar 1696 Grietje Vernoy, 8 chn. Jacob was alive in 1687 & in 1710 but is not named in Tjerck's Will in Anjou's abstracts nor in George C DeWitt's transcription to idiomatic English.

8   RACHEL deWIT alive in 1738 m Cornelius Bogardus, 8 chn.

9   LEUCAS deWIT estimated b circa 1672 banns 22 Dec 1695 m 23 Dec 1695 Annatje Delva/Delval (DRCK:512) d/o Jannetje Hillebrants & her 2nd hus Anthony Delva/Telba/Delga/d'Elva/Dulleva. Annatje was said to be Spanish & Roman Catholic. Her half-sis, Jannetje Le Seur d/o Jannetje Hillebrants & Francois Le Seur/Lozier/Lesier, is also an ancestor of those of us descended from Debora, Geertruy Persen & siblings. Luycas was joint owner with his father of the sloop Saint Barbara & its Skipper. Anjou's abstract of wills gives the spelling as Luycas, which may indicate how the will was signed. Pro 09 Mar 1703 (UCPR 1:65) 4 deWit chn.

10 PEEK deWIT circa 1674 (d 1741) m1 Jan 01 1698 Marytje Janse Vandenburgh (NYGBR 17:255); banns 01 Dec 1723, m2 21 Dec 1723 Maria Teunis/Deunies (DRCK:545) 6 chn.

11 TJERCK deWIT in his Pa's will was to receive 1/2 the home place & land after paying each of the others 1/12 shares. He was alive in 1687. By 1716/17 when Pro started he would possibly be at least 36 to 40. Andries' son Tjerck was 29. There seems to be no trace of him. Grandson Tjerck Probated Grampas' will.

12 MARRITJE deWIT m1 03 Nov 1700 Hendrick Hendricksen Kortreght j/o (DRCK:516) b & res Kingston, 1 ch.
     She m2 banns 06 Sep 1702 Jan Macklin/John MacLean (DRCK:516) b Scotland, 5 chn.

13 AEFJE deWIT d/o Ti(e)rck Claasz bp 14 Feb 1684 sp (uncle, aunt & hus) Lucas Andriesz, Cornelis Switz, Jannetie deWit (DRCK:20) as "Aagje" she m 23 Aug 1712 Jan Paling (sic) [DRCK:526] s/o Henry Pawling & Neeltje Roosa (Eefje, Aefje translate as Eva; the Dutch used "i" & "j" "f" & "g" interchangeably). In John Pawling's Will in Philadelphia Co PA his wife was Ephia, likely an English version of her name (NYGBR 17:254/5) 7 chn.

Notarial Papers 1 and 2, 1660-1696 p69,70 Power of attorney from Tjerck Claessen deWitt to Jan Albertsen. On this day, the 9th of June 1661, appeared before me, Dirck van Schelluyne, notary public and before the hereinafter named witnesses, Tjark Claesz deWith, husbandman, dwelling in the Esopus, who hereby constitutes and appoints Jan Albertsz, master shoemaker, his brother-in-law, who intends to go to Holland, his special attorney to demand, collect and receive from his other brother-in-law named Pieter Janz, dwelling at Oosterbmus in Oost Vrieslant, amicably, or if need be by means of judicial proceedings, such rents as said Pieter Jansz owes him for the use of a certain piece of land obtained by the principal on the death and decease of his late father; for receipts acquittance to grant and with said money to pay some of the principal's debts, as far as the amounts will reach; also to best advantage of the principal to lease the said land, preferably to his brother-in-law Pieter Jansz, if he desires it and is willing to pay as much rent as anyone else; and furthermore all things to do and to perform in this matter that may be needful and may seem advisable, the principal promising at all times to hold valid whatever by said attorney shall be done and performed in the premises without any contradiction, provided that the attorney be holden to make a proper return of his transactions and receipts. Thus done and executed in Beverwyck in New Netherlands, in the presence of Hendrick Jochemsz and Louwys Cobes, as witnesses hereto called.

                              Tierck Clasen Witt

Hendrick Jochemsz
Lodouicus Cobes
                       D. V. Schelluyne, Not. Pub. 1661

In these Notarial papers other transactions of interest on p 61/2,71,86,90 261/2

THE WILL OF TJERCK CLAESZEN DeWITT (OU 8:18/22)

(Contributed by George G DeWitt, translated from the Dutch).
(Spelling inserts from UCPR 1:56/7)
IN THE NAME OF THE LORD, AMEN
Be it known to every one of these, that on this fourth day of March in the year of our Lord one thousand six hundred and eighty seven I, the undersigned, Tjerck Clase DeWitt of Kingstowne in the county of Ulster, being sick of body but my mind remaining completely sound, the Lord be praised therefor, considering the shortness and frailty of man's life, the certainty of death, and the uncertainty of the hour of it, and being desirous to put all things in order, do make this, my last will and testament, in the form and manner hereafter written, now by these revoking, annulling and making naught all such testament or testaments, will or wills heretofore made or attempted to be made, by word or writing, and this alone shall be taken to be my last will and testament and otherwise none.

<u>Imprimis</u>. I commit my soul to God Almighty - my maker, and to Jesus Christ my Redeemer, and to the Holy One my Sanctifier, and my body to the earth from whence it came to be buried in a Christian like manner, and there to lie till that my soul and body shall be raised at the last day to enjoy the blessings of immortality which God in his mercy, through the sole merits of our Saviour, has promised and made known to all that sincerely, from the heart, believe in Him. And touching such temporal estate of land, houses, Negroes, goods, horses, beasts, debts, gold, silver coined and uncoined, etc. as it has pleased the Lord heretofore to lend to my use, I order, bequeath and dispose of it as follows: It is my will and desire that my wife Barbara remain in possession of the whole of my estate during her life, to have the same for her own use, and on the death of my said wife, the remainder of my estate, together with that which may be gained thereon and at the time accumulated, shall be distributed among my heirs as hereafter written.

<u>Item.</u>   I give to my eldest son, Andries DeWitt his assigns, heirs or administrators, the lawful one twelfth part of my whole estate, and that my aforesaid son, on the death of my said wife, shall have and possess for him and his assigns or heirs forever, the lawful half part of the land, houses, etc. belonging to me <u>provided</u> that the same shall be appraised by impartial persons, on oath, and that he pay to my other heirs thereout according to that which they shall be entitled to. Also as I have land in Kocksinck paid for, and since then a grant of the Government and Council of this province for a great part authorized, also, with a piece of land, (near the little Esopus, acquired in company with William De Meyer, which) (sic) of Kocksinck and Little Esopus, I have given to my aforesaid son and confirm, even without his being obliged to pay any money to my other heirs.

<u>Item.</u>   I give to my youngest son Tierck DeWitt or his assigns, heirs or administrators, the lawful twelfth part of my whole estate, and that my aforesaid son, on the death of my wife, shall have and posses for himself, his assignor heirs, forever, the lawful half of the lands, houses, etc. belonging to me upon the condition to bind himself to pay to my other heirs according to that which they shall be entitled to be paid thereout, to be appraised by impartial persons, on oath.

<u>Item.</u>   I give to my son John DeWitt or his assigns, heirs or administrators, the one twelfth part of my whole estate, in manner as above mentioned; Also that my said son, out of the money belonging to me, shall receive, for the purchase of land, five hundred bushels of wheat, without returning anything for it to my other heirs.

<u>Item.</u>   I give to my son Lucas DeWitt or his assigns, heirs or administrators, the lawful one-twelfth part of my whole estate, in the manner aforesaid. Also I built, during the last year, the half of a sloop, which sloop is and shall be the property of my said son or his assigns without his being obliged to return or pay anything to my other heirs.

<u>Item.</u>   I give to my son, Peek DeWitt or his assigns, heirs or administrators, the lawful one-twelfth part of my whole estate, in the manner aforesaid.

Item. I give to my daughter Tjaatje the wife of Mattys Mattysen, or her assigns, heirs or administrators, the lawful twelfth part of my whole estate, in the manner aforesaid.

Item. I give to my daughter, Jannetje wife of Cornelius Switz, the lawful twelfth part of my whole estate, with these conditions, that if my aforesaid daughter shall die without leaving any children, then all the said part shall be the property of my heirs, to be equally divided between them.

Item. I give to my daughter Gertruy or her assigns, the lawful twelfth part of my whole estate in manner aforesaid, to be held by my said daughter without paying anything for it to my heirs. [There is no mention of her hus Hendrick Schoonmaker].

Item. I give to my daughter Rachel or her assigns, or heirs the lawful part of my whole estate in the manner aforesaid, with the condition, that my said daughter's share shall be decreased one hundred pounds for the benefit of my heirs, which is what my daughter's husband, Cornelius Bogardus, owes me for the one-eighth of a brigantine, desiring however that the child of the said Bogardus, named Barbara, shall receive, out of the aforesaid one hundred pounds, fifty pieces of eight.

Item. I give to my daughter Marritje her assigns or heirs, the twelfth part of my whole estate in manner aforesaid.

Item. I give to my daughter Aaghe or her assigns or heirs, the lawful twelfth part of my whole estate in manner aforesaid.

Item. It is my will and desire, that if any of my heirs shall die before coming of age, then that those shares shall be equally divided among my heirs.

Item. I appoint my executrix of this my last will and testament, my aforesaid wife Barbara DeWitt.

Item. I desire that this my last will and testament shall be completely fulfilled and executed as thus made, at my house, the day and year above noted.

   TJERCK CLAESZEN DeWitt   L.S. (lawful signature)

Signed, sealed, and declared by Tjerck DeWitt this to be his last will and testament, in the presence of
                   JACOB RUTSEN
                   ABRAHAM LAMETER
                   WILLIAM DE MEYER

The certificate of Robert Hunter, Esqr. "Captain General and Governor Chief of ye Provinces of New York, New Jersey, and Territories depending thereon, in America, and Vice Admiral of the same. &c., sets forth, that on the 26th day of December, before William Nottingham, Gent'n, by me thereunto authorized, the last will and testament of Tjerck DeWitt, was proved, approve, and allowed by me, having, while he lived, and att ye time of his death, goods, chattels, and creditts, in divers places within this Province, and the administration of all and singular, ye goods, chattels and creditts of ye s'd Dec'd, & his will and testament, in any manner or way concerning the same, was granted unto Barbara DeWitt, ye executrix in ye s'd last will and test'm't named."
   In test Jany 26th, 1710.
(In the old Georgian calendar, the new year began in March.)

Dick Schemoes, j.p.

Note in this translation # 7 Jacob DeWitt is not listed. From the Genealogical Society of Utah, an abstract transcription by Louise Hasbrouck Zimm "Earliest Deeds of Ulster County NY, Liber BB 1688-1718" page 444 Jacob DeWitt of Rochester, yeoman, quitclaim unto [grandson] Tjerck DeWitt of Corp. K[ingston] yeoman, from all manner of action, etc. and demands whatsoever in Law and Equity, concerning what is due unto me by said Last will and testament of my father Tjerck Clasen DeWitt deceased, Except the 10 acres of land being part of my said father's farm which Tjerck DeWitt has this day Conveyed to me except my 1/12 part of the house in the Town of Kingston, which did belong to my father's Estate. (Signed) in Kingston 3 November 1716, Jacob DeWitt (mark). Wits: John Beatty, John Wood, Junr., W. Nottingham.

A letter to Mr John DeWitt.

"Your favor enclosing letters from my grandfather to the Hon Charles G DeWitt, and the letter from Mr Sutherland DeWitt (of Elmira NY) is received. The letters of my grandfather are of great interest to me as they were written in the office I now occupy. I have had copies made of the same, one of which I shall send to my father, George G DeWitt, who is living in Nyack, now in his eighty second year, and another I enclose to you." This letter discusses Dutch Heraldry and George's research overseas, indicating it's likely the American coat of Arms used by Sutherland DeWitt was done by an American sign painter who was commissioned by Andries DeWitt, but was the painter's invention probably using the Harlem Coat of Arms with his own additions. It is not registered in Dutch Heraldry. George invited Sutherland to call at his office or house #70 East 55th Street. In 1867 George travelled in Holland with "my uncle your cousin, Edward DeWitt who wkas my predecessor in this office . . . Since his death in 1872, I have taken up the same subject. I have been in Holland five times. " George says the Belgian or Antwerp Peter DeWittes came from Spain, the name being Candidus, Spanish for white. He found a North Holland family with another Coat of Arms different from the Dordrecht DeWitts. He said the DeWitt motto "of our branch of the family was `Fortis Et Fidus' (Strong and Faithful)". George places Esens as being "Essens where Krupp's gun factory is now located" not Esens, East Friesland, the reason his research was not successful. There is mention of much discussion with Thomas Evans who was working on compiling the DeWitt family. Evan's work was published in the New York Genealogical and Biographical Record as previously noted. He placed Tjerck's birth as the same year as John DeWitt, Grand Pensionary of Holland, which was 1625.

From a letter written 16 Jan 1890 by George G DeWitt, Law Office of
DeWitt, Lockman & DeWitt, #88 Nassau Street, New York (DG:317/9).

Tjerck DeWitt's stone house. The remolding changed its character.
There were three sections. The door was moved from left end to what is now the front.
It appears the upstairs may have been added with the first changes made possibly
when Andries DeWitt was killed by a falling beam.

Author Vona (DeWitt) Smith

Notes on Barbara Andriessen's family

ANDRIES LUYCASZEN b 1519 Fredrickstad, Denmark (NGSQ 57: 288) was a Skipper. His wife was Jannetje Sebyns. Deacons's Account Book at Albany states Jan Andiesz rented the large poll (shroud) for buriel of his mother 30 December 1676.

1. Geertuy Andriessenborn 1619 d 1682, "of Doesburg, Gelderland" arrived in the new world in 1642, w/o Hendrick Albersen alias Harry Alberts, b 1613 d 1648, an Englishman returning from Europe. He was Ferrymaster at Bevewyck (O'Callaghans' History of the New Netherlands). Geertruy m2 the next ferry master at Beverwyck, Jacob Jansen Stol (alias Slycoten, Slicoten) also from Doesburg & m 3 Aert Martensen Doorn of Wel, Doesburg , a tailor res in Albany.
2. Hendrick Andriessen/Dries/Driez b 1621, arrived with sister Gertrude. He m Maritje Dam, a widow, res in Albany.
3. Lucas/Luykas Andriessen , Skipper on the Hudson River, res in New Amsterdam m 20 Nov 1655 Aefje Laurens. Note the youngest child of Lucas' sister Barbara and Tjerck deWitt was bp Aefje [Eva].
4. Marritje Andriessen m in 1647 Jan Janz Breestede from Denmark.
5. Jan Andriessen b 1635 was a cooper at Albany& not to be confused with a reprobate Irishman called by the same name [really John Anderson].
6. Christian Andriessen appears in joint deeds with Lucas and Gertrude, d in the 2nd Esopus massacre 07 June 1663. "List of killed at Wildwyck . . Soldiers, Christian Andriessen, on the street" (DHSNY 4:42).
7. Barbara Andriessen b Amsterdam d 06July 1714 Hurley NYI in New Amsterdam m 24 Apr 1656 Tierck Claszen deWith (MRDNA:20).

NYGBR 62:148/9/274.   **Ulster County NY Tax Lists 25 March 1709/10**

"The Inhabitants Resident Sojourners and freeholder in ye County of ulster their Reall & personall Estates are rated & assessed by ye assessors Chosen for ye Same the 9th day of December 1709; and to pay at ye rate of four pence and three & a halfe farthing pr pound, towards paying the sd County's proportion in ye Six thousand pound Act viz:-"

	£ Pounds	Pounds	s	p	fl (farthing)
Anthony Tilba (Delva)	5	0	2	0	1 1/2
The Estate of Tjerck d'Witt	360	7	6	3	-
Barbara deWitt	25	0	10	1	3 1/2
Mattys Mattyse	100	2	0	7	2
Andries deWitt	180	3	13	1	2
Jacob deWitt	135	2	14	10	1/2

NYGBR 62:282   21 Feb 1711/12

The estate of Tjerck DeWitt	400	1	9	2	0

NYGBR 62:278/9   Ulster County Tax List

Andries de Witt	4 Chimnys & 3 slave		0	10
Jacob de Witt	2 fyreplaces & 1 slave		0	4

GENERATION 3

deWit

1.1.9 LUYCAS/LEUCAS/LUYKAS deWit m Annatje Delva

1. JANNETJE DeWIT * b 06 Mar 1697 (fr R N Bahl) bp 07 Mark 1697 Kingston sp (ma's half bro & sis) Jan Lesier, Rachel Lesier (DRCK:49) m 19 Sep 1717 Cornelis Langendyk (DRCK:533) s/o Pieter Janse Langendyk & Geertie Cornelis, bp 10 Jul 1693 in NYC (UCPR 1:66) res near Mt Marion NY.
2. BARBARA deWITT bp 12 Nov 1699 sp Tjerck deWit, Sara Roosekrans (DRCK:57). Barbara is not in Leucas' will in 1703 (UCPR 1:65) **dy.**
3. JAN deWIT bp 08 Dec 1700 sp (grprts) Tjerck Classe deWit, Barbara deWit (DRCK:60) m banns 26 Sep 1731 Ariaantje [Harriet] Oosterhout (DRCK:561) d/o Gysbert Oosterhout & Marretjen Bogaard, bp 09 Mar 1712 sp 'Tjerk Mathysz, Ariaantjen Oosterhout (DRCK:97; OFG:37) res Catskill T Greene Co NY.
4. LEUCAS/LUYCAS deWIT bp 05 Sep 1703 sp (uncle, aunt's hus, grma) Andries deWit, Cornelis Bogardus, Barbara deWit (DRCK:70) m 17 Jan 1729 Catrina/Catha Cathrina Roosa (DRCK:556) d/o Evert Rosa/Roosa & Tiet(je) Van Ette[n] bp Hurley NY 16 Sep 1709 sp Arien Roosa jr, Antje Roosa (DRCK:87). On the west side of the Plattekill across from the Peter Winnie grant, Luycas bought 51 acres 24 Feb 1728 (EHS:94). He is presumed to have built a house. Would it be the one, which was a stronghold in the Revo in the possession of his son Capt Jan/John DeWitt? It was a Dutch stone house, destroyed by fire in the 1980's. Antie Delva m2 banns 31 Mar 1706 Gerrit Bunschoten (DRCK:522). Gerritie/Geeretie Van Bunschoten bp 19 Jan 1707 sp Teunis Elias, Marretie van Bunschoten (DRCK:79). Antony Van Bunschooten bp 11 Sep 1709 sp Elias Van Bunschooten, Sarah Jansze (DRCK:85). Solomon Van Bunschoten bp 18 Nov 1711 sp Jan Lesier, Catalyntjen t'Broek (DRCK:96). Antjen Dulleva m3 26 Oct 1721 Hendrik Roosekrans (DRCK:540)

The court records for Ulster County present us with an interesting case but not the eventual disposition of it. "Meeting of the Justices, 27 Sept 1693 Catrina De Duyster charges that she is with child by Luycas deWitt and that he promised to marry her; he pleads not guilty; case is continued".

"Session for Ulster and Dutchess Counties, Mar 1693/4 Jacomyn Elting, midwife, swears that Catrina De Duyster said that Luycas DeWitt was the father of her child. As said Luycas is at present out of the province, his father Tjerck DeWitt is ordered to give bond that the child shall not be a burden to the parish" (NGSQ 61:276).
[We'll never know who swore the truth but chances of good child support were certainly better then than today, if a prosperous father was named].

Tjerck's Will 04 Mar 1687 left [this] Leucas 1/2 of a sloop he and Leucas built last year. "Luycas DeWitt appears to have been engaged in trade: The Record of a Bill of sale for the sloop St. Barbara, built in 1686, to Capt Daniel Hobart of Barbados for £200, is found in the Registers Office in the City of New York" (DG).

WILL OF LUYCAS (LEUCAS) DeWITT
dated Feb 15, 1702/3, and written in Dutch (UCPR 1:65/6)
(In the Old Georgian Calendar the New Year started with March. It was proved 22 days after it was written.)

My Eldest son Jan shall have, in advance, as his birth right, being my eldest son, when he reaches majority, out of the whole estate the sum of £5.

My wife Antie, shall have the just half of the residue in house, land, real and personal property, as well all that is coming to me from my father, as his testament will show.

My children, i.e., my son Jan and my daughter Jannetje, and my wife Antie, who is at present with child, shall have half (as before).

If my wife should remarry, she is to appoint guardians over the minors and to deliver to them one half part of the estate. If she remains unmarried she is to possess everything.

Signed by the testor.
TEUNNIS ELLISEN (his mark)
TEUNIS TAPPEN
JAN HEERMANS JUER
C BOGARDUS

(Cornelius Bogardus, Teunis Tappen, & Jan Heermans Junior, appeared before the Court, March 9/10, 1703/4 proving the will).

GENERATION 4

If a couple traces back to DeWitt ancestry more than once, m is {m} indicating this fact. Numbering used is the first parent chronologically. Both numbers are given but the one to be used in succeeding generations is underlined.

LANGENDYK

1.1.9.1 JANNETJEN deWITT m Cornelis Langendyk

1. GEERTRUY LANGENDYK b 22 Jun 1718 sp (ma's half bro) Jan Lesier, Calentyntjen ten Broeck (DRCK:122). In 1742 Geertje Langendyk & Peter Wenne Jr are sp for a Merkel ch's bp & in 1743 Geertje & Lucas Langendyk are sp for uncle Luykas deWit & Catrina Roosa's ch (DRCK:267).
2. LUCAS LANGENDYK bp 31 Mar 1723 sp Abraham Louw and his mother's half sister Jannetje LeSieur (DRRC:146) dy.
3. LUCAS LANGENDYK bp 07 Nov 1725 sp uncle & ma's half-sis Luycas deWit, Geeritjen Van Bunschooten (DRCK:159) & (tbstn b 17 Oct 1723 d 04 Apr 1797 ae 74 d 74-02-17) m 20 Apr 1756 Christina Woolven/Wulfin/Wolf (DRCK:610) b 25 Nov 1734 d 12 Jan 1806 ae 72-02-17 both bur Langendyk Cem (OGUC:264) res Mt Marion NY.
4. PETRUS LANGENDYK bp 30 Jun 1728 sp (ma's aunt) Johannes Wynkoop, Rachel Bogardus (DRCK:175) Will 05 Oct 1775 Pro 25 Oct 1784 (NYHSC 36:333) m 11 Nov 1765 Catharina Falkenburg at the Germantown DRC d/o Hieronymus Falkenburg/Van Valkenburg & Maria Elizabeth Mejer, bp 05 Jan 1741 sp Johannes Meher, Catharina Mejer (K&S:5 [Ft:113]) d after 1789. She m2 Jacobus Winne.
5. ANNETJE LANGENDYK b ca 1731, bp page is missing, as Annaatje m banns 02 Feb 1753 Arent/Arend Winne/Wenne (DRCK:606) s/o Pieter Winne jr & Antjen Markel bp 05 Sep 1725 sp Johannes Traphagen, Jannetje Pier (DRCK:158).
6. CATRINA LANGENDYK bp 02 Sep 1733 sp (ma's uncle) Peek deWit, Marytje Overpag (DRCK:198) m Lowy Balbon.
7. MARIA LANGENDYK bp 06 Jun 1736 sp Thomas Beekman, Judik Beekman (DRCK: 218) m Richard/Rutsert Borhans s/o Wilhelm Borhans/Burhans/Borrahans & Catharina Davenport, bp 09 Jun 1747 sp Rutsert Devenport, Johanna Devenport (K&S:11). So Richard is 11 years Maria's junior (BG:176,183,202).
8. JANNETJE LANGENDYK bp 19 Nov 1738 sp Broer Dekker, Marietje Lauresse (K&S:4) no marriage found. In 1755/57/60 Jannetje Langendyk, once with bro Lucas, twice with bro Petrus sp at bp of sis Annetje Langendyk & Arent Winne's chn (K&S:19,23,26).

Jannetjen (deWitt) Langendyk

GENERATION 5

If a couple traces back to DeWitt ancestry more than once, m is {m} indicating this fact. Numbering used is the first parent listed chronologically. Both numbers are given but the one to be used in succeeding generations is underlined.

LANGENDYK
1.1.9.1.3 LUCAS LANGENDYK m Christina Woolven/Wulfin/Wolf
1. CORNELIS LANGENDYK bp 26 Dec 1756 sp (pa's bro & sis) Petrus Langendyk, Maria Langendyk (K&S:22) dy.
2. CORNELIS LANGENDYCK bp 14 Sep 1758 sp (aunt & uncle) Petrus Langendyk, Maria Langendyk (K&S:24). Note names of prts and sp seem to be reversed by the minister according to records at the "Bronck House" Lib in Coxsackie, info from Marilyn K Walker of Saugerties NY (Cornelis b 27 Aug 1758 d 02 Sep 1838 ae 80-00-06 bur Langendyk Grd [OGUC:264]) m 13 Oct 1781 Johanna Wulfin/Wolven/Wolf both b res Saugerties (K&S:247). Cornelis served in the Revo.
3. JOHN LANGENDYK bp 26 Nov 1761 sp Jan Wulfin, wf Grietje Muller (K&S:28) res Kingston, j/o m banns (DRCK: 651) 02 May 1786 Maria Kernyrk b 1761 d/o Rynbeck d/o Hieronymus Carnryk/ Kernyk/Carenyk & Anna Fuhrer, (FT 3:26). On 06 Jul 1799 John Langendike, wf Maria Carnryke are on the CH membership list for Shokan (BRSRC:65). In Dec 1797 his pa left John "all realty at Chocan [Shokan]". John's Will refers to grchn John Elsworth, Maria Swarwout, dau Christina, grdau Mary Ann Burger. Exs: sons-in-law Peter Ekert, Henry Weeks (fr FSUHL).
4. MARIA LANGENDYK b 22 Sep 1764 bp 14 Oct 1764 Loonenburg, Greene Co (Athens) sp (her uncle & aunt) Petrus Langendyk, Maria Langendyk (NYGBR 84:93, MRAWC:124) m1 20 Feb 1783 James Ransom (K&S:248) of New England who d 05 Aug 1821 Greene Co (FT:79). James Ransom/Remson of Blue Mtn m2 05 Oct 1800 <u>1.1.9.1.5.1.3.</u> Catharina Winne (K&S:255) d/o Petrus Winne & m1 Maria Langendyk (indicated by bp sponsors & naming patterns; & fr BG:179). Catharina's chn are listed under her number.
5. LUCAS LANGENDYK bp 13 Jan 1768 sp Jan Brink, wf Gritjen Wolf (K&S:38) assumed dy.
6. LUCAS LANGENDYK bp 06 May 1771 sp Jan Brinck, wf Gritjen Wolf (K&S:45) m Lenah Schoonmaker/Schumacher; inherited his pa's Kingston T property. She m2 06 Jun 1816 Isaac Waldron (fr MWK).
- C LANGENDYK b 06 Dec 1773 d 12 Aug 1775 dy (OGUC:264).
7. ADAM LANGENDYK bp 09 Aug 1774 sp Adam Wolf, Maria Hommel (K&S:52) **dy.**
8. ADAM LANGENDYK bp 25 Apr 1777 sp Adam Bonloni, wf Gritje Brink (K&S:58) d 15 Jul 1798 ae 21 bur Langendyk cem (GIUC:2) **single**.

Lucas Langendeck, farmer, Kingston NY, Will 31 Jul 1797. Bequest to wife Christina with income from the estate for widowhood. To daughter Maria wife of James Remsen, furniture and all "my wife brought from her father" [not named]. To son John all realty at Chocan [Shocan], Lucas all realty in Kingston and balance of personality. Maintenance to son Adam. Exs: son Cornelius, son-in-law James Remson [Ransom]. Witnesses: Benjamin Snyder, Sara Brink, Hendricus Wynkoop of Town of Kingston. Probate: 04 Dec 1797 p45/6/7 (AWUCK Liber C:3).

LANGENDYK
1.1.9.1.4 PETRUS LANGENDYK m Catharina Falkenberg/Faleckenburg
1. CORNELIS P LANGENDYK bp 08 Apr 1766 sp (uncle & wf) Lucas Langendyk, wf Christina Wolf (K&S:36) & (d 17 Jul 1836) m banns 26 Jun 1788 Christina/Christeintje Snyder (DRCK:656) b 04 Feb 1767 d 1845 d/o Zachariah Snyder/Sneider/Schneider & Margaret Fiero. K&S:48 has Margrit d/o Zacharias Snyder & Margret Furo bp 13 Jul 1772 sp Willem Eeling & Margaret Spean. Her Will 27 Mar 1845 Pro 28 Apr 1845.
2. PETRUS LANGENDYK bp 13 Jan 1768 sp Johannes Valkenburg, (his aunt) Maria Langendyk (K&S:38) **dy.**
3. MARIA LANGENDYK bp 10 Apr 1769 sp Hieronymus Falkenburg, Lydia Falkenburg (K&S:41) m banns 18 Feb 1790 Jacobus Van Etten (DRCK:659).
4. PETRUS LANGENDYK bp 06 May 1771 sp (aunt & hus) Richard Borrhans, wf Maria Langendyk (K&S:45) m Sophia Schaart d/o Petrus Schaart/Short & Alida Edwards, b 01 Nov 1787 sp Hendrick Schaart, Sophia Sneider (K&S:86).
5. CATHARINA LANGENDYK b 16 Dec 1773 bp 20 Jan 1774 sp William Kockburn, wf Catharina Trombauer (K&S:50) **dy.**

Petrus Langendyck Will 05 Oct 1775 Pro 24 May 1784. Chn Cornelius ae 18, Petrus 15, Maria 14 & Petrus provided for "my sister-in-law Annetje's dau who lives with me". Exs: wf Catherine & bro-in-law Christian Valkenburg; among Wits: Petrus A Winne, Arent Winne, of Saugerties (NYHSC 36:333).

Catharina Valkenburg w/o Petrus Langendyk m2 08 Aug 1778 Jacobus Winne, jm, bp 09 Jan 1757 both of Katsbaan (DRCK:639) s/o Pieter Winne & Arriantje Van Etten, sp Jacobus Van Etten & wf Catharina Cool. Their chn were James b 1779, Catharina b 1781, Cobus & Ariantje b 1785. Catharina Valkenburg & Jacob Winne were sp/o her grson Petrus Langendyk bp 17 May 1789 s/o Cornelis Langendyk & Christientje Snyder (K&S:90).

Jannetjen (deWitt) Langendyk

WINNE
1.1.9.1.5 ANNAATJE LANGENDYK m Arent/Arend Winne/Wenne

1. PETRUS A WINNE bp 01 Jul 1753 sp (ma's bro & sis) Petrus Langendyk, Maria Langendyk (K&S:18) & (d 1801/2) m1 Annetje Du Boys b 29 Mar 1749; m2 31 Jul 1785 Catharina/Catrina/ Catharintje Borhans/Burhans both Ulster Co (K&S:250) d/o Willem Burhans & Catharine Davenport, b 12 Oct 1755 (BG:183). Winne Grd near Saxton NY lists a Petrus Winne b 1731 d 04 Jun 1801. One wonders, noting his Will, if the weathered stone was b 1751; Katy Winne d 1838 also bur there (OGUC:230).
2. JANNETJE/JANTJE WINNE/WENNE bp 31 Mar 1755 sp (aunt & uncle) Lucas Langendyk, Jannetje Langendyk (K&S:19) b/res at Kerkenland [Churchland] of Kingston m 29 Nov 1775 Hans/Johannes Markel/Merkel/Marcle (DRCK:634, UCPR 2:181).
3. CATHARINE WINNE bp 02 Oct 1757 sp (uncle & aunt) Petrus Langendyk, Jannetje Langendyk (K&S:23). She & bro Cornelis seem to be sp in 1780's for bro Petrus A's ch.
4. CORNELIS LANGENDYK WINNE bp 07 Apr 1760 sp (ma's bro & sis) Petrus Langendyk, Jannetje Langendyk (K&S:26). Cornelis & sis Catharina Winne are wits at bp as sp/o bro Peter's ch in 1780. This Cornelis is not traced. Butler's Rangers lists Sgt John Maracle & Cpl Carne Winney on the Loyalist (British) side (BR:117) in the Revo & a Cornelis & Arent Winne were on the American side. Cpl. Corn'ls Winney res Home District, Butler's Rangers, Stamped Book Niagara, S.P.L.N., 1786 (CSUC:276). One Peter Wynney, Cpl. King's Rangers is also recorded (CSUC:329).
5. ARENT/AREND/AARON WINNE bp 13 May 1672 sp Mathies Merkel, wf Margriet Keel (K&S:29) jm [young man] with a certificate m1 06 Jan 1788 Christeintje/Styntie/Christina Jong/Young jd [young woman] both r/o Kingston (DRCK:655) m2 Maria Bouck.
6. MARIA WINNE bp 08 Sep 1764 sp (ma's bro & sis) Petrus Langendyk, Maria Langendyk (K&S:32) m Peter Emrigh.
7. ANNATIEN WINNE bp 03 Aug 1768 sp Jacob Trumper, Annatien Trombauer (K&S:40) m Abraham Jonngh/Young.
8. GERTJEN/GEERTJE/CHARITY WINNE bp 26 Aug 1771 sp Frederich Rauh, wf Catharine Van Nette (K&S:46) {m} banns 05 May 1793 1.1.9.4.7.1 Hendrikus/Henricus Osterhout (DRCK: 665) Kingston s/o Jannetje DeWitt & Jacobus Osterhout bp 24 Oct 1770 sp Hendricus Mejer, Annetjen Osterhout (K&S: 44;OFG:18).
9. SARAH WINNE bp 09 Aug 1774 sp Willem Mejer wf Saartjen Nieuwkerk (K&S:52 & fr EBSD).

BALBON/BALDON
1.1.9.1.6 CATRINA LANGENDYK m Lowy Baldon

1. MARIA BALBON bp 10 Apr 1769 sp aunt Annetje Langendyk's & hus Arent Winne, & grma Jannetje DeWitt (K&S:40).

BURHANS
1.1.9.1.7 MARIA LANGENDYK m Richard/Rutsert Borhans/Burhans

1. CATHARINA BORHANS b 07 May 1768 bp 01 Jun 1769 sp Wilh Borhans, Catharina Davenport (K&S:41) & (d 16 Feb 1842 ae 73-09-09 bur with her two chn Schoub Grd between Saxton & Blue Mtn [OGUC:278]) m 03 Jun 1799 Lodewyck Schop/Schoub (K&S:254) b 28 Feb 1775 of Shandaken/Shandeca (7 yrs her jr) d 17 Sep 1860. He m2 Harriet Purdy, res Saugerties (BG:176,183,202).
2. JANNETJEN BORHANS bp 29 Oct 1771 sp Petrus Borrhans, wf Catharina Falkenburg (K&S:46) & (tbstn b 11 Aug 1769 d 18 May 1853 ae 83-09-07 [OGUC:278]) m 14 Jul 1798 William (H) Legg Jr (K&S:253) s/o Corneles Legg & Annatjen Osterhout, bp 09 Aug 1774 sp William Leg, wf Sarah Wolfen (K&S:53) & b 26 Aug 1774 d 10 Feb 1820 ae 45-05-15 both bur Mountain View Cem Saugerties (BG:176,183,202).
3. RICHARD BORHANS bp 25 Apr 1777 sp John Burhans, Catrintje Burhans (K&S:58 BG:183) ma would be 41; family statements say he d before 1798, single, Parents Richard & Maria appear as sp at a bp of a ch of Cobus Osterhoud & Jannetje DeWitt in 1781 & for Petrus A Winne & Catharina Borhans in 1786 but no more chn have been found for them. 1790 NY census p71 Kingston T Ulster, Richard Borhans 1-0-2-0-2. Explanation on next page.

Jannetjen (deWitt) Langendyk

GENERATION 6

If a couple traces back to DeWitt ancestry more than once, m is {m} indicating this fact. Numbering used is that of the first parent listed chronologically. Both numbers are given but the one to be used in succeeding generations is underlined.

1790 USA Census lists: Free white males over 16 including heads of families / Free white males under 16 / Free white females including heads of families / All other free persons / Slaves.

LANGENDYK

1.1.9.1.3..2 CORNELIS LANGENDK m Johanna Wolven/Wolf
1. CHRISTINA LANGENDYK bp 01 Jan 1783 sp (her grprts) Lucas Langendyk, Christina Wolven (K&S:71).
2. JAN LANGENDYK bp 04 Jul 1784 sp Hans Wolve, Marretie Brink (K&S:77). The History of Greene County says he was b 15 Jun 1784 d 24 Jan 1846 (HGC:442) as John of Plattekill m 18 Oct 1806 Elisabeth Dumond of Great Imbougt District (K&S:260) d/o Catharine Van Orden & John Baptist De Mond /Dumond Jr b 31 May 1789 bp 12 Jun 1789 sp David Dumond, Elizabeth Dumond (CDDGG:41, HGC:442) d 01 Jan 1864 [Catharine Dumond m2 Henry DeWitt 1.1.9.4.3.4, so he is Elizabeth's step-pa]).
3. MARIA LANGENDYK bp 26 Jun 1788 sp (aunt & hus) James Remsy/Ransom, wf Maria Langendyk (K&S:88) m Peter Wynkoop.
1790 NY Census Kingston Town, Ulster Co. p171 Cornelis Langendyk 1-2-2.

LANGENDYK

1.1.9.1.3.3 JOHN LANGENDYK m Maria Kernryk/Carenryk
1. ANNATJE LANGENDYK bp 12 Aug 1786 sp John Wolf, Regina Kernryk (K&S:83) m 08 Sep 1802 Peter Elsworth at The New Paltz Reformed CH res Shokan.
2. CHRISTINA LANGENDEK bp 19 Apr 1788 sp (grprts) Lucas Langendyk, Christina Wolf (K&S:87) at Marbletown, as Christianna m1 16 Nov 1809 Jonas Burger res Olive NY (MSRUC:214) m2 Peter de la Montange (fr MKW).
3. SARAH/SARA/SALLY LANGENDYK bp 08 Jan 1791 sp Johannes Carenrygh, Annatie Carenrygh (K&S:95) m 29 Oct 1809 Peter Eccert (MSRUC:214, fr MKW). On 11 Nov 1820 Sarah Longendike w/o Peter Ackert is on the CH membership list for Shokan (BRSRC:67).
4. JOEL LANGENDEK b 15 Feb 1793 (fr SFUHL) bp 10 Apr 1793 in Woodstock sp Petrus Kernryk, Margritje Krans (DRCK:440) d 16 Nov 1793 bur Shokan.
5. MARY/POLLY LANGENDYK b 19 Apr 1803 bp 01 May 1803 sp John Langendyk Jr & Mary Langendyk at Shokan (BRSRC:4) & (d 08 Jun 1870 ae 72-08-00) m 06 Dec 1839 Henry Weeks b 1793 in 1855, State Census, res Olive NY d 1896 bur Shokan (fr FSHUL).

RANSOM

1.1.9.1.3.4 MARIA LANGENDYK m James Ransom
1. SARY/SARA/SALLY Ransum bp 22 Nov 1783 sp (uncle) John Langedyk (sic) & Sara Ransum (K&S:75) m Job Gillespie.
2. JOSEPH RANSOM bp 18 Jun 1786 sp Joseph Ransom, Lydia Ransom (K&S:83) as Joseph Remsen of Blue Mtn m 27 Apr 1806 Elizabeth/Elisabet Snyder/Sneider (K&S:259). Ulster Co Gen So Pub 1:14 02 Jul 1988 Item: 30 Apr 1853 Saugerties Telegraph. Mrs Elizabeth Ransom d 24 Apr 1853 Malden of Dropsy in her 70th yr ae 69-06-13 (OCUC:287).
3. CHRISTINA RANSOM/RENSEN bp 17 May 1789 sp (grprts) Lucas Langendek, Christintje Langendek (K&S:90) & (d 1860 ae 70-08-00) m 08 Feb 1807 Levi Meier/Meyer/Myer (DRCK:680) both of Kingston (DRCK:680, [later of Durham T Greene Co]) b 07 Mar 1777 d 17 Dec 1860 ae 70-03-19 bur Blue Mtn Cem Saugerties T (OGUC:245; BG:47,192).
4. JAMES RAMSON bp 27 Feb 1792 sp (uncle) Cornelius Langendek, Jannetje Burhans (DRCK:435) & (Pro 30 Apr 1855) m 11 Jun 1815 Leah Valkenburg/ Valk.
5. MARIA RANSOM b 08 Apr 1795 bp 10 May 1795 sp (uncle & wf) Lucas Langendyk, Lena Schoenmaker (K&S:108) & (d 07 Apr 1854 ae 59) m as Polly Remsen 29 Dec 1824 Christian A Fiero at Saugerties (K&S:273) s/o Abraham Firo & Sarah Rechtmeyer, b 27 May 1795 bp 28 Jun 1795 sp Coenrad Rechtmeyer, Maria Firo (K&S:109) d 23 Apr 1841 ae 45-10-43 both bur Katsbaan Cem (OGUC:282).
6. CATHARINA/CATY RANSOM /RAMSAY b 22 Feb 1798 bp 10 Mar 1798 sp Pieter J [?A] Winne, & Catharina Borhans (K&S:120) as Caty m 15 Oct 1818 Tjerk/Dirk Osterhout both/o Saugerties (K&S:268) Osterhout family in the Ulster Co Gen So (OUCGS:25) has Dirk bp 1769 m 1818 Catharina Ransom. The Commemorative Biographical Record of Ulster County say he was b 1793 (CBRUC:1132). He was probably Tjerck b 29 Sept 1793 s/o Teunis Osterhoud & Maritje Louw. As Dirk he m 1818 Cath Ransom.

James Rensen/Ransom m2 1.1.9.1.5.1.3 CATHARINA WINNE – note Catharina's children numbering
1. 1.1.9.1.5.1.3.1 PETRUS RENSON b 05 May 1801 bp 14 May 1801 sp Cornelis Winne, Annetje Borhans (K&S:134).
2. 1.1.9.1.5.1.3.2 ANNATJE REMSEN b 18 Feb 1803 bp 10 Apr 1803 sp Peter P Winne, Catharina Winne (K&S:141).
3. 1.1.9.1.5.1.3.3 LUCAS LANGENDYK REMSEN b 05 Mar 1805 bp 28 Apr 1805 no sp (K&S:148).

Jannetjen (deWitt) Langendyk

THE DIFFERENT NUMBERING IS BECAUSE THE LINE OF DESCENT IS THROUGH CATHARINE WINNE

Jeremiah Remsen married 08 May 1808 Jane Wells both Blue Mountain (K&S:261). <u>The Burhans Genealogy</u> says James Ransom married 3rd Jantje Wells (BG:179) daughter of Hendricus Wells and Margrieta Burhans. 6 chn of this union are traced (BG:179,183). They are listed here to help distinguish them from Ransom offspring who are DeWitt descendants (FT:80). John Henry Ransom born 1809, Samuel Wells Ransom 1812, Zackariah Backer Ransom 1814, David Ransom 1816, Margaret Remson (sic) 1819, Jane Ransom 1821. Note: of the 2nd family Annatje & Lucas are not in the will, perhaps dy.

James Ransom of Durham Town, Greene County NY, Probate 23 Nov 1821. Heirs: wife, chn <u>Sarah, Christina, James, Mary, Caty, Peter,</u> John, Samuel, Zacharia, David, Margaret, Joseph and embryo (sic) yet unborn. Mary w/o Joel Fiero, Caty w/o Tyark Osterhout. Exs: John Wells, Levi Meyer, Tjark Osterhout, Wits: Peter A Snider, Hannah Snyder, John Wells (AWGNY 1:23).

LANGENDYK
1.1.9.1.3.6 LUKAS LANGENDYK m Lenah Schoonmaker/Schumacher
1. LUKAS LANGENDYK bp 08 Jan 1792 sp (grprts) Lucas Langendyk, Christintje Wolfen (K&S:98) m 16 Apr 1815 Annetje Schoonmaker, both Saugerties (K&S:264; fr MKW).
2. CATHARINA LANGENDYK b 11 Nov 1806 bp 28 Feb 1813 sp Hendrick Wolven, Catharina Schumacher (K&S:171).
3. MARGARETTA LANGENDYK b 14 Mar 1810 bp 28 Feb 1813 sp (pa's cousin & wf) Jan Langendyk, Elizabeth Dumont (K&S:171).
4. PETRUS P LANGENDYK b 02 Oct 1812 bp 28 Feb 1813 sp Wilhelmus Emerick, Margaret Schoonmaker (K&S:171) {m} 03 Jan 1833 Catharine Decker <u>1.1.9.4.1.2.1</u> b 03 Apr 1814 d/o Annetje Langendyke & John Decker d 06 Apr 1874 ae 60-00-03 bur Pine Grove Cem about 4 miles west of Saugerties Village (GIUC:9; fr MKW).

LANGENDYK
1.1.9.1.4.1 CORNELIS P LANGENDYK m Christina/Christeintje Snyder/Sneider/Schneider
1. PETRUS LANGENDEK bp 17 May 1789 sp (grma & 2nd hus) Jacobus Wenne, Catharina Falkenberg. He was alive in 1845. Did Petrus marry?
2. ANNATJE/HANNAH LANGENDYK/LANNANDICK bp 14 May 1791 sp Isaak Post, Catharina Sneider (K&S:95) & (d 18 Jun 1862 ae 72-02-15) m John I Decker b 13 Dec 1783 d 29 Aug 1851 ae 67-08-16 both bur Pine Grove, Saugerties T (GIUC:8; WHS).
3. MARGRITJE/MARGARETTA LANGENDYK bp 04 May 1793 sp (uncle) Petrus Langendyk, Margritje Sneider (K&S:100) m Isaac Decker (fr MKW).
4. ZACHARIAS LANGENDYK b 13 Mar 1796 bp 10 Apr 1796 sp Izaak Snyder, Zusanna Kern (K&S:112) m1 Anna Hogan; m2 Barbara Ann & res Woodstock NY (fr MKW)
5. JAMES LANGENDYK b 13 May 1798 bp 03 Jun 1798 sp (aunt & hus) Jacobus Van Etten, Maria Langendyk (K&S:121) & (d 16 Mar 1878) m 19 Feb 1817 Sarah/Sally Burhans b 04 Dec 1797 d ? Aug 1845 (K&S:266) d/o Tjerck Burhans & Catharine Dederik, both bur Mt Marion Cem (BG:37 & fr MKW).
6. CORNELIS S LANGENDYK b 15 Nov 1800 bp 01 Jan 1801 sp Joseph Miller, Catharina Fero (K&S:132) & (bur Mt Marion Com Cem as b 16 Dec 1800 (d 09 Mar 1832 ae 31-03-24) m Mary A Blackwell d/o William Blackwell & Christina Doll, b 11 Apr 1803 d 16 Jan 1875 (BG:54, fr MKW).
7. CATY/CATHARINE LANGENDYK b 08 Aug 1803 m 26 Sep 1819 John P Winne both/o Saugerties (K&S:268) ma's Will says she m a Winne.

Will of Christine Langendyke (p316/21) 27 Mar 1845 Pro 28 Apr 1845 mentions Peter Longendyke, Annatie w/o John Decker, Peter A Winne of the T/of Saugerties, Zachariah Longendyke of Woodstock, James Longendyke T/of Kingston, Peggy wf/o Isaac Decker, guardian of William S Longendyke & Cornelius E Longendyke, minors of the T/of Kingston and George Winne, Christina Margaret Winne, Angeline Winne, Silas Winne, John Winne, Hannah Winne all minors res in Saugerties, being kin of the late Christine Langendyke of Saugerties, summoned to appear 17, March 1845. Will p319 says grandsons William Snyder Langendike & Cornelius Edgar Langendike are s/o Cornelius S Langendike, dec. Clothing to Blandina Decker d/o Isaac Decker & my 3 daus Peggy, Caty, Annatje. Will presented 28 Apr 1845 Exs: Levi Blackwell, Jeremiah Russel.

VAN ETTEN
1.1.9.1.4.3 MARIA LANGENDYK m Jacobus Van Etten
1. MARIA VAN ETTEN bp 24 Oct 1790 sp John Van Etten, Maria Van Etten (K&S:94) m William Emory.

LANGENDYK
1.1.9.1.4.4 PETRUS LANGENDYK m Sophia Schaart
1. PETER LANGENDECK bp 22 Aug 1804 sp Peter Miller, Annatje Schaart (DRCK:481) m 23 Apr 1821 Maria Plass b 1805 (fr NY 1855 Census; BG:88,145).

Jannetjen (deWitt) Langendyk

WINNE
1.1.9.1.5.1 PETRUS A WINNE m1 Annatje Du Boys/Dubois
1. ANNATJEN WENNEN/WINNE bp 20 Aug 1770 sp (grprts) Arend Wennen, wf Annatjen Langendyk (K&S:43) both res under the jurisdiction of Kingston m banns 21 Jan 1787 Wilhelmus Burhans/Borhans (DRCK:653) s/o William Burhans & Catharine Davenport, bp 25 Jun 1765 (K&S: 34; BG:176). William Burhan's sis, Catharine, m as his 2nd wf Petrus A Winne, Annetjen's father; bro Richard Burhans m Petrus A Winne's aunt Maria Langendyke (BG:176).
2. CHRISTINA WENNE bp 02 Feb 1773 sp (grprts) Lucas Langendyk, Christina Wolf, not in pa's will (K&S:48) presumed **dy**.
3. CATHARINA WINNE bp 10 May 1775 sp (pa's uncle & wf) Petrus Langendyk, Catharina Falkenberg (K&S:54). Catharina, as his 2nd wf, m 05 Oct 1800 James Remsen/Ransom of Blue Mtn (K&S:255) wd/o Maria Langendyk (1.1.9.1.3.3).
4. PETRUS WINNE bp 23 Nov 1777 sp William Tembord, Marteitje Duboys (K&S:59) alive in 1802.
5. JANNETJE WINNE bp 1778 Loonenburgh (Athens NY) dy.
6. CORNELIS WENNIE bp 07 May 1780 sp (uncle & aunt) Cornelis Wenne, Catharina Wenne (K&S:64) (d ae 23).

m2 Catharina/Catrina/Catharintje Burhans/Borhans

7. MARIA WINNE bp 26 Feb 1786 sp (ma's bro & pa's aunt) Richard Borhans, Maria Langendyk (K&S:82) **presumed dy.**
8. JANNETJE/JANE WENNE bp 28 Jun 1787 sp John Burhans (her aunt) Maria Wenne (K&S:85) at Saugerties m 24 Apr 1808 John Emmerich/Emerick (K&S:261) s/o Peter Emmerich & Maria Wolven. This family is said to have moved to Auburn NY (BG:183,204; FT 7:35).
9. SARAH WINNER/WINNE b 21 Oct 1788 bp 21 Jun 1789 sp (grprts) Arent Winner, (sic) Annatje Langendyk (K&S:91; BG:183) **presumed dy.**
10. AARON WINNE bp 20 Jun 1791 sp (uncle & wf) Aaron Winne Jr Catharina Yong (K&S:96) m Polly Curtis (BG:183/4,204).
11. WILLIAM WINNE b 03 Aug 1794 bp 17 Aug 1794 sp Samuel Borhans, wf Catharina Beer (K&S:105) & (d 28 Nov 1879 [OGUC:279 as 1794-1878]) m Mary C Eligh d/o William Eligh & Maria Bair, b 07 Oct 1810 bp 17 Nov 1810 sp Samuel Burhans & Catharina Beer (K&S:163) d 08 Jan 1845 bur Winne Family Cem, Adam Wolven farm, Saxton book recorded 1930 (BG:184; OGUC:279).
12. JOHANNES WINNE b 03 Nov 1796 bp 04 Dec 1796 sp Johannes Markel, Margaritha Winne (K&S:115) not in the Will, **presumed dy.**

Petrus Winne's Will dated 27 Dec 1800 Pro 26 Apr 1802 mentions his ma Annetje, names of his first family, Annetje, Peter, Cornelius, Catharine, w/o James Ransom & their chn, Arent, William, Jannetje, grchn Marytje & Annatje Burhans. Property divided among his 7 chn. Maria would have been 16, Sarah 14, Johannes 6 when the will was Pro & are not mentioned; presumed deceased.

MERKEL
1.1.9.1.5.2 JANNETJE WINNE m Johannes/Hans Merkel
1. ANNATJE MERKEL bp 06 Sep 1777 sp (grprts) Arent Winne, wf Annatje Langendyk (K&S:59).

After the American Revolution:
On 28 June 1785 a session of the Court of Oyer and Terminer and General Goel Delivery for Ulster County N.Y., opened at Kingston with Robert Yates, a Justice of the Supreme Court and (five named) Commissioners on the Bench and twenty-two Grand Jurors. The Grand Jury brought in indictments of misprision of treason against the following: Luke Dederick, John Merkell, Cornelius I Winne, Peter J Winne and Peter P Winne and others. On 06 Jul 1785 they were ordered to give bail £300 each and each £150 for their appearance at the next court (NGQ 61:61).
(Merriam-Webster Pocket Dictionary: "misprision - misconduct or corrupt administration especially by a public official"). It must have held a different meaning under that Court.

The Treaty of Paris 3 Sept 1783 signed by John Adams, Benjamin Franklin, and John Jay, recommended to Congress the return of rights and property of the Americans who were losers in the war. The treaty was ignored and Loyalists were denied property rights and imprisoned. The people listed above had returned to the USA to take their families back to Canada. In the American Revolution the property of Loyalists was confiscated; they had no rights whatsoever. They could be beaten, murdered, their assets stolen.

Butler's Rangers lists Sgt John Marcale & Cpl Corn Winney on the Loyalist side in the Revo & a Cornelis & Arent Winne were on the American side. Cpl Corn'ls Winney resided Home District (ON), Butlers Rangers, Stamped Book Niagara, S.P.L.N., 1786 (CSUC:276). Peter Winney, Cpl. King's Rangers (CSUC:329) identification welcomed.

Jannetjen (deWitt) Langendyk

WINNE
1.1.9.1.5.5 ARENT/AARON WINNE Jr m1 Christeintje/Styntie/Christina Jong/Young
1. HANNAH WINNE b 07 Jan 1793 (d 05 Nov 1831) m 18 Mar 1809 Hendrikus Burhans b 18 May 1789 d Burlington IA 10 Feb 1878 (BG:105;180,194). He m2 24 Nov 1834 Mary Bouck wd/o Peter Burhans.
2. SEFEYA WINNE bp 06 Feb 1790 Catskill Ref Low Dutch CH d/o Arondt (sic) sp (aunt Maria's hus) Petrus Emrigh, Mareytje Jongh (NYGBR 86:222) **dy.**
3. SARAH WINNA b 13 Feb 1795 bp 22 Feb 1795 Durham sp Jeremiah Jongh, Annatie Winna (RDCOH:3) m 28 May 1813 Josiah Dutcher (RDCOH:47).
4. SAPHIA/SOPHIA WINNE b 30 Jan 1798 bp 03 Feb 1798 sp (aunt's hus) Peter Emerich, Maria Young (RDCOH:7) m 22 Jan 1815 Henry Knoll (RDCOH: 47) Oak Hill, Durham T Greene Co NY.
5. JANE WINNE b 22 Apr 1800 bp 25 May 1800 sp Peter Beck, Elizabeth Young (RDCOH:11) m 09 Nov 1816 Stephen Sprigs (RDCOH:47).

m2 24 May 1834 Maria Bouck wd/of Peter Bunker

EMRIGH
1.1.9.1.5.6 MARIA WINNE m PETRUS Emrigh
1. MARIA EMRIGH bp 29 Feb 1788 Catskill sp (uncle & wf) Arent Winne, Christeyntje Winne (CDGGC:39). Did Maria Winne d after one ch or did they just move?

JONNGH/YOUNG
1.1.9.1.5.7 ANNATIEN/HANNAH WENNE m Abraham Jonngh/Young
1. PETER JONNGH b 20 Jun 1795 bp 11/12 Jul 1795 sp Peter Becker, Elizabeth Jonngh (DRCOH:4).
2. HOSEA YOUNG b 30 Jan 1798 bp 03 Feb 1798 sp (aunt & hus) Hendrick Oosterhoudt, Geertie Winna (RDCOH:7).
3. CORNELIUS YOUNG b 21 Feb 1800 bp 13 Apr 1800 no sp (RDCOH:11)
4. JONAS YOUNG b 20 Mar 1803 bp 29 May 1803 no sp (RDCOH:16).
5. MARIA YOUNG b 07 May 1805 bp 25 May 2805 no sp (RDCOH:20).
6. HANNAH YOUNG b 25 Jan 1812 bp 23 Feb 1812 (RDCOH:34).

OSTERHOUT
1.1.9.1.5.8 GERTJEN/CHARITY WINNE {m} Hendrikus Oosterhoudt
1. ANNATJE OSTERHOUD b 29 Oct 1793 bp 10 Nov 1793 sp (grprts) Arent Winne & Annatje Langendyk (K&S:103) ma Geertje Wenne.
2. JANE OSTERHOUT b 29 Apr 1795 bp 14 Jun 1795 sp (aunt & hus) Abrm Jonngh, Annatie Vinne/Winne (sic [RDCOH:3, CH rec p42]) ma Geertie Vinne.
3. JAMES OOSTERHOUDT b 08 Mar 1797 bp 28 May 1797 sp (uncle & wf) Aaron Winna, Tyne (Christina) Young (RDCOH:6, CH rec p47) ma as Geertie Winna.
4. PETER OOSTERHOUDT b 17 Jan 1799 bp 10 Feb 1799 sp (uncle) James Oosterhoudt, Maria Young (RDCOH:9, CH rec p54) ma as Charity Winna.
5. CORNELIS OSTERHOUT b 11 Dec 1801 bp 07 Feb 1802 sp (uncle & aunt) Cornelis Winne, Catharina Winne (K&S:136) ma as Geertje Winne.
6. SARAH OSTERHOUT b 29 Sep 1803 bp 04 Dec 1803 no sp (RDCOH:18) ma as Charity Winna.
7. SOPHIA OSTERHOUT b 15 Jul 1805 bp 08 Sep 1805 no sp (RDCOH: 20, CH p76) ma as Charity Winna.
8. HENDRICK OSTERHOUT b 09 May 1807 bp 17 Mar 1807 no sp (RDCOH:24, CH p83) ma Charity.
9. TINE OSTERHOUT b 21 May 1809 bp 23 Jul 1809 no sp (RDCOH:28).
10. CHARITY CATHARINE OSTERHOUT b 31 Dec 1810 bp 21 Apr 1810 no sp (RDCOH:32) ma Charity Winne. Transcript in Salt Lake Library copied from page 98 of the Records of the Reformed Dutch Church in Oak Hill, Durham Town NY) There are the occasional birth/baptismal errors in the minister's records or in copying. Hank Jones, Palatine authority says <u>Geertje translates as Charity</u>.

<u>Osterhout Family Genealogy</u>, origin not recorded, bought by the author from the Ulster County Genealogical Society, lists DeWitt Osterhout & wf Elizabeth Monk & 5 chn. 3 chn with the same names on that list were bp at Oak Hill belonging to Hendricus Osterhout & wife Geertjen/Charity Winne. The bp 23 Feb 1786 of a Marretie at Katsbann is a ch/o Benjamin Osterhout. Perhaps Henry was nicknamed "DeWitt" causing some of the confusion. Hendricus res in Saugerties T Ulster County NY then Oak Hill Durham T Greene Co NY.

SCHOOP
1.1.9.1.7.1 CATHARINA BORHANS m Lodewyck/Ludewick Schop/Shop/Shoub
1. RITCHART BORHANS SCHOP b 27 Jul 1799 bp 08 Sep 1799 sp Lodewyk Schop (grma) Maria Langendyk (K&S:127) & (d 15 Mar 1810 ae 10-09-00) **dy.**
2. JAN LODOWYCK SCHOP b 26 Dec 1802 bp 08 Feb 1803 sp (uncle) Jan Langendyk, Sara Remson (K&S:140) d 30 Jun 1862.
3. PETRUS POST SHOP/SCHOP/SHOUB b 15 May 1806 bp 21 Aug 1806 sp Peter J Post, Maria McKensie (DRCK:488) & (d 04 Jul 1849 ae 43-01-19) both Saugerties m 26 Dec 1835 Susanna Valk/Falk/Valck, Wits: John A Valk/Falk,

Jannetjen (deWitt) Langendyk

   Catharine Mouer (K&S:281). Susanna was d/o Jacob Valk & Nellie Osterhoudt b 16 Oct 1820 d 16 Mar 1880 ae 59-05-00 (BG:202,303).
4 MARIA CHRISTINA SCHOP b 03 Feb 1809 bp 26 Mar 1809 sp (aunt & hus) William Legg, Jannetje Burhans (K&S:157) d 15 Jun 1810 ae 00-05-13 **dy.**

LEGG

1.1.9.1.7.2 JANNETJEN BORHANS m William H Legg

1 RICHARD BORHANS LEGG b 30 Nov 1798 bp 09 Dec 1798 sp Samuel Legg & (aunt) Catharina Borhans (K&S:124) & (d 06 Jun 1858 ae 59-07-07 [OGUC:236]) He m Abigail Scribner d/o Chauncy Scribner b 16 Aug 1803 d 21 Aug 1867 both bur Mountain View Cem (BG:202/3; FT:56).
2 CORNELIS W LEGG b 09 Sep 1802 bp 03 Oct 1802 no sp (K&S: 138) d 11 Aug 1882 **single.**
3 WILLIAM HENRY LEGG b 07 Feb 1809 bp 26 Mar 1809 sp Hendrick Legg, Jannetje Rust (K&S:157) & d 29 Aug 1864 ae 54-06-22 bur Shoub Family Grd between Saxton & Blue Mountain (OGUC:278) **single.**

Jannetjen (deWitt) Langendyk

GENERATION 7

LANGENDYK

1.1.9.1.3.2.2 JAN/JOHN LANGENDYCK m Elizabeth Dumond
1. CORNELIUS LANGENDYCK b 11 May 1808 bp 25 May 1808 no sp (K&S:155) & (d 09 Dec 1885 in NYC of smallpox [GIUC:2]) m1 20 Dec 1827 Jane A Dumont d/o Jacobus Dumont & Johanna Ostrander b 01 Jan 1805 and they resided Imbought Dist. d 27 Apr 1848 ae 43-01-27 in child birth of toxemia. Jane was adm to Plattekill RDC 4 Sep 1846 on cert fr Flatbush. (PRDC 1:70) Cornelius of Plattekill m2 26 Apr 1851 Jane (Carnright) Schoonmaker of Saugarties by Rev R A Chalk (ST) b 1817 wd/o John Schoonmaker; their chn William, Elizabeth, John (PRCFU:27; fr MKW).
2. MARGARETTA LONGENDYKE b 14 Mar 1810 * m Teunis Van Gaasbeck.
3. ELIZABETH OSTERHOUT LANGENDYCK b 10 Aug 1811 bp Aug 1811 sp aunt & hus Hendrick DeWitt & Catharina Dumont (K&S:165) (bur Tonger Cem Olive Town NY) m Isaac Trowbridge (fr MKW).
4. CATY/CATHARINE LANGENDYCK b 1812 (d 13 Jun 1886 bur Catskill) m Andrew Ackert b 1807 Dutchess Co NY. Caty joined the Plattekill CH adm cer fr Flatbush 07 Dec 1838 dis 10 Jul 1865 to Catskill (PRDC:74).
5. HENRY LANGENDYCK b 16 Feb 1816 bp 20 Mar 1816 no sp (K&S:182) & (d 08 Oct 1890 [OGUC:252]) m Cornelia Post d/o Peter Post & Jane Myer, b 13 Jul 1816 d 13 Jan 1882 both bur Mt Marion Com (Plattekill Cem) Henry's adm (to Plattekill DRC) 07 Dec 1838 on cert fr Flatbush, dis to RDC Catskill read m 15 Dec 1844 cert fr Catskill (PRDC:74).
6. JOHN LANGENDYCK Jr b 08 Mar 1818 & (d 28 Dec 1878 bur Catskill Cem) Ulster Co landowner, farmer & a dentist res Greene Co (census 1855) m Eliz Ann Sax both Ulster d/o Benjamin Sax & Margaret Hover b 17 Feb 1825 bp 04 Sep 1825 (CDDGG:97) d 29 Mar 1896 bur Catskill Cem (fr MKW). Benjamin Sax's will proved 24 Jun 1876 names dau Elizabeth w/o John Langendyck (AWGNY 2:91; NYDCG:148)).
7. JOANNA LANGENDYCK b 28 May 1820 (RDCFU:15) d 05 Dec 1896 bur Catskill Cem as was Christina & Jane.
8. CHRISTINA MARIA LANGENDYCK b 28 Nov 1823 d 20 Feb 1909.
9. JANE ELIZABETH LANGENDYCK b 05 Jun 1826 (d 15 Feb 1897).
10. MARGARET ANN LANGENDYCK b 04 Jun 1829 (RDCFU:25) m John H Post s/o Peter Post & Sarah Grant, b 1829 d 20 Jan 1882.
11. SARAH RACHEL LANGENDYCK b 09 Dec 1831 (RDCFU:28) d 22 Jun 1863 ae 31.

John Langendyck of Catskill Pro 09 Mar 1846. Heirs: wf Elizabeth, sons Cornelius, Henry & John Jr, dau Margaret Ann, Sarah Rachel, Joanna, Christina Maria, Jane Elizabeth, Caty wf/o Andrew Acker. Exs: wife Elizabeth and son John. Wits: James Powers, Abel Brace and Benjamin Sax (AWGNY 1:75).

Catherine Ackert of Catskill Pro 04 Oct 1886. Heirs: Joanna Longendyke, niece Christina/Tiny. Ex: Joanna Longendyke; Wits: J A Griswold & Irving Osborn both of Catskill (AWGC 1:blurred)

Joanna Longendyke of Catskill Pro 08 Feb 1897. Heirs: sis Mary A Post, Jane E & Christina M Longendyke. Exs: Jane E & Christina Longendyke; Wits: W I & Annie C Jennings of Catskill. Jane E Longendyke of Catskill Pro 10 Jan 1898. Heir: sis Christina M Longendyke; Wits: W I Jennings & Emory Chase of Catskill.

ELSWORTH

1.1.9.1.3.3.1 ANNETJE LANGENDYK m Peter Elsworth
1. JOHN LANGENDYK ELSWORTH b 16 Jan 1804 bp 19 Feb 1804 Shokan sp (grprts) John Langendyk & Mary Kernryk (BRSRC:5).
2. MARIA ELSWORTH b 16 Jan 1807 bp 30 Mar 1807 sp Theophilus Elsworth, Maria Wiest (BRSCR:6) m Swartwout (John Langendyk's will).

BURGER/de la MONTANGE

1.1.9.1.3.3.2 CHRISTINA/CHRISTIAANA LANGENDYK/LANGENDEK m1 Jones Burger.
1. SALLY BURGHER b 14 Jun 1815 bp 06 Sep 1819 Shokan (BRSRC:16).
2. ELIZA BURGHER b 1818 m Peter W Lane b 1816 (fr FSUHL).
   m2 Peter de la Montange

ECKERT/ACKERT

1.1.9.1.3.3.3 SARAH/SALLY LANGENDYK/LONGENDIKE/LONGENDYCE/LONENDYKE m Peter Eckert/Eccert
1. JOHN LANGENDYK ECKERT b 13 Mar 1811 bp 09 Jun 1811 Shokan sp John Langendyk, Mary Kernryk at Shokan (BRSRC:10) (d 25 Sep 1850 ae 39-06- 00).
2. MARIA ACKERT b 04 Jun 1817 bp 03 Aug 1817 (BRSRC:14) m Jacob Bush. CH membership list Jacob Bush & wf Maria Eckert removed from Shokan 24 Mar 1855 (BRSRC:70)
3. ISAAC DAVIS ACKERT b 12 Jun 1821 bp 19 Jul 1821 (BRSRC:17) m 09 Jun 1847 Sarah Ann Dubois b 1825. (There was an older man in the same area & same name)

Jannetjen (deWitt) Langendyk

4   NEHEMIAH SMITH ECKERT b 28 Nov 1827 bp 22 Jun 1828 (BRSRC:18) not in 1860 NY census index.
5   SARAH JANE ECKERT b 15 Mar 1832 bp 01 Jul 1832 (BRSRC:18) m John Bryn b 1832 (fr MKW).

WEEKS

1.1.9.1.3.3.5 MARY/POLLY LONGENDYCK m Henry Weeks

1   JOHN J WEEKS b 1834.
2   JENNE WEEKS b 1837.
3   HENRY J WEEKS b 1840.
4   PRISCILLA J WEEKS b 1842.
5   FRANCES WEEKS b 1847 (fr MKW).

GILLESPIE

1.1.9.1.3.4.1 SARY/SARA/SALLY RANSOM/RAMSON/RANSEM/REMSEY m Job Gillespie

1   MARG/MARGARET SUSANNAH GILLESPIE b 18 Jun 1808 bp 17 Jul 1808 sp Levi Meyer, Christina Ransom (K&S:155).
•   MAGDALENA GILLESPIE b 18 Apr 1810 bp 17 Jun 1810 no sp d/o "John" Gillespie & Sally Ransom (K&S:161).
2   JOHN RANSOM GILLESPIE b 26 Jun 1812 bp 02 Aug 1812 no sp (K&S:169).
3   HARRISON GILLESPIE b 20 Mar 1815 bp 14 May 1815 no sp (K&S:179) d 04 Nov 1817 ae 01-08-00 (OGUC:274.
4   LYDIA CATHARINE GILLESPIE b 09 Dec 1819 bp 20 Feb 1820 no sp (K&S:190).
5   MATILDA JANE GILLESPIE b 29 Nov 1822 bp 02 Feb 1823 no sp (K&S:197)
6   WYNTJE CHRISTINA GILLESPIE b 11 Apr 1826 bp 14 Apr 1826 no sp K&S:203).

RANSOM

1.1.9.1.3.4.2 JOSEPH RANSOM m Elizabeth/Elisabet Snyder/Sneider

1   MARIA RANDSOM bp 16 Oct 1806 no sp (DRCK: 489) & (a possibility a Maria m Philip Hendricks & had son John Persal b 25 Jun 1832 [DRCFU:29]).
2   ANN ELISA RAMSOM bp 13 May 1808 sp Cornelius Minckelaer, Cataline Sneider (DRCK:494) Eliza Remsey m 30 Mar 1834 John P Foland both Saugerties Wit: Miron Bosworth, Abraham Hommel no sp (K&S:280).
3   SALLY SUSANNA RUNSON b 22 Aug 1809 bp 09 Mar 1809 sp James Runson, Polly Runson (SPLWC:36) m Abraham J Hommel.
4   DEBORAH CATHARINA RANSOM bp 28 Dec 1815 mother not named (K&S:181).
5   DAVID JOEL RANSOM b 10 Sep 1817 bp 30 Nov 1817 no sp (K&S:187) & (d 07 Nov 1841 ae 24-02-06 [OGUC:287]) m Eliza C Valkenburgh d 20 Dec 1853 ae 29-03-28 bur Katsbaan Cem.
6   * PETER BACKER RAMSAY b 11 Jan 1821 bp 15 Apr 1821 no sp s/o Ramsey & Elizabeth Snyder (K&S:193).

MYER/MEYER

1.1.9.1.3.4.3 CHRISTINA RANSOM/REMSEN/RAMSAY m Levy/Levi Myer/Meier/Meyer

1   CHRISTINA ANGELINE MEYER b 16 Oct 1810 bp 09 Dec 1810 sp William Meyer, Rachel Meyer (K&S:163) & (tbstn Katsbaan Cem b 14 Dec 1816 d 01 Mar 1905 [OGUC:287]) m Barzilla Ransom b 17 Sep 1813 d 04 Jun 1884.
2   NELSON MEYER b 19 Apr 1814 bp 29 May 1814 no sp (K&S:175).
3   RACHEL MARIA MEYER b 20 Jan 1816 bp 09 Feb 1817 no sp (K&S:186).
4   SALLY CATHARINE MYER b 07 Jul 1821 bp 12 Aug 1821 no sp (K&S:194) at Saugerties m 16 Oct 1845 Edgar W Burhans b 15 Jan 1820 s/o Johannis Burhans & Clarissa Peck (BG:191).
5   WILLIAM MERROL MYER b 14 Oct 1826 bp 17 Dec 1826 no sp ma as Remson (K&S:204) at Saugerties m Louisa E Charity Vedder b 25 May 1827 d/o Aaron H Vedder & Elizabeth Sparling (BG:47). Louise lived in Schoharie 1880.
6   REBECCA MYER b 08 Jun 1833 m 12 Jan 1847 William Alexander Vedder b 27 Sep 1820 s/o Aaron H Vedder & Elizabeth Sparling (BG:47).

RANSOM

1.1.9.1.3.4.4 JAMES RANSOM Jr m Leah Valkenburg/Valk

1   CATY RANSOM bp 31 May 1812 b 11 May 1812 no sp (K&S:168) in ma's Will as Catharine m Patrick McCoy.
2   MELVINA/LAVINA RANSOM b 12 Mar 1815 bp 11 Jun 1815 no sp (K&S:179) in pa's Will as Lavinia Snyder, deceased, his Pro 30 Apr 1855. Lavina m Emund Snyder and her son was Ransom Snyder.
3   JONAH RANSOM
4   ABIJAH RANSOM
5   RHODA RANSOM
6   ELIZABETH RANSOM m David Richmond.
7   LEAH RANSOM m James Sylvester Snyder s/o Peter A Snyder, b 06 Jul 1815 bp 06 Aug 1815, both belonging to ancient families (OU 3:69,77). "Mrs Snyder was engaged in the boarding business. She & her son William are respected by all. Her daughter Mrs Strong & son Wilbur also kept boarders".
8   CHARLOTTE RANSOM m Samuel Tual.
9   SALLY RANSOM m Hiland Richmond.

Jannetjen (deWitt) Langendyk

James Ransom of Durham Pro 30 Apr 1855. Heirs: wf Leah, sons Jonah & Abijah, daus Rhoda, Elizabeth wf/o David Richmond, Leah wf/o James Snyder, Charlotte wf/o Samuel Tual, Sally wf/o Hiland Richmond, Catharine M wf/o Patrick McCoy, grdsn Ransom Snyder s/o deceased dau Lavinia. Exs: wife & son-in-law Samuel Tual. Wits: Lyman Wilcox & M B Mattice (AWGNY 1:104).

Leah Ransom of Durham Pro 15 Nov 1869. Heirs, sons Jonah & Abijah, daus Catharine McCoy, Sally Richmond, Elizabeth Richmond, Leah Snyder, Charlotte Tuell & Rhoda. Exs: Samuel Tuell & Rhoda. Wits: William Pierce, Samuel Rusk (AWGNY 2:44).

FIERO/FEERO
1.1.9.1.3.4.5 MARIA/POLLY RENZOM/RANSOM/REMSEN m Christian A Fiero

1. ANN CATHARINE FIERO b 06 Apr 1826 bp 07 May 1826 no sp (K&S:203) m Zacharia Backer Ransom s/o James Ransom & m3 Jane Wells b 31 Sep 1814 res Malden NY d at Malden 06 Sep 1883 ae 69-05-06 bur Katsbaan (OGUC:287) farmer at Katsbaan (BG:215; FT:79).
2. SARAH FIERO b 10 Feb 1829 bp 15 Mar 1829 (K&S:208) d 03 Feb 1832 dy bur Katsbaan Cem (OGUC:289).
3. MARY ELIZABETH FIERO b 12 Feb 1833 bp 31 Mar 1833 no sp (K&S:216) m James Vanderbilt.

Will of Christian Fiero 14 Aug 1840 Pro 04 Jul 1841 wife Mary, 2 minor daus; Joshua Fiero appointed legal guardian 22 Jun 1841, provision for Christian's ma. Exs: Mary Fiero & Tjerck Osterhout (GCPR Liber K:227)

Mary Ransom Fiero's Will 31 May 1854 Pro 18 Apr 1854 (GCPR Liber N: 120) provides for her mother-in-law. In 1855 state census Sara Fiero, age 88, was living with Zachariah and Ann Ransom family (FT:80).

OSTERHOUT
1.1.9.1.3.4.6 CATHARINA/CATY RANSOM/RAMSEY/RAMSON/RAMSEY m Tjerck Osterhout

1. ANNA MARIA OSTERHOUT b 19 Dec 1818 bp 21 Nov 1819 no sp (K&S:190).
2. CORNELIUS OSTERHOUT b 12 May 1822 bp 16 Jun 1822 no sp (K&S:195).
3. JOEL FIERO OSTERHOUT b 22 Jun 1824 bp 01 Aug 1824 no sp (K&S:199).
4. TJERCK LOW OSTERHOUT b 01 Aug 1826 bp 03 Sep 1826 no sp ma ? Ransom (K&S:204) & (d 15 Feb 1907 of Saugerties m Wed 26 Aug 1846 Sarah Alida Ingraham of Kingston, Wits: Dumont Ingraham, Abram M France (PRDC 1:3) b 27 Dec 1825 d 27 Apr 1890, 25 Apr 1890 CH rec (OGUC:253). Sarah Alida Ingraham b 27 Dec 1825 w/o Tjerck Low Osterhout adm 05 Dec 1856 on conf Platteskill CH; (PDRC:74).
5. SARAH ELIZABETH OSTERHOUT b 20 Mar 1833 bp 28 Apr 1833 no sp, ma Ramsay (sic [K&S:216]) d 21 Dec 1906 m Peter Snyder b 01 Mar 1825 d 24 Apr 1904 (CBRUC:1131/2). Both bur Mt Marion Com Cem (OGUC:255; CBRUC:1132/3) res Hurley.

LANGENDYK
1.1.9.1.3.6.1 LUCAS/LUKAS LANGENDYK m Annatje Schoonmaker

1. SALINA ANN LANGENDYK b 19 Mar 1816 bp 23 Mar 1816 sp John Shoemaker, Annatje (K&S:182).
2. JAN SCHOONMAKER LONENDYKE b 11 Jun 1817 bp 06 Jul 1817.
3. ALMIRA/ELMIRA LANGENDYKE b 23 Jun 1819 bp 01 Aug 1819 (fr Arthur Kelly, Christ's Evangelical Lutheran CH Germantown, Columbia Co) & (d 13 Jun 1896 item "Saugerties Records") m Alfred Schoonmaker s/o Godfrey Schoonmaker & Catharine Schoonmaker, b 18 Jun 1819 d 15 Aug 1895.
4. LUCAS SCHOONMAKER LANGENDYK bp 02 Jul 1821 m Harriet Meyndertzen d/o Johannes Meyndertzen & Maria Swart.
5. PAUL LONGENDYKE bp 09 Sep 1827 (Rhinebeck CH Rec)
6. UNNAMED SON b 15 Feb 1829.
7. UNNAMED SON b 11 Sep 1830.
8. ROBERT LANGENDYKE d 14 Sep 1834 Trinity CH Rec.
9. MARY LONGENDYKE (SF 3:227).
10. JOHN LONGENDYKE (SF 3:227)

LANGENDYK
1.1.9.1.3.6.4 PETRUS P LANGENDYK {m} 1.1.9.1.4.1.2.1.Catharine Decker

1. HIRAM LONGENDYKE b 05 Dec 1833 d 08 Jan 1865 in the South in Hospital, member of the 7th Regt NY Vol in the American 2nd Civil War.
2. SOPHIA JANE LONGENDYKE b 20 Jul 1838 (d 14 Jan 1910) m 25 Dec 1858 David Lorr Myer d 1888. They moved to Bridgeville DL, established a thriving nursery business, both bur Bridgeville Cem.
3. RACHEL ANN LONGENDYKE b 23 Jul 1839 d 26 Nov 1864 ae 23-05-04 (fr MKW) bur Herrick's Bridge, Town of Saugerties or b 23 Jun 1839 d 26 Dec 1862 (fr AWLM).
4. LYDIA EMMALINE LONGENDYKE b 11 Jul 1841 d 26 Nov 1864 ae 23-04-14.

Jannetjen (deWitt) Langendyk

5   BENJAMIN <u>FRANKLIN</u> LONGENDYKE b 09 Sep 1843 (d 01 Sep 1909) m1 09 Nov 1870 Mary E Jones by Rev W D Buckelow at Blue Mountain CH Saugerties d/o Benjamin Jones; (BMRC:59) she d ? Dec 1873. "On 16 Oct 1873 notice is hereby given that my wife Mary Elizabeth has left my bed and board; signed Benjamin F Langendyk". Note within 2 months of the notice Mary died. Benjamin m2 09 Dec 1874 Margaret Ann Kleiber d/o John Kleiber & Victoria Loerzel; they are bur Bridgeville DL Cem (fr AWSM; MKW).

6   M C D LANGENDYKE b 19 Jun 1850 d 28 Jun 1853 ae 03-00-12.

DECKER

1.1.9.1.4.1.2 ANNETJE/HANNAH LANGENDYK/LANENDICK m John I Decker

1   CATHARINE DECKER b 03 Apr 1813 bp 18 May 1813 no sp (K&S:172) & (d 06 Apr 1874 {m} 03 Jan 1833 <u>1.1.9.1.3.6.4</u> Peter Longendyke at Woodstock Ref CH, s/o Lucas Longendyke & Lena Schoonmaker, b 02 Oct 1812 d 06 Apr 1871 both bur Pine Grove (Herricks Bridge) Cem Saugerties NY.

2   PETER HENRY DECKER b 05 Jan 1816 bp 05 Feb 1816 Woodstock Ref CH (WHS 14:25) d 21 Mar 1841 ae 25-06-16 bur Mtn View Cem, Village of Saugerties (GIUC:8).

3   HARRIETTA DECKER b 06 Sep 1818 Woodstock Ref CH (WHS 14:25).

4   HANNAH MARIE DECKER b 15 Nov 1821 bp 25 Feb 1821 (<u>sic</u>) no sp (K&S:193) m Sat 21 Sep 1844 Andrew Carle, Wit: John Decker, Capt Peter H Brink (PDRC:2).

5   JEREMIAH RUSSEL DECKER b or bp 26 Jun 1824 Woodstock Ref CH (WHS 15:17) 1905 bur Pine Grove Cem ae 80-08-00.

6   JANE MARGARET DECKER b or bp 12 Aug 1826 Woodstock Ref CH (WHS 15:20).

7   C0RNELIS S DECKER 13 Nov 1828 bp 19 Dec 1828 Woodstock Ref CH m Nov 1854 Mary M Wolven d/o Martin Woolven.

8   SOPHIA DECKER bp 23 Jul 1834 Woodstock Ref CH.

DECKER

1.1.9.1.4.1.3 MARGRITJE/MARGARETTA/PEGGY LANGENDYK/ LONGENDIKE m Isaac P Decker

1   CORNELIUS LANGENDYK DECKER b 16 Jul 1812 bp 08 Aug 1812 sp (grprts) Cornelis Langendyk, Christine Snyder (K&S:169).

2   ANNATJE DECKER b 03 Aug 1814 bp 11 Nov 1814 no sp (K&S:177).

3   JANE CATHARINE DECKER b 11 Apr 1817.

4   BLANDINA DECKER b or bp 05 Apr 1819 Woodstock Ref CH (WHS 15:11).

Isaac Decker m2 Jane Catherine Post and had Catherine b 05 Aug 1821; William b 06 Jun 1824; Ann Marie b 28 Jan 1827 bp 14 Jun 1827; John b 18 May 1830; Cornelia b 05 Nov 1832 (WHS 15:14).

LANGENDYK

1.1.9.1.4.1.4 ZACHARIAS LANGENDYK m1 Ann/Anna Hogan

1   JANE CATHARINE LONGENDYKE b or bp 05 May 1819 (WHS 15:12).

2   ABRAHAM SNYDER LANGENDYKE b 15 Oct 1822 no bp date (s/o Anna Hoogan & Langendyke no sp (K&S:195) m1 Elizabeth, m2 Barbara Ann

3   CHRISTINA C LANGENDYK b 27 Jun 1824 at Woodstock (d 01 Aug 1883) m James Vandeburgh b 18 Mar 1828 d 02 Jan 1890 (GIUC:23) note grma Christina Snyder wf/o Cornelis Langendyk. Jan Langendyck & Elizabeth Dumont at Catskill had a dau Christina also.

4   CORNELIUS CULVER LONGENDYKE b 15 Apr 1825 d 04 Feb 1829 ae 03-09-20.

5   ZACHARIAH LONGENDYKE b 06 Sep 1827 d 03 Feb 1829 ae 01-04-28.

6   SYLVESTER LANGENDYKE b 06 Sep 1827 d 21 Mar 1829 ae 01-06-15.

LANGENDYK

1.1.9.1.4.1.5 JAMES LANGENDYK m Sara/Sally Burhans

1   CORNELIUS LONGENDYKE b 28 Aug 1817 bp 28 Sep 1817 sp (grprts) Cornelius Langendyk, Christine Snyder (d 30 Aug 1841 ae 24-00-02 bur Finger Grd Mt Marion (OGUC:248) also called Plattekill Cem [GIUC:6]) m 15 Aug 1840 Maria Catherine Tipp b 22 Nov 1816 d 06 Dec 1846 d/o James Tippp & Catharine Du Bois. She m2 John Hervey, their dau Elizabeth b 1844.

2   JOHN BURHANCE/BURHANS LONGENDYKE b 03 Nov 1819 at Esopus (WHS 15:11 1805/27) m 25 Aug 1850 Amelia Moulton, b 11 Mar 1829 d 06 Feb 1905 d/o Russel Moulton & Tryphenia Colburn (BG:53; fr MKW).

3   TJERCK LONGENDYKE b 25 Jul 1821 at Flatbush (RDCFU: 17) & (d 20 May 1888) m 3 Oct 1844 Catharine Ann Middaugh b 18 Oct 1826 at Woodstock d 10 Mar 1879 d/o Geo Middaugh & Elizabeth Ann Lane (BG:53).

4   SARA LONGENDYKE b Flatbush 17 Sep 1823 (BG:53).

5   CHRISTINA LONGENDYKE b 24 Mar 1826 (d 18 Dec 1906) m 29 Nov 1876 Peter Fonda wdr at Tivoll, **no chn.** (BG:53) s/o Matthias Fonda & Elizabeth Segendorf of Glasco, b 09 Dec 1821.

6   JAMES LONGENDYKE b 1833 d 1884 **single.**

7   SOLOMON LONGENDYKE

8   PETER HENRY LONGENDYKE b 1816 m1 Elizabeth Sparling d/o John Sparing & Ann Terwilliger (fr FSUHL) m2 Jane C

Jannetjen (deWitt) Langendyk

9 SARAH JANE LONGENDYKE b 1834.
10 MARY ELIZA LONGENDYKE b 02 Jun 1837 at Kingston (d 21 Aug 1921) m 07 May 1859 Levi York wdr b Saugerties 30 Oct 1817 s/o Moses York & Elizabeth Barks (BG:53)
11 HARMON LONGENDYKE b ? Oct 1840? d ae 2 **dy.**
12 MELISSA LONGENDYKE b 02 Jan 1845 m 02 Apr 1864 Pliny L Bovee b 02 Apr 1843 s/o Jacob Bovee & Sophia Barton various family members (BG:37,53,98/9,100,156).

LANGENDYK
1.1.9.1.4.1.6 CORNELIS S LANGENDYK m Mary A Blackwell
1 WILLIAM SNYDER LONGENDYKE b Rhinebeck 04 Jan 1828 (PDRC:38) & (d 15 Nov 1907) m 12 Apr 1854 Sarah Burhans, b Kingston 13 Jul 1834 d 16 May 1916 d/o Solomon Whitaker Burhans & Catharine Carle (OGUC:252/3, BG:54) William, Sarah & son William Floyd adm 11 Feb 1870 on cert fr ME CH Glasco NY.
2 CORNELIUS EDGAR LANGENDIKE b 02 Feb 1830 (d 08 Aug 1895) {m} 22 Jan 1857 1.1.9.1.3.2.2.5.2 Elizabeth Catherine Langendyck b 12 Jul 1838 d 25 Nov 1911 d/o Henry Longendyke & Cornelia Post. Her adm (to Plattekill CH) 05 Dec 1856 on conf, dis to Flatbush 01 Sep 1883 (PDRC:74).

WINNE
1.1.9.1.4.1.7 CATHARINA/CATY LONGENDYKE m John P Winne
1 CHRISTINE/CRISTINE MARGARET WINNE b or bp 06 Dec 1820 Woodstock (WHS 15:14).
2 PETER ABRAHAM WINNE b or bp 19 Jan 1823 Woodstock **dy** (WHS 15:16).
3 GEORGE WINNE b/bp 04 May 1825 Woodstock (WHS 15:19).
4 HANNAH WINNE b 26 Oct 1825
5 ANGELINE WINNE
6 SILAS WINNE
7 JOHN WINNE (fr BG:183).

LANGENDYK
1.1.9.1.4.4.1 PETER LANGENDYK/LONGENDIKE m Maria Plass
1 AMOS LONGENDIKE
2 CHRISTINA CATHARINE LONGENDIKE b/bp 27 Jun 1824 (WHS 15:17) {m} James Van Etten DeWitt.
3 CHRISTOPHER C LANGE\NDKE b 22 Jan 1827 (WHS 15:20) d 06 May 1898 tbstn ae 69-03-14 [FT:96; OGUC:252]) m1 03 Jun 1854 Maria Catharine Short, both of Saugerties, Wits: Peter D Short, Jane Langendyk (PRDC:8). Maria was d/o Jeremiah Short & Margaret Brink, b 08 Aug 1830 d 20 Aug 1854 ae 24-00-12, two months after marrying, bur France Family Cem Woodstock (GIUC:37). He m2 Lavina C Carle wd/o John Snyder b 23 Dec 1832 d 14 Apr 1896 ae 63-03-22 bur with Christopher at Mt Marion Cem (OGUC:252).
4 JANE MARIE LONGENDIKE b 02 Jun 1831 m 25 Oct 1856 Abraham Vanaken both of High Wood (BMRC:54).
5 CORNELIUS P LONGENDIKE/LARNEDYKE b 04 1834 m 12 May 1857 Elizabeth Ann Decker d/o David Decker of High Wood (BMRC:55).
6 MICHAEL LONGENDIKE ca 1836 (in Woodstock CH Rec fr WHS) of High Wood m 04 Jul 1857 Julia France d/o Wilhelmus F France (BMRC:55).

BURHANS
1.1.9.1.5.1.1 AANETJEN WENNIE m Wilhelmus Burhans
1 ANNETJE BURHANS bp Saugerties 05 Jan 1788 sp (grpa & wf) Petrus A Winne, Catharina Burhans (K&S:87) m Abram Matholomie/Bartholomew.
2 MARITJE BURHANS mentioned in her grpa's Will (BG:176).

RANSOM
1.1.9.1.5.1.3 CATHARINA WINNE m James Ransom
1 PETRUS RENSON b 05 May 1801 bp 14 May 1801 sp (ma's bro) Cornelis Winne, Annetje Borhans (K&S:134).
2 ANNATJE REMSEN b 18 Feb 1803 bp 10 Apr 1803 sp Peter P Winne, Catharina Winne (K&S:141).
3 LUCAS LANGENDYK REMSEN b 05 Mar 1805 bp 28 Apr 1805 no sp (K&S:148)
• **James Ransom m3 Jane Wels**. Note last lines p27, Gen 6.

WINNE
1.1.9.1.5.1.6 CORNELIS P WENNIE m Elizabeth Backert/Baker/Barker
1 PETRUS (CORNELIUS) WINNE b Quarryville, Saugerties b 07 Jan 1803 bp 09 Jan 1803 sp (uncle) Peter P Winne, Maria Baker (K&S:140) & (d 22 Aug 1877 bur Katsbaan Cem [OGUC: 290]) m Catherine Myer bp at Saugerties b 02 Jun 1805 *d 07 Mar 1856 d/o David Myer. His stepfather raised Petrus; he was a farmer, bought 48 acres fr Conrad Fiero owned later by his grchn (fr BG:183).

EMMERICH
1.1.9.1.5.1.8 JANNETJE/JANE WINNE m John Emmerich
1 MARIE EMMERICH b 05 Sep 1808 Saugerties (FT:35).
2 LEVI EMMERICH b 10 Feb 1811 bp 28 Apr 1811.

Jannetjen (deWitt) Langendyk

WINNE
1.1.9.1.5.1.10 AARON WINNE m Polly Curtis

3 SALLY CATHARINE EMMERICH b 01 Feb 1813 bp 18 Apr 1813 (BG: 183/4, 205).

1. JAMES AARON WINNE b 31 May 1833 (BG:183,204) m 05 Jan 1882 Maria Hold b 09 Apr 1855 d/o Augustus Hold & Margaret Burger.
2. WILLIAM HENRY WINNOW b 05 Nov 1838 m 22 Feb 1859 Nellie Sophia Van Steenbergh b 15 Nov 1843 d/o Andrew Van Steenbergh & Hannah Maria Hommel, res near Catskill.
3. MARY JANE WINNE m Francis C Benjamin s/o Augustus Benjamin.
4. ANGELINE WINNE m Thomas Post s/o Abraham Post (fr BG:183/4, 204).

WINNE
1.1.9.1.5.1.11 WILLIAM WINNE m Maria C Eligh

1. MARY CATHARINE WINNE b 04 Mar 1813 at Catskill m 09 Jan 1853 Abraham Schoonmaker s/o Peter S Schoonmaker & Catharine Wolven lived Quarryville, NY.
2. LANY JANE WINNE b 24 Sep 1835 m James Oliver Goodwin b 27 Jan 1827 s/o Edwin Goodwin & Elisabeth Morris.
3. MARGARET ELIZABETH WINNE b 15 Jun 1839 m 04 Jul 1861 Joseph Bond b 15 Sep 1837 s/o John Bond & Mary Croeder. They lived Palenville NY.
4. WILLIAM WINNE b 21 Dec 1842 (d 24 May 1902) m 10 Dec 1868 Emeline Lasher d/o Elisher & Jane Dederick b 04 Dec 1851 d not recorded (OGUC:279).

BURHANS
1.1.9.1.5.5.1 HANNAH WINNE m Hendrick Burhans

1. DENSLOW BURHANS b 14 Aug 1820 bp 30 Oct 1825 (RDCOH:43).
2. AUGUSTUS HENRY BURHANS b 10 Jan 1829 bp 22 Mar 1829 (RDCOH:44).

KNOLL
1.1.9.1.5.5.4 SOPHIA WINNE m Henry Knoll

1. AARON WINNE KNOLL b 02 Sep 1816 bp 13 Oct 1816 (RDCOH:40).
2. SALLY MELVINS (?) KNOLL b 11 Sep 1821 bp 30 Oct 1825 (RDCOH:43).
3. HENRY KNOLLE m 07 Apr 1825 Sophia Frare (RDCOH:48).

SCHOP
1.1.9.1.7.1.3 PETRUS POST SCHOP m Susanna Valk/Falk/Valck

1. CHAUNCEY LODEWYCK SCHOUB b at Albany 29 Mar 1838 m 04 Oct 1855 Anna Maria Mower d/o Andrew Mower & Hannah Hommel b 28 Nov 1836 d 04 Feb 1890 ae 53-02-09 Mower Family Cem Manorville, a dist North of Blue Mountain (BG:248).
2. NELLIE CATHARINE SCHOUB b 28 Feb 1843 m 20 May 1865 Peter Merritt b 01 Sep 1838 s/o Stephen Merritt & Hannah Clum (BG:248).
3. IRA HARVEY SCHOUB b 18 Sep 1847 m 28 Oct 1873 Catharine Sage d/o John Sage & Bridget Gallagher, b 01 Apr 1858 lived Palenville NY (BG:248).

LEGG
1.1.9.1.7.2.1 RICHARD BURHANS LEGG m Abigail Scribner

1. SILAS W LEGG m 10 Mar 1855 Margaret Wood.
2. ALONZO O LEGG b 1834 (d 22 Mar 1860) m 04 Jul 1857 Jane Ann Morris d/o Eli Morris of Palenville NY. She m again.
3. JULLIETTE LEG b 1831 (d 10 Dec 1879) m 04 Jul 1863 Lewis Rider b 20 Jul 1840 s/o Isaac Rider & Margaret Gray b 10 Jan 1840.
4. MARY EMILY LEGG
5. CORNELIUS HENRY LEGG b 15 Jan 1844 m1 Clara Haines b 07 Jan 1846 (d 16 Oct 1878) d/o Abraham Haines & Maria Britt m2 07 Jun 1881 Gertrude Kerr b 20 Feb 1860 d/o Robert Kerr & Margaret Haines of Tannerville NY res Tannersville NY (all BG:248).

Jannetjen (deWitt) Langendyk

GENERATION 8

If a couple traces back to DeWitt ancestry more than once, m is {m} indicating this fact. Numbering used is that of the first parent listed chronologically. Both numbers are given but the one to be used in succeeding generations is underlined.

LANGENDYCK
1.1.9.1.3.2.2.1 CORNELIUS LANGENDYCK m1 Jane A Dumond

1 JOHANNA ELIZABETH LONGENDYKE b 25 May 1828 (fr MKW, RDCFU: 23) ma as Jane Van Alston. Is this difficult handwriting or late recording by Rev from memory? At Flatbush DRC Johanna m 04 Sep 1845 Benjamin Rilyea/Relyea b 1826. He m2 01 Jan 1867 Sophia Lewis.

2 SIMEON PETER ALSDORF LANGENDYCK b 17 Dec 1830 (RDCFU:27) d 27 Sep 1900 ae 69-09-07 [Saugerties Rec fr MKW]) m 06 Sep 1851 Lucinda Harriet Felten both of Saugerties, Wit: Frances Myer, Levi D Myer, b 18 Feb 1831 High Wood d 20 Jun 1913 (DRCFU 1:7, BG:112) & in the Saugerties Telegraph, d/o Zachariah Felten & Elizabeth Ackert (Seamon Rec fr MKW)

3 JAMES DUMOND LONGENDYKE b 30 Jun 1833 (d 30 May 1884 NYC [fr MKW]) at Mt Marion m 25 Jan 1855 Harriet Maria Plass/Plof Wits: Barent G Van Aiken, John P Myer (PRDC: 9) Wit: Barent G Van Aiken, John P Meyer b 23 Jun 1837 d/o Sebastian Plass & Catherine Brink, d 01 Feb 1873 ae 35-07-08 bur Mt Marion Com Cem (OGUC:252; family fr MKW).

4 JOHN OSTRANDER LANGENDYCK b 04 Jun 1835 (d 03 Jan 1917) m 04 Apr 1857 Elizabeth Van Aken b 07 Oct 1839 d/o Solomon Van Aken & Jane M Joy, Saugerties d 20 Mar 1915 both bur Wildwyck Cem. Her bros were Lewis & Solomon Van Aken. John adm 27 Feb 1857 on Conf (to Plattekill RDC) dis 20 Jun 1891 to First Presb Kingston NY (PRDC:75).

5 MARY CATHERINE LONGENDYKE b 24 Aug 1837 (d 03 Jun 1917 bur Old Trumpbour Farm Cem [fr MKW]) of Saugerties m Sat 22 Jan 1853 Egbert Van Buerin/Buren, wits: Andrew D Van Buren, Henry Longendyke, (PRDC:8 lists the groom as Egbert Van Buren of Kingston). He was b 15 Mar 834 d 08 Apr 1885.

6 MELINDA/MALINDA JANE LANGENDYCK b 27 Jun 1840 (RDCFU: 36) & (d 19 Nov 1859 ae 19 bur Old Trumpbour Farm, Langendyke Cem one mile west of Mt Marion [OGUC: 264]) m 02 May 1857 Ephriam Magee/Myer both of Saugerties Wit: Godfrey Majer/Mejer, Maria Margaret Van Aken (PDRC:9). Melinda Jane Langendyke adm 05 Dec 1856 on Conf to Plattekill, dis to Blue Mtn 25 May 1859 (PRDC:74).

7 RACHEL ANN LANGENDYCK b 30 Jun 1843 Kingston NY (d 02 Nov 1915 ae 72-02-29 bur Wildwyck Cem) {m} 05 Sep 1857 <u>1.1.9.4.8.2.9.1</u> Alexander Kiersted Low both of Saugerties, Wits: Silas Carle, Elizabeth Low (PRDC:9) b 07 May 1834 (BG:130) s/o Abraham Low & Margaret Eva Brink. Cdn listed under Pa's number Gen. 8 p 146.

* CHRISTINE LANGENDYCK b 27 Apr 1848 bp 29 Apr 1848 (PDRC: 28) & (d 01 Jul 1904) her ma d in ch b (GIUC:2). Cornelius Langendyke & Jane A Dumond adopted this ch.

m2 26 Apr 1851 Jane (Carnright) Schoonmaker.

8 SARAH MARGARET LONGENDYKE b 31 Mar 1852 bp 16 May 1852 (PRDC:32).

9 CAROLINE LONGENDYKE b 17 Jan 1854 bp 18 Jun 1856 (PRDC: 34).

10 CORNELIUS HENRY LONGENDYKE b 07 Mar 1856 bp 25 May 1856 (PRDC:36) d 25 Oct 1913 ae 57-07-00 Kingston bur Catskill Cem (#50875 NY State Rec.

11 CORNELIA MARIE LONGENDYKE b 08 Sep 1857 bp 11 Mar 1858 (PRDC:38).

12 CHARLES EDGAR LONGENDYKE b 18 May 1860 bp 15 Sep 1861 (PRDC:41).

TROWBRIDGE
1.1.9.1.3.2.2.3 ELIZABETH OSTERHOUT LANGENDYCK m Isaac Trowbridge

1 LUCAS TROWBRIDGE b 26 Mar 1839 (d 25 Jul 1892) m 27 Mar 1866 Sara Louise Keator b 28 Oct 1842 d 15 Jun 1911.

2 MARY JANE TROWBRIDGE b 20 Mar 1837 m 20 Feb 1862 Gilbert Gomalia Vandermark (fr MKW).

LANGENDYKE
1.1.9.1.3.2.2.5 HENRY C LANGENDYKE m Cornelia

1 PETER HENRY LONGENDYKE b 05 Sep 1835 d 09 May 1837.

2 ELIZABETH CATHERINE LANGENDYKE b 12 Jul 1838 (d 25 Nov 1911 West Landing NY) {m} 22 Jan 1857 <u>1.1.9.1.4.1.6.2</u> Cornelius Edgar Langendyk s/o Cornelius S Longendyke & Mary Blackwell, b 02 Feb 1830 d 08 Aug 1895 ae 65-06-06 Heath NY (fr MKW, OGUC:252) Chn under Pa's number Generation 8 p 41.

3 SARA JANE LONGENDYKE b 23 May 1841 Mt Marion (d 30 Jan 1918 Saugerties) m 20 Oct 1859 Silas Carle both of Saugerties, wits: Cyrus Carle, Charlotte Decker (PRDC:10). He d before 1918.

4 CORNELIA ANN LONGENDYKE b 26 Nov 1842 (d 07 Apr 1920 Ruby NY) at St Pauls Luth CH m 03 Nov 1881 George W Pettinger b 22 Sep 1815 d 07 Mar 1895 (fr MKW).

5 JOHANNAH MARIA LANGENDYKE b 02 Feb 1846 bp 05 Apr 1846 Mt Marion CH (PDRC: 26) as Jeanna M Longendyck w/o Isaac Van Aken adm 05 Mar 1865 on conf (to Plattekill DRC) (d 02 Jan 1911 ae 65-11-00 bur Wildwyck Cem) m 06 Sep 1865 Isaac Jason Van Aken both of Saugerties wits: Charles A Longendyke, Henry Felten (PRDC:11) Isaac

Jannetjen (deWitt) Langendyk

s/o Solomon Van Aken & Jane Marie Joy b 03 Mar 1845 bp 13 Apr 1845 (BMDC:25) res 66 Liberty St Kingston. Joanna M Longendyck w/o Isaac Van Aken adm 05 Mar 1865 on Conf (to Plattekill DRC) d 1910.

6 JOHN ABRAHAM LANGENDYKE b 23 Apr 1849 bp 22 Jul 1849 (PRDC: 29) & (d 30 Nov 1908 Ruby NY [fr MKW) m 04 Dec 1867 Mary Amelia Low of Kingston, no Wits (PRDC: 12) b 1849 Ruby NY d 1929 both bur Mt Marion Cem (OGUC: 252)
7 HARRIET LANGENDYKE b 26 Sep 1852 bp 28 Nov 1852 (PRDC:33) m 02 Dec 1868 Rufus Carle b 07 Jan 1849 bp 03 Jun 1849 s/o Eli Carle & Leah Catharine Plass (PRDC:29).
8 MARY ALICE LANGENDYKE b 04 Nov 1854 bp 22 Apr 1855 (PDRC 1:35) m 08 Jan 1873 Alfred France both of Kingston at the home of Corn Langendyke wit: Jacob H France, F B Low (PDRC 1:15). Alfred b 30 Jul 1850 BP 29 Sep 1850 Ruby NY (PDRC 1:30) s/o William H France & Nellie Snyder, d 08 Oct 1920 Ruby NY.
9 MARGARET ALIDA LANGENDYKE b 20 Dec 1856 bp 27 Feb 1857 (PDRC 1:36) & (d 04 Sep 1878) of Saugerties, m 04 Dec 1878 Henry Richtmyer of Catskill at Plattekill CH $5.00 (PRDC:17) b 30 Jul 1850 Catskill NY.
10 PETER POST LANGENDYKE b 28 Aug 1859 bp 21 Sep 1860 (PDRC 1:40) & (d 25 Mar 1940) fr MKW) m 01 Jun 1882 Eudora Valk d/o William C Valk & Marion Wolven, b 17 Jan 1861 Woodstock NY d 13 Sep 1935 both bur Old Woodstock Cem.
11 EMMA AMELIA LANGENDYKE b 03 May 1864 bp 14 Mar 1865 (PRDC:44) m 29 Jul 1883 Ira Britt b 1863 Kingston NY, s/o Edgar Britt & Susan.

LANGENDYKE

1.1.9.1.3.2.2.6 JOHN LANGENDYKE m Eliza Ann Sax
1 MARGARET E LANGENDYKE b 1844 m Emerick.
2 JOHN B LANGENDYKE b 23 Apr 1847 Shandaken (d 06 Jun 1911) m 23 Dec 1890 Emily Persen d/o John Persen & Fanny Jane, b 18 Nov 1849 d 03 Mar 1905 both bur Catskill.
3 JANE C LONGENDYKE b Feb 1850 d 27 Aug 1852 **dy.**
4 HENRY A LANGENDYKE b 1853 d 04 Apr 1880 ae 27 bur Catskill Cem.
5 MARY F LONGENDYKE b 1855 (d 06 Dec 1888) m Franklin Martin.
6 CORNELIUS A LANGENDYK b 24 Apr 1858 (d 17 Apr 1924) m Anna M Petrie b 31 Mar 1872 Westerly RI d 07 Jun 1928 both bur Wildwyck Cem.
7 SARAH LONGENDYKE b 14 Apr 1863 d 18 Mar 1864, bur Catskill Cem **dy.** In the 1855 Greene Co. NY State census Elizabeth is 66, Christina 32, Jane E 28, Margaret 26, Sarah R 23, all lived with John (fr MVK).
Henry A Langendyke of Catskill Will Pro 16 Sep 1880, heir mother Eliza Ann, Ex: bro Cornelius A Wits Abram Rightmeyer & Fred Werner both of Catskill (AWGNY 3:120).

POST

1.1.9.1.3.2.2.10 MARGARET ANN LANGENDYKE m John H Post
1 ELLIOT E POST b 13 Apr 1858 Catskill NY (d 12 Aug 1915 NY) m Christina Massino d/o William Massino & Catherine Smith, b 17 Dec 1862 Smith Landing d 11 Jun 1932 Troy NY.
2 PETER L POST b 1862.

ECKERT

1.1.9.1.3.3.3.3 ISAAC DAVIS ECKERT Jr m Sarah Ann DuBois
1 MARY A ECKERT b 1850.

HOMMEL

1.1.9.1.3.4.2.3 SALLY SUSAN RANSOM * possibly m Abraham J Hommel
1 * CHARLOTTE HOMMEL b 28 Sep 1835 bp 15 Nov 1835 (K&S:220).

BURHANS

1.1.9.1.3.4.3.4 SARAH CATHARINE MYERS m Edgar W Burhans
1 MARY JANE BURHANS b 11 Nov 1846 d 24 Jan 1847.
2 FRANK W BURHANS b Saugerties 26 Dec 1847 North Hudson NY m 10 Aug 1869 Marcelia Eliza Walker.
3 GEORGE BURHANS b 05 Nov 1853 d 13 Feb 1857.
4 MARY M BURHANS b 26 Sep 1855 Warrenburgh NY m1 12 Nov 1879 James Henry Mixter s/o John Mixter & Hannah March, b 23 Nov 1857. He m2 24 Jun 1886 Charles Warren Putnam s/o James Madison Putnam & Rhoda Smith b 05 Mar 1847 Moriah NY.
5 HIRAM BURHANS b 18 Dec 1857 d 14 Mar 1859.
6 CLARA C BURHANS b 17 Sep 1859 Warrenburgh NY m 02 Oct 1879 George W Powell of Findley OH s/o Daniel Powell & Elizabeth Rauch b 30 Sep 1848, res Moriah NY (fr BG: 119).

SNYDER

1.1.9.1.3.4.4.2 MELVINA/LAVINA RANSOM m Edmund Snyder
1 RANSON SNYDER (fr BG:119)

SYNDER

1.1.9.1.3.4.4.7 LEAH RANSOM m James Sylvester Synder
1 MARGARET E SNYDER m ? Beman moved to PA.

Jannetjen (deWitt) Langendyk

2   MARY J SNYDER
3   SARAH SNYDER
4   WILLIAM SNYDER One dau was "Mrs Strong" (OU 3:69,77)

RANSOM
1.1.9.1.3.4.5.1 ANN/ANNA CATHARINE FIERO m Zachariah Backer Ransom
1   CHARLES A RANSOM b 25 Sep 1845 Katsbaan (d 08 May 1922 Malden NY)at Trinity CH Lime Rock CT m at 11 o'clock 18 Dec 1878 Marly Louisa White d/o Charles White & Rebecca Calkin b 09 May 1851 Sharon CT d 01 Jun 1917 Malden bur Katsbaan Cem.
2   CLARENCE RANSOM b 02 Nov 1847 d 16 Dec 1847 ae 00-01-14 **dy**.
3   SARAH C RANSOM b 20 Dec 1848 m 11 Oct 1871 Jacob Henry France s/o William France & Nellie Snyder, b 17 Nov 1846 bp 31 Jan 1847 Plattekill Ref CH.
4   SAMUEL RANSOM b 08 Sep 1852 d 22 Oct 1852 ae 02-00-08 **dy.**
5   JAMES F RANSOM b 19 Feb 1860 d 27 Feb 1863 ae 02-00-08 **dy.**
6   HENRY T RANSOM b 08 Oct 1867.

In 1855 Greene County NY census Zachariah had 25 acres improved, 10 acres unimproved, $2,000 cash value of farm, $350 value of stock, $150 value of tools. The Ulster County Genealogical Society collection of "Family Trees" is very interesting & useful reading.

OSTERHOUDT
1.1.9.1.3.4.6.4 TJERCK LOW OSTERHOUDT m Sarah Alida Ingraham
1   ARIETTA OSTERHOUDT b 13 Oct 1847 bp 12 Dec 1847 (PRDC:28).
2   EMMA CATHERINE OSTERHOUDT b 05 Jul 1850 bp 22 Sep 1850 (PRDC:30).
3   WILLIAM OSTERHOUDT b 30 Sep 1852 bp 27 Feb 1853 (PRDC:33).
4   MARTIN SCHENK OSTERHOUDT b 16 Dec 1854 bp 31 Aug 1856 (PRDC:46).
5   NELSON OSTERHOUDT b 22 Dec 1857 bp 04 Jul 1858 (PRDC:38).
6   MARY ALICE OSTERHOUDT b 14 Sep 1860 bp 18 Oct 1861 (PRDC:41).
7   ANNA ELIZABETH OSTERHOUDT b 27 Aug 1863 bp 26 Mar 1864 (PRDC:43).

SYNDER
1.1.9.1.3.4.6.5 SARAH ODTERHOUDT m Peter Synder
1   CHARLES A SNYDER b 09 Sep 1852 m1 Mary Jane Felter b 12 Jan 1845 only d/o Levi Felter & Jane Weeks, d 25 May 1882 ae 37-02-13 bur Mt. Marion Com Cem (OGUC:255). He m2 Louisa Burhans b 19 Nov 1845 (1.1.9.4.2.5.2.8) d/o Geeritje Newkerk Van Keuren & Edward Burhans. Since DeWitt desc Charles Snyder m twice, his number is followed to maintain numbering of sibling.
2   CORNELIA ANN SNYDER m Henry W Schoonmaker d by 1896.
3   SARAH ELIZABETH SNYDER m John O Osterhout.
4   EMMA CATHARINE SNYDER m Ten Eyck Myer.
5   MARY LOUISA SNYDER m William H Myer.
6   GEORGE B SNYDER
7   WESLEY RANSOM SNYDER b 31 Aug 1866 bp 11 Apr 1867 (PRDC:46) m Sarah V K Osterhout.
8   PETER L SNYDER b 15 May 1870 (d 13 Mar 1907 bur Mt Marion Com Cem [OGUC:255]) m Julia Daily.
9   EDWIN C SNYDER
10   WILLIAM SNYDER d before 1896. Family listed in (CRBUC:1132/3)

SCHOONMAKER/SHOEMAKER
1.1.9.1.3.6.1.3 ALMIRA LANENDYKE m Alfred Schoonmaker/Shoemaker
1   WILLIAM SHOEMAKER b 1845.
2   JOHN SHOEMAKER b 1849.
3   NINA L SHOEMAKER (fr AWSM).

MYER
1.1.9.1.3.6.4.2 SOPHIA JANE LONGEDYKE m David Lorr S Myer
1   JAMES HARVEY MYER b 16 Sep 1859 bp 01 Jan 1860 Blue Mtn CH bur Bridgeville DE.
2   LYDIA ANN MYER bp 24 May 1862 (BMRC:22) ma as Sophia Jane Longindych.
3   HARVEY MYER bp 24 May 1862.
4   EMMA MYER
5   FEMALE MYER (fr AWSM).

LONGENDYKE
1.1.9.1.3.6.4.5 BENJAMIN FRANKLIN LONGENDYKE m1 Mary E Jones
1   THEODORE FREDERICK LONGENDYKE b 05 Jan 1872 (family bible) bur Bridgeville DE mLettieE Short(fr MKW)
2   CELIA JANE LONENDYKE b 20 Feb 1873 (d 1945 m ?   Lomas; 2 daus.
m2 09 Dec 1874 Margaret Ann Kleber/Klieber.

Jannetjen (deWitt) Langendyk

3   SARAH EMMA LONGENDYKE b 17 Mar 1876 d 24 10 1878 bur Bridgeville.
4   VICTORIA ANN LONGENDYKE b 22 Aug 1877 (d 30 May 1963) m S Z Wunderman no chn.
5   FRANCES ELLEN LONGENDYKE b 27 Aug 1878 (d 25 Apr 1914) m Charles L Miller.
6   MINNIE AUGUSTA LONGENDYKE b 01 Aug 1881 (d 06 Aug 1972) bur Bridgeville DL Cem) m Arthur N Stuart.
7   WILLIAM F LONGENDYKE b 04 Jan 1884 (d 10 Jun 1958) m Anna McMurray.
8   MARGARET JANE LONGENDYKE b 17 Sep 1887 (d 22 Jan 1914) **single**.

LANGENDYK

1.1.9.1.4.1.2.1 CATHARINE DECKER {m} Peter P Longendyk

          Children are with their Father's underlined number Generation 7

LANGENDYKE

1.1.9.1.4.1.4.2 ABRAHAM SNYDER LANGENDYK m Elizabeth

1   ERWIN LANGENDYK m Elizabeth (fr MKW).

VANDERBURGH

1.1.9.1.4.1.4.3 CHRISTINA C LONGENDYKE m James Vandeburgh

1   SARAH I VANDEBURGH b 16 Jun 1862 High Woods, Saugerties T NY (d 20 Nov 1884 Fishcreek NY bur Millertown NY) m ? Perkins.

LONGENDYKE

1.1.9.1.4.1.5.1 CORNELIUS LONGENDYKE m Marie Catharine Tipp

1   CORNELIA ANN LONGENDYKE b 02 Nov 1841 bp 11 Jan 1842 (d 28 Jun 1917 Utica NY) m 10 Feb 1861 George C Lowe b 30 Sep 1832 s/o Jacobus Lowe & Ann Carle, d 04 Feb 1900 (fr MKW, BG:98, FSUHL).

LONGENDYKE

1.1.9.1.4.1.5.2 JOHN B LONGENDYKE m Amelia Moulton

1   JOHN VAN HORN LONGENDYKE b 20 Aug 1851.
2   CHARLES MILTON LONGENDYKE b 03 Aug 1853.
3   HENRY MONROE LONGENDYKE b 01 Mar 1856 Springfield MA (d 12 Jul 1936 ae 80-04-11 Kingston NY bur Woodstock NY [fr MKW]) m 25 Dec 1877 Emma Stall (Lown) b 18 Nov 1854 d/o Henry Stall and Maria Finger. (fr MKW) Emma's ma d & she was adopted by her Uncle Lown, & desired her name be given as Lown, d 1915 bur Woodstock.
4   GEORGE ORLANDO LONGENDYKE b 21 May 1858.
5   ANDREW ADEN LONGENDYKE b 27 May 1860 m 01 Jan 1880 Mary Colman.
6   ELLA CHRISTINA LONGENDYKE b 27 Jan 1865 m 10 Nov 1879 Richard Anson b 23 Mar 1855 s/o Henry Anson & Catharine Robertson.

LONGENDYKE

1.1.9.1.4.1.5.3 TJERCK LONGENDYKE m Catharine Ann Middaugh

1   MARIA CATHARINE/KATIE LONGENDYKE b Woodstock 02 Jul 1845 (d 26 Oct 1885 bur Woodstock Cem) at Saugerties m 03 Jan 1867 James Merchant b 21 Jan 1843 s/o William Merchant & Ann Hurl/Hearl b 16 Jul 1845 d 14 Nov 1918 Saugerties bur Mtn View Cem as were Charles & George.
2   CHARLES EDGAR LONGENDYKE b Kingston 24 Jun 1850 d 24 Dec 1851.
3   GEORGE ALFRED LONGENDYKE b Kingston 13 Jan 1853 d 10 Oct 1858.
4   CHARLOTTE/LOTTA DELILAH LONGENDYKE b Kingston 20 Mar 1854 m 24 Jan 1882 William H Hurl s/o Samuel Hurl & Maria Maby b 31 Jan 1850 NYC (fr MKW, Info BG:98/9).

LONGENDYKE

1.1.9.1.4.1.5.8 PETER H LONGENDYKE m1 Elizabeth Sparling

1   GROSS LONGENDYKE b 1841.
2   CLARISSA LONGENDYKE b 1844.
3   MARY HELEN LONGENDYKE b 14 Oct 1847 Marbletown NY.
4   GERRAS LONGENDYKE b 1850.
     m2 Jane C
5   ERASTUS LONGENDYKE b 1858.
6   RACHEL LONGENDYKE b 1859.

YORK

1.1.9.1.4.1.5.10 MARIE ELIZA LONGENDYKE m Levi York

1   JENNIE YORK b 05 May 1860 m William Ziegler s/o Louis Zeigler & Caroline Wurster, b 03 Apr 1858 NYC d 13 May 1923 ae 64-11-10 at Saugerties T NY.
2   CARRIE YORK b 28 Feb 1863 d 16 Aug 1865.
3   EMMA YORK b 22 Jan 1866.
4   JOHN YORK b 13 Dec 1867.
5   GEORGIANNA YORK b 03 Sep 1871.

Jannetjen (deWitt) Langendyk

6   GEORGE YORK b 03 Sep 1871 m Sarah Miner d/o Oliver Miner & Debbie Doyle, b 1878.
7   CHARLES T YORK b 30 Sep 1876 d 12 Mar 1881.
8   FLORENCE L YORK b 31 Aug 1879 d 28 May 1881 (Info (BG:99).

BOVEE
1.1.9.1.4.1.5.12 MELISSA LONGENDYKE m Pliny L Bovee
1   FRANKLIN BOVEE b 20 Dec 1864/5 (d 15 Mar 1916 ae 50-02-25 Saugerties bur Chestnut Hill Cem) m 14 Oct 1895 Grace DeWitt d/o Isreal DeWitt & Mary Young (FSUHL).
2   FREDERICK BOVEE b 18 Jun 1868 d 19 Apr 1880 **dy.**
3   NELSON BOVEE b 04 Dec 1879.
(chn b West Saugerties, Ulster Co NY BG:99)

LONGENDYKE
1.1.9.1.4.1.6.1 WILLIAN SNYDER LONGENDYKE m Sarah Burhans
1   WILLIAM FLOYD LONGENDYKE b 26 Jan 1855 Glasco NY bp 15 Jun 1856 (PRDC: 36) & (d 13 May 1914 Newburgh NY) at Hy Yorks m 22 Jul 1879 Sarah Ellen/Ella Van Aken York both/o High Wood cost $5 Hy Yorks (PRDC: 17) d/o Henry Van Wagenen York & Hannah Margaret Van Aken, b 01/2 Sep 1859 d 21 May 1936. (fr MKW).
2   CHARLES LONGENDYKE b 13 Jan 1857 Shokan NY (d 18 Sep 1838 ae 81-03-05) m at Glasco Meth CH m 29 Dec 1881 Anna Catherine Weeks d/o Holly Hoyt Weeks II & Elizabeth Marie Burhans b 06 Sep 1860 (fr MATS) d 14 Mar 1935 both bur Mt Marion Cem, res Glasco Ulster Co NY Charles adm same as father, dis to 6th Ave Meth CH Brooklyn NY 22 May 1911.
3   ALICE LONGENDYKE b 28 Jun 1860 bp 29 Nov 1860 (PRDC: 40) d 05 Dec 1861 ae 01-06-07) **dy,**
4   ADDISON LONGENDYKE b 02 Nov 1862 bp 10 Mar 1863 Glasco Meth CH (d 13 Feb 1916) m 28 Nov 1889 Mattie Frazer Glasco Meth CH rec b 1867 Glasco (all fr MKW).
5   ARTHUR LONGENDYKE b 19 Dec 1864 bp 24 Mar 1865 Glasco Meth CH d 21 Apr 1880 ae 15-04-02 **dy.**
6   JASON LONGENDYKE b 13 Apr 1867 bp 13 Aug 1867 Glasco Meth CH (d 26 Feb 1946) m 18 Jun 1896 Leah Margaret York d/o Emory York & Emma Carle b 09 Apr 1877 d 10 Feb 1964.
7   CORA LONGENDYKE b 11 May 1870 bp 01 Jul 1870 (d 13 Jan 1947) m 13 Dec 1888 Solomon Van Aken York s/o Henry York & Hannah Margaret Van Aken b 19 Apr 1864 (MKW has Apr) bp 05 May 1864 Flatbush Ref CH d 29 Jan 1929.
8   VICTOR LONGENDYKE b 07 Aug 1876 (d 30 Mar 1950 Saugerties) m 20 Nov 1902 Annie Van Aken York b 05 Nov 1876 d 01 Jul 1964 Saugerties (Info fr BG:100/56/7)

LONGENDYKE
1.1.9.1.4.1.6.2 CORNELIUS EDGAR LONGENDYKE {m} 1.1.9.1.3.2.2.5.2 Elizabeth Catherine Longendyke
1   EDWIN LONGENDYKE b 29 Jul 1860 bp 29 Nov 1860 (PRDC: 40) d 24 Jan 1862 ae 01-05-26 Flatbush Landing (OGUC:252) **dy.** bur Mt Marion Com Cem.
2   ELVINA/ELLA LONGENDYKE b 26 Jan 1862 bp 08 Oct 1862 d/o Cors E Langendyk & Elizabeth C Longendyk (PRDC:42) m Charles Cramer s/o Phillip Cramer & Christina Hopeman b 15 Apr 1858.

DeWITT
1.1.9.1.4.4.1.2 CHRISTINE CATHERINE LANGENDYKE {m} 1.1.9.4.2.3.5.2 James Van Etten DeWitt
1   CATHERINE DeWITT b 30 Nov 1849 bp 06 Dec 1849 (PRD:26).

LONGENDYKE
1.1.9.1.4.4.1.3 CHRISTOPHER LONGENDYKE m1 Maria Catharine Shortt; He m2 Lavina C Carle
1   LOUISA/<u>LAVERSIA</u> LANGENDYKE b 23 Nov 1861 bp 22 Jun 1862 (d 1951 bur Mt Marion Cem) fr <u>The Saugerties Telegraph</u> m 19 Oct 1882 Ezra Short s/o Abraham H Short & Julia Maria Kipp, b 03 Dec 1859 Saugerties NY d 28 May 1914 bur Mt Marion.
2   TITUS LONGENDYKE b 22 Aug 1863 m 11 Mar 1885 Martha Vredenburg b 15 Sep 1862 d 22 Sep 1936 bur Wiltwyck Cem Kingston NY

LONGENDYKE
1.1.9.1.4.4.1.5 CORNELIS P LONGENDYKE m Elizabeth Decker
1   MARY ELLEN LONGENDYKE b 10 Oct 1857 bp 28 Mar 1858 (PRDC: 38) m 23 Sept 1875 Jonathan C Meyer (Saugerties Telegraph).
2   WILLIAM ADDISON LONGENDYKE b 15 Apr 1860 bp 22 Jul 1860 Plattekill Ref CH (PRDC: 40) d 12 May 1914 Newburgh NY.
3   CYRUS MITCHELL LONGENDYKE b 25 Apr 1872 bp 11 Jan 1873 Plattekill Ref CH (d 1942) (PRDC: 52) m 28 Jun 1899 Ella France d/o Henry France & Elizabeth C Wolven b 1873 d 1962.

LONGENDYKE
1.1.9.1.4.4.1.6 MICHAEL LONGENDYKE m Julia France
1   WILBUR LONGENDYKE b 06 Apr 1858 bp 26 Jun 1859 (d 30 Apr 1913 ae 55-00-24 (Saugerties Rec) m 15 Dec 1881 Mary A Carle d/o Walter Carle & Mary S Carle (NY State Rec #2324) b 25 May 1857.

Jannetjen (deWitt) Langendyk

2   NORMAN LONGENDYKE b 25 Jun 1862 bp Jan 1863 Plattekill Ref CH (PRDC: 43) (d 21 Oct 1932 ae 70-03-26 bur Wildwyck Cem) m Mary.

WINNE

1.1.9.1.5.1.6.1 PETER CORNELIUS/CORNELIUS PETER WINNE m Catharine Myer

1   JOHN VALENTINE WINNE b 03 Nov 1830 (K&S:279) bp 22 Aug 1877 (d 24 May 1893) active in the Katsbaan community m1 18 Oct 1854 Eliza Catharine Kemble (K&S:279) d/o John Peter Kemble, b 15 Sep 1833 d 15 May 1868 (CBRUC:452; OGUC:290). He m2 06 Jun 1872 Anna Sax d/o John P Sax, b 25 May 1831 d 27 May 1900 ae 69-00-02 (OGUC:290).

2   CATHARINE WINNE b 26 Dec 1836 d 18 Mar 1860.

SCHOUB

1.1.9.1.7.1.3.1 CHAUNCEY L SCHOUB m Ann Marie Mower

1   ROSALIA ANN SCHOUB b 10 Dec 1856, m 14 Jan 1873 William Craft b 10 Jan 1851 s/o John Craft & Catharine Seward (BG:303).

SCHOUB

1.1.9.1.7.1.3.2 NELLIE C SCHOUB m Peter Merritt

1   IRA DeWITT MERRITT b 26 Mar 1866.

2   IDA PENOLA MERRITT b 31 Dec 1867 (BG:303).

SCHOUB

1.1.9.1.7.1.3.3 IRA HARVEY SCHOUB m Catharine Sage

1   CHAUNCEY ULYSSES SCHOUB b 31 Jul 1874

2   CHARLES SCHOUB b 29 Mar 1876.

3   JESSE SCHOUB b 15 Feb 1878 (BG:303).

LEGG

1.1.9.1.7.2.1.1 SILAS W LEGG m Margaret M Wood

1   WILLIAM C LEGG (BG:303).

RIDER

1.1.9.1.7.2.1.3 JULIETTE LEGG m Lewis Rider

1   EMMA RIDER b 01 Jun 1865 d 28 Nov 1874.

2   IRA RIDER b 16 Aug 1867.

3   EDWIN RIDER b 06 Dec 1868 (BG:303).

LEGG

1.1.9.1.7.2.1.5 CORNELIUS HENRY LEGG m1 Clara Haines

1   CORA LEGG b 1867.

2   CARRIE LEGG

3   ABBIE LEGG b 1869.

4   NELLIE LEGG b 1871.

5   ABRAHAM LEGG b 1873.

6   ALFRED LEGG b 1875.

7   CHARLES LEGG b 1877.

m2 07 Jun 1881 Gertrude Kerr

8   MAUDE HAINES LEGG b1887 BG:303, Info FT:56).

GENERATION 9

If a couple traces back to DeWitt ancestry more than once, m is {m} indicating this fact. Numbering used is the first parent listed chronologically. Both numbers are given but the one to be used in succeeding generations is underlined.

RILYEA
1.1.9.1.3.2.2.1.1 JOHANA ELIZABETH LONGENDYCK m Benjamin D Relyea
1. SARAH JANE RELYEA b 31 Jul 1846 d 16 Apr 1848 ae 01-09-16 bur Old Trumpbour Farm Mt Marion NY (GSIUC:2) bur Langendyke Grd one mile west of Mt Marion, likely same Cem, reading of weathered tbstn, abandoned Cem.
2. PRISCILLA CATHARINE RILYEA b 20 Jun 1848 bp 14 Aug 1848 (PRDC:28).
3. ANDREW DUBOISE RELYEA b 25 Aug 1851 bp 21 Mar 1852 (PRDC:32) m 10 Sep 1868 Elizabeth Catherine Lewis both of Saugerties wits, Charles Lewis & Sarah Link (PRDC:13).
4. JANE ELIZABETH RELYEA b 16 Jun 1856 bp 12 Oct 1856 (PRDC:36) m Silas C Newkirk.
5. MARY MARGARET RELYEA b 24 Jun 1859 bp 01 Mar 1861 (PRDC:41).
6. JOHANNA RELYEA m Charles Newkirk (fr MKW).

LONGNEDYKE
1.1.9.1.3.2.2.1.2 SIMON PETER LONGENDYKE m Lucinda Harriet Felten
1. MARY AGNESS LONGENDYKE b 01 Feb 1864 bp 08 May 1864 (PRDC:44) m 14 Nov 1883 Lewis York both of Saugerties wit: (bro) Solomon V York & Emma J Felton (PDRC:180) s/o Henry York & Hannah M Van Aken, b 18 Mar 1861 bp 24 Nov 1861 (PDRC:42).

LONGENDYK
1.1.9.1.3.2.2.1.3 JAMES LONGENDYK m Harriet Maria Plass
1. LILLIAN ADELADE LONGENDYCK b 20 Dec 1855 bp 28 Sep 1856 d 07 Jan 1857 (PRDC 1:36).
2. FRANKLIN DUMOND LONGENDYCK b 14 Oct 1857 (d 17 Jul 1915) m 13 Jun 1882 Ella Short b 23 Dec 1862 d 31 Jan 1928 (fr MKW).
3. LELIAN/LILLIAN ADELAIDE LONGENDYCK b 14 Oct 1860 bp 10 Mar 1861 (d 17 May 1930, fr MKW) m 26 Sep 1878 Watson J Short (BMRC:62) s/o Abrm H Short & Julia Kipp, b 14 Aug 1859 (PRDC:44).
4. ELMER LONGENDYCK b 13 Jul 1861 d 20 Sep 1862 **dy**.
5. DWIGHT SEBASTIAN LONGENDYCK b 28 Sep 1863 bp 08 May 1864 (PRDC 1:44) {m} Cora Agness Longendyke (1.1.9.1.3.2.2.1.4.6) d/o John O Longendyke & Elizabeth Van Aken, b 21 Nov 1867, bp 22 Aug 1869 (fr MKW) (PRDC:48).
6. HENRY A LONGENDYKE b 13 Nov 1866 d 06 Dec 1867 **dy** (fr MKW).
7. MAGGIE/LELITIA/MARGARET LONGENDYCK b 24 Sep 1869 bp 30 Jul 1871 (PRDC:50) m John Short.
8. JAMES E LONGENDYCK b 24 Jan 1873 d 03 Mar 1873 **dy** (fr EBSD).

LANGENDYCK
1.1.9.1.3.2.2.1.4 JOHN O LANGENDYK m Elizabeth Van Aken
1. JASON LONGENDYCK b 17 Jun 1858 bp 22 Aug 1858 (PRDC:38) m 20 Apr 1879 Sarah Emma Dubois, d/o Henry Dubois & Frances Wolven.
2. EMMA JANE LONGENDYCK b 28 Feb 1860 bp 12 May 1860 (PRDC:40) m 12 Dec 1878 Charles H Benn b 10 Apr 1852 s/o George A Benn & ? Bear.
3. MARY ELLEN LONGENDYCK b 05 Feb 1862 bp 22 Jun 1858 (PRDC:42) m 20 Oct 1879 Leonard Myers DuBois, s/o Henry Dubois & Frances Wolven (fr MKW, DuBois Book).
4. FORDYCE LONGENDYCK b 25 Mar 1864 bp 08 May 1864 (PRDC:44) m 29 Mar 1882 Elizabeth Windfield b 03 Jan 1862 d/o George Windfield & Rebecca Sparling.
5. IDA ANN LONGENDYCK b 24 Dec 1865 bp 22 Feb 1866 (PRDC:45) m 25 Jun 1884 Samuel Van Gaasbeck DuBois b 03 Sep 1885, s/o Harry Dubois & Rebecca Van Gaasbeck.
6. CORA AGNESS LONGENDYKE b 21 Nov 1867 bp 22 Aug 1869 (PRDC:48) {m} 05 Aug 1885 (BG:164) Dwight Sebastian Longendyke (1.1.9.1.3.2.2.1.3.5) s/o James Dumond Longendyke & Harriet M Plass, b 28 Sep 1863.
7. ARRIETTA LONGENDYKE b 28 Dec 1869 d 07 May 1870 **dy**.
8. EDWARD OTIS LONGENDYKE b 29 Apr 1871 bp 10 Aug 1871 (PRDC:50) **dy**.
9. NETTIE MAY LONGENDYKE b 27 Jul 1873 (PRDC:53).
10. SOLOMON LONGENDYKE b 10 Mar 1876 bp 04 May 1876 (PRDC:54) m Mary Kay (fr MKW).

VanBUERIN
1.1.9.1.3.2.2.1.5 MARY CATHERINE LONGENDYKE m Egbert Van Buren/Van Buerin
1. ANGELINE Van BUREN b 22 Jan 1854 bp 18 Jun 1854 (PRDC:34).
2. JENNIE Van BUERIN m Oliver Percy Maxwell.

Jannetjen (deWitt) Langendyk

MAGEE
1.1.9.1.3.2.2.1.6 MELINDA LONGENDYKE m Ephriam Magee
1   GODFREY MAGEE b 01 Jan 1858 bp 28 May 1858 (PDRC:38).

LOW
1.1.9.1.3.2.2.1.7 RACHEL ANN LONGENDYKE {m} 1.1.9.4.8.2.9.1 Alexander K Low
Children are with their Pa's underlined number Generation 8.

LANGENDYK
1.1.9.1.3.2.2.5.2 ELIZABETH CATHERINE LANGENDYKE {m} 1.1.9.1.4.1.6.2 Cornelius Edgar Langendyk
Children are with their Pa's underlined number Generation 8.

Van AKEN
1.1.9.1.3.2.2.5.5 JOANNA MARIA LONGENDYKE m Isaac Jason Van Aken
1.   EDWARD OTIS Van AKEN b 14 Nov 1866 bp 09 Apr 1867 (PRDC:46).
2.   MARY ELIZABETH Van AKEN b 29 Jul 1870 bp 02 Nov 1870 (PRDC:49).
3.   RUFUS CARL Van AKEN b 31 Jul 1875 bp 04 May 1876 (PRDC:54).

LANGENDYKE
1.1.9.1.3.2.2.5.6 JOHN A LANGENDYKE m Mary Amelia Low
1.   CHARLES LAURIN LANGENDYKE b 22 Sep 1868 bp 11 Jun 1869 (PRDC:48).
2.   CARRIE STEVENS LANGENDYKE b 17 May 1876 bp 09 Oct 1876 (PRDC:54) m Clyde I Gaddis (fr MKW).

FRANCE
1.1.9.1.3.2.2.5.8 MARY ALICE LONGENDYKE m Alfred France
1.   CHARLES HENRY FRANCE b 25 Oct 1873 bp 05 Jul 1874 (PDRC:53).
2.   LUELLA FRANCE bp 05 Jun 1875 (PRDC:53).

LANGENDYKE
1.1.9.1.3.2.2.5.10 PETER POST LANGENDYKE m Eudora Valk
1.   FANNIE E LONGENDYKE m Arthur R Elwyn.

SNYDER
1.1.9.1.3.4.6.5.1 CHARLES A SNYDER m1 Mary Jane Felter
1   WILLIAM SNYDER b 13 Jul 1873 d 25 Mar 1882 dy.
2   ANNA MAY SNYDER b 24 Jan 1875.
3   LUELLA SNYDER b 10 Dec 1878.
m2 14 May 1884 Louisa Burhans (1.1.9.4.2.5.2.8) b 19 Nov 1845 (BG:490)
THIS IS A PUZZLE SINCE LOUISA WOULD BE AGE 39, THEN SHE HAD SIX PREGNANCIES!
4   MARIA SNYDER m Richard Tappen.
5   CATHARINE ANN SNYDER m Ephriam Burhans
6   SARAH J SNYDER m John Kneiffer
7   ELIZABETH SNYDER **dy**, twin of
8   EDWINA SNYDER m George Sagendorf
9   CLINTON SNYDER m Emma Sagendorf
10   HEZEKIAH SNYDER m Sarah M Merritt. The Snyder Biography is from CBRUC:1132/3.

LONGENDYKE
1.1.9.1.3.6.4.5.1 THEODORE FREDERICK LONGENDYKE m1 Mary E Jones, m2 Lettie E Short
1   DOROTHY LONGENDYKE m George Hutton (fr MKW).

MILLER
1.1.9.1.3.6.4.5.5 FRANCES ELLEN LONGENDYKE m Charles L Miller
1   MARGARET E MILLER m Amos Burke.
2   VICTORIA L MILLER m Granville Messick.
3   (male)

STUART
1.1.9.1.3.6.4.5.6 MINNIE A LONGENDYKE m Arthur N Stuart
1   WILLIAM A STUART b 26 May 1912 (15 Apr 1979) m Peg Cassel.
2   ANNA WILHELMINA STUART b 22 Aug 1915 m Neil Malestein.

LONGENDYKE
1.1.9.1.3.6.4.5.7 WILLIAM F LONGENDYKE m Anna McMurray
1   ELIZABETH LONGENDYKE **single** (fr MKW).
2   FLOYD LONGENDYKE b Oct 1903 Kingston NY (d 13 Jan 1904 bur Wildwyck Cem.

LONGENDYKE
1.1.9.1.4.1.4.2.1 ERWIN LONGENDYKE m Elizabeth
1   NETTIE C LONGENDYKE b 1867 m 15 Oct 1892 Allen Van Valkenburg (Kgtn newspaper).
2   CHARLES LONGENDYKE b 1870.

Jannetjen (deWitt) Langendyk

LOWE
1.1.9.1.4.1.5.1.1 ORNELIA ANN LONGENDYKE m George C Lowe
1. EMMA LOWE b 14 May 1862.

LONGENDYKE
1.1.9.1.4.1.5.2.3 HENRY MONROE LONGENDYKE m Emma Stall (Lown)
1. JAMES HENRY LONGENDYKE b 12 Feb 1879 bp 13 Sep 1879 Woodstock CH (d 31 Aug 1946 ae 67-06-18) m Christine S German d/o Christian German, b 26 Sep 1880 Brooklyn NY d 03 Dec 1936 both bur Woodstock NY Cem.
2. LOUELLA LONGENDYKE b 08 Jan bp 10 Jan 1885.
3. NINA BELLE LONGENDYKE b 26 Jun 1884 bp 06 Jun 1885 (d 10 May 1943 Saugerties NY bur Woodstock Cem NY) m Harry G German.
4. HAZEL LONGENDYKE b 1890 (d 1915) m ? Teitter.
5. MARGARET M LONGENDYKE b 1882 Woodstock, in Kingston NY. He m 08 Aug 1912 William Van Bramer s/o William Van Bramer, b 1891 PA.

MERCHANT
1.1.9.1.4.1.5.3.1 MARIA CATHARINE/KATIE LONGENDYKE m James Merchant
1. WILLIAM T MERCHANT b 03 Mar 1870 Saugerties NY (d 17 Oct 1933 bur Mt Marion Cem) m 10 Oct 1892 Blanche E Fellows d/o John Fellows & Mary Houseley (fr MKW).

HURL
1.1.9.1.4.1.5.3.4 CHARLOTTE/LOTTA DELILAH LONGENDYKE m William W Hurl
1. LESTER W HURL b 22 Apr 883.
2. PERCY L HURL b 20 Jun 1884.

ZIEGLER
1.1.9.1.4.1.5.10.1 JENNIE YORK m William Ziegler
1. BLANCHE E ZIEGLER b 1887 d 1969.
2. JANE ZEIGLER b 1892 d 14 Feb 1982 bur Mt View Cem **single**.
3. WILLIAM WURSTER ZEIGLER b 23 May 1896 (d 22 Oct 1964 bur Mt View cem) m1 Margaret Ann Leide b 15 Jun 1906 d 09 Sep 1939; He m2 21 Feb 1945 Helen Elizabeth Martino.
4. EMMA LOUISE ZEIGLER b 1903 d 14 Aug 1965 bur Mt View Cem **single**.
5. MARJORIE ZIEGLER b 1907 (d 17 Dec 1964 bur Mt View Cem) m Carlton Strieder.

LONGENDYKE
1.1.9.1.4.1.6.1.1 WILLIAM FLOYD LONGENDYKE m Sarah Ellen/Ella Van Bramer York
1. MARTHA/MARHTA/MATTIE CORA LONGENDYKE b 16 Feb 1880 bp 10 Jul 1880 (BG:157 [d 1920]) m Judge Robert Lee Robertson of San Antonio TX (fr ESD).
2. ERLE HARVEY LONGENDYKE b 04 Feb 1882 bp 08 Jul 1882 Mt Marion (PRDC:57) & (d 1946) m 06 Jan 1904 Marie L Hart (Flatbush CH Rec) d/o Charles Hart & Mary Steigert, b 1883 d 31 Mar 1976 bur Mt Marion Cem, Saugerties T NY (fr ESD).
3. WILLIAM FLOYD LONGENDYKE II b 27 Jan 1892 (d 31 Jan 1917 Newburgh NY (alternate info [fr Mays] d 19 Jan 1919at Newburgh NY) bur Mt Marion Saugerties T) m 1912 Mildred Jane Netherton of Germantown, NY b 27 Jan 1893 d 08 Sep 1942 (fr ESD).

LONGENDYKE
1.1.9.1.4.1.6.1.2 CHARLES LONGENDYKE m Anna Catharine Weeks
1. ARTHUR LONGENDYKE b 26 Jun 1884 bp 02 Mar 1887 Glasco Meth CH (d 14 Sep 1926) Hasbrouck Heights, NJ) m 29 Jun 1907 Sarah Esther Cole d/o Charles William Cole & Sarah Esther Shultis, b 25 Jul 1884 Peekskill NY d 22 Mar 1960 Troy NY (fr ESD).
2. GRACE LONGENDYKE b 17 Aug 1886 bp 02 Mar 1887 Glasco M E CH d 06 Aug 1891 ae 05-11-20 bur Mt Marion Cem Saugerties T (OGUC:252).
3. HOWARD C LONGENDYKE b 04 Aug 1892 Saugerties T (d 18 Jun 1969 Brooklyn NY) m Ethel McManus d 20 Jan 1969 Brooklyn (fr ESD).
4. CORA BLANCHE LONGENDYKE b 27 Oct 1896 (d 08 Dec 1969) m Chester Bell d 06 Dec 1976 both bur Mt Marion.

LONGENDYKE
1.1.9.1.4.1.6.1.4 ADDISON LONGENDYKE m Mattie Frazer
1. MABEL LONGENDYKE b 18 Jun 1890 bp as an adult Glascoe Meth CH (d 28 Mar 1983 Saugerties) m Fred W Collins & div. He d 30 Jun 1964 (fr ESD).
2. ETHEL LONGENDYKE b 22 Jun 1896 Kingston NY (d Dec 1912 bur Wildwyck NY) m Harry Grasekamp.

LONGENDYKE
1.1.9.1.4.1.6.1.6 JASON LONGENDYKE m Leah Margaret York
1. NATHAN LONGENDYKE (originally Emery) b 06 Jan 1898 (Saugerties Rec fr MKW) d 17 Dec 1960 **single**.

YORK
1.1.9.1.4.1.6.1.7 CORA LONGENDYKE m Solomon Van Aken York
1. MYRTLE ALICE YORK b 26 Sep 1894 (d 28 Jul 1978) m 14 Sep 1921 Richard George Shortt s/o John F Shortt & Catherine Marguerter Friedrich (fr York-Longendyke Family Bible pub American Bible Society 1882) b 14 Jan 1902 d 13 Feb 1960 bur Mt Marion Cem (fr ESD & MAYS).

LONGENDYKE
1.1.9.1.4.1.6.1.8 VICTOR LONGENDYKE m Annie Van Aken
1. STANLEY LEON LONGENDYKE b 28 Feb 1903 bp 04 Sep 1904 Plattekill CH m 17 Mar 1925 Evelyn Lucille Feldman b 18 Jan 1904 Ramsey NJ d 03 Sep 1982 Tuscon AZ bur Mt Marion Cem Saugerties T NY (fr MKW).

CRAMER
1.1.9.1.4.1.6.2.2 & 1.1.9.1.3.2.2.5.2.2 ELVINA/ELLA LONGENDYKE m Charles Cramer
1. VIOLA BELLE CRAMER b 24 Nov 1888 bp 02 Jun 1889 Flatbush Rec (fr MKW).

LONGENDYKE
1.1.9.1.4.4.1.6.1 WILBUR LONGENDYKE m Mary A Carle
1. JENNIE LONGENDYKE b 11 Sep 1882 (in 1915 Kingston Dir).
2. MAUD EVA LONGENDYKE b 28 Apr 1890 d 02 Sep 1892 ae 02-04-04 bur Mt Marion cem. (OGUC:252)

LONGENDYKE
1.1.9.1.4.4.1.6.2 NORMAN LONGENDYKE m Mary
1. MYRTLE LONGENDYKE b 09 Jan 1888.
2. BLANCHE D LONGENDYKE b 1893.

WINNE
1.1.9.1.5.1.6.1.1 JOHN VALENTINE WINNE m1 Eliza C Kemble
1. AIDA WYNCOOP WINNE b 02 Oct 1855.
2. ELIZABETH DEDRICK WINNE b 16 Jun 1858.
3. CATHERINE COLLIER WINNE b 14 Dec 1862
4. HEZEKIAH WINNE b 07 Dec 1866.
   m2 06 Jun 1872 Ann Sax.

Jannetjen (deWitt) Langendyk

GENERATION 10

If a couple traces back to DeWitt ancestry more than once, m is {m} indicating this fact. Numbering used is the first parent listed chronologically. Both numbers are given but the one to be used in succeeding generations is underlined.

RELYEA
1.1.9.1.3.2.2.1.1.3 ANDREW DUBOISE RELYEA m Elizabeth Catherine Lewis
1. MAGGIE RELYEA b 1869.
2. DAVID HENRY LEWIS RELYEA b 1878 bp 10 Aug 1878 Flatbush CH Rec Ulster Co NY m 26 Oct 1898 Mary L Pomeroy b 1878 Woodlawn (NJ or NY) (fr MKW).

NEWKIRK
1.1.9.1.3.2.2.1.1.4 JANE ELIZABETH RELYEA m Silas C Newkirk
1. GEORGE ARTHUR NEWKIRK b 18 Nov 1882 bp 27 Apr 1887.
2. PETER EDWARD NEWKIRK b 30 Jun 1885 bp 27 Apr 1887.
3. JANE ELIZABETH NEWKIRK b 01 Dec 1889.
4. RALPH DUBOIS NEWKIRK b 20 Dec 1897 bp 08 Oct 1899 (fr MKW).

NEWKIRK
1.1.9.1.3.2.2.1.1.6 JOHANNA RELYEA m Charles Newkirk
1. ERNEST NEWKIRK b 1887 m Mabel Jones.
2. ISSAC NEWTON NEWKIRK b 05 Jul 1891 Glerie (d 09 Nov 1918) m Sophia M Hommel d 23 Mar 1975 both bur Mt Marion NY.
3. CHRISTIAN PAUL NEWKIRK **single**.
4. EDWARD J NEWKIRK b 1894, at Palenville NY m Laura Etta Mauterstock (fr MKW).

YORK
1.1.9.1.3.2.2.1.2.2 MARY AGNESS LONGENDYKE m Lewis York
1. CLARENCE YORK b 30 Nov 1884 bp 17 Jul 1886 Plattekill Dutch Reformed CH (d 08 Aug 1919 bur Mt Marion Cem ae 34-08-06) m 18 Oct 1909 Inez Lasher b 27 Feb 1887 d 30 Sep 1971 bur Mt Marion Cem. d/o George Lasher & Louisa Shortt. Inez Lasher m2 01 Feb 1922 Howard C Post.
2. EDITH MAY YORK b 26 Jul 1887 bp 14 Jul 1888 (PRDC) [bur Mt Marion Cem] m Abraham Coles.
3. HENRY YORK b 02 Jun 1892 bp 29 Apr 1893 (PDRC) [d 10 May 1959 bur Mt Marion Cem] St Mary's CH rec m1 03 Jul 1915 Anna Connelly d/o George H Connolly & Sarah J Clark, d 16 May 1922; Henry m2 24 May 1924 Anna Herring d/o Frederick Herring & Theresa Lamelein, b 29 Jan 1892 d 12 Apr 1957.
4. LEWIS YORK Jr b 29 Dec 1903 bp 21 Jun 1905 (PRDC) [d Dec 1980 bur Mt Marion Cem] m Genevieve. (info fr MKW).

LONGENDYKE
1.1.9.1.3.2.2.1.3.2 FRANKLIN DUMOND LONGENDYKE m Ella Short
1. CORNELIUS DUMOND LONGENDYKE b 18 Jul 1883 NYC bp 10 Jan 1884 (PRDC) [d 25 Sep 1938 Saugerties T NY bur Mt Marion cem] m 07 Jun 1905 Cressie Lasher d/o George Lashur & Louisa Short b 29 Feb 1884 bp 05 Sep 1884 Woodstock NY d 31 Jan 1971 Kingston bur Mt Marion Cem.
2. WATSON LeROY LONGENDYKE b 05 Feb 1885 bp 20 Sep 1885 (DRCFU fr MKW) [d 10 Apr 1946]. At the bride's home he m 29 Jun 1909 Emma Lena Carle d/o Nathan Carle & Martha York, b 22 Aug 1882 Saugerties d 06 Dec 1968.
3. MARY HOWELL LONGENDYKE b 20 Jun 1886 bp 04 Jan 1887 (PRDC) [d 14 May 1976 Elmira NY bur Pine City NY] m 04 Feb 1906 Richard France Hunt b 12 Jan 1880 d 20 Jul 1963 bur Pine City NY.
4. PEARL LEONA LONGENDYKE b 06 Mar 1888 during a blizzard, bp 05 May 1889 (RDCFU) [d 24 Oct 1927 Saugerties bur Mt Marion Cem] at Bayonne NJ. She m 20 Sep 1916 Raymon/Rex Vala s/o Raymond Vala & Amy, b 19 Jun 1880 d 08 Oct 1966.
5. CLAUDE SHELDON LONGENDYKE b 02 Sep 1889 (d 21 May 1979 Kingston bur Mtn View Cem) m 05 June 1915 Susie Shultis d/o Sherman Shultis & Elizabeth Broadhead b 12 Jul 1894 d 26 Oct 1978 Kingston bur Mtn View.
6. JENNIE EVELYN LONGENDYKE b 15 Nov 1891 Saugerties T d 22 Jan 1906 bur Mt Marion cem.
7. CECIL KENNETH LONGENDYKE b 23 Aug 1893 Saugerties (d 25 Nov 1943 Schenectady NY) m 27 Aug 1917 Eva E Patell b 26 Jul 1893 Malone NY d 26 Jan 1992 Schenectady NY.
8. ALICE LILLIAN LONGENDYKE b 28 May 1896 bp 05 Jun 1910 (DRCFU [d 19 Jun 1971 Saugerties]) m1 24 Dec 1914 Raymond Benton b 15 Nov 1895 Kingston d 14 Mar 1984, at Saugerties. She m2 20 Mar 1943 William H Quigley b 15 Sep 1888 NJ d 06 Jul 1951 Saugerties both bur Mt Marion Cem.
9. STANLEY CLIFTON LONGENDYKE b 26 Jul 1898 Saugerties (d 07 May 1941 Saugerties). At Brooklyn NY m 26 Apr 1924 Mildred Luhman b 09 Apr 1904 Brooklyn d 18 Dec 1985 Kingston.
10. HAROLD ROOSEVELT LONGENDYKE b 26 Jun 1900 Saugerties d 02 Sep 1905 Kingston bur Mt Marion, **single**.

Jannetjen (deWitt) Langendyk

11 AMY SOPHIA LONGENDYKE b 05 Aug 1902 Saugerties (d 28 Apr 1992 Saugerties) at Saugerties m 11 Oct 1942 Frank Provenzano s/o Joseph Provenzano & Catherine Martino b 08 Sep 1914 Glasco NY d 30 Jan 1965 Woodstock NY both bur Mt Marion.
12 NETTIE EVA LONGENDYKE b 09 Oct 1905 Saugerties (d 05 Nov 1973 Kingston bur Mt Marion) at Saugerties m1 22 Jun 1925 Harold McAdam Kamp s/o John C Kamp & Louise Marie Wahl b 02 May 1896 Buffalo NY d 06 Aug 1958 Kingston bur Mt Marion Cem; at Lexington SC m2 26 Jun 1943 George V Swart s/o James Swart & Anna Roosa, b 14 Oct 1917 Saugerties d 21 Jan 1990 Kingston bur Mt Marion Cem.

SHORT

1.1.9.1.3.2.2.1.3.3 LILLIAN A LONGENDYKE m Watson J Short

1 FRANKLIN WATSON SHORT b 12 Jul 1881? bp Jan 188? (PRDC:56) d 01 Nov 1888 High Woods NY, diptheria, bur Mt Marion ae 07-03-20.
2 ETHEL MAY SHORT b 23 May 1886 bp 04 Jan 1887 (PRDC d before 1931) m George Ingram.
3 SARAH KATHRYN/KATIE SHORT b 1 Sep 1889 bp 30 Mar 1890 (PRDC CH rec d 23 Dec 1964) m 07 Oct 1909 Arthur Backus b 18 Feb 1885 d 04 Nov 1957.
4 WARREN HELMUS SHORT b 2 Sep 1892 bp Nov 1894 (DRCFU d Schenectady NY) m Eva Sherman (fr MKW).
5 MARGARET LILLIAN SHORT b 16 Feb 1894 bp Nov 1894 (DRCFU d 19 Dec 1979) m James Gaddis b 1885 d 1975.
6 LEWIS MONTGOMERY SHORT b 26 Jan 1898 bp 30 Jan 1903 (ODCKU:101 d 1956 Kingston bur Montrepose Cem) m Leona Prindle.
7 CHESTER ROOSEVELT SHORT b 03 May 1900 bp 30 Jan 1903 (ODCKU:101).
8 CLAUDE LAMONT SHORT b 04 Mar 1902 bp 30 Jan 1903 (ODCKU:101 the three bp at Bethany Chapel) m Ruth Erikson.

LONGENDYKE

1.1.9.1.3.2.2.1.3.5 DWIGHT SEBASTIAN LONGENDYKE {m}Cora Agnes Longendyke (1.1.9.1.3.2.2.1.4.6)

1 EMMA MAY LONGENDYKE b 24 Nov 1886 bp 26 May 1889 (Plattekill CH Rec) & (d 29 Nov 1915 ae 29-00-05) in Hurley NY CH Rec m 16 Aug 190? Harley John Palen s/o John H Palen & Sarah Emily Hogan, b 07 Jul 1885 bur Hurley Cem. He m2 Mary Howard.
2 SARAH ADELAIDE/ADDIE LONGENDYKE b 20 Feb 1889 bp 26 May 1889. Brought up by Aunt Let (fr MKW) & (d 31 Jan 1967) m1 08 Mar 1908 Leslie Bush; m2 Walter Adams div 1939.
3 LEETTA WATSON LONGENDYKE b 17 Jul 1891 (d 17 Aug 1970) in Hurley CH Rec m 23 May 1909 Arthur Beesmer s/o George W Beesmer & Katie A Krom, b 06 Jul 1884 d 12 Mar 1952.
4 MABEL RADCLIFFE LONGENDYKE b 10 Aug 1893 (d 30 Nov 1978) m 18 Aug 1915 John Wojciehowski.
5 JAMES DUMOND LONGENDYKE b 03 Jun 1896 m ? Aug 1916 Susan A Polhemus/Purhamus ("A Tree Grows in Ulster") b 17 Mar 1898 d 24 Sep 1979. She m2 23 Feb 1925 Arthur H Brown.
6 FRANKLIN DWIGHT LONGENDYKE b 17 Nov 1898 (twin of James) & (d ? Dec 1949 bur Woodstock NY) m 08 Oct 1920 Eva Beesmer d/o George W Beesmer & Katie A Krom, b 24 Sep 1896 d 11 Apr 1952 bur Woodstock Cem.
7 MARGARET LETITIA/MARGIE LONGENDYKE b 01 Apr 1901 (d 04 May 1931) m 14 Dec 1919 Albert Wolfersheim.
8 JOHN OSTRANDER LONGENDYKE b 13 Aug 1907 (d 18 Nov 1978) m Aletha Anna May Delevan d/o Edwin V Delevan & Laura Hoffman (all fr MKW).

BENN

1.1.9.1.3.2.2.1.4.2 EMMA J LONGENDYKE m Charles H Benn

1 HERMAN F BENN b 30 Jun 1879 d 12 Oct 1881 ae 02-03-12 bur West Camp NY.
2 RAYMOND BENN b 1881 m Mary ? b 1888.
3 MAGGIE BENN b 10 Mar 1883 at West Camp.
4 NETTIE BENN b 1890.
5 KATIE M BENN b 1891.

DeBOIS

1.1.9.1.3.2.2.1.4.3 MARY ELLEN LONGENDYKE m Leonard Myers DuBois

1 FRANKLIN DuBOIS b 29 Jun 1881 (DuBois Book #3392).
2 LOTTIE MAY DuBOIS b 10 Apr 1884 d 28 Apr 1889 ae 5 bur Wildwyck Cem Kingston NY (DuBois book #3393).
3 MABEL DuBOIS b 1895.
The American Descendants of Chretien DuBois of Wicres, France by William Heidgerd. Huguenot Historical Society. New Paltz NY, Vols.

LONGENDYKE

1.1.9.1.3.2.2.1.4.6 CORA AGNES LONGENDYKE {m} 1.1.9.1.3.2.2.1.3.5 Dwight Sebastian Longendyke
Children are with their father's underlined number Generation 8.

Jannetjen (deWitt) Langendyk

LONGENDYKE
1.1.9.1.3.2.2.1.4.9 SOLOMON/SOL LONGENDYKE m Mary Kay
1. FRED LONGENDYKE b 26 Feb 1896 (d 04 Aug 1954) m Catherine Schnider d/o Jacob Schnider & Mary E Reis b 23 Apr 1897
2. ETHEL LONGENDYKE b 1898.
3. HILDA E LONGENDYKE b 14 Jul 1911 bp 03 Sep 1911 Clinton Ave CH Rec #769.

GADDIS
1.1.9.1.3.2.2.5.6.2 CARRIE STEVENS LONGENDYKE m Clyde I Gaddis
1. PERCY WINFIELD GADDIS b 29 Sep 1897 bp 07 Jan 1899 Plattekill CH Rec, m at Saugerties 04 Apr 1926 Alice Josephine Marsden d/o George Marsden & Mary E Aldrich b 09 Dec 1904 Providence RI.
2. HAROLD IRVING GADDIS b 29 Jan 1907 At Ruby he was bp 22 Nov 1908 Plattekill CH Rec m Eleanor Delores Kidd d/o David M Kidd & Edna A St John, b 10 Jan 1909.
3. HELEN ELIZABETH GADDIS b 03 Mar 1910, At Saugerties she m 30 Mar 1929 George F Seyler s/o Wendell Seyler & Catherine Ebell.

ELWYN
1.1.9.1.3.2.2.5.10.1 FANNIE E LONGENDYKE m Arthur R Elwyn
1. CATHERINE ELWYN b 07 Jun 1908.

MESSICK
1.1.9.1.3.6.4.5.5.2 VICTORIA L MILLER m Granville Messick
1. MARGARET/PEGGY MESSICK m Amos Burke.

LONGENDYKE
1.1.9.1.4.1.5.2.3.1 JAMES HENRY LONGENDYKE m Christianna German
1. JAMES MONROE LONGENDYKE b 03 Jan 1907 NYC (d 28 Feb 1992 Morrisville NC) m Adele Frantz b 11 Jan 1903 d 24 Aug 1991 Raleigh NC.

GERMAN
1.1.9.1.4.1.5.2.3.3 NINA BELLE LONGENDYKE m Harry German
1. LILLIAN L GERMAN b 24 Dec 1906 d 29 Aug 1934 ae 27-09-05 at a TB hospital single.

ZIEGLER
1.1.9.1.4.1.5.10.1.3 WILLIAM WURSTER ZIEGLER m1 Martaret Ann Leide
1. MARJORIE ZIEGLER b 27 Jan 1928 m 20 Sep 1948 Herbert G Chaffe Jr.
2. JANE M ZIEGLER b 22 May 1934 at Saugerties Ref CH m 20 Sp 1953 William J Kiernan.
3. WILLIAM CHARLES ZEIGLER b 21 Sep 1939 m Carolyn Marrozziti.
   m2 21 Feb 1945 Helen <u>Elizabeth</u> Martino.
4. HELEN LOUISE ZIEGLER b 21 Jun 1950 m 14 Aug 1977 John Eric Paulsen.
5. ANN MARGARET ZIEGLER b 10 Nov 1951 m 27 Oct 1977 Randall Geyssens.
6. ELIZABETH EVELYN ZIEGLER 16 May 1956.

ROBERTSON
1.1.9.1.4.1.6.1.1.1 MARTHA CORA LONGENDYKE m Robert Lee Robertson
1. ROBERT LEE ROBERTSON Jr
2. HAMILTON GOODMAN ROBETSON
3. FLOYD CLAY ROBERTSON

LONGENDYKE
1.1.9.1.4.1.6.1.1.2 ERLE HAVEY LONGENDYKE m Marie L Hart
1. HAROLD KENNETH/DICK LONGENDYKE b 22 Mar 1904 bp 21 Jun 1904 Pattekill CH Rec (d 07 Aug 1983 ae 79-05-18). At 12 Alcazar Ave. he m 1927 Janet McLean.
2. GLADYS MILDRED LONGENDYKE b 1905 (d 1946) m Harrison Barnes.
3. ERLE WILLIAM LONGENDYKE b 15 Dec 1907 Ruby NY (d 10 Aug 1982) m Mildred Nickerson b 31 Dec 1911 d
4. ? Jan 1981.
5. CLIFFORD H LONGENDYKE b 09 Nov 1911 (d 26 Aug 1976) served in C.S.F. in WW II m Jeanne W b 1925.
6. ELLA LONGENDYKE b 09 Mar 1917 m1 Frederick Edlefsen; she m2 Oscar/Tex Holt.

LONGENDYKE
1.1.9.1.4.1.6.1.1.3 WILLIAM FLOYD LONGENDYKE II m Mildred Jane Netherton
1. WILLIAM FLOYD LONGENDYKE III b 26 Apr 1914 m 26 Nov 1936 Germaine Lucy McDermott.

LONGENDYKE
1.1.9.1.4.1.6.1.2.1 ARTHUR LONGENDYKE m Sarah Cole
1. MIRIAM ESTHER LONGENDYKE b 19 Aug 1909 (d 20 Dec 1986 Sidney NY bur Mt Marion NY) m Robert B MacDonald b 16 Jan 1906 Sidney NY d 1975.
2. STUART ARTHUR LONGENDYKE b 21 Jul 1915 Brooklyn m1 Helen Lamphere; m2 Eleanor Sanderson.

LONGENDYKE
1.1.9.1.4.1.6.1.2.3 HOWARD LONGENDYKE m Ethel McManus
1   LAURA LONGENDYKE b 27 Jul 1917 m Arthur Kear.
2   ELWOOD LONGENDYKE b 10 May 1919 m Mary Duffy.
3   JOHN LONGENDYKE b 26 Feb 1923 (d 14 Apr 1973) m Charlotte Brossen.

COLLINS
1.1.9.1.4.1.6.1.4.1 MABEL LONGENDYDKE m Fred W Collins
1   ROBERT COLLINS b 17 Jul 1917 m Joan Elizabeth Fear b 15 Jun 1934.
2   EEANOR COLLINS b 14 May 1922 m George Wendell Faust b 04 Jul 1920 d 1983.

SHORTT
1.1.9.1.4.1.6.1.7.1 MYRTLE ALICE YORK m Richard George Shortt
1   HAROLD LEWIS SHORTT b 23 Nov 1922 m 25 Sep 1949 Marie Shirley Hill b 25 Nov 1929.
2   ETHEL BLANCH SHORTT b 10 Jan 1924 m 30 Jun 1946 LeRoy Donaldson b 20 Jul 1924.
3   VIVIAN JANETTE SHORTT b 1925 d 23 Dec 1932 ae 07-05-14 bur Mt Marion.
4   DOROTHY ELOISE SHORTT b 25 Aug 1930 m1 25 Mar 1951 Francis X Stenson b 08 Feb 1920 (d 21 May 1979) m2 25 Aug 1984 Max Hofman b 17 Mar ?   (EBSD).

LONGENDYKE
1.1.9.1.4.1.6.1.8.1 STANLEY LEON LONGENDYKE m Evelyn Lucille Feldman
1   EILEEN LONGENDYKE b 25 Apr 1925 bp 04 Jul 1925 First Congregational CH & m there 15 Oct 1945 Henry Antonelli s/o Henry Antonelli, b 17 Nov 1921 (fr ESD: MKW).

Jannetjen (deWitt) Langendyk

GENERATION 11

LONGENDYKE
1.1.9.1.4.1.6.1.1.2.1 HAROLD K LONGENDYKE m Janet McLean
1. HAROLD JOHN/JACK LONGENDYKE b 1927 m1 ? m2 Kay Violette.
2. JAMES LONGENDYKE
3. DENNIS LONGENDYKE
4. JOSEPH EUGENE/JOE LONGENDYKE
5. GWEN LONGENDYKE m Myron Rossi.
6. ELLA LONGENDYKE m ? Holt (fr MAYS).

BARNES
1.1.9.1.4.1.6.1.1.2.2 GLADYS MILDRED LONGENDYKE m Harrison Barnes
1. HELEN MARIE BARNES
2. HARRISON B BARNES

LONGENDYKE
1.1.9.1.4.1.6.1.1.2.3 ERLE WILLIAM LONGENDYKE m Mildred Nickerson
1. JANICE LONGENDYKE
2. KAY REBECCA LONGENDYKE

LONGENDYKE
1.1.9.1.4.1.6.1.1.2.4 CLIFFORD H LONGENDYKE m Jeanne
1. CLIFFORD H LONGENDYKE b 1947.

EDLEFSEN/HOLT
1.1.9.1.4.1.6.1.1.2.5 ELLA LONGENDYKE m1 Frederick Edlefsen
1. DAWN EDLEFSEN b 19 Apr 1935 m Fred Brinner.
2. MARIN EDLEFSEN b 30 Jul 1937 m Ida C Savoie.

m2 Oscar/Tex Holt

LONGENDYKE
1.1.9.1.4.1.6.1.1.3.1 WILLIAM FLOYD LONGENDYKE III m Germaine Lucy McDermott
1. JEANNE ALICE LONGENDYKE b 11 Feb 1938 m 25 Oct 1958 Francis A Chauncey.
2. JANET GERMAINE LONGENDYKE b 07 May 1942 m 07 Jul 1962 M Richard Kalter.

MacDONALD
1.1.9.1.4.1.6.1.2.1.1 MIRIAM ESTHER LONGENDYKE m Robert B MacDonald
1. ROBERT DUNCAN MacDONALD b 04 Jan 1936 m1 Nancy Baker; m2 Mary Ellen Bruhn.

LONGENDYKE
1.1.9.1.4.1.6.1.2.1.2 STUART ARTHUR m1 Helen Lamphere
1. ALLEN LONGENDYKE b 22 Jul 1951.

m2 Eleanor Sanderson

LONGENDYKE
1.1.9.1.4.1.6.1.2.3.2 ELWOOD LONGENDYKE m Mary Duffy
1. THOMAS LONGENDYKE
2. BRIAN LONGENDYKE

LONGENDYKE
1.1.9.1.4.1.6.1.2.3.3 JOHN LANGENDYKE m Charlotte Brossen
1. JOHN LONGENDYKE Jr
2. LYNNE LONGENDYKE

COLLINS
1.1.9.1.4.1.6.1.4.1.1 ROBERT COLLINS m Joan Elizabeth Fear
1. JAMES ROBERT COLLINS b 22 Jul 1969.

FAUST
1.1.9.1.4.1.6.1.4.1.2 ELEANOR LONGENDYKE m George Wendell Faust
1. GEORGE RANDALL FAUST b 18 Nov 1947 m Cathy Cowan.
2. ROBERT THOMAS FAUST b 19 Apr 1951.
3. VIRGINIA ANN FAUST b 31 Oct 1952 m Michael Bradford.
4. ELIZABETH JAN FAUST b 11 Nov 1958.

SHORTT
1.1.9.1.4.1.6.1.7.1.1 HAROLD LEWIS SHORTT m Marie Shirley Hill
1. RANDY RICHARD SHORTT b 11 Feb 1956 m 17 May 1981 Susan Pare.
2. DALE RAYMOND SHORTT b 07 May 1958.

Jannetjen (deWitt) Langendyk

DONALDSON
1.1.9.1.4.1.6.1.7.1.2 ETHEL BLANCHE SHORTT m Leroy Donaldson
1. BEVERLY DONALDSON b 25 Dec 1948 m 08 Jun 1968 Kenneth Skidmore b 30 Dec 1944.
2. KATHLEEN DONALDSON b 31 Dec 1949 m 08 Aug 1970 Walter Skidmore b 30 Dec 1944, twin of Kenneth.
3. ROGER MARK DONALDSON b 11 Mar 1956 d 12 Mar 1956.

STENSON/HORMAN
1.1.9.1.4.1.6.1.7.1.4 DOROTHY E SHORTT m1 Francis X Stenson m2 Max Hofman
1. DENNIS STENSON b 18 Mar 1952 m 06 May 1978 Barbara Kleeman b 20 Nov ? .
2. PATRICIA ANN STENSON b 15 Mar 1953 m 03 Jul 1983 Robert Maxwell.
3. MARIE V STENSON b 15 Nov 1961.
4. PATRICK STENSON b 17 Sep 1963.
5. BRIDGET STENSON b 21 Nov 1966.

ANTONELLI
1.1.9.1.4.1.6.1.8.1.1 EILEEN LONGENDYKE m Henry Antonelli
1. HENRY VICTOR ANTINOLLI b 02 Sep 1945 m 03 Jun 1967 Susan Mary Keigher b 14 Oct 1945; m2 ? Nov 1986.

GENERATION 12
BINNER
1.1.9.1.4.1.6.1.1.2.5.1. DAWN EDLEFSEN m Fred Binner
1. MARK FREDERICK BINNER
2. ELLINE DAWN BINNER
3. LYNELLA ANN BINNER (info fr EBSD).

EDLEFSEN
1.1.9.1.4.1.6.1.1.2.5.2 MARTIN EDLEFSEN m Ida C Savoie
1. FREDERICK HERMAN EDLEFSEN
2. KIRSTEN MARIE EDLEFSEN (fr EBSD).

CHAUNCY
1.1.9.1.4.1.6.1.1.3.1.1 JEANNE ALICE LONGENDYKE m Francis A Chauncy
1. TRINA CHAUNCY b 05 Aug 1959.
2. LIA CHAUNCY b 23 Feb 1961.
3. KIMBERLY CHAUNCY b 07 Aug 1962.
4. CHARLES CHAUNCY b 25 Oct 1963.
5. DANIEL CHAUNCY b 05 Jul 1972 (info fr EBSD).

KALTER
1.1.9.1.4.1.6.1.1.3.1.2 JANET GERMAINE LONGENDYKE m Richard M Kalter
1. DAVID KALTER b 11 Aug 1963 (fr EBSD).

MacDONALD
1.1.9.1.4.1.6.1.2.1.1.1 ROBERT DUNCAN MacDONALD m1 Nancy Baker; m2 Mary Ellen Bruhn
1. CHRISTINE DIANE McDONALD b 29 Jul 1966.
2. SEAN EAN McDONALD b 10 Jan 1969 (info fr EBSD).

FAUST
1.1.9.1.4.1.6.1.4.1.2.1 GOERGE RANDALL FAUST m Cathy Cowan
1. AMANDA FAUST b ? Jan 1972 (fr EBSD).

HILL
1.1.9.1.4.1.6.1.7.1.1.1 RANDY RICHARD SHORTT m Susan Pare
1. KELLI ANN SHORTT b 24 Feb 1987 (fr EBSD).

SKIDMORE
1.1.9.1.4.1.6.1.7.1.2.1 BEVERLY DONALDSON m Kenneth Skidmore
1. KENNETH RICHARD SKIDMORE b 26 Jan 1969.
2. BETHANNE SKIDMORE b 12 Feb 1970.
3. SEAN AUSTIN SKIDMORE b 05 Feb 1982 (info fr EBSD).

SKIDMORE
1.1.9.1.4.1.6.1.7.1.2.2 KATHLEEN DONALDSON m Walter Skidmore
1. STACY COLLEEN SKIDMORE b 06 Oct 1974.
2. KIMBERLY ANN SKIDMORE b 03 Jan 1977 (fr EBSD).

ANTONELLI
1.1.9.1.4.1.6.1.8.1.1.1 HENRY VICTOR ANTONELLI m Susan Mary Keigher
1. LISA MARIE ANTONELLI b ? Nov 1986 (fr EBSD).   *THE END*

GENERATION 4

Please note – Generation 1 Nicholaas/Class deWitt starts on pages 15-16. Generation 2, Tireck Clafen DeWitt is pages 18-21. Generation 3 is Luycas DeWitt page 22. This work is tracing the ancestry of Luycas DeWitt's three surviving children. They have been tabulated so that the information appears separately for each one.

DeWIT

1.1.9.3 JAN deWIT m Ariaantjen Osterhout

1. MARIA DeWIT bp 16 Feb 1735 DRC Catskill sp Ludwig Blanck, Marytche Blanck (NYGBR 86:16) m 10 Apr 1757 Christian (K&S: 245) s/o Pieter Winnen/Winne & Antjen/Antje Van der Merken/Merkel bp 12 Oct 1735 sp Chistiaan Meyer, Geertruy Stefanus (DRCK:213) res Kingston & then Saugerties.

2. PETRUS DeWIT bp 26 Dec 1737 at Katsbaan sp Henrich ?, Grietje (K&S:3) m Rachel Van Leuven. Petrus became a member of the RDC Rochester T 10 Nov 1769 (RRCAU:232). Peter & wf Rachel Van Lowen are sp at the bp of Rachel d/o Maria DeWit (Peter's sis) & Christian Winne 23 Oct 1774 in Saugerties T (K&S:54). The author has not succeeded in contacting Cora E Nelson, deceased (last found at Tumwater WA) a descendant of John Van Leuven DeWitt. We place Petrus & Rachel in this line on the basis of family baptismal connections continuing even after they moved to Rochester T & negative evidence of belonging elsewhere.

3. JOHANNES DeWIT bp 25 Dec 1739 sp (possibly pa's cousin & sis) Tjerk deWit, Jannetjen deWit (DRCK: 244) m1 Maria Rothersdorf; m2 27 Oct 1781 Ann Snyder (K&S:247).

4. EZECKIEL DeWIT bp 27 Sep 1741 sp (pa's uncle) Beek (sic [Peek]) deWit, Mareitje Overbach (DRCK:255) m 06 Apr 1760 Maria Keller (K&S:245) d/o Jacob Keller & Barbara Hein/Heyn bp 22 Apr 1739 sp Velde Keller, Margriet Hein (DRCK:239). In 1758 in Ulster Co NY Ezekiel was a Pvte ae 17 in the Seven Years War in the WVA Militia in the Revo in the Compendium of American Genealogy (CAG 6:398) They lived in Kingston in 1762. By 1768 they settled with 10 other families at Turkey Foot, now Confluence PA. Peter Keller moved to PA also; his Will WA Co PA. Ezeckiel moved to Buffalo Creek, Hopewell T Washington Co PA before 1776 where he was appointed constable that year. There in 1778 he had a tavern and was in the Pittsburg fighting (DFUSC:63). He was a Pvte in the WVA Militia in the Revo (CAG 6:398). The census of 1781 for Hopewell T WA Co PA lists for Ezekiel 400 acres of land, 2 horses & 4 cows valued at 177 £. At Harrisburg PA there is a land patent for 400 acres for Ezekiel DeWitt dated Feb 24, 1782 and said to have been granted originally in Ohio Co VA. Before 1775 in Ohio Co Ezekiel was a slaveholder. The transcript of the Ohio Co VA record ends with 01 Sep 1780 when the County seat was withdrawn to Wheeling (now WVA). State boundaries changed in this time period. Boyd Crumine's Records of old Virginia Courts contain numerous mentions of Ezekiel deWitt of which the following are examples: At a Court held for Augusta Co at Pittsburg Jan 16, 1776 Ezekiel deWitt is app'ted a Const(able) in the room of J Carpenter. In Compliance with which (order of VA General Assembly) and certain other instructions.... directing him....to summon the several landholders within said Co Ohio to meet at the house of Ezekiel DeWitt on Buffalo Creek on the Dec 27 last as well as for the purpose of electing and constituting a committee in and for the said Co Court to be held in the future, within sd Co. Which was done accordingly. Nov 3 1778 Ord that Ezekiel DeWitt, Jeremiah Murr and others, or any three of them view the most convenient way for a road from the Court House to Annanish Davis's Mill and make report....to the next Court. Ordered that Ezekiel DeWitt do act as overseer for the opening of the road from Bogg Mill to the Court House and that he summon the Tithables within three miles of the South of sd road to work thereon.
On the motion of Ezekiel DeWitt, ordered that his mark (for cattle) a crop of the near ear be recorded (fr KWS; CCD2) In the West Virginia Society, Sons of the Revolution p446 elected to membership, Ezekiel's descendant Herbert Johnson DeWitt, Terra Alta, Preston Co, West Virginia State #714 (DFUSC:153).

5. CORNELIS DeWIT bp 26 Dec 1743 sp Willem Dorner & wf Anneke Osterhout (K&S: 7) m Marietje Osterhout. Cornelis & Maritje were sp at bp of Sara Winne d/o Maria deWitt & Christian Winne 12 May 1776 Kingston & were sp for bro Benjamin's son Cornelis at Schaghticoke, Albany Co (Rensselaer Co) b 04 Sep 1783. It's not known if they had chn or where they went.

6. BENJAMIN DeWIT bp 26 Dec 1745 sp Efraim Van Keuren, Elisabeth Borhans (DRCK:281) m 1775 Maria d/o Lewis & Annetje (Quackenbos) Veile, bp Albany NY 24 Feb 1754. Benjamin res in Herkimer Co in 1800 census.

7. WILHELM/WILLEM DeWIT bp 26 Dec 1747 sp Theunis Osterhout wf Catharina Leg (K&S:11) m1 Maria, m2 Catrina d/o Johann Jury & Catrina (Spaan) Overbaugh/Overbag/Overbagh, bp Catskill Jan 1754.

8. JACOB DeWIT bp 28 Mar 1749 sp Jacob Brink, wf Marietje Elig (K&S:12).

9. ARIE DEWIT bp 30 Mar 1752 sp (pa's cousin & wf) Arie Van Etten, wf Christina Dewit (K&S:16).

Recognizance 26 Feb 1767 of Jan DeWitt, yoeman and Arieanentje (sic) his wife, and Christian Fiero, all of Kingston, for Jan and Ariaentje DeWitt to appear in court and keep the peace, especially toward John Walker of Kingston, schoolmaster (NGSQ 61:295).

GENERATION 5

If a couple traces back to DeWitt ancestry more than once, m is {m} indicating this fact. Numbering used is the first parent listed chronologically. Both numbers are given but the one to be used in succeeding generations is underlined.

WINNE
1.1.9.3.1 MARIA DeWITT m Christian Winne

1. ARRIANTJE WINNE bp 26 Dec 1757 sp (grprts) Jan Dewit & wf Arriantje Osterhout (K&S: 23) as Ariaantje of Shandaken NY m banns 22 Jul 1777 Ignatius/Igneas/Ignas Dumond (DRCK:637) res in Bakatakan (sic) s/o Peter Dumond/Dumont/Dumon & Maria Wagenen, bp 23 Sep 1753 as Ygenas sp Jacobus Dumon, wf Catharina Schuyler (DRCK:318). There were 2 Ignatius Dumonds b in 1753 but Olde Ulster & Family Trees indicate this one. Peter Dumond and two other men set out from the Hudson Valley in 1762 in the autumn, locating near an Indian Settlement (now Arkville) and purchasing farms. These four pioneer families were the first permanent settlement on the East Branch of the Delaware River (OU 4:154/5; Ft:31) 1800 census has Egnus Dumond as in Delaware T NY. Another item: Ignatius Dumond was the first settler on the present site of Margaretville in 1784 where he owned a farm, which he sold for £100. He then went back in the woods seven miles to the present new Kingston. The valley was covered with heavy primitive forest and the first six families, of which he was one, were compelled to blaze their way on trees to be able to find their way back (OU 4:155).
2. JONATHAN WINNE bp 16 Apr 1759 sp Johannes DeWit, Heiltje Osterhout (K&S:25) m1 Eve Van Wagenen; m2 Ann/Anny Davis b 03 Jan 1758.
3. CORNELIS WINNE bp 04 Oct 1760 sp Cornelis Brink, wf Annaatje Winne (K&S:27) m Elizabeth Martin/Martha/Masten/Marta.
4. MARIA/MARIAH WINNE/WINNER/WINNOW bp 03 Jul 1762 sp (her uncle & wf) Ezechiel Dewit, Maria Keller (K&S:29) Family Tree says she m Petrus Jong (FT:124). Her family as sp/o her chn's bp indicate she m Conrad Wespel/Wisper (maybe both men).
5. LUCAS WINNE bp 29 Jan 1764 sp Lucas Langendeik, wf Christina Wolvin (K&S:31) m1 Maria Oakley/Oaklie d/o Rutgert Oakley & Alida Schert bp 15 Sep 1765. Richard Oakley's Will 27 Sep 1791 Pro 01 Jun 1792 left two farms at Marbletown T Ulster Co equipment & stock to dau Mary w/o son-in-law Lucas Winner (sic) who was one of the Exs: (UCPR 2:95). He m2 1792 Rachel Davis.
6. ANNATJE WINNE bp 28 Jan 1766 sp Cornelis Brink, Annatje Brink (K&S:35) m Benjamin Bush.
7. FREDERIK WINNE bp 13 Jan 1768 sp (ma's cousin & wf, the wd/o his uncle Frederick Winne) Jan Dewitt & wf Anna Merytje DeWitt (K&S:38) m Maria Fotler.
8. LISABETH WINNE bp 19 Sep 1769 sp Peter Winne, wf Arriantje Van Etten (K&S:41).
9. CATHARINA WINNE/WINNER bp 05 May 1773 sp Tobias Myer, Catharina Louw (K&S:49) of Zcaherties (sic Saugerties) banns 25 Jun 1791 m in July Aldert T Roosa b Hurley, both res Rochester (RRCAU:192).
10. RACHEL WINNE bp 23 Oct 1774 sp (uncle & wf) Petrus DeWitt, wf Rachel Van Lowen/Leuven (K&S:54) m Elias Beck/Peck (FT:123).
11. SARA WINNE bp 12 May 1776 sp (uncle & wf) Cornelius DeWit & Maritje Ostrout (DRCK:379) m Mache Koons.

"In 1797 Christian Winne wrote his Will leaving his farm to his son Cornelis, whereon he did live, during the term of his certain lease for three lives, granted unto him by Margaret Livingston". He also mentions his other chn, his wf Maria and grchn. They res in the T of Woodstock NY (OU 5:360; FT:124).

Mention is made of Winne men in New York in the Revolution. 1st Regt Ulster County under Col Johannes Snyder, Arent, Arent jr., Benjamin, Cornelis, Jacobus, James, John, Peter, Peter jr, Peter A, Peter J. In the 3rd Regiment under Colonel Levi Pawling & Colonel John Cantin were John, Peter I. Land Bounty rights were granted to Arent, Arent jr, Johannis of the 1st Regiment and Henry jr of the 2nd Regiment.

DeWITT
1.1.9.3.2 PETRUS DeWITT m Rachel Van Leuven

1. JOHN VAN LEUVEN DeWITT bp 13 Feb 1765 sp John Van Leuven, Urceela Van Leuven (RRCAU:13) & (d 06 Nov 1845 Grahamville, Sullivan Co NY) m Peggy d/o Richard Carman & wf Sally of New Paltz NY b 18 Jan 1768 d 02 Jan 1859 both bur Clareyville NY (fr CEN). Richard Carman's will (Ulster Co NY Abstracts Liber D p4 04 May 1801 Pro 14 Jun 1814 names Peggy wf/o John V DeWitt.
2. SAMUEL DeWITT b 27 Oct 1768 bp 27 Nov 1768 sp Daniel Van Leuven, Maraboff Harker (RRCAU:16).
3. MARIA DeWITT b 31 May 1771 bp 23 Jun 1771 sp Frederick Rosenkrantz, Maria Depuy (RRCAU:19).
4. RACHEL DeWITT bp 24 Sep 1780 no sp (MSRUC:43).
5. ELIZABETH DEWITT b 22 Oct 1786 bp 31 Dec 1786 sp Timothy & Ann Wood at New Paltz (DRCNP).

deWITT
1.1.9.3.3 JOHANNES deWITT m1 Maria Rothersdorf

1. MARIA DeWIT bp 09 Oct 1773 sp (grprts) John Dewitt, wf Adriaantje (K&S:50).

Jan deWitt

2   JOHANNES DeWITT bp 20 Oct 1783 (prts Johannis Wyet, Maria) sp John Webber, Peggy Brandow (NYGBR 86:153) m2 Annatje/Ann Snyder
3   ANDREW DeWIT b 25 May 1783 sp Johannis M Snyder, Hyltje Osterhout/Oosterhoud (K&S:73).
    Of Jan DeWitt (1.1.9.3) and Arriaantje Osterhoud's nine children found none was called Jeremiah. His son's Johannes and William lived in the Catskill district. Johannes had a son Andries baptized 1783 in Saugerties NY. William had a son Jeremiah born 1779.

* Private Printing of Rowlely-King and Allied Families, sources not listed, gives the following information: (it doesn't seem to agree with above) "at that time (1790) our ancestor, John, was in Hempfield Township, Westmoreland County, PA. In 1777 Ezekiel DeWitt of Ohio Co VA took the Oath of Allegiance. He owned 400 acres of land in Washington County PA in 1781. A Jeremiah DeWitt signed a petition for a new state circa 1780 in southwestern Pennsylvania. Peter DeWitt was also there during the Revolutionary War. He was taxed for land in Bedford Co in 1783 as a non-resident. During this period counties were being formed and boundaries changed quickly. Even the boundary claims along the southern border of what is now Pennsylvania were in dispute with Virginia. Many groups who migrated were members of the same family, or neighbors. Very few came alone. So always the question, where did they move, and with whom?" "If one were selecting the family group which came to the southwestern Pennsylvania area it could be the sons of Jan DeWitt & Ariantje Osterhoudt. It is with this line of reasoning that we submit our line of descent." So far this author hasn't found connecting links.

DeWITT

1.1.9.3.4 EZEKIEL deWITT m Maria Keller
1   PETER DeWIT b 1762 NJ m Rebecca Whetsell (fr DDD & MELD) moved to the present Co of Somerset PA, to Pleasant District, Preston Co VA, (CAG 6:398) on to Hampshire Co, Clarke Co KY, settled Roaring Creek in 1795 (DFUSC:153/63). He was thought to have moved from New Jersey with his father when a lad of 12, to Pennsylvania, and from that state to what is now Pleasant District, Preston County. He married Rebecca Whetsell and settled on Roaring Creek about 1795. In the Virginia census he is listed in Hampshire County as head of a family of five. The partial destruction of the Monongalia county records and the complete destruction by fire of the Preston County records in 1869 leave little data available on Peter DeWitt. However, it is thought he moved with his family several years later to Clarke County KY where on October 18 1833, he made oath to an application for pension. In this application he states that on June 15 1775, he volunteered in Capt. Michael Oresap's company, and giving in some detail his experiences while on duty as a private soldier, ranger and spy, in an enemy's country filled with Tories and Indians. Several incidents mentions in the application are confirmed in Lowdermilk's History of Cumberland. Signed in his own hand Peter DeWitt follows the affidavit of Thomas Boon. On an old envelope, it is recorded Peter DeWitt, who was a private in the company commanded by Col. McDonald, in the Virginia line for 6 months.
2   HENRY DeWIT m Sarah Friend d/o John Friend of Sang Run Preston Co MD in 1800. John Friend Sr m in VA Kerrenhappuch Hyatt (she d 13 Oct 1798 [DFUSC:151]). In the mountains the late snow storms and frosts in 1817 caused a complete failure of crops. This was known as "the year without summer" so Henry and others moved to Carroll Co OH.
3   JOHN DeWIT m Katharine Quick. Cornelius Quick's Will in WVA 17 Sept 1787 Pro 07 Feb 1792 names dau Katharine & among the Exs: John DeWitt (P-DR:143; DFUSC:131) Records of RDC & Presby CH at Smithfield PA.

DeWITT

1.1.9.3.6 BENJAMIN deWIT m Maria Veile.
1   JOHANNES DeWIT b 23 Jul 1776 sp (uncle) Johannes DeWit, Elizabeth Fort (NYGBR 61:85).
2   LEWIS VIELE DeWIT b 05 Oct 1778 bp 04 Jan 1778 sp Lewis Viele, Annatie Quakingbos (NYGBR 61:296).
3   ANNETIE DeWIT b 08 Mar 1781 sp Teunis Viele, Elizabeth Viele (NYGBR 61:296).
4   CORNELIS D WIET b 04 Sep 1783 sp (uncle & wf) Cornelius D Wiet, Maria Osterhout, Schaghticoke T Rensselaer Co NY (NYGBR 61:296) & d (05 Dec 1853) m1 Lydia b 1796 d 02 June 1827 ae 33 bur Mile Strip, Fenner NY. **m2 Lois Gaylord** d/o Thomas Gaylord of New Hartford T Oneida Co, b 1784 d 14 Dec 1860 ae 76-03-16 (Madison Co Clerk's Office Grantee Book 67 p 303/5 02 Oct 1832). Cornelius & Lois (1850 Monroe Co census as Louisa) bur East Baptist CH Reeves Rd, Henrietta NY (fr VDM & tbstn, Township Historian) SLC 017745 Henrietta Town Supervisor 1809-1870 Wm H Peck <u>Monroe Co NY Landmarks, Biographies & Family Sketches 1895</u>.
5   ARIAANTJE DeWIT b 19 Sep 1786 bp 01 Jan 1786 sp Igenars Kip, Sara Kip (NYGBR 61:416) presumed dy,
6   SYBRANT VIEL DeWITT b 09 Aug 1788 bp 10 Aug 1788 sp Sybrant Viele, Lena Novel (NYGBR 61:425)
7   ARIANTJE DeWIT b 03 Oct 1790 bp 10 Oct 1790 sp Petrus Fort, Maria Viele (NYGBR 63:55) 1790 census NY p42 Schaghticoke, Albany Co (later part of Rensselaer Co) Benjamin DeWitt 1-4-2, indicating 1 dau d; #7 b after census taken 1800 census NY Benjamin DeWitt was in Herkimer Co NY.

    Index of Deeds Onandaga County NY 1774-1870. Grantor Index N460 page 589 31 July 1813 John DeWitt & Sybrant DeWitt in the Town of Oppenheim, County of Montgomery and Lewis DeWitt of County of Saratoga to Daniel Kellog of Town of Marcellus, County of Onandaga - for $60.00 ¼ part of a parcel of land in Sempronius and Spafford being in the

Counties of Cayuga and Onandaga being known on the map of the Military Township made by the Surveyor-General by Law No:11 containing 450 acres. Signed by Lewis DeWitt, Sybrant DeWitt and John DeWitt. Witnesses: also listed.

DeWITT

1.1.9.3.7 WILLEM DEWIT/DeWITH m1 Maria

1. CATHARINA DEWITT/DeWITH bp 17 Jan 1778 sp John Walker, Catharina Walker (NYGBR 86:150, CDDGC:27). History of Greene County has Catharina a d/o William with the other chn.

m2 19 Apr 1802 Catrina Overbaugh/Oberbag

2. JEREMIAS/JERIMA DeWITH/DeWIT bp 06 Sep 1779 sp Jeremia Overbagh, Elizabeth Diderick (NYGBR 86:151 DRC Catskill; CDDGG:28) from the Flats m 19 Apr 1802 Susannah Mower/Mouer, Blue Mtn (K&S:257) res Catskill.
3. MARIA DeWIT b 02 Feb 1782 bp 03 Mar 1782 Linlithgo, Columbia Co sp Petrus Porker, Marytje Porker (BRLC:72).
4. ANNATJE/HANNAH DeWIT bp 06 Jun 1784 sp Hansie Overbag, Annatje Conjes (K&S:76; HGC:434).
5. JOEL DeWIT bp 30 Apr 1786 sp Petrus Overbag, Cathrin Fiero (K&S:82).

Jan deWitt

GENERATION 6

If a couple traces back to DeWitt ancestry more than once, m is {m} indicating this fact. Numbering used is the first parent listed chronologically. Both numbers are given but the one to be used in succeeding generations is underlined.

DUMOND

1.1.9.3.1.1 ARIAANTJE/ARRIANENTJE/ARIANTJE WINNE/WENNER m Ignas/Ignatius/Igneas Dumond

1. WILLEM DUMONT bp 04 Jul 1779 sp Willem Schmit, Elisabet Van Wagenen (DRCK:389) m Rachel Delamater.
2. MARIA DUMONT bp 19 Nov 1780 sp (grprts) Christian Wenne, Maria Wenne (DRCK:394) m 13 Jun 1799 Harmonus Dumond Jr s/o Harmonus Dumond & Jannetje Brink, b after his father was mistakenly shot & killed as a Tory, bp 01 Nov 1778.
3. CATHARINA DUMON bp 02 Jun 1782 no sp (MSRUC:46) m ? Van Aken.
4. JACOBUS/JAMES/COBE DUMONT bp 06 Oct 1784 no sp (DRCK:406) & (d ? Apr 1871) m Jane Ann Yaple ("parents of the late William W Dumond, who assisted this writer in this work").
5. IGNEAS DUMOND Jr m Anna Delamater (OU 4:155).
6. CORNELIUS DUMOND bp 04 Mar 1788 no sp called "King" (DRCK:419) & (d ? Oct 1869) m Mary Yaple (sis of Jane Ann) "Grprts of the late Dr Cornelius J Dumond who had the Dumond records searched, established".
7. SELLIE DUMOND bp 09 Jun 1789 (DRCK:424).
8. PETRUS DUMOND bp 14 Sep 1790 (DRCK:429) **dy**.
9. ANNA DUMOND
10. CHRISTIAN DUMOND m Martha Beaman.
11. HARRIET DUMOND
12. ABRAHAM DUMOND m Elizabeth Sprague.
Five of the children & added info from Olde Ulster (OU 4:155).

Ignatius Dumond was the first settler on the present site of Margaretville in 1784 where he owned a farm, which he sold for £100. He then went back in the woods seven miles to the present New Kingston. The valley was covered with heavy primitive forest and the first six families, of which he was one, were compelled to blaze their way on trees to be able to find their way back (OU 4:155).

WINNE

1.1.9.3.1.2 JONATHAN WINNE m1 Eve Van Wagenen

1. CHRISTIAN WENNIE bp 11 Feb 1785 sp (grprts) Christian Wenne, Maria Dewitt (DRCK:407).
m2 Ann/Anny Davis/Davies b 03 Jan 1758.
2. ELIZABETH WINNE bp 05 Jul 1789 sp Jacobus Keater, Elizabeth Keater Marbletown (MSRUC:64).
3. CORNELIA WINNE bp 06 Feb 1791 sp Cornelia Wynkoop (MSRUC:65).
4. JACOBUS DAVIS WINNE b 10 Apr 1793 sp Jacobus Davis, Polly Davis (MSRUC:70).
5. FREDERICK WINNER b 25 Jun 1795 bp 19 Jul 1796 no sp (MSRUC:72).
6. POLLY/MARY WINNE b 18 Aug 1799 Rochester no sp (RRCAU:59).
7. SALOMON WINNE b 03 Dec 1801 bp 03 Jan 1802 no sp (RRCAU:63).
8. CORNELIUS WINNAN b 09 Mar 1804 bp 25 Mar 1804 sp (RRCAU:70).
9. ANNATJE TERWILLIGER WINNER b 25 May 1809 bp 17 Sep 1809 no sp (MSRUC:121).

JONATHAN b 1759 & bro CORNELIS b 1760 are sons of CHRISTIAN WINNE & MARIA DEWIT. The following compilation is based on information in Family Tree (FT:59). Otherwise it's hard to distinguish between their offspring.

Jonathan's chn	Cornelis' chn
Christian 1785, Elizabeth 1790	Sellie 1788, Catharine 1791
Cornelia 1791, Jacobus Davis 1793	Elizabeth 1790, Lucas 1791
Frederick 1795, Polly 1799	Christian 1795, Cornelius 1799
Salomon 1801, Cornelius 1804	Benjamin 1801, Polly 1803
Annatje Terwilliger 1809	Peter 1806, Annatje 1809
	Henry 1813

WINNE

1.1.9.3.1.3 CORNELIS WINNE m Elisabet Martin/Matha/Marthe/Masten/Marta

1. SELLIE/SARAH WENNE bp 25 Jun 1788 sp Johannes Martin, (aunt) Elisabet Wenne (DRCK:420) m Thomas Swartout Jr, Shokan.
2. ELISABET WENNE bp 07 Feb 1790 no sp (DRCK:427) m Joel Freligh.
3. CATHARIN WINNE b 04 Jul 1791 bp 30 Aug 1791 sp (aunt & hus) Aldert Roosa, Catharina Winne ma Elizabeth Masten (MSRUC:67) m John Swartout.

Jan deWitt

4. LUCAS WINNE bp 30 Aug 1791 no sp bp 1793 sp Lucas Winne & wf.
5. CHRISTIAN WINNE b 12 Jul 1795 sp (grprts) Christiaan Winne & Maria (DeWitt) Winne (RRCAU:516) & (d 23 Jan 1872 ae 77) m Anna Longyear b 1796 d 14 Sep 1875 ae 79 both bur Hudler Cem, Mt Tremper (GIUC:25; CBRUC:1291).
6. CORNELIUS WINNOW/WINNE b 29 Mar 1799 bp 12 Aug 1799 no sp ma Elizabeth Martha (MSRUC:89) & (tbstn b 1797 d 11 Oct 1866 ae 69 [GIUC:191]) m Eva Bush d/o Thomas Bush & Lena Longyear, b 1800 d 15 Nov 1872 ae 72 (FT:59) both bur Winne Farm east of Shandaken, T Shandaken, Ulster Co (GIUC:19). Shokan is in Olive T Ulster Co NY.
7. BENJAMIN WINNOW/WINNE b 14 Aug 1801 bp ? Sep 1801 Shokan (BRSRC:2) & (tbstn b 1802 d 06 Jan 1855 ae 53) m Maria Gulneck b 14 Feb 1802 d 18 Aug 1869 ae 67-06-04 both bur Hudler Cem, Mt Tremper (GIUC:25).
8. POLLY WINNOW/WINNE b 06 Sep 1803 bp 05 Nov 1803 (BRSRC:4).
9. PETER WINNOW/WINNE b 27 Feb 1806 bp 31 May 1806 (BRSRC:6).
10. ANNATJE WINNOW/WINNE b 15 Jul 1809 bp 17 Sep 1809 (BRSRC:8).
11. HENRY WINNE b 15 Jul 1813 bp 05 Feb 1815, prts Cor's Winner & Elizabeth Motte (sic) [tbstn b 21 Sep 1813 d 13 Feb 1856 ae 42-04-23 bur Winne Farm east of Shandeken as was bro Cornelius] * as Henry G Winne m Maria G Hudler b 14 Feb 1802 d 18 Aug 1869 ae 67-06-04 (GIUC:25).

WESPEL
1.1.9.3.1.4 MARIA/MARIAH WINNE/WINNER/WINNOW m Conrad/Coenrad Wespel/Wisper
1. COENRADT WIPPELAR/WISFELAR bp 25 Apr 1782 sp (uncle & grma) Lucas Winne, Maria DeWitt (MSRUC:46).
2. ANTJE WESPEL b 09 Jun 1789 no sp (DRCK:424).
3. JOHANNES WESPLE b 20 Oct 1790 sp Catharina (RRCAU:42).
4. SARA WISPEL b 20 Aug 1799 bp 16 Feb 1800 (BRSRC:1).
5. ABRAM WISPER b 13 Oct 1801 bp 18 Apr 1802 (BRSRC:3). * may have m2 Peter Jong (FT:124).
    1810 Census Woodstock, NY Conrad Wespel 1-1-0-1 0-0-0-1
    1810 Census Woodstock, NY   Wespel 0-0-0-0 2-2-1-1

WINNE
1.1.9.3.1.5 LUCAS WENNE m1 Maria Oakley/Oklie
1. JOHN WINNE bp 29 Feb 1784 Marbletown no sp (MSRUC:49).
2. ALIDA WINNE bp 13 May 1786 sp Richard Oakley, Alida Short (MSRUC:53). An Alida Winnow & Peter Clute had Jacob b 19 Jul 1806 bp 03 Aug 1807, no proof of connection.
3. HENRI WENNE bp 15 Oct 1788 sp Henri Oaklie, Rachel Oaklie (DRCK:421).
    m2 1792 Rachel Davis.
4. JAMES WINNER b 1795 bp 31 Jan 1796 by Rev Dirk Romeyn no sp (MSRUC:74).
5. LUCAS WINNOW b 17 Mar 1798 bp 08 Apr 1798 no sp (MSRUC:83).
6. MIRIAM WINNE b 23 May 1800 bp 15 Jul 1800 no sp (MSRUC:91).

BUSH
1.1.9.3.1.6 ANNATJE/HANNAH WINNE/WYNNER m Benjamin Bush
1. MARY BUSH b 06 Mar 1793 bp 30 Jun 1793 no sp (MMW:204).
2. ANNY BUSH b 06 Mar 1794 bp 14 Sep 1794 no sp (MMW:206).
3. JOHN BUSH b 25 Oct 1795 bp Sept/Dec 1800 (RRCAU:61).
4. ALDERT BUSH b 08 Aug 1799 bp Sept/Dec 1800 (RRCAU:61).
5. JONATHAN WINNE BUSH b 08 Feb 1801 (RRCAU:62).
6. ELIZABETH BUSH b 06 Nov 1802 bp 03 Apr 1803 (RRCAU:67).

WINNE
1.1.9.3.1.7 FREDERIK/FERDERICK WENNE m Maria Fotler
1. FREDERIK WINNE bp 09 Jun 1789 sp Conrad Meisner, Maria Catharina Fotler (DRCK:424) bp same day as a child of each of Frederik's sisters Ariantje (1.1.9.3.1.1) & Maria (1.1.9.3.1.4).

ROOSA
1.1.9.3.1.9 CATHARINE/CATRINA WINNE/WINNER/WINNOW m Aldert T Roosa/Rosa
1. JOHN ROSA b 30 May 1792 sp John Roosa, Rebecka Roosa (RRCAU:46)
2. NATTE ROOSA b 13 Feb 1794 sp John Crispell, Rebeka Rosa (RRCAU:49).
3. CATRINA ROOSA b 03 Apr 1800 no sp (RRCAU:60).
4. LUCAS WINNE ROOSA b 05 Jan 1802 no sp (RRCAU:64).
5. RACHEL ROOSA b 07 Aug 1804 bp 02 Sep 1804 no sp (MSRUC:106).
6. NANCY HASBROUCK ROOSA b 31 May 1806 bp 29 Jun 1806 no sp (MSRUC:111).
7. ANNE ROOSA b 20 Apr 1809 bp 11 Jun 1809 sp Peter Hoffman, Ann Lounsberry.
8. ELIZABETH ROOSA b 30 Sep 1814 bp 26 Feb 1815 no sp, d/o Aldert Roosa & Catherine Winner (MSRUC:137).

Jan deWitt

BECK
1.1.9.3.1.10 RACHELWINNE/WINNOW m Elias Beck/Peck
1   JOHN BECK bp 12 Aug 1798 **no chn** sp (DRCK:460).
2   POLLY BECK b 01 Aug 1799 bp 07 Oct 1799 Shokan (BRSRC:1).

KOONS
1.1.9.3.1.11 SARA WINNE m Mache/Meche Koons
1   CATHARINA KOONS bp 09 Jan 1794 sp Jost Koens (MSRUC:68).

DeWITT
1.1.9.3.2.1 JOHN VAN LEUVEN DeWITT m Peggy Carman
1   SARAH DeWITT b 07 Nov 1791. Sarah, Peter & Richard were bp 18 Feb 1798 (MSRUC:82).
2   PETER DeWITT b 30 Apr 1795 (MSRUC:82) & (d 03 Aug 1877 Clareyville, Sullivan Co NY) m Mary b 01 Jan 1802 d 08 Jul 1853 ae 46-06-07. Both bur Clareyville, Sullivan Co. In 1875 census Neversink, Sullivan Co Peter as ae 75, retired farmer, res with Matthew Van Aken ae 46, wf Mary ae 34.
3   RICHARD CARMAN DeWITT b 19 Nov 1797 (d 19 Dec 1889 Neversink bur Grahamville) m Margaret Van aken d/o Levi Van Aken & Mary Hoornbeck b 09 Sep 1822 d 11 May 1910 Grahamville NY.
4   ABRAM/ABRAHAM DeWITT b 23 Apr 1800 bp 29 Jun 1800 (MSRUC:91) m1 Mary Dolson d 1832; m2 Elizabeth Gillet d 1866; m3 Sally (Gray) Depuy wd/o S W Depuy & sis/o John G Gray. It is said Abram's Will Pro 28 Sept 1884 not found in Ulster Co.
5   CALEB DeWITT b 1806 (d 07 May 1894 Grahamsville T Sullivan Co) m Henrietta (all fr CEN).

DeWITT
1.1.9.3.4.1 PETER DeWITT m Rebecca Whetsell
1   BARNEY DeWITT b 1790 MD as Barnabus he m 08 05 1823 Jane McKee b 1803 PA, James Smith MG officiating res Richland T Knox Co OH (DFUSC:198). 1850 census Barnabus Dewitt ae 60 was in MD, farmer, chn b OH Charles 26, Eliza 17, Milan 12, Elizabeth 11, Margaret 6.
2   WILLIAM DeWITT m Mary Du Casteel (sibling listed DFUSC:63).
3   JOHN DeWITT bp 02 May 1793 (d 07 Oct 1869 bur Hoyes Garrett Co MD) m1 Sarah Hartman d/o John Hartman (DFCUS:63/4). He settled on a farm near Crossroads, Hoyes PO (known as Johnstown [fr CCD]). Allegheny MD info fr IGI, (DSFU:153 & 1850 Census Allegheny Co MD). John DeWitt, at the age of nineteen, and his brother HENRY (1.1.9.3.4.7) probably seventeen, served as private soldiers during the war of 1812 in Capt. Matthes McGown's 4th^h Reg., VA Militia, June 29, 1814, until their company was mustered out at Lambert Point, near Norfolk, VA. John DeWitt Sr. son of Peter, came back from Virginia about 1828; m2 Louisa Casteel b 1797 dau of Shadrack Casteel, Jr. For $200.00 John bought of the heirs of James H. McFadon, of Baltimore, Military Lots, 1664, 1665, 1680 and 1682, at the cross roads. Later it was known as Johnstown, in honor of Pioneer John DeWitt, now Hoyes, Garrett county. His log house, now completely demolished, was on the road leading to Friendsville. This house should have been preserved as a monument (as should others) to those who braved the dangers of an unsettled country, fighting off wild animals, Indians, the warring French & in blazing a new trail. The home of the later D O DeWitt was built near the site of the old log house.
4   HENRY DeWITT b 1795 Preston Co WV m Elizabeth Jackson d/o Samuel Jackson b 1791, Preston Co WVA. Elizabeth was a descendant of Ephrian Jackson 1658-1732, one of the oldest and most prominent Quaker Families in Pa. Henry was a Pvte Preston Co WVA Militia 1815 (CAG 6:398). 1850 Census Preston Co names his first 6 chn (DFUSC:156).
5   PETER DeWITT b 1795 WVA Sarah Casteel b 1805 MD. (fr MELD & DDD; DFUSC:63, 153 & 1850 Census Allegheny Co MD).
6   SAMUEL DeWITT m 1830 Dorcas Du Casteel res Preston Co MD about 1830, Garrett Co about 1850.
7   SUSAN DeWITT at Allegheny MD m 10 Nov 1845 Archibald Casteel lived Sang Run (IGI).
8   RICHARD DeWITT b Preston Co WVI, served in War of 1812.
9   JOSEPH DeWITT b 1804 Sang Run MD (d there 1865) m Elizabeth Casteel b 1806 MD d/o Shadrack Casteel Jr from Bedford Co PA. Preston Co WVA 1850 Census names the first 8 chn.

From Mrs William DeWitt "The DeWitt Family" Published 1915 in the Oakland <u>Republican</u> Garret County MD In this 5 pg article she says "The DeWitt family is one of the oldest families in America and among the earliest settlers of what is now Somerset County PA & Preston County WVA and Garret County, MD".. "It is thought he (Tjerck) was the son of * Capt Claes Jansy deWitt who was the skipper of the ship `De Liefde' and a grandson of Capt Jan DeWitt who came to this country early in the 16$^{th}$ century (sic) and who sailed up the Hudson river in the ship `Little Fox' in the year 1614". Claes died before 1661 (DFUSC:62/6). Note * Claes Jansy deWitt estimated to be about 60 at that time. [refer to p 13].

DEWITT

1.1.9.3.6.4 CORNELIUS DeWITT m1 Lydia   ?
1. WILIAM CHEVALIER DeWITT (fr 1855 State Census res Henrietta 20 yrs) b 1812 (d 31 Jan 1872 bur Henrietta NY m Sarah Ann ?   b Dutchess Co NY (fr VDM).
2. CORNELIUS SHERMAN DeWITT b 01 Dec 1813 Madison Co (d 21 Jul 1885 Henrietta) m Susan Lincoln b 31 Aug 1816 Saratoga Co NY d/o William Lincoln & Rachel Works, d 01 Oct 1894 Rochester both bur Mt Hope Cem Rochester NY. NYS Census 1855: Cornelius ae 20, Susan ae 25 res Monroe Co.
  m2 Lois
3. JENNETT DeWITT b Aug 1830 m ?   Williams.
4. SARAH L DeWITT b Aug 1830 (d 18 Sept 1885 ae 55-01-00 in Los Angeles bur Maplewood Cem Henrietta NY) m Daniel Jones (fr VDM Sarah's Obit Rochester paper UA S26 1885 [2-3]. SLC 017745 Henrietta Town Supervisor 1869-70. Wm H Peck. <u>Monroe County NY Landmarks, Biographies and Family Sketches.</u> 1895. Research by Virginia (DeWitt) McCambridge.

DEWITT/DeWITH

1.1.9.3.7.2 JEREMIAH/JEREMY/JEREMIAS DeWITH/DeWITT m Susannah Mower/Mouer
1. MARIA DeWITT b 21 Aug 1802 bp 12 Sep 1802 sp John Vedder, Christina Vedder (CDDGC:62) Catskill.
2. PETER DeWIT b 22 Apr 1804 bp 27 May 1804 sp George Brant, Margaret Brant (CDDGC:64).
3. WILLIAM/WILHELM DeWITT b 23 Feb 1806 bp 19 Apr 1806 St Pauls CH West Camp NY sp (uncle) Joel Dewitt, Lena Roos (LCWC:35) m Sarah b 1820. Probably same man in 1855 Census Greene Co. William DeWitt b 1814 (note younger wf) landowner, farmer, and both res Windham T Greene Co NY 14 yrs   (NYDCG:80).
4. ANN ELIZABETH DeWITT b 16 Apr 1808 bp 19 Jun 1808 sp Stephen Mauser, Susan Margaret Mower (K&S:155].

Jan deWitt

GENERATION 7

SWARTOUT
1.1.9.3.1.3.1 SELLIE/SARAH WENNE m Thomas Swartout Jr
1. JACOB SWARTOUT b 06 Feb 1810 bp 22 Mar 1810 (BRSRC:9).

FRELIGH
1.1.9.3.1.3.2 ELISABET WENNE m Joel Freligh
1. ANN ELIZA FRELIGH b 25 Feb 1811 bp 17 Mar 1811 no sp (K&S:163).
2. MOSES FELIGH b 28 Nov 1812 bp 25 Dec 1812 no sp (K&S:170).

SWARTOUT
1.1.9.3.1.3.3 CATHARIN WINNE m John Swartout
1. CORNELIUS WINNOW SWARTOUT b 04 Dec 1809 bp 22 Apr 1810 (BRSRC:9) Shokan.
2. WILLIAM SWARTOUT bp 11 Nov 1811 (BRSRC:11).

WINNE
1.1.9.3.1.3.5 CHRISTIAN WINNE m Anna/Annatje Longyear
1. CORNELIUS WINNER b 30 Jul 1817 bp   Jan 1818 at Shokan pa as Christeyon Winner (BRSRC:14 [d 1897]) m1 Susan A Boice b 1817 d 1859; m2 14 Sep 1860 Margaretta K Simpson b 1828 d 1897 all bur Hudler Cem Mt Tremper (GIUC:25) m in <u>Saugerties Telegraph</u> paper.
2. ISIAH <u>DAVID</u> WINNE b 18 Jul 1819 bp 07 May 1820 of Shandaken (BRSRC:16) note (tbstn b 1818 d 1902 ae 79 yr G.A.R.) m1 19 Dec 1842 Angeline Longyear b 03 Jan 1817 d 18 Feb 1871 both bur Mt Tremper Cem (GIUC:27) m2 Adaline Dimmick, d/o Warren Dimmick & Mary Sands of Deleware Co **no chn** (CBRUC:1291/2).
3. WILLIAM WINNE
4. HENRY WINNE d before 1896.
5. BENJAMIN J WINNE b 29 Dec 1826 Shandaken (CBRUC:195/6) m 1849 Sarah J Simpson d/o Peter & Jane Simpson.
6. ELIZA ANN WINNE at Shokan as d/o Christian Winne, m 01 Nov 1847 James William O'Neal s/o James, all of Shandaken (BRSRC:43).
7. SARAH WINNE
8. CHRISTIAN WINNE
9. JEMIMA WINNE
10. CALVIN WINNE

Henry, Benjamin & Eliza were deceased in 1896 when the book was published (CBRUC:195/6).

WINNE
1.1.9.3.1.3.6 CORNELIUS WINNOW/WINNE m Eva Bush
1. SALLY ANN WINNE
2. HENRY WINNE of Shanaken, there m 25 Jan 1844 Magdalene Bush d/o Cornelius Bush of Olive (BRSRC:42) a Henry T Winne of Shandaken m 26 Jun 1851 Elizabeth Davis of Olive (BRSRC:44)
3. THOMAS WINNE
4. LANEY WINNE
5. MARY CATHARINE WINNE b 08 Aug 1826 (d 26 Mar 1864 ae 37-07-18 bur Hudler Cem Mt Tremper [GIUC:25]) m Edward Wood both bur Huddler Cem Mt Tremper (FT:59).
6. JOHN L WINNE b 21 Mar 1833 bp 06 Jul 1833 (BRSRC:19).
7. HANNAH WINNE b 14 Dec 1834 bp Aug 1835 (BRSRC:20) d 01 Mar 1851 ae 15-02-17 (GIUC:19).
8. GEORGE WINNE b 23 Dec 1836 bp 18 Jun 1837 (BRSRC:20) & (d 1860) m Mary Jones d/o Lucus Jones & Sally Ann Jones of West Shokan.
9. CHRISTIAN WILLARD WINNE b 12 Sep 1841 (BRSRC:22).
10. PETER C WINNE bp 21 Aug 1842 (BRSRC:22) s/o Cornelius Winne jr.
11. JAMES WINNE b 14 May 1844 bp 23 Aug 1847 ma as Eave (BRSRC:23).
12. IRA WINNE b 10 Aug 1846 bp 23 Aug 1847 (BRSRC:23).
13. TH(E)ODORE (R) WINNE b 23 Oct 1848 bp 20 Jul 1851 (BRSRC:24).

"Theodore R Winne, Cornelius, his wf Eve, dau Hannah, sons George & Henry are all in a small cemetery back of Mount Pleasant Cemetery in Shandaken, NY. George & Eve Winne petitioned the courts in the matter of Admin of Cornelius Winne's Estate as he left no will" (FT:59).

WINNE
1.1.9.3.1.3.7 BENJAMIN WINNE m Maria Gunlock
1. ALFRED WINNE b 23 Sep 1829 (d 05 Oct 1880 ae 51-00-13) m Kelly ? .

Jan deWitt

WINNE

1.1.9.3.1.3.11 HENRY WINNE possibly Henry G *m Maria G Hudler
- a MILTON HUDLER WINNE b 21 Oct 1853 d 03 Dec 1854 ae 01-01-13 as s/o Henry W Winne; same plot as Henry's brother Benjamin.

DeWITT

1.1.9.3.2.1.2 PETER DeWITT m Mary ? .
1. SARAH A DeWITT b 1830.
2. STEPHEN DeWITT b 1832.
3. MARY E DeWITT b 1836 m Matthew Van Aken.
4. PEGGY D DeWITT b 1838.
5. ABRAHAM DeWITT b 1842 all fr CEN).

DeWitt

1.1.9.3.2.1.3 RICHARD CARMAN DeWITT m Margaret Van Aken
1. DAVID DeWITT b 1840 Neversink, Sullivan Co NY, invalid, **single**
2. CYNTHIA JANE DeWITT b 14 Jun 1841 m Edgar Alonzo Perkins (notation by Cora E Nelson "my grandmother"). Info fr CEN family pages, Seattle Gen So.
3. POLLY DeWITT b 1842 Neversink.
4. CALEB DeWITT (possibly the line of Jan DeWitt & Arriantje Osterhout) b 1847 Neversink m Eliza Jane Smith b 1836. In 1880 Caleb ae 75 was living in Neversink, Sullivan Co with Margaret DeWitt ae 58.
5. MARGARET DeWITT b 1850 Neversink m Henry Armstrong.
6. NELLIE DeWITT b 1854 Kerhonkson, Ellenville, Ulster Co NY d 10 May 1940 **single** (all fr CEN).

DeWitt

1.1.9.3.2.1.4 ABRAM DeWITT m1 Mary Dolson
1. UNNAMED DeWITT
2. SALLY DeWITT m Capt Daniel Gillet res New York.
3. JOHN DeWITT res New York.

m2 Elizabeth Gillet d 1866; during Elizabeth's lifetime Abram adopted Cynthia Jane Gillet DeWitt d/o William Gillet, who m William Parks.

m3 Sally (Grey) Depuy wd/o S W Depuy & sis/o John G Gray (all fr CEN).

DeWITT

1.1.9.3.2.1.5 CALEB DeWITT m Henrietta ?
1. JOHN DeWITT b 1834.
2. THOMAS DeWITT b 1834.
3. BLANDINA DeWITT b 1838.
4. ANN DeWITT b 1840.
5. ABRAHAM DeWITT b 1842
6. JEREMIAH DeWITT b 1844.
7. SARAH DeWITT b 1848.
8. CHARLES DeWITT b 1850 all fr CEN).

DeWITT

1.1.9.3.4.1.3 JOHN DeWitt m1 Sarah Hartman
1. JOSEPH DeWITT D.D. b 1818 (d 13 Jan 1892 ae 71 with Julia bur Hoyes MD Meth CH Cem) m1 02 Jun 1843 Mary Jane Thayer b 1821 d 1846; m 2 Julia Robinson b 1821 d 28 Jan 1892. Rev Joseph was a well-known Methodist preacher and Judge of the first Orphan's Court of Garrett Co.
2. REBECCA DeWITT m Samuel Martin (DFUSC:64). Rebecca and Samuel Martin were the grpts of Robert ("Bob Martin." "Fighting Bob"- AEF King, who lost his only bout, one out of sixty, to Gene Tunney). Bob retired from the ring due to ill health. He was champion of AEF during the world war in the International Games in 1919, held in Pershing Stadium in France. In 1920 he married the charming and altogether lovely Mary Elizabeth Bird. Their engagement and wedding was international news. Notice of the wedding was also published in France. Pictures of the young couple were taken by Underwood & Underwood for publication in the nation's press.
3. CHRISTINA DeWITT b 1821 (d 12 Mar 1902 ae 81) m Elijah Cress Matheny b 1821 s/o Absolm Methany & Susan Cress (fr GCHSO:6; fr Mrs WD). All issue b Garrett Co MD. The Preston Co Journal Thurs 20 Mar 1902. Obit: Methany, Christine DeWitt d 12 Mar 1902 ae 81 wf/o EC Methany and well known in different sections of the County. She was a mother of 12 children.
4. SUSAN DeWITT m 21 May 1836 Michael Kilbaugh/Colbauch, Allegheny (IGI).
   m2 Louisa Casteel
5. SARAH ANN DeWITT m 04 Sep 1843 William Browning (IGI).
6. LOUISA DeWITT m 15 Mar 1855 Albert Cook at Allegheny Co MD (IGI).

7   JOHN DeWITT b 1828 (d 1912) m Harriet Collier had 6 chn (fr Mrs WD). John succeeded his father on the Johnston farm. On 17 Jul 1855, for $55 he deeded to William Casteel, Truman West, John Waggoner, Jonathan Friend and Nathan Casteel, trustees, Lot 2 in Johnston on which to build a house or place of worship. On this lot was built a log church (probably erected with the help of Martin, Barney, Peter and Henry. The DeWitts were strong men). Long since torn down and on its site a new M.E. church has been built. In the cemetery close by is the grave of John, Sr and the burial ground of other DeWitts.

8   ARCHIBALD CASTEEL DeWITT b 1832 (d 1913) at Allegheny Co m 04 Jan 1856 Mary Browning b 1834 d 1919 (fr Latter Day Saint's IGI; fr MGCG; fr Mrs WD).

DeWITT

1.1.9.3.4.1.4 HENRY DeWITT m Elizabeth Jackson

1   SAMUEL DeWITT b 1824 (DFUSC:156) m Mary J House b 1829 Preston Co WV, 1850 census.
2   WILLIAM DeWITT b 09 May 1826 Preston Co WV {m} Sarah Ann DeWitt (1.1.9.3.4.1.9.3) b Garrett Co MD 09 May 1824 (fr Mrs WD in DFUSC: 64/5) d/o Joseph DeWitt & Elizabeth Casteel.
3   GEORGE DeWITT b 1828 m1 ? Martin; m2 ? Wilhelm (fr Mrs WD)
4   NANCY DeWITT b 1830 (d 1905) {m} Thomas DeWitt (1.1.9.3.4.1.9.4) b 1831 d 1902. Thomas was religiously inclined, good natured, & generous to a fault, also something of a Philosopher (fr Mrs WD).
5   JAMES DeWITT B 1831 m * Louisa Friend (which James?).
6   RICHARD DeWITT b 1835 m1 Mary Ellen Whetsell; m2 Mary Price Burns. He was a war vet of 1864 & pa of 17 chn. His 1st wf gave birth to triplets in 1865.
7   JANE DeWITT m Thomas Ashley.
8   REBECCA DeWITT m J Bucklow (fr DFUSC:156 & 1850 Preston Co WVA Census).

DeWitt

1.1.9.3.4.1.5 PETER DeWITT m Sarah Casteel

1   PETER DeWITT b 1828/9 m Silvia b 1833 res near Selbysport 1860 census.
2   ELIZABETH DeWITT b 1831.
3   REBECCA JANE DeWITT b 1834 Allegheny Co m 06 Dec 1852 Patrick H McCabe.
4   ELIZA DeWITT b 1835.
5   SARAH DeWITT b 1837.
6   JOSEPH DeWITT b 1840.
7   CATHERINE DeWITT b 1842 (fr DFUSC:153 & 1850 Census Allegany Co MD).

DeWITT

1.1.9.3.4.1.6 SAMUEL DeWITT m Dorcas Castell/DuCasteel

1   JOHN HARRISON DeWITT b 1844 Maryland, son of Samuel & Dorcas (Castell) DeWitt of French & Irish parentage, He m 1870 Martha Wees d/o John & Mary Rennix Wees (d 1894) m2 1897 Minnie d/o Joseph Hinchman, chn were Zuella, Raymond, Anna Grace, James Holland, Mary Alice, Albert S., Stanley Congo, Emma. (fr Mrs WD in DFUSC:153; HRC:370). John was raised from the age of 3 years by the Fitzwaters of Beverly. He was in the Confederate Army, was twice wounded, once in shoulder at Martinsburg, again in the knee at Beverly during Hill's raid and was taken prisoner and sent to Camp Chase. He returned to Beverly in 1865. He took part in the battles of Berryville, Antietam, Winchester, Williamsport, Droop Mountain, Allegheny, Greenbrier, Fisher Hill, Strasburg and others; was elected Justice of the Peace in Beverly District in 1880, and was twice elected, holding office twelve years. Moved to Elkins in 1898. 1884 J.H. DeWitt, Justice of the Peace (HRC:226, 370, DFUSC:153).

DeWITT

1.1.9.3.4.1.9 JOSEPH DeWITT m Elizabeth Du Casteel

1   JAMES DeWITT b 1826 m 18 Apr 1856 Louisa Friend b 1813 d 1925 d/o Isreal Friend & Doracs Willison.
2   WILLIAM DeWITT b 1297 Preston Co WV (d 1899) m Anne Mattingly; all chn b Garrett Co MD (fr Mrs WD).
3   SARAH ANN DeWITT b 1829 (d 1896) {m} 1.1.9.3.4.1.4.2 William DeWitt s/o Henry DeWitt & Elizabeth Jackson. .
4   THOMAS DeWITT b 1831 {m} 1.1.9.3.4.1.4.4 Nancy DeWitt b 1830 d/o Henry DeWitt & Elizabeth Jackson. Thomas was religiously inclined, good natured & generous to a fault, something of a b 1827 (fr Mrs WD in DFUSC:65/6, fr DDD, CCD & MELD). Chn b Garrett Co MD, ae slightly different 1880 census.
5   ARCHIBALD CASTEEL DeWITT b 13 Jun 1837 at Allegheny MD m 30 Jun 1858 Hannah Ellen Chambers, had 7 chn (fr DF, IGI, OHSC:8, DFUSC:66).
6   RICHARD DeWITT b 1841 m Elizabeth Casteel. Chn b Garrett Co MD.
7   REBECCA DeWITT b 1846).
8   SUSAN DeWITT at Allegheny MD m 10 Nov 1848 Thomas Browning (IGI).
9   HULDA DeWITT m Daniel Maulin (b dates fr DFUC: 155 & 1850 Allegheny Co MD Census).

Jan deWitt

Mrs William DeWitt, "The DeWitt Family" Pub 1915 in the Oakland "Republican", Garret County MD.

Oakland County Surrogate Court: Liber C, folio 56

Will of Joseph DeWitt In the name of God, Amen, I Joseph DeWitt of Allegheny County in the State of Maryland, being sick and weak in body, but of sound and disposing mind, memory and understanding considering the certainty of death and the uncertainty of the time thereof, and being desirous to settle my worldly affairs and thereby be the better prepared to leave this world when it shall please God to call me hence do therefore make and publish my last will and testament in manner and form following, that is to say, First and principally I commit my soul unto the hands of the Almighty God, and my body to the earth, to be decently buried at the discretion of my wife, and after my debts and funeral charges are paid, I devise and bequeath as follows: viz: I give and bequeath to my dear wife Elizabeth my plantation wherein I now dwell, known and distinguished as Lot No. 40 on hundred and sixteen (4116) containing forty nine acres more or less (having sold one acre off of said Lot to William DeWitt) to her the said Elizabeth during her life and after her decease to our children to be equally divided between them, And whereas the property which I now Possess, hath been chiefly acquired by the joint industry and frugality of my wife and myself and thinking some additional to the above bequeast necessary, the better to enable her to live with convenience and comfort, I do, therefore give and bequest unto my said wife Item, one mare, Item Nine Sheep, Two Milch cows and all my household and kitchen furniture with my beds and bedding. Ratifying and confirming this and none other, to be my last will and testament. In testimony whereof, I have hereunto set my hand and affixed my seal, this 25th day of February in the year of our Lord One thousand Eight hundred and sixty-five.

    Signed, sealed, published and declared by   Joseph DeWitt (seal)
    Joseph DeWitt (sen) the above named testator, as and for his last will and testament, in the
    presence of us, who at his request, in the presence, and in the presence of each other, have
    subscribed our names as witnesses thereto
        D Harrison Friend
        Wilbur Browning
        his X mark
        Archibald Casteel

Oakland MD County Surrogate Court: Liber 26, folio 31

The heirs and devisees of Joseph DeWitt, deceased in 1868 joined in a deed to convey a certain piece of land to William Browning.

William DeWitt and <u>Sarah DeWitt</u> his wife
<u>William DeWitt</u> and Ann his wife
<u>Archibald DeWitt</u> and Hannah E his wife
<u>John DeWitt</u> and Mary his wife
<u>Richard DeWitt</u> and Elizabeth his wife
<u>Thomas DeWitt</u> and Nancy DeWitt his wife
Thomas Browning and <u>Susan DeWitt</u> his wife
Daniel Mauline and <u>Huldah DeWitt</u> his wife
Children of Joseph DeWitt and Elizabeth (du) Casteel signing the above deed are underlined.

DeWITT
1.1.9.3.6.4.2 CORNELIUS SHERMAN DeWITT m Susan Lincoln

1. AZRO DeWITT b 1838 d 15 Sept 1846 bur East Baptist CH Cem Reeves Rd Henrietta NY. Chn all b at Henrietta, Munroe Co NY (all research fr VDM).
2. GEORGE A DeWITT b 1840 m 20 Oct 1868 Emeline Coleman d/o Samuel B. Coleman & Mary Ann Chase, b 04 Aug 1847 d 31 Jan 1934 (MCNYL:HH).
3. MEDORA DeWITT b 1843.
4. ARTHUR DeWITT b 1845 d 05 Oct 1850 bur E Baptist CH Cem Henrietta.
5. LILLIAN DeWITT b 1847.
6. MARY DeWITT b Dec 1850.
7. NELLY E DeWITT b 1856 (all fr VDM).

DeWITT
*1.1.9.3.8.2.3 WILLIAM DeWITT m Sarah

1. WILLIAM H DeWITT b 1840.
2. GEORGE DeWITT b 1842.
3. EMILY JANE DeWITT b 1844.
4. FAUNELLE DeWITT b 1846.
5. EDWIN DeWITT b 1848.
6. FRANKLIN DeWITT b 1850.
7. ISABELLA DeWITT b 1852.
8. MINERVA DeWITT b 1855 d 9 months **dy** (1855 Census Greene Co NY).

Jan deWitt

GENERATION 8

WINNE
1.1.9.3.1.3.5.1 CORNELIUS WINNER/WINNE m 1 Susan A Boice
1 ANNA ELIZABETH WINNE b 30 Aug 1843 d 21 Oct 1854 ae 11-01-21 **dy**.
2 GIDEON BOICE WINNE b 24 Dec 1851 d 04 Oct 1852 ae 00-09-10 **dy**.
3 LOREN WINNE b 1856 d 23 Aug 1877 ae 21.
   m2 14 Sep 1860 Margaretta K Simpson
4 ALVIN WINNE b 06 Apr 1861 d 07 Apr 1861 ae 21-00-01 (fr CBURC:195/6).

WINNE
1.1.9.3.1.3.5.2 ISIAH DAVID WINNE m1 Angeline Longyear
1 ISAAC WINNE b 31 Oct 1843 (BRSRC: 25) (d 18 Oct 1886 GIUC:27) m1 Betty Lasher b 30 Sep 1851 d 25 May 1877 ae 31-07-15; m2 Martha E Myers b 20 Feb 1855 d 26 Aug 1885..
2 JOSEPHINE WINNE b 04 Nov 1845 (d 1876) m Chauncey Keater.
3 ALONZO WINNE b 09 Feb 1847 (d 19 Nov 1925) m Elizabeth Bryant. He was the prop/o the "Eagle Hotel" Kingston NY.
4 ELISABETH WINNE b 08 Aug 1850.
5 ANNA WINNE b 03 Sep 1852 **dy**.
6 ISIAH D WINNE b 08 Jun 1854.
7 CHISTIAN WINNE b 07 Nov 1856 m Sarah Lasher (1 ch Addie).
8 ANDREW A WINNE b 01 Apr 1859 bp 04 Mar 1860 (d 1922 GIUC:27) m Kate Moninger (all fr CBRUC:1292).
   m2 Adeline Dimmick, no chn.

WINNE
1.1.9.3.1.3.6.2 HENRY WINNE m1 Magdalene Bush, m2 Elizabeth Davis
1 FRANCIS WINNE bp 05 Dec 1862 Shokan (BRSRC:26).
2 ANN WINNE b 19 Oct 1869 bp 05 Mar 1870 (BRSRC:27).

WOOD
1.1.9.3.1.3.6.5 MARY CATHARINE WINNE m Edward Wood
1 WILLIS WOOD b 10 Feb 1854 d 07 Dec 1858 ae 04-10-28.
2 CHAUNCY WOOD b 14 Apr 1856 d 14 Dec 1864 ae 08-08-00.

WINNE
1.1.9.3.1.3.6.8 GEORGE WINNE m Mary Jones
1 JOSEPHINE WINNE m Johnson Every s/o Peter Every & Elizabeth Bell (FT:59)

WINNE
1.1.9.3.1.3.7.1 ALFRED WINNE m Kelly
1 AARON WINNE d 15 Nov 1858 ae 02-03-21 "I'm going to die mother", he calmly said (GSIUC:25).
2 FERRIS WINNE d 06 Apr 1860 ae 02-00-01.
3 ANNA WINNE d 18 Mar 1865 ae 02-00-28.

DeWITT
1.1.9.3.2.1.3.4 CALEB C DeWITT m Mrs Eliza Jane Smith
1 GEORGE WASHINGTON DeWITT b 1870 Libertytown, Sullivan Co NY (d ? Mar 1958).
2 MILES DeWITT b 1872 same place (d ? Jul 1942) m, had a dau Mildred who m Fred L Budd, Livingston Manor, Sullivan Co NY. Mildred (DeWitt) Budd didn't know anything about family background (fr CEN). Stepchn Horatio Smith b 1858, Mary Smith b 1860.
3 FRANK A DeWITT b 1874 d Livingston Manor Sullivan Co NY.

DeWITT
1.1.9.3.4.1.3.1 JOSEPH DeWITT m1 Mary JaneThayer
1 MARTHA DeWITT b 1843.
2 SARAH DeWITT b 1845.
   m2 1848 Julia Robinson b 1821
3 LORETTA DeWITT b 1849 dy
4 EMILY V DeWITT b 1850 d 1921 bur Hoyes MD Meth Cem.
5 CLINTON DeWITT b 27 Oct 1851 (d 17 Dec 1895 bur Hoyes Meth Cem [MGCG]) m 01 Aug 1872 Margaret Shock.
6 MINERVA DeWITT b 1852 d 1938.
7 FREEMAN DeWITT b 1855 d 1950.
8 DELIA DeWITT b 1856 d 1950.
9 ALICE DeWITT b 1858 (fr Mrs W DeWitt in DFUSC).

MATHENY
1.1.9.3.4.1.3.3 CHRISTINA MATHENY m Elijah Cress Matheny
1. JOHN METHENY b 1836 **dy.**
2. GEORGE W MATHENY b 1837.
3. REBECCA MATHENY b 1839.
4. RACHEL MATHENY b 1839.
5. SARAH ? SUSAN METHENY b 1841.
6. JOSEPH M MATHENY b 1843.
7. MARY A MATHENY b 1845.
8. GEORGE MATHENY
9. JOANNE MATHENY
10. JANE MATHANY
11. BROOKS MATHENY
12. UNNAMED **dy.**
13. UNNAMED **dy.**   All issue b 1850 Census Preston Co WVA (fr Mrs W DeWitt in DFUSC:156).

DeWITT
1.1.9.3.4.1.3.7 JOHN DeWITT m Harriet Collier
1. PROF ALEXANDER DeWITT b 1850 near Hoyes Allegheny Co now Garret Co MD (d Nov 1933 near Frostburg MD) m G J Frayee. He was a noted teacher & Prof of Garrett Co and it is reported he had a complete genealogy of the DeWitt family in his possession (OHSC:9).
2. CHARLES WHITFIELD DeWITT b 1852 Garrett Co MD (d 28 Dec 1932 bur Hoyes Meth Cem MGCG) m Emma Boyer b 15 Mar 1861. Whitfield's Will was written 20 Aug 1925 see p 70.
3. PERRY DeWITT d 1856 **dy**
4. WEBSTER DeWITT b 1860.
5. DAVID OWEN DeWITT b 1868 OR B CA 1868 (d 16 Jun 1936) m Letitia Friend b 1870 d 1914 both bur Hoyes Meth Cem; had 5 sons 1 dau..
6. MINNIE DeWITT m Daniel Thayer had 3 daus (DFUSC:152)

DeWITT
1.1.9.3.4.1.3.8 ARCHIBALD CASTEEL DeWITT m Mary ?
1. MARY DeWITT b 1855.
2. HORACE DeWITT b 1856.
3. LOUISE DeWITT b 1859.
4. SADIE DeWITT b 1864 m Hamel Casteel.
5. SUSAN DeWITT b 1866.
6. VESPIE DeWITT b 1869.
7. ARTHUR DeWITT b 1872.

DeWITT
1.1.9.3.4.1.4.1 SAMUEL DeWITT m Mary J House
1. EDWARD P DeWITT b 1846 m 09 Feb 1865 Harriett L Clay in Allegany Co MD
2. ELIZABETH DeWITT b 1848.
3. WILLIAM DeWITT b Tunnelton WVA (fr DFUSC:1850 Preston Co WVA Census).

DeWITT
1.1.9.3.4.1.4.2 WILLIAM DeWITT {m} Sarah DeWitt (1.1.9.3.4.1.9.3).
1. BALTUS DeWITT b 1858 Preston WVA (d 1900) m1 Ella Spindler d/o Jonathan Spindler & Deborah Pysell b 1861 Preston (fr GCHSC:5). He was educated at Frostburg Normal School but became a jeweler at Terra Alta & later added a photographer's establishment. He m2 Lillie Barnes.
2. ALICE DeWITT m Henry Spindler s/o Jonathan Spindler & Deborah Pysell/Beissel of Brandonville WVA. (All DFUSC:64/5 fr Mrs W DeWitt).

DeWITT
1.1.9.3.4.1.4.3 GEORGE DeWITT m1 ? Martin, m2 ? Wilhelm
1. JOSEPH DeWITT (fr DFUSC: Mrs W DeWitt)

DeWITT
1.1.9.3.4.1.4.4 NANCY DeWITT {m} Thomas DeWitt (1.1.9.3.4.1.9.4).
1. GEORGE DeWITT b 26 Jun 1854 (d 12 Jan 1894 fr typhoid fever) m 22 Dec 1874 Mary Jane Sanders d/o John Frederick Sanders (an early Garret Co MD res) & Elizabeth Baker of Morgantown VA, b 01 Nov 1850 d 12 Nov 1895. They res on the old Sanders farm, a gov't land grant of 800 acres. All Chn b Garrett Co MD. Of interest to several lines is John Frederick Sanders b 03 Sep 1825 in Osnabruck, Germany (now Austria) d 17 Aug 1904 & wf Elizabeth Baker b 09 Sep 1830 d 06 Feb 1897k, & their 13 chn. Research on George DeWitt, dau Arlene & her husband Daniel D DeWitt was done by Daniel Darwin DeWitt & wf Margaret Evelyn Lane of Sequim WA, fr their Bible & family

Jan deWitt

records (fr DDD & MELD). Fifty years ago, George and Mary lived at Sang Run, which was then almost a dense woods. Afraid to leave their house at night, they used to call the dogs close to frighten away the bears and rattlesnakes. Not all the pioneers stayed in the days of '49. A few years later they moved about five miles from Oakland to the Underwood community. With help he hewed immense trees to build a new house and barn for his family. Being in ill health he was little able to stand such work long. In this house of their own making was born their youngest child, William, in a family of eight. DeWitt was a God-fearing man giving to his neighbors rather than taking from them. Hard work resulted in a run down condition. He contracted typhoid fever and died at the age of 42, leaving his wife to carry on. Determined to keep her family together, with courage and fortitude she set to work with a will. She had willed to do too much. A frail body soon broke under the heavy burden. There was no lovelier spinner or weaver in all of Garret Co than Mary Jane DeWitt. Old Peter Gortner would have no one else to spin for him. The wheel she used is in the possession of the Breuningers of Sunnyside. Mary Jane DeWitt died in 1895, buried at the side of her husband within eleven months after his death, leaving seven children, one baby having died, aged two years. (DFUSC: 65/6)

2   LOUISE DeWITT m   ?   Casteel.
3   SOPHRONIA DeWITT m   ?   Lowdermilk.
4   MAUSELL DeWITT b 1859 Garrett Co MD.
5   ISABELLA DeWITT b 1854   "   "   "
6   ELIZABETH DeWITT b 1855   "   "   "
7   RUFUS DeWITT b 1860 Garrett Co m1 Margaret Sanders d/o John Frederick Sanders & Elizabeth Baker, b 09 Sept 1860 Garrett Co MD d 26 Feb 1892; m2 Betty Welch. They had 7 chn.
8   LAFAYETTE DeWITT b 1861 m Theresa Savage, chn b Garrett Co MD. They had 7 chn.
9   MATTHEW DeWITT b 1864 (d 1911) m Fanny Ferguson. They had 9 chn.
10   WILLIAM DELPHIA DeWITT m Ina McCroby. They had 10 chn.
11   SUSAN DeWITT {m} Harris DeWitt (all fr DDD & MELD).

DeWITT

1.1.9.3.4.1.4.6 RICHARD DeWITT m1 Mary Ellen Whetsell; m2 Mary Ann Price Burns
1   ELIZABETH DeWITT
2   SAMUEL DeWITT
3   REBECCA DeWITT
4   SARAH DeWITT
5   ODESSA DeWITT
6   HENRY DeWITT
7   MIKE DeWITT b 1865 WVA.
8   JOHN DeWITT b 1865 WVA.
9   ADALINE DeWITT b 1865 WVA.
10   ISAAC ROBERT DeWITT b 1870 VA (d 1957) m 1894 Cynthia Ann Dunbar.
11   JOSEPH DeWITT
12   BRIDGET DeWITT
13   ALBERTA DeWITT
14   OSCAR DeWITT
15   BORDMAN DeWITT
16   AMY DeWITT
17   FOSTER DeWITT

DeWITT

1.1.9.3.4.1.5.1 PETER DeWITT m Silvia ?
1   HENRY DeWITT b 1851.
2   EMMA DeWITT b 1855.

DeWITT

1.1.9.3.4.1.6.1 JOHN HARRISON DeWITT m1 Martha Wees, m2 Minnie Hinchman
1   ZUELLA DeWITT
2   RAYMOND DeWITT
3   ANN GRACE DeWITT
4   JAMES HOLLAND DeWITT
5   MARY ALICE DeWITT
6   ALBERT S DeWITT
7   STANLEY CONGO DeWITT (DFUSC:153).
8   EMMA DeWITT (all HRC:370).

DeWITT

1.1.9.3.4.1.9.1 JAMES DeWitt m Louisa Friend
1. MARGARET/MAGGIE DeWITT m ? Lowdermilk.
2. MARY VIRGINIA DeWITT m Emmanuel Custer III res Hoyes MD.
(fr Mrs Wm DeWitt "The DeWitt Family" pub in 1915 in the Oakland Republican, Garrett Co MD)

DeWITT

1.1.9.3.4.1.9.2 WILLIAM DeWITT m Anne Mattingly
1. FRANCIS DeWITT b 1852 **dy,**
2. LUCRETIA/TERESA DeWITT b 1854.
3. JEROME DeWITT b 1854/5.
4. EDMUND DeWITT b 1858.
5. ABEL DeWITT b 1859.
6. JAFFERSON DeWITT b 1862.
7. FRANCES DeWITT b 1868.
8. ELLEN DeWITT b 1871.
9. WILLIAM DeWITT b 1875.

DeWITT

1.1.9.3.4.1.9.3 SARAH DeWITT {m} 1.1.9.3.4.1.4.2 William DeWitt
Children are with their father's underlined number Generation 8.

DeWITT

1.1.9.3.4.1.9.5 THOMAS DeWITT {m} 1.1.9.3.3.1.9.4 Nancy DeWitt
Children are with their mother's underlined number Generation 8.

DeWITT

1.1.9.3.4.1.9.5 JOHN DeWITT m Margaret Hauck
1. SARAH DeWITT b 1858 ae 22 in 1880 census m Joe Sines (fr CCD).
2. WILLIAM LUCIEN DeWITT b 08 Aug 1859 in census date 1860 (d 15 May 1923) m 16 Feb 1891 Catharine Elizabeth Sanders at res of George W DeWitt by Rev A Nichols, res Swallow Falls Dist, 1900 census at Ryan's Glade Garrett Co. Catharine d 11 Dec 1942.
3. MATTIE DeWITT b 1864 m Stephen Friend.
4. CHARLES DeWITT b 1866) m Mary/May Savage.
5. DANIEL DeWITT b ca 1872 Oakland MD {m} Arlene DeWitt 1.1.9.3.4.1.9.1.2 d/o George DeWitt & Mary Jane Sanders b 18 Jan 1880 d 13 Mar 1964. Arlene m2 Joe Weaver; m3 Otto Newbraugh.
6. JOHN DeWITT b 1875 m Amy Friend.
7. CLIFFORD DeWITT b 1878 m Dacie Friend bur Hoyes Rural Cem, no dates (fr MGCG).
8. LULA DeWITT b 1879 m Gilbert Friend.
9. ELLA DeWITT m Frank Fries.
10. FANNIE DeWITT m Rehl Friend (all fr DDD, CCD2, MELD).

DeWITT

1.1.9.3.4.1.9.6 ARCHIBALD CASTEEL DeWITT m Hannah Ellen Chambers.
1. EMMA DeWITT b 1857
2. ELIJAH DeWITT b 1858.
3. ZURA DeWITT b 1860.
4. CHAMBERS DeWITT b 1861 m 1890 Emma Laura Merrill.
5. HENRY DeWITT b 1863.
6. EDWARD FINLEY DeWITT b 1865 Hoyes, Garrett Co MD m 15 Jun 1892 Amy (sic) Elizabeth Lepley d/o John Lepley & Susan Reiber of Larmer T Somerset Co. Ed was an insurance and real estate broker in 1908 of Scottsdale in Westmoreland Co PA. He was a veteran of the Civil War. Both parents survive & live in Meyersdale, PA. He was president several years ago of the DeWitt Reunion held annually for the descendants of Ezeckiel DeWitt. (Some of this information was recorded about 1933).
7. HIRAM COLFAX DeWITT b 20 Apr 1870 Hoyes, Garret Co MD (IGI) & (d 1948) m Verna Graves, res Deer Park MD. One of their chn was Violet who served as Sec of the DeWitt Runion for several yrs.
8. ARCHIBALD DeWITT b 20 Apr 1870 same as Colfax.
9. IDA DeWITT b 1873 m Robert Snyder.
10. STELLA DeWITT b 1875 (d 1937) m 1894 M C Montague.
11. VADA DeWITT m Luther Nine.
12. ETTA DeWITT
13. MARY DeWITT
14. JACOB DeWITT (fr OHSC:8).

DeWITT

1.1.9.3.4.1.9.7 RICHARD DeWITT m Elizabeth Casteel
1. WILLIAM DeWITT b 1857.
2. JAMES DeWITT b 1860
3. ELIJAH DeWITT b 1862
4. SARAH DeWITT b 1874. Chn b Garret Co MD.

DeWITT

1.1.9.3.4.6.4.2.2 GEORGE A DeWITT m Emeline Coleman.
1. FREDERICK A DeWITT b * 1869 (d 20 May 1903 bur Mt Hope Cem Rochester NY) m (* Claribel) Hagerman d 31 Aug 1971.
2. BYRAN GEORGE DeWITT b 23 Jul 1871 Henrietta NY (d 15 Jul 1944) at Henrietta m 18 Feb 1896 Alice Newton b 20 Aug 1872 at Henrietta d/o William Newton & Emily F Schuyler, d 05 Sept 1927 both bur Maplewood Cem Henrietta.
3. EUGENE C DeWITT b ? Jul 1874 (d ? Aug 1907 at Henrietta) m Florence Weeks.
4. EDITH DeWITT b 28 Jul 187(*5) d 24 May 1966 m James McNall.
5. MEDORA DeWITT b 15 Jul 1878 (d 30 Sep 1962 Rochester) m Hiram M Colwell.
6. IDA (DAISY) DeWITT b 28 Dec 1880 (d 09 Jul 1953 m F Clark Stone (fr VDM).

Jan deWitt

GENERATION 9

If a couple traces back to DeWitt ancestry more than once, m is {m} indicating this fact. Numbering used is the first parent listed chronologically. Both numbers are given but the one to be used in succeeding generations is underlined.

Winne

1.1.9.3.1.3.5.2.1 ISAAC WINNE m1 Betty Lasher, m2 Martha E Myer
1. CHAUNCEY WINNE
2. ALONZO WINNE
3. DAVIS WINNE
4. MAY WINNE
5. HARRY WINNE

KEATER

1.1.9.3.1.3.5.2.2 JOSEPHINE WINNE m Chauncey Keater
1. HURVEY KEATER
2. ANGIE KEATER

EVERY

1.1.9.3.1.3.6.8.1 JOSEPHINE WINNE m Johnson Every
1. EMERSON EVERY
2. RAYMOND EVERY
3. ARTHUR EVERY
4. JOELLA EVERY
5. ALICE EDNA EVERY
6. GEORGE EVERY
7. WILLIAM CARLTON EVERY
8. OTIS EVERY
9. ANNA MAE EVERY

DeWITT

1.1.9.3.4.1.3.7.1 PROF ALEXANDER DeWITT m G J Frayee
1. OLIVE DeWITT m Charles Riddle res Pittsburgh PA; 1 son.
2. CLARENCE DeWITT m Adele White res New York; 2 chn.

DeWITT

1.1.9.3.4.3.7.2 CHARLES WHITFIELD DeWITT m Emma Louise Boyer
1. MAUDE DeWITT (d 24 Jan 1933) m John Brennaman; 3 daus, 1 son.
2. MARY ELLEN/MAY DeWITT m George Brennaman; 1 son.
3. SADIE DeWITT m Richard Friend; 2 sons.
4. FREDIA DeWITT m William Spoerline; 2 sons 1 dau, note Frederick in will.
5. CHARLES WHITFIELD DeWITT (d 21 Oct 1976) m Mary Anita Gillespie.

Wills 1931-40. D 99. Will written 20 Aug 1925 Charles Whitfield DeWITT, Hoyes Garrett Co MD. All real and personal property to son Whitfield DeWITT; conditions are: provide for my wife Emma Louise, specifies given, to Mary Ellen Brenneman $1000.00, to Sadie L Friend $1000.00, Frederick Spoerline (s/o Freda DeWITT & William Spoerline) $1000.00. Ex: son Whitfield DeWITT. Wit: W A Smith, D O Smith.

CASTEEL

1.1.9.3.4.1.3.8.4 SADIE DeWITT m Hamel Casteel
1. HARLAND CASTEEL

DeWITT

1.1.9.3.4.1.4.2.1 BALTUS DeWITT m Ella Spinder
1. LULA ETHEL DeWITT b 31 Jan 1887 at Terra Alta m 1909 Darius Earl Methany of Philadelphia s/o William Methany & Emma King, b 24 Sep 1877 Pisgah WVA (DFUSC:65)
2. HERBERT JOHNSON DeWITT b 21 Mar 1892 of Terra Alta, Preston Co WVA SAR #714, (d 05 Jan 19_7 m Winona Eichelberger d/o William Eichelberger & Rose Maize (DFUSC:65). Herbert was an electrical engineer & had charge of the largest companies in the bituminus coal industry. He was a Mason & belonged to the SAR, res Morgantown WVA, then in 1969 Clarksburgh WVA.
m2 Lillie Barnes

DeWITT

<u>1.1.9.3.4.1.4.4.1</u> & 1.1.9.3.4.1.9.4.1 GEORGE DeWITT m Mary Jane Sanders
1. JOHN T DeWITT b 16 May 1867 (d 21 Aug 1961) m Rebecca J Thomas b 14 Mar 1884 d 31 Jan 1954 (DFUSC, GCFSC).
2. ARLENE DeWITT b 18 Jul 1880 (d 13 Mar 1964) {m} Daniel D DeWITT (1.1.9.3.4.1.9.5.5) her 1st cousin once removed, s/o John DeWITT & Margaret Hauck, b ca 1872 Oakland MD.

Jan deWitt

3 CYRUS E DeWITT b 09 Jul 1882 m Lulu Bradford/Brafford.
4 TRUMAN A DeWITT b 11 Oct 1884 (d 22 Nov 1941) m Bertha Lee. Truman's Will 1931-40 E 191 estate to wife. She is Ex. 09 Jan 1941.
5 GEORGE A DeWITT b 05 Oct 1886 (d 22 Jul 1962) m Mabel Frankhauser.
6 BENJAMIN H DeWITT b 26 Mar 1889 (d 25 Dec 1959) m1 Ruth Stahl; m2 Nellie Henline. Will 1951-60 G 120 leaves estate to wf Nellie, at her decease to 3 chn & stepson or if she remarries to all my chn. If she renounces provisions & takes statutory 1/3, remainder to my 3 chn. Ex: Beatrice E Sanders 09 Sep 1952.
7 DAISEY ADELINE DeWITT b 12 Apr 1891 d 16 Feb 1892 **dy.**
8 WILLIAM H DeWITT b 04 Mar 1893 (d 08 Oct 1980) m 04 May 1913 Jenny June Christy of Piedmont WVA.

DeWITT

1.1.9.3.4.1.4.4.7 & 1.1.9.3.4.1.9.4.7 RUFUS DeWITT m1 Margaret Sanders
1 ALBERT DeWITT m Lou Seymour.
2 ELSIE DeWITT m Walter Savage.
3 LEO DeWITT m Bessie Brady.
4 LESTER DeWITT m Amy Wilson
  m2 Betty Walsh.
5 BOYD DeWITT
6 CLARENCE DeWITT
7 AUBRY DeWITT

DeWITT

1.1.9.3.4.1.4.4.8 & 1.1.9.3.4.1.9.4.8 LAFAYETTE DeWITT m Teresa Savage
1 FREDERICK DeWITT
2 NELLIE DeWITT
3 TROY DeWITT; one Troy Bruce DeWitt b 07 Sep 1898 (d 20 Oct 1974) m Cora Mae ? b 01 Jan 1904 d 18 Sep 1978 Booming Rose Cem Friendville MD.
4 ALMA DeWITT
5 ANNA DeWITT
6 LlOYD DeWITT
7 FOSTER DeWITT

DeWITT

1.1.9.3.4.1.4.4.9 & 1.1.9.3.4.1.9.4.9 MATTHEW DeWITT m Fanny Ferguson
1 WALTER DeWITT b 1886.
2 ARTHUR DeWITT b 23 Mar 1880.
3 CELIA DeWITT
4 ADA De WITT
5 DORA DeWITT
6 ROBERT DeWITT
7 GUY DeWITT
8 GEORGE DeWITT
9 GILBERT DeWITT
10 ALICE DeWITT

DeWITT

1.1.9.3.4.1.4.4.10 & 1.1.9.3.4.1.9.4.10 WILLIAM DELPHIAS DeWITT m Ina McCorby
1 CLYDE DeWITT
2 ORR DeWITT
3 MYRTLE DeWITT
4 THOMAS DeWITT
5 BLISS DeWITT
6 MILTON DeWITT
7 LAWRENCE DeWITT
8 EFFIE DeWITT
9 MARTHA DeWITT
10 UNKNOWN DeWITT

DeWitt

1.1.9.3.4.1.4.6.10 ISAAC ROBERT DeWITT m Cynthia Ann Dunbar
1 MICHAEL DeWITT
2 SARAH DeWITT b 01 May 1896 m Charles Wesley Huggins (DFUSC).
3 THOMAS DeWITT
4 ESTHER DeWITT

5 GEORGE DeWITT
6 RUTH DeWITT
7 IRA DeWITT
8 PAULINE DeWITT
9 EDNA DeWITT

CUSTER

1.1.9.3.4.1.9.1.2 MARY VIRGINIA DeWITT m Emmanual Custer 111
1 ALICE CUSTER m William/Willie Friend
2 HOMER DELPHIA CUSTER b ? May 1874 m Francis Maude Friend of Sang Run MD b 1831 d 1925. Rev Harrison Ford m them. They res in Garret Co MD.

DeWITT

1.1.9.3.4.1.9.5.2 WILLIAM LUCIAN DeWITT m Catharine Elizabeth Sanders
1 CHARLES ROBERT DeWITT b 12 Oct 1892 (d 23 Apr 1916 bur Sang Run MD) m 29 Sep 1913 Emma Annie DeWitt, **no chn.**
2 MARY ELIZABETH DeWITT b 21 Jun 1893 m 31 Dec 1913 Gilbert Weimer.
3 JOHN WILLIAM DeWITT b 22 Apr 1897 near Shallow Falls Garrett Co MD (d 17 Jan 1949 both bur Silver Knob MD) m 01 May 1917 Emma Vida Ashley near Crellin MD by Rev Joseph Everhart. She was the d/o Eusebuis Winfield Ashby & Sarah Rebecca Strawser, d 23 Apr 1987 both bur Gortner Cem (MGCG). John was a coal miner; he worked in many coalmines in MD & WVA, finally operating one near Kingwood WVA employing about 30 men. In 1934 he built a home near Crellin, helped establish the Assembly of God Church, serving as Deacon & Sunday School Supt for many years.
4 CHARLOTTIE ELLEN DeWITT b 26 Aug 1899 (d 1968) {m} 03 Aug 1920 William DeWitt.
5 DAVID ARTHUR DeWITT b 1901 (d 04 Aug 1942) both bur Gortner Cem. m 09 Apr 1923 Rena Wilson.
6 DAISY LUCRETIA DeWITT b 10 Apr 1903 (d 18 Apr 1981 bur Gortner Cem) m1 25 Dec 1917 William Marshall McCabe (GCHSO:11) m2 Joseph Lynch; m3 Ernest Maybe (GCHSO:11 & ALDFG:8/9).

DeWITT

1.1.9.3.4.1.9.5.4 CHARLES DeWITT m Mary Savage
1 DONALD DeWITT
2 CURTIS DeWITT
3 DAYTON DeWITT killed during WWI in France; had 1 dau.

DeWITT

1.1.9.3.4.1.9.5.5 DANIEL DeWITT {m} 1.1.9.3.4.1.4.1.2 Arlene DeWitt
1 ERVILLE COLUMBUS DeWITT b 1897 Sang Run MD (d 04 Apr 1976) m1 ? Feb 1917 Amanda Blanche DeBolt, b 09 Oct 1891 Marion Co WVA (d 1918) d/o Spencer DeBolt & Emma Wright; m2 Elsie Clark; m3 Helen ? .
2 LLOYD DeWITT b ca 1903 (d 1938 in a mine accident) m Bertha Friend b 1902 d 1972.
3 OAKEY DeWITT m Belle Shank.
4 GEORGE WHIRLEY DeWITT **dy**, of tuberculosis.
5 CARL DeWITT d in prison.
6 HOWARD DeWITT b 22 Jul 1910 (d 1988) m Nell Joseph had 2 chn.
7 MARGARET DeWITT m Ray Campbell **no chn**.
Arlene DeWitt m2 Joe Weaver; m3 Otto Newbraugh. (Chn #2-#7 b Oakland MD (all fr DDD & MELD).

DeWITT

1.1.9.3.4.1.9.5.6 JOHN DeWITT m Amy Friend
1 LOU DeWITT
2 VERNA DeWITT

DeWITT

1.1.9.3.4.1.9.5.7 CLIFFORD DeWITT m Dacie Friend
1 GERTRUDE DeWITT m Gilbert Friend.

DeWITT

1.1.9.3.4.1.9.6.4 CHAMBERS DeWITT m E Laura Merrill
1 LURA DeWITT m Robert Echart.
2 MERLE DeWITT
3 GLADYS DeWITT
4 BRYDON DeWITT
5 EVANS DeWITT
6 VERDO DeWITT

DeWITT
1.1.9.3.4.1.9.6.6 EDWARD FINLEY DeWITT m Amy (sic) Elizabeth Lepley
1. CLYDE C DeWITT
2. ELLEN IRENE DeWITT
3. EDNA L DeWITT deceased (all info DFUSC:154).

DeWITT
1.1.9.3.4.1.9.6.7 HIRAM COLFAX DeWITT m Verna Graves
1. VIOLET DeWITT

DeWITT
1.1.9.3.6.4.2.2.2 BYRAN GEORGE DeWITT m Alice Newton
1. EUGENE NEWTON DeWITT b 01 May 1898 Henrietta NY (d 22 June 1947 Rochester NY) at Rochester m 16 Feb 1922 Clara N Hondorf d/o Herman E Hondorf & Josephine Widener.
2. MILDRED DeWITT b 28 Feb 1900 (d 03 Jul 1974) m 28 Nov 1925 Donald McGhee.
3. BEATRICE LUCILLE DeWITT b 04 Jul 1901 (d 1928 bur Maplewood) at Jacksonville FL m 22 Apr 1926 Basil George Baldwin.
4. WARREN DeWITT b 30 Nov 1902 (06 Dec 1983 Sarasota FL) m 31 Dec 1927 Edna Rumsey (all info fr VDM).
5. SHERMAN DeWITT b 05 Jul 1904 (d 22 Jun 1979 Rochester) m ? Oct 1928 Genevieve Connelly d 1960'S.

GENERATION 10

If a couple traces back to DeWitt ancestry more than once, m is {m} indicating this fact. Numbering used is the first parent listed chronologically. Both numbers are given but the one to be used in succeeding generations is underlined.

DeWITT

1.1.9.3.4.1.3.7.2.5 CHARLES WHITFIELD DeWITT m Mary Anita Gillespie.
1. HAROLD G DeWITT res McHeny MD.
2. WILARLIE DeWITT m John Houser res Middletown OH.
3. ANITA DeWITT m Thomas Brobst res LaVale MD.
4. CHARLES H DeWITT b 15 Sep 1923 (d 28 Oct 1974) m Valetta L Ruehl. Oakland, Garrett Co MD.

METHENY

1.1.9.3.4.1.4.2.1.1 LULA ETHEL DeWITT m Darius Earl Metheny
1. WILLIAM BLAKE METHENY res Philadelphia PA.

DeWITT

1.1.9.3.4.1.4.2.1.2 HERBERT DeWITT m Winona Echelberger
1. EVELYN R L DeWITT b 03 Oct 1918.
2. LEONA DeWITT b 21 Feb 1924.

DeWITT

1.1.9.3.4.1.4.4.1.1 JOHN T DeWITT m Rebecca J Thomas
1. MARY DeWITT b 31 Aug 1902 (d 30 Apr 1964) m 29 Sep 1929 Fisher Schaeffer b 1894 d 1952.
2. ROY DeWITT b 04 Jan 1904 d 05 Nov 1905 **dy**.
3. ETHEL DeWITT b 12 Aug 1905 d 31 Jan 1906 **dy**.
4. DELLA DeWITT b 18 Nov 1909 m ? Welch, Crellin MD (GCHSC).
5. EVELYN DeWITT b 04 Feb 1912 m1 Cecil Wilt; m2 Alvery Clark.
6. WILLARD DeWITT b 28 Feb 1917 (d 13 Jan 1949) m Esther Hollis of Terra Alta WV.
7. SYLVIA IRENE DeWITT b 12 Apr 1922.

DeWITT

1.1.9.3.4.1.4.4.1.2 ARLENE DeWITT {m}1.1.9.3.4.1.9.5.5 Daniel DeWitt
Children are with their Father's underlined number Generation 10

DeWITT

1.1.9.3.4.1.4.4.1.4 TRUMAN DeWITT m Berth Lee
1. RALPH DeWITT m Marie Ashby, Crellin MD.
2. VELMA VIRGINIA DeWITT m Elwood Adams, Crellin MD.

DeWITT

1.1.9.3.4.1.4.4.1.5 GEORGE A DeWITT m Mabel Frankhauser
1. CATHARINE DeWITT m Joseph Bolinger of Morgantown WV.
2. PAUL DeWITT
3. FRANCES DeWITT
4. HELEN DeWITT

DeWITT

1.1.9.3.4.1.4.4.1.6 BENJAMIN H DeWITT m Ruth Stahl
1. CLEO BELLE DeWITT b 08 Jun 1911 m 24 Dec 1932 Earl Lee.
2. GEORGE ELWOOD DeWITT (d ? Dec 1979) m Irene James, Kempton WV.
3. BERNICE ELAINE DeWITT b 18 Jan 1917 m George Sanders.
m2 Nellie Henline

DeWITT

1.1.9.3.4.1.4.4.1.8 WILLIAM H DeWITT m Jenny June Christy
1. JEAN FRANCIS DeWITT b 24 Jun 1924 Morgantown WV.

DEWITT

1.1.9.3.4.1.4.4.7.1 ALBERT DeWITT m Lou Seymour
1. MARVIN DeWITT
2. RAYMOND DeWITT
3. IRENE DeWITT
4. ELSIE DeWITT
5. WILLARD DeWITT
6. LEONA DeWitt

HIGGINS
1.1.9.3.4.1.4.6.10.2 Sarah DeWitt m Charles Wesley Higgins
1. ROBERT WESLEY HIGGINS
2. GEORGE HIGGINS
3. ANNABEL HIGGINS
4. BETTY HIGGINS
5. CHARLES EDWARD HIGGINS
6. LINSEY HIGGINS

CUSTER
1.1.9.3.4.1.9.1.2.2 HOMER DELPHIA CUSTER m Frances Maude Friend
1. CHARLES ARTHUR CUSTER b 13 Dec 1897 m Marther Ogger.
2. VIRGINIA ALICE CUSTER b 05 Dec 1899 m Masom Myer.
3. LULU MAE CUSTER b23 Dec 1901 m 04 May 1962 Alfred Franklin Bittner.
4. HOMER RAE CUSTER b 05 May 1904 m Ellen Hhostittler.
5. GEORGE ROOSEVELT CUSTER b 21 APR 1906.
6. LAURA MAUDE CUSTER b 17 Aug 1908 m Argyle Myers.
7. ELMA GERTRUDE CUSTER b 11 Mar 1911 m Gordon D Abittir.

WEIMER
1.1.9.3.4.1.9.4.5.2. MARY ELIZABETH DeWITT m Gilbert Weimer
1. ALFRED WILLIAM WEIMER b 27 Dec 1914 d 09 Sep 1938, **no chn.**
2. MABEL ELIZABETH WEIMER b 19 Apr 1916 m Arnold Savage, **no chn.**
3. LESTA? EVELYN WEIMER b 05 Aug 1918 m Aubrey Savage, 6 daus.
4. GLADYS IRENEWEIMER b 17 May 1920 m Edward Sereck, 4 chn.
5. SAMUEL CARROL WEIMER b 19 Mar 1922 d 10 Apr 1936.
6. ALFREDA WONDELL WEIMER b 16 Apr 1924 m ?   , 1 dau.
7. ALMA MAXINE WEIMER b 25 Jul 1926 m Hebdem, 2 chn.
8. OLIVER EDWARD EUGENE WEIMER b 24 mar 1929, **no chn.**
9. EVERETT BOYD WEIMER b 19 July 1930 m   ?   , 3 daus 1 son.
10. BETTY WEIMER b 28 Feb 1933 d 23 Sep 1936.

DeWITT
1.1.9.3.4.1.9.4.5.3 JOHN WILLIAM DeWITT m Emma Viola Ashby
1. STANLEY WILLIAM DeWITT b 12 Aug 1918 m 31 Aug 1941Betty Louise Rodeheaver. He was a coal miner & heavy equipment operator.
2. HAROLD EDWARD DeWITT b 25 Oct 1921 m 04 Nov 1942 Audrey Frazer. He had a bearing & transmission business in Cumberland MD.
3. MARIE EVELYN DeWITT b 06 June 1924 (d ? Jan 1974) m 10 Jan 1940 Clester Bryon Skipper. Marie was a sales clerk & worked for a Commission on Aging.
4. EMMA LORETTA DeWITT b15 Sep 1926 M 06 Aug 1950 Loraine C Sines. As well as housewife Emma was a bookkeeper & Real Estate Agent.
5. WANDA CAROLINE DeWITT b 13 Mar 1930 m 25 Oct 1951 Paul Kenneth Steiding. She was a homemaker & clerical worker.
6. BETTY LOUISE DeWITT b 23 Oct 1932 m 25 Aug 1952 Delano Ramsey Martin b 12 Feb 1933.
7. CLIFFORD CARLETON DeWITT b 18 Feb 1935, Deputy Court Clerk 195559 –1978, Clerk of Circuit Court for Garrett Co 1978 –1990.
8. JAMES ROBERT DeWITT b30 Dec 1939 m 25 Sep 1956 Linda Rae Hulk. He was a paper mill worker, store clerk & coal drying operator; 1 son Craig.
9. PEGGY LEE DeWITT b 02 Feb 1942 (d 26 Feb 1974 (m 18 Jun 1967 Claude Randall McCartney. Peggy was a housewife & beautician (all ALDFG:9/10).

DeWIT
1.1.9.3.4.1.4.9.2.4 CHARLOTTE ELLEN DeWITT {m} William DeWitt
1. ROY EDWARD DeWITT b 06 Feb 1922 d 1976.
2. EVELYN ELIZABETH DeWITT b21 Sep 1923 m Tobe Welch.
3. VIRGIE MARIE DeWITT b 30 Jan 1926 m Cecil Welch.
4. ALBERTA MARIETTA DeWITT b 08 Nov 1929 d 24 sep 1944.
5. WILLIAM BOYD DeWITT b 03 Apr 1931.
6. OLIVER BLISS DeWITT b 27 Aug 1923.
7. LORRAINE CATHERINE DeWITT b 13 Nov 1935.

DeWITT

1.1.9.3.4.1.9.5.2.5 DAVID ARTHUR DeWITT m Rena Wilson
1. ARTHUR WILLIAM DeWITT b 25 May 1928, Balto Policeman.
2. GLADYS DeWITT b 30 Mar 1934.

McCABE

1.1.9.3.4.1.9.5.2.6 DAISY LUCRETTA DeWITT m1 William Marshall McCabe
1. BEULAH FRANCES McCABE b 08 May 1920 m Lester B Shockey, 3 chn.
2. DENVER PAUL McCABE b 22 Nov 1922 m Winona George, 3 chn.
3. DARRELL CARLTON McCABE b 20 Jul 1925 m Gloria Lawanna Staunegar, 3 chn.

DeWITT

1.1.9.3.4.1.9.5.5.1 ERVILLE COLUMBUS DeWITT m1 Amanda Blanche DeBolt
1. DANIEL DURWARD DeWITT b 17 Mar 1918 Morgantown WVA, m1 Pearl Mae Dean; m2 Margaret Evelyn Lane. **m2 Elsie Clark**
2. ERVILLE DARWIN DeWITT b 10 Dec 1920 Morgantown, m1 Kay; m2 06 Dec 1964 Jean, **no chn** (fr MELD).

BALDWIN

1.1.9.3.6.4.2.2.2.3 BEATRICE LUCILLE DeWITT m Basil George Baldwin
1. DEAN DeWITT BALDWIN b 30 Jan 1931 in Ohio m 14 Jun 1953 Dolores Y Coleman b 10 Aug 1931 (fr VDM).

DeWITT

1.1.9.3.6.4.2.2.2.4 WARREN DeWITT m Edna Rumsey
1. WARREN DeWITT Jr (fr VDM).
2. CAROL DeWITT

DeWITT

1.1.9.3.6.4.2.2.2.5 SHERMAN DeWITT m Genevieve Connelly
1. JOAN DeWITT d in the 1960's (fr VDM).

GENERATION 11

DeWITT

1.1.9.3.4.1.3.7.2.5.4 CHARLES H DeWITT m Valetta L Ruehl
1. Lt RUSSELL DeWITT with US Army in Honolulu.
2. RONALD DeWITT Riverdale.
Oakland Garrett Co MD Estate No 5327 Charles H DeWitt; names his parents Whitfield & Anita (Gillespie) DeWitt; stepchn Mrs Sharon Reed res Somers NY, George H Kinsley, res LaVale; sis Mrs Thomas Bropst, LaVale, Mrs John Hauser Middleton OH, bro Harold G DeWitt res McHenry MD.

ARBITTER

1.1.9.3.4.1.9.1.2.2.7 ELMA GERTRUDE CUSTER m Gordon D Arbitter
1. BERNICE ELMA ARBITTER b 02 Dec 1930 m Rollin M Binkley II.
2. HELEN MARIE ARBITTER b 23 Jan 1943 m Albert Tacon.

DeWITT

1.1.9.3.4.1.9.5.2.3.1 STANLEY WILLIAM DeWITT m Betty Louise Rodeheaver
1. CARL EDWARD DeWITT b 28 Sep 1942 d 05 Jan 1957.
2. NANCY CAROL DeWITT b 06 May 1944.
3. TERRY LEE DeWITT b 03 Sep 1945.
4. STANLEY WILLIAM DeWITT Jr b 23 Sep 1946
5. DARRELL WAYNE DeWITT b 11 Jan 1949.
6. DONALD RICHARD DeWITT b 21 May 1954.
7. MICHAEL ALLEN DeWITT b 07 Feb 1962 (all ALDFG:9).

DeWITT

1.1.9.3.4.1.9.5.2.3.2 HAROLD EDWARD DeWITT m Audrey Frazer
1. HAROLD EDWARD DeWITT Jr b 03 Aug 1948 m Deborah Nelson.
2. PATRICIA ANN DeWITT b 21 Oct 1949.
3. REBECCA SUE DeWITT b 24 Mar 1951. (all ALDFG:9)

SKIPPER

1.1.9.3.4.1.9.5.2.3.3 MARIE EVELYN DeWITT m Clester Bryon Skipper
1. WILLIAM CARROLL SKIPPER b 11 Oct 1948 m 08 Jul 1972 ?, a minister.
2. SHERRY LYNN SKIPPER b 11 Jan 1951 (all ALDFG:10).

SINES

1.1.9.3.4.1.9.5.2.3.4 EMMA LORETTA DeWITT m Loraine C Sines
1. KEITH LORAINE SINES b 16 Sep 1951 (all ALDFG:10).
2. DIANA RAE SINES b 18 Aug 1955 m1 01 Sep 1973 Robert D Liller; m2 07 Apr 1980 Victor Della Mea.

STEIDING

1.1.9.3.4.1.9.5.2.3.5 WANDA CAROLINE DeWITT m Paul Kenneth Steiding
1. PAUL KENNETH STEIDING Jr b 17 May 1961 (all ALDFG:10).

MARTIN

1.1.9.3.4.1.9.5.2.3.6 BETTY LOUISE DeWITT m Delano Ramsey Martin
1. DAVID KENT MARTIN b 10 Jul 1953 m 14 Jul 1974 Frances L Friend.
2. PHILLIP JEFFREY MARTIN b 03 Jul 1956.
3. LINDA RAE MARTIN b 23 May 1959 (all ALDFG:10).

DeWITT

1.1.9.3.4.1.9.5.2.3.8 JAMES ROBERT DeWITT m Linda Rae Rulk
1. LAURA RENEE DeWITT b 21 Jul 1969.
2. AMY ELIZABETH DeWITT b 02 Aug 1977.
3. ROBERT ANTHONY DeWITT b 05 Oct 1985 (all ALDFG:10).

McCARTNEY

1.1.9.3.4.1.9.5.2.3.9 PEGGY LEE DeWITT m Claude Randall McCartney
1. RANDI SUE McCARTNEY b 24 Apr 1968.
2. JOHN RANDALL McCARTNEY b 12 Feb 1970 (all ALDFG:10).

DeWITT

1.1.9.3.4.1.9.5.5.1.1 DANIEL DURWARD DeWITT m1 Pearl Mae Dean
1. DANIEL DARWIN DeWITT b 09 Aug 1942 Warren OH.
m2 Margaret Evelyn Lane
2. RICHARD JAMES DeWITT b 20 Nov 1946 Spokane WA.
3. MARGARET ANN/PEGGY De WITT b 18 Jun 1949 Spokane WA.
4. SUSAN ELURA DeWITT b 02 Apr 1951 Spokane WA (fr DDD & MELD).

DeWITT

1.1.9.3.4.1.9.5.5.1.2 ERVILLE DARWIN DeWITT m1 Kay DeWitt
1   ROBERT DeWITT b 15 Mar 1950 Morgantown WVA (fr DDD, MELD).
    m2 Jean, **no chn.**

GENERATION 12

ARBITTER

1.1.9.3.4.1.9.1.2.2.7.1 BERNICE ELMA ARBITTER m Rollin M Binkley II
1   ROLLIN M BINKLEY III b 22 Mar 1960.
2   TACON BINKLEY
3   RHONDA MARIE BINKLEY b 16 Jan 1965.

TACON

1.1.9.3.4.1.9.1.2.2.7.2 HELEN MARIE ARBITTER m Albert Tacon
1   MARALISA TACON b & d 07 Jul 1970.
2   ANDREA LEE TACON b 25 Feb 1972

SAVAGE

1.1.9.3.4.1.9.5.2.3.1.2 NANCY CAROL DeWITT m Kenneth Savage
1   CHRISTINA LYNN SAVAGE b 08 Oct 1966.
2   KIMBERLY ANN SAVAGE b 29 Sep 1968
3   TRACY RENEE SAVAGE b 13 Aug 1970.
4   JENNIFER MARIE SAVAGE b 03 Aug 1976.

DeWITT

1.1.9.3.4.1.9.5.2.3.1.3 TERRY LEE DeWITT m Nancy Henline
1   JON DAVID DeWITT 31 Oct 1969.
2   JAMEY DEREK DeWITT b 27 Nov 1974.
3   JEREMY DANIEL DeWITT b 05 Dec 1976.
4   JUSTIN DARIN DeWITT b 17 Jun 1979.

DeWITT

1.1.9.3.4.1.9.5.2.3.1.4 STANLEY WILLIAM DeWITT Jr m Karen Lantz
1   CHAD RYAN DeWITT b 04 Apr 1975.
2   LARISSA SHEREE DeWITT b 17 may 1976.

DeWITT

1.1.9.3.4.1.9.5.2.3.1.5 DARRELL WAYNE DeWITT m1 Susan Wilcox; m2 Angel ? .
1   DILLON DeWITT

DeWITT

1.1.9.3.4.1.9.5.2.3.1.7 DONALD RICHARD DeWITT m Cindy Smith
1   DANIELLE DeWITT
2   NICOLE DeWITT

DeWITT

1.1.9.3.4.1.9.5.2.3.2.1 HAROLD EDWARD DeWITT m Deborah Nelson
1   NATHAN DeWITT b 26 Nov 1974.
2   KEVIN DeWITT b May 1978.

FOLEY

1.1.9.3.4.1.9.5.2.3.2.2 PATRICIA ANN DeWITT m Timothy Foley
1   TRISTA ANN FOLEY

SKIPPER

1.1.9.3.4.1.9.5.2.3.3.1 Rev WILLIAM CARROLL SKIPPER m Conna Brigham
1   CANDACE M SKIPPER b 10 Oct 11976.
2   KEVIN DeWITT Skipper b May 1978.
3   STACEY J SKIPPER b 26 Oct 1977.

LILLER/DELLAMEA

1.1.9.3.4.1.9.5.2.3.4.2 DIANE RAE SINES m1 Robert D Liller
1   KACEY D LILLER b 06 Dec 1975.
2   TORY D LILLER b 19 Sep 1979.
    m2 Victor Dellamea
3   NICOLE B DELLAMEA b 06 Feb 1981.

STEIDING
1.1.9.3.4.1.9.5.2.3.5.1 PAUL KENNETH STIEDING m Lisa Gift
1   EMILY MARIE STEIDING

MARTIN
1.1.9.3.4.1.9.5.2.3.6.1 DAVID KENT MARTIN m Frances L Friend
1   RYAN DAVID MARTIN b 07 Aug 1989.

SMITH
1.1.9.3.4.1.9.5.2.3.8.1 LAURA RENEE DeWITT m Darrin Smith
1   CRAIG SMITH b 11 Jul 1986.

DeWITT
1.1.9.3.4.1.9.5.5.1.1.1 DANIEL DARWIN DeWITT m1 Anne Baxter
1   RENAE DeWITT b 15 May 1964.
     m2 Janet Cato
2   BRIDGETT DeWITT b 13 May 1971 Spokane.
3   JENNIFER DeWITT b 30 Nov 1973 Spokane (info fr DDD).

DeWITT
1.1.9.3.4.2.9.5.5.1.1.2 RICHARD JAMES DeWITT m Roberta Raymond
1   JUSTIN COLBY DeWITT b 23 Aug 1971 New Bedford MA (fr DDD).

EASTLUND
1.1.9.3.4.1.9.5.5.1.1.3 MARGARET ANN/PEGGY DeWITT m Donald R Eastlund
1   ERIK JAMES DANIEL EASTLUND b 17 Mar 1980 Spokane WA.

TIEMANN
1.1.9.3.4.1.9.5.5.1.1.4 SUSAN ELURA DeWITT m Gregory James Tiemann
1   SAMANTHA ELURA TIEMANN b 23 Jan 1986 Bellevue WA (fr DDD).

DeWITT
1.1.9.3.4.2.9.5.5.1.2.1 ROBERT/BOBBY DeWITT m Diane ? .
1   ROBIN DeWITT b 1984.

GENERATION 13

GIFFORD/BIRCH
1.1.9.3.4.1.9.5.5.1.1.1.1 RENAE DeWITT m1 Bobby Gifford
1   TARA GIFFORD b 15 Feb 1985.
2   DANIEL GIFFORD b 30 May 1986.
     m2 Frank Birch
3   ROBERT BIRCH McMORRIS b 23 May 1989 (all fr DDD).

THE END

Leucas deWit

GENERATION 4

Please note – Generation 1 Nicholaas/Class deWitt starts on pages 15-17. Generation 2, Tireck Clafen DeWitt is pages 18-21. Generation 3 is Luycas DeWitt page 22. This work is tracing the ancestry of <u>Luycas DeWitt's</u> three surviving children. They have been tabulated so that the information appears separately for each sibling.

If a couple both trace back to DeWitt ancestry more than once m is {m} indicating this fact. Numbering used is the first parent listed chronologically. Both numbers are given, but the one to be used in succeeding generations is underlined.
To keep the chronology of LEUCAS' descendants #3 EVERT and #5 LUCAS are the exceptions.

DeWitt

1.1.9.4 LEUCAS/LUYKAS deWIT m Catrina Roosa

1. ANNAATJEN deWIT bp 05-Oct-1729 sp (pa's half bro & sis) Anthony Buntschooten, Geeritjen Buntschooten (DRCK:183) m banns 15 Oct 1756 Johannes Diederick j/o both res Albanie (this part became Greene Co [DRCK:610]).

2. JAN LUCAS deWIT b 04 May 1731 bp 04 May 1736 sp (aunt's hus) Cornelis Longendik, Jonge Longendik (K&S: 2:DR:258/9) & (d 27 May 1803 ae 72-01-09) at Newtown Zion Luth CH Loonenburg {m} banns 13 May 1758 Anna Marytje deWit (DRCK:614) d/o Peek deWit & m2 Anna Maria Teunis at same CH bp 15 Apr 1730 sp Christian Meyer & wf Antje (NYGBR 82:21) d 01 Jul 1814 ae 84-03-23 both bur Mt Marion Cem (OGUC:263; GIUC:3). Anna Maria was [the wd/o Frederick Winne s/o Pieter Winne jr & Antje Merkel] bp 22 Sep 1723 sp Jan Ostroud jr, Catrina Winne (DRCK:148). Frederick, Arent & Christian Winne were bros. John L deWitt was a Capt in the Revo. His stone house was fortified. He was storing arms for the Rebels/Patriots. Jan's b date may be suspect since Evert was bp in 1733, yet Jan is not bp until 1736 d 1801, perhaps an adjustment in his age in relation to his wf.
(USA records accept Jan as the elder).

3. EVERT deWIT bp 25 Nov 1733 sp (ma's bro & sis) Jacobus Roosa, Lea Roosa at Coxsackie (DRCK:199) (d 1801) {m} Geertruy Persen d/o Abraham Persen/Paarsen & Catrina Schoonmaker, bp 19 Jan 1735 sp (ma's grparents) Hendrik Schoonmaker & Tryntjen Oosterhout (DRCK: 207). In the Revo Evert may have been gunrunning for the British (fr PJDS). After the British burned Kingston & people were hanged he realized the danger and went down the Hudson to the British lines and served as an "Armed Boatman" based on Staten Island. He was among the Loyalist refugees transported from New York by the British Navy to what became the Maritime Provinces in Canada. As Everitt Dewett in Ship's Lists which show him and 2 males over ae 10 were aboard the Spring Fleet in 1783 suggesting he, Henry & Peter were evacuated first (ELSJ:195) [? wife Geertruy & dau Catherine not listed]. Sons John & Jacob would have moved with their Regts. DeWitt Land Grants were on the Oromocto River, Sunbury Co NB (LONB:276). In 1791 Burton Par Sunbury Co NB Can tax list includes Evert & sons Henry, Jacob & John. More info Gen 5.

4. MARYTJEN d WIT bp 07 Mar 1736 sp (ma's sis & hus) Jacob Oostrander, Marytjen Roosa (DRCK:216).

5. LUCAS deWIT bp 20 Aug 1738 sp Thobyas van Steenbergen, Zara Paarsen (DRCK:234) & (d 1820 DAR vol 22 p 72 lineage No 21192) {m} Debra Persen 1.1.6.12.6 bp 26 Feb 1737/8 at Catskill sp Martin Gerritsen van Bergen & Debra Van Bergen, her prts Abraham Paers/Persen & Catrina/Catharyina Schoonmaker `who moved to Raritan NJ' (they bought property there, proof not found so far that they moved there) (NYGBR 86:17; HGC:435/6). Lucas & family res Oak Hill, Durham, Greene Co NY. Lucas had a mill on the Katskill & was a Lt in the Revo but seemed to waver between which side to stay with. He had an older bro on each side. One Lucas was arrested for drinking a toast to King George III (MCDDC: 689/90). By 1778 Lucas would have been ae 40, his father Lucas, if alive, ae 73, his nephew, Evert's son Lucas ae 20. Info in Gen 5.
<u>Absracts of Wills of Greene Co NY Vol 1</u>
Lucas DeWitt of Freehold: Pro Sept 29 1820. Mentions his wf Deborah, sons Jacobus, John, Peter, daus Caty wf/o Jeremiah Young, Deborah w/o William West. Ex: Jacobus [ie James], John, Peter. Wit: John Plank Jr, Jeremiah Plank, James Battersell (AWGC:11).

6. ABRAHAM deWIT bp 15 Feb 1741 sp (ma's bro) Abraham Roosa, Annaatjen Kool (DRCK:251).

7. JANNETJEN deWIT bp 31 Jul 1743 sp (pa's cousins) Luykas Langendyk, Geertjen Langendyk (DRCK:267) {m} Jacobus/Cobus s/o Hendrik Osterhout & Johanna DeWitt bp 27 Jan 1745 (OFG:17).

8. RACHEL deWITT bp 22 Aug 1745 sp (ma's bro & sis) Arie Roosa, Rachel Roosa (K&S:9) m Abraham Low s/o Petrus Abrahamse Louw/Lau/Low & Mareitje Van Keuren, bp 23 Jan 1743 sp Abraham Louw, wf Jannetje Lesier, d 28 Nov 1812, res Saugerties.

9. CATHARINA deWITT bp 05 Sep 1748 sp Samuel Wels & wf Marietje Osterhout (K&S:12). A Catharina Dewitt & Jan Ostrander are sp at the bp 29 Mar 1764 of Catharina's bro (#5) Lucas' ch Jacobus. Zion Lutheran CH Loonenburg (Athens NY) p130 a Catrina Dewitt & Mathew Halenbek had Annatie b 02 Mar 1775 bp 24 Feb 1776 sp Evert deWitt wf Gertrow; p138 a Catrina deWitt & Barent Ebberts had Evert b 11 Apr 1778 bp 19 May 1778 sp Evert deWitt absent, wf Gertruyd.

10 PETRUS deWITT bp 02 Nov 1755 sp (pa's cousins) Petrus Langendyk, Maria Langendyk (DRCK:324) Petrus jm m 16 Nov 1775 Maria Hommel jd at Caaspan (Katsbaan; DRCK:634; fr CES).
Nothing further found on Petrus and his wife but perhaps the search should be in Canada as a Petrus DeWitt was granted Loyalist Land in New Brunswick, Canada. In a petition along with Evert DeWit and his sons John and Jacob (in 1783 Petrus was age 28, his namesake nephew just age 13). This nephew, Peter, Evert's son, in his Ontario Petition for land, said he accompanied his father to New Brunswick after the American Revolution and resided there 20 years but never drew or applied for any land there and that he returned to New York in 1803, moved to Ontario in 1811. This indicates he probably lived with his parents and presumably left after his mother's death. A Peter DeWitt died in a house fire 18 Aug 1827. Abraham Dewett and John Brown were administrators of his estate 28 Oct 1827.

Leucas deWit

GENERATION 5

If a couple both trace back to DeWitt ancestry more than once m is {m} indicating this fact. Numbering used is the first parent listed chronologically. Both numbers are given, but the one to be used in succeeding generations is underlined.

DIEDERICK

1.1.9.4.1 ANNAATJEN deWIT m Johannes Diederick

1 ABRAHAM DIEDERICK bp 21 Aug 1757 sp Jas Jager, wf Elisebetha Wieler (BRRCG:40).

2 LUCAS DIEDERICH bp 12 Feb 1760 sp (uncle & aunt) Lucas Dewit, Jannetje Dewit (K&S:26) & (d 03 Jan 1808 Long Point ON [WLD:8]) m Lucretia Persen d/o John Persen. As Lucas Tedrick, he was a Sgt in Butler's Rangers, served 6 yrs, was in the Niagara area where there was a Jacob Dedrick but then settled Walsingham T Norfolk Co ON. The Loyalist Gazette Autumn 1976 p17 Query asking for info on Lucas Dederick in the roster of Capt Peter Hare's CO on 30 Nov 1783 as a Cpl ae 22-06-00 single. "Lucas Dedrick came from Pennsylvania and was of German descent " (PSLPS: 35). He settled at Long Point in 1793. Stories in Gen 6.

3 * CHRISTIAN DEDRICK b 1775 m Elizabeth b 1784. Their chn were: John b 1801, Elias b 1803 & Lucas b 1806 (LPS:58). In 10 Sep 1807 Christian bought 150A & 50A in Woodhouse T Norfolk Co ON from Samuel Ryerse 03 Nov 1815 & old to Samuel Cooper 50A of the 1st purchase.

DeWitt

1.1.9.4.2 JAN LUCAS deWIT {m} Anna Marytje/Marytjien (DeWit/Dewit) Winnie

Chn/o Frederick Winne m Anna Maritje DeWit
Petrus Winne bp 23 Apr 1753 sp (ma's sis & hus) Arie Van Etten, wf Christina Dewit (K&S:17) m 14 Jun 1781 Sara Wolven (K&S:247).
Benjamin Wenne bp 31 Mar 1755 sp Matheus Wenne, wf Grietje Henriks (K&S:20).
Mareitje Wenne bp 23 Feb 1757 sp Pieter Wenne, Anna Maria Dewit (K&S:22).

1 JOHN DeWIT bp 07 Apr 1760 Katsbaan sp (uncle & wf) Ezechiel Dewit & Maria Keller (K&S:26; d 19 Feb 1816 bur Mountain View Cem Saugerties) m 06 Jul 1782 Mary Breesteed/Braisted/Busteed d/o Peter Breesteed & Sara Mynderse, b 09 May 1766 d 18 Oct 1853 bur Germantown Cem NY (P-DR:258). Simeon P DeWitt in a letter to A V DeWitt written in 1886 says of John I "I can well remember his features. He had the most commanding physiognomy of any DeWitt I've seen -- when once seen, never to be forgotten." He adds that John I was an intellectual man; that he owned a sloop which he used commercially on the Hudson River; that he prospered & at last sold his sloop & purchased property, mills and farms at Catskill (P-DR:258). The Peltz-DeWitt Record contains more information & John I Dewit's picture.

2 RACHEL DeWIT b 27 Jun 1761 bp 04 Jul 1761 sp (pa's bro & sis) Lucas Dewit, Rachel Dewit (K&S:28) & (d 11 Mar 1840 ae 78-08-11) m 17 Feb 1782 Johannes Van Leuven/Leeuwen (K&S:247) s/o Peter Van Leuwen & Jannetje Bekker, b 07 Mar 1753 (LCMC:55) bp 15 Apr 1753 sp Petrus Hofman, wf Catharina van Aalstein (DRCK:316) d 15 Jan 1805 ae 51-10-08 both bur Van Leuven Ground, Spalding Lane 1/2 mile south of Saugerties (OGUC:278/9). John Van Leuven was a soldier in the Revo War.

3 ABRAHAM/ABRAM DeWIT b 20 Jan 1763 bp 07 Feb 1763 sp Petrus Oosterhout, Maritje Brink (K&S:30) or b 01 Feb 1763 (P-DR:256/7) & (tbstn says d 09 Dec 1845 ae 82-09-23 [OGUC:3]) m1 01 Jul 1786 Catharine Dedrick (CBRUC:574) d/o Matthew Dederick & Maria Emmerick, b 27 Jun 1764 West Camp Saugerties bp 29 Jul 1764 Germantown d 18 Mar 1845 ae 70-09-21 both bur DeWitt Ground (his pa's place) later called the Lowther farm Cem at Mt Marion 1/2 mile west of the railway station (GIUC:3, HGC:426) m2 09 Nov 1837 Ann Pells, both of Saugerties wits: John Pells, Henry Ostrander (K&S:282) b 1788 d 19 Nov 1839 (OGUC:249). Will, 1855 census in Gen 6.

4 JOSEPH DeWIT b 14 Nov 1765 bp 28 Jan 1766 sp Petrus Post, Saertje Cole, d 1768. In the Pletz-DeWitt Record a ch is said to have been bp this date called Joshua (K&S:35) **dy,**

5 MARIA DeWITT bp 19 Apr 1768 sp (aunt Annetje Dewit's hus & her sis) Johannes Diederick, Jannetien Dewitt, (K&S:39) (d 1859) at Catskill, Greene Co m 20 Jun 1802 Levi Van Keuren (NYGBR 92:98) s/o Abraham Van Keuren & Garritse/Gerritje Nieukerk/Nieuwkerk, b 06 Dec 1767 bp 30 Dec 1767 sp Levi Pawling, wf Helena Burhans (CDDG:113; DRCK:358) d 1822 both bur Mt Marion Com Cem (OGUC:256). Maria Dewitt w/o Levi Van Keuren adm cert 07 Dec 1838 fr Flatbush (to Plattekill CH) d 1858 (PRDC:70). In looking at Maria's bp one wonders what happened to Aunt Annetje DeWitt b 1779 w/o Johannes Diederick.

6 ANDREW DeWIT bp 01 Feb 1775 sp Johannes Myer jr, wf Sallytjen Schneider (K&S:54) or (b 10 Jan 1775 (P-DR:257) or (tbstn b 20 Nov 1774 d 08 Sep 1793 bur DeWitt Grd, Lowther Farm [OGUC:263]) **dy.**

1790 NY census p171 Kingston, Ulster, John L DeWitt 3-1-3 & 4 slaves
1790 NY census p171 Kingston, Ulster, John I DeWitt 1-2-1 & 2 slaves

Peltz, W.L.L. Peltz-DeWitt Record: Some of their Companies Albany. 1948. American Historical Company, Inc. New York 420 pp. and two supplements, is a beautifully done family story, with photos, of John Lucas DeWitt descendants. Supplementary reading for all this line, copy in the New Platz Library. Author has a copy and 2 supplements.

DeWitt

1.1.9.4.3 EVERT deWIT {m} 1.1.6.1.2.5 Geertruy/Gerthroy/Gertrude/Gertruat Persen [for continuity 1.1.4.3 used]

1. LUCAS EVERT DeWITT b 02 Oct 1756 (NYGBR 22:5/6) at Loonenburgh Zion Luth CH by Domini Epiph, m Sep 1780 Elizabeth Van Loon b 04 Mar 1756 (NYGBR 73:118) d/o Jacob & Catherine Van Loon. 1790 Census p27 Frehold T Albany Co (now Durham T Greene Co) Lucas DeWitt jr 1-3-2- so 1st 3 boys 1 girl b by 1790. Luke DeWitt located on Con 2 Lot 15 Kingston T Frontenac Co On. Newspaper extractions, Kingston ON Gen So: Luke DeWitt attempting to change the boundary line between his & Amos Ansley's land Con 2 Lot 15 Kingston T, Kgtn Gaz 13 Aug 1813. Another item: Old Mr DeWitt of Con 6 of Ernestown d June 1852. Luke would have been 96, son John ae 66. John DeWitt res on Con 7 Lot 36 Ernestown Twp L&A Co ON.

2. ABRAHAM DeWITT bp 26 Dec 1757 sp (maternal grprts) Abraham Persen, wf Catrina Schoonmaker (K&S:23) **dy**

3. JAN/JOHN HENRY DeWITT b 15 Jan 1759 bp 28 Jan 1759 Linlithgo, Columbia Co NY sp (grprts) Abraham Persen, wf Catharina Schoonmaker (BRLC:27) & (Inventory of his estate 27 Nov 1801 Blissville Par Sunbury Co NB Can). He was in the 3rd NJ Volunteers, Land Grant at Oromocto, moved to Prince William, York Co NB (LONB:276) m 1801 Phoebe DuRose/DuRoss d/o Charles Durose who had enlisted in Capt Christopher Yates CO, raised in Albany Co, 2nd New York Regt to fight in the Seven Years War (French & Indian War) 1756-63 Officer who enlisted him 22 Apr 1761 was Lieut Ten Eyke on 20 Apr, Muster Roll 20 May 1761, ae 26, b Eng, labourer (sic) stature 5'6", complexion dark, eyes blue, hair brown (NYHSC:372). Afterwards Charles located in a Soldier's Settlement called the "Old Georgia District" on the east side of Lake Champlain (NYHSC:372). Charles was a Sgt in the King's American Regt in the Revo, Land Grant Oromocto South Branch, Sunbury Co NB. His second petition in 1810 said " the present Grant (1790) was burned over & was incapable of supporting his family which included children and grandchildren." His grdson Luke DeWitt was living on the second Grant in 1832; he sold it to Guy Alexander in 1841. Family tradition that Phoebe's son John Henry was "b in Georgia" (disproved by considerable research) is oral history & is evidence of John's ma's "Old Georgia District NY" place of birth.

John Henry (King) DeWitt

4. HENRICUS/HENRY DeWITT b 13 Mar 1761 (HGC:436) bp 27 Dec 1760 sp (ma's bro & sis) Jan Persen, Debra/Debora Persen (K&S:28) & (d 13 Apr 1830 Catskill NY). Henry at ae 35 m 19 Nov 1796 as the 3rd hus/o Catharina Dumon d/o David Dumon & Margaret Van Orden, bp 10 Mar 1767 sp Jacobus Dumon, wf Catharine Schuyler (K&S:37). Catharina m1 John Baptist Dumond, a dau Elizabeth Dumont b 1789. She m2 John Langendyk 1.1.9.3.1.2 Catharina m2 24 Jan 1795 Teunis Vandenberg of Bethlehem. Henry DeWit went to New Brunswick Can with his father in 1783, returned & lived out his life in the Catskills (HGC:436,443/4). The people who compiled family history in 1932 listed 5 chn for Henry, adding Jacob & Samuel, but no other record of them been found.

5. ABRAHAM DeWITT bp 26 Jan 1763 sp Nicolaes Tromphoude, Maria Tromphouder (CDDGC:13). In the 1851 Census Lincoln Parish, Sunbury Co NB he is ae 88 living with his dau Phoebe DeWitt & son-in-law Isaac DeWitt. 1851 Census Lincoln Par Sunbury Co NB lists him as Isreal but family insist his name was Isaac. One Abraham in Ulster Co NY m Catharina Kriesler in NY their dau Gertrout b 25 May 1789 bp 30 May 1789 NYGBR 85:83. Evert's Abraham m Caroline Tucker d/o Solomon Tucker (fr desc's family rec in NB). Abraham petitioned for land in Sunbury Co NB 1793 1804/9/10 (U of NB Archives). He was appointed to do 6 days roadwork.

6. CATHERINE/CATHARINA/KATE DeWITT bp 26 Jun 1765 sp Jacobus Persen, Catharina Persen (K&S:34) m 21 Mar 1785 Samuel Boone s/o William Boone & Ruth Hill, b RI 09 Mar 1764 d 04 Nov 1848 res near Fredericton Jct NB (fr ACB).

7. JACOB DeWITT b 1766 bp 22 Oct 1768 sp Samuel Provost, Elsje Staats, at DRC Coxsackie, Greene Co NY (NYGBR 88:211) & (d 08 Jun 1826 Tapleytown Saltfleet T Wentworth Co ON. He m1 Salome Tucker d/o Solomon Tucker & had 3 chn. He m2 Mrs Abigail (Cram) Kinney b 1777 Maugerville NB d 1861 ae 84 bur beside Jacob, wd/o Isreal Kinney & d/o Loyalist Robert Cram a Boston Shipbuilder recorded in Saint John NB harbour with a wf, 1 son, 7 daus in 1775. Robert joined Davidson's shipyard at Maugerville NB. Abigail repeated family stories she was told about their adventures during the Boston Tea Party. She m3 06 Jul 1828 David Pearson (d 14 Jan 1844 ae 77-03-00 Brant Co ON; Cem Rec at Brantford Museum ON) in a double wedding with her son John. Evert Dewitt's sons Lucas and Abraham operated two family farms in the Great Imbought District of Greene Co NY while John and Jacob worked on Their father's boat on the Hudson River. After the British attacked Kingston NY Evert joined the Loyalist cause on Staton Island as an Armed Boatman, John enlisted in the New Jersey Volunteers, and Jacob joined Col. Edmund Fanning's Kings American Regt (LSCRW Vol 3:92/3/4}. The 1779 list shows Jacob as a Grenadier [flag bearer]. He served in North Carolina and Georgia. He was on leave in New York State and then was recruiting there. Jacob went with his regiment to Saint John in what became New Brunswick, settled on the Oromocto River, Sunbury

Parish. In 1824 Jacob, Abigail and their children moved to Upper Canada, (Ontario) Saltfleet Township, Wentworth County. He had cancer of the face and knew he hadn't much longer to live. His brother Peter had settled in Chippewa ON in 1811. Both Jacob & bro Peter had grdaus who were six feet tall; their pictures included. Jacob felt the good Farm land in Ontario would be a better opportunity for his & Abigail's children. He settled in Tapleytown and after having been badly flooded once in New Brunswick, he looked at the escarpment and chose the top area. He & Abigail are buried in Tapleytown United Church Cemetery. My (Vona's) grandfather Jonathan, said to have had 1 lung died from pneumonia at age 25 is buried beside him [fr VED S]. The DeWitts had been in America about 150 years.

ABIGAIL (CRAM) KINNEY DeWITT PEARSON   **JACOB DeWITT GRVE STONE**

8   PETER deWITH bp 24 May 1770 Zion Luth CH Loonenburgh (Athens NY) sp (uncle & wf) Janse deWith, Anna Maria Dewit [NYGBR 84:96; K&S:258]) returned from NB Can to Greene Co NY. At ae 34 Peter m 04 Dec 1804 Annetje/Hannah/Annie Snyder wd/o Paul Sacks/Sax (K&S:258). Annetje lived to ae 102, bur Drummondville Cem, Niagara Falls ON. A list for 24 Jan 1799 gives Paul Sax as dead, removed from the Catskill DRC Membership (CDDGC:122).

New Brunswick, Canada Archive Film #1328 Sunbury Co Probate Rec 1786-1896 Wills 1786-1829. P88 # 11 Evert Dewitt In the Name of God Amen I Evert Dewitt of the County of Sunbury and Township of Burton being weak in body but of sound memory (Blefsed be God) do this eighteenth Day of October in the year of our Lord one thousand Eight hundred one make and publish this my last Will and Testament in manner following (that is to say) First my desire is that all my whole Estate both real and personal be left in the hands of my dear wife for her support until her Decease. Then my desire is the remainder of my property that is left (if there be any) be Equally Divided in Seven shares between my seven Children viz. Luke, John, Henry, Jacob, Abraham, Peter and Catherine in such manner as to make an Equal Division among the whole. I make and ordain Son Jacob Dewitt and Samuel Boone my fole Executors of this my Will and Testament in Trust for the Intent and purpose in this my Will contained in Witnsfs whereof I the said Evert Dewitt have to this my last Will and Testament set my hand and Seal the day and year above Written Signed Sealed and Delivered

Lawrence Mersereau   his
Joshua Thomas   Evert + Dewitt
Martha Thomas   mark

Leucas deWit

LIST OF THE PROPERTY OF THE LATE EVERT DEWITT, DECEASED
taken this 26th day of November 1801

	£.	s.	p.
Lot N 1 homestead	50	0	0
Lot N 3 Birch Point	20	0	0
Lot N 5 called fick Lot	40	0	0
A note of hand the amount	9	4	7
1 Do	5	11	6
1 White faced Cow 12 yrs. old	5	0	0
1 Black Do	4	10	0
1 Red Do	4	0	0
1 Yearling Bull	1	5	0
1 Yoke Oxen	19	0	0
1 Brown Mare 6 year old	14	0	0
1 Bay yearling Colt	8	10	0
11 Sheep at 10/	5	10	0
2 Hogs	0	15	0
1 Hide	0	8	0
1 Spring Colt	6	0	0
1 Large Saw	1	5	0
1 Small Do	0	6	0
2 Muskets	0	15	0
1 Iron Kettle	0	5	0
3 Steel Traps 10/	1	10	0
1 Salmon Net	0	5	0
1 pair Snow Shoes	0	12	6
1 Chain 2 Axes	0	18	0
2 Casks	0	8	0
2 fork Shovel	0	10	0
1 Large Wheel	0	7	6
Cask Due	1	15	0
1 Plough Irons & Clevis	2	0	0
Ox Staple & ring	0	5	0
Post Ax & frow	0	8	0
1 Small Ax	0	2	6
50 bushels Oats at 2 S. per bushel	5	0	0
4 bushels Wheat at 6	1	4	0
9 Do Rye at 4	1	16	0
£	215	6	7

CODE: £ Pound, s Shilling, p Pence, Do Ditto.

The undermentioned articles belonging to the Estate of the late Evert Dewitt were added after the original Inventory was given to me.

WM. HUBBARD, Surrogate & Registrar

1 hide leather u 1/2 1/c .	0	12	9
1 Do u.	0	12	9
1 Green Hide 11 & 1/4 at /c	5	7	0
10 1 Colt	3	0	0
10 1 Calf	1	5	0
10 1 Red and Red.g		0	0
1 --------	3	0	0
£	13	16	11

Leucas deWit

Inventory of Evert's property 26 Nov 1801 value £215 6s 7p filed 12 Mar 1802. Appraisers Lawrence Mersereau, Clapman Smith, Joshua Thomas; Exs: Samuel Boone, Abraham DeWitt. Hubbard Papers, New Brunswick Museum, Saint John (fr-KLAD).

Filed this 12th day of March, 1802

INVENTORY OF	Lawrence Mersereau	}
EVERT DeWITT	Chapman Smith	} Appraisers
ESTATE	Joshua Thomas	}

EXECUTORS } SAMUEL BOONE
           } ABRAHAM DeWITT

You swear that the within Inventory by you exhibites and figures contains a just & true appraisment of all and singular the goods, chattels & effects which Evert Dewitt, late of Burton, in Sunbury County, died judged of in said County or for as they were sworn unto you by Jacob Dewitt & Samuel Boone, Executors of said Estate according to the best of your ability & judgment so help you God.

Sworn before me this 23rd day of July 1803   LAWRENCE MERSEREAU
                                                  WM. HUBBARD by Register,

You swear that this Inventory contains all the goods, chattels and effects which Evert Dewitt, died, seized & possessed of which have come to your knowledge and of mind & shall hereafter appear you will remember account thereof.

SWORN before me this 12th day of March 1804   SAMUEL BOONE
                                                  WM. HUBBARD
                     by Register.   JACOB DeWITT

The 3rd Annual Report of the State Historian, New York, p827.
    In the 1767 militia list under Captain Jacob Halenbeck's Company includes Evert Dewitt and Jan Persen.
The Early History of Saugerties . . for early Saxton & Asbury "The Dutch settlers had a native scent for fertile lands and soon learned what was to be had at the foot of the mountains. Somewhere in the vicinity of the iron bridge of 1900, on the road from Saugerties to Woodstock. . the farm of Capt Jeremiah Snyder. . just north is Lawerence Winne . . north of Winne's a half mile is the house of Evert DeWitt. . a little farther north is Aaron Winne. Proceeding north over what will be in the coming years the Saxton flats we pass in succession the houses of Luke DeWitt, Johannes Rowe, William Burhans, Michael Plank and John Burhans before reaching the Albany county line, soon to become Greene County. John Burhans, William Burhans, Johannes Rowe, Johannes Plank jr and Frederick Rowe jr will become ardent Loyalists" (EHS:97).
    Family tradition says Evert had a sloop on the Hudson River for many years (as did his Roosa ancestors) & probably transported goods for the British. According to Phoebe Jane (DeWitt) Smiths' stories told by her grandmother Abigail, Evert was gun running for the British and made a good deal of money. Remember Abigail's husband Jacob worked with his father. After the executions in Kingston he realized their danger and sailed down the Hudson to British lines and served during the war as an "Armed Boatman" from Staten Island. Lucas and Abraham continued to live in the Great Imbought District of Greene Co NY. Two of Evert's Coxsackie farms were confiscated in 1783. (Note the extended area of Coxsackie in that era.). His sons, John in the New Jersey Volunteers, Jacob in the King's American Regiment, probably enlisted on Staten Island, an early army staging area.
    At the end of the first American Civil War when the British Forces withdrew from New York, Evert's family were among the refugees of 1783 who were transported by the British Navy to Nova Scotia. The next year the area on the Oromocto River where they located, became part of newly formed New Brunswick. Fourteen years later Evert & wife must have visited their old home area, quite a holiday for those times. Son Hendrick, who returned to New York State, and his wife had a daughter baptized in the Katsbaan & Saugerties Reformed Church named Geertrui born 26 Oct 1797 bp 26 Nov 1797 sponsors EVERT DeWIT and GEERTRUI DeWIT indicating they were present at the baptism (K&S:119). At the Zion Lutheran CH, Loonenburg (now Athens) NY Evert DeWitt and wife Gertroud were sponsors at a baptism 12 Mar 1775; Evert deWitt absent and wife Gertroud again sponsors at a baptism 12 Aug 1778; then Evert deWitt absent & wife Gertruyd sponsors 09 May 1779. For their son Lucas and wife Elizabeth's daughter Gertroud's baptism 14 Feb 1782 sponsor Evert deWitt and wife Gertroud were present (NYGBR 84:150,158/9 85:74)

Evert Dewitt, Tory, his family warned to remove from state; Gertruyd, wife of Evert warned to remove from the state (MCDDC:523,674,676,689, 690,699,724) Luke/Lukas Dewitt/DeWit of Great Imbocht, farmer, charged with disaffection, warrant issued for his arrest, arrested & committed, examined & recommitted, released on bail. Deserters from the Continental Army . . . Luke DeWitt of this County [Albany] . . . and they being severally brought before us and be resolved they be committed. Ordered that a Mittimus be made out against them. (MCCDD:680) Luke/Lukas Dewitt Jr of Coxsackie, farmer, arrested and committed, released on bail (MCDD:680, 724/5). Abraham Dewitt/Dewit/DeWit charged with the intention to join the enemy, to be apprehended, sent under guard to Catskill, released on bail (MCDD:685,705,720/1). Bail was £100.

NB Archive film #1328 Sunbury Parish Wills 1786-1829; Probate Records 1786-1896. There is a story that Evert and his son John drowned, falling through the ice of the Oromocto River. Evert's Will written 01 Nov 1802 was executed 05 Nov 1802. It names his son John in the bequests. It would be unusual for a will to have been written and both drown within four days, but John did die about that time. Inventory of Evert's property 26 Nov 1801 value £215 6s 7p filed 12 Mar 1802. Appraisers Lawrence Mersereau, Clapman Smith, Joshua Thomas; Executors: Samuel Boone, Abraham DeWitt. Hubbard Papers NB Museum Saint John (KLAD).

deWitt
1.1.9.4.5 LEUCAS deWITT/DeWITT {m} Debra Persen
1. JACOBUS DeWITT (Jacobus translates as James) bp 29 Mar 1764 sp Jan Ostrander, Catharine Dewitt (K&S:31) res Durham, Greene Co NY (d 14 Oct 1831 Norfolk Co ON) m Catherine Edwards, moved to Can in 1818.
2. CATHRINA DeWITT b 22 Jan 1766 bp 28 Jan 1766 sp Jacob Peersen, Cathrina Peersen (K&S:35) & (d ? Jun 1820) m Jeremiah Young (HGC:436).
3. JOHN DeWITT "s/o Lucas DeWitt Jr" bp 03 Aug 1768 sp John Pearsen, Jannetjen DeWitt (K&S:40) res Durham. ("Jr" indicates grpa Lucas b 1703 was alive since Lucas s/o Evert would have been 12 yrs old.) at Greenville Presby CH m 18 Apr 1802 Hannah Egbertsen/Abbison/Egburts (both of Durham) bp 24 Oct 1784 d/o Cornelius Egbertsen & Rebecca. It's presumed John d before 1855 state census as by then Hannah, ae 70, res with son Isreal.
4. PETER DeWITT b 1770 lived Durham m 25 Jan 1795 Jannetje/Jane Person d/o Jacobus Persen & Eva Queen, bp 01 Jun 1777 Germantown NY (HGC:436).
5. DEBORAH DEWITT b 1772 m1 William West; m2 20 Sep 1813 Chester Spencer (RDCOH:47).
6. ABRAHAM DeWITT bp 25 Apr 1777 sp Abraham Perce, Leah Falk (K&S:58) **dy.**
7. ABRAHAM DeWITT bp 27 Oct 10 1780 RDC Germantown, Columbia Co NY (IGI) **dy.**
8. ABRAHAM DeWITT bp 05 Sept 1783 RDC Germantown Columbia Co (IGI but not in HGC) Above info & dates fr Oram DeWitt's Bible Records.

1790 NY census p27 Luke Dewitt Freehold, Albany 3-1-3
1790 NY census p27 Luke DeWitt Jr Albany, Freehold 1-3-2 Freehold became Durham, Greene Co NY; Evert DeWitt's bro & Evert's son. Jr in that time period, the younger of two men with the same name, father and son were "elder & younger".

Lucas DeWitt of Dewittburgh, Freehold Town Albany County Will Probate 29 Sep 1820. Heirs: wife Deborah; sons Jacobus (James when translated) John, Peter; daus Caty w/o Jeremiah Young & Deborah w/o William West. Executors: sons Jacobus, John, Peter. Witnesses: John Plank Jr, Jeremiah Plank, and James Satterall.

Extract from the <u>Kingston Daily Freeman</u> 12 Jul 1901 (NY). "The Oak Hill, Greene County Record contains the following which is of local interest because of the connection between the person referred to and one of the oldest families in Ulster County. In connection with the death of Isreal DeWitt, recently, it may be of interest to many younger residents to know that the first actual settlement in this Town was made at Oak Hill by Lucas DeWitt and others about 1770 or 1772. Lucas DeWitt Jr., was the son of Lucas DeWitt who lived in the Town of Hurley, Ulster County, previous to forming the settlement known as Oak Hill. Lucas DeWitt Jr took possession of the farm, which had for so many years been conducted by his grandson. His first house was a log building, which occupied a plot of ground now used as a garden. In those early days they were obliged to go to Catskill and Leeds to have their grain ground, but in time Lucas DeWitt built a mill dam near the upper bridge and attached a hand mill to the water power, which became the first grist mill in town. The settlement at that time was known as Dewittsburgh or Dewittville. In 1776, the Indians became troublesome and the settlement was abandoned; the people returned to Ulster County. But in 1782 they again returned and Lucas DeWitt recovered his grist mill which he had stored in a hollow log several years before, and it did service again until it was replaced by a more modern one built on the banks of the Catskill. The log house was removed about this time and replaced by the one so long occupied by Isreal De Witt" (DeWitt. Godwin: 454 pp, Buffalo NY Public Library).

OSTERHOUT
1.1.9.4.7 JANNETJEN DeWITT m Jacobus/Cobus Osterhout
1. HENDRICUS OSTERHOUT bp 24 Oct 1770 sp Hendicus Mejer, Annetjen Osterhout (K&S:44) {m} 05 May 1793 <u>1.1.9.1.5.8</u> Geertje/Geertien/Charity Winne/Winna/Wenne (DRCK:665) d/o Annatjen Langendyck & Arent Winne, bp 26 Aug 1771 sp Frederich Rauh, wf Catharina Van Ette[n], (K&S:46; OFG:18).
2. CATHARINE/CATHERINA OSTERHOUT bp 15 May 1773 sp (grprts) Luycas Dewit, wf Catharina Ros(a) in (K&S: 49) & (d ? Jun 1820) m Cornelis Hoff <u>possibly</u> s/o Michael Hooft & Maria Frans, bp 09 Feb 1786 sp Cornelis Frans; this makes a 13 yr ae difference & by 1816 Catharina would be ae 41.

Leucas deWit

3   MARIA OSTERHOUT bp 20 Feb 1776 sp Cornelius Dubois wf Marytje Ostrout (sic) (K&S:56) * m 18 Mar 1794 Silvanis Kess of Blaauw Berg (Blue Mountain [K&S:251; OFG:15]). Maria's bro named a son "Silvans". Note a Maria Osterhout m Herman Beer. <u>Osterhout Family genealogy</u> says Maria m Benjamin Coddington. Benjamin bp 28 Jun 1758 s/o Christopher Coddington & Maria Oosterhoudt (RRCAU:7) had banns 02 Nov 1792 with Maria Rosekrans (RRCAU:193) and m 24 Jan 1793 Maria Osterhoudt in Rochester T Ulster Co. This suggests he m a wd named Maria Osterhout Rosekrans or a Maria Rosekrans Osterhout. Our Maria is 18 years younger & less than 18 yrs old when this m took place. Our Osterhouts were in Saugerties & then Oak Hill, Durham, Greene Co NY.

4   LUCAS OSTERHOUD/OUSTERHOUT b 06 May 1778 bp Zion Luth CH Loonenburg on Ascension Sunday at Kisked sp (uncle & wf) Lucas & Debora deWitt (NYGBR 84:157) m 21 Aug 1800 Jacomeyntie/Jacomntje Young both of Blue Mountain (K&S:255).

5   JACOBUS/COBUS OUSTERHOUD/OSTERHOUT bp 25 Feb 1781 sp (ma's cousin & hus) Richard Borhans, Maria Langendyk (K&S:66) m Eunice/Teunis Sharp/Ferp (OFG:18). You will have noted usage in that era - "f" for "s" and "fs" for "ss".

6   MARTINUS OSTERHOUT bp 13 Aug 1786 sp Martinus Homel/Hommel, Margaret Wels (K&S:83). 1790 NY census p183 Rochester, Ulster Co Jacobus Osterhout 3-0-1

LOUW

1.1.9.4.8 RACHEL DeWITT m Abraham Louw/Lau/Low 1

1   ABRAHAM DeWITT LOUW/LOW bp 08 Sep 1764 sp (likely aunt Annetje DeWit's hus) John Diederich, Jannetje Lau (K&S:33) presumed **dy**.

2   ABRAHAM DeWITT (LOUW) bp ? Jun 1765 sp John Diederick, Jannetje Law (K&S:34) m banns 26 Feb 1784 Elisabet/Elizabeth Schaert/Scort/Short/Sjart (DRCK:648).

3   PETRUS LOUW bp 13 Jan 1768 sp Petrus Louw, wf Lena Kierstede (K&S:38) **dy.**

4   MARYTJE LOUW bp 22 May 1770 sp Tjerk Louw, wf Annatje Wolfin (K&S:42) m 17 Feb 1794 Petrus Elmondus Van Bunschooten both Plattekill (K&S:251).

5   PETRUS LOUW bp 03 Feb 1773 sp Petrus Louw, Helena Kiersteden (K&S:49) (d 21 Mar 1855 ae 82-11-09 bur Plattekill Cem) m 18 Aug 1794 Elisabet/ Elizabeth Conjes/Conyes/Coenius/Cunyes both Kingston (DRCK:667).

6   ELISABETH LOUW/LOW bp ? Jan 1776 sp Jacobus Louw, Elizabeth Thomas (DRCK:378) m 13 Jun 1793 Johannes Bakker Jr/Baker/Becker both j/o Kingston (DRCK:665).

7   CATHARINA LOUW bp 29 Apr 1778 sp Tobyas Mejer & Catharina Louw (K&S:60) m Willem Widdeker/Whitaker. 8

8   JAN/JOHN A LOUW bp 17 Sep 1780 sp (uncle & wf) Jan DeWit, Anna Marytje DeWit (K&S:64) & (d 16 Apr 1828 Poughkeepsie) m 11 Mar 1804 Helena/Lena Felton both res j/o Kingston (DRCK:676) d/o Philip Felton/Velton & Margritta Cool, bp 18 Feb 1785 sp Matheis Felton, Lena Felton (DRCK:407) d ? Mar 1825 Jerome Twp Union Co OH. Probate of Will of Philip Felton 04 Aug 1825 three years after his death, by son Philip Felton living in the State of OH (UCPR 1:176/77 John A Low had gone east for Philip Felton's Will & died of Consumption there.

9   RACHEL LOUW /LOW b 06 Apr 1783 sp (aunt & hus) Jan Van Leuven & Rachel DeWit (K&S:72) & (d 26 Jul 1843 ae 59-04-29 [OGUC:247]) m 06 Mar 1803 Zacharias Conyes of Platteskill (K&S:258) b 15 Oct 1777 d 07 Jul 1863 both bur Finger Grd near Residence of Clinton Finger of Mt Marion NY. Zacharias Conyes d Jun 1863 & wf Rachel Louw both admission to Plattekill CH on a certificate from Flatbush 07 Dec 1838 (PDRC:67,74).

10   WYNTJE LOUW bp 20 Nov 1785 sp Jan Ette, Maria Van Etten (K&S: 81) m 05 Jun 1803 Laurens Felten/Velten both Plattekill (K&S:258) s/o Philip Felten & Margrit Cool, bp 11 Aug 1782 sp Benjamin Felten, wf Annatje Kieffer (DRCK:399; UCPR 1:176/7).

11   JANNETJE LOUW bp 19 Apr 1788 sp Ephriam Mejer, Jannetje Louw (K&S:87) Jannetje of Plattekill (Mt Marion) m 18 Jan 1807 Tjerck/Shark Schoonmaker of Blue Mountain (K&S:260) s/o Edward Schoonmaker & Elisabeth Weathaker/Whitaker bp 18 May 1783 sp Shark Schoonmaker & Jannetje Breesteede (K&S:73) in 1811 resided on Main St in Saugerties but moved to Metz, Cayuga Co NY.

12   LEVI LOUW bp 28 Aug 1790 sp David Mejer, Mareitje Louw (K&S:93) m Margaret Kool/Cole.

1790 NY census p183 Rochester, Ulster Co, Abraham Low 3-0-1
1790 NY census p172 Kingstown, Ulster Co, Abraham Low 2-1-3 others 2
1790 NY census p39 Saratoga, Albany Co, Abraham Low 3-1-6; only this last one fits the children of Rachel DeWitt & Abraham Louw would have by 1790; research needed.
1790 NY census p183 Rochester, Ulster Co, Abraham Low

Leucas deWit

GENERATION 6

If a couple both trace back to DeWitt ancestry more than once m is {m} indicating this fact. Numbering used is the first parent listed chronologically. Both numbers are given, but the one to be used in succeeding generations is underlined.

DEDRICK
1.1.9.4.1.2 LUCAS DEIDERICK/DEDRICK m Lucretia Persen

* ?? Samuel Dedrick b 24 May 1790 (d 03 Sep bur Bayview cem Port Rowan On ae 67-03-10) m Sarah (Norfolk Museum). Capt John Backhouse list 1st Batt (LPS:253) Samuel appears as a Sgt 25 Apr to 24 May 1812).

1 JOHN DEDRICK b 1789 (d 07 Aug 1833 [his will]) m Harriet Fick b 1798 d 02 Jun 1875 (Br Can Newspaper 09 Jun 1875) res Walsingham T Norfolk Co ON (PSLPS:35; Dedrick file #739 Eva Brook Donley Museum, Simcoe ON).

2 CORNELIUS DEDRICK b 1789 (d Aug 1860) m Nancy Spurgin/Spurgeon b 1796 d 21 May 1887 (PSLPS:35). He was a Deacon at Port Rowan Baptist CH for 52 yrs res Walsingham T. Both bur Port Royal Cem fr Bk #5 Walsingham Cem Rec at Simcoe Museum. Nancy's pa was Col William Spurgin J.P., Esquire, wf Ann, fr NC where he lost a large estate. He joined Lord Cornwallis in the fighting. His application for losses is a long list. In Canada he was appointed J.P. for London Dist, Com for Highways and Chairman of the District Court (LPS:202/3). He d 13 Aug 1806. Nancy, named in his will, as w/o Cornelius Dedrick & as d/o a Loyalist received her land grant 14 Jan 1840 in Charlotteville T Norfolk Co.

3 CATHARINE DEDRICK m1 as his 2nd wf Austin Stearns; no chn. He had a son John. "For many years the old Stearn's Hotel in Port Rowan was one of the best known public-houses in the country and the name will always remain a familiar one in the history of the old and pleasantly situated village" (PSLPS:36). Catharine m2 Abraham Countryman, a carding mill operator in Walsingham, b 1799 d 07 Mar 1877. There were 4 more various Abraham Countryman marriages (PSLPS:36,462,536). Catherine's OR (Order-in-Council as a daughter of a Loyalist, for land grant) was in Walsingham T 14 Apr 1831 (LPS:249)

4 HANNAH DEDRICK at Walsingham m 14 Mar 1814 John Backhouse b 1793 (1851 census) d 04 Sep 1783 ae 83, 2nd s/o John Backhouse & Margaret Longbottom. They were m by JP Thomas Bowlby Wits: Samuel Cooper, Abraham Backhouse (ON Reg: 43 London Dist; PSLPS:536/7). They settled on the old homestead. Hannah's OC [Land grant - Order In Council] was 21 Nov 1815 Walsingham T.

5 JAMES DEDRICK m Elizabeth Edwards (fr FVD, FDSS).

6 LUCAS DEDRICK b 1804 (d 24 Dec 1883 ae 79-06-00 [PSLPS:36]) m Catherine d/o Christian Rohrer & Anna Baumwart, b 1807 d 08 Feb 1875 ae 67-04-00 (PSLPS:36; in Christian Messenger CBBMD 11:9; dates are tbstn Rec fr Bayview [Port Rowan] Cem Walsingham T Norfolk Co ON in Eva Brook Donnely Museum Simcoe ON).

Before settling in Norfolk Co ON Lucas Dedrick was in the Niagara area where a Jacob Dedrick located. Lucas established his homestead in 1793 on the elevation fronting the Big Creek Marsh that extended out into Lake Erie, a short distance east of the present Port Rowan. Lucas' choice of this particular land may have been influenced by a previous visit to the area when, as a member of Butler's Rangers, he took refuge at the mouth of Big Creek during a bad storm while enroute from Buffalo to Detroit. In addition to the erection of his log cabin, Lucas proceeded to clear an area of land for future agricultural crop that would supplement his diet of wild game that included the ducks, turkey and deer numerous in the region. That fall he sowed the acre of ground that was still thickly studded with stumps with the wheat seed he had brought with him.

The following June a party of UE Loyalists settlers arrived at the mouth of Big Creek. Being low on provisions, they watched with much interest and anxiety as the field of wheat matured to it's ripening stage. Although fish and game were readily available, they had no flour with which to make bread and no store from which to purchase any. When harvest arrived, the visitors assisted with the threshing, which yielded sixty bushels of wheat. Thirty bushels were transported to the nearest gristmill located on the Niagara River. John McCall owned the boat that took the grain away to the mill and eventually returned with the flour, which Lucas Dedrick distributed equally among them without reckoning of payment. Mrs J C Backus, in researching the History of Port Rowan said this first wheatfield was planted where the Bayview cemetery now stands.

The Indians in the area were peaceable and friendly and later when Lucas Dedrick constructed a bridge over the stream, which now bears his name, Dedrick Creek, they assembled on the crude structure and held high carnival.

Upon completion of the survey of Walsingham Township in 1797 Lucas received his patent for the 200 acres he had settled upon four years earlier. When he established his homestead he had no idea that his cabin and pioneer wheat field location would become the future site of Bay View Cemetery where many of his descendants would be interred. Although the exact spot of his burial is unknown, the place where his home was erected has been suggested by the discovery of broken bits of crockery that surfaced during improvements to the cemetery.

During the summer of 1794 John Parsens/Persen, father-in-law of Lucas Dedrick, settled on land Northeast of Murphy's Creek adjoining Lucas Dedrick's property. As a Loyalist supporter, John petitioned the Government for permission to be granted the land he had settled upon and improved during the previous year. He was successful in gaining title to 400 acres. Lucas' ma, Annetje DeWitt, had an uncle John Persen but there has been no success tracing either family just prior to the Revo (fr FVD, FDSKS & GDS; LFGR:180/8).

Leucas deWit

In July 1797 Lucas petitioned the Land Board seeking an additional grant for his wife. As a d/o Loyalist John Peresen Lucretia was eligible for a Grant of mentions his wife Lucretia, notes eldest son John, Cornelius, daus Hannah & Catharine & younger sons James & Lucas. Ex: wife, son John & John Persen. There was an Inventory (WLD:8).

Film Walsingham T Papers (000190).

Order in Council 25 May 1808 Lucas Dedrick for Marsh in Walsingham. Enter in OC Book no 3 p155 RS WI 07 Apr 1810.

Film Walsingham T Papers (000191).

In Council 25 May 1808. Ordered that Lucas Dedrick of Walsingham do obtain that part of the marsh in the T of Walsingham, which he's opposite to Lot no 15 in the front Concession of that T.

To acting Surveyor Genr John and Cornelius Dedrick were confirmed as heirs to this Marsh lot of 79 1/4 acres.

DEDRICK

1.1.9.4.1.? * CHISTIAN DEDRICK m Elizabeth ?
1. JOHN DEDRICK b 1801.
2. ELIAS DEDRICK b 1803.
3. LUCAS DEDRICK b 1806; *Connection of this family a possibility, not proven*.

DEWIT

1.1.9.4.2.1 JOHN I DeWIT m Mary Breesteed/Braisted
1. PETER BREESTEED DeWITT b 23 Feb 1783 bp 24 Feb 1784 sp Andrew Breesteed, Maria Mynerse (K&S:75) m Hannah Levina (P-DR:258/9). London Dist Mar 1800-1833 fr Norfolk Co ON, Jeremiah Wolfen m 06 Jun 1812 Catherine Wolfen at Walsingham, Wit: Peter Br DeWitt. Peter Breestede DeWitt was in the Norfolk Militia, Flank Coy 1st Regt 1812 under Lt Col J Ryerson. He left the Regt on his return from the capture of Detroit and went to the Home District, his place of residence
2. JOHN DeWIT b 15 Dec 1788 bp 11 Jan 1789 Catskill sp Meindert Meinersen, Maria DeWit (K&S:89) & (d 11 Oct 1831) m1 Jan 1810 Sarah d/o Tjerck & Jane (Breestede) Schoonmaker (ma's sis) b 29 Oct 1788 Saugerties d 11 Nov 1824 New Brunswick NJ; (P-DR:258-9). He m2 20 Sep 1825 Anna Marie Bridgen, his first cousin, d/o Charles Bridgen and Lena Ten Eyck. She was b 10 Oct 1796 d 12 Apr 1843 Albany NY (P-DR:260). Rev John DeWitt was a prominent clergyman who served in many Parishes and capacities. His career and family are mentioned in 15 various pages of the Peltz – DeWitt Record including his portrait. "John DeWitt was said to have had knowledge of nine languages including Hebrew and Arabic. He was a student of botany and had musical talent. He was an eloquent speaker, of fine appearance and cheerful temperament, somewhat over medium height" (P-DR:223).
3. ANDRIES DeWITT bp 08 Dec 1793 sp John Van Leuven, Ragel DeWitt (K&S:103) **dy,**
4. WILLIAM HENRY DeWITT b 27 May 1804 bp 10 Jul 1804 no sp (K&S:145) & (d 25 Mar 1886) m 01 Nov 1826 Catharine b 26 Jul 1805 d/o Jacob Ten Broeck/Tenbroek of Clermont, Columbia Co NY. Jacob's Will 03 Feb 1829 Pro 11 Jun 1829 Ex: William H DeWitt of Catskill (P-DR:259; Barber's Abstract of Wills Columbia Co Vol 3-5 p8). History of Albany p525 says, in 1844 William H DeWitt was Vice President of the Columbia Bank of Hudson NY. In the 1850 Federal Census William's ma Mary ae 84 res with him. In 1858 William was a Germantown JP. In the 1875 State Census William H was 71, a farmer, belonged to the Germantown Ref CH wf Catherine M ae 69, dau Ada ae 31.
5. CHARLES T DeWITT b 13 Jan 1807 bp 01 Mar 1807 no sp (K&S:45; CDDGC:70) & (d 14 May 1880) res Germantown m 15 Oct 1840 Jane C Ashley b 1816 (P-DR:259). In 1847 Charles was a JP at Germantown. In 1855 State & 1860 Federal Census he was a teacher & a scholarly man but eccentric.
6. HORACE DeWITT b 02 Sep 1808 (bur Olive NY) m Eve ?.

VAN LEUVEN

1.1.9.4.2.2 RACHEL DeWIT m John Van Leuven
1. MARYTIE/POLLY VAN LEUVEN b 16 Dec 1783 bp 11 Jan 1784 sp (uncle) Abram DeWit, Maria DeWit (K&S:75) & (d 22 Oct 1832 ae 48-10-06) m 30 Oct 1805 Rev Peter A Overbagh of Bethlehem as his 2nd wf (MRRCC:5) s/o Abraham Overbagh & Rachel Freligh, b 17 Oct 1779 bp 30 Oct 1779 DRC Catskill NY d 20 Feb 1842 ae 62-04-03 bur Van Leuven Grd Barkley Heights, Saugerties NY (OGUC:278). He m1 22 Sep 1801 Sally Overbagh d/o Peter Overbaugh & Sarah Dubois; m3 12 Jun 1838 Helen Tappan d/o Peter Tappan & Elizabeth Crannel.

John Van Leuven of Kingston (no date) to wf Rachel 5000 (sic) & land & furniture. To only daughter, Polly Van Leuven, all lands. On her death without issue same "to all my bros & sis" not named, & bro Zacharias share "to all his chn" not named, & share of sis Margerit "to her chn" not named. Exs: said wf & friend John T DeWitt, Jacob Marius Groen & Henry Johnson. Wits: Benjamin Snyder, Tjark Schoonmaker Jr of Kingston, Yoeman, & William H Diederick. Pro 12 Aug 1805 (AWGNY Liber D:68-80).

DeWITT

1.1.9.4.2.3 ABRAHAM DeWitt m1Catharine Dederick/Dideriks
1. LEVI DeWITT b 28 Jul 1788 bp 09 Aug 1788 sp George William Diederik, Maria Dewitt (K&S:88) & d 30 Mar.
2. ANN ELIZABETH DeWITT b 06 Jun 1790 bp 28 Jun 1790 (d 06 Feb 1868 ae 67-08-00) m Seth K Otis res Flatbush, Ulster Co NY. Her pa's Will 1846 names Ann Eliza w/o Seth K Otis & her several chn but in 1855 she res with her bro John at Windham, no mention of hus or chn.

Leucas deWit

3   MARITJE DeWITT b 26 Dec 1791/2 (HCH: 426) bp 08 Jan 1792 sp Matthie Diedrick, Maryte Falkenberg (K&S:98) & (d 13/14 Aug 1877 ae 85-07-18) m Jonas s/o John & Maria (Falkenbourg) Van Etten, b 18 Apr 1793 (MDVEB) bp 04 May 1793 sp Johannes Falkenbourg, d 15 Dec 1877 ae 84-07-18 (84-07-27 MDVEB) both bur Meyers Grd Mt Marion NY near the Railway Stn (OGUC:263). Jonas served in the War of 1812 (CBRUC:122). His wf Maria adm to Plattekill CH 07 Dec 1838 on cert fr Flatbush (RRDC:70). Bible Record. Saugerties Ref CH copied 28 Apr 1974. Holy Bible Pub 1818 by M Carey & sons. Inscription: "Nov 11, 1818 Abraham DeWitt bought this Bible from James Woodruff; given $5.00. I gave it to Maria DeWitt for a present - wife of Jonas V Etten".
4   CHARLES DeWITT b 1793 (belongs in the family according to the 1855 census Greene Co NY).
5   ANDRIES DeWITT b 26 Nov 1794 bp 14 Dec 1794 (K&S:107) sp Schie/Kezekiah Wynkoop & wf Elizabeth Dederiks (d 13 May 1887 ae 82-05-17 m ? Aug 1815 Mary/Polly Van Etten b 26 Dec 1791 d 13 Aug 1877 ae 85-07-10 (MDVEB) res Saugerties; Polly DeWitt w/o Andrew DeWitt was excommunicated 28 Jul 1823 fr the 2nd Presbyterian CH of Durham in the village of West Durham (CDDGC:232). Andrew DeWitt Sr adm to Plattekill CH 07 Dec 1838 on cert fr Flatbush (PRDC:70).
6   JAN DeWIT b 11 Dec 1797 bp 10 Jan 1798 sp Jan L DeWit & Pallie Van Leuven (K&S:119). As John I in 1855, a widower, landholder, farmer b Ulster, lived Windham. Ann, Charles, and Elizabeth res with him.
7   ELIZABETH DeWITT b 06 Jun 1799 bp 07 Jul 1799 sp Jan L DeWitt, Pallie Van Leuven (K&S:127) m James Otis (HGC:426).
8   RACHEL DeWITT b 11 Apr 1802 bp 21 Apr 1802 no SP d 23 Oct 1805 (K&S:137).
9   SIMON PETER DeWITT b 03 Feb 1808 (CBRUC:574) bp 12 Feb 1809 no sp (K&S:156) or (tbstn b 08 Jan 1809 d 21 Jan 1889 ae 90-11-18) & {m} 16 Nov 1843 Harriet DeWitt (1.1.9.4.5.3.6) [HGC:426] d/o John DeWitt & Hannah Egbertsen b 17 Feb 1817 Oak Hill, Greene Co NY d 17 Apr 1885 ae 68-02-00 (PDR:255/6/7/60; OGUC:249). Simon inherited the Jan L DeWitt farm, later called the Lowther Farm, both bur there. Simon P DeWitt member #59 adm (to Plattekill RDC). **m2 Anna Pels both of Saugerties.**

Record of Wills 1846-Ulster County New York Surrogate Court Abraham DeWitt Will 20 May 1835 Probate 09 Feb 1846 names Andrew, Simon Peter, Maria wife of Jonas Van Etten; 3 grandchildren: Abraham H, Moses and (first born) Catherine DeWitt, offspring of my son Levi, deceased (children are Catherine, Abraham H & Moses) daughter Ann Eliza wife of Seth K Otis (her several children). Exs: sons Andrew & Simon Peter.

Windham Greene Co NY 1855 Census, John I DeWitt b 1795 wdr, land-holder, farmer, also bro Charles b 1793, sis Ann b 1790, Elisabeth b 1799, all b Ulster res Greene since 1834. They res in the house of Raimond Winchell (NYDCG:80).

VAN KEUREN
1.1.9.4.2.5 MARIA DeWITT m Levi Van Keuren
1   ANNA MARIA VAN KEUREN b 03 Apr 1803 bp 15 May 1803 sp Pieter DeWitt, Polly Van Leuven (K&S:141).
2   GERRETJE NEWKERK VAN KEUREN b 06 Jul 1804 bp 18 Aug 1804 (DRCK:481) & (d 17 May 1885) m 15 Feb 1831 at Kingston, Edward s/o Cornelius & Maria (Tenbroeck) Burhans, b 11 Mar 1804 d 30 Apr 1858 (BG:469,490).
3   ANDREW DeWITT VAN KEUREN bp 02 Sep 1807.
4   PETER HENRY VAN KEUREN b 25 Dec 1808 Fatbush, Ulster Co NY (DRCFU:1) & (d 1864 bur Mt Marion Com Cem) m Sally A Reynolds b 1808 d 1896 (OGUC:256).
5   CHARLES VAN KUREN b 1811 bp Flatbush, Ulster (DRCFU:5) & (d 1896). Capt Charles Van Keuren of Kingston NY, at Plattekill m Sat 27 Sep 1845 Sarah Crispell/Chrispell of Woodstock Wits: Capt Peter H Brink, Rev Thomas C Strong (PRDC:3) tbstn as Crispell b 1816 d 1898. Sarah was bp & both, on conf, Admitted to the Plattekill DRC 03 Sept 1869; both bur Mt Marion Com Cem (OGUC 256; PDRC:48,61/9).
6   MARIA VAN KEUREN bp 20 Jul 1813 Flatbush, DRC Ulster. 1810 Census Kingston NY Levi Van Keuren

DeWITT
1.1.9.4.3.1 LUCAS EVERT DeWITT/DEWID m Elizabeth Van Loon
1   GERTROUD DeWITT bp 14 Feb 1782 sp Evert DeWitt, wf Gertroud (NYGBR 85:74) indicating Evert was home & at the Zion Luth CH in Loonenburg (Athens NY) for this bp; in other bp during the Revo his wife is sponsor & he is listed as absent.
2   JACOB DEWID b 17 Jun 1784 bp 22 Aug 1784 sp Albert Van Loon, wf Maria (NYGBR 85:78).
3   JOHANNES DeWITT b 08 Oct 1786 bp 31 Dec 1786 sp Johannes Plank, wf Catherina (NYGBR 85:80) & (17 Jan 1851 ae 67. John wdr ae 66 res with dau Elizabeth & hus John Graham.
4   ABRAHAM DeWITT bp 03 Jun 1789 Albany NY (d 27 Feb 1868 ae 80) m Ella Rebecca b 08 Jan 1788 d 14 Apr 1884 ae 96-03-06 both bur Wilton Cem On. Abraham had a Crown Land Grant 11 Jun 1836 Con 7 Lot 35 Ernestown T L&A Co of 250 acres; Deed 10 Apr 1865; Will 04 Apr 1867 names his chn. Deed of his land to son John 17 Jul 1777 (in his name until 12 Nov 1900).

Leucas deWit

5   EVERT DeWITT b 1791/3 (1851 Census says b in Can, may be wrong since sis Catharine b 1798 in Durham T NY not in 1861 Census. Evert may have died as son Henry ae 17 is listed as farmer with his mother & the family in Sophiasburg T Census L&A Co). He m 29 Oct 1818 Catherine b 1803 near Kingston ON d/o John & Catharine (Buck) Horning. A morgage on 100 acres being bought by an Evert Dewitt of Kingston T for the eastenmost half of Lot 7 Con 1 Richmond T L&A Co on 26 Feb 1842 was discharged by Cert No 130 entered & filed L&A Co 23 Jan 1855 either by Evert or his heirs.

6   LUCINDA DeWITT m 11 Aug 1811 Joshua Anderson. His Will at Fredericksburgh Twp L&A Co ON 12 Jun 1825 Pro 07 Jul 1826.

7   PETER DeWITT bp 25 Sep 1796 Durham, Oak Hill, Green Co NY. IGI no other info.

8   CATHARINE DeWITT b 26 Sep 1798 bp 24 Feb 1799 sp Henry De Witt, Catharine Dumond (NYGBR 87:53; CDDGC:55).

DeWITT

1.1.9.4.3.3 JAN/JOHN HENRY DeWITT m Phoebe Du Rose

1   MARY G DeWIT bp 06 Mar 1788 Maugerville Anglican CH Maugerville NB (MACNB: 2 copied by CB) m 22 Sep 1809 John Bailey s/o Benjamin Bailey & Susannah Wanty, b 26 Nov 1785 d 18 Mar 1863 res Newcastle Creek, Queens Co NB Can, Will written 22 Sep 1859. (Some records name Mary G as Mary Elizabeth; 1851 census wf Elizabeth b 1851) He m2 Elizabeth b 1787. (1851 census)

• PHOEBE DeWIT bp 06 Mar 1788 (MACNB:2 not identified).

2   ABRAHAM PERSEN DeWIT b 31 Dec 1788 Blissville Par Sunbury, Co, South Branch of the Oromocto River bp 10 Jun 1792 Maugerville Anglican CH NB (MACNB:28, fr Mrs. CB) & (d 14 Feb 1866 ae 77-01-14 Maxfield ME (fr by KG) petition for land Sunbury Co 1793, 1804/9/10 (U of NB Archive) m Nancy S Smith b 24 Mar 1793 d 25 Sep 1863 ae 70-05-09 both b Oromocto River NB Can & bur Maxfield ME Cem south side of Piscataguis River. In 1812 Abraham was appointed to do 6 days roadwork. He was a farmer & lumberman, moved to Maxfield, Penobscot Co ME in 1822. Research by Mrs Thomas Franklin.

3   THOMAS DUROSE/DUROWS DeWIT b 09 Jan 1791 bp 10 Jun 1792 Maugerville Anglican CH (MACNB:28 fr Mrs.) & (d 23 Jun 1871 Seboeis ME; 1830 census Maxfield ME) at Burton Par Sunbury Co NB, m1 08 Apr 1817 Hannah C Seeley Burton Par NB (both b Oromocto River) license fr John Hazen, Justice of Quoram (NB Archive; MLNB, CB) d/o Ezekiel & Rebecca (Thomas) Seeley, 1830 census Maxfield ME b 05 Jul 1803 d 23 May 1846 ae 43-10-18 d & bur Whitney Ridge (R3T8) Seboeis Plantation ME, (tbstn fr BVH); Thomas DeWitt m2 Mary/Polly A (Lyford) Smart b NH d ae 94 (wd/o John Smart, their son Charles Lyford Smart).

4   JOHN/KING DeWIT b 03 Apr 1793 bp 05 Jul 1796 Anglican CH Maugerville NB (MACNB:45 fr CB) & (d 10 Jan 1890 Avondale NB) m by license 15 Oct 1815 m 24 Oct 1815 Annie d/o Daniel & Annie (Morgan) Wood (MLNB; fr KLAD) b 07 Jun 1794 d 15 Apr 1889 both bur Baptist CH Avondale NB (Waterville). Info & tbstn recorded by Lester D Mallory. They lived at French Lake then Waterville. John was a farmer and also worked as a lumberman & for a time kept a hotel. He was healthy & vigorous. He was said to have been called "King" DeWitt because of his great strength. He was long lived perhaps age 90 in a picture taken of him when a very old man, provided by George DeWitt of Ardrie AB.

5   GERTRUDE/GERTRYD DeWIT b 1795 Blissville NB bp 05 Jul 1796 Maugerville Anglican CH (MACNB:45, CB) & (d 1896 bur Presque Isle ME) m Clapman s/o Clapman & Susannah (Bailey) Smith, b 1795 d 1871. Clapman conducted services for early Baptist settlers at Mill Settlement NB. In 1829 he helped build a house, which Hon Horace Smith now owns at Hoyt. They moved to Presque Isle ME in their later years d & bur there. Clapman's death was said to have been brought on earlier by his homesickness for NB.

6   ANNA MARIA DeWIT bp 07 Jul 1797 (MACNB:49, CB) m 15 Oct 1818 Seth Farrow/Feero moved to Southampton Par York Co NB (IGI).

7   CHARLES DeWIT b 1799 bp 02 Jul 1801 (CSNB:13; MACNB:65, CB) & (d after 1871) farmer in Mill Settlement West (Hoyt) area m Hannah b 1806 d/o Lemuel & Mary (Tracy) Nason, b 13 May 1806 d 09 Apr 1840 both members 09 Apr 1840 of Blissville Baptist CH. (Hannah's sister Sarah Nason b 1796 m Evert Boone (fr KLAD; MWD; census)

8   LUKE DeWIT bp 02 Jul 1801 (d 10 Mar 1876 ae 76 Will 02 Feb 1876) both of Burton Par m 13 Jan 1827 Mary Wood b 1815 d 02 Feb 1881 ae 66 both bur Blissville Cem Hoyt NB (fr LDM; MWD). Bp copied by Cleadie Barnet fr the Maugerville Anglican Church Rec 1787-1805.

Leucas deWit

Hubbard Papers, New Brunswick Museum, Saint John.
Appendix H Administration Bond N 20 Filed Nov 6 1801. List of property of the late John De Witt, deceased, taken 27th day November 1801:

	£ (pounds)	s (shillings)	p (pence)
4 Heifers, each 3 10 0	14	00	0
1 Bull	2	5	0
1 Cow, red	3	10	0
1 " brindle	4	0	
1 " pied	4	10	
1 " red	4	10	
1 " deep red brindle	4	10	
3 Calves	2	10	
1 Heifer	2	10	
1 Black Horse	11	0	
1 Bay Mare	16	0	
20 Sheep - 10/	10	0	
Homestead farm	40	0	
Upper farm	70	0	
3 Hogs - 5/	2	15	
1 Chain	0	5	
1 Ax	0	7	6
1 Shovel	0	5	0
Writing to Amount	23	0	0

     her   Jacob DeWitt   )
Phebe X DeWitt   Clapman Smith) Apprisors (sic)
     Mark   Joshua Thomas)
Lawrence Mersereau

DeWIT
1.1.9.4.3.4 HENRICUS/HENDRIKUS/HENRY DeWIT m Catharina Dumond

1   GEERTRUI/GITTY DeWIT b 26 Oct 1797 bp 26 Nov 1797 sp Evert DeWit & Geertrui DeWit (K&S:119; HGC:442) & (d 03 Apr 1867) m 31 Aug 1816 Peter James s/o James/Jacobus & Christina (Eman) Overbagh, b 05 Sep 1795 d 15 Jan 1870 (HGC:442).

2   TEMPERENCE DeWIT b 29 Apr 1800 bp 25 May 1800 sp Hendricus Borhans, Temperence Du Mon (K&S:130) & (alive in 1883) m 20 Feb 1822 Henry b 04 Sep 1790 (d 13 Jul 1863) s/o William & Catharine (Ten Broeck) Van Orden (HGC:442).

3   ELSE/ALICE DeWITT b 19 Sep 1805 m Benjamin Winne. (HGC:436,442,443)

Henry Dewitt's petition in 1787 in New Brunswick, Canada reads "Henry Dewitt, Loyalist . . . That I, with several others did Memorial to Your Excellency last spring for a Tract of land on the Oromocto. The lot fallen to your humble Petitioner proveth to be a burnt Piece of Land entirely without wood or arable, whereas in the front of your Petitioner on the opposite side of the Creek, there lyeth a small vacant gore of intervale, it being entirely too small for any Person to settle on, your humble Petitioner therefore prayeth the favour that your Excellency and the Right Honourable Council would be pleased to grant The favour to Annex the said small Gore of Intervale to the said Lott without which indulgence the said lot will be entirely useless as there is not timber sufficient even to build a House thereon . . . Henry DeWitt".

Henry DeWitt of Catskill, Will, Probate 05 Jun 1830. Heirs: three daus, Elsie wife of Benjamin Winne, Gitty wife of Peter Overbagh, Temperance wife of Henry Van Orden. Executors: son-in-laws Benjamin Winne and John Langendyke of Saugerties. Witnesses: James Powers, Joseph Hyde and Caleb Day. Witness to Codicil: Caleb Day, William Van Vechten and Chester Hull, Jr (AWGNY 1:34).

Catharine DeWitt of Catskill, Will, Probate 22 Mar 1856 [widow of Henry DeWitt] heirs: three daughters, Elizabeth (daughter of John Baptist Dumond] wife of John Langendyck of Saugerties; Temperance wife of Henry Van Orden of Catskill and Elsie wife of Benjamin Winnie. Catharine's pa is mentioned as David Dumond. Exs: son-in-law Benjamin Winne and John Langendyck. Wit: James Powers, Caleb Day and G Van Bergen (AWGNY 1:107); no reference to daughter Gitty, alive until 1867.

DeWITT
1.1.9.4.3.5 ABRAHAM DeWITT m Catherina Kriestler ???

GERTHROUT DeWITT b 25 Mar 1789 bp 30 May 1789 sp Jorgan Schram, wf Annatie, Zion Luth CH Loonenburg, Greene Co NY (NYGBR 85:83). <u>Possibly</u> the same man who married Caroline Tucker.
m Caroline Tucker

Leucas deWit

1. PHOEBE DeWIT b 1807 m 20 Dec 1806 Issac DeWit (1.1.9.4.3.7.3) b 1802 d 1884) both of Lincoln Co NB (SCMC:#368 fr Mrs CB). NB Census misread Issac as Isreal & wf Phoebe.
   ? * SOLOMON DeWIT bp 11 Jan 1801 no age given, received land with Peter & cousin Thomas Or was Solomon s/o Jacob, who was also a son-in-law of Solomon Tucker but there is no family "memory" of him in Jacob's descendants.
   ? * PHILIP DeWITT also received land, unidentified.
   ? * PETER DeWIT bp 11 Jan 1801 Maugerville Anglican CH Rec 1787-1805. Pg 65 #1218 28 Aug 1827 NB "Gazette d 18th inst Salmon River house fire, Peter Dewett". #1328 30 Oct 1827 Est Peter Dewett, Burton Par NB Can, Admin [? s/o] Abraham Dewett, John Brown 28 Oct 1827, or was the man who d in the fire Evert & Abraham's bro Peter b 1755. m Mary/Maria DeWit
   ? * NANCY DeWIT m 08 May 1826 Solomon Tracy (SCMC:#348). She does not belong to John or Henry. This leaves her possible parent as the senior Peter (no known chn) Jacob (unknown to his desc) or possibly Abraham.

BOONE

1.1.9.4.3.6 CATHARINA/KATE DeWIT m Samuel Boone

1. JOHN BOONE b 1786 d 1812. John drowned at the mouth of the Morency in 1812 by going through ice while crossing the river to return a borrowed chain to Richardson Webb (the Pioneer). John was a soldier in the 104th Regt and was home on leave when it happened.
2. EBENEZER BOONE b 1787/88 bp 11 Jul 1788. He was a schoolteacher in the 1851 census in Linclon Par Sunbury Co. Ebenezer was lame. He d of a fever at Sunpoke, NB.
3. ABRAHAM BOONE b 1789/90 bp 03 Jan 1791 d 1813/4 was in the 104th Regt, which made the snowshoe trip from Fredericton NB to Quebec City PQ departing in groups, 13-17 Feb 1813. Over a thousand men were involved and the distance was 370 miles. From Quebec the troops were conveyed to the Niagara war area. From an account of the Tracy Family written by John Colby Tracy (1855-1937) quote "Abram Boone may have served under General Brock and it is said he was the largest man in the 104th Regt. Legend tells us Abram died in a chimney corner while roasting beef on a bayonet in either 1813 or 1814 at or near Lundy's Lane". He choked on a piece of meat (PJDS).
4. MURRAY BOONE b 1791 bp 17 Jun 1792 (drowned Dec 1823) m 01 Jan 1817 Elizabeth/Betsy youngest d/o Isreal & Abigail (Cram) Kinney. His Will was Pro Jan 1824. Elizabeth/Betsy m2 James Nelson; m3 Capt Benjamin Haverlon. The 20 Jul 1824 issue of NB Royal Gazette "Estate of Murray Boone of Lincoln Parish, Sunbury Co. Administrator: Samuel Nevers" (fr ACB)
5. HENRY BOONE b ca 1794 (d Oct 1848) m 13 Nov 1828 Mary Ann d/o William & Ann (Boone) Hayward, Samuel's brother res Blissville. After Henry's death his single bro James lived with this family on the Tracy NB area property.
6. EVERT/EVERIT/EVERETT DEWITT BOONE b 1795 bp 05 Jan 1798 (MACNB:53) m 07 Nov 1814 Sarah Nason b 12 Apr 1791 d/o Lemuel Nason & Mary Tracy. The couple was both of Lincoln Par Sunbury Co (SCMC:#46) then res Par of Blissville, Sunbury Co NB.
7. WILLIAM BOONE b 1795 bp 05 Jan 1798 (MACNB:53, Mrs CB) m 27 Oct 1817 Mary Cogswell (d 10 May 1866) d/o Capt Cogswell & wf Hannah (Boone) Rose, b 1795, res Tracy but in 1836 had no children in school there. In 1851 they are in Burtts Corner area, Par of Douglas, York Co NB with them Hannah Cogshale ae 83 (fr ACB).
8. SAMUEL BOONE b 11 Nov 1798 bp 02 Feb 1801 (MACNB:65) & (d 19 May 1855 ae 56) m Hannah/Ann d/o Jonathan & Rachel (Webb) Tracy, (fr ACB) b 22 Jul 1813 d 25 Sep 1871 res Gladstone Par Sunbury Co NB Can bur Pioneer Cem Tracy NB. Gladstone Par came into existence 03 Nov 1874; until 1834 it was the rear part of Lincoln Par, 1837-74 it was part of Blissville Par (fr ACB).
9. JAMES BOONE b 1802 **single** d 1871/81 res Blissville. James res with Ann & family (bro Henry's family [CSNB:110].

Bps are in Maugerville Anglican CH rec fr Cleadie Barnet. Info br Allen C Boone, RR# 3 Oromocto NB.

"The Bearer Jacob DeWitt being about to change residence from thr Providence of New Brunswick to that of Upper Canada, I do certify that he is an American Loyalist of reputable Character and entited to favourable consideration of His Majesty's Government to which he intends moving. Dated at New Brunswick the 22nd Day of June 1824 ---

W. H. Blifs
Administrator of the Government"

DeWITT

1.1.9.4.3.7 JACOB DeWITT m 1 Salome Tucker

1. MARTHA/PATTY/? FREDERICKA DeWITT (fr KLAD) b 20 Jan 1791 bp 31 Jul 1798 (MACNB:58) (b 1790 fr KALD:1795 in 1851 census) & (d 1877) m 08 Aug 1813 John Nason b 06 Jan 1790 d 1852, s/o Lemuel Nason & Mary Tracy. They are bur Pioneer Graveyard, Tracy NB Can. Martha was known to take a text & preach a sermon; she also used to sing. They were great singers, music lovers & for their education, gifted speakers (fr ACB: KLAD)

- GERTRUDE DeWITT bp 31 Jul 1798 (MACNB:58) family stories say there may have been more chn. If Martha, not a DeWitt name, was named for Salome's mother, Gertrude for Jacob's mother would be logical. Alternative theory, Abraham's Gertrude could have d & a 2nd ch so named.

2. JACOB DeWITT bp 18 Jul 1801 (MACNB:65) & (d 1881) m 29 Aug 1829 Betty Creekmore (SCMR:#463 fr ACB) res Gladstone Par Sunbury Co NB.

3. ISAAC DeWITT b 1802 (d 1884) {m} 20 Dec 1826 1.1.9.4.3.5.2 Phoebe DeWit b 1807 d/o Abraham DeWit & Caroline Tucker (SCMC:#386). (SCC p 8 said) Isaac & Phoebe died 2 weeks apart.

m2 Mrs Abigail Cram Kinney/Kenny

4. JOHN DeWITT b 12 Mar 1808 Sunbury Co NB (d 29 Oct 1879 ON) at Tapleytown ON m 06 Jul 1828 Phoebe d/o Samuel Nevers, b 20 Mar 1809 Maugerville NB d spring 1883 Port Dover ON, bur there beside son Judson & his wf Eliza (fr Family Bible MJPSM). They res in a log house Lot 10 Con 6 Saltfleet Twp Wentworth Co ON (fr HBS to ICSP).

5. JONATHAN P DeWITT b 23 Dec 1809 Gladstone Par Sunbury Co NB Can (d ? 1904 Grande Ledge MI [fr SC] but his wd is with their dau in 1900), at Grimsby ON Anglican CH m 30 Sep 1834 Caroline Jane Corey b 25 Dec 1816 Gagetown NB (adult bp at St Lukes Anglican CH Burlington ON) & (d 1904 MI) d/o Morris Corey & Sarah Lounsbury, both Saltfleet T ON, bondsman James Nash, tailor, John C Pettit, yoeman (MBO:318) res Brant ON then Grand Ledge MI. (Can 1851 Census Oakland Twp Brant Co ON list of chn). Prof Stanley Corey used material from typescript "The American Family of Corey" by Charles Estabrook Corey b 1853 Dumfries ON. LDS Film # 1240709 Eaton Co MI for 1900: Olelol A Walker wf Antinnett (faint, hard to read & sounded) b ? Oct 1862 ae 37 m 12 yrs, got citizenship 1875, res US 24 yrs, dau Eliza S b ? Oct 1896 in MI ae 3, pa b NY, ma b Can in same house Caroline J Dewitt, ma, b ? Dec 1815 d ae 84, 13 chn, 9 living, b NB Can, pa b Eng (sic) ma b Wales (sic). Her grma Abigail Cram's nationality was said to be Welsh, still not proven. Her pa, Morris Corey, was b North Castle, her ma Rye both places in Westchester Co NY & both prts were of Eng Ancestry. Info from Prof Stanley Cory of Kent OH & Green Valley AZ acquired previous research collected before 1903 more done by 1927. He has worked 35 yrs on all Corey Loyalist desc.

JOHN DeWITT

6. PRUDENCE DeWITT b 1810 Sunbury Par NB, of Saltfleet Twp & at Ancaster ON m 02 Mar 1829 Jacob Neff b 1804, yoeman, of Barton, Twp ON Con 6 Lot 13 100 A) bondsmen John Findlay & James Chep, both Ancaster, merchants (MBO:138). Can New Connexion religion. His parents were John Neff & Magdalen Burkholder. Prudence's mother, Abigail Cram, res with this family after 1860 (fr NG; census).

7. SARAH/SALLY DeWITT b 1812 Gladstone Par NB (d 1903 bur Picton ON, Cem Rec there) at Hamilton ON m 01 Aug 1834 James Nash, both of Saltfleet Twp, bondsmen Ira Holton, physician, Thomas Kerr, mariner, (MBO:138). James was b 1812 USA came to Can ae 6, became a Tailor and Merchant at 22 King St Hamilton ON (MBO:348) res 71 Main St, but in 1863 no longer in the city directory. In 1851 census Abigail res with them.

8. ABIGAIL DeWITT b 1814 d 03 Dec 1831 bur family plot Ker United CH Cem (used to be Meth) Tapleytown ON **dy,**

9. THOMAS DeWITT b 1818 (date in 1851 Census in New Brunswick, m1 28 May 1839 Harriet d/o Charles Moore & Elizabeth, b 1818 Saltfleet Twp ON d 14 Feb 1847 of Consumption; m2 Sarah J b 1866 UC NCM religion. (1861 census Harwich T Kent Co ON). He was a blacksmith at Morpeth Twp then res Howard Twp Kent Co ON. In later census he was a foreman in a carriage factory.

10. GEORGE DeWITT b 1818 (census [alive in 1903 & said to have reached ae 92 fr ISD]) at Grimsby ON Anglican CH m 28 Sep 1840 Mary Charlotte Corey b 20 Oct 1822 Gagetown NB d/o Morris Corey & Sarah Lounsbury (Anglican Rec McMaster U Hamilton ON. Mary was bp as an adult at St Luke's Ch Burlington ON. Her Loyalist prts

Leucas deWit

are bur there. On the back of the tbstn of grdau Caroline (DeWitt) & hus John H Martin is inscribed "In memory of Mary and George DeWitt, Grandparents of Hie and May Norton their wishes filled".

Abigail Cram & Isreal Kenny Jr's chn were:

Isreal Kenny b 1796 (d 14 May 1856 Jacksonville NB) m1 08 Mar 1816 Mary Tracy; m2 Jane Everett De Grass.

James Kenny m Ansie Chapman.

Susie Kenny m Samuel Havens. In 1851 census at Hamilton Ruth Havens ae 2 lived with Murray Boone's daus Elizabeth & Ruth, suggesting she was an orphan.

Betsy Kenny m 01 Jan 1817 Murray Boone (1.1.9.4.3.6.3 [SCMR:#103]) fr ACB) s/o Catharine DeWitt & Samuel Boone m2 James Nelson; m3 Capt Benjamin Haverlon. Each hus was one military rank higher than her previous one.

Annie Kenny m James Drake (fr ACB, possibly another military man).

Abigail (Cram) Kenney DeWitt married 1st, 06 Mar 1793 Isreal Kenny Jr (E W Bell. Isreal Kenny and His Descendants 1944) at Tapleytown ON, married 3rd 06 Jul 1828 David Pearson born 14 Oct 1766 died 14 January 1844 age 77 buried Mount Pleasant Pioneer Cemetery, Brant County ON; next grave Hannah Pearson died 13 Mar 1828 age 51, also an infant daughter died 13 Mar 1823 age 11 months. Abigail had a double wedding with her son John DeWitt [oral history recorded in 1933 by people whose parents knew Abigail and were John's children]. Witness: Thomas DeWitt, identity unknown. According to census their son Thomas was age 10 at that time though census can be inaccurate. Perhaps Thomas was a relative of Jacob DeWitt or one of the Sussex County N J DeWitts who lived in the Hamilton ON area at that time.

A Kenney grandson from NB visited Abigail for her 80th birthday, so she ironed a shirt for him and they went to have their pictures taken, copy of hers included here. After searching years in New Brunswick, some of the Robert Cram lines were found in Norfolk Co ON, there before 1815. Research done in 1932 by a group of DeWitt descendants state Abigail had six children when she married Jacob. They still remember her stepchildren disliked her because she reported any misbehavior to Jacob who was very strict. It was said her New England family disapproved of her marriage to Jacob DeWitt. Jacob served in the King's American Regiment. At age thirteen, on 15 Nov 1779, he was in Col Edmund Fanning's Grenadier Company at Lloyd's Neck New York. This would be the flag bearers, tallest men in the Regiment. His Unit was in the Southern Campaign, though he is listed as on furlough Feb to Apr 1781 from Capt Thomas Chapman's Company at Georgetown SC, then as recruiting in NY for Chapman. His company was at Savannah Georgia April till June 1781 (LSCRW 3:89,91, 104). Jacob died 08 Jun 1827 at Tapleytown ON. Oral history says he had at one time been flooded out by the Oromocto River and came to believe his children would have better opportunities in Ontario. In 1824 "knowing he had not long to live" he moved his family to the Hamilton area along with the Samuel Tapley and Morris Corey families. Family sources say Jacob had cancer of the face (PJDS). He looked at the Lake Ontario escarpment and decided he wanted no land near any lake that could rise, so he located on Mud Road above it `on the Mountain' (a local colloquialism). The frame house, in very bad condition, still stands.

MOVING FROM NEW BRUNSWICK TO UPPER CANADA

From Margaret Stockton of Woodstock ON comes this account of the trip from New Brunswick to Ontario. It does not mention the Vails or the Morris Corey family who came about the same time (two Corey daughters married two of Jacob DeWitt's sons). Morris' 1837 application for a grant of the land he lived upon at Burlington Beach says he had been there thirteen years. His brother, Thomas Corey with some of his family was in the same district (Elgin County, Ontario) as the group described next. Abigail Cram Kinney DeWitt Pearson had Cram relatives in Norfolk County before 1815

Margaret writes: All reports of the trip from New Brunswick indicate 1824 (refer to Jacob's Loyalist recommendation) but have no other proof of this. Perhaps the Tapley's and others were there earlier. The Stocktons came from the area of Smith's Creek, King's County, New Brunswick. But the Tapleys, Nevers, Kenny/Kinneys, Churchill, McGees, Grays all came from below Hartland, Carleton County, I believe. The only mutual family was the Sipperells, some of whom lived in Kings County and others in Carleton County I wonder if it was through them that the Stocktons and Nevers met. The Innis family came from Kings County. In Ontario they married with the Sipperells. But legend says that William Stockton was not aware that John Innis lived across the road until the sound of the axe bought them together. James Innis, son of John, was in Blenheim ON in 1822.

Through the Innis family, who have some old letters written from Blenheim Township Ontario to New Brunswick, comes the following information. "We were in Boston Bay out of site (sic) of land with forty eight passengers on board when we run a foul of an American Schooner. The wind was very high. The Captain's brother was killed on board the American schooner. But O the cries that was on board". "New York is a very beautiful and very large town. My road to Canada was very short. Every day was something new to be seen. I come 333 miles in the canal through a settled part of the States. I see fifty acres of land in one place covered over with salt flats where they dry it with the sun. They call it the Onandaga Salt Works. After I left New York, I was in many a town before I got where I live now"...

The Stocktons did lose an infant on the journey and supposedly her body was given to the Indians on Long Island for burial. There has to be some truth to the story.

I have an account from the memories of one of the Stockton girls who made the journey, in which she claims to have traveled most of the way in a sailing vessel and when the waves became so bad they feared they would be swamped, they cast a horse overboard. For three days and three nights it swam along side the vessel until it sank from sight (???).

It was a caravan of families, most of whom were Baptist. In South of Sodom published in 1983 by the South Norwich Historical Society, is the following ... "a caravan of some fifty families ... This caravan was led by a man by the name of Revely and consisted of such well known family names as the Stocktons, Nevers, Holdens, Sipperells, Wingardners, Mercers, DeWitts and Mudge as well as Innis". They sure kept together or rather in touch in Ontario because Sipperells married Innis; Winegarden married Nevers; Revely married Sipperell; Mercer married Gray, married Innis; DeWitts married Nevers; Stockton married Nevers on arrival.

After traveling all those miles on the Erie Canal, somehow they arrived at Tapleytown. Samuel Nevers, father of Phoebe, etc. made a home there for several years. Phoebe married (John DeWitt) and lived there. Mary Nevers married John Burkholder and lived in Saltfleet. Harriet daughter of William J Stockton and Ann Nevers, married in 1838 Enoch Burkholder, lived in Saltfleet or Barton Township at first, then eventually in South Norwich, Norfolk County ON. This account of the horse is hers. (End of account.)

Descendants wonder why their ancestors moved and how they chose just that destination. From these tales and documents you see the DeWitts in New Brunswick kept in touch with Henry when he returned to the United States and other relatives in New York, with Luke on the Bay of Quinte ON, and considering Jacob's destination and Loyalist recommendation, with Peter at Chippewa ON. Peter received his Ontario land grant 14 Feb 1823 and may have communicated this information to Jacob who took steps to take with him proof of his Loyalist standing. Jacob was a Loyalist in his own right because of Military Service. As children of a Loyalist each child of his was entitled to 200 acres, available until 1840, a fact they must not have known since none received their grants as sons or daughters of a Loyalist though it was seldom Ontario granted land to New Brunswick Loyalists. Remember too, Evert and wife visited Greene County NY in 1798. You will see that some of Evert's brother Lucas' family located in Norfolk County ON.

DeWitt Clinton, Governor of New York State, was later bankrupt. His Papers are now in the Guelph ON University Archives. In the War of 1812 it is said he got in touch with his Canadian relatives seeking information. It would be interesting to follow up this story.

DeWITT

1.1.9.4.3.8 PETRUS/PETER DeWITT m Mrs Annetje/Hannah/Annie Snyder Saxe/Saks

John P Saxe b 08 Oct 1792 d 16 Jun 1870 (UCCBR: 280).
Benjamin Saks b 18 Dec 1794 bp 18 Jan 1795 sp Benjamin Snyder, Annatje Brink (K&S:107).
Paulus Sax b 13 Apr 1800 bp 11 May 1800 sp Petrus P Sax, Elizabeth Sax s/o Annatie Snyder, husband deceased Last winter (NYGBR 86:54).

1. MARIAH DeWITT b 31 Oct 1805 (tbstn 1806) bp 12 Jan 1806 sp Henry Dewit, Catharina Dewit (CDDGC:68) d 08 Feb 1883 bur Drummond Hill Cem Niagara Falls ON **single** tbstn recorded by author.
2. CATHERINE DeWITT b 01 Mar 1807 bp 14 Jun 1807 (CDDGC:71) & (d 05 Sep 1881) at Chippewa ON m 02 Jul 1829 Francis Bogardus, both of Stamford Twp ON (OPR 8:154) s/o Cornelius F Bogardus & Zipporah Anderson b 16 Apr 1794 d 05 Sep 1881 res Chippewa ON (OPR 8:154) both bur Glen Meyer Cem Norfolk Co ON.
3. HENRY DeWITT b 31 Jul 1808 bp 09 Oct 1808 sp Peter DeWitt & Hannah Snyder (CDDGC:73) & (d 12 Apr 1898 bur Drummond Hill Cem) at Chippewa ON m 13 Dec 1854 Isabella Cropley both of Chippewa ON (CMBMD:2) b 1831 in NB d 28 Oct 1916 Montrose, Stamford Twp ON. Henry built the First Baptist CH at Lundy's Lane, Drummondville at his own cost. In a quarrel with his Cropley brother-in-law he shut it down at one time. Baptist & Anglican Archives are both stored at McMaster's U Hamilton ON.
4. EVERT DeWITT b 10 Feb 1811 bp 20 Apr 1811 no sp (K&S:164) d 16 Sep 1899 bur Drummond Hill Cem **single.**
5. ANNATJE DeWITT b 25 Oct 1812 bp 11 Nov 1812 no sp (K&S:170) **dy.**
6. PIETER DeWITT b 11 Aug 1814 bp 31 Aug 1814 sp Petrus Van Vlierden, Jane Kerelvas (K&S:176) & (d 12 Jan 1900 bur Drummond Hill) at ae 62 m 29 Feb 1876 Charlotte Dell, no family. Drummond Hill Cemetery Niagara Falls ON, recorded by author. (JJ -- Joyce Jewett, Buffalo NY). Jewett was originally DeWitt. Why the change?

- A JOHN DeWITT b 1807 married Jane Dell; his ancestry unproven. 1860 census for 12th Ward, Buffalo NY has John Dewitt age 53, a Cooper, owns real estate, born NY, wife Jane age 40, born Canada. John is in the State 1865 census but not in the City Directory in 1868. Jane Dell Dewitt died 10 Dec 1875, Administration of her estate of $300 states she has no husband, sister, mother, or father alive; a brother, Masten Dell is at Chippewa ON, names of other brothers - unknown (fr JJ). One John DeWitt son of William DeWitt and Mary was bp 19 May 1807 Niagara ON by Rev Robert Addison (OPR 3:24). Whether or where William and John fit is unknown.
MSS "Street (Samuel) Papers" 1828 letter, Robert Dickson, Niagara to Samuel Street sending subpoena tickets stating the witness for the Dell Case is Peter DeWitt September 16, 1828.

John H DeWitt was of particular interest because of the sensational newspaper items about him in the Niagara

Chronicle and reprinted in other papers. He seemed to have been involved in the 1837 Rebellion when William Lyon McKenzie fled to the US. "It is beyond a doubt that John H DeWitt, whose trial we give below, was a leading instrument, if not the actual planner, of most of the outrages, which took place on the frontier five years ago. From information, the accuracy of which is not to be questioned, it appears that in addition to the offences for which he has been incarcerated for life, he and a man named Wheeler were the parties by whom Brock's Monument was blown up by the same men was Dr Mewburn's barn burnt down. DeWitt and a man named Caswell were the destroyers of the Chippewa Church and DeWitt and Benjamin Lett were the persons who set fire to Mr Henry Miller's barn. The following, received during the late Assizes, from the active and intelligent officer at Buffalo, give the names of several parties by whom the house of the Rev Mr Anderson was robbed . . . ." (Census and Administration from Joyce S Jewitt, Hamburg NY; she and her husband compiled and published "Genealogical Extractions of Canadians in Erie County NY". He is a descendant of Tjerck DeWitt, Andries line, through Garton DeWitt, Loyalist to Cornwall ON. Their family name had been changed from Dewitt to Jewitt.

Upper Canada Land Petitions "D" Bundle 13, 1820-1823 (RG 1, L 3, Vol. 156, pt. 1) p45,45a,45b.
To his Excellency Sir. Peregrine Maitland K.C.B. Lieutenant Governor of the Province of Upper Canada –
In Council
The Petition of Peter Dewitt of the Township
Of Stamford, Yoeman
Humbly Shewith

That your Petitioner is a native subject of his Majesty being born at Hudson in the late Province of New York in the year 1771 -- (sic) That your petitioner's father served His Brittannic Majesty during the greatest part of the American Revolutionary War -- That at the Peace of 1783 your Petitioner with his father went and Settled in the Province of New Brunswick where your Petitioner resided 20 years after which he returned to Hudson and came into this Province in the year 1811 where he has since resided. That your Petitioner from having a large family to support and unable to purchase land is therefore anxious to receive some from your Excellency and he has never drew or applied for any in New Brunswick therefore prays that Your Excellency may be pleased to Grant him upon as favourable term as possible such portion of the waste lands of the Crown as to Your Excellency may seem meet and Your Petitioner as in duty bound will ever pray -- -- --   LS (lawful signature)
Stamford Peter Dewitt (his handwriting) January 9: 1823

I certify that Peter Dewit a neighbor of mine is a most industrious and good moral man and that I verily believe what Peter Lampman States in the annexed certificate as the loyalty of the Petitioner and his father, to be Correct
Thomas Clark J.P.
D 13   Petition of Peter Dewitt No. 45 for a Grant of Land Gov House 1st February 1823 Referred to the Sur [Surveyor] General for his Report for the Information of the Hrnbl [Honourable] Ex [Executive] Council by Command W Hilten I do not know that the Petitioner has received any land or order for land
Sur Office   Thos Ridout
3 Feb 1823   Surgne [Surveyor General]
Entd in Land Book   page 366
In Council 6th February 1823 recommend for one or two hundred acres as ----
I of Petitioner PM Order after 14 February 1823 WDP

DeWITT
1.1.9.4.5.1 JACOBUS/JAMES DeWITT m Catharine Edwards

1 JACOBUS/JAMES DeWITT b 29 Apr 1795 bp 14 Jun 1795 sp Peter DeWitt & Jane Persen (RDCOH:3 [Reformed Dutch Church Oak Hill Durham T Greene Co NY]) res Walsingham T Norfolk Co ON in 1818 (d 14 Oct 1831) m Gertrude b 1795/6 USA. They res at Port Royal ON. In 1851 census Gertrude is with her son Edgar. She was Baptist
2 LUKE/ELUCAS DeWITT b 01 Oct 1797 bp 08 Oct 1797 (grprt) sp Lucas DeWitt & Deborah Persen (RDCOH:7) res Durham T Greene Co NY m Mary/Polly Williams b 1794. He received a Quit Claim 10 Apr 1834 at Walsingham ON but later returned to the States. His Cemetery Plot number at Fairview Cem, Annawan IL is Lot #235.
3 CHARLES DeWITT b 17 Mar 1800 bp 04 May 1800 no sp (RDCOH:11) wf maybe was Elizabeth b 1798 d 1871 Charlotteville Twp Norfolk Co ON.
4 SALLY ANN DeWITT b 16 Nov 1802 bp 19 Dec 1802 no sp (RDCOH:15).
5 WALTER DeWITT b 24 Mar 1805 bp 14 Apr 1805 no sp (RDCOH:20) m 31 Dec 1834 Catherine Burger both Walsingham by banns, wits Edward Dickenson, Henry Barrett (NCMR:64 taken fr London Dist (ON) Mar Rec 1833-55). He was a Baptist, a wdr in 1851 census, his chn res with others.
6 ELIZA JANE DeWITT b 09 Feb 1807 bp 15 Mar 1807 no sp (RDCOH:23).
7 JANE DeWITT b 27 Mar 1809 bp 09 Apr 1809 no sp (RDCOH:27).
8 EDWARDS DeWITT b 22 Jul 1811 bp 04 May 1811 (sic) no sp (RDCOH:33).
9 IRA DeWITT b 23 May 1814 bp 26 Jun 1814 no sp (RDCOH:37).

Leucas deWit

YOUNG
1.1.9.4.5.2 CATHARINE DeWITT m Jeremiah/ Jeremy Young
1. SALLY YOUNG b 02 Feb 1804 bp 18 Mar 1804 no sp (RDCOH:19).
2. NANCY YOUNG b 18 Jul 1807 bp 09 Aug 1807 no sp (RDCOH:24) ma is 41, no other chn found.

DeWITT
1.1.9.4.5.3 JOHN DeWITT m Hannah Egbertsen/Abbison/Egburts
1. PETER DeWITT b 13 Jan 1803 bp 13 Feb 1803 Durham, Greene Co NY no sp (RDCOH:16) d before 1844 wf not recorded. Note his pa's Will in GEN 6
2. AARON CORNELIUS DeWITT b 21 Jan 1804 bp 10 Feb 1804 no sp (RDCOH:19). *Found an Aaron B Dewitt wf Maria Dupuy son John Charles b 20 Jun 1834 (DRCFU:34).
3. HENRY DeWITT b 22 Jul 1807 bp 09 Aug 1807 no sp (RDCOH:24) m Eliza Ann b 1811 Rensselaer Co NY res Greene Co 16, yrs State Census 1855 Greene Co NY, Henry DeWitt landholder, farmer, butcher, b Durham T Greene Co NY (NYDCG:80).
4. MARGARET/PEGGY MARIA DeWITT bp 06 Nov 1809 m Gideon Howland, (Bible rec as Margaret [RDCOH:29; fr OLD]).
5. DANIEL DeWITT b 24 Dec 1814 bp 25 Aug 1814 (RDCOH:38) m Catherine Pike res Waldron, Orange Co NY.
6. HARRIETT DeWITT b 02 Jun 1817 bp 30 Nov 1817 no sp Oak Hill, Durham T Greene Co (RDCOH:41) & (d 17 Apr 1885 ae 68-0-00) {m} 16 Nov 1843 (HGC:426) 1.1.9.4.2.3.9 Simeon/Simon Peter DeWitt (K&S: 268) s/o Abram DeWitt & Catharine Dederick, b 03 Feb 1809 bp 12 Feb 1809 (K&S: 156) d 21 Jan 1899 ae 90-11-18. Both bur on the DeWitt Farm, Mt Marion.
7. ADELIA ANN/DELLIA DeWITT b 22 Feb 1820 bp (RDCOH:41 (d 1893]) m 1840 Blake Wales Jr s/o Dr Blake Wales & Phoebe Reynolds, b 1815 d 1884.
8. ORLEAN DeWITT based on pa (John)'s Will. 1855 census lists Isreal's nephew who res with him, called Orlean DeWitt ae 10 b 09 Sep 1843 Schoharie but lived in Greene since 1850 suggesting he was an orphan. Added info Orlean m Jerusha Case (DFUSC:98 fr. DAR 52:242 #51552).
9. ISREAL DeWITT b 01 Jan 1823 bp 03 May 1823 (RDCOH:42) & (d 1900) m Elsie Thorne b 1839 res Durham T Greene Co NY. Note the 16 yr ae difference.
10. ALEXANDER/ELEXANDER DeWITT b 01 Oct 1826 bp 03 Dec 1826 (RDCOH:43) The Bible record seems to show "ORLEAN De WITT b 09 Sep 1843 m Jerusha Case" as a child of John & Hannah; not so, as Hannah would be 57 by then. More info under Isreal, Generation 7.
John DeWitt of Durham Will Pro 22 Jan 1844 heirs wife Hannah, sons Isreal, Alexander, Orlean, Henry, Daniel, daus Maria wf/o Gideon Howland, Delia wf/o Blake Wales, Harriet, deceased, son Peter's heirs--Edward, Albert, Mariah, John. Exs: Orlean DeWitt, Daniel Jones, Isreal DeWitt (AWGNY 1:70).

DeWITT
1.1.9.4.5.4 PETER DeWITT m Jane Person
1. ANNETJE DeWITT b 01 Oct 1795 bp 01 Nov 1795 sp Isaac Van Garder, Annatie Queen (DRCOH:4).
2. JACOBUS DeWITT bp 17 Sep 1798 Katsbaan.
3. ABRAHAM DeWITT b 24 Sep 1800 bp 07 Dec 1800 no sp (DRCOH:12).
4. LUCAS DeWITT b 03 May 1803 bp 29 May 1803 no sp as "Lucas IV" (DRCOH:16).
5. ELIZA DeWITT b 08 Nov 1806 bp 11 Jan 1807 no sp (RDCOH:23).

WEST/SPENCER
1.1.9.4.5.5 DEBORAH/DEBBE DeWIT m1 William West
1. ELIZABETH WEST b 10 Jan 1795 bp 22 Feb 1795 sp Peter West, Elizabeth Richtmeyer (RDCOH:3).
2. WILLIAM WEST b 18 Aug 1798 bp 26 Aug 1798 no sp (RDCOH:8).
3. CATHERINE WEST b 25 Dec 1800 bp 11 Jan 1801 no sp (RDCOH:12).
4. PETER WEST b 29 Mar 1803 bp 08 May 1803 no sp (RDCOH:16).
5. JANE WEST b 15 Feb 1805 bp 14 Apr 1805 no sp (RDCOH:19).
6. SALLY ANN WEST b 08 Jan 1807 bp 01 Feb 1807 no sp (RDCOH:23).
7. JAMES WEST b 14 Feb 1811 bp 04 May 1811 no sp (RDCOH:33).
8. SILENCE ESTHER WEST b 09 Jul 1812 bp 15 May 1814 no sp (RDCOH:37).
   m2 1813 Chester Spencer
9. JAMES HORATIO SPENCER b 22 Apr 1814 bp 10 Jul 1814 (RDCOH:37).

OSTERHOUD
1.1.9.4.7.1 HENDRICUS/HENDRIKUS/HENDRICK/HENRY OSTERHOUT/OOSTERHOUDT {m} 1.1.9.1.5.8 Geertje/Charity Winne/Winna
Children are with their Mother's underlined number Generation 7.

HOFF
1.1.9.4.7.2 CATHARINA OSTERHOUT m Cornelis Hoff
1. PIETER HOFF b 17 Jan 1811 bp 16 Mar 1811 no sp (K&S:163).

2   WILLIAM HOFF b 22 Sep 1813 bp 19 Dec 1813 no sp (K&S:174).
3   JAN HOFF b 09 Jun 1816 bp 14 Jul 1816 no sp (K&S:183).

Early History of Saugerties "between Katsbaan and Saugerties the house of Hendrick Osterhout where long afterwards will dwell Cornelius Hoff"... "Before we reach the vicinity of the Katsbaan Church we come into a great forest of imimmense white oaks for a mile each way over the flats toward West Camp. Trees are tremendous girth, height and age. Few will still remain in 1900 by the Katsbaan Church but the spreading forest will be cleared by the great grandson of Cornelis Hoff who will reside in 1900 on the Canoe Hill Road" (EHS:88,101). West Camp became Loonenburgh, then Athens NY.

KESS
1.1.9.4.7.3 MARIA OSTERHOUT * m Silvanus Kess
1   JANNETJE KESS b 02 Sep 1798 bp 25 Sep 1798 sp Samuel Kess, Deborah Kess (K&S:123)

OSTERHOUT
1.1.9.4.7.5 LUCAS OSTERHOUD m Jacomina/Jacomyntje Jongh/Young
1   MARIA OSTERHOUT/OOSTERHOUT b 07 Nov 1800 bp 22 Feb 1801 (K&S:133).
2   JACOBUS OSTERHOUT b 02 Dec 1802 bp 15 Mar 1803 sp Jacobus Osterhout & Annatje Young (K&S:141).

OSTERHOUT
1.1.9.4.7.6 JACOBUS/COBUS OSTERHOUT m Eunice/Teunis Sharp/Ferp
1   CATY MARIA OSTERHOUT b 21 May 1811 bp 10 Nov 1811 sp Samuel Burhans & Catharina Beer (K&S:166).
2   SILVAN JEREMIAS OSTERHOUT b 05 Sep 1813 bp 30 Jan 1814 sp Jacobus Burhans, Eunice Sharp (K&S:174).

LOUW
1.1.9.4.8.2 ABRAHAM DeWITT (LOUW JR) m Elisabet/Elizabeth Schaert/Scort/Short/Sjart
1   ANNATJE LOW bp 14 May 1786 sp Hendrick Short, Marytje Low (K&S:82).
2   RACHEL LOUW b 20 Apr 1788 sp (grprts) Abraham Louw, Rachel De Witt (K&S:87) m 06 Mar 1803 Zacharias Conyes both Plattekill (K&S:258).
3   PETRUS LOUW bp 28 Aug 1790 sp Petrus Louw, Catharina Schaart (K&S:93).
4   MARIA LOUW bp 30 Feb 1793 sp Ebenezer Roosa, Rachel Schaart (DRCK:438).
5   WILLEM LOUW b 19 Mar 1795 bp 24 May 1795 sp (aunt & hus) Willem Wideker, Catharina Louw (K&S:108).
6   ELIZABETH LOUW b 18 Sep 1797 bp 05 Nov 1797 sp (aunt & hus) Johannes Bakker Jr Elizabeth Louw (K&S:119).
7   LEA LOUW bp 20 June 1800 no sp (DRCK:466).
8   WYNTJE LOUW b 03 Nov 1802 bp 31 Jan 1803 sp (uncle & aunt) Levi Louw, Wyntje Louw (K&S:140) & (d 20 Nov 1871 ae 67-11-17) m 24 Jan 1824 Jonas Meyer, both Saugerties (K&S:272) b 30 Mar 1803 d 30 Jul 1860 ae 57-10- 00 both bur Saugerties Mountain View Cem (OGUC:238).
9   ABRAHAM A LOW b 28 Aug 1806 (d 01 Dec 1863) at Saugerties info Burhans Genealogy (BG:45) m Margaret Eva Brink d/o Robert Livingston Brink & Elizabeth Falkenburgh, (PRDC:74) b 02 May 1812 d 29 Dec 1884 (BG:45,73/4). Abraham A Low adm (to Plattekill RDC) CH 27 Dec 1846 on conf d 1863 (PRDC:74).

VAN BUNSCHOOTEN
1.1.9.4.8.4 MARYTJE LOUW m Petrus Elmondus Van Bunschooten
1   SAARTJE VAN BUNSCHOOTEN b 31 Oct 1794 bp 03 Jan 1795 no sp (K&S:107).
2   LAKIE VAN BUNSCHOOTEN bp 14 Jun 1799 at Woodstock no sp (K&S:125).

LOUW
1.1.9.4.8.5 PETRUS LOUW m Elisabet/Elizabeth Coenius/Conjes/Conyes/Cunyes
1   ELIZABETH LOUW b 28 Feb 1796 bp 19 Mar 1796 sp (grprts) Abraham De Witt Louw, Elizabeth Sjord/Scort (K&S:112).
2   PEGGIE LOUW b & bp 27 Jan 1798 sp Frederick Conjes, Grietje Schneider (K&S:120).
3   ANNATJE LOUW b 21 Jun 1801 bp 11 Jul 1801 no sp (K&S:134).
4   LUCAS ELMDORF LOW b 05 Nov 1816 (DRCFU:10). Where did they live the 15 years between the chn b in Katsbaan/Saugerties & the Flatbush bp?

BAKKER
1.1.9.4.8.6 ELISABETH LOW m Johannes Bakker/Baker Jr
1   ABRAHAM BAKKER b 16 Apr 1798 bp 16 May 1798 sp (grprts) Abraham Louw, Rachel DeWit (K&S:121).
2   ANNATJE BAKKER b 24 Oct 1800 bp 06 Dec 1800 sp Jan Mains, Annatje Bakker (K&S:132).
3   ELIZABETH BAKER b 13 Jan 1803 bp 18 Feb 1803 sp Johannes Baker, Elizabeth Wolven (K&S:140).
4   JOHANNES BECKER b 22 Apr 1808 bp 05 Jun 1808 sp John Valkenberg, Neeltje Snyder (K&S:155).
5   PETRUS BACKER b 04 Dec 1810 bp 21 Jan 1811 no sp (K&S:163).
6   NELLY BACKER b 07 Apr 1813 bp 16 May 1813 no sp (K&S:172).

WHITAKER
1.1.9.4.8.7 CATHARINA LOUW m Willem/William Widdeker/Whitaker Jr
1   ELIZABETH WIDDEKER b 29 Sep 1795 bp 08 Nov 1795 sp (uncle & wf) Petrus Louw, Elizabeth Conjes (K&S:110).
2   LEVI WITTAKER bp 20 May 1798 sp (uncle & aunt) Levi Louw, Weintje Louw (DRCK:459).

Leucas deWit

3   JAN WIDDEKER b 26 Aug 1800 bp 17 Sep 1800 sp Jan Post, Annetje Volland (K&S:131).
4   PETRUS WITTAKER bp 26 Jan 1804 sp Petrus Wittaker Jr, Margrit Minckelaer (DRCK:479).
5   RACHEL WITTAKER bp 07 Sep 1806 sp (grprts) Abraham Louw, Rachel Dewitt (DRCK:488).
6   WILLIAM WHITAKER b 22 Jan 1812 bp 16 Feb 1812 no sp (K&S:167).

LOW

1.1.9.4.8.8 JAN A LOW m Helena/Lena/Lany Felton
1   LUCAS LOUW bp 20 Dec 1805 no sp (DRCK:486) m 06 Mar 1828 Margaret Sagar.
2   TOBYAS LOUW bp 14 Dec 1808 no sp (DRCK:495).
3   MARGARET/PEGGY/PAGY LOUW b 07 Jul 1809 (WHS 14:20) m 28 Nov 1828 Levi Sagar.
4   JOHN LOUW m 17 Feb 1831 Mary Jackson.
5   POLLY LOUW b 01 Sep 1814 b 12 Oct 1814 no sp (K&S:177). LMB says Peggy & Polly may be one person.
6   CHARK/TJIRCK LOUW (Tierck/Tjerck was pronounced Charick) b 11 Mar 1817 Katsbann, Ulster Co NY & (d 25 May 1896 of Bright's Disease bur Buxton Cem Watkin's Christian CH, Dover Twp Union Co OH). At Dover m 25 Nov 1843 Charlotte McClung d/o Joseph McClung & Margaret Conner. [WHS 14:25]. She d 26 Nov 1852 bur Old Darby T Union Co near Plain City, Madison OH. He m2 26 Nov 1853 Phoebe Jane Beck b 15 Jul 1837 bp 27 Jan 1838 d/o Abraham Beck & Mary Jane Doty also of Dover T. Phoebe d of Consumption 28 Apr 1866 bur with her hus (fr LBM research Union, Madison OH Rec, IGI, m certificate, Newspapers).
7   ELIZA LOUW b Pickaway or Madison OH m 11 Aug 1844 Washington Taylor.

CONYES/CUNYES/COENIUS

1.1.9.4.8.9 RACHEL LOUW m Zacharias Conyes
1   ANNA ELIZABETH CONYES b 04 Aug 1804 bp 09 Sep 1804 sp Elizabeth Low (K&S:146). * An Eliza Conyes w/o John Anderson, adm 04 Sep 1857 on conf at Plattekill dis 12 Jan 1858 to RDC 23rd St. NY d & bur at Platterkill, 01 Dec 1882 (PRDC:69).
2   PEGGY/MARGARET COENIUS bp 24 Sep 1807 sp Frederick Coenius, Peggy Snyder (DRCK:492) m Peter Brink. Margaret (Conyes) adm 05 Dec 1856 at Plattekill CH on conf at F Lowes (PRDC:69).
3   RACHEL JANE CONYES b 13 Aug 1810 bp 23 Sep 1810 no sp (K&S:162).
4   JACOB HENRY CUNIAS b 22 May 1818 (DRCFU: 12) & (d 08 Jul 1886) m Cornelia Osterhoudt b 12 May 1822 d 07 Jun 1895 both bur Mt Marion Cem (OGUC:251) Cornelia Osterhoudt w/o Jacob Henry Conyes adm to Plattekill DRC 04 Jun 1841 on conf (PRDC:680) d 07 Jun 1895.
5   SALLY/SARAH CATHERINE CUNIAS b 17 Nov 1822 (DRCFU:19) & (tbstn b 17 Oct 1822 d 02 Dec 1885). Sarah Conyes adm to Plattekill CH on conf 02 Jun 1877 (PRDC:77) m 17 Jul 1847 Elias Osterhoudt (PRDC:4) both of Saugerties Wit: Frederick B Low, S Ferguson, b 26 Jul 1821 d 19 Jan 1896 bur Mt Marion Com Cem (OGUC:253)

FELTEN/VELTEN

1.1.9.4.8.10 WYNTJE/WENTCHE LOW m Laurens/Larance Velten/Felten/Felte
1   ZACHARIAS FELTEN b 21 Feb 1806 bp 06 Apr 1806 sp (aunt & hus) Zachariah Coenius, Rachel Louw (DRCK:486) m Elizabeth Ackert (PRDC:25).
2   POLLY FELTEN b 17 Aug 1809 (WHS 14:20).

SCHOONMAKER

1.1.9.4.8.11 JANNETJE/JANE LOUW m Tjerck E Schoonmaker
1   CHRISTIAN SCHOONMAKER b 16 Apr 1808 bp 08 May 1808 sp David Schoonmaker, Sarah Valkenburg (K&S:155) & (d 27 Nov 1875 bur Round Top Cem Cairo NY) m 29 Sep 1833 Silvia Marquiet b 30 Jan 1809 d 20 Dec 1894 (P-DRS:396).
2   RACHEL SCHOONMAKER b 01 Nov 1809 bp 06 Dec 1809 sp (grprts) Abraham Louw, Rachel DeWitt (K&S:159).
3   SALLY ELIZA SCHOONMAKER b 01 Sep 1811 bp 03 Oct 1811 sp Petrus Low, Sarah Hommel (K&S:165).
4   ABRAHAM EDWARDS SCHOONMAKER b 07 Apr 1813 bp 03 Jun 1813 sp Edward Schoonmaker, Annetje Schoonmaker (K&S:172) d 04 Jul 1848 Poughkeepsie.
5   TJERCK SHOEMAKER b 25 May 1816 bp 29 Jun 1816 sp Jan Shoemaker, Christina Reghtmeyer (K&S:183).
6   JOHN BRINCK SCHOONMAKER b 06 Nov 1820 (WHS 15:18)

LOUW

1.1.9.4.8.12 LEVI LOUW m Margaret Kool/Cole
1   ABRAHAM LOUW b 11 Nov 1811 bp 03 Dec 1811 sp Zachariah Kool, Betsy Kool (K&S:166).
2   JAMES LOUW b 18 Mar 1815 bp 18 Apr 1815 no sp (K&S:178) m Margaret.
3   RACHEL ANN LOUW bp 03 Apr 1819 (DRCFU:14) of Kingston m 24 Mar 1860 Titus Van Hovenburg of Saugerties Wit: James Low, Richard France (PDRC:10).

GENERATON 7
DEDRICK

1.9.4.1.2.? * SAMUEL DEDRICK m Lucy Watt

* THERESA DEDRICK b res Walsingham Norfolk Twp Co ON , by Rev W H Haviland m 15 Mar 1868 James R Backhouse b res Malahide Co, Wit: Mark Watt. **Placing of this family is unknown.**

*JAMES W DEDRICK (as son of Samuel, Bayview Cem Port Dover ON) b 13 Mar 1865 (d 17 Jul 1939 ae 74-04-01) m Inez b 1869 d 05 Apr 1939 ae 70. Their son *Roy was b 20 Dec 1888 (Bayview Cem Rec).

DEDRICK

1.1.9.4.1.2.1 JOHN DEDRICK m Harriet Fick

1 JOHN DEDRICK
2 CHARLES DEDRICK inherited the front part of the old homestead.
3 ABRAHAM/ABRAM DEDRICK b 1819 Canada West s/o John Dedrick [d 07 Aug 1833] & Harriet, res Bayham T Norfolk Co ae given as 27 m 21 Dec 1862 Maryann Park b 1830 ae as 16 res Walsingham CW, by J Clulton, wit: John A Stearn (NCMR: 312). Abram is not in the will but he would be only 14 though perhaps he had left home. Jane & Susan also are not mentioned. The 1898 Pioneer Sketches of Long Point Settlement might be in error or they were disinherited or dy. A copy of the original Will might help.
4 WILLIAM DEDRICK. There are 2 William Dedricks. One at Port Rowan m 07 Oct 1855 Helen M Hutchinson 3rd d/o A W B Hutchinson, Esq, at the res of the bride, by Rev Wm McDermond (NCMR:162).
5 CATHARINE DEDRICK m Benjamin Welch s/o Zeal Welch & Hannah Mead, res in Walsingham. Benjamin m2 Rebecca Jewel (PSLPS:446)
6 JANE DEDRICK. One Jane m 25 Dec 1850 Abraham Countryman both of Walsingham, by H Fitch; wit: W T Hollingwood, William Dedrick (note a bro William [NCMR:112]). In Walsingham T there were two men, Abraham Countryman on Con A lots 14 & 15 and Abraham J Countryman on Con A Lot 8 s/o Philip Countryman Con A Lot 9, in the 1867 Norfolk and Oxford Gazetteer.
7 HANNAH DEDRICK b 1827 d 04 Apr 1899 Port Rowan ON **single** (Br Can Newspaper 12 Apr 1899).
8 HARRIET DEDRICK
9 SUSAN DEDRICK (this family fr PSLPS:35).

Wills of the London District 1800-1839 London District Surrogate Registry Norfolk Hist So. Editor William Yeager 1977 p 223 John Dedrick Walsingham d 07 Aug 1833 at Walsingham. Will 01 Apr 1831 wf Harriet/Hariet; son John, Charles, youngest son William, daus Catharine, Jane, Hannah. Exs: bro Cornelius Dedrick, friend Hugh A B Michael, wife Harriet Dedrick. There were 2 Jane Dedricks. One m 25 Dec 1850 Abraham Countryman both of Walsingham, by H Fitch, W T Hollingwood, William Dedrick (NCMR:112).

DEDRICK

1.1.9.4.1.2.2 CORNELIUS DEDRICK m Nancy Spurgin/Spurgeon

1 LUKE DEDRICK. One Lucas Dedrick m Jemima Backhouse (PSLPS:537). Will 16 Jul 1844 of Henry Webster Town of Simcoe mentions Jemima Dedrick w/o Lucas Dedrick, d/o Thomas Backhouse, Esq & Amelia Young LPS:225).
2 SAMUEL DEDRICK b 24 May 18 ? (d 03 Sep 18[58] ae 67-03-10, impossible! his father was 3 in 1791; maybe a weathered tbstn, 1888 more likely or a typographical error; Bayview Cem, Port Rowan ON fr Norfolk Museum) m1 Sarah; Samuel Dedrich of Walsingham m2 26 Oct 1846 Lucy Watt of Charlotteville by W McDermond, wit: Henry Killmaster, Isaac Brown (NCMR:98). Lucy m ae 25, b 25 Jul 1821 d 21 Sep 1892 ae 67- 01-27 bur Bayview Port Rowan Cem.
3 WILLIAM W DEDRICK b 1823 (LPS:58)
4 HANNAH C DEDRICK b 08 Apr 1824 Port Rowan (d there 03 Apr 1901) ae 37 (she lost 3 yrs!) m 27 Mar 1864 Ethiel Davis ae 40, b 1824, by S McConnell, wit: Auston Didrick (sic) (NCMR: 230 Elgin Co M Reg 1858-69.
5 SALLY DEDRICK; a Sarah Dedrick m 01 May 1851 John D Backhouse, both Walsingham, s/o Thomas Backhouse & Amelia Young, by H Fitch, wit: J B Culver, Thomas Backhouse (PSLPS:537; NCMR:116 Talbot Dist M Reg 1837-57)
6 AUSTIN DEDRICK b 1835 (d 04 Sep 1906 ae 71) b/r Walsingham m 24 Dec 1865 Melissa Dench b/r Port Rowan d/o Isaac Dench & Margaret, b 1844 d 1921. They were m by W H Haviland, wit: Joseph Raymond (NCMR:342) both bur Bay View Cem Port Rowan ON.
7 NANCY LUCRETIA DEDRICK b 1826 (LPS:58) as Nancy Lucretia d/o Cornelius Dedrick & Margaret (sic) m 15 Dec 1858 Joseph Cattle, both Walsingham, s/o John Cattle & Ann, by J de Poors, wit: John H Backhouse, Austin C Dedrick (her bro [NCMR:267 fr Norfolk Co Reg 1858-69]).
8 JERUSHA JANE DEDRICK b 1827, youngest dau of the late Deacon C Dedrick & Nancy, all of Walsingham CW, at ae 26 m 23 Dec 1863 Thomas M Smith ae 24 of Canada West b 1829, at the r/o the bride's ma, by Rev Joseph Clulton Wit: Austin C. Dedrick (NCMR:168, 322). Note a Thomas Smith is also given as m Lucretia Backhouse d/o John Backhouse & Hannah Dedrich.
9 LOUISE J DEDRICK b 1837 (LPS:58).

There are 2 William Dedricks. One at Port Rowan m 07 Oct 1855 Helen M Hutchinson 3rd d/o A W B Hutchinson, Esq at the res of the bride, by Rev Wm McDermond.

Leucas deWit

STEARNS/COUNTRYMAN

1.1.9.4.1.2.3 CATHARINE DEDRICK m1 Austin Stearns

Austin Stearns had a son John by a previos m & **no chn** with Catherine.

m2 Abraham Countryman

1. VALETTA/VIOLET COUNTRYMAN of Port Rowan m Edward Backhouse s/o William Backhouse & Hannah McMichael, (PSLPS:536) moved to Bowling Green KY.
2. FEDELLA/ADELLA COUNTRYMAN m 12 Nov 1852 John Alexander Coates, G J Ryerse M Reg 1831-37; wit: Simon Maybe, Hubbard Davis (NCMR:59,122).

* An Abraham Countryman m2 23 Dec 1832 Clarissa Woodroof, both Walsingham, by W McDermond; wit: Corns Dedrick, Wm Franklin (NCMR:27, London Dist M 1800-33). Their dau dau Helen b 1834 at ae 27 m 12 Aug 1861 Robert Biddle ae 23 (NCMR:299,395)
* An Abraham Countryman yoeman, wdr, applied 25 Mar 1837 to m3 Lucy Smith, spinster, both Walsingham (NCMR: 436 Upper Canada M Bonds). Their chn were Lavina m ? Dibble & Nettie m Louis Fick

BACKHOUSE

1.1.9.4.1.2.4 HANNAH DEDRICK m John Backhouse Jr

1. LUCRETIA BACKHOUSE m 30 Apr 1832 Thomas Smith, both Walsinghem, Banns, wit: R Young, John Smith (PSLPS:536, NCMR:62 London M Reg 1833-55).
2. EMMA BACKHOUSE m Frederick Bouck (PSLPS:536).
3. JOHN DEDRICK BACKHOUSE m 03 Aug 1841 Sarah Ann McDermand (both Walsingham) b 1818 d 11 May 1876 d/o William McDemand, by Elder Joseph Merrill, Baptist CH Bayham; wit: Isaac Titus, John Backhouse (NCMR:70 London Dist M Reg 1833-55, PSLPS:536/7). John inherited the homestead.
4. ADELAIDE BACKHOUSE m 26 Sep 1855 Abram Brando, both Walsingham, by W McDermand, wit: Thomas Brando, Henry Killmaster (NCMR:137 Talbot Dist M Reg 1837-57).
5. CORNELIUS BACKHOUSE **single.**
6. MARY ANN BACKHOUSE m John Alexander (PSLPS:536).
7. HANNAH BACKHOUSE b 1827 (d 08 Jul 1861 ae 33-1-21 bur Port Rowan Cem). One Hannah m 21 Mar 1850 Frederick La Fortune both Walsingham by H Fitch, wit: John A Stearns, Thomas Backhoouse (PSLPS:536/7, NCMR:112).

DEDRICK

1.1.9.4.1.2.5 JAMES DEDRICK m Elizabeth Edwards

1. THOMAS DEDRICK twin of
2. JOHN W DEDRICK b 1829 (d 04 May 1900 ae 71) m Susan Elizabeth Miller b ca 1828 d 28 Nov 1909.
3. ELIZABETH DEDRICK of Walsingham m 20 Aug 1845 Edward Eager of Charlotteville by William McDermond, Wit: James Dedrick, Michael Landown (NCMR:99).
4. JANE DEDRICK
5. SALOME DEDRICK of Walsingham m 19 Apr 1854 William Ward, Charlotteville by H Fitch, wit: Jeremiah Johnson, Jacob Sovereign (NCMR:130). An Obit for a Mrs Ward in <u>Norfolk Newspaper Record</u> the "Simcoe Argus". Extracted by William Yeager 1986, p9 11 Feb 1886 news New Delhi. The funeral of Mrs William Ward (who died at her residence here on Fri last).
   There were 2 Janes. One Jane Dedrick m 25 Dec 1850 Abraham Countryman both Walsingham, by H Fitch wit: T H Hollingwood, William Dedrick NCMR:112. The other Jane seemed the probable one since her brother was Witness.

DEDRICK

1.1.9.4.1.2.6 LUCAS DEDRICK m Catherine Rohrer

1. CATHARINE DEDRICK b 1824 d 09 Sep 1857 in her 33rd yr. Catharine & Emma were witnesses at a wedding 12 May 1855 (NCMR:137) both bur family plot Mt Pleasant Cem.
2. CORNELIUS DEDRICK b 03 Jun 1827 (d 03 Nov 1854 ae 27-05-00) * at Charlotteville m 12 May 1852 Miss Caroline Brown both Walsingham, by A Duncan (NCMR:158). One Caroline Ditrick m 17 Oct 1855 James C Newkirk both Walsingham, by M Swan, wit: William S Brown, Hannah S Warisi (NCMR:136).
3. LUKE DEDRICK b 1829 d 13 Dec 1882 53rd yr, s/o Mrs Luke Dedrick (Br Can Newspaper 20 Dec 1882).
4. MARY DEDRICK b 1832 d 10 Mar 1842 10th yr **dy,**
5. NANCY AMELIA DEDRICK b 1832 d 16 Feb 1921 ae 79-11-00.
6. EMMA DEDRICK b 1837 d 25 Feb 1838 ae 1 yr **dy,**
7. EMMA E DEDRICK b 1838 d 12 Oct 1907 69th yr.
8. REBECCA DEDRICK
9. GEORGE W DEDRICK b 1853 d 03 Apr 1928 75th yr **single**, on the farm. All of Lucas Dedrick's chn settled in Walsingham T Norfolk Co ON.

DeWITT
1.1.9.4.2.1.1 PETER BREESTEED DeWITT m Hannah Levina
1. ANDREW DeWITT b & bp 02 Sep 1807 sp (grprts) John DeWitt, Maria DeWit (K&S: 151). One Andrew m Elizabeth Finney, communicants at Plattekill CH in 1848 (RRDC:61)
2. HORACE DeWITT bp 02 Sep 1808 m Eve at Hancock, Delaware Co NY in 1886. London Dist Mar 1800-1833 Norfolk Co ON, Jeremiah Wolfen m 06 Jun 1812 Catherine Wolfen at Walsingham one wit was Peter Br Dewitte.

DeWITT
1.1.9.4.2.1.2 Rev JOHN DeWITT D.D. the elder {m} Sarah Schoonmaker
1. SILAS JOHN DeWITT b 12 Jun 1810 (d 13 Oct 1859 Millstone NJ) m 03 Feb 1842 Louise Van Doren b 19 Mar 1824 d/o Dr Garrett Van Doren (P-DR:259).
2. JAMES DeWITT b 12 Mar 1812 d 03 Oct 1832 in China **single**. (P-DR:291)
3. JOHN CLINTON DeWITT b 20 Apr 1814 at Flatbush Ulster Co (DRCFU:9) & (d 21 Oct 1845 NYC) m 22 Oct 1835 Elsie Van Dyck b 05 Sep 1809 d/o Abraham Van Dyck & Catharine Bronk of Coxsackie d 01 Aug 1885 Selkirk. Clinton was a lawyer, moved to NYC in 1840 (P-DR:260).
4. MARY DeWITT b 20 Apr 1816 d 08 Apr 1818 **dy.**
5. MARY DeWITT b 19 Feb 1819 (d 15 Jan 1903 at Albany) m1 1843 Stephen Van Dyck b 1818 d 04 Apr 1846 ae 28; m2 17 Mar 1852 Philip Peltz at Coxsackie (P- DR:299).
6. JOHN DeWITT b 27 Jan 1820 d 20 Dec 1820 **dy.**
7. JOHN DeWITT D.D. the younger b 29 Nov 1821 (d 19 Oct 1906 Irvinton NY bur Evergreen Cem New Brunswick NJ) m 09 Jun 1847 Charlotte Lee Gillett b 20 Aug 1826 at Westfield MA d Dec 1893 d/o Hervey Gillett & Sophronia Spalding Lee (P-DR:260/7). Rev John remained in New Brunswick, NJ, graduating from Rutgers in 1838 and from the Seminary in 1842. The churches he served were Ridgeway MI, Ghent NY, Canajohorie NY, Millstone NJ. In 1863 he was named Prof of Biblical Lit in New Brunswick Seminary for 21 yrs and 8 more as Prof of Helenistic Greek.
8. SARAH DeWITT b 26 Jan 1824 (d 11 Sep 1894) {m} 30 Nov 1844 Tjerck Schoonmaker b 19 Mar 1820 d 27 Aug 1884 both bur Mt Marion Cem (fr Mt Marion tbstn P-DR Sup p356). Sarah DeWitt w/o Tjerck Schoonmaker adm (to Plattekill CH) on conf 29 Nov 1866) (PRDC:84).
(Chn Clinton to Theodore b Millstone NJ).
   m2 Anna Marie Bridgen
9. CHARLES BRIDGEN DeWITT b 18 Jul 1826 d 19 Aug 1827 **dy,**
10. HELEN LANSING DeWITT b 19 Sep 1827 New Brunswick NJ d 16 May 1903 Englewood NJ at Albany m 24 Nov 1847 Rev Ashbel Green Vermilye b 6 Sept 1822 Princeton d 08 Jul 1905 Englewood NJ s/o Rev Thomas E Vermilye & Elizabeth B Hazard.
11. CHARLES DeWITT b 07 Jan 1829 d 22 Sep 1829 **dy.**
12. ANNA MARIA DeWITT b 28 Mar 1830 Bound Brook NJ (d 01 Aug 1869 Spencer MA) m 25 Dec 1862 at Newburyport Rev James Cruickshanks b 12 Nov 1828 Haddington Scotland d 1889 s/o James Cruickshanks, came to America ae 12 res Chelsea MA (P-DR:312).
13. EDWARD LANSING DeWITT b 24 Nov 1813 d 02 Nov 1832 **dy.**

DeWITT
1.1.9.4.2.1.4. WILLAM HENRY DeWITT m Catherine Maria Ten Broeck/Tenbroek
1. JACOB TEN BROECK DeWITT b 29 May 1828 bp 23 Nov 1828 (CDDGC:102 & d1876) at b Brooklyn NY m 1851 Juliet Louise May b 1831 d 1873.
2. MARY JANE DeWITT b 22 Mar 1830 m 27 Oct 1851 Benjamin Townsend Hoagland b 1829 d 1890 s/o Col Benjamin R Hoagland, res Brooklyn NY.
3. JOHN DeWITT b 14 Aug 1832 d 23 Aug 1834 **dy,**
4. MARTIN VAN BUREN DeWITT b 19 Apr 1835 m 1864 Jane C Hover b 1840 d 1912 d/o Jonas Hover & Anna Sturges.
5. HELEN CHRISTINA DeWITT b 09 Apr 1838 m 29 Apr 1858 Everlin Beckley Hamlin b 14 Aug 1836 s/o Charles Roger Hamlin & Sarah Buckley **no chn,**
6. CATHARINE ANN DeWITT b 03 Apr 1841 (in 1870 census Catharine ae 29, a teacher) m 09 Sep 1873 at Germantown Isaac Carthart b 14 Mar 1815 s/o George Carhart & Mary Herbert of Brooklyn res at Germantown NY **no chn,**
7. ADA TEN BROECK DeWITT b 23 Jan 1843 (in 1870 census Ada ae 26, teacher) m 01 Feb 1883 Charles H Hover s/o Chauncey Hover & Julia Elmendorf **no chn,**
8. EUGENE B DeWITT b 12 Jul 1846 (d 1931) m 24 Jul 1870 Barbara Rosa Lasher b 1844 d 1923 d/o George T Lasher & Hannah Berringer.
Wills Columbia County, New York: Index 1 & 2; 1886 S p.201. William H DeWitt. Will 12 Apr 1883 Pro 17 Jun 1886 all real & personal property to wf Catharine Marie. Exs: dau Ada wf of Charles H Hover & son Eugene. Wills Columbia County, New York: Index 5; 1896 K218 p442. Catharine M DeWitt dated 22 Dec 1892 Town of Germantown recorded 25 Apr 1896 widow of William H DeWitt. $300.00 to Jane C DeWitt for my son Martin V B

DeWitt to be used by her for their joint use as she deems fit & proper. To grandchildren Frank H DeWitt & Ada B Hinckey, children of my son Jacob B Dewitt deceased, $100.00 each. Residue equally to daughters Mary Jane Hoogland, Helen C Hamlin, Kate A Carthart, Ada Hover & son Eugene. Exs: Eugene DeWitt & Ada Hover.

DeWITT

1.1.9.4.2.1.5 CHARLES T DeWITT m Jane C Ashley
1. MARY G DeWITT b 1843
2. DORR DeWITT b 1845.
3. ELIZA DeWITT b 1847
4. FRANKLIN DeWITT b 1849.
5. EMMA DeWITT b 1851.
6. JANE ANN DeWITT b 1853.
7. ROSE DeWITT b 1857 (all CDDGC:70).
   Wills Columbia Co NY Index 1 & 2; 1880 Q 426;
   Charles DeWitt, Germantown dated 13 May 1880 Pro 10 Jul 1880 estate to William H DeWitt & wf Catharine M DeWitt. Exs: George H Rockefeller & Eugene DeWitt. This will is signed with an "X" indicating some disability. Whatever happened to his wife and seven children since his brother and wife are his heirs?

DeWITT

1.1.9.4.2.1.6 HORACE DeWITT m Eve ? .
1. GEORGE DeWITT b 1837.
2. MARY DeWITT b 1845.
3. MATHEW DeWITT b 1847.
4. CHARLOTTE E DeWITT 1848.
5. JOHN C DeWITT b 1849 (all CDDGC:70).

OVERBAGH

1.1.9.4.2.2.1 MARYTIE VAN LEUVEN m Rev Peter A Overbagh
1. JOHN VAN LEUVEN OVERBAGH b 22 Oct 1806 Saugerties (PWHS:17) & (d 03 Oct 1853) m 06 Jan 1824 Caroline Verplanck b 07 Mar 1807 d 27 Nov 1895.
2. RACHEL ANN MARIE OVERBAGH b 03 Mar 1810 bp 03 May 1810 (RDCFU:3) & (d 13 May 1865 at Saugerties) at Katsbaan m1 08 Nov 1827 Stephen Nottingham Ostrander b 1804 d 1840 at Coxsackie, res Marbletown s/o Rev Henry Ostrander & Jane Nottingham; he became a doctor. Rachel was badly beaten by her husband 16 Jul 1839, confined to bed for a week before she could be moved. She left and filed a Bill of Complaint. Stephen's Will 09 Nov 1839 left his estate to his sister. He had Dropsy. It was said he took opium at that time. An out of Court settlement was reached on the estate. Rachel, at Kingston, m2 02 Jan 1842 her cousin Solomon Freligh Overbagh b 1819 d 16 Aug 1844; m3 19 Feb 1846 Capt William Teunis Swart b 20 Apr 1804 s/o Teunis Swart. William ran a sloop on the Hudson Glasco to NYC. He outlived his wife, d 06 Mar 1884 bur Wildwyck Cem.
3. TITUS OVERBAGH b 12 Apr 1813 d 12 Jun 1828 **dy**.
4. SARAH MARGARET OVERBAGH b 19 Sep 1818 Flatbush (d 08 Jun 1874 [RDCFU:12]) m Peter Osterhout.
5. LOUISA OVERBAGH b 11 Apr 1821 (d 26 Oct 1842) m 16 May 1840 Elijah Dubois (HGC:434/5; NYGBR 92:237) at Coxsackie.

DeWITT

1.1.9.4.2.3.1 LEVI DeWITT m Sarah/Sally Frolich/Freligh
1. ABRAHAM HENRY DeWITT b 15 Mar 1817 (RDCFU:11) d 19 Dec 1874 ae 57-09-04 (MDVEB).
2. JANE CATHARINE DeWITT b 23 Feb 1820 (RDCFU:15) m 12 May 1848 Lemuel Cunyes. As Catharine Jane w/o Leml Conyes adm 01 Mar 1861 on cert fr Flatbush (to Plattekill CH [PRDC:71]).
3. MOSES FRELIGH DeWITT bp 13 May 1822 (d 18 Jan 1879 ae 56-10-15 [MDVEB]) m 09 Nov 1850 Mary E Martin of Saugerties by the Rev RA Chalker (HGC:434/5).

OTIS

1.1.9.4.2.3.2 ANN ELIZABETH DeWITT m Seth K Otis
1. LUZILLA/LURETTA SOPHIA OTIS b 28 Nov 1829 (RDCFU:25) ma as Eliza.
2. CORA ELLEN OTIS b 18 Jan 1844 d 21 Jul 1866 ae 22-06-03 (MDVEB).

Abraham DeWitt's Pro in 1846 named dau Ann Eliza wf/o Seth K Otis "and her several children." Ann, Charles & Elizabeth all res with bro John DeWitt in 1855 Census; all said to have been in Windham from 1834.

VAN ETTEN

1.1.9.4.2.3.3 MARITJE DeWITT m Jonas Van Etten
1. CATHERINE MARIA VAN ETTEN bp 26 Feb 1813 m 20 Dec 1832 Samuel Freligh Woolven (RDCFU:91) b 14 Mar 1810 d 28 Jun 1894 ae 84-03-14.
2. SALLY ANN MARIA VAN ETTEN b 05 Oct 1816 bp 05 Nov 1816 no sp (K&S:185).
3. MARGARET ELOISA (ELIVA in the Bible) VAN ETTEN b 26 Nov 1819 as Peggy Eliza at Flatbush (RDCFU:15).

4 JOHN ABRAHAM VAN ETTEN b 17 May 1824 (MDVEB). John A Van Etten d 19 Sep 1855 ae 31-04-02 [OGUC:263] m Rachel C Myers d 16 Jan 1872 ae 41-10-03.

5 RACHEL CHRISTINA VAN ETTEN b 17 Sep 1829 (d 28 May 1898 bur Lowther Farm Mt Marion (GIUC:3) m Fred Miles.

6 MARTHA JANE VAN ETTEN b 21 Oct 1831 (DRCFU:26) bible b 21 Oct 1832 d 26 Apr 1872 ae 42-04-28) m George J Cornish.

The Bible Record lists Winslow DeWitt Van Etten b 15 Mar 1854, presumed son of John A Van Etten. The next entry is John Abram Van Etten b 19 Dec 1885.

DeWITT
1.1.9.4.2.3.5 ANDRIES/ANDREW DeWITT m Mary/Polly Van Etten

1 ANN ELIZA DeWITT b 27 Nov 1818 (RDCFU:13 ma as Sally) {m} Jeremiah Wolven; note Ann Eliza Dewitt w/o Jeremiah Wolven adm 03 Sep 1848 on Conf d 18 Mar 1866 ae 47-03-20 (b 29 Nov 1818 [PDRC:70]).

2 JAMES VAN ETTEN DeWITT b 17 Feb 1821 (DRCFU:17) {m} (1.1.9.1.4.4.1.2) Christina Catharine Langendyke b/bp 27 Jun 1824 (WHS) d/o Peter Langendyk & Maria Plass. Saugerties Telegraph 1848-1852: 08 Dec 1949 issue. "On Tuesday afternoon Mr. James DeWitt of this town hung himself, 25/26 years of age, leaving a wife and three small children, the youngest four days old." Death Records of Ulster Co NY 1847-1850 p59. James DeWitt d 04 Dec 1849, of Saugerties, ae 28, farmer, suicide (ch bp PDRC:30; WHS:17).

3 ABRAHAM DeWITT b 12 May 1823 (d 19 Oct 1881 ae 58-08-07) m Rebecca C Van Aken b 1824 d 10 Apr 1891 ae 66-06-16 both bur Mt Marion Com Cem (OGUC:251).

4 PETER DeWITT b 1825 m Helen James both of Saugerties Wit: Jacobus Carle, Mrs Jacobus Carle (as Hellen Griswold [DFUSC:99 DAR Rec] & as Ellen G James). Peter Dewitt adm (to Plattekill CH) 01 Jun 1855 on conf dis to ME CH of Saugerties (PDRC:70). Helen James w/o Peter DeWitt adm 03 Dec 1858 dis to ME CH etc.

5 HENRY DeWITT b 1837.

DeWITT
1.1.9.4.2.3.9 SIMON/SIMEON PETER DeWITT m Harriet DeWitt 1.1.9.4.5.3.6

1 CLINTON DeWITT b 11 Oct 1844 d 21 Jul 1861 ae 16-10-16 **single**. 1861 Saugerties Telegraph Obits p15 21 July: Esopus Creek, one and a half miles above this village, Clinton DeWitt, 17, son of Simeon P DeWitt & John W Dowling, 16, son of James Dowling of Plattekill, in this town, drowned.

2 HOWARD DeWITT

3 ISREAL A DeWITT b 1850 "music dealer Chillicothe, OH" (CBRUC:574).

4 HELEN G DeWITT b 18 Mar 1846 d 21 Oct 1882 ae 36-07-03 **single**.

5 SMON PETER DeWITT d ae 30-11-18 on the farm.

6 CATHARINE/KATE DeWITT m 21 Nov 1877 Christopher S Lowther s/o James Lowther & Eliza Allin. Catharine's father inherited the 108-acre farm handed down from John L DeWitt, & as a general farm & extensive fruit growing, became known as the Lowther Farm.

7 DANIEL DeWITT b 02 Jun 1848 bp 13 Feb 1849 d 15 Apr 1867 ae 18-02-02 on the farm, **single**.

8 SARAH E DeWITT

BURHANS
1.1.9.4.2.5.2 GERRITJE NEWKERK VAN KEUREN m Edward Burhans

1 MARIE BURHANS b 23 Oct 1831 m 08 Sep 1857 Richard Wynkoop Tappen s/o George Tappen & Anna, Kierstedt Brocton NY. b at Kingston 22 Jan 1798 and d 14 Sep 1866 at Brocton, NY.

2 CATHARINE ANN BURHANS b 10 Feb 1833 m 25 Aug 1858 Ephriam Burhans b 29 Apr 1829 s/o James Burhans & Margaret Burhans.

3 SARAH JANE BURHANS b 19 Oct 1834 m 24 Dec 1856 John Kiefer b 16 Jul 1835 s/o John Kiefer & Louisa Heiser.

4 ELIZABETH BURHANS b 31 Mar 1837 m 31 Mar 1864 George Sagendorf b 29 Dec 1835 s/o Jeremiah Sagendorf & Catharina Clum.

5 EDWINA BURHANS b 31 Mar 1837 d 04 Aug 1837 twin of Elizabeth **dy**.

6 CLINTON BURHANS b 02 May 1839 m 24 Mar 1887 Emma Sagendorf b 07 Aug 1843 wd/o Jacob Elias Finger, d/o Jeremiah Sagendorf & Catharina Clum.

7 HEZEKIAH S BURHANS b 15 Nov 1843 (d 31 Mar 1884) m 02 Oct 1867 Sarah Merritt b 22 May 1848 d/o Caleb Merrit & Henrietta Houghtaling. Mr Burhans was a res of Kingston NY & held a number of positions of trust in that place. The year before his death he was Supervisor of the town.

8 LOUISA BURHANS b 19 Nov 1845, as his 2nd wf {m} 14 May 1884 1.1.9.1.3.4.6.5.1 Charles Albert Snyder b 09 Sep 1852 s/o Sarah E Osterhout & Peter Snyder, (all BG:490). He m1 Mary Jane Felton (d 1882) only d/o Levi Felton & Jane Weeks. EXCEPTION: Since Charles m twice his number is followed to maintain sibling numbering. This family is also listed in the Jannetje DeWitt Langendyk line Gen 8 & 9.

Leucas deWit

DeWITT

1.1.9.4.3.1.3 JOHHANES DeWITT m Martha ? .

1. ELIZABETH DeWITT b 17 Jan 1817 Canada West (d 10 Jun 1895 Glendale ON (fr BDP) m John Graham b 1811 Ire EM Religion d 17 Jan 1853 of Dropsy in the morning, bur Waterloo Cem Kingston T Frontenac Co ON). John farmed Con 18 Lot 1 & Con 6 Lot 12 Kingston T. John DeWitt wdr ae 66, res with this family 1851 census. News item: "Old Mr. DeWitt Con 8 of Ernestown d 1853".

Newspaper per extractions, Kingston Gen Soc card file: John Dewitt was the premium winner at the annual Frontenac Agricultural Show at Waterloo (fr Kgtn Chn [Chronicle] 17 Oct 1823). Elected Roadmaster for the Western pt Con 6 Kingston T Road master, Kgtn Chn & Gaz 01 Jan 1834; letter at Kingston Post Office Kgtn CH & Gaz (Kingston Chronicle & Gazette) 30 May 1845.

DeWITT

1.1.9.4.3.1.4 ABRAHAM DeWITT m Ella Rebecca ? .

1. LUKE DeWITT b Jul 1813 in USA m Eleanor/Ellen b Dec 1813 Ernestown T L&A. Luke is listed in the 1865 Atlas but not in 1878. He is in the 1851 agricultural Census. Luke had Con 3 Lot 5 L&A, Westbrook PO, Rel WM, Kingston T Frontenac Co ON. He had Con 1 Lot pt 42/3/4 Camden T L&A, 200 A, 78 in crop, 100 cult, 20 pasture, 2 garden or orchard, 10 woods or wild, 18 A wheat-216 bu, 5 barley-40 bu, 6A rye-110 bu. There were 3 M at school, 1 F, res in log house.
2. HIRAM DeWITT b 1815 in 1861 in Ernestown T L&A Co ON, Wesleyn Methodist res with John Simons & wf, **single**. Hiram had a deed for Con 3 Lot 23 Ernestown T 30 Jun 1852. He had a mortgage for Con 6 Lot 43/20 Apr 1859 & the Deed 16 Sep 1862, also Ernestown.
3. ELIZA DeWITT
4. MARTHA DeWITT
5. ABRAHAM DeWITT b 1821 m Ann b 1832, 5 chn in 1851 census. He res with Abraham Sr in 1861; presumed to have lost his family in an epedemic & may have predeceased his pa. Abraham Sr received a Crown Land Grant of 200 acres Con 7 Lot 35 Ernestown T 11 Jun 1836.
6. ANN DeWITT
7. FRANCES/FANNY DeWITT b 1826 (d 20 Nov 1871 ae 45 bur Wilton Cem Stone for Frances was missing in 1990) m 14 Nov 1846 Benjamin Hicks, both of Ernestown T by Rev George Goodson, b 1826 d 1871 bur Wilton Cem Ernestown L&A Co ON (McDowall M Reg).
8. AMANDA DeWITT b 1827 (d 23 Oct 1904 at Harrowsmith ON) m Thomas D Hicks b 1821 d 03 May 1857 bur Harrowsmith Cem Portland T Frontenac Co ON, a carpenter & builder.
9. CAROLINE F DeWITT b 1827 There was a Caroline DeWitt, a Professor in Milton, m 22 Dec 1847 Titus Simon Detlor of Napanee by Rev. Mr. Beynon Wesleyen Meth. Caroline F would be too young.
10. JOHN G DeWITT b 1834 (d 13 Mar 1912 ae 78 [L&A Cem Vol 2 Wilton Cem p2]) m Angeline Caton b 1842 Ireland d 11 Sep 1895 ae 53 fr Typhoid Fever bur Wilton Cem. Ella Rebecca DeWitt res near her chn in 1871. In 1881 she lived with John. John had Con 7 Lot 36 Ernestown T L&A; William Caton is listed on Con 7 Lot 35.
11. JANE DeWITT b 1839 of Ernestown Canada West, at ae 22, m 28 Jul 1861 Edward Thomas Shewell s/o Edward Shewell & Eliza, Ernestown T ON, ae 21 b Can West (CMRF:102).
    One Ann Duitte, unidentified, b 1826 d/o Elizabeth Duitte in the 1861 Census for Pittsburg T Frontenac Co m James Reid b 1822 Scot, farmer, and chn: 1 William b 1850, Elizabeth b 1852, and James b 1854.
    Newspaper Extractions, Kingston Gen So. Abraham Dewit/Dewitt mentioned in notice of a lost pocket book containing notes of hand Kgtn Gaz 06 Feb 1813; letter at the Bath PO Kgtn Chn 14 Jul 1820, again Kgstn Chn letter at the Bath PO 13 Oct 1820; 13 Apr 1821 list of British letters at the Kgstn PO; Kgtn Chn & Gaz 10 Sep 1831, 17 Oct 1831, 24 Sep 1831; Letter remaining at Bath PO Kgtn Chn & Gaz 12 Sep 1838; same 15 Dec 1838. Ellen Dewit Letter at Kgtn PO Chn & Gaz 11 Sep 1844.

DeWitt

1.1.9.4.3.1.5 EVERT/EVERETT DeWITT m Catharine Horning

1. GEORGE HIRAM DeWITT b 1820 Kingston T FrontenacCo ON (d 1881 in Oregon) m Lydia Louise Bott, b 1823 d 1901 OR USA. They res Camden East T Con 1 prt Lot 37/8 200 A Cultivated, 60 in crops, 40 A pasture, 120 wild or woods in 1851; 3 M in School, 1 F, log house 1 storey. Moved to Oregon. Newspaper extractions by the Kingston Gen So, letter for George at the Kingston PO 22 Nov 1843, another 10 Jan 1844.
2. WILLIAM LUKE DeWITT b 1823 Can West (d 1907 bur Glenwood Cem, Picton ON) Con 1 Pt 5 east part, West Green Point, Sophiasburg Pr Ed Co ON. He & m1 Samantha Alelia Cronk b 1841 had a dau when she was 16/17. He m2 Phoebe b 1823, in the 1861 census lists dau Samantha b 1858. In 1871 census with Samantha b 1857 ae depending on the month of the census was recorded. He m3 Jemima Foster b 1826 d 1925 bur Glenwood Cem Picton ON. His will left his property equally to his wife & to his natural dau Samantha, b 1857 d 1948 d/o Samantha Alelia Cronk b 1841, to each receive half his estate as tenants in common. Pro 15 Mar 1909.

Leucas deWit

3   JOHN DeWITT b 1825 Can West (bur Oakwood Cem Gaines MI) m Melinda Oliver b 01 Dec 1829 Deseronto ON d 1919 at Guilloz, Detroit MI both bur Oakwood Cem Gaines MI d/o Frederick Oliver & Diancy Woodcock. They farmed Con 1 SW of Green Point Lot 20, Sophiasburg, L&A Co, 75 acres on Long Reach. He is on the map 1863 & not there in 1878 (family info fr CFD).
4   JANE DeWITT b ca 1827 m 22 Nov 1846 Asa Oliver both of Richmond Twp, L&A ON by Rev Goodson. Researching has turned up no record of chn b to Evert & Catharine for several yrs; perhaps the family lived in the USA for awhile or several chn **dy,**
5   MARY DeWITT b 1841.
6   HENRY DeWITT b 1844 lived Prince Edward Co ON map 1863.
7   LYDIA DeWITT b 1847.
8   CATHARINE DeWITT b 1850 (from census her mother would be 47). In the 1861 Census for Sophiasburgh (C-1070) Evert in not with the family, presumed deceased. Henry ae 17 is listed as a farmer.

Newspaper extractions by Kingston Gen So Everit DeWitt Letter at Kingston PO Kgtn Gaz 13 Oct 1818, 20 Oct 1818, 27 Oct 1818; Kingston T Found a steer, Kgtn Chn 11 Oct 1822, 20 Dec 1822, elected as a road master for the western part Con 3 Kingston Twp Kgtn Chn 07 Jan 1825 again 09 Jan 1830, letter at Kingston PO Kgtn CH 04 Dec 1830; letter fr United States at Kingston PO Kgtn Chn & Gaz 07 Jun 1834, Evert Dewit/Dewitt Letter at Kgtn PO Kgtn Chn & Gaz 05 Dec 1835, 07 Dec 1836, letter fr US same 08 Sep 1838, to consult lawyers if necessary re claims for compensation for property damage resulting from the construction of the Kingston-Napanee road. Kgtn Chn hr & Gaz 25 May 1839, Evert/Everet/ Everit Dewit/Dewitt Application be made to him for the position of teacher in the school house in the T of Kingston on Con 3 in Kgtn CH & Gaz 09 Jan 1841 to 16 Jan 1841, elected Road Master for Kgtn T Kgtn Chn & Gaz 23 Jan 1841.

BAILEY
1.1.9.4.3.3.1 MARY G DeWITT m John Bailey

1   ABRAHAM W BAILY b 1808 (d 27 Mar 1867 bur Bapt Cem Newcastle Creek NB m 24 Jul 1822 (fr ACB) Margaret Mitchell b 1813. He was a Baptist Deacon.
2   JOHN T BAILEY b 1812 (d 1883) m 29 Aug 1844 Lavinia Jane Scribner b 1817 d 1895 both bur Blissville Cem Hoyt NB. Dates fr 1851 census Blissville Par Sunbury Co NB (CSNB:10) tbstn & family rec (fr KLAD).
3   PHOEBE ELIZABETH BAILEY b 1811 (d 02 Feb 1872 ae 61 tbstn Blissville Cem) m James W Seely b 1807 d 01 May 1883 ae 76 (collected by KALD fr JS, SLBG, tbstn, fr ACB).
4   CHARLES J BAILEY b 28 Jan 1815 (d 14 Jan 1911) m 14 Dec 1837 Rachel Webb b ca 1819. Info fr 1851 census Blissville Par Sunbury Co NB. (CSNB:10). Charles was a lumberman.
5   GIDEON D BAILEY b 25 Feb 1817 Oromocto (d 20 May 1879) m1 02 Feb 1843 Hannah Branscombe d 1854 of Waterborough NB wits: W Duncan, W Perley, John Y Bailey (QCNBM:101) d 1854; m2 Rachel Branscombe b 1821 d 1903.
6   EPHRIAM M BAILEY
7   MATILDA BAILEY m Thomas H Kelly.
8   BENJAMIN STUDLEY BAILEY m Hannah Seeley (fr MAH).
9   LUKE E BAILEY b 1837 a mill owner (1851 Census Sunbury Par NB, fr SCBG).

DeWITT
1.1.9.4.3.3.2 ABRAHAM PERSEN DeWITT m Nancy S Smith

1   JOHN DeWITT b 24 Jul 1814 Oromocto River NB Can res Presque Isle ME (d 29 May 1901 Maxfield ME) by William I Lee JP m1 09 Oct 1845 Mahala L Page (Augusta ME State Archives). She was b ? Jul 1826 d 05 Aug 1866 ae 39-11-22, chn b Maxfield. In 1861 John was Selectman & Constable. He held all positions in Town Of Maxfield at various times. m2 Betsy J ? b 28 Jan 1818 b 28 Oct 1897 (History of Penobscot Co ME & Census Rec) (SCMR by KBG).
2   LYDIA DeWITT m David Holbrook of Maxfield.
3   DAVID T DeWITT b 1817 Oromocto River NB m1 Winifred Vaughn went to Presque Isle ME; m2 Hannah Briggs (1850 Maxfield ME Census) res in Presque Isle ME.
4   HENRY DeWITT b ? Jun 1820 d 12 Dec 1839 ae 19-06-00 bur Maxfield.
5   PHOEBE DeWITT
6   NANCY DeWITT
7   CHARLES DUDLEY DeWITT b 1830 Maxfield ME. Thomas P Bunker JP m 22 Jul 1851 Bethia G Buswell b ca 1833 b Maxfield, res Presque Isle (m rec microfilm at Augusta ME State Archive copied July 1982) (fr BBVH).
8   MARY ELIZABETH DeWITT b 09 Feb 1832 Maxfield (d 28 Sep 1919 ae 87-07-19) m Moses Greenleaf Smart of Howland ME, bro/o Charles Smart, no issue. Mary's death certificate states she d at Howland ME having res their 45 yrs, previously of Maxfield ME. Her mother is given as Lydia Smith, not Nancy, parents both from NB. Cause of death Mitral Regurgitation & senility. This suggests Abraham Peren DeWitt may have m a second time.

9   PHOEBE S DeWITT m John Tolpa of Bangor ME.
10   CHRISTIANA S DeWITT m John Burham of WI. Seboeis Plantation was originally Whitney Ridge ME.

DeWITT
1.1.9.4.3.3.3 THOMAS DUROSE DeWITT m1 Hannah C Seely

1. RUFUS DeWITT b 16 Aug 1820 (IGI has 17 Aug 1820 Blissfield Northumberland NB) & (d 23 Mar 1897 ae 76-07-07 bur Medford Cem) m1 Olive Smart d/o John Smart, b 1833 d 1854 ae 21 bur Sebois Cem; m2 Susan Roberts b 1832 d 12 Aug 1888. In 1850 census listed with bro James, as 'lumberman' res with John Healy, Innkeeper. Chn b Lowell, Penobscot ME.
2. JAMES DeWITT b 1822.
3. PHOEBE ELIZA DeWITT b 01 Apr 1823 Sebec ME (d of pneumonia 12 Mar 1897 Seboeis ME) m 02 Apr 1840 Charles Lyford Smart b 20 Oct 1816 d 27 Oct 1862 of typhoid fever on the steamship "Catawba" en route home from military service in the Civil War. He was the s/o John Smart & Mary (Polly) Lyford.
4. THOMAS DeWITT b 22 Jul 1825 d 23 Dec 1849 ae 24-05-01 Seboeis.
5. JOHN G DeWITT b 02 Jun 1829 in ME d 22 Feb 1850 ae 20-08-20 Seboeis.
6. REBECCA JANE DeWITT b 12 Feb 1837 d 19 Jun 1855 ae 18-04-07 Seboeis.
7. EZEKIEL DeWITT b 1834; 1840 census there are seven chn, only heads of families named. Ezechiel is not listed there in the 1850 census.

m2 Mary/Polly A Lyford Smart,
In 1813 Thomas DeWitt, John Bailey, Abraham De Witt, Calvin Hathaway, John DeWitt, William Smith got grants of land on Shin Creek west of the SW Oromocto River Branch in New Brunswick.

DeWITT
1.1.9.4.3.3.4 JOHN [KING] DeWITT m Annie Wood.

1. DANIEL DeWITT b 27 Jul 1817 Blissville Par Sunbury Co NB {m}1 04 Dec 1838 Catharine/Katie Boone (1.1.9.4.3.6.4.1) d/o Murray Boone & Elizabeth Kenney, b 1818; m2 Uphanie Ho. "My mother visited Daniel as a ch & remembers pumpkin pie for breakfast" (fr LDM).
2. JOHN HENRY DeWITT b 27 Jun 1820 French Lake North Branch of the Oromocto River NB m Mary E Seeley b 1829. They res Victoria Corner near Hartland, Carleton Co NB and petitioned for land 1838 in Blissville. He was a lumberman in 1851, 1861. Their chn were b in Blissville (fr Census, LOM).
3. BETHUEL DeWITT b 09 Feb 1823 French Lake NB m Mary E Smith d/o Stephen Smith & Polly Seely, b near Fredericton NB, Par/o Lincoln, Sunbury Co. He bought the farm of John Mallory in Carleton Co NB but followed his son to ME & d 1915 at Presque Isle ME, chn b Par/o Blissville Sunbury Co
4. LUKE E DeWITT b 18 May 1825 (d 03 Jun 1909 bur Jacksons Corners Co NB) m1 26 Sep 1848 Rebecca Seeley; d/o James Seeley b 1832 d 1871 (fr KLAD, LDM).
m2 Mrs Euphemia Hendry (undated Obit clipping fr GMD) & she moved to Waterville Carleton Co, her funeral Waterville United Baptist CH, Hendry chn & grchn listed.
5. ANNA JANE DeWITT b 27 Feb 1830 at Blissville (d 07 Nov 1918) m 16 Oct 1849 William E Hoyt of Woodstock, Carleton Co NB b 1825 Post Master at Rosedale NB; all chn b Carleton Co NB, order unknown. William Hoyt came fr Hoyt Station near Fredericton NB (fr LDM).
6. PHOEBE E DeWITT b 11 Jun 1832 (d 1908) m Robert Moffat. All chn b Blissville.
7. EZEKIEL DeWITT b 23 Jan 1833 (d 29 Jan 1880 bur Simonds NB) m1 Irene S Smith; b 1843 d 10 Oct 1866 ae 23; **m2 Frances E DeWitt** b 1850 d 16 Jan 1933 ae 83. (Simonds is 4 miles up stream from Hartland, Carlton Co NB, on the west side) res in St Thomas, Carlton Co.
8. GEORGE MORGAN DeWITT b 16 Jan 1835 North Branch Oromocto (d 07 Nov 1918 Avondale NB & wf bur United Baptist CH Waterville) m 10 May 1860 Angeline Hoyt at Sunbury Co b 09 Mar 1837 Hoyt Station d 12 Jun 1928; chn b Waterville, Carleton Co NB. Info in family Bible of Ruth (DeWitt) Estey copied 14 Jan 1962 now in res of George DeWitt, Airdrie AB. <u>The Holy Bible Containing The Old And New Testament Translated Out of The Original Tongues.</u> Cruden's. Philadelphia. A J Holman: 1879. Sold by Thompson and Company, Woodstock NB.
9. THOMAS ORRIN DeWITT b 07 Oct 1837 (d 27 Mar 1908) m Annie Belyea b 13 Sep 1837 Windsor Co NB d 29 Apr 1928 both bur in the Blissville Baptist Cem Hoyt Station NB (fr MWD). The Rev Thomas Orrin DeWITT was educated at the University of New Brunswick and ordained as a Baptist Minister. He left some notes about his father, which his dau Mabel Sweet gave to Dr Mallory. They had been copied on a typewriter from the handwritten originals.

JOHN [KING] DeWITT 1793 –1890 by KATHERINE LORENA (ALEXANDER) DeWITT
John's son Thomas wrote down the story and passed it on to his daughter Mabel Sweet.

Individually and co-operatively several persons have been researching the history of the family whose surname, at least in New Brunswick, is currently most often spelled 'DeWitt'. In early provincial records the spelling is usually 'DeWit' though there are also other variations. Some of these researchers who are also RURAL EDITION READERS may be already acquainted with the following material, but for the benefit of others it is submitted.

John DeWitt who was born in Blissville in 1793 is one of the more interesting of the older family members. He was the son and grandson of Loyalists who came from Greene County, New York, in 1783 to what was then Nova Scotia, and who eventually settled on the shores of the South Oromocto. There is only one family of record named Dewit among the Loyalists of this province. It was headed by Evert (late an armed boatman of Staten Island who ran contraband for the British) and his wife Gertrude. "Our sons and a daughter [Catherine] accompanied their parents" [Henry and Peter were on a Ship's list with Evert]. Jacob, a veteran of the King's American Regiment and John, a veteran of the 3rd New Jersey Volunteers may have traveled with their Regiments. [Abraham was not mentioned but he was also in New Brunswick].

John Dewit married Phoebe Durose (sometimes given as Duross). Phoebe's mother also named Phoebe, was born in the Old Georgia District, a Soldier Settlement Grant on Lake Champlain, now part of Vermont. Her father was Charles Durose who received his land for service in the NY Provincial Army in the Seven Years war [French and Indian war 1756-63]. Charles was a Loyalist Seagent in the Revolution. John Henry DeWitt was a land grantee of the area. It is their son John, who is the subject of this article.

John was one of seven children born to their parents, none of whom were yet in their teens when their father died in 1891. How the family survived is unknown, but John at least, early showed an enterprising nature. At the age of 16 and already a member of the militia, he petitioned for a grant of land 'on the southwest branch of the Oromocto River about a mile below the mouth of Shin Creek, commonly called the Ash Meadow'. His petition was granted October 14, 1811.

John then began a career as a farmer and lumberman. Somewhere along the way he acquired the nickname 'King' and it was as 'King Dewit' he was known to most of his contemporaries. In maturity he was a man with leadership qualities and definite opinions, which he had no hesitation in expressing. He was also was possessed of great energy and physical strength. As evidence of the last, according to a family tradition, he once killed a bull with a single blow of his fist. His physical stamina and agility lasted into old age for his son, Rev. T.O. DeWitt, recounted the story of a visit to his father when the latter was 76 years of age. At that time King demonstrated how he could jump in the air from the floor and crack his heels together.

When he was 21 years of age John married Annie Wood of the Branch Lake vicinity. Their first home was on the farm known as 'The Bill Morrow Place'. Shortly after they moved to another location at Waterville and kept an Inn for some ten years. Winters John spent cutting the pine lumber of which there was a good supply near at hand. One can but speculate that if the inn business were in any way brisk, Annie must have been one busy lady, for King's time must have been largely taken up by his other pursuits.

To King's youngest child, Rev. T.O. DeWitt, we are indebted for an account of his father's journey made to Canada [Ontario] and New York State in 1830. The purpose in going was to see some land to which a relative had a claim. King left Fredericton in January in company with the man carrying the mail by dog team to Quebec. By late evening of the second day they had reached Tobiqaue where they spent the night in a wigwam. The next day they reached Grand Falls and so they traveled along until they came to Simes Bear, Madawaska. There they stopped with the widow of one of the soldiers of the 104 Regiment and were treated well. The next night was very different as they stopped with a French family and an attempt was made to rob King. There were several men about the place and King became suspicious of their intentions, though he could understand none of their language. His room was over the kitchen and he could hear whispering so he decided not to go to bed. He barricaded his door as best he could and sat on the bed to wait. Sure enough they came. He heard a stumble on the stairs and a fumble at his door as he sat with his single-barreled horse pistol in this hand. He fired two shots – one through the door – and had no more trouble. At daybreak he set out without waiting for breakfast and traveled on alone for the mail carrier had left him there.

He arrived at a place called 'Bay Canty' (Bay of Quite) and fell in with a coloured man named Carter, who directed him to the home of his uncle, L. E. DeWit. There King spent the night and the following day set out for Utica. From there he proceeded to Albany and to a place called Catskills where he located his Uncle Henry. He remained there for about a week and many came to see the man from Nova Scotia, as New Brunswick was often called.

On his way, King contracted measles, but never stopped traveling. He crossed the North River and set out for Boston, walking the whole distance. From Boston, he took passage on a sailing vessel and after beating about for several days in dense fog; they arrived at Eastport, Maine. King crossed over to New Brunswick and set out along the Old St.Andrews Road, spending a night at McDougall's on Shin Creek. From there he proceeded to the old block house where Linus Seeley lived and on to John Bailey's, then back to Hartt's Mills and on to his home at French Lake, arriving about the middle of March, having made the journey in less than three months and mostly on snowshoes.

In 1837, John and Annie with their family of seven sons and two daughters moved to the North Branch Oromocto where they settled on the Back Tracy Road as it is now called. The family is said to have acquired two lots on one of which, was a frame house, one of those that had escaped the fires of 1825, known as 'The Miramichi Fire'. The house still stands and is the

Leucas deWit

home of Elsa and John Tracy. In 1869, Luke DeWit, one of King's sons, and his wife Rebecca deeded the property to Lynas (sic) Tracy, who was John's Grandfather.

Seven years later, the DeWitt family moved again, this time to the South Branch where they took up residence in a frame house on the site of the present home of the Wallace Smiths. The old house is long gone and was replaced by a new one. It is unlikely that all the children of John and Annie accompanied them, for some of the older sons were doubtless married by this time.

When the 1851 Census was taken, John, his wife Ann, daughter Phoebe, and sons George, Thomas and Ezekiel were members of one household. Sons Daniel, Luke, Bethuel and John were all married and all living in Blissville Parish, but at that time Gladstone was included. Daughter Ann does not appear under the name DeWitt; she too may have married or it may be she simply happened to be away from home at the time of the census taking.

John DeWitt continued his farming and lumbering work with his sons seemingly closely allied. The only unusual incident reported concerning his lumbering is to the effect that at one time he was taking cargo of deal [wood or a board of fir or pine] to Saint John by river. He engaged a pilot to take him through the Reversing Falls, but the craft upset and King was thrown into the water. He managed to reach and climb Split Rock where he clung until rescued.

Once more the family moved, this time in 1853 when they went to Carleton County. The married sons may not have moved immediately, but they were shortly to be found in the fairly near vicinity of their parents' new home. The only note that has appeared so far about their business undertakings is one that tells of King DeWitt, when in his 60's lumbering for Charles Connors up the Becaquimec Stream where he was said to have 'made a good year'.

Both King and Annie lived to a remarkable old age. She died in 1889 at the age of 95, while he lived in the following year, dying at age 97. Their gravestone, bearing only their names and dates stands in the Baptist Cemetery, Waterville, Carelton Co, New Brunswick.

King and Annie's many descendants are by this time scattered through Canada and the U.S. They are sometimes called the Carleton County Branch of the family, but this is only partly true. Not a few of their direct descendants live in South Sunbury. A granddaughter, Phoebe DeWitt, married George Scott and established the family home on Gore Road on the farm presently owned by the John Halls. Three of the 12 Scott children married and settled in the vicinity. Winslow and Elizabeth (Mrs. Stanley McCracken) at Fredericton Junction and Clarissa (Mrs. Elgan O.Smith) at Hoyt. Their descendants in three generations live or have lived in the area.

Another of King and Annie's granddaughters Delilah married David H. Kirkpatrick. Their six children all lived in Hoyt or Juvenile. Mrs. Parker Graham, Mrs. Cliff Lewis, Mrs. Ernest Kirkpatrick and Raymond Kirkpatrick still survive while children Grant and Allison are deceased. Delilah's descendants, too, extend to the third generation.

Several persons have remarked that no record among the official papers could be found concerning King DeWit(t). This may solve the problem, since the name given him at his christening ceremony in the Maugerville Church was JOHN.

SMITH
1.1.9.4.3.3.5 GERTRUDE DeWITT m Clapman Smith

1 PHOEBE SMITH b 1826 m 05 Sep 1846 Thatcher Smith (SCMR, SDVSW) b 1822 (both 1851 Blissville Census) then lived Presque Isle.
2 DANIEL SMITH b 1828 Blissville, Sunbury Co NB farmed near Hoyt Stn NB m Charlotte Smith d/o Stephen Smith & Polly Seely, b 1835 [She was a sis/o Mary Smith m to Bethuel DeWitt]. Daniel & family moved to Spraque Mills ME; both are bur there.
3 NANCY SMITH b 1832 (d 1916) m 25 Nov 1852 Warren Smith, by Rev Jacob Gunter, Blissville, b 1818 d 1902 (? 1912). "Went to school in Mill Settlement, lived at Hoyt buried Blissville Baptist Cemetery" (SDVSW:3). Chn b Blissville, Sunbury Co NB. They moved to Presque Isle ME between 1851 & 1860 (family info DVSW:3). Warren, Thatcher & Charlotte Smith were chn/o William Ellis Smith & Mary of East Machias Me, unrelated to this Smith family (info fr KLAD)
4 MARY SUSANNE SMITH dy bur Blissville Baptist Cem.)
5 MARY ANN SMITH b 1835 (d 1923) m Alexander Wooden b 1833 d 1914 both bur Blissville NB Baptist Cem. Alexander wrote poetry, led the singing at the Mill Settlement East Baptist Church. They celebrated their 50th wedding anniversary 01 Jan 1907 and received $50 in gold from their son, James. All chn b Mill Settlement NB (family info fr MWD; SDVSW:2).

Walter Patterson built a house in 1829 for Clapman Smith Jr and Gertrude/Gitty DeWitt. Daniel lived in it at one time. For more than 150 years it was a well-known residence in the Valley of the South Branch of the Oromocto River at what is now known as Hoyt NB. Ownership remained in the Smith family, the final owner being Horace B Smith who had the house razed after a fire severely damaged it on New Years Eve1986. Typical of the structure of the homes in rural New Brunswick at the time it was built. The house was little changed in appearance over the years as shown in the picture taken in 1943. Horace B Smith provided the picture.

Leucas deWit

DeWITT

1.1.9.4.3.3.7 CHARLES DeWITT m Hannah Nason

1. JOHN L DeWITT b 1824 (d 16 Apr 1907 Howland, Penobscot Co ME bur Randall Ridge Cem, Maxfield ME) m 1850 Lucretia D Emery d/o Deacon Joseph Emery & Lydia Bryer, b 1830 Howland ME d 1902 bur N side of Piscataguish River. In 1850 Howland ME census John, **single**, lived with the Emerys 1870 & 1880 at Maxfield.
2. CHARLES DeWITT b 1828 still **single** ae 32 d 1904.
3. MARY DeWITT b 1830 m Henry Crombie/Crummue b 1831 res Juvenile Blissville Par NB 1871.
4. ABRAHAM THOMAS DeWITT b 1832 (d 1904) m Mary Patterson b 1834 d 1912; Abraham was a shoemaker, res opposite the Cem in Fredericton Jct NB.
5. LUKE EMERY DeWITT b 01 Dec 1833, known as Luke Em (d 17 Nov 1899 NB) m 20 Sep 1858 Rachel E Mersereau b 01 Jul 1835 d 12 Jul 1912 (fr KLAD. The info on a loose white sheet in the De Witt Family Bible in possession of Ronald & Katherine DeWitt & fr RDB). Both are bur Blissville Cem Hoyt NB.
6. GEORGE F DeWITT b 1836 in 1851 census not in 1861.
7. ISREAL W DeWITT b 1838 **single** ae 33.
8. PHOEBE ANN DeWITT, b 1840 (d 1920) m Thomas Bell b 1826 d 20 Oct 1911 both bur Juvenile NB (fr KLAD, MWD).
9. HANNAH E DeWITT b 1841 (d 1917) m 2nd Sept 1864 Fred Kingston b 1846 (1851 Census) d 1921 both bur Blissville NB (fr KLAD, MWD)
10. JEREMIAH/JAREMIAH WILLIAM DeWITT b 1844 (d ca 1881 ae 37) Rev Samuel Downey, Free Christian Baptist Minister at Bissville NB, m 19 Jul 1869 Mary Matilda Hay (Wit: Isabella Buckingham, A T De Witt & Thomas Bell) d/o William Hay & Sarah, b 1845 probably Harvey NB (fr LCB). She belonged to CH of England. They res at Blissville, then Island Falls ME. He was a common labourer, cook, & a CH Sextant. Lottie (DeWitt) Hardin said, " Grandfather was a diabetic. He used to take a ten quart pail of water to bed and drink it during the night" (fr AMS)
11. GIDION HAMILTON DeWITT b 1846 Blissville NB m1 21 Dec 1872 Elizabeth Johnson b 1846 both of Blissville (fr VSNBN 06 Jan 1873) res South Branch of the Oromocto. Elizabeth d 06 May 1872 ae 26. Gideon m2 Mrs Hannah Jane Nason. In 1871 Isreal DeWitt lived with them (fr KLAD, MWD, 1871 census).
12. CLARA JANE DeWITT b 1848 at Blissville.
13. MARY ISABEL DeWITT b 1850 m Obadiah Buckingham.

DeWITT

1.1.9.4.3.3.8 LUKE DeWITT m Mary Wood

1. JOHN DeWITT b 12 Dec 1827 Blissville NB (d 18 Aug 1903 Blissville) m1 Chloe C Hoyt b 1831 d 1862 bur Blissville Cem d/o George Hoyt & Mary (fr KLAD). He m2 28 Dec 1865 Dorothea Sinclair b 1836 Lincoln Par Sunbury Co NB d 1873. These chn were split up and raised apart form each other. John m3 Annie Bailey b 1851 d 1932 **no chn**.
2. MARY J DeWITT b 1830 Blissville NB m Joshua Webb b 1824 Blissville NB (Census fr KLAD) s/o Joshua Webb (d 19 May 1884 ae 94) & Sophia Jones (d 23 Apr 1881 at 80 fr tbstn Blissville Cem Hoyt NB).
3. ELIZABETH DeWITT b 1832 (d 15 Sep 1912 at 82 yrs) m Andrew Mersereau b 1827 d 08 Jun 1882 ae 55 (fr tbstn Blissville Cem Hoyt NB).
4. DANIEL WOOD DeWITT b 1834 Blissville NB (d 1912 ae 78) m Emma Ann Webb d/o Joshua Webb & Sophia Jones b 06 Dec 1833 d 02 May 1868 both bur Blissville Cem all chn b Blissville. Daniel was a lumberman & as a wdr lived with son John (fr KLAD).
5. MARGARET A DeWITT b 1841 (d 08 Aug 1929) m after 1871 John Murphy b 1841 d 1923 all bur Blissville Cem (fr KLAD).
6. DAVID W DeWITT b 17 Mar 1846 (d 08 Aug 1884) m Margaret A Hoyt b 1847 d 1933 both bur Blissville Cem NB.

OVERBAG

1.1.9.4.3.4.1 GEERTRUI/GITTY DeWITT m Peter James Overbag

1. JAMES OVERBAGH b 03 May 1817 bp 14 Sep 1817 no sp (CDDGG:83).
2. HENRY DeWITT OVERBAG b 27 Feb 1821 bp 08 Apr 1821 no sp (CDDGG:89). Register of members received at Catskill 05 May 1821 Peter J Overbag & Gitty DeWitt (CDDGG:129).

VAN ORDEN

1.1.9.4.3.4.2 TEMPERENCE DeWITT m 1822 Henry Van Orden.

1. JACOB TEN BROECK VAN ORDEN b 04 Nov 1822 bp Jan 1823 (CDDGG:92) m Catharine Sax d/o Benjamin Sax.
2. HENRY DEWITT VAN ORDEN b 13 Mar 1824 bp 24 Jun 1824 (CDDGG:95).
3. SAMUEL VAN ORDEN b 22 Aug 1828 bp 23 Nov 1828 (CDDGG:102).
4. CATHARINE CHRISTINA VAN ORDEN m ? Badeen.

Henry Van Orden of Catskill Will Pro 24 Aug 1863. Heirs wf Temperance, sons Samuel & Henry, dau Catharine Christina Badeen (mentions his pa as William). Exs: wife & sons Jacob T B & Henry DeWitt; Wit: William H Van Orden & Mary Van Orden (AWGNY 2:12).

Leucas deWit

Benjamin Sax of Catskill, Will Pr 24 Jun 1876. Heirs dau Eliza Ann, wf/o John Langendyke & Catharine wf/o Jacob T B Van Orden. Exs: Son-in-law, John Langendyke & Jacob T B Van Orden Wit: Rufus H King & D K Olney both of Catskill (AWGNY 2:91).

WINNE

1.1.9.4.3.4.3 ELSJE DeWITT m Benjamin Winne.
1 JOHN WINNE bp 15 Jan 1832 (CDDGG:108) presume **dy**.
   Benjamin Winne of Catskill Will Pro 02 Feb 1863. Heirs wf Elcy, adopted dau Ann P Winne, formerly called Ann Pratt. Exs: Peleg C Mattoon & Rufus H King. Wit: Joseph Hallock & Frederick Hill (AWGNY 2:10).

DeWITT

1.1.9.4.3.5.2 PHOEBE DeWITT {m} Isaac DeWitt (1.1.9.4.3.7.3)
1 SALOME DeWITT b 1827 **single.**
2 HENRY DeWITT b 1829 (d 06 Nov 1919 ae 91 bur Tracy NB Cem) m1 Mary Ann Nason b 1833 Rusagonis NB (d 05 Mar 1854 in ch b), {m}2 11 Nov 1858 Mary Jane Nason (1.1.9.4.3.7.1.3.3) b 1842 d 28 Feb 1906 at Tracy NB both bur Tracy Cem d/o John Nason & Abigail Grass (fr IMWH & ACB).
3 JEREMIAH DeWITT b 1831 at Lincoln Co NB {m} 08 Oct 1856 Adeline Nason (1.1.9.4.3.7.1.3.1) d/o John Nason & Abigail Grass, b 1839.
4 NANCY DeWITT b 1832 **single.**
5 CATHARINE/KATIE DeWITT b 1836 m George Rowe.
6 ISAAC DeWITT b Nov/Dec 1839 m Hannah/Ann Boone b 1847 d Oct/Nov 1920. They res Rusagonis NB then McAdam, York Co NB (fr grchn WD & MD. They do not mention Melvin or Jaspeth).
7 JACOB DeWITT b 1843. (fr ACB)
8 CHARLES DeWITT b 1851l (info fr IMWH & ACB). SCC group info 1944 says 8 chn but names just 5.

BOONE

1.1.9.4.3.6.4 WILLIAM/MURRAY BOONE m Elizabeth/Betsy Kinney.
1 CATHERINE BOONE b 1818 {m} 04 Dec 1838 <u>1.1.9.4.3.3.4.1</u> Daniel DeWitt s/o John DeWitt & Annie Wood, b 27 Sep 1817. Par of Blissville, Sunbury Co NB.
2 SUSAN(AH) BOONE m Samuel Havens.
3 ELIZABETH BOONE b 1822 **single** in 1851, dressmaker. She d 19 Jan 1867 ae 45, bur Tapleytown United CH Cem in the DeWitt plot.
4 RUTH BOONE b 1824 milliner (fr HBS, ACB).
   Boone Brook NB is named for this family. In 1851 census at Hamilton ON, Ruth Havens age 2, born NB is living with Elizabeth and Ruth.

BOONE

1.1.9.4.3.6.5 HENRY BOONE m Mary Ann Boone
1 CATHARINE BOONE b 1829 (d 1851) m 19 Dec 1850 George Webb s/o George Webb & Nancy Jones, b 1825.
2 ANN BOONE b 1833, as his 2nd wf m1 George Tracy s/o Jeremiah Tracy Jr & Mary Webb, b 24 Sep 1812 d 31 Mar 1870. (George Tracy & his 1st wf Mary's chn fr 1851 census, are George E b 1842, Frederick H b 1854, Basheba b 1848). Ann m2 George Nason (1.1.9.4.3.7.1.3.2).
3 HANNAH BOONE b 1836 (d 01 Mar 1866) m 04 Jun 1854 John Mersereau later called "Deacon John" b 1822 d 1899. She was his 2nd wf of three.
4 JAMES E BOONE b 1838 (d 23 Nov 1890) m 1857 Basheba/Bashie Whitman d/o James Whitman & Maria Nevers Boone, b 1838.

BOONE

1.1.9.4.3.6.6 EVERETT DeWITT BOONE m Sarah Nason.
1 GERTRUDE BOONE b 1815 m 21 Jun 1834 Jarvis Harris s/o Abram Harris & Martha Thomas.
2 JOHN BOONE b 1817 (d 1896) m Hannah Boone (1.1.9.4.3.4.7.1) d/o William Boone & Mary Cogswell, b 1819. All chn b Blissville Par, Tracy area (fr EMB, grdau of John Boone line above in 1965).
3 LEMUEL BOONE b 1819. Before 1851 Lemuel moved to New Orleans d there of brain fever.
4 SARAH BOONE b 1821 (d 1871/81) m1 29 Jun 1837 William A Carr b 1813 of Geary NB d 1864. She m2 01 Aug 1870 as the 3rd w/o George Kingston b 1807 London Eng. In 1881 George was thinking of marrying again but the prospective bride would not have him.
5 MARY BOONE b 1823 (d 1840) m 13 Jul 1839 (fr ACB) Charles Alexander b 1810 near Five-mile-town, Girlaw T Co Tyrone, Ire. He came to NB with the family in 1822 s/o Thomas Alexander & Jane Little. Mary took her baby to church the next Sunday after birth, as was the custom. She caught cold and died ae 17 days old **dy** (fr KLAD).
6 EVERETT BOONE b 1825 Blissville NB m 12 Sep 1844 Mary Thomas 1822 (1851 census b 1828). All chn b Blissville NB.
7 WILLIAM <u>MURRAY</u> BOONE b 1827 m Hannah Nason b 1823.
8 SAMUEL BOONE b 1830 no info in 1851.

Leucas deWit

9 ABIGAIL BOONE b 23 Jun 1832 Blissville Sunbury Co NB (d Nov 1917) m Lemuel Nason b 22 Sep 1831 Tracy Sunbury Co (d 21 Jul 1885 McAdam) s/o Lemuel Nason Sr (1797 - 1871) & Annie Dunlop (b 1802) of North Branch of Oromocto (fr ACB & Alexander Family Rec).

BOONE
1.1.9.4.3.6.7 WILLIAM BOONE m Mary Cogswell
1 HANNAH BOONE b 1819 {m} 03 Oct 1839 1.1.9.4.3.6.6.2 John Boone b 1817.
2 SAMUEL BOONE b 1823 m Temperance b 1829.
3 RUTH A BOONE b 1826.
4 MARY A BOONE b 1831.
5 JOHN BOONE b 1832.
6 GEORGE BOONE b 1834 (all fr ACB).

BOONE
1.1.9.4.3.6.8 SAMUEL BOONE m Hannah Tracy
1 JOHN C (or E) BOONE b 1832 m 30 May 1854) Sarah Tracy.
2 RICHARDSON BOONE b 1834/5 m 28 Jul 1858 Annis Shirley b 23 Sep 1834.
3 JAMES/JONAS BOONE b 1838 at Tracy NB m Emeline Mott b 1845.
4 RACHEL BOONE b 1843 m Robert Waters.
5 CHARLES BOONE b 1845 m Victoria ? .
6 WILLIAM BOONE b 1850.
7 HANNAH LEVINA BOONE b 1852 d 09 Aug 1867 ae 14 of consumption (fr ACB).

NASON
1.1.9.4.3.7.1 MARTHA/PATTY DeWITT m John Nason
1 ISAIH NASON b 08 Jan 1812 (Fire story says b 1814) d 1838 (cem 1815-1838) **single** (? SCC says "remarried").
2 ISACK/ISAAC NASON b 1815 - 2 chn John b 1843, Haywood b 1848 in 1851 census listed as sons, but not whose sons. They can't belong to John and Martha, possibly grdsons.
3 JOHN M NASON b 04 Sep 1816 Blissville Par, Sunbury Co NB (d 1879) m 17 Feb 1838 Abigail Grass b 1815.
4 MARY NASON b 10 Aug 1818 Blissville Par Sunbury Co NB m 07 Dec 1836 George Tracy (2daus, 1 son)
5 NANCY NASON b 29 July 1820 or d 29 Sep1820 **dy** (fr SCC).
6 ZACKARIAH NASON b 20 May 1823 (d ae 72) m Mary Jane Clark. He was a Doctor d Kansas City ae 72 (fr SCC).
7 LEMUEL NASON b 09 Feb 1826 m Martha Murphy.
8 EPHRIAM/EPHEREM NASON b 02 Jan 1828 (d 02 Sep 1898) at Blissville m 12 Oct 1852 Elizabeth S Grey b Nov 1827 d 18 Mar 1917. Zackariah stayed with Ephriam at one time & eventually became unbalance mentally. "He would be up much of the night raving".
9 ANNIE/ANN NASON b 16 Jul 1832/3 at Blissville Par Sunbury Co NB (d 1926) m 08 Oct 1856? Isreal/<u>Aaron</u> Philips b 1831 d 1901. In 1851 Census all chn b Blissville (SCC doesn't include #3, all fr ACB).
John Nason the elder's sister Hannah b 1806 m Charles DeWitt. John lived with son Ephriam in 1851 Census.

Phillips, Miriam L. <u>Facts and Folklore. Tracy and the Little Lake Area.</u> Fredericton: Capital. 1985 (Permission granted) to reprint)

THE FIRE OF 1825

"The fall of 1825 was warm and dry, and October 7 was no exception. A lumber crew employed by Thomas Hartt of Hartt's Mills, a community founded at First Falls, approximately four miles downstream from Second Falls, the site on which Tracy now stands, paused for dinner. They `boiled' on the banks of the Yoho Stream, a tributary about five miles to the west. After finishing they put the fire out and, briefly noting a stiff northwest wind had risen, moved back to the `cut'. However, a small spark apparently missed when the fire was extinguished, began to glow. By four-thirty in the afternoon, this small spark, fed by the wind, had become a raging inferno.

Tall trees exploded with a roar, as the fire, steadily increasing in size, swept down the North Branch Stream, devouring everything in its path. Homestead after homestead succumbed to the flames as the inhabitants fled to the sanctuary of the river. The inferno, however, was not to be left unchallenged. Resting high on the south bank of the river, about seven miles east of the fire's origin, stood the John Nason homestead. He was the son of Samuel Nason and Mary (Tracy) Nason, and grandson of Lemuel Nason, and grandson of Pioneer Jeremiah Tracy. The house - large for its time (25 ft by 40 ft) was lovingly constructed of 7 by 15 inch hand-hewn pine, dovetailed together. Endowed with two fireplaces, one with an oven in the kitchen and the other on the opposite end, it was the pride and joy of Martha (DeWitt) Nason, wife of the presently absent John. It was her home and would not be surrendered easily.

Mother of five, with `one on the way', being five months pregnant with son Lemuel, she waited apprehensively. From the first smell of smoke in the early afternoon, she had anticipated its arrival. Blessed with a substantial area of lush green aftergrass surrounding the house and westward, she had realized the greatest danger lay with the wind. Flaming firebrands, flung skyward by the hungry tongues of fire, would be carried forward as vanguard for the broadening front.

With the help of her two eldest sons Isiah, eleven, and nine-year-old John, she had made ready to do battle. She again reviewed her preparations. Every container that would hold water had been filled. The stock was all tethered near the house. An extra ladder was placed against the house and a spare roof ladder added. Finally, with daughter Mary, age seven, having been repeatedly instructed in the care of her sister Nancy, age five and two-year-old brother Zachariah, she was ready.

The wind had seemed to pause for a brief time. Suddenly it stiffened and warmed by the fire, exploded with a roar. The battle had begun. Time seemed an eternity long as sparks and flaming debris filled the air with smoke and heat. Firebrand after firebrand rained down, as the fire raged furiously. Suddenly it was over. Her house still stood. She won!

Gathering her soot-stained family about her, she gave thanks to God. Her home was safe. Later when asked about her ordeal, she would modestly reply, "I just poured water over the ridgepole".

Almost three miles wide, the fire swept downstream to Second Falls, devouring everything in its path. Homes, stores, and lumber mill--even the wood in the milldam fell victim to flames. The inhabitants, mostly women and children since the menfolk were away to the woods working, without exception took to the river. Families, with few personal belongings, huddled in the millpond and under the face of the dam. One mother, a Mrs Thomas, with her day old infant, was seen pouring water over herself and her tiny infant in an attempt to keep cool. The heat from the fire was so intense it killed fish in the shallow water. Although human casualties are unknown, it is said that as one mother in panic hastened to the water, her tiny infant slipped unnoticed from its wrappings and succumbed to the flames.

Mary (Phillips) Tracy had the presence of mind to place silver and gold coins, needed to pay the mill crew, in a small trunk which her two sons carried down to the river, thus saving it, to the relief of her returning husband.

When the day dawned that October 8, 1825, nothing was left untouched. The breeze, that only yesterday carried the mixed odors of drying apples, preserving pumpkins, freshly baked bread, and roasting meat, now carried the sharp, bitter stench of burned wood and cloth - and dreams.

Thirty-nine-year-old mill owner Jeremiah Tracy stood in the midst of the still smoking ashes of what had been a thriving sawmill, and surveyed the blackened landscape. Though only in operation a short time, already the `Tracy Mill' was making the difference between obscurity for the village and a certain degree of prominence. But now what? His wife and eight children were safe and he was well and able; should he rebuild and start over? He was standing at a `crossroad'; which road would he take? On his decision was to rest the fate of this tiny village and the direction of the lives of its future generations.

The fire (sometimes thought erroneously to be the 1825 Miramichi Fire) was to continue on its destructive course through Hartt's Mills until it finally burned itself out on the banks of the main Oromocto River. It had burned over an area of approximately 80 square miles. The effect of this `burn' would be untold hardship for the survivors of these North Branch communities.

Yet they were of hardy stock, descended from men and women who had the fortitude to leave their native England in order to keep their faith intact and to provide a better future for their families".

Martha (DeWitt) Nason was the author's great aunt.
(Note: the DeWitt's were in New Netherland by about 1638, but Martha's mother's people were English.)

DeWITT

1.1.9.4.3.7.2 JACOB DeWITT m Betty/Betsy Creekmore
1 ANNIE DeWITT b 1830 m George Mott.
2 MORRENDY/MERANDA DeWITT b 1831 m George Tucker.
3 JOHN E DeWITT b 1835.
4 MARTHA F DeWITT b ? 1838 ? m1 Oliver Slote/Sloat (fr ACB) or she m Oliver Tucker (fr KLAD).
5 ELIZABETH ANN DeWITT b 1840 m Oliver Tucker. *
6 SARAH DeWITT b 1845 m Oliver Tucker. * (SCC 1934 rec shows both Elizabeth & Sarah m Oliver Tucker).
7 JACOB I DeWITT b 1848 d a young man.
8 GEORGE F DeWITT b 1851 m Henrietta Moore (all fr ACB).
9 HANNAH DeWITT m   ?   Perkins (SCC does not list John or Elizabeth).

DeWITT

1.1.9.4.3.7.3 ISAAC DeWITT/DUIT {m} 1.1.9.4.3.5 Phoebe DeWitt
Children are with their father's underlined number Generation 7.

DeWITTT

1.1.9.4.3.7.4 JOHN DeWITT m Phoebe Nevers
1 JACOB DeWITT b 31 Mar 1829 bp 16 Mar 1865 (d 03 Sep 1917 bur Tapleytown) farmed L9 C6 Saltfleet T Wentworth Co ON, m1 31 Oct 1854 Elizabeth Lee b 19 Jun 1829 d 13 Feb 1857 d/o John Lee & Mary; m2 24 Jun 1858 Elizabeth (Soules) Green b 01 Jan 1829 d 1871 bur Tapleytown; wd/o John Green s/o "the Scout" Billy Green & d/o Benjamin Soules & Mary E Green, Saltfleet, m3 Harriet E Kintzel b 1835 d 1901 bur Max Binkley Family Cem. Elizabeth Soul's son, George Green was with them in 1851 Census. He was a "contrary fellow", eventually res with sis Jane (DeWitt) Smith & smoked out her kitchen every morning lighting the fire (fr HBS, ICSD).

Leucas deWit

2   HIRAM DeWITT b 13 Sep 1830 bp 04 Aug 1861 at Saltfleet m 30 Nov 1868 Margaret Conlon b 1840 res L 6 C 6 Saltfleet. Margaret was orphaned ae 5 coming from Ireland & she was raised by Thomas Mulholland family (fr EM). They res Tweedside ON.

3   ABIGAIL DeWITT b 12 Oct 1832 Saltfleet T (d 15 Jan 1906 in her 74th yr) m 17 May 1853 Sylvester Thomas (Bible as Tiffany) Pettit b 14 Aug 1829 Binbrook T Wentworth Co On s/o Aaron Pettit, d 1912. They and dau Jane are bur Mapleton Cem South Dorchester T. After Sylvester died a large stone was erected in the Mapleton Cem near Belmont ON (fr ICSP). Aaron Petitt bought each of his sons one hundred acres to farm (as had his father Thomas for Aaron & his bros). Abigail was described as 'a tall, slender, strong woman with red hair and I fear a temper to match'. Robert Percy Richard says his mother inherited the auburn hair, as did several cousins. Sylvester was an apiarist as was his son Morley. He and moved to Aylmer ON in 1904, but Morley and his two sisters stayed at the home in Binbrook. The family history as related by Ruth Olive Ryder states they were Pennsylvania Dutch and not desc from "the Judge" in New Jersey. Perhaps a wife's family's stories in a previous generation have resulted in a crossover attributed to the Pettits.

4   RHODA DeWITT b 01 Dec 1834 (d 1906) single in 1861 working for Charles Marshall m James Alexander Chambers Freel, bp 08 Nov 1812 d 22 Jun 1884 s/o James Freel & Ann/Nancy Chambers (fr ICSP). They lived L 99 C 14 (on Lake Erie) Howard T Kent, bur Anglican CH Morpeth, Kent Co ON (fr ICSP).

5   ANN ESTHER DeWITT b 18 Sep 1836 (d 07 Feb 1923) m 19 Oct 1858 Samuel Joseph H Armstrong of York Co ON b 08 Aug 1832 s/o Samuel Armstrong & Ann Kidd both b Ireland, d 27 Jun 1912 Samuel left his family in the early 1830's and no word was ever heard of him again according to Gladys R Hyland. Ann & Joseph both bur Tapleytown Cem. They res Lot 9 Con 2 West York (fr "Samuel Armstrong History" by MA to ICSP).

6   JOHN DeWITT Jr b 01 Aug 1838 Norwich ON (d 30 Jul 1899 Napinka MB) by license by Rev Philander Smith at Tapleytown Meth E CH m 16 Mar 1865 Eunice Churchill b 16 May 1844, s/o Isaiah Churchill & Mary Freel of Norich, Norfolk Co ON, d 29 Mar 1925 Napinka, MB res L 8 C 5 Saltfleet, moved spring of 1880 to 3 mile from Waterford, Lambton Co ON & in 1887 to MB (fr EJDL, MTD). All chn b Tapleytown ON. Added note: Isaiah Churchill was b 06 Feb 1807 Carleton Co NB, West Bank of Saint John s/o Nathaniel Churchill & Eunice. The family moved to Ontario in 1831. He m 09 Jul 1838 Mary Freel b 31 Oct 1807.

7   PRUDENCE DeWITT b 06 May 1840 d 25 Oct 1846 ae 05-06-01 bur Tapleytown **dy.**

8   SAMUEL DeWITT b 24 Apr 1841 d 11 Dec 1910 **single**. He was in MI possibly to visit sis Abigail; worked in a sawmill (fr JDW). He was believed to be of the gay persuasion.

9   ARTHUR DeWITT b 22 May 1843 **single.**

10   PHOEBE JANE DeWITT b 25 Mar 1845 Tapleytown bp ca 1860 (d 28 May 1929 Fruitland ON) m 12 Jan 1867 John Wesley Smith b 22 Jun 1843 s/o John Smith & Jane Atkins of Winona ON, d 27 Dec 1926 Orlando FL both bur Fruitland, res L 9 C 2 Saltfleet, built a white frame house on Hwy #8 (fr ICSP & HBS).

11   MARGARET J DeWITT b 09 Jun 1847 m Arthur Kelton, lived San Diego (fr ICSP).

12   HENRY DeWITT b 03 Feb 1850 d 15 Aug 1854 **dy.**

13   JUDSON ADANIRIUM DeWITT b 22 Jul 1852 Tapplytown (d 1916 bur Alamogordo NM) m 21 Nov 1876 Eliza Ann Johnson b 05 Dec 1852 Forestville, Norfolk Co ON d 25 Jan 1943 Kansas City MO d/o Richard Lawrence Johnson. They res Port Dover ON, Forestville, Stratford ON, Racine WI, Alamogordo NM. (fr ICSP)

14   MARTIN LUTHER DeWITT b 23 Mar 1856 lived Long Point ON (fr EJDL).

Excerpt from 1932 material written by Howard B Smith, son of Phoebe Jane (DeWitt) Smith, grandson of John DeWitt & Phoebe Nevers. Phoebe Jane was six feet tall, wore men's boots, the only ones that fit. The children liked to slip into her bedroom and take a peek at her highly polished shoes.

John DeWitt was a tall man, said to have been the same height as Abraham Lincoln and George Washington, 6' 4" in his stocking feet. He was a very powerful man. During the rebellion of 1837, as a cavalryman stationed at Hamilton, it was his duty to quell any drunken brawls among the soldiers. To prove his strength he offered, at the Hotel, to carry upstairs as many as could cling to his back. Four men took up the offer and he carried them upstairs.

Pheobe Jane DeWitt m John Wesley Smith

Leucas deWit

My grandmother, Phoebe Nevers met John DeWitt at an apple-paring bee. She was seventeen and he was nineteen when they married. She never had any schooling because there were no schools. But she could catch a sheep, sheer it, convert the wool into yarn and clothe and outfit a person, either man or woman. When they were married her mother-in-law took the son's clothes and gave them to a poor man in the neighborhood who had lost his wife and had no winter clothes, saying that John had a wife who could outfit him for winter and had all summer to do it.

Phoebe (Nevers) DeWitt learned to read and write and figure by going over the lessons with her children when they were going to school and got to write a very good hand and composed a good letter. Their books were the Bible from which they learned reading and spelling, Dabough's Arithmetic and an American Geography which described Canada as a country lying to the north, covered in ice and snow most of the year and inhabited by bands of wild roving Indians and wild animals. Phoebe DeWitt was a very kind disposition person and would always go to the help of anyone who was sick. It was quite common to see a man coming into the yard on horseback and leading another horse for grandma to go back with him and nurse his sick. They would come sometimes as far as fifty miles away. Grandfather objected sometimes to her going but she never refused if she was able to go. She used a lot of the Indian remedies; one, in the case of a bad bruise, was apply hot vinegar or fruit juice, which would draw out the inflammation. For diptheria take the skin of a rabbit or a small cat, something very light, put the flesh part next to the neck with the fur side out to keep the body heat in and draw out the poison. I saw these two remedies applied in two cases where the children were given up and they pulled through and are living today, fifty years afterwards.

Samuel Nevers lived on the Oromocto River and in winter used to take his produce to market to Saint John, on his back, by skating down the Morocco River and then down the Saint John River, about one hundred miles. In the summer he went by canoe. One time when he was coming back in the summer in his canoe, he started out after dinner for home and as it was a moonlight night, he paddled from noon until the moon went down about midnight, then he pulled into shore. He turned his canoe upside down and crawled under intending to go to sleep until morning. He heard in the distance what he thought was a child crying a long way off. As he listened it began getting nearer and finally he heard it in the bushes. He grabbed up his belongings as he could see this dark object. He paddled to the middle of the river and it followed him along the shore, turning out to be a panther. He lived to be well over a hundred. I have his picture taken on his 100th birthday.

DeWITT

1.1.9.4.3.7.5 JONATHAN P DeWITT m Caroline Jane Corey.
1. SARAH ANN DeWITT b 1836, as his 2nd wf m Henry Townsend, Brant Co ON, b1817 d 20 Jan 1880 Pro 31 Jan 1880 (DFUSC: census, b dates of chn 1851 Census Brantford C11&113)
2. LEVY/LEVI DeWITT b 1837.
3. JONATHAN DeWITT b 1839 Saltfleet T Wentworth Co ON res Brantford a Pump Maker m 19 Nov 1864 Carolin Fick of Walsingham (by D Griffin Wit Albert Brantford) b 1840 Bayham T res Walsingham T Elgin County Marriage Register 1858-69 d/o Joad & Joanna Fick both Norfolk Co ON (NCMR:231). His religion is WME hers Baptist (1871 census reel C-9908 South Norfolk, Middleton).
4. MARY CHARLOTTE DeWITT b 06 Apr 1842 bp 09 Dec 1861 by W W Clark at Brantford ON, m 27 Sep 1864, John Horning by Rev James McAlister of Meth New Connexion b 1843 res Brantford T ON s/o of Joseph Horning & Harriet. John was a mechanic (MNNR:23).
5. MORRIS C DeWITT b Jul 1845 Brant Co ON. In Santa Cruz Co CA 1900 census p105 Morris C DeWitt. He m 1870 for 30 yrs, wf 3 sons 3 daus, owned his house, (per record in 1900 Santa Cruz Co CA), b Can E (US lists E-Can.- Eng, or F-Can.- French) as were his prts. Naturalized citizen in 1879, occupation was a Thresher.
6. JAMES DeWITT b 1847 (Can census, 18422 US census). LDS film #1254577 MI 1880 Eaton Co, E 1/2 Oneida Village of Grand Ledge MI, James Dewitt white male ae 39, a stone mason, b Can, prts b NB. He m Henrietta b 1852 in MI white female ae 28, keeping house, her prts b NY, family res Grand Ledge MI.
7. EDWIN DeWITT b 1849.
8. FRANCIS A DeWITT b 1853.
9. JACOB M DeWITT b 1855. LDS film # 1244975 MI 1900 Jacob N DeWitt white male ae 46 b ? Nov 1854 Can, citizenship pending, m Minnie C Hamlin b ? May 1859 MI ae 41, res Linden Ave Lansing, Ingham Co MI in 1900. Her ma Roancy Hamlin b ? Jul 1836 NH ae 62 lived with them (US census).
10. GEORGE HARMER DeWITT b 1858 (d 06 Aug 1908 res Guelph ON bur Municipal Cem) m Mary who d 05 Dec 1908. George was a carpenter, could sign his name, bought his Stuart St house 03 Jun 1878 sold it 26 Jul 1889, both bur in free graves, no chn found.
11. ANTINETTA DeWITT b ? Oct 1862, moved to MI 1875 US citizen * 1878 (faint film) m 1870 Olelio Walker, In Benton T Eaton Co MI, her ma ma with this family b ? Dec 1815 ae 84 (bp as 26 Dec 1816), 13 chn 9 living.
12. HENRIETTA DeWITT b 1864. Some of the family lived in Alpena MI that I met by chance in Simcoe ON).

NEFF

1.1.9.4.3.7.6 PRUDENCE DeWITT m Jacob Neff
1. ABRAHAM NEFF b 1832 Barton T Wentworth Co ON m 30 Nov 1859 Helen/Alena Hill, d/o John Hill &Margaret, b Ire 1838. They lived Con 6 Lot 13 Barton T. Abraham was a carpenter (fr ICSP; census).
2. SARAH ANN NEFF b 1835.

Leucas deWit

3   JAMES BRENNAN NEFF b 19 Aug 1839 (d 27 Jun 1913 at the Hotel Dieu Hospital St Catherines ON) m1 1870 Sarah Howard b 1839 d 27 Dec 1869 bur Overholt Cem Humberstone T Welland Co ON. James went to high school in Hamilton ON, College in Philadelphia, became a member of the College of Physicians & Surgeons of ON 10 Apr 1878 res Port Colbourne, Humberstone T Welland Co ON in 1871 Census. All infants bur in the Overhold Cem (fr ICSP & family rec). James m2 10 Apr 1878 Charlotte Omstead of German desc b 1839 d 14 Dec 1895. He m3 Catherine Peterson (no chn) d/o Robert Peterson & Catharine Hiscott. Jessie and her husband Fred Montgomery had her father James & his 3rd wf live with them until they d, bur St Catharines Victoria Lawn Cem.

4   THOMAS DeWITT NEFF b 1842 (fr ICSP).

NASH

1.1.9.4.3.7.7 SARAH DeWITT m James Nash MP

1   GEORGE D NASH b 1834.

2   PRUDENCE NASH b 31 May 1835 d 23 Sep 1835 bur Stoney Creek Cem.

3   JOSEPH PLATT NASH M.D. b 1838 obtained his license 03 Oct 1874, practitioner in Wroxeter On, Marshall MI, Brooklyn NY & Picton ON in 1858 (info in Illustrated Historical Atlas of Prince Edward County) m 1858 ? Sittzer b 1838 of Auburn NY. His mother res with him. He d in Pr Ed Co ON. His will says "I Joseph Platt Nash of the Town of Picton in the County of Prince Edward, Physician . . . . to my mother during her natural life all my Real and Personal property and after her death . . . . to my brother James M Nash" dated twenty-eighth day of March AD 1881.

4   N J CHRISTIE NASH b 1840 d 07 Mar 1849 bur Stoney Creek, Hamilton.

5   JANE ANN NASH b 1848 d ae 20 **single**.

6   CECELIA NASH b 1849 d 1869 ae 20, a pianist.

7   JAMES M NASH b 1851.

8   F H NASH b 1853.

DeWITT

1.1.9.4.3.7.9 THOMAS DeWITT m1 Harriet Moore

1   LEREIGH J DeWITT b 1845.

2   MAHALA DeWITT d 18 Aug 1846 ae 7 yr 6 mo bur Burkholder United CH Cem Mohawk Rd East, Hamilton ON.

3   THOMAS DeWITT b 1846 2, was mo old when his mother d. He was a carpenter Sombra T ON in census. m2 Sarah J.

4   PRUDENCE DeWITT b 1849.

5   JULIA DeWITT b 1851 tailoress.

6   JOSEPH DeWITT b 1857.

7   FLORENCE DeWITT b 1859.

8   WILLIAM DeWITT b 1861.

9   ALENITH DeWITT b 1863 female.

10   MARY J DeWITT b 1866.

DeWITT

1.1.9.4.3.7.10 GEORGE DeWITT m Mary Charlotte Corey.

1   FREDERICK NELSON DeWITT b 14 Dec 1841 Tapleytown ON (d 27 Feb 1909 Newdale MB) m1 01 Oct 1866 Margaret Jameison Wit: Prudence DeWitt & Jameison Cunnington, b 06 Jun 1838/9 Saltfleet d (tbstn) 17 Feb 1871 bur Tapleytown, d/o John Jameison & Jane. Fred moved west in 1877, finally settling at Newdale, Harrison Municipality, MB Section 7 Township 16 Range 20. This was on the edge of the village. He had a dairy farm and a cheese factory (fr ACCH). He m2 03 Apr 1872 Susannah Gammage b 13 Oct 1842 d 14 Dec 1907 Newdale MB (tbstns recorded by author). "We have hair wreath made by Susannah, the center part is all made from family hair (fr Ava Harris)". Prudence is in a wedding picture with them.

2   GEORGE DeWITT b 1843 (d 08 Oct 1869 bur Tapleytown) m 1868 Elizabeth Martin (fr ACH).

3   SARAH PRUDENCE DeWITT d at birth **dy**,

4   PRUDENCE SARAH DeWITT b 1846 (d 1917) m1 Louis Berg, m2 Jaby Harris. Prudence & sisters Eliza & Florence had businesses in Hamilton ON & Chicago IL called "DeWitt Flowers" (Chicago 1906 Directory). They were most talented. They made from goose feathers a wreath of white roses, buds & leaves around an engraved pewter plaque in a deep frame for their brother which read "Jonathan DeWitt Age 25 At Rest". Prudence had **no chn**. She's bur in her bro Charles DeWitt's plot at Fruitland ON.

5   CHARLES WILBERT DeWITT b 1849 (d 16 Nov 1926) bur Fruitland ON. The family had preserved a letter of sympathy written 06 Jan 1927. Charles m Julia Ann Horning b 11 Mar 1850 d 1927, d/o Jeremiah Horning & Charity Smith (G Ralph Horning's Bible). They lived at DeWitt sideroad & #8 Hwy Saltfleet T Wentworth Co ON. This fruit farm is now a subdivision called "DeWitt Heights" (fr CCD1, cem rec)

6   ELIZABETH/ELIZA DeWITT b 1851 m Albert Trato b 1846 s/o Christa Trato & Sofa moved to Battle Creek MI, home address in 1906 was 241 W 46th Pl, Chicago IL (fr ICSP & M)

7   EUNICE DeWITT b 1853 m ? Bloomer. Helen Trato said they had two chn (fr HBS).

8   CAROLINE/CARRIE DeWITT b 1855 (d 16 Dec 1896 ae 41) m John H Martin b1858 d Mar 1880 in his 23rd yr

both bur DeWitt plot Tapleytown United CH Cem.
9. FLORENCE DeWITT b 1857 (alive in Chicago in 1906) wd & in business, m Smith Fred Lucas or? Fred Smith Lucas. In 1906 Chicago Directory under "DeWitt Sisters Flowers" are Prudence Berg, Eliza Trato, Florence Lucas (they made remarkable goose feather flower wreaths) 237 W 46th PL but in 1911 Florence appears as wd/o Smith Lucas at 5418 Aberdeen Chicago IL.
10. JONATHAN DeWITT b 23 Dec 1859 (d 16 Feb 1885) m 17 Oct 1882 at the bride's home, Selena Horning b 04 Nov 1857 d 22 Oct 1929 bur the Trinity United CH Cem Hannon ON d/o Ira Smith Horning & Dorothy Oliphant (fr ISD family rec).
11. MARGARET/MAY A DeWITT b 1860 m Steven Parsons b NB. They moved to Battle Creek MI according to Helen Burke Trato (fr HBT).
12. SARAH/SADIE DeWITT b 1860, **single,** lived with sisters in Chicago, then Battle Creek MI. <u>1851 Agricultural Census Saltfleet T Wentworth Co ON.</u> George DeWitt. Con 6 Lot 16, 84 A - 44 A under Cult, 44 under crop, 40 A Wood or wild, 10 A wheat - 300 bu, 4 A peas - 20 bu, 1 A in buckwheat, 5 A - 7 bundles or tons of hay, hay, 45 lbs wool, 30 fulled cloth yards, 35 flannel yards, 2 bull oxen or steer,
4 milk cows, 2 calves. 2 horses, 14 sheep, 4 pigs, 200 lbs butter, 4 barrels or cwt beef, 19 barrels or cwt of pork, Clay soil.

Jonthan DeWitt

BOGARDUS
1.1.9.4.3.8.2 CATHERINE DeWITT {m} Francis Bogardus.
1. CORNELIUS BOGARDUS b 05 May 1830 (d 31 Dec 1902 bur McNab Cem WHERE) m1 14 May 1853 Elizabeth Beard b 1832 d 27 Jul 1867. He m 2 1867 Martha Brady b 26 Mar 1845, d 1910.
2. MARIA BOGARDUS b 22 Nov 1831 (d 1916) m ? Hewett.
3. PETER BOGARDUS b. 11 Aug 1833 (d 1916) m 1857 Matilda Fair.
4. CORNELIA BOGARDUS b 08 Apr 1835 m ? Howey.
5. HENRY BOGARDUS b 23 Jan 1837 Niagara Falls ON (d 10 Apr 1913 Clinton IL) m1 29 Nov 1862 Rachel Packard d 15 Dec 1872 at Colorado Springs CO, m2 10 Jan 1875 Margaret A McCullough b 1850 Antrim Ire d 03 Sep 1935 at Clinton IL.
6. PHILLIP BOGARDUS b 10 Jun 1838 at Niagara Falls ON (d 22 Nov 1902 *? OR d 1918 bur St Catharines ON). He m ae 25 on the 15 Dec 1863 Elizabeth Phipps ae 18 (b 1845) of Louth d 31 Oct 1911 bur Victoria Lawn Cem St Catherines ON, d/o John Phipps and Elizabeth. Co M Rec 1858-1869 Vol 19 Lincoln & Welland Co p 9. There seems to be a transcribing error. He d either ae 58 or 76)
7. UNNAMED BOGARDUS b 08 Nov 1841 d 16 Aug 1842 **dy,**
8. ADORUM BOGARDUS b 07 May 1843 Niagara-on-the-Lake ON (d 26 Mar 1928 at Virgil, Niagara-on-the-Lake) at East Saginaw MI m 15 Oct 1872 Christine Spencer b 16 Jun 1843 d 1893.
9. BENJAMIN BOGARDUS b 27 Apr 1845 m Eliza I b 1844.
10. CYNTHIA BOGARDUS b 02 Mar 1847 m ? Sutton.
11. CATHARINE BOGARDUS b 12 Apr 1850.
12. FRANCIS BOGARDUS b 01 Jun 1852 m Phoebe b 1857 d 27 Sep 1900 (all fr WBB).

DeWITT
1.1.9.4.3.8.3 HENRY DeWITT m Isabella Cropley.
1. PETER RICHARD DeWITT b 12 Jul 1856 (d 15 Dec 1921) m 29 Feb 1876 Charlotte Dell d/o Henry Dell & Elsie Pettit, d 30 Mar 1902 ae 76, **no chn.**
2. MARY ANN DeWITT b 10 Sep 1858 d 22 Jun 1909 ae 51 bur Drummondville Cem **single.**
3. ISABELLA/BELLA DeWITT b 1861 (d 28 Dec 1949 ae 88 bur First Baptist CH, Lundy Lane). She moved to the USA and is believed to have m Frank R DeWitt of Peoria IL who d 19 Jan 1911 bur York St Cem Hamilton ON. Isabella was bp as an adult 16 Nov 1885. In 1897 she is a member of First Baptist CH Niagara Falls ON & res Montrose near Chippewa ON, next listing in 1920, 1926 & 1928 Lundy's Lane. Frank DeWitt b IL was bur Sec "K" Row 4 Grave 20A Hamilton ON, last address York St, Hamilton, wf (?) <u>Marie B DeWitt</u> (note Isabella's older sis Mary Ann b 1858, **single,** a teacher).

Leucas deWit

When Isabella left the children with the Childrens Aid Society she did not use her correct name. Frank was said to have "belonged to one of the NB Can DeWitts & that he was a boxer". In the Hamilton City Directory he was a labourer & a carpenter (info & Bella's Will, fr grdson JD [James DeWitt] res Chippawa, cem rec fr ICSP & research by VEDS Baptist Rec McMaster U Hamilton ON).

4   HENRY DeWITT b 14 Jan 1864 d 16 Mar 1865 ae 01-02-02 **dy**. Family info fr grdson James DeWitt, Chippewa ON.
5   CHARLES H DeWITT b 10 Sep 1868 d 15 Jul 1921 **single**. Welland Co ON Liber N Folio 475, Will 31 Dec 1919 Pro 16 Jan 1922. He had a great deal of property in MB, SK and in Welland Co ON, most of it left to Bella (fr VEDS).

DeWITT

1.1.9.4.5.1.1 JACOBUS/JAMES DeWITT m Gertrude ? .

1. JANE DeWITT b 1819 (d 05 Oct 1903 at Port Royal ON m Rev I M Chapman. Jane paid for O D DeWitt's tbnstone.
2. ADELINE DeWITT b 1820/1827 (2 census). In 1871 Adeline res with Sarah Logan b 1815 & a Jane DeWitt b 1825.
3. EDWARD H DeWITT b 02 Oct 1824 d 04 Sep 1825 **dy**.
4. DIANTHA DeWITT b 1826.
5. MARIA DeWITT; Henry Logan m 21 Aug 1842 Maria deWitt of Walsingham. Norfolk Co ON by W McDermand Wit: Ratio Spencer, James DeWitt (note James Horatio Spencer s/o Debra DeWitt & Chester Spencer).
6. ORAM DAY DeWITT b 1830/1 (d 07 Feb 1897) m Charlotte b 1833 d 01 Apr 1881.
7. EMILY DeWITT b 23 Nov 1833 d 25 Oct 1842 **dy**.
8. SEBE DeWITT (female) b 1836.
9. EDGAR DeWITT b 1838/9 Walsingham m 23 Dec 1863 Cecelia Fick b 1841 d/o Frederick & Sarah Fick of Houghton T, Norfolk Co ON. In Walsingham in 1871 in one house were Sarah Logan (ae 56) b 1815, Jane Dewitt (ae 46) b 1825, Adeline Dewitt (ae 46 or 51) b 1820 or 27, all b ON, Baptist & Dutch.

DeWITT

1.1.9.4.5.1.2 LUKE/ELUCAS D DeWITT m Mary/Polly Williams.

1. HARRIETT ELIZABETH DeWITT b 04 Jun 1820 Durham T Greene Co NY (d 20 Aug 1868 at Kewanee IL bur Fairview Cem, Annawan IL) at Walsingham T Norfolk Co Can, she m1 18 Nov 1843 Adam Beam b 23 Mar 1823 Wits: W Lamport, John Bower CW (Canada West ie ON) Adam was bur Lot #136 above, was farmer & other occupations (fr LWB). In G J Reyerse "Marriage Register 1831-37" both of Walsingham (NCMR: 89). She m2 ? Franklin (census, family rec).
2. HENRY DeWITT b 20 May 1824 Durham, Greene Co NY (d Annawan IL) m at Walsingham T Norfolk Co ON 05 May 1847 Sarah Ann Nelson.
3. PERMILLY DeWITT b 13 Jan 1827 Durham, Greene Co NY.
4. PLATT DeWITT b 27 Aug 1830 Durham, Greene Co NY (d 13 Oct 1875 bur Fairview Cem Lot 298 Annawan, Henry Co IL). At Annawan he m 13 Oct 1875 Louise Wilhemina Bunge b 17 Oct 1855 Melzow Ger d 18 Jul 1923 Annawan.
5. IRA DeWITT b 27 May 1833 Walsingham (d 08 Dec 1863 Annawan Cem Lot 235).
6. ANTOINETT DeWITT b 04 Dec 1837.

The DeWitt Family was in the milling business in Durham NY, in Canada at Walsingham Township, Norfolk County 1833-1849, then Annawan, Henry Co IL. Data from bible of Platt DeWitt provided by Omar DeWitt, Grand Ledge IO.

DeWITT

1.1.9.4.5.1.5 WALTER DeWITT m Catherine ? .

1. DELIA S DeWITT b 1838. Note a possibility, <u>Talbot Dist Mar Reg</u> Peter Smith, Walpole m 08 Feb1855 <u>Re</u>delia DeWitt by J Williams, Wit: Alexander Shaw, John Hanson (NCMR:134).
2. WILLIAM DeWITT b 1841.
3. THERON DeWITT b 1846 Walsingham.

DeWITT

1.1.9.4.5.3.1 PETER DeWITT wf not recorded. Note his pa's Will in GEN 6.

1. EDWARD DeWITT s/o Peter DeWitt.
2. ALBERT DeWITT
3. MARIA DeWITT
4. JOHN DeWitt

DeWITT

1.1.9.4.5.3.3 HENRY DeWITT m Eliza Ann ?

1. ADELINE DeWITT b 1836 Greene.
2. WARREN H DeWITT b 1847 Greene.

Under "other" mentioned in census is black servant Matilda Buskirk 9 yrs.

HOWLAND

1.1.9.4.5.3.4 PEGGY MARIA DeWITT m Gideon Howland

1. HELEN HOWLAND m Jarrius Bissel Strong (DFUSC:98). (DAR Vol 22 p 72 lineage 21192).

Leucas deWit

DeWITT
1.1.9.4.5.3.5 DANIEL DeWITT m possibly Catherine Pike
1   SARAH DeWITT b 10 Mar 1839

DeWITT
1.1.9.4.5.3.6 HARRIET DeWITT {m} 1.1.9.4.2.3.9 **Simon Peter DeWitt**
Children are with their Father's underlined number Generation 7.

WALES
1.1.9.4.5.3.7 ADELIA ANN/DEILIA DeWITT m Blake Wales.
1   ALEXANDER DeWITT WALES b 1848 (d 1920) m 1876 Lizzie Hall Hart b 1852 d 1899.

DeWITT
1.1.9.4.5.3.8 ORLEAN DeWITT m Jerusha Case.
1   ORLEAN DeWITT Jr b 1845 Schoharie m Laura McColley (DFUSC:98).

DeWITT
1.1.9.4.5.3.9 ISREAL DeWITT m Elsie E Thorne.
1   HANNAH W DeWITT b 1858 Oak Hill NY m Henry T Waterbury (DFUSC:98). DAR Lineage 44:81 #43212 traced through Hannah.
2   MARY VAN BUREN DeWITT b 1860 m Charles Waterbury.
3   EDWARD DeWITT b 1861.
4   GEORGE CLARK DeWITT b 1866 m Maude Minot.
5   MANLEY DeWITT b 1868 m Mary Wilson.
6   NELLIE DeWITT b 1869 m Will Thorn.
7   JOHN DeWITT b 1871 m Hattie Van Aken.
8   CORDELIA DeWitt **dy.**
Isreal DeWitt single, landowner, farmer ae 31 lived Durham Town, Greene County NY. In the household mother Hannah age 70, brother Daniel age 39 - furnace man, aunt Mariah Egbertsen age 51, nephew Orlean DeWitt age 10 born Schoharie, res Greene for 5 years; other mentioned Henry Scutt farmer, age 26 born Schoharie, res Greene 26 yrs (NYSCG:80).

MEYER
1.1.9.4.8.2.8 WYNTJE/WYNCHE LOUW m Jonas Meyer.
1   ANNA MARIA MEYER b 07 Jul 1824 bp 15 Aug 1824 no sp (K&S:199).
2   SARAH ELIZABETH MEYER b 08 Jun 1828 bp 06 Jul 1828 no sp (K&S:207).
3   AMELIA MEYER b 01 Nov 1830 bp 05 Dec 1830 no sp (K&S:211) d 07 Apr 1844 ae 13-05-06 Mountain View Cem (OGUC:237) **dy**, Ulster Co NY.
4   ABRAHAM LOW MEYER b 15 Jul 1833 bp 25 Aug 1833 no sp (K&S:216) & (d 30 Nov 1900 ae 67-04-15) m Lea E Dile b 07 Dec 1850 d 16 Aug 1876 ae 35-09-09 (OGUC:237).
5   RALPH MEYER b 01 Feb 1836 bp 24 Mar 1836 no sp (K&S:220) m Sarah A ?.
6   ANGELINE MEYER b 03 Mar 1839 bp 05 May 1839 no sp (K&S:225).
7   ASA MEYER b 14 Jul 1842 bp 09 Oct 1842 no sp (K&S: 227) & (d 25 Apr 1857 ae 14-09-12 (OGUC:237) **dy.**
8   HENRY CLAY MEYER b 09 May 1846 bp 04 Oct 1846 no sp d 12 Mar 1897 ae 50-10-08 (OGUC:237).

LOW
1.1.9.4.8.2.9 ABRAHAM A LOW m Margaret Eva Brink
1   ALEXANDER KIERSTED LOW b 07 May 1834 {m} 05 Sep 1857 Rachel Ann Longendyck (1.9.1.3.1.2.2.1.7) b 03 Jun 1843 d/o Cornelius Longendyck & Jane Dumond, both Saugerties Wit: Silas Carle, Elizabeth Low (BG:73). .
2   ELIZABETH LAVINA LOW b at Flatbush Ulster Co NY 01 May 1835/6 m 15 Aug 1863 William D Bossard b 07 Apr 1838 s/o George Bossard & Rebecca Relyea (BG:74).
3   WILLIAM VAN SANTFORD LOW b 09 Nov 1837 m 05 Jan 1861 Mary Elizabeth Moran b 30 Mar 1842 d/o Dennis Moran & Dorcas A Porter (BG:74).
4   ABRAHAM LOW b 1841 d 1843 **dy.**
5   REBECCA M LOW b 13 Apr 1850 m 12 Aug 1868 Clark Davis, wdr, s/o Martin Davis & Caroline Lockwood, b 27 Jun 1835, res Fishkill Creek near Saugerties (BG:74).

LOW
1.1.9.4.8.8.6 CHARK LOW (Tierck/Tjerck was pronounced Charick) **m1 Charlotte McClung.**
1   LEVI LOW b 30 Mar 1845 Union Co OH (d 14 Mar 1927) m 24 Dec 1868 Annis B Laird (by James Ketch J.P.) b 1852 PA (fr LBM marriage Certificate, picture of Levi, 1880 census, Union Co Rec).
2   MARY JANE LOW b 21 Feb 1847 Union Co (d 1907) m Isaac Conklin.
m2 26 Nov 1853 Phoebe Jane Beck Dover T Union Co d/o Abraham Beck & Mary Jane Doty b 15 Jul 1837 or ? bp 27 Jan 1838 Union Co d of Consumption 28 Apr 1886 bur with hus (fr LMB search IGI, OH family rec newspapers) Chn b Union Co OH.
3   SYLVESTER LOW b 08 Dec 1854 d 30 Dec 1882.

Leucas deWit

4   SARAH ELIZA LOW b 16 Feb 1857 (d 03 Jun 1929) m ? Tossey.
5   JOHN LOW b 19 Apr 1860 d 31 May 1939.
6   FLORA BELL LOW b 05 Jun 1863 d 03 May 1919.
7   ELMER CHARK LOW b 30 Apr 1866 d 02 Oct 1941.
8   MARTHA JANE LOW b 07 Jul 1868 (d 06 Dec 1878) m ? Herd.
9   SAMUEL H LOW b 05 Dec 1870 d 06 Dec 1878.
10 ALMENA LOW b 20 Apr 1874 d 15 Apr 1877 (fr LMB research IGI, OH family rec, New Papers).

CONYES/CUNYES/COENIUS/CONJES

1.1.9.4.8.9.4 JACOB HENRY CONYES m Cornelia Osterhoudt.
1   HENRY SANFORD CONYES b 19 Aug 1840 bp 09 Oct 1840 (PRDC:21). Sanford H Conyes m 13 Jun 1867 Rachel Weeks both of Saugerties, Wits: Mrs S T Cole, Mary Felten (PRDC:12).
2   JASON CONYES b 21 May 1842 bp 03 Jul 1842 (PRDC:22).
3   MELLISA CATHARINE CONYES b 05 Oct 1844 bp 17 Nov 1844 (PRDC:25).
4   SARAH ANN CONYES b 14 Aug 1846 bp 11 Oct 1846 (PRDC:26).
5   GEORGE CONYES b 29 Jan 1849 bp Apr 1849 (PRDC:29) d 15 May 1849 ae 00-03-16 **dy**.
6   WILLIAM HAWLEY CONYES b 06 Mar 1850 bp 01 Jun 1850 (PRDC:30).
7   JAMES DEMAREST CONYES b 05 Sep 1854 bp 01 Dec 1854 (PRDC:34).

OSTERHOUDT

1.1.9.4.8.9.5 SARAH CATHERINE CONYES m Elias Osterhoudt
1   PETER CONYES OSTERHOUDT b 26 Oct 1848 bp 26 Nov 1848 (PRDC:28).
2   JOHN OSTERHOUDT b 28 Jul 1851 bp 19 Oct 1851 (PRDC:32).
3   AMELIA ELIZA OSTERHOUDT b 30 Jan 1855 bp 10 Jun 1856 (PRDC:36).

FELTEN

1.1.9.4.8.10.1 ZACHARIAS FELTEN m Elizabeth Ackert.
1   RACHEL ANN FELTEN b 13 Jan 1845 bp 30 Mar 1845 (PRDC:25).

SCHOONMAKER

1.1.9.4.8.11.1 CHRISTIAN SCHOONMAKER m Silvia Marquiet
1   MARTIN DOW SCHOONMAKER b 21 Oct 1834 (d 04 Aug 1918) m 28 Feb 1876 Jane Carberry Smith b 09 Jan 1850 Crum Castle, Cork Ire d 28 Aug 1932.
2   MARY E SCHOONMAKER b 27 Sep 1836 (d 18 Aug 1906) m Willis Finch b 30 Jun 1826 d 08 Aug 1900 bur Round Top Cem Cairo NY.
3   GEORGE P SCHOONMAKER b 08 Apr 1839 (d 1911) m 20 Jun 1880 Cinderella Hines d 29 Jan 1918 Jericho KS.
4   CHARLES A SCHOONMAKER b 26 Feb 1841 d 23 Feb 1862 in the Army during the Civil War.
5   WALTER SCHOONMAKER b 24 Sep 1848 (K&S:155) & (d 15 Dec 1935) m Esther Garrison d/o John Garrison & Catherine Somes, b 03 Jul 1850 d 13 Nov 1926 bur Round Top Cem Cairo NY **no chn** (P-DRS:396).

LOUW

1.1.9.4.8.12.2 JAMES LOUW m Margaret ? .
1   CATHARINE ELIZABETH LOW b 27 Jun 1839 d 30 Jan 1844 ae 05-07-03 bur Asbury Meth CH Gnd (OGUC:267) A James Low m 23 Jun 1866 Cornelia Felten of Kingston, Wits: Mrs S T Cole, Catherine Legg (P- DR:10).

GENERATION 8

If a couple both trace back to DeWitt ancestry more than once m is {m} indicating this fact. Numbering used is the first parent listed chronologically. Both numbers are given, but the one to be used in succeeding generations is underlined.

WELCH
1.1.9.4.1.2.1.5 CATHARINE DEDRICK m Benjamin Welch
1. ABRAHAM WELCH
2. WILLIAM WELCH
3. MADISON WELCH
4. HARRIET WELCH
5. SUSAN WELCH
6. JANE WELCH

Benjamin Welch m2 Rebecca Jewell & had 2 more chn.

DEDRICK
1.1.9.4.1.2.2.6 AUSTIN DEDRICK m Melissa Dench
1. LUCY DEDRICK b1865 d 20 Nov 1867 ae 12 **dy.**
2. WARREN SPURGEON DEDRICK b 1861 d 1946.
3. JOSEPH DEDRICK d 02 Oct 18 ? .
4. JENNIE MAY DEDRICK d 03 Sep 1866 ae 04-06-00 **dy.**

DEDRICK
1.1.9.4.1.2.5.2 JOHN W DEDRICK m Susan Elizabeth Miller
1. ABRAM STEPHEN DEDRICK b 11 Nov 1869 (d 02 Sep 1956) m 29 Jan 1898/9 Olive Procunier d/o David Procunier & Katherine Van Waggoner b St Williams ON 08 Sep 1875 d 31 Aug 1961. They lived on Con 1 of South Walsingham T Norfolk Co ON six miles west of Port Rowan until 1904 when they purchased the Procunier farm at St. Williams to which an extensive two-storey addition was added constructed of Procunier bricks. There had been a brick manufacturing business on the property for two generations. The kilns were torn down soon after they moved (fr FVD).

DeWITT
1.1.9.4.2.1.2.1 SILAS JOHN DeWITT m Louise Van Doren
1. JOHN DeWITT b 25 Sep 1844 d 15 Jan 1863 in VA.
2. MARY LOUISE DeWITT b 25 Oct 1846 d 29 Mar 1848 **dy.**
3. KATRINE DeWITT b 11 Aug 1848 New Brunswick NJ m 13 Jan 1870 George R Williamson of LaFayette IN.
4. FRANKLIN DeWITT b 20 Nov 1850 d 27 Apr 1851 **dy.**
5. GARRET DeWITT b 22 Nov 1854 d 26 Jul 1874 **dy.**
6. CHARLES SILAS DeWITT b 20 Sep 1856 d 1857 **dy.**

DeWITT
1.1.9.4.2.1.2.3 CLINTON DeWITT m Elsie Van Dyck.
1. ABRAHAM VAN DYCK DeWITT b 11 Aug 1836 Coxsackie (d 26 Mar 1912 at 255 Hempstead St New London CT) m 09 Jan 1896 Grace Hallam Learned d/o Rev Robert Coit Learned, b 14 Mar 1854 Canterbury CT d 16 Jan 1935 New London CT.
2. JOHN CLINTON DeWITT b 10 Dec 1837 Coxsackie (d 03 Sep 1862 Alexandria VA, an officer in the Union Army) m 1859 Lucy M Whipple, **no chn.** She m Charles T Warren.
3. KATHARINE DeWITT b 04 Oct 1842 Brooklyn NY (d 03 Jan 1932) m 18 Jan 1868 William Law Learned d 20 Sep 1904 **no chn.** "Mr Learned was, for more than thirty years, Justice of the Supreme Court of NY, residing at Albany, and was for nearly twenty years, Presiding Justice of the General Term of that Court".(Katherine's Lineage DAR 20:340 #19930, DFUSC:91).
4. MARY LOUISE DeWITT b 18 Jan 1845 Brooklyn (d 08 Feb 1902 Hamilton, Bermuda). At Albany she m 05 Jan 1875 John Treadwell Norton a lawyer from Albany s/o John Pitkin Norton & Elizabeth Pepood Marvin b Albany 13 Aug 1850 d 12 Jan 1932 (all fr P-DR:293).

VAN DYCK/PELTZ
1.1.9.4.2.1.2.5 MARY DeWITT m1 Stephen Van Dyck
1. ABRAHAM VAN DYCK d ae 15 months **dy.**
2. SARAH VAN DYCK b & d same day **dy.**

m2 1852 Philip Peltz.

3. JOHN DeWITT PELTZ b Coxsackie 26 Jun 1853 (twin of Sarah Peltz) bp 07 Oct 1853 Coxsackie (d 07 May 1904 at 323 Station St, Albany of typhoid fever). John, a lawyer, m1 24 Apr 1881 Mary Marvin Learned b 16 Apr 1856 Albany NY, 23 Nov 1888 Colorado Springs Co, d/o Hon William L Learned & Phoebe Rowland Marvin. John m2 05 Apr 1894 Catharine Barnard Walsh d/o of Augustus H Walsh & Laura Spenser b 02 Jul 1862 d 17 Mar 1924 Albany.
4. SARAH PELTZ b Coxsackie 26 Jun 1853 **single**, d Coeymans, NY 16 May 1883 (P-DR: 270,299).

Leucas deWit

5 RICHARD CLINTON PELTZ b 19 Sep 1857 bp 20 Nov 1857 at his father's CH at d Paterson NJ 23 Jan 1859 (all read P-DR:299). There is much detail in the Pletz - DeWitt Record & Supplements.

DeWitt
1.1.9.4.2.1.2.7 Rev JOHN DeWITT Jr D.D., LLD, LittD m Charlotte Lee Gillett
1. CHARLOTTE GILLET DeWITT b Coxsackie 20 Mar 1848 (d 01 Sep 1927) m 15 Jan 1880 Theophilus Calhoun Dunn s/o Dr. Theophilus Calhoun Dunn b Newport 19 Mar 1837 d East Orange NJ 27 Nov 1918.
2. CLINTON DeWITT b 26 Feb 1851 (d 12 Dec 1929 at Saugerties (P-DR:301) {m} 1 18 Jan 1891 Mary D Schoonmaker d/o 1.1.9.4.2.1.2.8.2 Tjerck Schoonmaker. She d 1916 while they res at 155 Harrison Ave, Jersey City NJ, no chn. He m2 12 Nov 1921 Mrs Antoinette Houghtaling of Saugerties who survived him. He attended Rutgers in 1870, a non graduate, had a Batchelor of Laws from NYU in 1874, later gave up legal practice & became a teacher (fr Rutger's Alumni Rec).
3. MARY DeWITT b 08 Apr 1853 d 27 Apr 1855 **dy**.
4. HERVEY GILLETT DeWITT b 26 Oct 1855 d 10 Feb 1857 **dy**.
5. SARA DeWITT b 05 Jan 1858 Millstone NJ (d 16 Dec 1945 Rye NY) at New Brunswick NJ, the brides father officiating m 05 Jan 1881 Franklin Townsend Lent BS MS (architect) s/o David B Lent & Louisa M b 03 Mar 1855 Poughkeepsie NY d 03 Dec 1919 Sterling MA. Their first 3 chn b New Brunswick NJ (more info on P-DR:301).
6. ARTHUR MASON DeWITT b 08 Mar 1862 d 08 Aug 1862 Tom's River NJ **dy**.
7. THEODORE FRELINGHUYSEN DeWITT M. D. b 17 Jul 1863 Millstone NJ (d 16 Jun 1946) at Cornwall-on – Hudson. He m, with his father officiating, 25 Sep 1890 Harriet Weston Matthiessen d/o E A Matthiessen, living in San Diego CA in 1946. The Children Clinton to Theodore were b Millstone NJ (P-DR:260/7, 270, 291, 300-06).
8. JOHN DeWITT b 20 May 1866 Saugerties (d 08 Oct 1927 bur Evergreen Cem New Brunswick NJ) m 1905 Ruth A Howland (more info on P-DR:304).
9. ELIOT LEE DeWITT b 01 Oct 1867 d 06 Jan 1871 **dy** (all P-DR:300/06 on Rev John DeWitt's Family).

SCHOONMAKER
1.1.9.4.2.1.2.8 SARAH DeWITT {m} Tjerck Schoonmaker.
1. HENRY WYNKOOP SCHOONMAKER b 07 Feb 1848 bp 16 Apr 1848 (PRDC:28) & (d ca 1891) m 19 Oct 1875 Cornelia Annie Snyder d/o Peter Snyder & Sarah Osterhout, b 1854 d 1925.
2. MARY DeWITT SCHOONMAKER b 06 Nov 1852 bp 27 Feb 1853 (PRDC:33) & (d 1916) {m} 18 Jan 1891 her cousin 1.1.9.4.2.1.2.7.2 Clinton DeWitt s/o Rev John DeWitt, the younger. Clinton was b 1851 d 1929 **no chn**.
3. JOHN DeWITT SCHOONMAKER b 11 Jul 1855 (DRCFU:45) & (d 13 Oct 1906 bur Colorado Springs CO, will pro 26 Nov 1906) m 27 Oct 1881 Cora E Wallace of High Woods, Ulster Co NY; res Littleton CO **no chn**.
4. JAMES CLINTON SCHOONMAKER b 13 Jun 1857 bp 04 Aug 1857 (PRDC:37) d 24 Jan 1884 **single**, bur Mt Marion Cem.
5. ABRAHAM TJERCK SCHOONMAKER b 13 or 24 Feb 1862 bp 08 Oct 1862 (PRDC:42) & (d 07 Dec 1947 bur Mt Marion) m 17 Nov 1890 Mildred Van Etten d/o William Gehi Van Etten & Angeline, b 09 Jun 1869 at Kingston NY P-DR:358).

VERMILYE
1.1.9.4.2.1.2.10 HELEN LANSING DeWITT m Rev Ashbel Green Vermilye
1. THOMAS EDWARD VERMILYE b 31 Oct 1848 (d 22 Sep 1934 after loss of eyesight at Wappingers Falls NY, bur Englewood NJ) at Schenectady NY m 19 May 1874 Susan Gertrude Vedder b 18 Mar 1842 of Schenectady NY d/o Nicholas Alexander Vedder & Annatje Marselis. Thomas was a member of the Holland Society, was with the Seventh Regiment NGNY, attended Rensselaer Polytechnical Institute and became a civil engineer. He was active in public affairs at East Orange NJ.
2. HELEN LANSING VERMILYE b 25 Mar 1853 Newburyport MA (d 29 Sep 1887 Englewood at Orange NJ) m 02 Oct 1878 George Long Hutchings) of NYC s/o Rev Samuel Hutchings & Elizabeth Coit Lathrop, b 13 Mar 1844 Clapham Park, London, England d 02 Dec 1937 Charleston SC. He m2 1890 Mrs Caroline (Gillender) Lane and m3 1931 Mrs. Elizabeth (Hammond) Goldsmith (all fr P-DR:309/10/11).
3. ELIZABETH BREESE VERMILYE b 13 Mar 1858 Newburyport d 18 Dec 1930 Asbury Park NJ.

CRUICKSHANKS
1.1.9.4.2.1.2.12 ANNA MARIA DeWITT m Rev James Cruickshanks
1. MARY STUART CRUICKSHANKS b 28 Nov 1865 Spencer lived 23 High St, Spencer MA, d 13 Sep 1949. "Mary studied and travelled in Europe for eight years; taught German and French at Williamsport, PA. She lived for about ten years at Montclair, with her cousin Elizabeth Vermilye and travelled with her several times to Europe, also spent two winters with her in Riverside CA".
2. JOHN DeWITT CRUICKSHANKS b at Spencer MA 12 Jul 1869 d ? Dec 1891 near Gibralter on his way to Naples (all P-DR:312).

Leucas deWit

DeWITT
1.1.9.4.2.1.4.1 JACOB TEN BROECK DeWITT m Juliet Louise May
1. KATE OSBORNE DeWITT b 03 Mar 1854 (d 19 Mar 1860) m 04 Jan 1874 Lorin W Lathrop.
2. ELIZABETH MAY DeWITT b 27 Jul 1855 d 11 Sep 1868 **dy.**
3. FRANK HUNTSMAN DeWITT b 17 Dec 1857 m 03 Apr 1878 Maria F Kerman.
4. ADA BELLE DeWITT b 25 Jul 1862 m 11 Aug 1882 Richard S Hickey (CDDGC:102).

HOAGLAND
1.1.9.4.2.1.4.2 MARY JANE DeWITT m Benjamin Townsend Hoagland
1. MARY ELIZABETH HOAGLAND b 21 Sep 1852 d 16 Apr 1853.
2. CHARLES TOWNSEND HOAGLAND b 21 Jun 1854 m Helen Viele Richmond.
3. DE WITT HOAGLAND b 20 Jun 1857 (d 18 Dec 1892) m 03 Feb 1886 Verina Bailey.
4. HELEN CORNELIA HOAGLAND b 04 Oct 1859 d ? May 1863.
5. GEORGE HOAGLAND d 14 Sep 1863.
6. JOHN WILLIAMS HOAGLAND b 15 Nov 1865 m 12 Apr 1893 Mary Alice Vrooman. Family res Brooklyn NY (CDDGC:102).

DeWITT
1.1.9.4.2.1.4.4 MARTIN VAN BUREN DeWITT m Jane Cornelia Hover
1. FREDERICK DeWITT b 15 May 1866.
2. MARY MAZIE DeWITT b 09 Aug 1868.
3. JENNIE JANE DeWITT b 21 Nov 1871.
4. CATHARINE/KATE DeWITT b 18 Jan 1874 d 12 Feb 1878 **dy.**
5. CORNELIA DeWITT b 01 Dec 1878 (CCDGC:102).

DeWITT
1.1.9.4.2.1.4.8 EUGENE B DeWITT m Barbara Rose Lasher.
1. BERTHA C DeWITT b 1871 m ? T(h)eller.
2. EUGENE DeWITT bp 27 Apr 1872 d 31 Jul 1872.
3. JESSIE C DeWITT b 1875 m ? Helsly.
4. HELEN DeWITT bp 08 Mar 1877 (d 18 Jun 1883) info in Town Clerk Rec p 88.
5. ISAAC C DeWITT bp 05 Dec 1882 d 06 Mar 1884 ae 01-03-00, info in Town Clerk Rec p 87 **dy.**
6. FRANCES C DeWITT b 1886 m John L Davies.
7. LOUISE M DeWITT m ? Weist (CCDGC:102).

OVERBAGH
1.1.9.4.2.2.1.1 JOHN VAN LEUVEN OVERBAGH m Caroline Verplanck.
1. MARIA VAN LEUVEN OVERBAGH b 10 May 1825.
2. ELENA V OVERBAGH b 08 Apr 1827 m Elias Dubois.
3. RACHEL ANN OVERBAGH b 03 Jan 1830.
4. PETER TITUS OVERBAGH b 01 Sep 1832 Flatbush, Town of Saugerties (d 18 May 1871) m 16 Dec 1858 Caroline Goldsborough Caldwell d/o John Sipple Caldwell & Rebecca Baker b 14 Jan 1839 Wilmington DL d 17 Oct 1915 Saugerties.
5. KERNLAUCK OVERBAGH b 07 Apr 1842 bp 01 Jul 1842 (RDCFU:21,22,25,29,37).

OSTRANDER/OVERBAGH/SWART
1.1.9.4.2.2.1.2 RACHEL ANN MARIE OVERBAGH m1 Stephen Nottingham Ostrander
1. TITUS OSTRANDER b 05 Sep 1829 (RDCFU:23) Rachel & son's pictures were painted by Philips in 1838.
2. MARIA LOUISA OSTRANDER b 05 Oct 1835 (RDCFU:32) m Theodore Hollenbach.

m2 02 Jan 1842 Solomon Freligh Overbagh.
3. PETER TEPPAN OVERBAGH b 20 Aug 1843 bp 18 Nov 1843 Marbletown d 23 Aug 1844 a week after his father, bur Van Leuven Grd Saugerties. (MSRUC:161)

m3 19 Feb 1846 Capt William Tunis Swart (RDFU:23, MSRU:61).

Rachel Ann Marie Overbaugh's Will dated Aug 1862, left the estate to her beloved daughter & Executor Maria Louisa Ostrander. Codicil Sept 1864 left son Titus three shares of Bank Stock, four pictures but not the Phillips, a silver cake basket for her secretary. Both children lived in NYC, probably Brooklyn. William Swart left his estate to stepdau Maria Louisa Hollanbach; Titus got $100. He seems to not be well thought of. There's a detailed explicit account in Family Trees (FT:71). From the "Kingston Democratic Journal" May 31, 1865 "Died - Swart - On Saturday May 13, last, Ann M Overbagh d/o Rev Peter A Overbagh (deceased) and wife of William T Swart, aged 55 years 2 months 10 days. Thus ended a strange and eventful life."

OSTERHOUDT
1.1.9.4.2.2.1.4 SARAH MARGARET OVERBAUGH m Peter P Osterhoudt
1. ALFRED OSTERHOUDT b 19 Feb 1839 (RDCFU:35).

Leucas deWit

2 MARY ELIZABETH OSTERHOUDT b 10 Feb 1843 bp 18 Jun 1848 (RDCFU:39).
3 LOUISA OSTERHOUDT b 24 Aug 1844 bp 13 Oct 1844 (RDCFU:38).

CUNYES/CONYES

1.1.9.4.2.3.1.2 JANE CATHARINE or CATHARINE JANE DeWITT m Jacob Lemuel Conyes
1 RACHEL CUNYES b 12 May 1848 bp 24 Sep 1848 (PDRC:28).
2 WILLIAM DeWITT CONYES b 30 Aug 1850 bp 16 Mar 1851 father as Jacob L Conyes (PDRC:31).

DeWITT

1.1.9.4.2.3.1.3 MOSES FRELIGH DeWITT m Mary E Martin
1 ABRAHAM HENRY DeWITT b 06 Sep 1851 bp 04 Apr 1852 (RDCFU:42) d 11 Feb 1856 **dy.**
2 ALICE DeWITT bp 20 Nov 1854 d 27 Jan 1846 **dy.**
3 WILLIAM DeWITT b 10 Jul 1856 **dy.**
4 GEORGE DeWITT
5 MILLARD MONTGOMERY DeWITT bp ? Jun 1860 Flatbush Ulster Co NY m1 20 Aug 1882 Ida G Lewis d 27 Mar 1906; m2 Mary Shepherd.
6 HATTIE EUDORA DeWITT bp 26 Sep 1871 (d 27 Oct 1903) m 12 Dec 1886 Austin P Whitney of Minden CT.
7 ARTHUR LESTER DeWITT bp 11 Jul 1875 m 03 Mar 1906 Carrie M Sietz b 22 Aug 1882 (HGC:434/5).

WOOLVEN

1.1.9.4.2.3.3.1 CATHARINE MARIA VAN ETTEN m Samuel Freligh Woolven.
1 ANNA MARIA WOOLVEN b 06 Jan 1835 m 25 Jun 1861 William Schermerhorn Van Hoesen.
2 ELIZABETH WOLVEN b 05 Aug 1842 d 28 Nov 1851 ae 09-03-23 (bible).

WOLVEN

1.1.9.4.2.3.5.1 ANN ELIZA DeWITT m Jeremiah Wolven
1 ANDREW DEWITT WOLVEN b 15 Feb 1846 bp 06 Sep 1846 (PRDC:26).

DeWITT

1.1.9.4.2.3.5.2 JAMES VAN ETTEN DeWITT m 1.1.9.1.4.4.1.1 Christina Catharine Langendyke
1 CATHARINE DeWITT b 30 Nov 1849 bp 06 Dec 1849 (PDRC:30).

DeWITT

1.1.9.4.2.3.5.3 ABRAHAM A DeWITT m Rebecca C Van Aken.
1 ANNIE DeWITT m Apr 10 1876 Albert Snyder both of Saugerties, at the house of Abram DeWitt; $10.00 (PRDC:16, DSTM).

DeWITT

1.1.9.4.2.3.5.4 PETER DeWITT m Helen James.
1 ALBERT JAMES DeWITT b 05 Apr 1855 bp 15 Jul 1855 (PRDC:35) m Violetta Turk.
2 MARY ALICE DeWITT b 15 Apr 1857 bp 12 Jul 1857 (PDRC:37).

LOWTHER

1.1.9.4.2.3.9.6 CATHARINE DeWITT m Christopher S Lowther
1 HELEN LOWTHER b 25 Jul 1880 m Lorraine B Wood, 82 Highland Ave Kingston NY (P-DR:255)

SNYDER

1.1.9.4.2.5.2.8 LOUISA BURHANS {m} 1.1.9.1.3.4.6.5.1 Charles Albert Snyder; m1 Mary Jane Felton , her chn
WILLIAM SNYDER b 13 Jul 1873 d 16 Aug 1874 **dy.**
ANNA MAY SNYDER b 24 Jan 1875.
LUELLA SNYDER b 10 Dec 1878.
Charles Snyder m2 14 May 1884 Louisa Burhans (BG:490)
1 MARIA SNYDER was the wd/o Richard Tappen in 1896.
2 CATHARINE ANN SNYDER m Ephriam Burhans.
3 SARAH J SNYDER was the wd/o John Kneiffer in 1896.
4 ELIZABETH SNYDER **dy** twin of
5 EDWINA SNYDER m George Sagendorf.
6 CLINTON SNYDER m Emma Sagendorf.
7 HEZEKIAH SNYDER d before 1896 m Sarah M Merritt (CBRUC:1132/3) no further info.

GRAHAM

1.1.9.4.3.1.3.1 ELIZABETH H DeWITT m John Graham
1 JOHN GRAHAM b 1834/5 (census 1851 Kingston T Frontenac Co CW).
2 MARGARET GRAHAM b 1837/8 m 08 Mar 1854 Ansom Totliff.
3 MARTHA M GRAHAM b 1838/9.
4 JOANNA GRAHAM b 1842/3 of Kingston T m 12 Dec 1867 James Gordon s/o Alex Gordon&Mary McCartney b 1840.
5 JAMES GRAHAM b 1847/8.
6 CHARLES A GRAHAM b 1849/50 of Napanee ON d 1895.
7 JOHN GRAHAM Jr b 1853 res Con 4 Lot 6 Kingston Twp m 29 Mar 1854 Martha Reid.

John Graham Sr was born 1811 in County Sligo, Ireland, and came to Canada with his family when he was 10. At age 19, he was converted to Episcopalian Methodist at the floating Bridge Camp Meeting. On the day of his majority he married Elizabeth Dewitt. His death occurred in Kingston Township January 17, 1853 age 42. He was buried in the cemetery at Waterloo. The widow was left with 6 children. Her mother and one child preceded the husband and father by but a few months. Mr Graham had served for nearly 20 years as leader, steward and exhorter (fr MNMP, 16 Feb 1853 p36).

DeWITT

1.1.9.4.3.1.4.1 LUKE DeWITT m Elenor ? .
1. JOHN C DeWITT b ? Jun 1836 Ernestown T L&A Co ON.
2. ABRAHAM <u>SEMORE/SEYMOUR</u> DeWITT b Jan 1839 Ernestown T res Sophiasburg T at ae 28 m 06 Jan 1868 Sarah A Alysworth d/o David Aylsworth & Nancy, b 1840 Ernestown res Odessa (CMRLA:11). Abraham of Napanee, mail carrier, sold 08 Feb 1870 to Luke Dewitt of Kingston T W1/2 of E1/2 of Lot 5 Con 3 Kingston T Western Addition, 50 acres for $1500. Wit: S O Clark of Ernestown T, same day Luke Dewitt & wf Eleanor obtained from Abraham Seymour Dewitt a morgage for $100.00 (fr land rec).
3. <u>ANNA</u> AMELIA DeWITT b 04 Jun 1843 bp #246 25 Dec 1849 Camden East T L&A Co ON (WMBLA:68,74 [tbstn 1845-1914 Cataraqui United CH Cem Frontenac Co ON Lot 15 Con 3]) res Kingston, at ae 24 m 24 Mar 1868 James Sproule b 1842 Kingston ON s/o Joseph Sproule & Ellen, d 1910 (CMRF:107).
4. LUKE ALBERT DeWITT b 11 Apr 1847 Camden East T bp #245 25 Dec 1849 minister Charles Taggart (Ann & Luke WMBLA:74).

HICKS

1.1.9.4.3.1.4.7 FRANCES DeWITT m Benjamin Hicks
1. JAMES HICKS farmed Con 5 Lot 35 Ernestown T L&A Co. ON
2. ALBERT HICKS b 1848.

DeWITT

1.1.9.4.3.1.4.9 JOHN G DeWITT m Angeline Eliza Caton
1. ETTA REBECCA DeWITT b 1871 near Bath d 26 Sep 1895 typhoid ae 26.
2. FREDERICK DeWITT b 11 Mar 1872 bp #653 30 Mar 1874 Ernestown T (WMBLA:101).
3. IRA DeWITT b 25 Apr 1874 bp #652 30 Nov 1874 Ernestown T L&A Co by A M McCann (WMBAL:101) d 26 Oct 1895 typhoid. Cem Rec Napanee ON Museum.
4. ALBERT DeWITT b 1882 d 01 Nov 1895 ae 13 from typhoid fever. Burials Wilton Cem Ernestown T.

DeWITT

1.1.9.4.3.1.5.1 GEORGE HIRAM DeWITT m Lydia/Lidia Louise Botts
   1851 Census; 3 M in school, 1 F, log house, 1 storey.
1. LIDDIA DeWITT b ? Sep 1844 Ernestown T L&A Co ON.
2. GEORGE DeWITT b 17 Mar 1845 Ernestown bp 13 May 1851 #49 at Camden E by C Taggart (WMBLA:69)
3. LUKE AUGUSTUS DeWITT b 01 Aug 1849 Camden T L&A Co d 07 Nov 1931 CA (IGI).

DeWITT

1.1.9.4.3.1.5.2 WILLIAM LUKE DeWITT & Samantha Alelia Cronk; m1 Phoebe; m2 Jemima Foster
1. SAMANTHA LUELLA DeWITT b 1857 (as Samantha Lambert d 1948 bur Glenwood Cem, Picton ON) m1 George O Hatch b 1850 d 1880, m2 E Lambert, dau b 1885. From William's Will & some info from the Picton Museum Curator about 1980. A quilt made by Samantha Cronk when she was ae 11 is on exhibit.

DeWITT

1.1.9.4.3.1.5.3 JOHN DeWITT m Melinda Oliver
1. CATHARINE E DeWITT b 1853 in census, not in bible, presumed **dy**.
2. IRA CLANCY/CHAUNCY DeWITT b 08 Nov 1856 Prince Edward Co ON (d 29 Nov 1919 a blacksmith bur Oakwood Cem, Gaines Genesee Co MI) m Martha Mary Fleming d/o William Fleming & Catherine Story, b 07 Apr 1855 d 17 Dec 1951 both bur Oakwood Cem Gaines MI ae 96. Early in their marriage they lived in Louisville, Kent Co ON Can. In the late 1880's they moved to Detroit MI & later settled north of Detroit at Gaines MI. He was the village blacksmith. At the time of his death Grand Truck Railway employed him as a Repair Foreman. Returning from work during a high wind he was struck by a falling object, possibly a large brick from a building, but when his body was found it was evident that he had been robbed (fr CFD & JFFGD).
3. ARMENTA DeWITT b 1859 (d 1914 bur Oakwood) m Caleb R Wood.
4. LUKE <u>ALBERT</u> DeWITT b 1865 (d 1917 bur Oakwood) m Emma Gotchalk.
5. HATTIE ELLEN DeWITT b 22 Jun 1866 (d 08 Mar 1853 bur Oakwood) m Albert Learst (fr CFD).

BAILEY

1.1.9.4.3.3.1.2 JOHN T BAILEY m Lavina <u>Jane</u> Scribner
1. ARAMENTA BAILEY b 1843 (d 11 Aug 1877 tbstn both Blissville Cem) m David Nason.
2. CHARLES A BAILEY b 1845.

3 OLIVE Y BAILEY b 1847 (d 1879) m Wellington Fowler (fr grdson Emerson Eldridge) (bur Blissville Cem).
4 LEONA BAILEY b 1849.
5 ANNIE BAILEY b 1851 (d 1932) {m} as his 3rd wf John DeWitt (1.1.9.4.3.3.8.1.) s/o Luke DeWitt & Mary Wood, b 12 Dec 1827 d 18 Aug 1903 **no chn** (bur Blissville Cem).
(fr KLAD, CSNB:10, tbstn, family records).

SEELY
1.1.9.4.3.3.1.3 PHOEBE ELIZABETH BAILEY m James Seeley
1 ADELINE SEELY
2 GEORGE SEELY
3 LUKE SEELY
4 ANN SEELY
5 PERLEY SEELY
(collected by KLAD, fr JS, tbstn).

BAILEY
1.1.9.4.3.3.1.4 CHARLES J BAILEY m Rachel Webb
1 HAYWARD D BAILEY b 1842.
2 MELISSA H BAILEY b 1844.
3 LEVINA A BAILEY b 1846.
4 SOPHIA BAILEY b 1848.
5 MARY A BAILEY b 1850.

BAILEY
1.1.9.4.3.3.1.5 GIDEON D BAILEY m1 Hannah Branscombe
1 GEORGE BAILEY
2 MARY E BAILEY
3 MARTHA BAILEY
m2 Rachel Branscombe b 1821 d 1903.
(CSNB:10, 1851 Census, Blissville Parish, Sunbury Co NB) No dates copied.

BAILEY
1.1.9.4.3.3.1.8 BENJAMIN STUDLEY BAILEY m Hannah Seeley
1 LESLIE OSBORNE BAILEY b 30 Jul 1854 Fredericton NB (d 25 Aug 1945 Winnipeg MB, he & wf bur Brookside Cem) at Harcourt NB (CH Reg #5255) m 29 Mar 1877 Mary Elizabeth Hannay d/o James Hannay & Christable Cail b 07 Dec 1855 Kingston NB d 07 Dec 1934 ae 79 Winnipeg MB (fr SCBG; MAH).
2 BLISS BONFORD BAILEY
3 GEORGE BAILEY
4 COLINDA BAILEY m Leslie J Wathen of Harcourt & had 2 chn.
5 OTTO A BAILEY b 03 Jan 1865 fr Obit date not recorded s/o Mr & Mrs Benjamin Bailey. He moved with his parents to Rexton when young. He enlisted in the Royal Canadian Regt during the Boer War, d at Sunny Brae (now part of Moncton NB) survivors - wife, dau Marion, 2 bros Bliss & Leslie & sis Mrs L J Wathem.

DeWITT
1.1.9.4.3.3.2.1 JOHN DeWITT m1 Mahala L Page
1 SAMUEL L DeWITT b 10 Nov 1850 d 01 May 1863 ae 12-05-21 **dy** (HPCM cem record).
2 VICTORIA A DeWITT b 20 Feb 1854 d 04 Mar 1862 ae 08-00-12 **dy** (HPCM cem record).
3 BRADBURY G DeWITT b 1857 res Medford ME (d 1942 Medford ME m Edith Thomas d/o Benjamin Thomas & Sarah Lancaster b 1866 Maxfield ME d 1943.
4 CHARLES H DeWITT b 1859 res Presque Isle (d 1932) m Lizzie S. b 1861 d 1933.
5 MARY J DeWITT m Marshall Fuller of La Grange ME.
6 ELLA DeWITT m Isreal H Bemis of Carmel ME.
7 EMMA DeWITT
m2 Betsy J ? b 28 Jan 1816 d 28 Oct 1897 (Info History of Penobscot Co ME & Cem Rec).

DeWITT
1.1.9.4.3.3.2.3 DAVID T DeWITT m1 Winifred Vaughn
1 VAUGHN DeWITT (one Vaughn H DeWitt, possibly a grson, d 28 Aug 1904 ae 01-10-00 bur Maxfield ME.
m2 Hannah Briggs
2 ASHAEL W/ISREAL W DeWITT b 06 Feb 1837 (d 01 Feb 1904 Maxfield) m Ellen ? .
3 SARAH E DeWITT
4 EDWIN G DeWITT
(1850 Mansfield ME Census)

DeWITT

1.1.9.4.3.3.2.7 CHARLES DUDLEY DeWITT m Bethia G Buswell
1. ELLA FRANCES DeWITT b 05 May 1852 Maxfield d 19 May 1853 **dy.**
2. JOHN COLBY DeWITT b 18 Aug 1862 Presque Isle ME (d 1949) in CA m 01 Nov 1897 Nettie Louise Houlton d/o Horatio Houlton & Melissa Jane Harvey, b 22 May 1868 Elk River MN d 25 Oct 1949 (fr BBVH).

DeWITT

1.1.9.4.3.3.3.1 RUFUS DeWITT m1 Olive Smart, m2 Susan Roberts
1. CAROLINE C DeWITT b 1855.
2. CHARLES A DeWITT b 1859.
3. PHEBE JANE DeWITT b 16 May 1862.
4. MARJORIE OLIVE DeWITT b 02 Jan 1872 (all chn b Lowell, Penobscot ME, fr IGI).

SMART

1.1.9.4.3.3.3.3 PHOEBE ELIZA DeWITT m Charles Lyford Smart.
1. LLEWELLYN BROOKS SMART b 20 Mar 1842 Sebec, Piscataquis Co ME, served in the Civil War (d 10 Mar 1935 Seboeis ME) was a Sharpshooter in the Civil War; at Howland ME m 08 Oct 1868 Flora Emma Sargisson d/o William Edward Sargisson & Mary L Higgins, b 26 Feb 1846 La Grange ME d 30 Nov 1922 both bur Seboeis ME.
2. CHARLES L SMART b 01 Feb 1851 Sebec ME (d 01 Jul 1928 Seboeis ME) m Allura S Fowles.
Info from vital stats, Civil War Rec, Pension Rec, tbstns, Charles Smart Sr's bro was Moses Greenleaf Smart m Mary Elizabeth DeWitt d/o Abraham P DeWitt & Nancy S Smith (fr BBVH).

DeWITT

1.1.9.4.3.3.4.1 DANIEL DeWITT {m} 1 Catharine/Katie Boone (1.1.9.4.3.6.4.1)
1. PHOEBE ANN DeWITT b 13 Jul 1840 Briggs Mills NB (d 13 Jul 1912) m 29 Oct 1859 George Scott res Briggs b 10 Dec 1819 Gagetown NB area d 12 Apr 1897 Fredericton Jct NB both bur Gladstone Cem; chn b Fredericton Jct. George was a farmer & long time invalid; the family was Baptist.
2. HENRY L DeWITT b 1842.
3. EUNICE DeWITT b 1844 **single.**
4. DANIEL <u>LUDLOW</u> DeWITT b 1846 m Lizzie Webb.
5. ADELINE M DeWITT b 1850 m George Briggs; no info found.
6. ABIGAIL DeWITT m Frank Shaw **no chn**.
7. DAVID DeWITT (d a young man) m Maggie Davis.
8. GEORGE DeWITT m wd Mrs Maggie (Davis) DeWitt his bro David DeWitt's wd.
9. BENEDICT DeWITT
m2 Uphanie Ho (fr LMD; KLAD).

DeWITT

1.1.9.4.3.3.4.2 JOHN HENRY DeWITT m Mary E Seeley
1. ANNA GUSTA DeWITT b 1852 m Norman Hoyt.
2. CARSON JANE E DeWITT b 1854 m E M Shaw of Victoria Corners NB.
3. MARSHALL R DeWITT b 1856 **no chn**.
4. ADDIE S DeWITT m 1888 Haddon P Birmingham both Victoria Corners.
5. ELIZA DeWITT m Sam Boyer had one dau, res Vancouver BC.
6. FREDERICK SEELEY DeWITT b 1860.
7. MARY E DeWITT b 1864.
8. JOHN H DeWITT b 1866.
They lived at Victoria Corner near Hartland, Careleton Co NB; Petition for land 1838 in Blissville; chn b at Blissville (fr Census LDM).

DeWITT

1.1.9.4.3.3.4.3 BETHEUL DeWITT m Mary E Smith
1. BABY DeWITT d at b **dy.**
2. CLOWES SHERMAN DeWITT b 1853 Oromocto area NB (d 01 Nov 1901 Presque Isle ME of pneumonia) m Georgie Ann Drake d/o Francis Drake & Emmeline Plummer, b 01 Jan 1854 Carleton Co NB, d 1922. The farm was the life and interest of Clowes.
3. ANNIE/HANNAH DeWITT b 1854 (alive 1931) {m} Melbourne Smith. (1.1.9.4.3.3.5.2.2.) s/o Daniel Smith & Charlotte Smith, b 1856 d 1926 res Presque Isle ME. Annie div him; he {m} 2 Adeline Scott (1.1.9.4.3.3.4.1.1.6.) d/o Phoebe Ann DeWitt & George Scott, **no chn** (fr LMD).

May DeWitt, when she was 85, wrote her son Lester Mallory her childhood memories of her grandfather Bethuel. She recalls him as rather stocky in stature, probably about five feet eight inches tall. He had a good deal of gray hair showing which had probably been black or very dark brown. His eyes were gray. Her grandmother told her that when younger and having a wonderful voice, and with a scarcity of organs, he "set the tunes in church meetings". By faith he was a Free Will Baptist and while not overly religious, observed the rules closely. She remembers a time when she was about seven years old that his white mare had gone to the lake to drink and became mired. Bethuel pondered on this for some time, then said 'This is the Sabbath, but I can't lose her', so he harnessed another horse and with a rope pulled the white mare out. He a not rather regular church attendant, which his wife Mary wished, but sometimes he would say that he did not feel well and would lie down on a couch in the kitchen. At that point his wife would remark that he would recover as soon as it was too late to go to church.

This surviving picture of four generations is of Mary E Smith died about 1915 w/o Bethuel DeWitt; George Drake 1854-1922 w/o Clowes DeWitt; May DeWitt 1882-1976 w/o Enrique Mallory; son Lester DeWitt Mallory 1904. A collection of this family's photographs was destroyed in a flood in British Columbia.

May DeWitt Mallory remembered her grandmother kept up the flower garden planted by the Mallorys, including Sweet William, Sweet Mary, Ribbon Grass and other old time flowers. She was past age four when, on 04 Mar 1887 the house burned down. It was a very large home built by the Mallorys in Rosedale and the grandparents and parents lived there together. On that cold and windy day her mother and grandmother had visitors and built a big fire. A spark lit on the roof. She recalled very clearly that she was by the window looking out toward the woods where her grandfather had gone for firewood, across a little brook that flowed from Rider Lake, when she saw him running toward the house. He had seen the flames on the roof. He put up the ladder to the roof but it was too late. She relates that she had gone twice to her grandmother's room and got behind the door and the second time was carried out, put on a snow bank and told to stay there. A fortuneteller by the name of Slack took her father's buffalo robe which had a big piece burned out of it, and put it on a cranberry bush. Soon her father, who had been helping a neighbor thresh oats, arrived with a sled full of men, but it was too late. Apparently all that was saved was a sewing machine and the buffalo robe.

They were given a room in a house of Fred Culberson while Clowes had a new house built. He could have only occupied it a few years, as he moved to Presque Isle ME and continued to farm. Bethuel farmed in Rosedale and later in life moved to Presque Isle ME, where his son had previously gone (fr LDM).

DeWITT
1.1.9.4.3.3.4.4 LUKE E DeWITT m1 Rebecca (Seeley) Hoyt
1   ELIZABETH MALVINA DeWITT b 1850.
2   PHOEBE D DeWITT b 1852 m   ?   Bailey.
3   JOHN FRED DeWITT b 1853 Carleton CO NB (d 10 Jul 1935) m Mary Welch all chn b Carleton Co NB.
4   JAMES ALONZO DeWITT b 1856 m Mary Churchill.
5   AUSTIN/OSCAR DeWITT b 1860 m Emma Gardener.
6   UNNAMED DeWITT b 1861.
7   MELVIN DeWITT b 1863 (d 1935) m Annie Culbertson.
8   ANNIE DeWITT b 1864 (d 04   ?   1958) m James McLeod b 1863.
9   THOMAS H DeWITT b 1867 d 03 Apr 1867 Blissville NB **dy.**
10 CHARLOTTE E DeWITT b 1867 d 17 Apr 1867 Blissville NB **dy.**
    m2 1884 Mrs Euphemia Hendry
11 GEORGE ARTHUR DeWITT killed ae 19 at Ignace ON while employed with the CPR (fr KLAD, LDM).

HOYT
1.1.9.4.3.3.4.5 ANNA/ANNIE JANE DeWITT m William E Hoyt
1   ALICE/?ALICIA ADELIA HOYT b 1850 (d   ?   Mar 1882 MT) m   ?   McKenzie.
2   ELSIE HOYT **single**.
3   SILAS HOYT m Maggie Haley of Houlton ME.
4   PHOEBE HOYT m   ?   Bailey.
5   CLEMENTE HOYT m George Haley.
6   BLANCHE M HOYT m   ?   Humphrey res Oregon City OR had a ch.
7   THOMAS HOYT m Barbara Neal res Rosedale NB Tom worked on railway out of Woodstock NB, had at least one dau. (fr LDM).
8   ANNA HOYT m   ?   Crockett (all fr LMD, KLAD).

MOFFAT
1.1.9.4.3.3.4.6 PHOEBE DeWITT m Robert Moffat, all chn b Blissville
1   MARGARET MOFFAT m Wellington Hoyt.
2   JOHN MOFFAT b 1853.
3   ANN MOFFAT b 1855.
4   ROSYNET MOFFAT b 1857.
5   GEORGE MOFFAT b 1859.

DeWITT
1.1.9.4.3.3.4.7 EZEKIEL H DeWITT m1 Irene S Smith; m2 Frances E
1   IRENE DeWITT m 1889 Odber Shaw.

Leucas deWit

2 JOHN DeWITT d in BC. A "Mr DeWitt" came to BC with the Overlanders from ON to the gold rush & has not been identified.
3 FRANK DeWITT res in Houlton ME.
4 WILLIAM DeWITT
5 MOUNT DeWITT m ? Tapley (fr MWD).

DeWITT

1.1.9.4.3.3.4.8 GEORGE MORGAN DeWitt m Angeline Hoyt

1 LYMAN GILBERT DeWITT b 22 Jun 1861 d 09 Jul 1888. He went to Montana at a young age & worked in the lumber camps, where he lost an arm. He looked in a bar, liked it, and bought it. He was said to have drowned. While fording a river someone shot him off his horse which went back to the barn. But Lyman was dead with a bullet in him, just as he was about to leave for home.
2 RUTH ANN DeWITT b 19 Mar 1863 (d 15 Mar 1956) bur Mt Pleasant Cem Toronto) m1 13 Oct 1885 Wilmot Clark, b 13 Oct 1885 (fr KLAD, LDM) m2 13 Oct 1905 Ernest Estay, in 1918 res Vancouver BC; 1943 Obit as Mrs R A Estay of Toronto.
3 JOHN WELLINGTON DeWITT b 02 Jan 1865 (d 15 Apr 1947) m 25 Jun 1902 Lizzie Bell Lipsett b 1873 d 28 Mar 1942 ae 69 bur Waterville Cem NB in 1918 they res Avondale NB (fr LDM).
4 PHOEBE ELIZA DeWITT b 10 May 1867 (d 08 Jan 1949 Waterville, Carlton Co NB) m 01 Nov 1886 Samuel R Hayden; d 1922 in 1918 res Riley Brook NB then res Presque Isle ME (fr LDM; Orbit fr GMD). Phoebe was Baptist.
5 EPPIE EUPHEMIA DeWITT b 29 Sep 1869 Waterville NB (d 23 Nov 1951) m 01 Apr 1887 Charles Gray (fr LDM). 1918 Obit lists a dau as Mrs C Craig of Woodstock NB. Perhaps this is a misquote from oral info; Saunders is as Sanders; in 1943 Obit as Mrs C H Gray of Jacksonville NB, 1949 in Vancouver.
6 GEORGE HOWARD DeWITT b 27 Jul 1871 (d 06 Oct 1958 Waterville NB) (in Geo's Obit his wf predeceased him) res Saint John NB m 24 Dec 1904 Lula M Drake d/o Sherwood Drake & Alice, b 1879 d 1950. An undated clipping: Waterville - The funeral of George H DeWitt of Epworth Park and formerly Saint John was held Thursday afternoon from Waterville Baptist Church here with service conducted by Rev Harold Merrill. Pallbearers were Hallie Gray, Ernest Culberson, Carl Culberson, and all nephews of Mr. DeWitt. A profusion of floral tributes was received. Interment was in Waterville Baptist Church Cemetery (fr EDS, GMD). George was a mechanic with the former NB Power Co. He was a charter member of the Masonic Lodge, Benjamin, No. 31, F and AM.
7 EMMA IDELLA DeWITT b 14 Apr 1873 (d 24 May 1943) m 21 Feb 1893 William E Culberson d 1960 (fr LDM), in 1918 res Waterville NB, she was Baptist. Obit also names 4 sons but not her 14 grchn, 4 sis, 4 bros.
8 ELIZABETH/BERTIE CLOE DeWITT b 02 Sep 1876 Wateville, Carleton Co NB (d 23 Jan 1952 Victoria Corner NB) m 20 Sep 1899 Guy Birmingham, in 1918 res Victoria Corners NB, 1949 Saint John. (fr LDM).
9 SAUNDERS WILMOT DeWITT b 12 Aug 1878 at home in 1918 m 03 Oct 1922 ?
10 ERNEST BARKER DeWITT b 29 Aug 1880 Avondale, Carleton Co NB, moved to Calgary, Alberta, Canada Apr 1919 (d Calgary AB 26 Feb 1976 bur Queen's Park Cem) m1 25 Oct 1905 Sarah/Sadie Eastman McLeod d/o J C McLeod & Etta, b 27 Apr 1880 d 11 Mar 1946. He m2 Faye Balmain Mersereau d/o John Mersereau of Rusagonis NB She died March 2000. In retirement both he and his brother Saunders resided in Calgary AB. They were ranchers & farmers. When he was nine when he and the rest of the family were at his grpa John DeWitt's bedside when he died.
Information copied by E. B. DeWitt from the Family Bible on 06 Apr 1966 was recopied by Ruth DeWitt Estay on 14 Jan 1962. The Bible transcriptions and Ernest's stories about New Brunswick, Cuba and Alberta were phoyocopied by a family member and generously given to the author by his son George DeWitt of Airdrie AB several years ago.

DeWITT

1.1.9.4.3.3.4.9 REV THOMAS ORRIN DeWITT m Annie Belyea

1 BURTON M/BERTREM DeWITT b 1871 d 18 Dec 1884, "Burton" on tbstn **dy.**
2 JOSEPHINE/MINNIE DeWITT b 24 Dec 1875 (d 04 Nov 1949 Blissville Cem) m ? Miles, **no chn.**
3 ALLEYNE DeWITT b 30 Jul 1876 (d 26 Feb 1956) m Hess, **no chn** (fr KLAD).
4 ORRIN LEE/ORRIE DeWITT b 21 Sep 1878 Blissville NB (d after 1962) m (fr LDM).
5 MABEL DeWITT b 20 Aug 1881 Blissville NB (d 10 Apr 1962) m Dr Charles F Sweet (fr MWD).

SMITH

1.1.9.4.3.3.5.1 PHOEBE SMITH m Thatcher Smith

1 FRED SMITH
2 RAINSFORD SMITH
3 MARY ANN SMITH b 1848.
4 NATHAN SMITH b 1850.
5 RANDALL/RANDOLPH SMITH
 (1851 Census, moved to Presque Isle ME by 1860)

SMITH

1.1.9.4.3.3.5.2 DANIEL SMITH m Charlotte Smith

1 ELLA SMITH m ? Daggett of Spraque Mills ME.

Leucas deWit

2   MELBOURNE SMITH b 1856 (d 1926) {m}1 Annie R DeWitt (1.1.9.4.3.3.4.3.3) d/o Bethuel DeWitt & Mary E Smith, b 1954 (alive in 1931) res Presque Isle ME, Annie div him, Melbourne was a bank president at Presque Isle; {m}2 Adeline Scott (1.1.9.4.3.3.4.1.1.) d/o Phoebe Ann DeWitt & George Scott, b 1870 d 1954 both bur Presque Isle ME, **no chn.**
3   MAY SMITH m Maylord Estes of Island Falls ME **no chn.**
4   CALVIN SMITH at Spraque Mills ME.
5   EFFIE GERTRUDE SMITH m Merrill Hoyt, **no chn.**

SMITH
1.1.9.4.3.3.5.3 NANCY SMITH m Warren Smith

1   ALEATHA SMITH b 1854 m Angus Riley.
2   DAVID O SMITH b 1841 Hoyt Blissville Parish, Sunbury Co NB {m} Delilah Scott (1.1.9.4.3.3.4.1.1.3) b 1864 d 1899 d/o Phoebe Ann DeWitt & George Scott. They res in Salt Lake City UT and all their chn were born there.
3   ELGAN OTIS SMITH b 1859 (d 1900) bur United Church Cem Hoyt {m} Clarissa Scott b 1862 d 1936/8 (1.1.9.4.3.3.4.1.1.2) d/o Phoebe Ann DeWitt & George Scott.
4   DANIEL F SMITH b 1861, at Witchita KS m 21 Mar 1889.
5   ELLA SMITH b 26 Feb 1864 (d 10 Jan 1940) at Blissville m 01 Jun 1891 (Prof) Charles Jones, by Rev W H Perry. Charles ran a business college at Brocton MA. They had 2 foster chn.
6   MAIDE SMITH b 1866 d 1867 bur Blissville Baptist Cem.
7   GERTRUDE SMITH b 1873, at Blissville m 01 Dec 1896 Fred Mason, Rev T O DeWitt officiating. (SDVSW: 3 & family info) all chn b Hoyt NB.

A LOVE LETTER TO MARY ANN SMITH FROM ALEXANDER WOODEN

"Dear Mary Ann

I want to know
Have you on earth another beau?
Or is there one more near your heart,
Pray tell me love if we must part?

When I first came up to this branch,
Some pretty girls I saw by chance;
They looked so charming I do declare
They drew my heart into a snare.

But when I saw their stately glance,
I thought for me there is no chance
Yet there is one about nineteen
Who lives across the South Branch stream?

Who's heart is free from this vain pride
Oh! If I had you for my bride,
Or if indeed you were in my arms,
You'd yield to me a thousand charms.

While on this earth I'd happy be
Forever blessed with love and thee
My bride, I said; but I'm too fast,
I should have left that for last.

In that I might have been more bold
Did I posses great stores of gold
But yet I hold that love sincere
Is far beyond great wordly gear.

And this I'm sure, on earth did dwell
None that would love you half so well;
I still remain your humble friend,
Your humble servant, "Alex Wooden".

"Apparently Alex and Mary Ann were quite happy though Mary Ann said her only regret was her surname was not 'Smith' as the others in the family all had that name. She must have been quite proud of her Smith ancestry for family legend reports Alex once observed to her "There must have been some other important people beside Smiths, to which she replied that the DeWitt's were prominent back in New York, where a DeWitt house had thirteen fireplaces" [not so!] fr KLAD)

WOODEN
1.1.9.4.3.3.5.5 MARY ANN SMITH m Alexander Wooden

1   LAVINA ALMA WOODEN b 08 Jan 1858 (d 19 May 1917) m Emerson Hoyt res Mill Settlement. She was a teacher, lived in Duluth MN (sic SDVSW:41).
2   JAMES N WOODEN b 1861 d 1937 **single** (Buried Blissville Cem Hoyt N.B.).
3   CHARLOTTE MELISSA WOODEN b 03 Mar 1864 (d 11 Jun 1951) m Frederick Welpley b 1855 d 1946 (SDVSW).
4   LUCINDA <u>GERTRUDE</u> WOODEN b 186 d 1871 **dy.**

Leucas deWit

5   ANNIE M WOODEN b 08 Oct 1866 (d 18 Dec 1850) at Mill Settlement m 25 Dec 1895 Joseph <u>Samuel</u> Van Wart by Rev T O DeWitt, b 27 Jan 1866 of Hampstead NB d 23 May 1944 Mill Settlement bur in private cem on the homestead at Pleasant Villa NB.
6   ROBERT WOODEN b 26 Jul 1872 Blissville NB (d 22 Feb 1944 bur Blissville Cem) m Mary Gardener b 1877 d 1958 bur Blissville Cem Hoyt N.B.
7   ALICE <u>ADELIA</u> WOODEN called "Delia" b 1875 Blissville NB (d 1952 Fredericton Jct NB) {m} Winslow Scott (1.1.9.4.3.3.4.1.1.7) of Fredericton Jct s/o Phoebe Ann DeWitt & George Scott b 22 Jun 1874 Fredericton Jct NB d 08 Dec 1948. All chn b Fredericton Jct (SDVSW:4)
    (all chn b Mill Settlement, NB family info fr MDW, SDVSW:2)

DeWITT

1.1.9.4.3.3.7.1 JOHN L DeWITT m Lucretia D Emery
1   CHARLES E DeWITT b 1851.
2   WILLIAM HENRY DeWITT b 23 Jul 1853 Medford ME d 10 Mar 1854 bur Randall Ridge Cem **dy,**
3   IDA MAY DeWITT b 1855 Medford ME (d 27 Oct 1917) m 1871 Charles Edward Thomas s/o Benjamin Thomas & Sarah Lancaster, b 05 Aug 1846 Maxfield ME (d 09 Jun 1915 both bur Maxfield ME Cem.
4   HANNAH J/BELL DeWITT b 1857 Maxfield ME. Rest of the chn b Maxfield.
5   WILLIAM HENRY DeWITT b 1858 ME d 10 Mar 1859 bur Randall Ridge Cem **dy.**
6   JAPHET S or L DeWITT b 1861.
7   EMERY J DeWITT b 1862 d 04 Sep 1889 bur Randall Ridge Cem, **single.**
8   ADA B/ADDIE DeWITT b. 1869.
9   CLINTON J DeWITT b 1871 d 03 Feb 1879 b Randall Ridge Cem **dy.**

CROMBIE

1.1.9.4.3.3.7.3 MARY DeWITT m Henry Crombie/Crummie
1   ANNIE CROMBIE b 1868.
2   MARCUS CROMBIE b 1869 (d 1941 dates fr tstn) res Juvenile NB m Ella May/Nellie Worden b 1868 d 1962 both bur Juvenile Cem Sunbury Co (fr KALD). Marcus' obit mentions 7 grchn, 2 ggchn, nieces, nephews & cousins attending funeral at Fredericton NB bur Patterson United Cem.

DeWITT

1.1.9.4.3.3.7.4 ABRAHAM THOMAS DeWITT m Mary Patterson
1   GEORGE DeWITT **dy.**
2   ESTELLA DeWITT **dy.**
3   GEORGE S D DeWITT **dy.**
4   THOMAS DeWITT **single.**
5   WILLIAM DeWITT b 1868 d 1943 Hoyt NB bur Hoyt Baptist CH cem in Parsons plot, **single.**

<u>From Religious Intelligencer 05 Nov 1890</u> "Dr. McAlpine who was beaten at Fredericton Jct recovered sufficiently to be taken home to Grand Falls. It was evidently a drunken spree". A reprint of an item that was in the Oct 26 1990 Gleaner tells of a severe beating suffered by Dr McAlpine of Grand Falls, his money stolen. He was found by a woman who heard him moaning lying in the road near her house at 2 a.m. At midnight he had been seen drinking with G Kingston & W DeWitt. His companions don't seem to have been blamed and there was no mention of a solution of the crime.

<u>From the Gleaner</u> In 1990 a daily paper, published in Fredericton was celebrating 100 years of Publishing every day is a Centential Corner column, gems from 100 years age appear. - - Dr. McAlpine of Grand Falls was seen drinking with G Kingston and W DeWitt about midnight on Saturday Oct 26 1890 - - about 2 Sunday morning Mrs. Kelly heard groans, went out to the road and found him Dr McAlpine - - on the highway near her house in a pool of blood - - badly beaton. He was terribly injured about the head, seventy-five dollars - - the doctor had - - were gone.

William was a real character, never married. They must not have been blamed for the McAlpine affair as they were around the area for years (fr KALD).

6   ANNIE DeWITT m Thomas Williamson.
7   HANNAH DeWITT m ? Shaw.
8   LAVINA DeWITT m Benison Parsons.
9   STELLA DeWITT m Stanley Cutler.

DeWITT

1.1.9.4.3.3.7.5 LUKE EMERY DeWITT m Rachel Mersereau
1   LYDIA ALFRETTA/ RETTY DeWITT b 10 JN 1860 at Saint John NB m 01 Sep 1888 Alonzo Sanford moved to Boston MA bur there (fr KLAD, RDB)
2   RANDAL PARKER DeWITT b 19 Sep 1862 (d 1946) at Orient ME m ? Aug 1890 Mae Colson (Colter?) (fr RDB)
3   GERENIA ANN DeWITT b 03 Nov 1864 (d 1929 bur Juvenile NB Cem) m1 03 Nov 1886 James Graham b 1855 d 1908 both bur Juvenile, NB Cem; m2 18 Sep 1912 William H Jones (fr RDB, KLAD).

Leucas deWit

4   JAMES AUSTIN DeWITT b 10 Jun 1866 res South Branch (Hoyt) on Luke E's farm (d 1946) Blissville (now Hoyt NB) m 29 Jun 1910 Stella May Mersereau d/o Orlo Mersereau of Blissville NB, b 1878 d Dec 1955 both bur Blissville Cem (all fr KLAD).

5   SCOULER BURTON DeWITT b 19 Dec 1868 Blissville (d 13 Sep 1934 Victoria Mills, Fredericton NB) at Saint John NB m 24 Oct 1900 Lottie R Davis d/o George F Davis & Margaret Touchborne b 1880 d 1962.Thet res Fredricton Jct both bur there in Gladstone Cem. They lived for some time at South Branch but later made their home on Gore Road, Fredericton Jct NB (fr KLAD & a clipping in their DeWitt Bible). Obit for Scouler DeWitt, engineer for the Fraser Co Ltd Mil at Victoria Mills, Fredericton NB. Names survivors wf former Lottie R Davis, 3 sons, Arthur of Saskatoon, Harold D & Ellis of Saint John, 3 daus Mrs Robert Cowie of Long Island, Mrs S J Butcher & Rheta E DeWitt of Saint John, 2 bros Austin of Central Blissville, Randall of Orono ME.

6   HANNAH CLEMENTINE DeWITT b 10 Feb 1871 (d 18 Apr 1891 ae 20 & her ch Mary d 29 Apr 1891) at Fredericton {m}1 28 Jul 1887 Austin Webb (1.1.9.4.3.3.8.2.1) b 1861 d 1945 s/o Mary J DeWitt & Joshua Webb, d 1947. (fr KLAD). He {m}2 Elizabeth DeWitt (1.1.9.4.3.3.8.4.5) d/o Daniel DeWitt & Emma Webb, b 1868 d 1953, all bur Blissville Cem.

7   ANDREW PARTLOO (sic) [PARTLOW]) DeWITT b 30 Apr 1878 d Farmington ME 26 Nov 1924 bur Blissville NB, **single.**

8   MELVINA AGNES DeWITT b 29 Nov 1879 (d 25 Jul 1914 bur Blissville Cem. Hoyt N.B.) m Fordice Rhoades res CA **no chn** (fr KLAD, RDB).

BELL

1.1.9.4.3.3.7.8 PHOEBE ANN DeWITT m Thomas Bell

1   BEN BELL m ? Buckingham (fr KLAD).
2   GEORGE MELVIN BELL m Lucinda Charlton (fr KLAD).
3   THOMAS D BELL, Rev (d Feb 1955) m1 Mary Kirkpatrick, m2 Ethel F Noble b in Maryland Par d/o late William J Noble & Ruth Smith (all fr KLAD).
4   CHARLES A BELL, Rev (d 1947) m Clara Kelly d 1980's (fr DMBN, KLAD).

KINGSTON

1.1.9.4.3.3.7.9 HANNAH DeWITT m Fred Kingston

1   IDA KINGSTON b 1866 (d 1948) m 20 April 1887 James Mersereau of Hoyt NB b 1858 d 1940 both bur Blissville Cem. Her residence Mill Settlement, his occupation baggage master NB railway northern division. Ida's twin was
2   ADA KINGSTON b 1866 m 20 Apr 1887 Manzer Webb of Tracy NB. Her residence Mill Settlement, his occupation Baggage master NB railway northern division (fr: IS)
3   RACHEL KINGSTON m ? Wood **no chn.**
4   ORLO KINGSTON m 27 dec 1894 Christina Boone, Religious Intelligencer 04 May 1887, bur Parsons Cem Hoyt NB
5   WILLIAM KINGSTON b 1880 (d 1936) m Ada Knorr b 1880 d 1965.
6   HANFORD KINGSTON m Agatha Eastwood **no chn** both bur Patterson Cem Hoyt.

DeWITT

1.1.9.4.3.3.7.10 JEREMIAH DeWITT m Mary Matilda Hay

1   CHARLES WILLIAM DeWITT b 21 Apr 1871 Blissville Par Sunbury Co NB (d 20 Dec 1936 ae 65 Island Falls ME) At Saint John NB m 15 Aug 1892 Rachel Ann Kirkpatrick d/o Walter Kirkpatrick & Elizabeth Harron, b 07 Oct 1874 Blissville d 29 May 1968 Houlton, Aroostock Co ME, both bur Island Falls Cem. Rachel was a Congregationalist. She had her left arm amputated 11 Aug 1966 at ae 91-10-00. Charles worked as a labourer, a cook & was a Sexton. 1891 Census Charles ae 37 res with Arthur & Ann Graham as a lodger after death of his father in Germantown Settlement NB.
2   ASA T DeWITT b 1874 m Nora Brown.
3   HANNAH DeWITT b 1877 Blissville NB m Hardy Nason of Fredericton Jct no surviving chn. He m2 Effie Josey
4   JEMIMA MARY/MAMIE DeWITT b 1879 (d 1954) m Frank Bunker b 1871 d 1943 bur Tracy Cem (fr AMS via KLAD).

DeWITT

1.1.9.4.3.3.7.11 GIDEON HAMILTON DeWITT m Elizabeth Johnson.

1   HANFORD DeWITT b 1868 Blissville.
2   ALICE MAY DeWITT b 1870.
    m2 02 Jan 1873 Blissville Hannah J Nason (KLAD, MWD, 1871Sunbury NB Census).

DeWITT

1.1.9.4.3.3.8.1 JOHN DeWITT m1 Chloe C Hoyt.

1   MELVIN DeWITT b 1861 d after 1871 **dy.**
2   WILLIAM DeWITT b 1866 d 1884 **dy.**
3   HARRY F DeWITT b 1869 d 1882 **dy.**
    m2 28 Dec 1865 DOROTHEA SINCLAIR.

Leucas deWit

4   ALFORD OTTY DeWITT m late in life, **no chn.** He was raised by John Murphy, res in ID, blinded in WWI.
5   ANNE FLORENCE DeWITT m George Dyer lived Providence RI.
6   ALBERT RANDOLFE DeWITT b 1872 Blissville (d 1937) m Elena J Charlton. b 1877 d 1960 both bur Blissville Cem. Albert was raised by Rev T O DeWitt.
    m3 Annie Bailey no chn. (fr KLAD; MWD)

WEBB

1.1.9.4.3.3.8.2 MARY J DeWITT m Joshua Webb

1   AUSTIN WEBB b 1867 (d 1945) {m} 1.1.9.4.3.3.7.5.6 Hannah <u>Clementine</u> DeWitt d/o Luke Emery DeWitt & Rachel Mersereau, b 1871 d 1891; {m}2 Elizabeth Phoebe DeWitt (1.1.9.4.3.3.8.4.5) d/o Daniel DeWitt & Emma Ann Webb, b 1868.
2   ELIZABETH WEBB m Asahel Seely b 1842 d 1917 both bur Blissville Cem.
3   WILBUR WEBB m ? .
4   ANNIE WEBB m ? Turtlotte.
5   MAUD WEBB m Lemont /Monty Gillespie (1871 - 1940) both buried Blissville Cem.
6   MINNIE WEBB m Walter Costello. These children are not in order by age (fr KLAD).

DeWITT

1.1.9.4.3.3.8.4 DANIEL WOOD DeWITT m Emma Ann Webb

1   ANN S DeWITT
2   LODEWICK DeWITT b 1860 (d 1947) m Lottie Whitenect (1879-1948) both bur. Blissville Cem.
3   FRASER DeWITT b 1863.
4   LESLEY W DeWITT b 1864.
5   ELIZABETH PHOEBE DeWITT b 1868 (d 1953) as a 2nd wf m 1.1.9.4.3.3.8.2.1 Austin Webb b 1867 d 1945.
6   JOHN DeWITT (fr KALD).

MURPHY

1.1.9.4.3.3.8.5 MARGARET A DeWITT m John Murphy.

1   WILLIAM MURPHY
2   HARRY J MURPHY (fr KLAD).

DeWITT

1.1.9.4.3.5.5.2 & 1.1.9.4.3.7.3.2 HENRY DeWITT m1 Mary Ann Nason

- UNNAMED DeWITT

    {m}2 Mary Jane Nason (1.1.9.4.3.7.1.3.3)

1   CHARLOTTE A DeWITT b 12 Jun 1860 (d 30 Jun 1931) m Frederick Harris s/o John Harris & Rhoda Tracy, b 1855 d 1926 (fr KLAD fr Sunbury West Historical Society).
2   HENRY <u>LEONARD</u> DeWITT b 03 May 1862 (d 18 Dec 1934) bur Tracy Cem) {m} Annabelle Harris (1.1.9.4.3.6.6.1.2.4) b 1865 d 04 Nov 1945 d/o Thomas Odber Harris & Mary Elizabeth Boone.
3   GEORGE <u>LYMAN</u> DeWITT b 19 Sep 1863 (d 10 May ?) m Carrie MacCowan b 1876 d 1945.
4   NEHEMIAH DeWITT b 26 May 1865 (d 28 Feb 1928) m Alice Drake b 1867 d 1961.
5   PHOEBE <u>MARIA</u> DeWITT b 18 Mar 1867 (d 11 Apr 1920 {m} Albion Harris (1.1.9.4.3.6.6.1.1.1) s/o Thomas Odber Harris & Mary Elizabeth Boone, b 1865 d 20 Apr 1952
    He m2 Mrs Penelope/Nellie Martin Sternley widow of Albert Sternley.
6   ANNIE JANE DeWITT b 09 Apr 1869 m Fred Tracy.
7   GELINA DeWITT b 06 Jan 1872 (d 20 Dec 1914) m Fred Phillips d 12 Apr 1926.
8   DAVID WESLEY DeWITT b 16 Sep 1873 (d 16 Apr 1946) m Rheta/Rita James.
9   JOHN B DeWITT b 28 Jun 1875 d 26 Apr 1876 **dy.**
10   ALFRED DeWITT b 23 Apr 1878 m Elva Burnett.
11   MINNIE DeWITT b 26 Jun 1881 (d 1981) {m} Sherman Harris (1.1.9.4.3.6.6.1.2.2) s/o Thomas Odber Harris & Mary Jane Boone, b 1873 d 02 Jan 1961 (fr IMWH 1865 – 1952 to KLAD & MDG Obit).

"Henry DeWitt was building a house in Rusagonis NB when his young wife (Mary Ann) died. He was quite depressed for a considerable time, but then he decided he was still a young man and should get on with living" (KLAD)

"The DeWitts lived on a farm at Sunpoke, then traded places with David Smith who had a farm on the Upper Tracy Road, above the Old Solomon Tracy place. Henry lived there until he was over ninety years of age. He had given part of his farm to his son Nehemiah and resided with his other son Henry <u>Leonard</u> on the homestead with his family of five daughters until my grandfather sold the farm to the Farm Settlement Board and moved down to the village of Tracy. I remember my grandfather Henry Leonard very well as a child. He wasn't very tall, just average height, walked with a spring in his step and had a great sense of humour. He used to sing and keep time with his hands and feet for the young people to dance when musical instruments weren't available. My grandmother always wore a dust cap in the morning and was very strict; she was a no-nonsense type of person. Before breakfast she always read the Bible and we had a prayer to begin the day.

Leucas deWit

My mother remembers Henry DeWitt's first ride in a car. It was a Pickle Ford (model T) driven by his son Nehemiah. She said he got in the back seat and hung on with both hands, scared of the great speed they were traveling. Henry DeWitt & Mary Jane Nason were buried in the Tracy cemetery; so are my grandparents, Leonard DeWitt and Annabelle Harris. The DeWitts were known for their long lives and strong constitutions" (fr IMWH).

DeWITT
1.1.9.4.3.5.2.3 & 1.1.9.4.3.7.3.3 JEREMIAH DeWITT {m} Adeline Nason (1.1.9.4.3.7.1.3.1)
1. ABIGAIL DeWITT m Whitfield Grass.
2. PHOEBE DeWITT b 1859 m Jeremiah Phillips.
3. CATHARINE SERIA DeWITT b 1860 m George Gehan/?Behan.
4. ANNA V DeWITT b 1868 m Wellington Phillips.
5. RAINSFORD M DeWITT b 1867.
6. ALICE A DeWITT b 1868 m Wesley Tucker.
7. LAURA JANE DeWITT b ? Mar 1870 m Henry Boehen.
8. SPAFFORD DeWITT m Maude ?

DeWITT
1.1.9.4.3.5.2.6 & 1.1.9.4.3.7.3.6 ISAAC DeWITT m Hannah/Ann Boone
1. ALMA DeWITT b 21 Jun 1867 m1 Joe Broderick, m2 Donald Stewart b 19 Jun 1871 **no chn**.
2. MELVIN DeWITT b 1869 d 1920.
3. JASPETH DeWITT
4. JEREMY DeWITT b Feb 1871.
5. MARY E /MAMIE DeWITT m Frank Lord, had 10 chn.
6. HERBERT DeWITT bachelor.
7. WILLIAM DeWITT **dy**
8. JEN/JENNIE DeWITT m Edward Batchelor, 4 chn.
9. BEATRICE THEODOSIA DeWITT b 04 Oct 1883 Three Tree Creek NB (29 Mar 1959 at McAdam NB) m 29 Sept 1899 Burton/Bert Wilbur Nason b 18 Jan 1874 d 17 Jul 1956 (both bur Rockland Cem McAdam) s/o of Isreal Nason & Sarah Ann Nason. Burton was a CPR Section man; all chn b McAdam.
10. FREDERICK ELLIS DeWITT b 09 Mar 1886 his pa's Three Tree Creek NB farm m Elizabeth Gallison d 1986.

On Nov 04 1986 The Fortnighter local paper carried an invitation to the whole town to attend Fred's 100th birthday celebration. The town offered their congratulations & were pleased to sponser refreshments. The paper repeated a 98th birthday interview. The family lived many years at 22 Spruce St, McAdam. Fred Had worked lumbering in the Canterbury at $14.00 a month for 18 to 20 hour days. In 1906 he got a job with the CPR in McAdam. In his last years the wage rose to $185.00 a month. He received his pension after 35 years with the Railway. Fred served overseas in WWI with the 42nd Black Watch and attended Rememberance Day when able. He was the oldest member of the McAdam Ashler Masonic Lodge. He said he is well taken care of by daus Eleanor & Leona. Sissy lives in Nova Scotia. He enjoys the paper, a bit of TV & cards, also mentioned many changes in his lifetime. He also spoke of the many fine young men in the town. Two things he has never done - drive a car or fly in an aeroplane.

11. ZORIAH/ZAIRA DeWITT m1 Margaret McKinnon, 3 chn. He m2 Amy Clark
12. GEORGE DeWITT b 1887 d 1969 m Regina Isobel Gallison (fr WD & MD).
13. NORMAN DeWITT b 1889 (d ae 92) res Milltown NB m Alameda Gallison 6 chn.
14. MARGARET DeWITT b 1891 m1 Thomas Bell 1 ch; m2 James Bell.
    The Village of McAdam donates to Wauklehegan Manor a chair in honour of each resident reaching the 100th birthday. Two would be for Frederick and Norman DeWitt (fr KLAD).

DeWITT
1.1.9.4.3.6.4.1 CATHARINE BOONE {m} 1.1.9.4.3.3.4.1 Daniel DeWitt
Children are with their father's underlined Generation 8.

TRACY/NASON
1.1.9.4.3.6.5.2 ANN BOONE m1 George Tracy
   m2 George Francis Nason (1.1.9.4.3.7.1.3.2)
1. WILLARD B NASON b 1867 (d 1914) m Mary Lawless (fr MWD).

MERSEREAU
1.1.9.4.3.6.5.3 HANNAH BOONE m John Mersereau (called Deacon John)
1. HENRY MERSEREAU m Emma Greensfield b NS.
2. RAINSFORD MERSEREAU m1 Alma Tracy b 1868 d 1901; m2 Bertha Philips.
3. GEORGIE MERSEREAU m George Brick Knowles bur Montreal QC.
4. ELIZABETH MERSEREAU b 1861 (d 1923) m Herman Tracy b 1861 d 1943 (fr KLAD & Tracy-Hartt Rec).

BOONE

1.1.9.4.3.6.5.4 JAMES E BOONE m Basheba Whitman
1. HERBERT P BOONE b 1861 d 07 Mar 1892.
2. MARY M/MARIAH BOONE b 1866 m Charles Weaver M.D.
3. BURTON H BOONE b 1868 m 1900 Lillie d/o Linus Tracy, b 1870 d 1921 buried Pioneer Cem Tracy N.B.
4. GEORGE F BOONE b 1879 **dy**.
5. ABSOLOM BOONE b 1873 **dy**.
* HARVEY BOONE (fr KLAD)
6. VIOLETTA BOONE b 1876 **dy** (all fr KLAD, ACB).
7. EDWARD A BOONE b 14 Sep 1876 (d 22 Sep 1936) m 1900 Brenda M Mitchell b 11 Aug 1880 d 11 Apr 1929.

HARRIS

1.1.9.4.3.6.6.1 GERTRUDE BOONE m Jarvis Harris
1. THOMAS <u>ODBUR</u> HARRIS b 1837 {m}1 Mary Elizabeth Boone (1.1.9.4.3.6.6.3) d/o Evert Boone & Mary Thomas, b 1850 both bur Pioneer Cem Tracy NB). m2 Mrs Bertha (Phillips) Davis wd/o Theodore Davis.
2. MARY ELIZABETH HARRIS b 1840 m1 ?   Durant; m2 John McCleary.
3. HANNAH HARRIS b 1842 m 06 Jul 1866 John McCleary.
4. REBECCA HARRIS b 1844 m James McCleary.
5. HAYWARD HARRIS b 1847 m Saphrona Nason.
6. WILLIAM C HARRIS b 1852 (d 1912) m1 Martha Phillips b 11 May 1856 d 28 Nov 1874 ae 17-09-00 m2 Martha McAuley (fr IMWH to KLAD).

BOONE

1.1.9.4.3.6.6.2 JOHN BOONE {m} Hannah Boone (1.1.9.4.3.6.7.1)
1. LILLAN BOONE b 1841.
2. SARAH BOONE b 1843.
3. HANNAH BOONE b 1845 m Charles Mott.
4. HENRY BOONE b 1847 (d 1933) m Mrs Mary (Meahan) McCleary wd/o Joseph McCleary.
5. VICTORIA ANNIE BOONE b 1849 not in 1861 census.
6. MARY ANN BOONE b ?   May 1851 {m} Isaac DeWitt.
7. JOHN L BOONE b 16 May 1853 (d 02 Dec 1918) m Sarah M Howland b 22 May 1866 d 29 Mar 1941.
8. GEORGE F BOONE b 1855 (fr ACB).

CARR/KINGSTON

1.1.9.4.3.6.6.4 SARAH BOONE m1 William A Carr
1. ABIGAIL CARR b 1838 (d 1927) m Samuel Shanks b 1834 d 1914 12 chn.
2. MARY ANN CARR b 1840 (d 1925) m Joseph Kingston res Fredericton Jct NB.
3. SARAH L CARR b 1843, visiting grpa Evert DeWitt 1851 census, d 18 Aug 1866 ae 23, **single**.
4. GEORGE OZIAS CARR b 1844 m Ruth Charlotte Boone.
5. MARTHA M CARR b 1846 m Hugh Case.
6. VICTORIA CARR b 1848 (d 23 Oct 1938 ae 90) m1 ?   Mersereau; {m}2 Charles Everett Boone (1.1.9.4.3.6.6.1) s/o Everett DeWitt Boone Jr & Mary Thomas, b 1845. No further info.
7. OTIS CARR b 1850 d 1886 at Geary NB **single**; "liquor killed him".
8. JAMES CARR b 1853 no info after 1861 census.
9. LEMSLEY <u>THOMAS</u> CARR b 1856 no info after 1861 census.
10. FRANCES <u>OLIVE</u> CARR b 1858 m ?   Megnon lived in CA.
11. LAURA CARR b 1860 at Burton m ?   Moore.
12. WILLIAM CARR b 1862 d 1934.

m2 01 Aug 1870 as 3rd w/o George Kingston (fr ACB).

ALEXANDER

1.1.9.4.3.6.6.5 MARY BOONE m Charles Alexander
1. THOMAS WILLIAM ALEXANDER b 1840 (d 1904) m 1862 Margaret Timmins d/o Peter Timmins & Sarah Scott, b 1841 Springfield, York Co NB d 1921 both bur Gladstone Parish Cem Fredericton Jct. NB, all chn b Fredericton Jct. He was a carpenter & the proprietor of a small woodworking shop and planing mill near the north end of the Hwy Bridge at Fredericton Jct NB.
Charles Alexander m2 Chloe Nevers, their chn were: John Little Alexander b 1843 d 1925, Charles Stuart Alexander b 1844 d 1934, Guy Warwick Alexander b 1845 d 1932, Mary Jane Alexander b 1847 d 1930, Joseph Frederick Alexander b 1849 d 1888, Charlotte Alexander b 1853 d. 1932, Samuel Duncan Alexander b 1854 d 1934; Anna Helena Alexander b 1864 (fr KLAD Alexander Family Rec). All chn were b in Fredricton Jct NB.

BOONE

1.1.9.4.3.6.6.6 EVERETT BOONE Jr m Mary Thomas
1. CHARLES EVERETT BOONE b 1846 {m} 1.1.9.4.3.6.6.4.6 Mrs Victoria (Carr) Mersereau d/o William Carr &

Leucas deWit

Sarah Boone, b 1848 d 1938 bur Rockland Cem, McAdam NB.
2 SARAH A BOONE b 1848 **dy.**
3 MARY ELIZABETH BOONE b 1850 {m} 1.1.9.4.3.6.6.1.2 Thomas Odber Harris b 1838 both bur Pioneer Cem Tracy NB.
m2 Mrs Bertha (Phillips) Davis wd/o Theodore Davis & had 10 more chn. Bertha had 2 chn fr her 1st m.
4 BURPEE BOONE b 1855.
5 DAYMAN (? DYKEMAN) BOONE b 1856 (fr ACB).

BOONE
1.1.9.4.3.6.6.7 WILLIAM MURRAY BOONE m Hannah Nason
1 REUBEN A BOONE b 1853 m1 ? McLaughlin.m2 Jenny ? m3 ?
2 SPAFFORD B BOONE b 1855.
3 ANNIE J BOONE b 1864.
4 OLIVE O BOONE b 1866.
5 BARLETTA ALEVILA BOONE b 1867.
6 MELBURN O BOONE b 1870 (fr ACB).

NASON
1.1.9.4.3.6.6.9 ABIGAIL BOONE d 1917 m Lemuel Nason 1831-1885
1 SARAH NASON b 27 Oct 1855 Tracy NB m Isreal Nason.
2 CELESTIA NASON b Aug 1856 m Darius Phillips.
3 NASON (female) b Aug 1858 d 1858 **dy.**
4 MARY DELILA NASON b 29 Aug 1860 m John Clifford.
5 VICTORIA NASON b 02 Sep 1862 m Benedict Pride (fr KLAD).
6 MANZER BOONE NASON b 21 Aug 1864 m Josie Vail.
7 HARVEY HENERY NASON b 13 Apr 1866 m Lydia Tracy.
8 EVERETT BOONE NASON b 28 Nov 1868 Harwood Creek (d 1948 at St Paul's Manse Fredericton NB m 1888 Anne Elizabeth Cowie (d 1941).
9 MOSES NASON d ae 18.
10 PENNELL E NASON b 04 Mar 1874 (d 1954) at McAdam m 1900 Ellen A Grass b 1883, both b at Tracy & d at McAdam (fr ACB, EAW).

BOONE
1.1.9.4.3.6.7.1 HANNAH BOONE {m} 1.1.9.4.3.6.6.2 John Boone
Children are with their father's underlined number Generation 8.

BOONE
1.1.9.4.3.6.8.2 RICHARDSON BOONE m Annis Shirley
1 SHERMAN W BOONE b 1860 Blissville became M.D. OBIT Newspaper Gleaner (Fredericton) May 28, 1936
Dr. Shermon W. Boone died at Presque Isle yesterday aged 77 after a long illness. He was born at Fredericton Jct. and when a boy came to Fredericton to live. Educated common schools and high school graduated University of New Brunswick 1883 with a BA degree, received M.D. degree from McGill University and soon after began practice of medicine in Presque Isle. He was a 32nd degree Mason and a member of the F.A.C.S.
Survivors: His wife and 3 sons, Dr. Storer Boone and Frank Boone of Presque Isle and Dr. Ralph Boone, Caribou ME he had two daughters Mrs. Vaughan Parsons and Mrs. George Cook of Presque Isle and one sister Mrs. Ida Hagerman, Keswick N.B. Buried Fairmount Cemetary Presque Isle, Maine.
2 IDA MAY BOONE b 1863 (d 1937) m 12 May 1886 Albert Hagerman b 1862 d 1906 ae 44, res at the mouth of Keswick, York Co NB (fr ACB).
3 ELLA J BOONE b 1865.
4 ANNIS L BOONE b 01 Mar 1869 d 15 Jul 1870 tbstn Pioneer Cem, Tracy as d/o R H & A S Boone.

BOONE
1.1.9.4.3.6.8.3 JAMES /JONAS BOONE m Emeline Mott
1 ELZER BOONE b 1865 Blissville NB.
2 TRIETHA BOONE b 1866 m1 Charles Webb; m2 Herman Tracy d 29 Mar 1943 (fr ABC).

NASON
1.1.9.4.3.7.1.3 JOHN M NASON m Abigail Grass
1 ADELINE NASON b 1839 (d 1925) {m} 08 Oct 1956 1.1.9.4.3.5.2.3 Jeremiah DeWitt s/o Phoebe DeWitt & Isaac DeWitt b 1831. Wits at the m were Aunt Annie Nason & hus Aaron Phillips.
2 GEORGE FRANCIS NASON b 1840 (d 1913 at Tracy NB) m1 08 Dec 1863 Eunice C Nason b 1841. George & Eunice both bur Pioneer Graveyard Tracy NB. Margaret Nason and George's bro Thomas were witness at George & Eunice wedding. George m2 Mrs Annie (Tracy) Boone 1.1.9.4.3.6.5.2 b 1847 d 1920 d/o George Tracy.
3 MARY JANE NASON b 1843 (d 1932 at Tracy NB) as his 2nd wife {m} 11 Nov 1858 1.1.9.4.3.5.2.2 Henry DeWitt b 1828 d 1919 s/o Phoebe DeWitt & Isaac DeWitt (5 girls & 3 boys).

Leucas deWit

4 THOMAS LEMUEL NASON b 1844 New Maryland, Blissville Par m1 23 Oct 1865 Margaret E Nason b 1849, m2 Mary Greer.
5 CHARLOTTE NASON b 1847.
6 MARTHA FINCH NASON b 1850 m Henry Burnett.
7 DAVID A NASON b 1853 m Henrietta/Nettie Grass (all fr ACB).

TRACY

1.1.9.4.3.7.1.4 MARY NASON m George Tracy
1 GEORGE E TRACY b 1841.
2 FREDERICK H TRACY b 1843.
3 BASHEBA TRACY b 1847 (all fr ACB).

NASON

1.1.9.4.3.7.1.8 EPHRIAM/EPHEREM NASON m Elizabeth S Grey
1 FRANCIS GILBERT/FRANK NASON b 20 Jan 1852 Blissville NB (d 1946 Tracy NB) m 21 Oct 1876 Sophia Bunker b 1857 d 1959 **note age**.
2 ZACHARIAH NASON b 27 Nov 1855 Tracy NB (d 1927 in KS) at Armourdale KS m 01 Jan 1891 Nettie Marie Fleming d/o Robert Fleming & Lucy Hovey, b Woodstock NB, one of the first suffragettes in the US. Zachariah was a lumberman when he injured his hip. He became a schoolteacher, met his wife, then took his M.D. at John Hopkins in 1888 & set up practice in Kansas (fr HS).
3 BENJAMIN JOHN NASON b 24 Dec 1857 (d 1929) at Fredericton Jct NB m 14 Jun 1887 Ada Nason by Rev G F Currie b 17 Aug 1868 d 23 Jun 1934.
4 MARTHA IDA NASON b 05 Jan 1859 (d 19 Nov 1952) **single**.
5 EDWIN E NASON b 18 Jan 1861 m Mattie Alexander.
6 MERRIT NASON b 18 Nov 1864 m Marie Prescot.
7 ELLA NASON b 17 Dec 1866 m James Kelly.
8 ANNIE A NASON b 17 Apr 1868 m Alfred Gibson (all fr ACB).

"Brother Zachariah stayed with Ephriam at one time & eventually became unbalanced mentally. He would be up much of the night raving. Ephriam & Elizabeth lost one child, buried over where Byron Nason's sawmill now stands along with a DeWitt baby, John B DeWitt b 28 Jun 1875 d 20 Apr 1876".

PHILLIPS

1.1.9.4.3.7.1.9 ANNIE NASON m Aaron Phillips
1 MELVIN PHILLIPS b 1851.
2 PHOEBE PHILLIPS b 1852.
3 MARY PHILLIPS b 1854.
4 MARTHA PHILLIPS b 1855.
5 IDA PHILLIPS b 1857.
6 ELIZABETH PHILLIPS b 1860.
7 LEAMON PHILLIPS b 1863.
8 JOHN PHILLIPS b 1866.
9 TERINE PHILLIPS b 1860, female (In 1871 Census all chn b Blissville).

DeWITT

1.1.9.4.3.7.3.2 & 1.1.9.4.3.5.2..2 HENRY DeWITT {m2} 1.1.9.4.3.7.1.3.3 Mary Jane Nason
Children are with their father's underlined number Generation 8.

DeWITT

1.1.9.4.7.4.3.3 & 1.1.9.4.3.5.2.3 JERMIAH DeWITT/DUIT {m} 1.1.9.4.3.7.1.3.1 Adeline Nason
Children are with their father's underlined number Generation 8.

DeWITT

1.1.9.4.3.7.4.3.6 & 1.1.9.4.3.5.2.6 ISAAC DeWITT {m] Hannah Boone
Children are with their father's underlined number Generation 8.

DeWITT

1.1.9.4.3.7.4.1 JACOB DeWITT m1 Elizabeth Lee
 m2 Mrs Elizabeth (Soules) Green
 Stepson George Green d 1930 (fr JD) m Rosanna Husey chn George, Mary and Walter who m Elizabeth Brown. Their dau m, res in B.C.
1 MARY DeWITT b 26 May 1859 m Henry Muir res Saltfleet L 9 C 6. Their son Frank (Francis) m & div but had a son Douglas res NF.
2 BENJAMIN DeWITT b 23 May 1866 d 1940 **single**.
 m3 Harriet E Kintzel,

DeWITT

1.1.9.4.3.7.4.2 HIRAM DeWITT m Margaret Conlon

All chn b L6 C6 family farm Tweedside Saltfleet T Wentworth Co ON.

1. CLARA DeWITT b 27 Dec 1867 d 1917 res 177 Jackson St E Hamilton ON, **single.**
2. SARAH DeWITT b 14 Dec 1871 d 1930/3 a nurse, d in Buffalo NY from a disease doing private duty **single.**
3. ANNA G DeWITT b 09 Dec 1873 (d ? Dec 1933 or 01 Jan 1934 bur Tweedside ON) m 1906 Frederick Skeleton of Saltfleet T ON d 1935.
4. NORMAN WENTWORTH DeWITT b 18 Sep 1876 at Tweedside (d 22 Sep 1958) m 1906 Katharine Ida Johnston d/o James Johnston & Margaret Ann Moffat. James Johnston was b 1839 in Ire of Scottish parents, moved to Hamilton in ON1855 & to IL in 1859. One son Norman DeWitt a B.A., Ph.D., FRSC. Professor of Latin Literature, Victoria College, Unvi. of Toronto, 1908, Emeritus 1944. He became a permanent resident of the United States in 1954, Ed: College Institute , Hamilton (Ont); Victoria College; University of Chicago; American School of Classical Studies in Rome; Fellow, University of Chicago 1901-8; Fellow American School in Rome, 1903-4; Professor of Classics, Lincoln (Illinois) College 1904-5; Instructor in Latin and Greek, Washington University, St. Louis, Mo, 1905-7; Professor of Greek, Miami Univ., Oxford , Ohio, 1907-8; Dean , Faculty of Arts 1923-28; Acting Professor of Classics , Cornell University, Ithica ,N.Y.,, Visiting Prof. Of Classics, Univ., of N.C., Chapel Hill N.C., U.S.A., 1947-48; President, Section IL., R.S.c., 1936; President, Classical Association of the Middle West and South (U.S. and Canada), 1838-39; Director , American Philological Assoc., 1938-40, Vice-Pres., 1946, Pres., 1947; Member of Management Committee, American School in Athens, 1939-41. Fellow of the Royal Academy of Mantua. Publications: The Dido Episode in the Aeneid of Virgil, 1906; Virgil's Biographia Litteraria, 1923; Ancient History, 1927: A Brief World History, 1934; Epicurus and his Philosophy. St Paul and Epicurus,1954; articles on classical subjects. Recreation: motoring Address: 143 Eleventh St., Lincoln, Illinois, U.S.A. 452x. Who's Who, 1951-1960. London: Adams & Charles, 1961.
5. SAMENA DeWITT b 09 Oct 1881 (d 1939) m 25 Oct 1905 Alfred Brigham Coleman in Canterbury Eng b 08 Nov 1865 d 25 Oct 1958 (fr ICSP & Mrs CAB). He was a building contractor. He developed Indian Point & built the Brant Inn in Burlington ON.

(Research ICSP fr Samena's dau Mrs C A Baines; Who's Who 1851-1960 London Charles Black Adams. 1961, fr Norman W DeWitt's chn).

PETTIT

1.1.9.4.3.7.4.3 ABIGAIL DeWITT m Sylvester Thomas (Tiffany in the Bible) Pettit

1. HIRAM PETTIT b 17 Mar 1854 (d 23 May 1935 CA) m Emma Jane Bryce b 1866 d after 16 Nov 1887. They res Belmont ON then moved to CA in 1904 (fr ICSP, HBS, HPSM). "He owned several thousand acres in the San Fernando Valley CA" (fr RPR).
2. HERMAN PETTIT b 15 Aug 1855 (d Sask) m Bertha/Beatrice Bruce (fr HPSM) res Saskatoon SK.
3. ALMEDA/MEDA PETTIT b 12 Nov 1856 of the T of South Dorchester Elgin Co (d CA) m 12 Jan 1881 Alexander Gracey at Tillsbury ON, res Fowler CA (fr HPSM).
4. MELVIN PETTIT b 13 Aug 1859 Binbrook T ON (d 27 Jul 1943 Kingsburg, Fresno CA) at Guelph ON m 14 Apr 1886 Anna A Kenney b 12 Feb 1864 d 05 May 1954 res CA.
5. SARAH PETTIT b 09 Jun 1861 had her M.D. at Ann Arbor she was one of the first woman doctors, m Oscar Roberts, **no chn.** "She (Aunt Sarah) and Uncle Oscar Roberts first went as missionaries to China, then when the Boxer Rebellion erupted, they paid a visit to Belmont ON (the one time I ever remember seeing her when I was under six). Then they went off to Africa. I used to have photographs of them in exotic settings" (fr HPSM) They died in Ohio
6. LOIS PETTIT b 07 Mar 1863 (d 26 Apr 1939 Aylmer ON at her dau Louise Arnold's home) m 17 May 1887 Richard Ferdinand Holtermann s/o Christian Ferdinand Holterman of Denmark (who owned a chain of general stores in ON) b 14 Apr 1860 Hamburg Ger d 10 Jun 1925 Fisherville ON (Bible d 26 Apr 1939 in ON) their summer home. "Richard was a well known Apiarist and taught at Ontario Agricultural College at Guelph ON, He taught Morley Pettit, brother of Lois. The Holtermann family is well documented to 1530 in Norway, Denmark, Sweden and Germany" (fr RPR).
7. RACHEL BEATRICE PETTIT b 20 Feb 1865 d 1891 CA res at Exeter ON with Jane & Morley. She was single.
8. JANE PETTIT b 16 Nov 1866 d 19 Mar 1899 from rheumatic fever, **single** bur Mapleton Cem Elgin Co S Dorchester T ON.
9. ESTHER PETTIT b 08 Feb 1871 d 26 Aug 1939 in ON (Bible) res in Georgetown.
10. MORLEY PETTIT b 24 Jul 1875 (d 13 Sep 1945 in Georgia) m Louise Risdon. He was an Apiarist (beekeeper) & taught at Ohio Agricultural College. "I have a lovely picture of Uncle Morley in his 20's - 6'4" tall. Because he supported his sisters, according to the old tradition, he never married till late in life; married his childhood sweetheart so the story goes. He spent his winters in Georgia" (fr HPSM).

"Sylvester Pettit walked from his father's home in Binbrook (near modern Hamilton ON) to Elgin County and near Mapleton and Crossley-Hunter he selected his 'wild land'. He and Abigail DeWitt married, went by oxcart to the land and erected a log cabin, cleared the land & planted it with the aid of his brothers George & John who lived in the Belmont area.

Leucas deWit

(This is extracted from a family letter dated 1952). They and their children lived in log cabins for almost twenty years until they could afford a proper house" (fr RPP).

FREEL
1.1.9.4.3.7.4.4 RHODA DeWITT m James Alexander Freel
1. MAGDALEN FREEL bur Anglican CH Morpeth T Kent Co **single**.
2. ANNIE FREEL **single**.
3. JOHN FREEL **single**. (all bur as above)

ARMSTRONG
1.1.9.4.3.7.4.5 ANN ESTER DeWITT m Samuel Joseph Armstrong.
1. RUTH LAWSON ARMSTONG b 1860 (d 1946 bur Mt Pleasant) m 1884 Thomas Wellington (Welly) Mulholland b 1853 d 1959 s/o Henry Mulholland & Jane Armstrong (all fr ICSP & her relatives).
2. SAMENA ARMSTRONG b 1863 d 1953 **single** res Tappleytown Saltfleet T Wentworth Co ON.
3. ANNIE ARMSTRONG b 1865 d 1951 **single** res Tappleytown.
4. BRUCE ARMSTRONG b 07 May 1867 d 12 Apr 1876 ae 08-11-05 bur dy Tapleytown Cem s/o S J & Anne Armstrong.
5. WILLOUGHBY DeWITT ARMSTRONG b 1869 (d 1959) m Violet Goodfellow res Pasadena CA **no chn**.
6. SAMUEL JOSEPH ARMSTRONG b 02 Apr 1878 m 29 Nov 1899 Selena Maude Clarke b 05 Mar 1877 (d 14 Mar 1968 bur Fifty Cem Stoney Creek ON. He left his family in the 1930's never to be heard of again (fr GRH).

DeWITT
1.1.9.4.3.7.4.6 JOHN DeWITT Jr m Eunice Churchill
1. HIRAM SYLVESTER DeWITT b 23 Apr 1866 Tapleytown ON (d 01 Dec 1924 Napinka MB) at Thorndale ON m 13 Jan 1892 Eliza Jane Logan b 09 Jan 1865 Thorndale ON d 19 Apr 1926 both bur Napinka Cem. First 2 chn were b where Hiram farmed on SE quarter section farm 21-4-25 but in 1899 they moved in to Napinka & lived in John DeWitt's house (fr EJDL, BB: 617/8).
3. MORGAN SAMUEL DeWITT b 10 Jul 1870 Tapleytown ON (d 10 Jul 1930 Napinka MB) m 31 Dec 1897 Emily Leigh b 31 Mar 1861 Orillia ON d 30 Sep 1960 Regina SK; chn b Napinka (EJDL, BB: 619).
4. JOSEPH HARRISON/DeWITT b 17 Mar 1872 Tapleytown ON (d 07 Jun 1959 Regina SK) m 24 Nov 1897 Katie Eleanor/Nellie Hall b 21 Nov 1876 Hull PQ d 27 Jul 1962 Regina.
5. ELINOR JANE/ELLA DeWITT b 13 Sep 1877 Tapleytown ON (d 29 Mar 1966 Winnipeg MB bur) m 14 Dec 1897 Robert Livesley b 09 Mar 1874 Florence ON d 30 Jun 1959 Winnipeg both bur Napinka; chn b Napinka. Ella taught school. They moved to Melita MB in 1908, to Winnipeg in 1940 to be near their children (info fr EJD, BB: 619).

Excerps quoting from Mildred Dodge's article (fr EJDL) in Bridging Brenda, a Municipal History Published October 1990. In January 1887, he (John DeWitt) took a trip to Manitoba, and as Mother (Eunice Churchill) had a brother living in Neepawa, he went there. He bought a farm, a quarter section of land with everything on it, stock, implements, and even a dog and cat, only a mile from Neepawa. My uncle looked after the stock while Father went back east and sold our farm there and one day in February we left behind us old Ontario. Father and Morgan left with a carload of settler's effects and Mother and the rest of us left the day after, but we were in Neepawa a week before them. The whole train consisted of settlers coming west, and they were snowbound for four days on the north shore of Lake Superior. We stayed at Uncle Nat's. Then when all arrived we moved to our new log house, with two rooms above and two below. The boys would go to the creek with a spear and a pitchfork and would bring home all the fish they could carry. Wild fruit was there in abundance too. After the crop was in that spring my father decided to look for more land to give the boys each a farm. Because all the good land was taken up around there, he took a trip over to Napinka district to see what was there and to visit some good friends of ours, the Pollocks.

Father got the section NW ¼ 21-4-25 which is two and a half miles from Napinka. It was raw prairie land (C.P.R.) and was bought for three dollars and twenty-five cents an acre. After the crop was harvested at Neepawa, we moved to our new location with a house 12 x 16. We had good years and bad years.

The first crop at Napinka, 1888, was frozen on the night of August 7th and 8th. Crops were ruined, acres were never cut, and what was cut and threshed was of little use. In 1889 it was very dry and crops were short. In 1890 and 1891 the crops were good and 1892 was extra good. By good management father was able to give to each of the boys a clear deed to a quarter section of land (160 acres).

Settlers kept coming in and all too soon all the land around here was taken up. Five years after we came the railway was built, before that our nearest town was Deloraine, only five years old. It was there we did our buying and drew our wheat. We also got wood for fuel from the Turtle Mountains. In 1891 the railroad was built from Souris, then called Plum Creek, and was operating in the fall. The train passed by every two or three days.

SMITH
1.1.9.4.3.7.4.10 PHOEBE JANE DeWITT m John Wesley Smith
1. NINORA/NINA ALEXANDRA SMITH b 04 Aug 1870, d 05 Nov 1952 at Winona m Cecil C Pettit s/o James Pettit & Ethelynder Smith res in a brick house on Hwy #8 across from Fruitland Christian Reformed CH **no chn**.
2. JOSHUA DeWITT SMITH b 25 Feb 1872 Winona ON (d ? Feb 1961 Greensville ON) m Sarah Jane Alway Smith.

Leucas deWit

3   ETHEL IONA SMITH b 01 Oct 1875 d 31 Oct 1931 of Albrights Disease. She was a very good shot & is bur Fruitland ON Cem, **single.**
4   ARTHUR WESLEY SMITH twin b 14 Mar 1880 Winona ON (d 26 Jun 1933 Vineland On m 13 Dec 1910 Adelaide Henry d/o Edwin Earl Martin & Margaret Augusta Henry, b 28 Jul 1881 d 09 Feb 1966, res Con 3 Lot 1 Vineland, Clinton T ON, his twin Howard.
5   HOWARD BLAKE SMITH twin b 14 Mar 1880 (d 26 Apr 1972 bur Fifty Cem Hwy & #8 Winona ON) at the Bath Hotel, Glasgow Scot m 22 Nov 1911 Edythe Reid d 06 Nov 1970.
6   ELIZABETH ANN/BESS SMITH b 14 Feb 1885 Winona ON (d 06 Mar 1966 bur Hamilton ON overlooking the Bay) as his 2nd wf m 20 Feb 1912 Howard Malcolm Sweeney s/o Sweeney & Belle K Lynch, b 23 Aug 1881 Beaver Falls PA d 20 Jun 1972. He worked & owned Union Drawn Steel, Hamilton ON. All chn born Lot 9, Con 2 Saltfleet Twp Winona. All res in a white house on #8 Hwy (all #5 HBS above & ICSP).

KELTON
1.1.9.4.3.7.4.11 MARGARET J DeWITT m Arthur Kelton
1   FRANK CORTEZ KELTON res in San Diego CA (Downs Syndrom).

DeWITT
1.1.9.4.3.7.4.13 JUDSON ADAIRIUM/ADANIRAM DeWITT m Eliza Ann Johnson
1   CLAYTON A DeWITT b 18 Apr 1879 Port Dover On (d ? Apr 1906 Stratford ON) **single.**
2   NORMAN BRUNSWICK DeWITT b 25 Oct 1880 Port Dover (d 02 Jul 1954 Alamagordo NM) m Alma Etta Pennington d/o Joseph Pennington & Ollie Daniel, b 09 Oct 1902.
3   THEODOSIA DeWITT b 05 Jun 1882 Forestville ON (d 15 Mar 1974) m 21 Mar 1907 Christian Frederick Schobert.
4   ETHEL DeWITT b 25 Nov 1883 Forestville (d 1903 Forestville) **single.**
5   LAURA BELL DeWITT b 23 Oct 1885 Forestville ON d 22 Jul 1979 Alamagordo m 26 Aug 1908 Andrew Sorenson.
6   CLARENCE DeWITT b 17 Jan 1888 Forestville d 29 Nov 1907 Alamagordo NM **single.** Clarence had TB & this was one reason the family moved to NM.
7   JEAN DeWITT b 28 Aug 1893 Forestville ON m 05 Mar 1916 Arthur Miller Wilkins s/o Stillman Eli Miller Wilkins & Alice Walker, b 20 Dec 1883 Jolin MO d 12 Mar 1954 Alamogordo NM, Div. (fr JDW)

TOWNSEND
1.1.9.4.3.7.5.1 SARAH ANN DeWITT m Henry G Townsend
1   CAROLINE SOPHIA TOWNSEND b 1859 m ? Piet.
2   ADA MAUDE TOWNSEND b 1865 (1851 Census).

DeWITT
1.1.9.4.3.7.5.3 JONATHAN DeWITT m Carolin Fick
1   ANNETTE/NETTIE DeWITT b 1864 m ? Heumann res Alpena MI.
2   ELMER DeWITT b 1867 m Libbie Fick, dau Lulu res Port Hope MI.
(1851 Census reel G-9908 South Norfolk, Middleton ON)

HORNING
1.1.9.4.3.7.5.4 MARY/CHARLOTTE DeWITT m John Horning
1   JOSEPH HORNING b 1868.

DeWITT
1.1.9.4.3.7.5.6 JAMES DeWITT m Henrietta ? .
1   VERNA A DeWITT b 1879 MI (US Census res Grand Lodge, E ½ Oneida T Eaton Co.)

DeWITT
1.1.9.4.3.7.5.9 JACOB M/? N DeWITT m Minnie C * Hamlin
1   ZARA C DeWITT b ? Nov 1879 MI m ? Mahones, res with prts.
2   XENOPHON DeWITT b ? Nov 1882 MI (family res Lancing, MI in 1900 - US Census 1900).

WALKER
1.1.9.4.3.7.5.11 ANTINNETT DeWITT m Oielio Walker
1   ELIZA A WALKER b ? Oct 1896 Bentch T Eaton Co MI.

NEFF
1.1.9.4.3.7.6.1 ABRAHAM NEFF m Helen/Alena Hill
1   HELENA A NEFF b 1861 res Hamilton ON **single** in 1932 City Directory.
2   ALICE NEFF b 1866.
3   IDA NEFF b 1870.

NEFF
1.1.9.4.3.7.6.3 JAMES BRENNAN NEFF m1 Sarah Howard
1   EDGAR NEFF **dy**
2   SUSAN NEFF **dy.**
3   ALFRED NEFF **dy.**
4   ARTHUR NEFF **dy.**

Leucas deWit

5   JAMES EDWIN NEFF b 24 Aug 1860 d 20 Sep 1935.
6   MARY ISOBEL/BELLA NEFF b 1862 m Robert Foster a contractor.
7   JESSIE NEFF b 1863.
    m2 10 Apr 1878 Charlotte Omstead
8   CHARLOTTE MAY NEFF **dy.**
9   JESSIE NEFF b 08 Sep 1872 (d 29 Oct 1954) m Frederick Montgomery b 1870 d 1940.
    m3 Catherine Peterson, no chn.

DeWITT
1.1.9.4.3.7.10.1 FREDERICK NELSON DeWITT m1 Margaret Jameison
1   GEORGE C DeWITT b 23 Nov 1867 went to Chicago, last heard from in CA. Niece Mae (Wilson) Boyes said she found his grave but did not say where, **single.**
2   JOHN HENRY DeWITT b 21 Apr 1869 d 1936 Winnipeg MN, **single.**
m2 03 Apr 1872 Susannah Gammage.
3   MARY CECELIA ANN DeWITT b 28 Dec 1875 Burford Twp Brant Co ON (d 12 Jun 1963 bur Dauphin MB) m 08 Jan 1896 William George Wilson s/o John Wilson of Belfast Ire & Margaret Baxter of Muddy York (Toronto) ON, b 14 Jan 1869 d 16 Jan 1945 Dauphin. Cecelia was a musician. She went with her parents to Newdale ae 2, but when she was 6 she was sent to ON for schooling and lived with her Aunt Prudence Sarah DeWitt.
4   PRUDENCE EMMA DeWITT b 04 Dec 1887 d 01 Jan 1888 Newdale **dy.**

DeWITT
1.1.9.4.3.7.10.2 GEORGE DeWITT m Elizabeth Martin
1   PRUDENCE De WITT m ? Lee, son Delmar Lee.

DeWITT
1.1.9.4.3.7.10.5 CHARLES WILBERT DeWITT m Julia Ann Horning
1   ELECTRA N DeWITT b 1879 d 10 Mar 1881 ae 00-09-20 bur Tapleytown **dy.**
2   FREDERICK WILBERT DeWITT b 1882 (d 1927) m Georgina Alma Dean Stewart b 20 Nov 1882 d 17 Sep 1969 bur Fruitland ON Cem res Lots 14 to 16 Saltfleet Twp ON. This family raised Charles' niece May Martin. She m Hiram Norton.

TRATO
1.1.9.4.3.7.10.6 ELIZABETH DeWITT m Albert Trato
1   CHRISTOPHER GEORGE TRATO b 1880 (d 1946) m 30 Mar 1904 Edith Lydia Compaigne b 1884 d 1969.
2   PANSY BLOSSOM TRATO m George Seth Swift.
3   ALBERT NELSON TRATO b 1887 (d 1967) m Vera Seume. In 1906 the DeWitt sisters, Prudence Berg, Eliza Trato and Florence Lucas had a business in Hamilton & in Chicago called "DeWitt Flowers", address 237 W 46th Pl Chicago. They made beautiful white goose feather flowers.
    Ira Smith DeWitt had a wreath of white roses and buds in a deep-glassed frame they made for Ira's father, their brother Jonathan. In the 1911 Chicago Directory p 373, lists "Dewitt Sister Flowers" (George Trato) 147 W 46th Pl.

MARTIN
1.1.9.4.3.7.10.8 CAROLINE DeWITT m John H Martin
1   MARY/MAY MARTIN b 18 Sep 1878 at Vinemount ON (d 26 May 1950 Tansley ON bur Palermo Cem Oakville ON) m 14 Feb 1900 Hiram George Andrew Norton b 09 Sep 1876 Tapleytown ON d 18 Aug 1947 Tansley ON. May was raised by her Uncle Charles Clifford DeWitt (fr CCD 1).

LUCAS
1.1.9.4.3.7.10.9 FLORENCE DeWITT m Smith Fred Lucas
1   a * FLORENCE LUCAS, Miss bkpr at 1750 Ashland Ave h 1738 N.
2   b * FRED LUCAS ins agt h 6614 Evans Ave (Chicago City Directory).

DeWITT
1.1.9.4.3.7.10.10 JONATHAN DeWITT m Selena Horning
1   IRA SMITH DeWITT b 27 Jun 1884 at Tapleytown (d 27 Mar 1966 Minnedosa MB bur 30 Mar 1966 Sandy Lake MB) at Newdale MB m 27 June1906 Edna Belle Barker b Aug 11 1883 Brookfield, Linn Co MO d/o Wilbur Jay Barker & Lovina Gertrude Judd, d 21 Dec 1968 Halton Centennial Manor, Milton ON bur White Chapel Memorial Gardens, Ancaster ON. In 1922 Edna was converted to the Seventh Day Adventist faith at a tent Revival meeting at Sandy Lake. In ill health, she lived her last 24 yrs with her dau Rhea.
    Selena Horning m2 Henry Ralston b 25 Feb 1852 wdr, his chn George & Annie; their chn Morris Albert Ralston b 20 Mar 1891

Ira Smith DeWitt m Edna Belle Barker

Leucas deWit

(d 1964 bur White Brick Cem Ancaster ON) m Emma Jane Binkley b 1875 d 1961 **no chn**. Ada Ralston b 29 Nov 1895 Barton T ON (d 15 Apr 1971 Binbrook bur Ancaster) m 15 Sep 1915 John Awry Daniels, had 10 chn.

PARSONS
1.1.9.4.3.7.10.11 MARGARETA/MAY DeWITT m Steven Parsons
1. FLOYD PARSONS.
2. DEWITT PARSONS.
3. PRUDENCE PARSONS m Robert Wilson (fr ICSP).

HEWLETT
1.1.9.4.3.8.2.2 MARIA BOGARDUS m ? Hewlett
1. JOB HEWLETT
2. ILYA HEWLETT
3. HARRY HEWLETT (info fr WBB)

BOGARDUS
1.1.9.4.3.8.2.3 PETER BOGARDUS m 1857 Matilda Fair
1. MARIA BOGARDUS
2. ANN BOGARDUS m ? St John (where?).
3. JOHN BOGARDUS
4. PHILLIP BOGARDUS
5. CYNTHIA BOGARDUS
6. HELEN AMELIA BOGARDUS b 23 Feb 1870.
7. FRANCIS BOGARDUS m 08 Jun 1910 Aida Maude Hill (info fr WBB).

HOWEY
1.1.9.4.3.8.2.4 CORNELIA BOGARDUS m ? Howey
1. CECILIA P HOWEY
2. JOHN HOWEY
3. FRANK HOWEY (info fr WBB).

BOGARDUS
1.1.9.4.3.8.2.5 HENRY BOGARDUS m1 Rachel Packard
1. JAMES EDWARD BOGARDUS b 16 Feb 1864 Clearnorth OH (d 25 Dec 1931 Los Angeles CA) m 1931 Los Angeles CA Leona L Earl b 1871 Piper City Il d 1951 Los Angeles.
2. EDWARD SHERMAN BOGARDUS b 08 Jan 1867 Clinton IL (d 12 Nov 1912 Clinton IL) m 05 Nov 1890 Hattie Hope Earl b 1873 Piper City IL d 1958.

m2 10 Jan 1875 Margaret A McCullough
3. LAURA BOGARDUS m Herbert Fennell.
4. HENRY ORVILLE BOGARDUS b Clinton MI (d 05 Jul 1950) m 10 Oct 1901 Grace Myrtle Bowen b 1882 d 1956.
5. ARTHUR DEWITT BOGARDUS b 04 Jun 1850 Clinton, IL d 05 Oct 1933 Clinton IL, **single**.
6. RUSSELL HERMAN BOGARDUS b 18 Mar 1884 m Beulah ? .
7. PHILLIP LEWIS BOGARDUS b 02 Jul 1887 Clinton IL (d 21 Jan 1950 at Effingham IL) m 02 Oct 1926 Alberta May Barnett b 1911 Matoon IL had a son. All but the 1st ch b Clinton IL.
8. UNNAMED MALE BOGARDUS dy (all but the 1st ch b Clinton IL. Info fr WBB).

BOGARDUS
1.1.9.4.3.8.2.6 PHILLIP BOGARDUS m Elizabeth Phipps
1. VIOLET MAE BOGARDUS b 1873 (d 23 Dec 1967) m Frederick Cale.
2. ARTHUR PHIPPS BOGARDUS b 27 Jul 1876 St Catherines ON (d Dec 1954) m 26 Nov 1905 Sarah Ann Wilson b 1877 Antrim ON d May 1958.
3. FREDERICK FRANCIS BOGARDUS b 28 Aug 1878 (d 1969) m 1910 Maude Hill.
4. CHARLOTTE BOGARDUS b 1880 (d 1941) m 27 Apr 1904 Harry Grafton Rowe Philip d 1952.
5. LENA GERTRUDE BOGARDUS b 04 Oct 1883 St Catherine ON m 04 Oct 1912 Charles Walter Cain b 1884 d 1940's; b m d St Catharines (research fr WBB).

BOGARDUS
1.1.9.4.3.8.2.8 ADORUM BOGARDUS m Christine Spencer
1. ASA BOGARDUS b 18 Sep 1874 **dy**.
2. IRA BOGARDUS b 14 Mar 1897 (d 1919) **single**.
3. IDA BOGARDUS b 30 May 1878 (d 20 Jan 1956) m Edward Arnold; they had a dau Irene Agnes.
4. ALBERT BOGARDUS b 25 Sep 1880 **single**.
5. LILLIAN BOGARDUS b 15 Feb 1883 (d 02 Aug 1967 Vineland ON) m Frank Arnold.
6. MABEL BOGARDUS b 19 Jun 1884.
7. DORA BOGARDUS b 28 Nov 1886 (d 27 Jun 1966) m Christian Frye.
8. JULIA BOGARDUS b 01 Aug 1888 (d 10 Mar 1971 bur St Catherines Cem ON) m Harry Mason.

Leucas deWit

9   ADORUM BOGARDUS b 30 Aug 1889 (d 1956 Barbados West Indies) at Sante Fe, Isle of Pines, in Cuba m 21 Sep 1913 Thusnelda W Warner.
10   LEWIS B BOGARDUS b 14 Jan 1891 d 01 Jul 1971 Palm Beach, FL **single**.
11   GRACIE BOGARDUS b 26 May 1893 d 1893 **dy** (all fr WBB).

BOGARDUS
1.1.9.4.3.8.2.9 BENJAMIN BOGARDUS m Eliza I   ?
1. LUCINDA BOGARDUS b 1878.
2. NORA BOGARDUS b 1880.
3. VERONA BOGARDUS m   ?   Van Velper.
4. ADORUM BOGARDUS
5. PETER BOGARDUS
6. BENJAMIN BOGARDUS (fr WBB).

SUTTON
1.1.9.4.3.8.2.10 CYNTHIA BOGARDUS m   ?   Sutton
1. ELVA SUTTON
2. HARRY SUTTON
3. NEALY SUTTON (fr WBB).

BOGARDUS
1.1.9.4.3.8.2.12 FRANCIS BOGARDUS m Phebe   ?
1. ANNA V BOGARDUS d 01 Oct 1900 (fr WBB).

DeWITT
1.1.9.4.3.8.3.3 ISABELLA/BELLA DeWITT m Frank DeWitt
1. WALTER DeWITT
2. ADDIE DeWITT b 1898/9. (From the Childrens Aid Society Hamilton Wentworth 2 Aug 1997) Addie was 12 on Apr 1 in 1911 Society Care to Feb 28 1914 then at Richmond Hill ON Hospital, then at the Ontario School in Orilla ON, then True Blue Orphanage until May 1930 discharged on probation. During the discharge period she had 2 illegitamate chn Joseph DeWitt in 29 May 1933, & John Martin DeWitt 14 Aug 1935 both in Orillia. They readmitted her to the school.
3. CLIFFORD DeWITT b 28 Apr 1901 was Ward of the Society 28 Apr 1911 because Bella DeWitt of 18 Garth St Hamilton a widow was unable to care for him & his siblings.
4. GRACE DeWITT b 1903 m 15 May 1922 Fred Russel. (From the Children Aid Society Hamilton Wentworth 2 Aug 1977) Grace placed in a variety of Foster Homes until 27 July 1921 she res with Mrs. H. Evans 29 Cumberland Ave Hamilton ON. She moved to Toronto 04 Jan 1922 res 392 George St Toronto.
5. JAMES DeWITT b Chicago IL.
6. ALBERT DeWITT dy. All the chn were b Chicago IL USA. (research ICSP, VEDS).

Clifford DeWitt s/o Isabella DeWitt & Frank DeWitt

In 1982 Jim DeWitt of Chippewa ON, who is a son of #3 Cliff, said 'Bella was his grdma. Three months after Frank DeWitt d at Hamilton ON, on the 28 Apr 1911 the 5 chn were placed with Children's Aid in the orphanage there by "Bella Smith". Isabella DeWitt reappeared at Chippewa as a single lady and joined the Church. Her father d in 1898, her mother in 1916.. She outlived a single bro & one bro who had no issue as well as two uncles, both single, all had farms. She must have inherited the properties since her will indicated she was wealthy for the times. She left 72 $1,000.00 bequests to assorted relatives, $5,250.00 to charities, money to keep the family graves up in perpetuity and the rest of her estate to her favourites but not a cent to the 5 orphanage chn. Jim said his pa introduced Bella to him as his aunt and when confronted later with the fact she was his grdma he was told to mind his own business. Jim never learned to read or write and was told by the lawyer handling the estate he would have to prove in court Bella was his grdma. He hadn't the finances at the time to pursue the matter. His house is on a lot of what was the original home farm. Jim gave us a copy of her will and a picture of Bella with Cliff. She was 6 feet tall.

BEAM
1.1.9.4.5.1.2.1 HARRIETT ELIZABETH DeWITT m1 Adam Beam m2   ?   Franklin
1. JAMES ALBERT BEAM b 17 Mar 1845.
2. CATHERINE ALMIRA BEAM b 10 Jun 1846.
3. EDGAR GENE BEAM b 19 Oct 1849.

DeWITT

1.1.9.4.5.1.2.4 PLATT DeWITT m Louise Whilhemina Bunge
1. FRANCES DeWITT b 13 Oct 1876 (d 12 Oct 1923 Kewanee IL) m 27 Feb 1901 Robert Duff.
2. EDWARD DeWITT b 26 May 1879 d 06 Mar 1881 **dy.**
3. JOHN HENRY DeWITT b 05 Jul 1881 Annawan, Henry Co IL (d 03 Mar 1964 Muskegan MI bur Whitehall MI). At Annawan he m 08 Sep 1904 Ollie May Moon b 05 Feb 1883 Annawan MI d 27 Jul 1959 Muskegon MI bur there. The family moved to Minnesota in 1911, to Michigan in 1916.
4. CHARLES DeWITT b 23 Feb 1883 (d 28 Feb 1955 Kewanee Public Hospital) m 08 Sep 1910 Mary Bentham.
5. WALTER DeWITT b 04 Jun 1885 (d 22 Nov 1974 Luther IL m 26 Dec 1912.   ?
6. MARIE/MAY C DeWITT b 18 Aug 1889 (d 29 May 1970 Kewanee IL) at Kewanee m 26 Dec 1912   ?
7. OSCAR DeWITT b 23 Dec 1891 d 16 Apr 1910 **dy.**
8. MABEL DeWITT b 18 Feb 1894 (d 10 Apr 1929 at Kewanee) m 09 Feb 1929 at Kewanee   ? (all fr OD).

STRONG

1.1.9.4.5.3.4.1 HELEN HOWLAND m Jarrius Bissel Strong
1. LOIS G STRONG b Black Lake NY, m John P Forbes (DFUSC:98) Lois' Lineage DAR 22:72 #21192.

DeWITT

1.1.9.4.5.3.8.1 ORLEAN DeWITT Jr m Laura McColley
1. LYDIA DeWITT b Kent Co DL m Franklin Gibbs Crispin (DFUSC:98) DAR Lineage 52:242 #51552.

DAVIS

1.19.4.8.2.1.5 REBECCA M LOW m Clark Davis
1. SANFORD DAVIS b 23 aug 1869 d 27 jun 1870 **dy.**
2. BERTHA DAVIS b 03 Feb 1872 d 12 Oct 1874 **dy.**
3. CHARLOTTE DAVIS b 13 Apr 1874 d 12 Oct 1874 **dy.**
4. MINERVA DAVIS b 28 Oct 1877.
5. MAUD DAVIS b 16 Feb 1880 res Fishkill Creek, near Saugerties NY (all fr BG: 131).

LOW

1.1.9.4.8.2.9.1 ALEXANDER KIERSTEDE LOW {m} Rachel Ann Longendyck (1.1.9.1.3.2.2.1.7)
1. RACHEL LAVINA LOW b 04 Aug 1859 d 03 Apr 1860 **dy.**
2. MARY ELIZABETH LOW b 12 Jun 1861 m 06 Nov 1878 David Cortland Hommel s/o William Hommel & Rachel Eliza Freleigh, b 15 Nov 1842 d 01 Dec. 1882. She m2 Eugene H Davis, res near Saugerties.
3. JAMES MILTON LOW b 28 Jul 1864 m 05 Nov 1885 Katie Van Buren b 22 Mar 1867 d/o Cornelius Van Buren & Sarah Roe.
4. LUCRETIA B LOW b 21 Apr 1870.
5. HATTIE GERTRUDE LOW b 09 Sep 1872.
6. SARAH MARGARET LOW b 21 Apr 1876.
7. TINE MABEL LOW b 28 Aug 1878
8. JOHN ADELBERT LOW b 19 Jul 1884 (all fr BG:130).

BOSSARD

1.1.9.4.8.2.9.2 ELIZABETH LAVINA LOW m William D Bossard
1. ALEXANDER BOSSARD b 18 May 1864.
2. WILSON BOSSARD b 29 Jun 1866.
3. AARON LAFAYETTE BOSSARD b 20 Sep 1868.
4. MARY E BOSSARD b 16 Aug 1871 (all fr BG:131).

LOW

1.1.9.4.8.2.9.3 WILLIAM VAN SANTFORD LOW m Mary Elizabeth Moran
1. WILLIAM E LOW b 27 Oct 1861.
2. ELEANOR J LOW b 02 Jan 1864.
3. GEORGE A LOW b 09 Jun 1865.
4. ELMER E LOW b 03 Feb 1867.
5. MARY A LOW b 17 Nov 1869.
6. FEMALE LOW b 17 Mar 1872 d 27 Mar 1872 **dy.**
7. MARGARET L LOW b 14 Sep 1873.
8. FANNIE A LOW b 12 Apr 1876.
9. SANFORD A LOW b 20 Feb 1878 (all fr BG:131).

LOW

1.1.9.4.8.8.6.1 LEVI LOW m Annis B Laird
1. CHARK ARMSTRONG LOW b 26 Apr 1869 Millcreek T Union Co OH (d 24 Jun 1953 Franklin Twp. Columbus Co. OH bur Union Cem) Union m 21 Jul 1892 Annie Lulu/Nellie Bland (Minister E E Cleland) d/o John Lewis Bland &

Nannie H McDowell, b 10 Sep 1874 Marysville T Union Co OH d 1902 & bur at Coffee (near Manchester IN) (fr LBM tbstns Chark's b rec, d rec, m cert, Anne Lulu's guardianship rec, photos)
2 CLARA DAISY LOW b 1871 OH.
3 ROSA MATILDA LOW b 1873 OH (fr MLMB).

CONYES
1.1.9.4.8.9.4.1 HENRY SANFORD/SANFORD HENRY CUNYES/CONYES m Rachel J Weeks
1 CARRIE L CONYES b 04 May 1870 bp 01 Sep 1870 (PRDC:49).
2 FRANCIS EDWARD CUNYES b 25 Nov 1878 bp 04 Feb 1881 (PRDC:56).

SCHOONMAKER
1.1.9.4.8.11.1.1 MARTIN DOW SCHOONMAKER m Jane Carberry Smith
1 GRACE SCHOONMAKER
2 ELIZABETH SCHOONMAKER b 1879.
3 WALTER SCHOONMAKER
4 LURA C SCHOONMAKER b 1883.
5 MARTIN F SCHOONMAKER b 1891 (fr PDRC: 12,21,22,25,26,29,30,34).
Family moved to Rock Island IL in 1856. Martin was President of Farmer's State Bank at Reynolds.

SCHOONMAKER
1.1.9.4.8.11.1.3 GEORGE P SCHOONMAKER m Cinderella Hines
1 WALTER W SCHOONMAKER b 1881.
2 MARY V SCHOONMAKER b 1882.
3 CHARLES W SCHOONMAKER b 1886 (fr PDRDC: ?)

Leucas deWit

GENERATION 9

If a couple both trace back to DeWitt ancestry more than once m is {m} indicating this fact. Numbering used is the first parent listed chronologically. Both numbers are given, but the one to be used in succeeding generations is underlined.

To keep the chronology of 1.1.9.4 LEUCAS' descendants #3 EVERT and #5 LUCAS are the exceptions.

DEDRICK
1.1.9.4.1.2.5.2.1 ABRAM STEPHEN DEDRICK m Olive Procunier
1. FRANCIS/FRANK VERNON DEDRICK b 06 May 1899 m1 25 Oct 1924 Phyllis Lucille Curtis b 22 May 1906 d 21 Apr 1936, m2 Pricilla Spera
2. FLORENCE MAY DEDRICK b 29 Apr 1904 (d 1986) m1 Charles Cecil Smithson b 1895 d 1944, m2 Calvin Stevens (fr FVD).

WILLIAMSON
1.1.9.4.2.1.2.1.3 KATRINE DeWITT m George F Williamson
1. MARY LOUISA WILLIAMSON b 06 Dec 1870 d 1873.
2. AMY WILLIAMSON b 18 Dec 1872.
3. IRENE WILLIAMSON b 10 Oct 1878.
4. GEORGE CLINTON WILLIAMSON b 09 Aug 1885 (fr FVD).

DeWITT
1.1.9.4.2.1.2.3.1 ABRAHAM VAN DYCK DeWITT m Grace Hallam Learned
1. ELSIE VAN DYCK DeWITT b 22 Nov 1896 (only child) New London CT (P-DR:298).

NORTON
1.1.9.4.2.1.2.3.4 MARY LOUISE DeWITT m John Treadwell Norton
1. ELSIE DeWITT NORTON b 06 Jan 1877 at 300 State St, Albany m 25 Feb 1905 John Read Pettit M.D. in Philadelphia d 1944. He was Lieutenant Commander Navy Medical Corps Reserve WW II.
2. JOHN TREADWELL NORTON b 19 Jul 1878 London d 27 Oct 1923 Albany, Chief Chemist Allegheny, Ludlum Steel Company, graduate of Albany Academy & Yale College.
3. KATHARINE DeWITT LEARNED NORTON b 01 Jun 1879 at Biarritz, m   Oct 1910 Gerald Holsman of Philadelphia (all P-DR:294).

PELTZ
1.1.9.4.2.1.2.5.3 JOHN DeWITT PELTZ m1 Mary Marvin Learned
1. WILLIAM LEARNED PELTZ b Albany m Katherine Hun. William was a lawyer & Author of Peltz-DeWitt Record: Certain of Their Companies.
2. PHILIP PELTZ d 26 Mar 1829 as a student, **single.**
   m2 05 Apr 1894 Catharine Barnard Walsh
3. JOHN De WITT PELTZ m Mary Ellis Opdycke. He was an executive with the American Red Cross, NYC P-DR:164).
4. CATHARINE WALSH PELTZ b Albany, Assistant Prof. NY State College for Teachers (all P-DR:164).

DUNN
1.1.9.4.2.1.2.7.1 CHARLOTTE GILLET DeWITT m Theophilus Calhoun Dunn
1. ELIOT DeWITT DUNN m 05 Oct 1910 Rhoda Deas. He was Vice President in 1946 of Cross & Brown Real Estate res 357 Melrose Pl, South Orange NJ.
2. THEODORE FRELINGHUYSEN DUNN b 14 Dec 1883 (P-DR:300).

LENT
1.1.9.4.2.1.2.7.5 SARA DeWITT m Franklin Townsend Lent BS, MS
   First 3 chn b New Brunswick NJ.
1. JOHN DeWITT LENT b 03 Nov 1881 New Brunswick NJ, m1 1916 Ruth Zubrod who d 1918, m2 Mildred Nadler. John won the Eliot prize at Harvard. He left before grad because of family business reverses. He was with the Western Clock Co, LaSalle IL, res Peru IL & by 1948 was retired.
2. ROSE DeWITT LENT b 16 Jul 1883 New Brunswick m Edmund V Lewis res NYC.
3. CHARLOTTE ELIOT LENT b at New Brunswick m Norton Blackstone Leo (d 1939) res Bronxville NY.
4. HARRIET DeWITT LENT b 18 Sep 1894 Cranford NJ m1 David Vinton Stahl div, m2 John Darrow Adams, b at New Brunswick, President of Provincetown Fisheries Inc, res 3 Kendall Lane, Provincetown PA.
5. THEODORE DeWITT LENT (d 1920) m 02 Apr 1916 Lillian Rosline (all P-DR:301-03).

DeWITT
1.1.9.4.2.1.2.7.7 THEODORE FRELINGHUYSEN DeWITT M.D. m Harriet W Matthiessen
1. HELEN DeWITT **dy.**
2. JOHN DeWITT b 06 Apr 1894 St Paul MN, grad Cornell 1917, officer US Air Corps in WWI, in WWII combat pilot, a Major, 355th Fighter Group, then in business NYC & Chicago. He m1 Dorothy Courtney Lee of Baltimore, {m2} Dorothy Peck, res in San Diego CA in 1945 (P-DR: 303).

DeWITT

1.1.9.4.2.1.2.7.8 JOHN DeWITT m Ruth A Howland
1. RUTH HOWLAND DeWITT grad U of Chicago 1914 as a lawyer, res with her mother Dallas TX.
2. CHARLOTTE DeWITT attended Chicago Art Institute, m Wayne Thomas, Aviation Editor, Chicago Tribune.
3. JOHN DeWITT grad/o U/o Pittsburgh School of Engineering in 1933, Coast Guard WWII, Radio Script Writer, m Miriam Boight. In 1948 they res 248 W 21st St NYC. Their dau Abigail DeWitt b 1941.
4. THOMAS HOWLAND DeWITT b 31 May 1918 NC, at Southern Meth School of Engineering 1938-41, Unitarian Religion, Lt US Air Corps WWII, m Ann Caroline Prior, res 1948 at 652 Galisteo St, Santa Fe NM (all fr P-DR:305).

SCHOONMAKER

1.1.9.4.2.1.2.8.1 HENRY WYNOOP SCHOONMAKER m Annie Snyder
1. SARAH GRACE SCHOONMAKER b 11 Dec 1876 & bp 23 Mar 1877.
2. JOHN DEWITT SCHOONMAKER b 16 Apr 1878 & bp 16 Aug 1878 (both PRDC:55).

VERMILYE

1.1.9.4.2.1.2.10.1 THOMAS EDWARD VERMILYE m Susan Gertrude Vedder
1. ASHBEL GREEN VERMILYE III (sic) b 27 Oct 1875 (d 03 Jan 1926) m Mary Belle Breed of Louisville KY, **no chn**. Ashbel was a building contractor; treasurer of the Humane Society for years.
2. GERTRUDE VEDDER VERMILYE b 26 Aug 1887 East Orange NJ m Col John Griffeth Booten b 01 Feb 1887 Delong IA US Army Retired, grad West Point 1911, Harvard Business School 1927. He was Purchasing Agent for Hollingworth & Whitney, Paper Manufacturers, res 267 Beacon St, Boston MA (P-DR:309).

HUTCHINGS

1.1.9.4.2.1.2.10.2 HELEN LANSING VERMILYE m George Long Hutchings
1. DEWITT VERMILYE HUTCHINGS b 18 Aug 1879 Orange NJ, at Riverside CA m 13 Sep 1909 Allis Hardenbergh Miller d/o Frank Augustus Miller & Isabella Demarest Hardenburgh, b 1882 Riverside, both chn b Riverside.
2. ELSIE LATHROP HUTCHINGS b 08 Dec 1886 Englewood NJ d 01 Apr 1888 (P-DR:310/11).

DUBOIS

1.1.9.4.2.2.1.1.2 ELENA V OVERBAGH m Elijah Dubois
1. CAROLINE LOUISA DUBOIS b 29 Oct 1846 bp 08 Jan 1847 (DRCFU:39).
2. CARRIE OVERBAGH DUBOIS b 05 May 1853 bp 03 Oct 1853 (DRCFU:43).

OVERBAGH

1.1.9.4.2.2.1.1.4 PETER TITUS OVERBAUGH m Caroline Goldsborough Caldwell
1. RICHARD BRINDLEY OVERBAGH b 21 Sep 1862 (d 04 Apr 1926) b/m/d all in Saugerties NY m 18 Sep 1894 Isabel Freligh d/o James A Freligh & Susan A Hoyt, b 1857 Coxsackie NY d 1942 Saugerties (fr RDCFU:37).

DeWITT

1.1.9.4.2.3.1.3.5 E. MILLARD MONTGOMERY DeWITT m1 Ida G Lewis
1. OSCAR DeWITT b 1890.
2. EARL DeWITT b 1899 (HGC:454/5).

m2 25 Dec 1906 Mary Shepherd

WHITNEY

1.1.9.4.2.3.1.3.6 HATTIE E DeWITT m Austin P Whitney
1. MILLARD G WHITNEY
2. CHARLES E WHITNEY
3. MICHAEL D WHITNEY
4. FRANCES WHITNEY b 1900 (HGC:435).

SNYDER

1.1.9.4.2.3.5.3.1 ANNIE/ANNA DeWITT m Albert Snyder
1. OTIS DeWITT SNYDER 28 Jan 1877, bp Jun 1877 (PRDC:55) Plattekill Reformed Dutch CH Ulster Co NY.
2. ROWENA SNYDER b 19 Sep 1880 bp 03 Sep 1881 (PRDC:56).

DeWITT

1.1.9.4.2.3.5.4.1 ALBERT JAMES DeWITT m Violetta Turk
1. BESSIE DeWITT b 1885 m1 Harley Granger Cowan. He m2 Alexander Charles Stark (PDRC:35).

HATCH/LAMBERT

1.1.9.4.3.1.5.2.1 SAMANTHA LUELLA DeWITT m1George O Hatch, m2 E Lambert
1. AMELIA ELIZA LAMBERT b 1885 (d 1931 from T B bur Solmesville ON) m J Seymour Putman (fr Museum at Picton). Her grpa bequeathed her $100.00.

DeWITT
1.1.9.4.3.1.5.3.2 IRA CLANCY DeWITT m Martha Mary Fleming

1. ARCHIE S DeWITT b 11 Apr 1883 Louisville Kent Co ON, d 16 Oct 1901 Gaines Genesse Co MI at 18 after an illness of seven weeks at Gaines, Genesse Co MI, bur Oakwood Cem. **single.**
2. WILLIAM JOHN DeWITT b 10 Feb 1885 Louisville Kent Co ON (d 05 Nov 1947 Highland Park MI) m 24 Aug 1910 Martha Whitehouse d/o John Henry Whitehouse & Martha Emma Sutcliffe b 09 Jun 1886 Anderson T Essex Co ON 24 Apr 1916 Detroit MI both bur Evergreen Cem, Detroit. William was a repairman & inspector for the Grand Truck Railroad; in later years an electrical seviceman for Briggs Mfg & the Ford Motor Company. He m2 16 Mar 1920 Hulda Victoria Whitehouse (Martha's sis) b 07 Jul 1897 Amherstburgh T Essex CO ON d 07 Oct 1966 Saginaw MI bur Evergreen Cem.
3. ROY C DeWITT b 09 Mar 1888 Gaines MI (d 06 Jul 1911ae 23 bur Oakwood Cem Gaines Genesee Co MI) and m Emma Jacobs d/o John Jacobs & Hattie b 08 Aug 1889 div Emma. She m2 a Mr Rogers, m3 William C Hanneman.
4. JEANETTE MAY/NETTIE DeWITT b 17 Jun 1889 Gaines, Genesee Co MI (d 11 May 1958 Bayport, Huron Co MI) m 14 Dec 1916 Charles Phillip Mellman b 26 Jan 1886 St Louis MO d 09 Aug 1968 both bur Oakwood Cem, Gines MI. He was employed 33 yrs as heat treatment foreman at Ford Motor Company before retiring in 1952 (info fr: CFD)

BAILEY
1.1.9.4.3.3.1.8.1 LESLIE OSBORNE BAILEY m Mary Elizabeth Hannay

1. ESTELLA MAUDE BAILEY b 08 Sep 1877 Harcourt NB (d 1961 Moncton NB) m 26 Jan 1898 John F R MacMichael s/o Alexander MacMichael & Elizabeth Hetherington, b 28 Jun 1874 d 17 Nov 1937 bur Elmwood Cem Moncton NB.
2. MABEL COLINDA BAILEY b 14 Jul 1879 Harcourt (d 17 Oct 1954 Burnaby BC bur there in Ocean View Cem) m Thomas Lyons b 10 Sep 1903 Winnipeg d 07 Mar 1969 ae 65 in Burnaby, bur Brookside Cem in Winnipeg MB. He worked for the Canadian Pacific Railway (CPR) Depot, **no chn.**
3. BENJAMIN STUDLEY BAILEY b ca 1881 **dy.**
4. BENJAMIN STUDLEY BAILEY b 09 Nov 1881 Harcourt (d 13 Aug 1951 Vancouver BC ae 69) at Winnipeg m 17 Apr 1906 Florence Amelia Passmore b 28 Dec 1885 London ON d 12 Apr 1957 ae 71 Vancouver, both bur Masonic Cem Burnaby.
5. LESLIE OSBORNE BAILEY b 07 Feb 1883 Brandon MB (d 16 Jun 1954 Winnipeg) at Grandview MB m 03 Jan 1907 Eva May Fisher d/o Alexander Fisher & Mary Dallas, b 24 May 1884 Winnipeg, d 25 Aug 1956 Vancouver BC bur Ocean View Cem Burnaby. This couple separated before 1945.
6. ETHEL MARY BAILEY 30 Mar 1885 Brandon d 21 Jan 1906 ae 21 bur Brookside Cem Winnipeg, **single.**
7. DOROTHY INEZ BAILEY b 22 Nov 1889 Brandon (d 31 Aug 1979 Winnipeg) at Niagara Falls m 07 Aug 1916 Anthony Philip Eckman, Dental Surgeon b 28 May 1884 Granite Falls MN d 20 Nov 1938 Winnipeg ae 54 bur Brookside Cem there.
8. GEORGE RUDOLPH BAILEY b 04 May 1891 Brandon d 25 Aug 1895 Winnipeg **dy.**
9. IDA PEARL BAILEY b 31 Jan 1894 Estevan SK when the family was on a holiday (d 27 Jun 1975 ae 81 Burnaby). At Winnipeg she m1 20 Sep 1915 Maurice Edmund Farwell b 22 Dec 1867 Orillia ON d 1936 Winnipeg. The m was annulled, as he was not div from his first wf Ida m2 07 Feb 1921 Frederick Alexander McDowell s/o Frederick McDowell & Ann Sutter, b 22 Oct 1893 Winnipeg, d 26 Jan 1962 Vancouver both bur Oceanview Cem Burnaby BC.
10. EWART GLADSTONE BAILEY b 08 May 1897 Winnipeg, at Kenora ON m 04 Sep 1920 Augusta Daisy Olive Bennett d/o Robert Bennett & Marion Walsh, b 12 Aug 1897 Cannington ON (fr SCBG, MAH, Cem Rec).

DeWITT
1.1.9.4.3.3.2.1.3 BRADBURY DeWITT m Edith E Thomas

1. HAZEL MAE DeWITT b 1890 d 19 May 1904 ae 14 **dy** (HPCM cem Rec).

DeWITT
1.1.9.4.3.3.2.3.1 ISREAL W DeWITT m Ellen ? .

1. HELENA R DeWITT b 11 Oct 1883 d 07 Feb 1904 bur Maxfield ME Cem **single.**

SMART
1.1.9.4.3.3.3.2.1 LLEWELLYN BROOKS SMART m Flora Emma Sargisson

1. EFFIE B SMART b 01 Jul 1869 Lagrange ME (d 1961 bur Seboeis Cem ME) m1 Robert Richardson, m2 Willie Crawford.
2. A T L SMART b 13 Mar 1871 Seboeis ME (d 27 Jul 1936 bur La Grange ME) m1 04 Jul 1920 Della McCutcheon; m2 Ida Bates Agrille.
3. ESTELLE E SMART b 01 Oct 1872 Seboeis m Currie Styles.
4. LAUREN W SMART b 12 Jul 1875 d 03 Apr 1892 **single.**
5. CHARLES BYRON SMART b 22 Aug 1877 Lagrange d 1958 **single.**
6. PHOEBE MAE SMART b 18 Aug 1881 Seboeis ME (d 25 Sep 1971 Old Orchard Beach ME) at Lagrange ME m 25 Oct 1903 Herman Adelbert Haskell s/o Samuel Lorenzo Haskell & Lucy Nason.
7. IDA FRANCES SMART b 02 Jun 1886 Seboeis ME m Lorenzo Styles (all fr BBVH).

SMART
1.1.9.4.3.3.3.2.2 CHARLES L SMART m Allura S Fowles
1. WALTER SMART
2. LOUISA SMART (fr BBVH).

NOTE: Phoebe Jane DeWitt Smith b 1845 was the granddaughter of Jacob DeWitt & his 2nd wife Abigail Cram Kinney DeWitt who moved to Ontario in 1824. Abigail told Phoebe that choices for marriage in New Brunswick were "Hingins, Hinglishmen or Relatives" so they chose Relatives. This reflects the attitude of the day.

SCOTT
1.9.4.3.3.4.1.1 & 1.1.9.4.3.6.4.1.1 PHOEBE ANN DeWITT m George Scott
1. HENRIETTA SCOTT b 25 Oct 1860 a teacher (d 25 Dec 1940) m Charles DeMerchant b 1860 d 20 Jul 1943 South Tilley NS; brought up several foster chn, **no chn** of their own.
2. CLARISSA SCOTT b 25 Aug 1862 (d 22 Jan 1938) {m} 21 Jul 1885 1.1.9.4.3.3.5.3.3 Elgan Otis Smith by Rev O DeWitt, s/o Nancy Smith & Warren Smith, b 03 Mar 1859 d 07 Apr 1900 Fredericton Jct NB bur Blissville Baptist Cem.
3. DELILAH SCOTT b 02 Jul 1864 (d 22 Oct 1899) {m} 09 Sep 1886 1.1.9.4.3.3.5.3.2 David O Smith s/o Nancy Smith & Warren Smith, b 1857; moved to Salt Lake City UT. He ran a bar; bur Mt Olivet Cem Salt Lake.
4. GEORGIANA SCOTT b 10 Jun 1866 (d 12 Sep 1947) m James Pike res Lynn MA, bur Harmony Grove Cem Salem MA, **no chn.**
5. WALTER SCOTT b 07 Apr 1868 d 1905 bur Gladstone Cem Fredericton Jct, **single.**
6. ADELINE SCOTT b 25 Mar 1870 (d 25 Jun 1954) as his 2nd wf {m} 1.1.9.4.3.3.5.2.2 Melbourne Smith b 1856 d 1926 res Presque Isle ME, **no chn.**
7. WINSLOW SCOTT b 22 Jun 1874 (d 08 Dec 1948) {m} 1906 1.1.9.4.3.3.4.4.7 Alice <u>Adelia</u> Wooden d/o Mary Ann Smith & Alexander Wooden, b 07 Jul 1875 d 01 Sep 1952.
8. WILLIAM B SCOTT b 04 Apr 1876 d 26 Mar 1903 bur Gladstone Cem, Fredericton Jct, **single.**
9. FLORENCE E SCOTT b 04 Sep 1878 (d 01 Feb 1905 bur Fredericton Jct) m 1897 Gilman Mersereau; div **no chn.**
10. FRASER SCOTT b 1879 (d 1890) **single.**
11. FRANK G SCOTT b 22 Dec 1880 (d 06 Mar 1947 Lynn MA) m Sadie Stevens b 05 Jul 1884 d 21 Mar 1945 bur Pine Grove Cem Lynn MA (SDVSW:4).
12. ELIZABETH/BESS SCOTT b 21 Mar 1883 (d 28 Dec 1952 bur Gladstone Cem) m Stanley McCracken b 28 Jun 1884 d 03 Jun 1976 bur Gladstone Cem, Fredericton Jct.

Phoebe Ann (DeWitt) Scott & Rachel (Mersereau) DeWitt w/o Luke Emery DeWitt were very good friends. On 12 Jul 1912 Rachel was struck by a train as she was walking along the CPR track from her son Austins on her way to visit another son, Scouler, at Fredericton Jct. She died within a very short time. Her friend Phoebe died that night. Phoebe's family used to say, of shock, on hearing of Rachel's death (all fr KLAD).

DeWITT
1.1.9.4.3.3.4.1.4 DANIEL <u>LUDOW</u> DeWITT m Lizzie Webb
1. COLEMAN/COLBY DeWITT b 1889 m 1917 Clara Lindsay b 1889
2. A son who lived a week.

EXCERPTS from TELEGRAPH JOURNAL, SAINT JOHN NB, November 2, 1884
If you ever get a chance to read this item you will find it's a wonderful story.

Colby, age seventeen, lied about his age and joined the Tenth Field Battery. Later his uncle from Maine persuaded him to go trapping with him. After a year in the woods he was left there with the dog while his uncle went to Boston with Two Thousand dollars in furs. The man squarndered the money and came back with nothing. Colby left and met Fred Agnew. They caught a freight train as far as Bathurst, nothing to eat, no money. They got jobs working in separate Bars. Then Colby worked for Albert Hinton and started learing the horse training business.

Colby and Lester Lindsay operated a livery stable and sold horses for Ned Hogan of Saint John who bought horses by the car load from Montreal and left some in Bathurst for the boys. At age nineteen he married Chester's sister, Clara age eighteen. Later Colby decided to buy a carload of horses from Montreal, hoping to make some money on them. The dealer was smuggling alcohol with the horses to New Brunswick. Colby whacked a Policeman with a chair when he was arrested and did a month in jail. To escape the disgrace to his family he decided to go to Boston. Ned Hogan loaned him the money for a ticket. He was very seasick on the voyage.

Colby stayed with his aunt and worked as a millwright. When he had a place, a table, two chairs and a bed he asked his wife to join him. They saved their money and returned to Woodstock to take care of his father (born 1846) until he died. They moved to Grand Falls NB and he sold horses on commission. Then they moved to Fredeickton where he had a livery stable with Chester Lindsay, but were forced to leave because of complaints about the smell.

Colby and a French speaking partner began trading in horses in Aciadia. They camped, traded horses, drove twelve miles and continued to repeat another twelve miles each day, camping and trading. He said horse traders wouldn't beat you, but a preacher was the worst and so were farmers. Colby believed in a code of honesty and raised his two sons to the same standard. At ninety-six he still trades a little, saying "You can't live on shoelaces". He still keeps four horses. He says he hasn't a regret in the world, but would do it all over again.

DeWITT

1.1.9.4.3.3.4.1.7 & 1.1.9.4.3.6.4.1.7 DAVID DeWITT m Maggie Davis
1. PARKER DeWITT b 1886 06 Feb 1959 ae 71 predeceased his wf) m Maizie Harris b 1891 d 18 Oct 1976 Wodstock NB (fr KLAD).
2. MARK DeWITT
3. JENNIE DeWITT m Carleton Burlock.
4. ANGELINE DeWITT m Arthur Mesereau.
5. DELILAH DeWITT b 188_ (d 1920) m David Kirkpatrick b 1870 d 1941 both bur United CH Cem Hoyt NB.

DeWITT

1.1.9.3.3.4.1.8 & 1.1.9.4.3.6.4.1.8 GEORGE DeWITT m Maggie (Davis) DeWitt
1. PHOEBE DeWITT m Lewis Briggs res 1982 Carleton Co NB d 1917 (Maggie's 2nd ch) (fr KLAD).

DeWITT

1.1.9.4.3.3.4.2.8 JOHN H DeWITT m   ?
1. ARTHUR M DeWITT b Woodstock NB d 22 Feb 1945, missing presumed dead WWII (fr KDM).

DeWITT

1.1.9.4.3.3.4.3.2 CLOWES SHERMAN DeWITT m Georgie Ann Drake
1. MAY L DeWITT b 06 Dec 1882 at the Mallory home Jacksontown, Carleton Co NB (d 08 Mar 1976 Kelowna BC) at Presque Isle ME m 24 Aug 1902 Enrique Mallory s/o John Leonard Mallory & Helen Plummer, b 24 Mar 1878 d 09 Nov 1965. They moved to Houlton ME in 1903 & Portland OR in 1905. May was b on the farm sold by John Mallory to Bethuel DeWitt. Despite the fact that Enrique's grdpa sold this farm to May's grdpa they lived only a few miles apart they did not meet until many years later on ME.

CLOWES SHERMAN DeWITT   **MAY DeWITT MALLORY (dau)**

May recalled a nice home at Presque Isle, a large barn with lofts for hay, and an 80 foot hay barn where cows and young stock were kept; at one side a boxed-in granary as well as sheds on the side of the barn and a large machine shed. She said the home was very dear to her. There being no mechanical refrigerators, ice was hauled from the river during the winter and packed in sawdust in the icehouse. There was a woodlot with maples and it was customary to tap the trees in the spring to make maple syrup.

Clowes was about five feet eleven inches tall and broad shouldered. He wore a mustache. His eyes were blue and looked "right through you". His hair was dark brown. He had no special personal habits. There is only one very small picture of him that remains from the vicissitudes of time. He certainly appears solid and dependable; "his word was as good as gold". His daughter related that he was very strict and she was obliged to eat what was put on her plate and no questions asked. His attitude toward religion was less severe than that of his father, but he attended the Baptist Church twice on Sunday and May had to attend Sunday School held in the schoolhouse on Sunday afternoons. He always had a fast driving horse and attended races nearby. When May was eleven or twelve years old he would put her in the sulky with the mare and urge her to see how fast she could go, but never in a race. One gathers that Clowes put some special emphasis on his daughter, or perhaps put her into a place a son would have fitted. By the time she was 11 she was the "boy" on the farm, raking hay & driving loaded wagons to the barn. From that time on she could drive a pair of horses as well as a man.

The cash crop was apparently mostly potatoes and ten or twelve acres were planted each year. When it came time to harvest, French Canadian came down to pick potatoes at three cents a barrel. In addition there was a man who came over a period of years to work at harvest time and who received $15.00 per month. There being no other facilities, they were given board and room.

Clowes is an evident transliteration of the Dutch Klass and indicated family traditions were still strong.
(Info fr <u>Some Descendants of Tjerck Classen DeWitt</u> by Lester De Witt Mallory, Guadaljara, Mexico, April 1980)

ENRIQUE MALLORY 1878 – 1965

The name Enrique, Spanish for Henry, was a far cry from the traditional English names current in Carleton County, New Brunswick in the 19th Century. It is said that it was bestowed at the suggestion of his Aunt Hannah, who had encountered it in a book she had read. It was given to her nephew who was called Enrik or Reek, and when the spelling of Enrique or Rique was used.

Enrique, the oldest of six children was born March 24, 1878 at the farm home of his father George Mallory. This farm was the 'old place' and next to that of his brother John.

Enrique had not lived on the 'new' place and spent his boyhood on the original farm. He went to the nearby school and I have no recollection of anything he said about it. George Mallory was a farmer, and while Enrique worked on the farm as a boy, he was a trader by inclination. An early venture was to travel about the countryside to buy young calves, which were not to be kept. He removed the hides, which he shipped to the firm of C.S. Page in Hide Park, Vt. Along the same line of endeavour, he bought hogs from time to time, which he sold to the packing plant, or as it was probably called in those days, the slaughter house.

There was a cheese factory in Jacksonville, New Brunswick and Enrique worked there in 1894 and 1895 (age 16 and 17) to learn the trade of cheesemaker. The factory worked four months each year during the flush milk season. For his work he received a pay of $12.50 per month and board. The cheese, he told me, was a Canadian Cheddar and was sold mostly in England at a price of 12 cents per pound.

In 1896, he went to Boston to work for a feed firm, which bought much hay and grain in Carleton County and had a retail outlet in Boston. There was an opening, which he was able to obtain. He boarded with the manager of the store. He spent the Summer in Boston and the Winter back on the farm. He returned to Boston in the Summer of 1897 in the same job, but caught typhoid fever and spent much of the Summer in the Massachusetts General Hospital. It has been noted earlier that his grandfather John and great uncle Ezekiel saw him in Boston in 1897.

In 1898 five young men left New Brunswick to join the Klondike gold rush, Enrique, Frank Miles (a cousin through the Plummer family) and three others. I recall father's mention of his son travelling down the Fraser River of British Columbia and seeing quantities of ducks on the water. From the rear of the train they shot at them with a Colt 41 revolver. The group proceeded to Victoria where Frank Miles had a sister. As I recall the story, the young men came to the conclusion that they would make their fortune, not in digging gold, but in cutting cordwood to sell to the river steamers. However, just at this time there occurred the great slide in the Chilicot Pass where many men on their way in were killed. Among those who died was a man from St. Andrews New Brunswick, who was a relative.

Frank Miles, who was married and had children, besides having run short of money did not wish to continue onward. He had previously worked in Great Falls, Montana together with a relative. The upshot of the trip was that Frank and Enrique went to Great Falls looking for work in the copper concentrator and smelter. Father related that while things were tight, they managed to get jobs 'on the jigs' at $2.75 per day, every day in the week with a shift of 13 hours at night and 11 hours during the day. This was in March 1898.

In the Spring of 1899, he joined two others in a gold rush – the Buffalo Hump rush in the Seven Devils Range in Idaho. Two pictures of this event survive, one of Enrique Mallory at age 21, dressed and armed for the wild west and the other is on route to the gold rush. The group were packing in by horse from Lewiston, Idaho to Miller Creek, an old placer mining camp, on the Salmon River, and includes the first house being built in Grangeville, Idaho, near to which they had camped.

They had outfitted in Spokane, Washington, which at that time was quite a mining and frontier center. He remembered that Mr. Davenport (of the Davenport Hotel) had a restaurant and a meal could be had for 10 cents. Father told me that the two others provided the money and he provided the know how. He added that they did not find gold. Father received his American naturalization papers in 1900. When I once looked at them and inquired how it was possible to become a citizen, with two years residence, he replied that in those days in Montana and when politics might be important, a lot of things could be done.

Following the unproductive search for fortune in gold, Enrique returned to Great Falls and his old job, staying until the Spring of 1901, when he went back East feeling half dead, possibly from overwork.

Concerning the working conditions of the copper industry, he mentioned that the hours were long and there was no vacation. He wanted to go duck hunting in the Fall and the only way he could, was in company with a friend.,to get his job and then get it back when he returned. These vacations were 10 days, both Spring and Fall at time of migration. They did pass shooting at Benton Lake and in reality, it was market hunting, for the sale of birds paid expenses. Father had two 10 gauge leveraction repeaters and a 12 gauge double. They received 75 cents per brace of mallards & $1.00 per canvasbacks.

He apparently was an excellent shot at flying game. This I never saw him do. Later in life I knew that in the hills, he could knock down grouse with a pistol that I could not use to hit a washtub. My brother Donald, an excellent snapshot at game and he would be asked to sight a rifle, which I saw him do when he was he was about 60 years old.

Upon returning to New Brunswick, in the spring of 1901, he went into the selling of Life Insurance at Woodstock and there spent the summer months. In the fall he went to Presque Isle and Fort Fairfield, Maine, with the Mutual Life of New York and did rather well, because it was a large established company and there were many Canadian friends resident in Maine.

He married May L. DeWitt of Presque Isle, Maine on August 24, 1902. Her father had emigrated from New Brunswick some years before and died of pneumonia in 1901. A son, Lester DeWitt Mallory was born at Houlton, Maine, April 21, 1904. A major change took place the next year and the reasons were never told to me. One presumes it was in keeping with the saying, that once a westerner always one. I also recall my mother's dislike of the long cold winters 'back East'. In 1905, the family, including Georgie DeWitt (Drake) my grandmother, moved to Portland, Oregon. Here father was agent for the Travelers Insurance Co. of Hartford and also one called the Continental Casualty Co. for which he had the states of Oregon, Washington and Idaho. There was some business arrangement with one or more railroads, which collected premiums. Offices were also maintained in Spokane and Seattle.

This business must have been quite worthwhile for some years. I remember that a number of agents worked for the office, which was located in a building opposite the Meyer and Frank Dept. Store. My mother kept the books and went to the office regularly on the streetcar with father. What happened I do not know, but father said that the business 'petered out' and in the fall of 1914, the family moved to Dalles, upstream on the Columbia River. I was 10 years old at the time and very distinctly remember the trip by sternwheel steamer and the scenery on the way. A number of changes followed in the next few years.

At Dalles, we lived on an orchard - a wonderfully grown area of some 40 acres of cherries and 10 of peaches. Cherries were profitable if one could get production. This was lacking on all sides. The Dalles, just east of the Cascades had a suitable climate and there were many orchards of about the same age, but no one was getting rich on them. Many theories were advanced concerning the reasons - usually soil deficiencies. I remember people going to the machine shops for metal scraps. Others drove iron spikes in the trunks, etc. The Oregon Agricultural College, so called then, at Corvallis was actively working on the problem and shortly found the solution. However, by the time it was learned, the Mallory family had been unable to survive and had moved on. The cause was the need for cross-pollination. Had we known it, we could have in a few years, done very well economically. The cherry orchard in full bloom in the Spring was an exceptional sight.

From Dalles, a move was made to Baker, in eastern Oregon, in the spring of 1916. A son, Donald was born there, March 23, 1916. Here, father bought and shipped fruit. Then in the following winter, another move was made to Calgary, Alberta, a fall and winter in the Cypress Hills, of which more later, and in the Spring of 1917, a major move of the household from Calgary to Naramata, British Columbia, again on a fruit farm. From this time forward there was buying and selling of orchard properties, the last sale in 1963 at age 85, when a young replanted apple orchard was becoming too burdensome and they retired to live near their son Donald, the grandchildren and great grandchildren.

Over the years there had been a variety of farm activities. Nursery stock was grown and sold. Two fruit ranches of considerable size, one in British Columbia, and one in Washington, were planted, partly grown and then sold because of lack of capital to carry them during the higher cost years of growth.

Fur farming was added at one time with efforts at raising foxes and mink. This was a considerable project extending over some years. A last effort in this field, undertaken perhaps less with the promise of profit than of interest was a basement colony of chinchillas. In this growth and reproduction were successful. Whether it was financially rewarding I do not know.

Father always had an interest in innovations, new ideas of new opportunities. He had the foresight or ability to see new or emerging opportunities. From time to time the family lived well and from time to time not so well. There was never much of a surplus. I remember one venture, which may now be virtually forgotten - the Pinless Clothesline Company. This was a clothesline made of galvanized spring steel wire in links about a foot long. These links had a sort of eyed openings through which corners of clothes could be put and then slid between the tight wire which was joined in the middle – sort of a flat bow knot looking arrangement. There was a small plant in Portland, Oregon, with cutting and bending jigs, soldering equipment, etc. I imagine there were Pinless Clotheslines scattered about Oregon and Washington, but the idea did not catch on.

At another time, there was direct mailing of packed fresh fruits and canned berries to customers on the Prairies. We sent out large quantities of price lists, etc. and in the summer would work into the night, taking fruit to the railway express or boiling the canned product the required time. I imagine the profit margin was ample, but the volume was not enough on which to get rich.

Enrique Mallory was about 5 feet 10 inches tall. His father George, about 5 feet 8 inches, grandfather John was described as 'tall' and great-grandfather William a 'small' man, perhaps 5 feet 7 inches. Enrique had two sons, Lester about 5 feet 11 inches and Donald at 6 feet. Enrique was of medium build, small boned and of spare build. So far as I know he was remarkably healthy most of his life. At the time of the burial of his brother Clarence, he suffered a heart injury. He was with this the rest of his life. It did not slow him down much until his late years when an enlarged heart affected his breathing, and he had to move about with a minimum of exertion.

In the last two years of his life he suffered lapses of memory and became enfeebled. In the fall of 1965, he went to the hospital in Penticton, British Columbia where he remained some two months and died on November 8, 1965 at the age of 87. Although the oldest of his family, he outlived his brothers and sisters. His younger brother Ray preceded him at the age of 79, only by a few days having passed away October 10, 1965.

SMITH
1.1.9.4.3.3.4.3.3 ANNIE DeWITT {m} Melbourne Smith (1.1.9.4.3.3.5.2.2)
1 FRANK ELWOOD SMITH b Presque Isle ME m Della Gartley; a son Clayton DeWitt (fr LDM).
2 PEARL MAY SMITH m   ?   McInnes; a dau Hycia McInnes (fr LDM).
3 EFFIE GERTRUDE SMITH a music teacher, m Merrill Hoyt, **no chn.**

BAILEY
1.1.9.4.3.3.4.4.2 PHOEBE DeWITT m   ?   Bailey
1 CATHARINE BAILEY m   ?   Carpenter.
2 EVA BAILEY m Bartlett Rockwell.
3 WILLIAM BAILEY m Alice Bell.
4 MURRAY BAILEY m Ruth Belyea had 2 dau (info fr KLAD; LDM).

DeWITT
1.1.9.4.3.3.4.4.3 JOHN FRED DeWITT m Mary Welch
1 HAZEL DeWITT m John Hanson.
2 GEORGIE DeWITT m1 ? Nason, m2 Ora O'Brien.
3 STANLEY DeWITT (d 1954) m Gertrude Crane.
4 LAURA DeWITT b Carleton CO NB m Perley Smith.
5 MATILDA DeWITT b Carleton CO NB m Roy Cluff .
6 BENJAMIN DeWITT b 1896 Carleton CO NB (d 26 Dec 1955) m Grace Boone.
7 JAMES LUKE DeWITT m Annie Lenentone.
8 JUDSON HALE DeWITT m Freda Whitten.
9 NELLIE RAY DeWITT m Russell Lawrence (info fr LDM).

DeWITT
1.1.9.4.3.3.4.4.4 JAMES ALONZO DeWITT m Mary Churchill
1 CLAUDE DeWITT m Mary Irvine. They res in Presque Isle ME.
2 JENNIE DeWITT had a dau Cynthia, lived possibly Boston (info fr LDM).

DeWITT
1.1.9.4.3.3.4.4.5 AUSTIN/OSCAR DeWITT m Emma Gardiner
1 CATHERINE DeWITT
2 MAY DeWITT (info fr LDM).

DeWITT
1.1.9.4.3.3.4.4.7 MELVIN DeWITT m Annie Culberson
1 J HENRY DeWITT (d 16 Jan 1962) m Lizzie Plummer.
2 E RAY DeWITT m Lulu Carpenter (info fr LDM).

McLEOD
1.1.9.4.3.3.4.4.8 ANNIE DeWITT m James McLeod
1 MELVINA McLEOD m Rev Van Wart.
2 PHOEBE McLEOD
3 WILLIAM McLEOD (info fr KLAD, LDM).

McKENZIE
1.1.9.4.3.3.4.5.1 ALICE/ALICIA ADELIA HOYT m ? McKenzie.
1 KENNETH McKENZIE b 18   ?.
2 HARRY McKENZIE b 1882 (info fr LDM).

The boys were raised by grpa William Hoyt & Anna J DeWitt in Woodstock NB. (fr LDM) Mother (May (DeWitt) Mallory believed (this family) went west and resided in Montana. When Kenneth was 7 and Harry 5 their ma died. The boys were put on a train with tickets pinned to their shoulders and sent to Woodstock NB. The only care they received they had from the train conductor. May DeWitt went to school with them and they lived with their grdprts, the Hoyts.

HOYT
1.1.9.4.3.3.4.5.7 THOMAS HOYT m Barbara Neal
1. IRENE HOYT m Odbur Shaw.
2. JOHN HOYT d in BC.
3. FRANK HOYT res Houlton ME.
4. WILLIAM HOYT
5. MOUNT HOYT m ? Tapley (Info fr LDM).

CLARK
1.1.9.4.3.3.4.8.2 RUTH ANN DeWITT m Wilmot Clark
1. JOHNSON W CLARK (d Anzac, AB ae 90) m Helen Lockhart.
2. DEBORAH CLARK (d before 1956) m Ernest Warriner.
3. EDNA NINA CLARK m Wallace T McAffie (info fr KLAD, LDM).

DeWITT
1.1.9.4.3.3.4.8.3 JOHN WELLINGTON DeWITT m Lizzie Bell Lipsett
1. GLEN DeWITT m Doris Peabody (fr LDM).

HAYDEN
1.1.9.4.3.3.4.8.4 PHOEBE DeWITT m Samuel R Hayden
1. SAMUEL HAYDEN **dy**.
2. ANNIE HAYDEN b 1887 m David A Aiton res Plaster Rock 1949.
3. HELEN HAYDEN b 1889 m James Plummer, had 3 chn.
4. FRANK G HAYDEN d 1892 m Grace Plummer, had 3 chn, res Upper Woodstock..
5. JAMES HAYDEN b 1894 m Jenny Caldwell, had 1 ch res Riley Brook.
6. SARAH HAYDEN m John E Quinn, had 2 chn, res Plaster Rock 1949.
7. RALPH HAYDEN m Joan Miller, had 2 chn res Nictau.
8. MARY HAYDEN m G N Hickey **no chn** res Plaster Rock 1949.
9. EDITH HAYDEN twin/o Evelyn, m Wilmot H Hathaway res Bathurst had 2 chn.
10. EVELYN HAYDEN (info fr LDM) the above were places in NB.

GRAY
1.1.9.4.3.3.4.8.5 EPPIE E DeWITT m Charles Gray
1. NINA GRAY m Duncan Hannah.
2. HALLIE GRAY m Edna Cuthbertson.
3. OTTO GRAY m ? Fallet
4. RHODA GRAY m Basil Harper.
5. SADIE GRAY
6. KENNETH GRAY
7. HELEN GRAY m Fred Peabody (info fr LDM).

DeWITT
1.1.9.4.3.3.4.8.6 GEORGE HOWARD DeWITT m Lulu M T Sherwood
1. EFFIE DeWITT m Otto Smith. Effie, a wd lived New Westminster BC 1982 **no chn**, she was interviewed by VEDS.

CULBERSON
1.1.9.4.3.3.4.8.7 EMMA IDELLA DeWITT m William Culberson
1. FAYE CULBERSON
2. FERNE CULBERSON m Louis Everett of Waterville NB (her ma's Obit).
3. ERNEST CULBERSON m ? Carpenter res Jacksonville NB.
4. CARLE CULBERSON m ? Everett of Waterville NB.
5. RONALD CULBERSON m ? Bert res Jacksonville (fr LDM).

BIRMINGHAM
1.1.9.4.3.3.4.8.8 ELIZABETH/BERITE DeWITT m Guy Birmingham
1. MARY BIRMINGHAM m Lorne Britton.
2. HAZEL BIRMINGHAM m Walter Hatfield (fr LDM).

DeWITT
1.1.9.4.3.3.4.8.10 ERNEST BARKER DeWITT m1 Sarah/Sadie Eastman McLeod m2 Faye Balmain Mersereau
1. ERNEST FRANKLIN DeWITT b 20 Apr 1905 St Stephen NB, funeral notice said he was accidentally killed 02 Feb 1925 near Crossfield AB. Family & friends from Crossfield, Airdrie & Inverlea attended the United Church funeral.
2. JOHN CAMPBELL DeWITT b 30 Sep 1907 St Stephen NB d 10 Aug 1909 **dy**.

Leucas deWit

3 ALICE ANGELINE DeWITT b 10 Aug 1909 St Stephen, m 17 Nov 1939.
4 GEORGE ELLIS DeWITT b 15 Aug 1911 St Stephen d Jan 1912.
5 JANET/JENNET DeWITT b 20 Jan 1913 d 20 Apr 1913 a twin b St Stephen bur Sayago Deablo, Cuba.
6 ANNIE LOUISE DeWITT b 20 Jan 1913 d 28 Oct 1913.
7 EDWARD McLEOD DeWITT b 21 Jul 1914 d Oct 1914.
8 ROBERT EARL DeWITT 14 Jan 1916 m 03 Aug 1942.
9 GEORGE McLEOD DeWITT b 22 Jul 1918 m 23 Jul 1942 (info fr LDM when visiting Ernest DeWitt in AB.

On a sheet of paper copied by "Ernest Senior." is this poem.

MY GET UP AND GO - GOT UP AND WENT

How do I know my youth has been spent
Because my get up and go has gone and went.
But in spite of all that I am able to grin
When I think what my get up and go has been

Old age is golden, I have heard it said,
But sometimes I wonder as I go to bed;
My ears in a drawer; my teeth in a cup;
My eyes on a table till I get up

As sleep dims my eyes I say to myself
Is there anything else I should put on the shelf?
But, I'm happy to say as I close the door
My friends are the same as in days of yore.

When I was young and my slippers were red
I could kick my heels 'way over my head.

When I was older my slipper were blue,
But I could dance the whole night through

Now that I'm older my slippers are black
I walk to the corner, and puff my way back.
So the reason I know my youth is spent
Is, my get up and go has gone and went
But I don't really mind when I think with a grin
Of all the places my get up has been

Since I have retired from life's competition
I busy myself with complete repetition
I get up each morning; dust off my wits;
Pick up the paper, and read the "Obits".
If my name is missing I know I'm not dead;
So I eat good breakfast, and go back to bed.

NOTES BY ERNEST BARKER DeWITT salvaged from a damp basement and deciphered where possible.

(I was) youngest of a family of 10, consisting of 5 boys and 5 girls. As was the custom in those days, I passed the fourth book, which is very little schooling as compared to today. While we were to school, father worked at the lumber camp in the winter, while mother kept the home fires burning with the help of the children.

The best money Sam and I made was trapping muskrats, which were worth 18 cents a pelt. Later when I was 16 and Sam was 18 we worked one winter on the Hartland Bridge built across the St. John River. This 2-lane bridge still stands 2¾ of a mile long. That was one of the coldest winters I have ever seen. We boarded at home because the bridge was only 2 miles away from home. We were paid $1.25 a day. This was a very dangerous job, the top span being 64 feet from the ice below. Henry (?Hany) Burmingham, one of the crew, fell from the lower span which was 34 feet to the ice and was severely injured.

We were always trapping in our spare time, fox skins being worth $4.00. They were crafty and cunning and not caught by many people. Skill and cunning was applied to catch our foxes. We only trapped 2 months, November and December because of the deep snow plugging our sets. We had set two lines, one west of home, the other east, each being about 50 miles long, and it took three days to visit them. My line was east of the St. John River. After my line was set I used to saddle a horse to visit them. The best trip I had was when I caught 16 the first day and, 9 the second and 8 on the last day. This was in 1896; if only someone was living there now that remembered that day! Of course after trapping foxes a few years, I could skin a warm fox in 3 minutes. All the foxes brought in that day was skinned ready to stretch.

Father and us 4 boys decided we needed more land. We bought the Welch farm adjoining our homestead, the Brown farm and then 8 miles away, the Simeson farm that was worth $5,000. John 36, George 26 said they would never marry until they had a farm. So father divided the land. John and George got the Welch & Brown farms plus father's homestead. Father, Sam & I moved to the Simeson place. Father was then 64; he told Sam & I to take over. We continued to fox hunt and feed cattle plus buying cattle and fur.

Farm boy's first experience. My first trip on the steamer Brose was from Sydney NS to Port Aux Basques Newfoundland 1908. (Sydney to Port Basques is still a main run between NS & NFLD) I left Saint John NB from our head office where we had a Wholesale Business. The steamer left CB of PM for Port Aux Basta from there on a narrow gage RY that took 2 days; on my arrival back to Port Aux Basta on the steamer Bruce in the morning when part way back on the Strait of Cansas we run into heavy ice flow and was held up for several hours and arrived at Sydney at dark.

Leucas deWit

Crossfield July 9/65. To whom it may concern. 19_1 I lived on the farm near Hartland (NB). Phoebe Hayden farmed at Riley Brook, Victoria County NB and Sam Hayden had some beef steers for sale there, three years old. I took the train from Hartland to Perth 40 miles. I took the train from Plaster Rock 28 miles, from there I went (?) with . . . to Riley Brook 32 miles.

I bought Sam's steers and a few from his neighbors, 10 head in all. I left Riley Brook . . . day on foot. Before I got to Perth I saw. . . S and told the farmer if he would come into Perth I would get the money to pay him. I had heard the name of Miles McCray, a blacksmith. I found. . . say that had heard of my father being a friend of his. Those times money was scarce but Mr McCray borrowed from a Grocery man and let me have it to pay the farmer. Aways along the road I saw another . I bought the cow from the owner & told him I would send him the money as soon as I got home . . home after 3½ days from Riley Brook a distance of 100 miles. I did this 100 miles alone on foot. In those days driving cattle on horseback was unheard of. (Ink blotches make much unreadable) . . . to receive hay & potatoes . . . the produce. My brother took a trip to . Asnonce by boat and called at Bermuda, St. To ias St. Kits, Barbadoes and Demerarra South America. He went to Nova Scotia, Cape Breton and to St. John Newfoundland. On my trip to & from St. John the steamer Bruce I was in, crossing the strait of Cansos run into an arctic ice flow; crossing we were all afraid, as the Captain, after 4 hours got then out so we went to North Sydney by dark. Five years later that steamer was lost on the same voyage in an ice flow. I was in Havana at that time and read about it's loss.

Our . . . . in St. John got on a train with William Thompson, Steam Ship Agent; they told me that Cuba was buying potatoes by schooner and if I would put on 3,000 bags of 50 lbs bu in one of their steamers for . on .. of our firm could have passage in the same boat for Havana for free. We put . . . cars of potatoes on . . . at St John 3,000 bu. and sent J. W. Clark and . . . to go. He found a good market in Havana for that shipment of potatoes to Cuba that left St. John. Clark had a tough job in this not knowing any of the Spanish language. He found a man by the name of C B (Delana or) Jelana that spoke French English and Spanish that . . . They sold the 3,000 bu. And began to book . . . . . to be sent to Cuba. It was a job to St. John to. ? . PTS many potatoes in Rio, sometime 25/30 Mar, after . . . organized in Havana. He came home as . . . . . . recommended to our N.B. Premier that the N.B. Sh . . . . should have a warehouse in Cuba. The premier instructed . . . . . to rent a warehouse for the . . . . . for $175.00 a month and looked after it for the Government. At times I went back to Havana instead of Clark. Soon as the Potato Dealers Firm . . d Cuba could use our potatoes they sent a representative to Havana by the name of Guy G. Porter. After I arrived in Havana Mr Jelana and I began to book orders fast; we were able to sell a 1,000 bu. cargo every ten days. That year we shipped 86,000 bu. to Cuba. After April the market fell off and I cabled our St. John office not to ship any more. But they was over anxious and sent me a 12,000 bu cargo by schooner. The cargo was in bad shape (? is short ?eaded) and the Captain was 28 days on the way. He missed the trade winds and the Cargo had spoiled. The Health Authorities in Havana forced us to go back to sea and dump our cargo. It cost $2200 and I paid ½ , $1100, the Firm the other ½.

The cargo was a complete loss plus the $100, the cargo cost $20,000 to $25,000 at St. John and the fgt had to be prepaid $6,000 so it was a hard bloe for DeWitt Bros. Ltd. I came home in June and we did some more financing to strengthen the Co. My father put up $5,000, bro. John $2,000 and Ernest . . . . . $1200. The next fall in Scht I went back to Havana with my wife and family with the first cargo shipped in late Sept 1910. The cargo was caught in a cyclone west side of Havana and the ship could not dock on account of high seas and had to stay out at sea for (? 2) days until the sea stilled. The cargo shifted and the potatoes a . . . .That sort of discouraged my b . . . . and I cabled home to come to Cuba. After we talked of . . . . we decided to go out in the country and try sugar cane and bananas. We found a sugar mill . . . that offered us land and $20,000 to plant with but we had to pay 25 per CT metric. We always figured we got a year to contract with this mill. My wife & family was . . . in Cuba. After 3 years of hard work and hard . . . . we had more debt af . . . to the mill. 1914 a revolution broke out in Cuba between the black and whites. We sent Sadie and family back to N.B. The Govt. soldiers brought my brother 12 army rifles and ammunition that we kept handy and every day the soldiers would come and consult us if we thought any of our men were rebels. We always had a gang of men working in our cane fields. We had 10 families living on our plantation. As soon as the First World War 1914 broke out we had a chance to sell our (control) . . . . out to a Cuban. He paid us $10,000 in $20 gold pieces. We always said we would get out of Cuba as soon as we could get out with our shirts on.

We had 500 acres of rough land that was always used to run hogs in. We usually had . . . cattle . . . in it. As soon as . . . got 150 lbs or so we would send a Cuban to shoot it and clean it in the brook and bring it to our house to cook up for our labourers. We always got 20 ct a lb and there was never enough to go around. After we sold our cane we had to get all our hogs & pigs out of the pasture. The hogs lived on wild fruit and royal palm berries and would get real fat. We called in our neighbors to help catch the hogs. We got 10 gallons of vino or wine and had the natives to barbecue 2 or 3 small pigs and loaded the pigs on carts and send to Dy Colonado 8 miles away to sell. It took all night to get to Colonado with our carts.

After our business went haywire in the potato business Mr. Ross, Mgr. B . . . t N.S. in Havana suggested to me that bro. & I go to western Canada. Twice while I was in Cuba I had a close call with some of our labourers. Once a Molatto pulled a knife on me. I held him off with rocks. The next time a Spaniard with a big watacco, something like a big hoe, but quick thinking saved me.

Material for this family was provided by George McLeod DeWitt. I was not given any information on their travel from Cuba to Alberta.

Leucas deWit

Calgary 7 March 1968

To Geo. We are getting better from the flue; it has lasted 2 weeks. Here is some old history that I will pass along. Since I came to Alberta 1919 I saw (4) Bad Blizzards. First 1919 2 May that killed thousands of cattle & sheep. It may happen again. Frank Leandymore's father, at the [D]ugan Ranch that storm killed thousands. Watch weather warnings and have a saddle horse handy and round up cattle at once. This weather is too good to last I am afraid. EBD

Saturday 20 ? 1969

To Geo. I wonder if you have did anything about your pump house before winter so that it will not freeze up like last winter, before cold weather begins. Water for beef cattle and outside cattle is very important. I forgot to ask you the other day when you were here.

All for now. EBD

(fr GMD) Added notes. "King DeWitt and 4 brothers weighed 1100 lbs". "Father, Uncle Sam & Johnson Clark sold baled hay, feed oats & shipped potatoes to Cuba, chartering boats. With one load the barge sank, tipped, rose at high tide; they lost the whole load, had to be dumped at sea, cost $30,000". "While living in Cuba they had 100 natives working in the sugar cane operation. It sold for 9, 10 cents a lb then down to 2 cents, next in the war year went up to 14 cents. The two brothers little children were buried there; cholera. Place had a dirt floor. The men carried swords & guns on their hip; when leaving they sold the revolvers." (I visited George DeWitt – VEDS).

DeWITT

1.1.9.4.3.3.4.9.4 ORRIN/ORRIE LEE DeWITT m ?
1   THOMAS DeWITT
2   JAMES DeWITT
3   MARVELL DeWITT
4   ELLEN DeWITT (fr LDM).

SWEET

1.1.9.4.3.3.4.9.5 MABEL DeWITT m De Charles F Sweet
1   THOMAS SWEET m Marion Charnley (fr MCD).

SMITH

1.1.9.4.3.3.5.2.2 MELBOURNE SMITH {m} 1.1.9.4.3.4.4.3 Annie DeWitt. He {m} 2 Adeline Scott (1.1.9.4.3.3.4.1.1.6)
Children are with their mother' underlined number Generation 9.

SMITH

1.1.9.4.3.3.5.3.2 DAVID O SMITH {m} Delilah Scott (1.1.9.4.3.3.4.1.1.3)
1   ARTHUR SMITH **single** lived Lynn MA when young.
2   IRVING SMITH b 1891 alive 1979.
3   BABY SMITH b 1899.
4   EUNICE SMITH
    "He had 3 sons, one died young, another poisoned himself because he failed exams at Harvard College, both bur at Utah" (SDVSW:3).

SMITH

1.1.9.4.3.3.5.3.3 ELGAN OTIS SMITH {m} Clarissa Scott (1.1.9.4.3.3.4.1.1.2)
1   EARL SMITH b 1886 Hoyt NB (d 1967) {m} Lottie Van Wart (1.1.9.4.3.3.5.4.5.1) b 1897 d 1967 both bur Blissville Cem Hoyt (all fr KLAD, VSK).
2   MARSHAL SMITH **dy.**
3   MYRTLE SMITH b 1890 d 1917 **single.**
4   ELLA SMITH b 1893 Hoyt NB (d 16 Dec 1978 m William Gourley d 1951 bur Cody's, Queens Co NB.
5   VIOLET SMITH **dy.**
6   ELGAN F SMITH b 1900 d 1990 {m} Blanche Wooden (1.1.9.4.3.3.5.4.6.2) 1903 - 1985 d/o Robert Wooden. Both Elgar & Blanche buried in Blissville **no chn.**

HOYT

1.1.9.4.3.3.5.5.1 LAVINA ALMA WOODEN m Emerson Hoyt
1   FRANK HOYT
2   ROY HOYT
3   JOHN HOYT
4   MARION HOYT
5   MYRTLE HOYT (fr KLAD)

WHEPLEY

1.1.9.4.3.3.5.5.3 CHARLOTTE MELISSA WOODEN m Fred Whepley
1   HAROLD WHEPLEY d 24 Apr 1983 **single.**
2   BLANCHE LOTTIE WHEPLEY b 06 May 1893 d 1980 **single.**
3   ALMA LILLIAN WHEPLEY m Erwin Amberg; a dau Loel Amberg.

Leucas deWit

4   GLADYS HELEN WHEPLEY b 09 Apr 1899 **single.**
5   ETHEL WHEPLEY b 05 Mar 1901 m 21 Nov 1931 Norman Jorgensen.

VAN WART
1.1.9.4.3.3.5.5.5 ANNIE MARY WOODEN m Joseph Samuel Van Wart
1   LOTTIE VAN WART b 1897 (d 1967) {m} 1.1.9.4.3.3.5.3.3.1 Earl Smith of Hoyt NB s/o Elgan Smith & Clarissa Scott b 1886 d 1967.
2   VIOLA GERTRUDE VAN WART m Waldo Dunn.
3   ALICE LILLIAN VAN WART bur Pleasant Villa Cem **dy.**
4   MABEL ALEXANDRA VAN WART a nurse, bur Pleasant Villa Cem **single.**
5   DELLA VAN WART b 1906 m Oct/Nov 1928 Frank McCorkle 1978 their Golden Anniversary at Hoyt NB.
6   VERA BERNICE VAN WART b 1909 m Charles King (all fr MDW, SDVSW:2).

WOODEN
1.1.9.4.3.3.5.5.6 ROBERT WOODEN m Mary Gardener
1   MAHLON WOODEN **single dy.** 1899 - 1926 bur Blissville Cem.
2   BLANCHE WOODEN {m} 1.1.9.4.3.3.5.2.3.6 Elgan F Smith.
3   GERTRUDE WOODEN m William Bell. Bur United church cem.
4   LILLIAN WOODEN single 1901 - 1968 bur Blissville cem (fr KLAD).

SCOTT
1.1.9.4.3.3.5.5.7 ALICE ADELIA WOODEN {m} Winslow Scott (1.1.9.4.3.3.4.1.1.7)
1   ROY W SCOTT b 05 Jan 1907 d 17 Oct 1907 **dy.**
2   GLADYS L SCOTT b 09 Feb 1908 (d 02 May 1983 bur Blissville Cem) was a lawyer Boston & Lynn MA m Clinton Elliott div **no chn.**
3   EDNA MARION SCOTT b ? Aug 1911, a nurse (d 26 Jul 1977) m Ernest Emerson d 1975.
4   FRANK RAYMOND SCOTT b 03 Feb 1915 d Feb 4 1997, bur Gladstone Cem Fredericton Jct at Fredericton Jct {m} 14 Feb 1942 Ida Vivian Mersereau 1.1.9.4.3.6.5.3.2.1 d/o Winslow Mersereau & Freda May Noble, b 1924 Tracyville NB.
5   EARL W SCOTT b 11 Jul 1917 Hoyt NB, bur Blissville cem Hoyt at First Congregational CH Concord NH m 21 Jan 1949 Mrs Marion (Richardson) Ferron (fr KLAD).

THOMAS
1.1.9.4.3.3.7.1.3 IDA MAY DeWITT m Charles Edward Thomas
1   WILLIAM CUSHING THOMAS b 02 May 1872 (d 1945 Dublin NH) m Caroline Bailey Pickering.
2   ANGIE THOMAS b 13 Dec 1875 (d 1942 Howland ME) m Harry Halsey.
3   WINIFRED IDA THOMAS b ? Aug 1897 (d 10 Mar 1897) m Harry Scott.
4   VERNON CHARLES THOMAS b 30 Mar 1881 (d 13 May 1956 Howland ME). (info fr LDM).

CROMBIE
1.1.9.4.3.3.7.3.2 MARCUS CROMBIE m1 Ellia May Worden
1   CHARLES CROMBIE m Clara McFawn d 1979 Bangor ME, res Bangor (bro's Obit Midland CA)
     m2 Azalene
2   FORD CHIPMAN CROMBIE b ? Nov 1910 (d 07 Nov 1990) res Hoyt NB m Phyllis Wright b Wirral NB res Juvenile NB (all fr KLAD). Undated Obit: bur Patterson United CH Cem Fredericton Jct NB.
3   DONALD L G CROMBIE d 1991 m Hazel Duplisea b Central Blissville NB D1998 res Saint John NB both bur Blissville cem Hoyt NB. Their son Claire B Crombie 1947-1953 bur Blissville Cem. (all fr FC via KLAD).

WILLIAMSON
1.1.9.4.3.3.7.4.6 ANNIE DeWITT m Thomas Wiliamson
1   BESSIE WILLIAMSON
2   WILLIAM WILLIAMSON (fr KLAD).

SHAW
1.1.9.4.3.3.7.4.7 HANNAH DeWITT m ? Shaw.
1   STELLA SHAW
2   WILLIAM SHAW (fr KLAD).

PARSONS
1.1.9.4.3.3.7.4.8 LAVINA DeWITT m Benison Parsons
    In one plot in the Hoyt Baptist Cem with Bennison & Lavina are Charles, George Erb, Percy H & Annie E Parsons, identified on the tbstns as chn of Bennison & Lavina. Charles Moore (hus of Margaret Parsons) William DeWit (Lavina's bro). Are the next plot grdau Marjorie E Parsons b 1920 d 1979, then Rudman & Stanley B Parsons as s/o above couple. One more plot is dau Mary w/o Ansley Bell. Fredericton Gleaner 17 Jan 1990 has Margaret (Parsons) Moore's obit. It seems to wrongly identify her as d/o Eligal B Parsons & Sarah L Dewitt in disagreement with their tbstn inscriptions (United Hoyt Baptist CH cem). Margaret (Parsons) Moore was survived by 2 daus, Marjorie & hus Walter Webb, & Mrs Dorothy Sine both of Ottawa; one sis, Blanch Parsons & bro Thomas Parsons, Mill Cove Nursing Home, their grchn are Lynda Sine, Ottawa, Paul Sine,

Leucas deWit

Langley BC & Allan Sine, Vancouver. Ggrchn are Trina & Sabrina Sine of Vancouver. Margaret Moore to be bur Hoyt United Baptist Cem in Spring.
1. ANNIE PARSONS b 1889 d 1975 **single**.
2. CHARLES A PARSONS b 1892 d 1918 **single**.
3. GEORGE ERB PARSONS b 1894 d 1927 **single**.
4. PERCY H PARSONS b 1896 (d 1944) m Edith Post.
5. MARY PARSONS b 1898 d 1986 m Ansley Bell res Hoyt, bur Hoyt United Baptist CH cem **no chn**.
6. MARGARET PARSONS b 1900 (d 1990) Fredericton Jct NB m Charles H Moore b 1896 d 1944, bur United Baptist CH cem. In Hoyt NB (fr KLAD).
7. STANLEY PARSONS b 1903 d 07 Jun 1989 ae 86 **single**, twin of
8. BLANCHE PARSONS b 1903 **single**.
9. RUDMAN PARSONS b 1907 d 1979 **single**.
10. THOMAS PARSON b 1911 m Addie Charlton d 1989, res Hoyt operated a store & lunchroom (all fr KLAD).

SANFORD
1.1.9.4.3.3.7.5.1 LYDIA ALFRETTA/RETTY DeWITT m Alonzo Sanford
1. EDITH SANFORD m Lev Dykeman.
2. MALCOLM ALONZO SANFORD m Daisy Elizabeth Sleep of Saint John NB, will res in Boston. Elliot bro of Malcolm was Best Man (fr KLAD newspaper clipping, no date).
3. ELLIOTT SANFORD m Betty both d in the 1970's, lived Melbourne FL; dau m R Whitney res Buffalo NY.
4. ADA DeWITT SANFORD m John Lawrence McMurrough of Stamps AK (fr KLAD newspaper clipping, no date).

DeWITT
1.1.9.4.3.3.7.5.2 RANDALL PARKER DeWITT m Mae Colter
1. MINNIE DeWITT m ? Jenkins res Brownville ME.
2. ZULA DeWITT m ? Bubar of Danforth ME res Houlton ME (fr RDB).

GRAHAM/JONES
1.1.9.4.3.3.7.5.3 GERENIA ANN DeWITT m1 James W Graham m2 William H Jones
1. A GRANT GRAHAM b 1896 d 1914 **single**.
2. LEOLA GRAHAM (bur Patterson United Cem) m Burton Kirkpatrick res Saint John, **no chn** (fr RDB).

DeWITT
1.1.9.4.3.3.7.5.4 JAMES <u>AUSTIN</u> DeWITT m Stella May Mersereau
1. RONALD WESLEY DeWITT b 23 Jan 1913 (d 02 Apr 1996) m1 Kathleen May Smith b 1921 d 1947 bur Blissville NB, m2 Katherine Lorena Alexander b 1917 of Fredericton Jct NB. Ronald took over his father's farm & woodlot (1946 to 1953) then worked for the Department of Defence. Next he worked for the CPR in the Block Signal Department for 15 years. Finally he moved to the NB Horticulture Nursery Department of Agriculture.
Katherine took her teachers training at the Fredericton Normal School and taught for a time. She joined the Womens Division of the Royal Canadian Air Force and trained at Rockcliff (Ottawa) and Trenton ON then to Patricia Bay Vancouver Island where the base had trenches dug in in case of a Japanese invasion. Her posting to Gander Nfd 1943 to 1945 was the most interesting station. From there as a Corperal she was discharged at Darmouth NS. At Acadia University she earned her MA in Economics and a Certificate in Secretarial Science. She was head of her Secretarial Department before retirement.
2. EMMA <u>VERNA</u> DeWITT b 1916 d 1972 Hoyt NB bur Blissville Cem there, **single**. Verna had a B.A., Bed, Med from UNB Department of Mathamatics and taught at Moncton High School (all fr KLAD).

DeWITT
1.1.9.4.3.3.7.5.5 SCOULER BURTON DeWITT m Lottie R Davis
1. LENORA AGNES DeWITT b 29 Nov 1901 Blissville (d in the 1990s) m 31 May 1930 Robert Alexander Cowie b 12 Jul 1901 d ? Apr 1989. Lenora res Perrysburg OH.
2. RUBY LILLIAN DeWITT b 06 Jul 1903 Fredericton Jct (as were the rest of the chn) predeceased by her hus (d 04 May 1984 bur Fernhill Cem, Saint John NB) m 1924 Samuel John Butcher d 28 Sep 1975.
3. ARTHUR RAYMOND DeWITT b 11 Apr 1905 Fredericton Jct NB (d 25 Jul 1977) at Saskatoon SK m 1932 Viola May Burton b 1905 Beverley MA.
4. RHETA EDYTHE DeWITT b 16 Mar 1907 m 1942 Weldon Havelock Fuller d 1999, Rheta predecessed him **no chn**.
5. HAROLD DAVIS DeWITT b 10 Jun 1909 at Saint John m 1942 Kathleen Doris MacLean d/o Percy B MacLean & Clotilda Ferris, b 1910 White Cove Queens Co NB (fr RDB, KLAD).
6. ELLIS SCOULER DeWITT b 30 Mar 1911(still living 11 Apr 2000) Fredericton Jct NB at Halifax m 1938 Lily Edna Maltby b 1917 Newcastle NB, (d ?) res Halifax NS, all chn b there (fr RLDB, KLAD).

WEBB
1.1.9.4.3.3.7.5.6 HANNAH <u>CLEMENTINE</u> DeWITT {m} 1.1.9.4.3.3.8.2.1 Austin Webb.
He {m}2 Elizabeth Phoebe DeWitt (1.1.9.4.3.3.8.4.5).
Exception: Children are with their father's underlined number Generation 9.

Leucas deWit

BELL
1.1.9.4.3.3.7.8.1 BEN BELL m ? Buckingham
1. ANNIE BELL (fr RLDB).

BELL
1.1.9.4.3.3.7.8.2 GEORGE MELVIN BELL m Lucinda Charlton
1. HATTIE BELL b 1896 (d 1961) m Harley Duplisea b 1896 d 1956 both bur Blissville.
2. ELDON BELL d 03 Apr 1887 m Ruby Harron of Hoyt NB, bur Blissville cem. Eldon Bell survivors; his only chn Mrs J. Bertram Wood (Verna) of Saint John, a sis Mrs Andrew Mersereau (Joyce) of Saint John, 3 grchn Edwin, Dennis both Saint John, Marilyn Wood & 5 Ggrchn.
3. JOYCE BELL b 1906 (d 1990 bur Blissville cem m William <u>Andrew</u> Mersereau s/o Georgianna Alexander & Sebastian Mersereau, b 1891 Juvenile NB d 1977.
4. DOROTHY/DORA MINNIE BELL b 1910 Fredericton NB (d 1980 bur Blissville Cem [fr a recording by KLAD] m Lee Gordon Nason b 1990 (fr DMBN, KLAD).

BELL
1.1.9.4.3.3.7.8.3 Rev THOMAS D BELL m1 Mary Kirkpatrick
1. BEAUMONT BELL m Ernest William Fox b Jacksonville NB. He d when the tractor he was driving overturned. He was 76. An undated obituary names his wf & 6 chn. He was bur Jacksonville Cem NB. Info fr Beaumont's cousin Dorothy Minnie (Bell) Nason (ie. DMBN).
2. ELMER WEYMAN BELL twin of Beaumont m ? res Pemaquid Harbor ME. Elmer died ae 93, of Orlando St, Sanford Maine, born Wirral NB son of Rev Thomas D and Mary Kirpatrick Bell. Veteran WWI 58th Howitzer Battery and served in England and France with the CEF. Surviors, his wife Louise H (Madden) Bell, son Thomas E of Orange Conn., 2 dau Muriel Tucket & Kathleen Costillo of Framingham Mass, 2 stepdau Carolyn Reilly, Framingham Mass & Chariotte Nasler, Holliston Mass, 2 brothers Rev George R Bell, Smith Cove NS, John of Ottawa, 2 sis Marion Morehouse of Fredericton NB, Inez J Bell Saint John, 20 grandchildren and 12 great grandchildren. Predecessed by first wife Estella Kitchen, twin sister Beaumont Fox, infant sister Geneva, his parents Rev Thomas D and Mary Bell. Obit Daily Gleaner Wed Aug 14, 1991. Employed CPR after the war, lived Sussex NB then a builder and carpenter in Framingham Mass and Pemequid Harbor Maine (all from Obit).
3. MARION BELL m Hinson Morehouse.
   m2 Ethel F Noble
4. INEZ BELL res Saint John NB (still there in 2000)
5. GEORGE BELL, Rev res Smith's Cove NB in 1975.
6. JOHN I BELL res Ottawa ON in 1975.

Obit in the <u>Telegraph Journal:</u> Saint John NB (abbreviated)
Mrs Ethel F Bell d 15 Feb 1975 at Saint John Hospital. Her husband, Rev Thomas D Bell d in Feb 1955. She was b in New Maryland [NB] d/o the late William J Noble & Ruth (Smith) Noble. She is survived by 1 dau, Miss Inez Bell of Saint John; 2 sons, Rev George R Bell of Smith's Cove NS & John I Bell of Ottawa; 2 step-daus, Beaumont (Mrs Ernest Fox) of Jacksonville NB & Marion (Mrs Hinson Moorehouse) of Upper Blackville NB; a step-son Elmer W Bell of Pemoquid Harbor ME; 16 grchn, 32 Ggrchn, nieces & nephews. Castle Funeral Home (Hillsley) Saint John was the undertaker. Burial was in rural cemetery after entombment. (fr DMBN, KLAD)

BELL
1.1.9.4.3.3.7.8.4 Rev CHARLES A BELL m Clara Kelly
1. SIMEON BELL (d 1970's) m twice lived in ME.
2. PAULINE BELL m Ed Waring res South Holland IL. In 1975 Clara res with Patricia d in the 1980's (fr KLAD). Pauline & Ed had two daughters. Patricia was one of them (fr DMBN, KLAD).

MERSEREAU
1.1.9.4.3.3.7.9.1 IDA KINGSTON m James Mersereau
1. VANCE MERSEREAU b 1888 d 1930 bur Blissville NB Cem **single.**
2. ROY MERSEREAU b 1890 b 1892 Blissville bur Blissville **single.**
3. LOUELLA MERSEREAU (d 1960's) m James McConnell. Lived in Maiine USA
4. ELDON MERSEREAU m1 Vera Willis d a young woman (fr KLAD & IMS); m2 Ethel Bell; m3 Stella Charlton.
5. ILA MERSEREAU d 17 Jan 1990 bur St Luke's Anglican CH cem 20 Jan 1990 Hoyt NB m Alfred Smith d 1975 (fr KLAD & IMS). Fredericton <u>Gleaner</u> 19 Jan 1990 obit for Ila (Mersereau) Smith Survivors are 2 daus Barbara w/o James Weston, Fairfield NB; Carol Carter of Hoyt; 2 sons Douglas Smith of Moncton NB; Everett Smith of Hoyt NB 16 grchn, 29 Ggrchn (fr IMS to KLAD).

WEBB
1.1.9.4.3.7.9.2 ADA KINGSTON m Manzer Webb
1. Irene Webb d 1978 (fr KLAD, MWD).

Leucas deWit

KINGSTON
1.1.9.4.3.3.7.9.4 ORLO KINGSTON m 27 Dec 1894 Christina Boone
1. MYRTLE KINGSTON (fr KLAD, MWD).

KINGSTON
1.1.9.4.3.3.7.9.5 WILLIAM KINGSTON m Ada Knorr
1. ULA KINGSTON m George Stackhouse.
2. ELLEN KINGSTON m ? Worden.
3. MALCOLM KINGSTON fr KLAD).

DeWITT
1.1.9.4.3.3.7.10.1 CHARLES WILLIAM DeWITT m Rachel Ann Kirkpatrick
1. WALTER DeWITT b ca 1894/5 **dy.**
2. LOTTIE VIOLA DeWITT b 16 Jun 1895 Blissville bp 07 Apr 1912 Hoyt Station, Blissville, Sunbury Co NB. (d 22 Feb 1988 at home Sherman St Island Falls ME); The Rev Charles Blackney, Wit: Ansil Baker, Gaspereaux Staton, Woodstock Carleton Co NB when Lottie m 05 Jul 1911 Forrest Fenwick Hartin b 23 Mar 1891 bp 01 Jul 1914 Forest City York Co NB d 31 May 1974 ae 83 at 3 am Military St Regional Hospital, Houlton ME funeral Island Falls Baptist CH, both bur Island Falls Cem (old Part) s/o Glen Stanley Hartin Sr. & Leah Emma Angeline Van Tassel, res Island Falls ME. His color white, complexion medium, height 5'8", weight 125 lbs, hair brown, (as ch blond) Eyes blue; came to the US with parents 01 May 1901. Lottie's marriage certificate gave ae as 18 though she was 16. She was a housewife, naturalized US citizen, and Baptist religion. She enjoyed television, her plants; favorite songs were hymns. She died suddenly of congestive heart failure.
3. BESSIE JEMIMAH DeWITT b 05 Jul 1896 Blissville (d 07 Jun 1967) m1 Harry Landers b 05 Dec 1885 d 24 Apr 1926; m2 Wallace Ireland.
4. DAVID IRVIN DeWITT b 20/25 Oct 1899 d 1919 flu epedemic.
5. RENA CATHERINE DeWITT b 07 Apr 1904 Crystal ME (d 16 Oct 1981) m James Parker **no chn.**
6. ASA STERLING DeWITT b 1909, an infant **dy.**
7. CHARLES BIGELOW DeWITT b 06 Jul 1914 Island Falls ME m1 Idres; m2 Dorothy d 22 May 1980, m3 Doris; **no chn.**

After, at age 37, his father died, Charles was a lodger with the Arthur and Ann Graham family in Germany Settlement NB. Their son Teed married Alice Kirkpatrick, a sister of Charle's wife Rachel Kirkpatrick. Charles was five feet five inches tall, with blue eyes, dark hair and light complexion. He was afraid of thunderstorms. My mother, Madeline [Viginia Hartin] Hill, said of him "Grandfather DeWitt was a stern, hard working man. I was always a little afraid of him. He had a razor strap that he threatened us with, if we bothered him. Of course he never used it". He was very ill his last days; died of cancer of the gall bladder and liver (fr AMS dau/o Madeline Hill via KLAD).

BUNKER
1.1.9.4.3.3.7.10.4 JEMIMA MARY/MAMIE DeWITT m Frank Bunker
1. GORDON BUNKER infant d 1913
2. RUBY BUNKER m Wm Thomason lives in Fredericton Jct.,
3. OLIVER BUNKER b 1906 d 1943
4. BURTON BUNKER b 1916 d 1978 m Kate, 7 chn. Katie Marie, Gerald, Brian, Ralph, William, Jones, and Wesley. (fr KLAD).

DeWITT
1.1.9.4.3.3.8.1.6 ALBERT RANDOLF DeWITT m Elena J Charlton
1. DOROTHY MAY DeWITT b 23 Mar 1895 Blissville (d 27 Jun 1967) m Talmage Earl Nason of Fredericton Jct b 1888, **no chn.**
2. DORA DeWITT b 1897 d 1900 Warren RI **single.**
3. EMMA FRANCES DeWITT b 27 Nov 1899 Warren RI (d 1982 bur Blissville Cem. Hoyt NB) res Saint John NB **single**
4. MARTHA WOODEN DeWITT b 23 Sep 1903 d 03 Oct 1990 bur Blissville, at White Rapids Manor Fredericton Jct NB, had res Fredericton NB, taught in the Public Schools of NB, finally was employed with the Correspondence Section of the NB Department of Education. She was active in NB DeWitt genealogical research; **single.**
5. JOHN HENRY DeWITT b 16 Jun 1905 Patterson Settlement, Sunbury Co NB (d 02 ? 1966 Saint John NB) m Irene Brown (fr MWD).
6. HAZEN ARNOLD DeWITT b 09 Apr 1910 Hoyt NB d 26 Jun 1984 m Grace Tracy of Tracy NB d 1993 bur in Tracy Cem NB, Grace res at White Rapids Manor, Fredericton Jct.

WEBB
1.1.9.4.3.3.8.2.1 AUSTIN WEBB {m} 1 Hannah Clementine DeWitt (1.1.9.4.3.3.7.5.6)
1. LILLIAN WEBB b 1890 m Charles Cochrane.
2. MARY WEBB b ? Apr 1891 d 29 Apr 1891 **dy.**
   m2 Elizabeth Phoebe DeWitt (1.1.9.4.3.3.8.4.5)
3. MINNIE WEBB b 1899 d 1989 Blissville cem. m ? Brown.

Leucas deWit

4   ELWIN WEBB b 1897 d 1971 m Nelle <u>Annabelle</u> Nason b 12 Mar 1902 d 11 Feb 1964 (fr KLAD).
5   MALCOLM WEBB b 1900 d 1945 m Mrs Vivian (Mersereau) Lyon b 1904 d 1972 wd/o Chester Lyon **no chn**.
6   GORDON WEBB b 1902 d 1988.
7   YERXA WEBB b 1902 m   ?   lived in BC.
8   DANIEL <u>FOSTER</u> WEBB b 1908 (d late 1900's bur Sussex NB) m Joyce, div **no chn**.
9   SANFORD WEBB b 1906 d 1929.
10   EVA WEBB b 1893 d 1928 **single** (info fr KLAD).

Exception: Children are with their father's underlined number to keep continuity of the family.

HARRIS
1.1.9.4.3.5.2.2.1 & 1.1.9.4.3.7.3.2.1 CHARLOTTE A DeWITT m Frederick Harris
1   ERNEST HARRIS b 1881 (d 1955) m Elizabeth Phillips b 1888 d 1934.
2   ARTHUR HARRIS m Hazel McIntosh (info fr KLAD).
3   LAVINA HARRIS {m} Albert Mersereau (1.1.9.4.3.6.5.3.1.2) s/o Henry Mersereau & Emma Greensleeves.

DeWITT
1.1.9.4.3.5.2.2.2 & 1.1.9.4.3.7.3.2.2 HENRY <u>LEONARD</u> DeWITT {m} Annabelle Harris (1.1.9.4.3.6.6.1.1.4)
1   FLORENCE MAY DeWITT b 06 Feb 1897 (d 19 Aug 1968) m1 Ralph Webb, m2 George Moffit.
2   MYRTLE EDNA DeWITT b 20 Mar 1899 (d 12 Oct 1979) m Chester/Bud Harris.
3   MABEL AMELIA DeWITT b 02 Apr 1901 (d 18 Nov 1860) m Hazen McCleary.
4   EDNA AMELIA DeWITT b 02 Sep 1905 (d 12 Jan 1982) m Trueman Wood.
5   STELLA LILLIAN DeWITT b 19 Apr 1909 m Erwin Abner Tracy. Stella lives at Fredricton Jct NB. Among her many hobbies are piecing & making quilts, acting as reporter for "Rural Edition" a mimeographed monthly published at Frederick Junction.

Chester Harris & Trueman Wood served overseas in WWI. Trueman was killed in a car accident, buried in Petitcodiac, West County NB. Chester Harris, Ralph Webb, Erwin Tracy were buried in Tracy Cemetery. Erwin Tracey was age 70, died subsequent to a pacemaker operation (info fr IMWH to KLAD).

DeWITT
1.1.9.4.3.5.2.2.4 & 1.1.9.4.3.7.3.2.4 NEHEMIAH DeWITT m Alice Drake
1   OTIS DeWITT m Florence Carr (family info fr KLAD by BDP).
2   ETHEL DeWITT b 1890 (d 07 Nov 1991 ae 101 at White Rapids Manor Grand Rapids Fredericton Jct NB) {m} Winsell Mersereau 1.1.9.4.3.6.5.3.1.4) s/o Henry Mersereau & Emma Greensleeves. Winsell predeceased his wife (fr KLAD out of the FREDERICTON GLEANER).
3   HELEN M DeWITT b 23 Apr 1900 m 11 Jun 1919 Winfield Webb (family info fr BDP to KLAD).

<u>RURAL EDITION</u> Pub in Fredericton Jct NB monthly, Issue #200 May 1990
THE HELEN WEBB RECOGNITION CELEBRATION SUNDAY APRIL 22ND 1990
    An extensive article tells of family and friends at the Tracy Baptist Church, celebrating Helen Webb's 90th birthday. Helen's mother, Alice, was a Church Deacon and member of the choir, as was her brother Otis. With training in voice and piano lessons, Helen joined the choir at age 12. She then followed after her mother as organist, remaining active for 70 years. Then she gave over to her daughter Glenna (Webb) Harris. Nehemiah DeWitt built the house where Helen Mersereau lived with her sister Ethel and bro Otis (now deceased).

HARRIS
1.1.9.4.3.5.2.2.5 & 1.1.9.4.3.7.3.2.5 PHOEBE <u>MARIA</u> DeWITT {m} Albion Harris (1.1.9.4.3.6.6.1.1.1)
1   LESLIE HARRIS **dy**.
2   WALTER HARRIS (d 1979) m Edith Wood (now deceased), #1 Son Ray & wife Helen (Tracy) live in Fredericton Jct. #2 Son Loyd deceased bur Armstrong Cem Geary NB
3   ALFRED/APPY HARRIS d prior 2000 m Madeline Golding d prior 2000 res Fredericton Jct NB son Leslie and his wife Lois O'Leary & family.
4   ELIZABETH HARRIS m Charles Acker who d before 1979 (fr IMWH to KLAD).
5   CHESTER/BUD HARRIS b 1896 (d 12 Oct 1978) {m} Myrtle DeWitt d/o Henry Leonard DeWitt & Annabelle Harris

HARRIS
1.1.9.4.3.5.2.2.11 & 1.1.9.4.3.7.3.2.11 MINNIE DeWITT m Sherman Harris (1.1.9.4.3.6.6.1.2.2)
1   RITA HARRIS (bur family plot Tracy NB) m1 Gordon Ryder, m2 John Hoyt.
2   TYLER HARRIS (d 07 Aug 1987 Oromocto Hospital) m Jennie Wood who d same day 07 Aug 1987 at White Rapids Manor, Fredericton Jct NB; double funeral at Tracy Baptist CH bur Tracy Cem (fr MWD, Obit).

NASON
1.1.9.4.3.5.2.6.9 & 1.1.9.4.3.7.3.6.9 BEATRICE <u>THEODOSIA</u> DeWITT m Burton Wilbur Nason
1   FREDERICK ALBERT NASON b 26 Jul 1900 McAdam NB CPR Section Man, at McAdam m 16 Apr 1924 Rachel Lily Cook d/o George Cook & Alice Orten b Essex Eng res McAdam in 1984; all chn b in McAdam.

Leucas deWit

2   WILBUR <u>EDGAR</u> NASON b 13 Feb 1904 McAdam NB (d 07 Nov 1965) self employed carpenter, at Saint John NB m 1924 Amanda E Ross d/o John Ross & Anne Morrissey, b 23 Oct 1904 Saint John d 02 Feb 1969 both bur Rockland Cem, McAdam. Chn #2-#12 b McAdam NB.
3   GERALD NASON b 07 Aug 1906, at McAdam m 1930 Alice Edna Moffit **no chn.**
4   GEORGE EARL NASON b ? Jul 1924 (d 26 May 1971) m 1960 Eleanor R DeWitt **no chn.**
5   ALMA EVELYN NASON b 07 Jul 1911 (d 01 Feb 1967) at McAdam. m 11 Aug 1938 John Sullivan s/o Scutormoris Divini Skidmore & Margaret Jackson Carson, (came from Aberdeen Scot as a small ch with his wdr father & adopted by James Sullivan & wf) b 09 Feb 1909 Lancashire Eng d 17 May 1984, CPR Car Man. 1 dau 1 son (fr RGD).

DeWiTT

1.1.9.4.3.5.2.6.10 & 1.1.9.4.3.7.3.6.10 FREDRICK ELLIS DeWITT m Elizabeth Gallison
1   LEONA DeWITT res Rothsay NB.
2   ANASTASIA DeWITT m Tom Gasper res Windsor NS.
3   ELEANOR DeWITT (d 14 Feb 1993 service & bur Rockland Baptist CH, McAdam NB (Gleaner Obit) res 22 Spruce St, McAdam NB m ? Nason.
4   BABY DeWITT (fr RGD).

DeWITT

1.1.9.4.3.5.2.6.12 & 1.1.9.4.3.7.3.6.12 GEORGE DeWITT m Regina Isobel Gallison
1   RITA DeWITT res McAdam NB.
2   MARGARET DeWITT {m} William DeWitt grdson of Isaac DeWitt & Annie Boone; 5 sons & 5 daus; 1981 in Montague PE.
3   WILLIAM DeWITT res McAdam.
4   FREDERICK DeWITT res McAdam.
5   ANNICE DeWITT res McAdam.
6   JEAN DeWITT res St Stephens NB.
7   GEORGE DeWITT Jr res St Stephens.
8   HORACE DeWITT (fr RGD).

MERSEREAU

1.1.9.4.3.6.5.3.1 HENRY MERSEREAU m Emma Greensfield
1   ERNEST MERSEREAU m Margaret Moore.
2   ALBERT MERSEREAU of Megantic QC {m} 1.1.9.4.3.5.5.2.1.3 Lavina Harris d/o Charlotte DeWitt & Fred Harris of Tracy.
3   FRED MERSEREAU m Vera Sisson of Tracy NB.
4   WINSELL MERSEREAU {m} 1.1.9.4.3.5.5.2.4.2 Ethel DeWitt b 1890 d 07 Nov 1991 at 101 d/o Nehemiah DeWitt & Alice Drake.
5   EDNA MERSEREAU m George Hawks d 1910.
6   CLARENCE MERSEREAU {m} Gertrude Tracy (1.1.9.4.3.6.5.3.4.3.2) d/o Gilbert Tracy & Elizabeth Latcham of Fredericton Jct NB. Gertrude was a grdau/o Elizabeth Mersereau & Herman Tracy (fr GMAW & KLAD)
7   HAZEL MERSEREAU m Harold Moore bro/o Margaret Moore who m Ernest Mersereau.

MERSEREAU

1.1.9.4.3.6.5.3.2 RAINSFORD MERSEREAU m1 Alma/Hannah Tracy
1.   WINSLOW JAMES MERSEREAU b 1892 (d 13 Sep 1979) res Tracy NB m 13 May 1914 Freda May Noble d/o Herbert Noble & Ida Bunker, b 26 Mar 1896 (all fr KLAD).
m2 Hannah Boone
2   CHARLES MERSEREAU m 1926 Lydia Phillips (1.1.9.4.3.5.5.3.2.?) of Tracy NB d/o Phoebe DeWitt & John Phillips. Lydia is a grdau/o Jeremiah DeWitt & Adeline Nason (fr KLAD).
m3 Bertha Philips
3   JOHN MERSEREAU m 27 Jun 1926 Sadie Mullen b Tracy NB (all fr KLAD).
4   HAZEN MERSEREAU m Beulah Nason **no chn.**
5   ALMA MERSEREAU m Angus Nason.
6   JENNIE MERSEREAU m Raymond Seely d 1977.
7   RAINSFORD MERSEREAU m Inez Segee.
8   HARRY MERSEREAU **dy.**

Obit in the <u>Gleaner:</u> 28 Dec 1979 Charles Rainsford Mersereau of Tracy, son of the late Rainsford Mersereau & Alma (Tracy) Mersereau. Survivors: his wife Lydia Phillips, son Paul P Mersereau of Saint John, step-daughter Mrs Theodore Mills of Tracy, stepson Robert Tracy of Sombra ON, half-sis Mrs Alma Nason of Tracy, half brothers John & Hazen Mersereau of Tracy, grandchildren, nieces & nephews. Service at McAdam's Funeral Home, Fredericton, buried Tracy Cemetery (fr KLAD).

Leucas deWit

KNOWLES
1.1.9.4.3.6.5.3.3 GEORGIE MERSEREAU m George Brick Knowles
1. RUSSEL KNOWLES
2. INEZ KNOWLES m ? Robinson and they had a dau Norma.

TRACY
1.1.9.4.3.6.5.3.4 ELIZABETH MERSEREAU m Herman Tracy
1. LORNE TRACY res Toronto m Eva Martin (fr GMAW).
2. YERXA TRACY res Toronto ON, in WWI m Evaline McDonald d 1976 Toronto.
3. GILBERT TRACY m 1913 Elizabeth Latcham of Carman MB, d 3 or 4 yrs ago (written 1979). They lived Creelman SK until 1926, then Tracyville NB & later at Fredericton Jct NB.
4. STELLA AMELIA TRACY (d 1949) m 1923 Harry Humphrey Gordon Alexander b 1893 d 1938 res Fredericton Jct NB (fr GMAW).

BOONE
1.1.9.4.3.6.5.4.3 BURTON HARVEY BOONE m Lillie Tracy
1. ROY ANGUS BOONE b 1893 m1 Lucy Phillips d 20 Nov 1916 ae 19, m2 Kathleen Jefferson.
2. LOREN GLIDDEN BOONE b 1902 d 11 Aug 1978 at his home in PA m Grace Smith, 2 sons, 2 daus.
3. GEORGE WESLEY BOONE b 1909 (d 08 Mar 1976) m Beatrice Webb (fr ACB).

BOONE
1.1.9.4.3.6.5.4.7 EDWARD A BOONE m Brenda M Mitchell
1. MERLE BOONE b 1902 m Rose Rhodes of England.
2. MONA BOONE b 1911 m Clayton Jones (fr KLAD).

HARRIS
1.1.9.4.3.6.6.1.1 THOMAS ODBUR HARRIS {m} 1 Mary Elizabeth Boone (1.1.9.4.3.6.6.3)
1. ALBION HARRIS b 1865 (d 1952) {m}1 1.1.9.4.3.5.2.2.5 Phoebe Maria DeWitt b 1867 d 1920, m2 Mrs Penelope (Martin) Sturney (fr KLAD).
2. THOMAS HARRIS m Ada Golding.
3. SHERMAN HARRIS {m} 1.1.9.4.3.5.2.2.12 Minnie DeWitt d/o Henry DeWitt & Mary Jane Nason.
4. ANNABELLE HARRIS b 08 Jan 1865 (d 04 Nov 1945) {m} 1.1.9.4.3.5.5.2.2 Henry Leonard DeWitt, b 03 May 1862 d 18 Dec 1943 s/o Henry DeWitt & Mary Jane Nason.

m2 Mrs Bertha (Phillips) Davis

5. MARY HARRIS m William Wentworth of Eastport ME.
6. ALMA HARRIS m Manzer Phillips.
7. LILLIE HARRIS m Edward Wentworth of Eastport ME.
8. GEORGE HARRIS **single.**
9. KENNETH HARRIS **single.**
10. ANDREW HARRIS m Lillian Clarke d 1983.
11. JAMES HARRIS m1 Mary Phillips; m2 Pearl Nason.
12. JENNIE HARRIS **dy.** (Perhaps it was Jennie who married Amos Wilson [fr KLAD]).
13. MYRTLE HARRIS b 1908 (d 1971) m Amos Wilson.
14. CHARLES HARRIS d of diptheria **dy.**

Thomas Odbur Harris adopted and raised his 2nd wife Bertha's chn; Lizzie Davis m Dellas Webb; Laura Davis m Remington Whelpley of Eastport ME.

HARRIS
1.1.9.4.3.6.6.1.5 HAYWARD HARRIS m Saphrona Nason
1. BENJAMIN HARRIS m Ada Mowat.
2. HOWARD (HAYWARD?) HARRIS **single.**
3. FRANK HARRIS m Bertha Scott.
4. ALMA HARRIS **single.**

HARRIS
1.1.9.4.3.6.6.1.6 WILLIAM HARRIS m1 Martha Phillips; m2 Martha McAuley. ? which mother.
1. HOWARD HARRIS m Martha Golding.
2. MABEL HARRIS m William Baker.
3. WILLIAM HARRIS m Ula Tracy.
4. STANLEY HARRIS m Elizabeth Moffatt.
5. BURPEE HARRIS m Dorothy Brown.
6. JARVIS HARRIS m Myrtle Harris.
7. MINA HARRIS m1 Wilmot Robinson; m2 Talmage Tracy.

Leucas deWit

ALEXANDER

1.1.9.4.3.6.6.5.1 THOMAS WILLIAM ALEXANDER m Margaret Timmins
1. IDA SARAH ALEXANDER b 1863 d 1947 m 1885 John Lang b 1936, res MA bur Fredericton Jct.
- CHARLES ALEXANDER **dy.**
2. LILLIE AGNES ALEXANDER b 1867, schoolteacher (d 1956) m 1898 Fenwick W Pride s/o Samuel B Pride & Matildy J Phillips, b 07 Sep 1861 d 1922 both b/m/d Fredericton Jct NB bur Gladstone Cem (fr DPP).
3. CHARLES FREDERICK ALEXANDER b 13 Jun 1870 (d 1906 bur Gladstone Cem, Fredericton Jct NB) m 1900 Lena Davis b Gloucester MA (fr KLAD).
4. BERTHA GENEVRA ALEXANDER b 1879 (d 1973) m 1900 Henry Harvey Stuart a teacher who d 1952, both bur Gladstone Cem, Fredericton Jct NB.
5. ESMOND ST CLAIR ALEXANDER b 1882 worked for the King Lumber CO, Chipman NB, retired 1955 moved to Fredericton Jct then Saint John NB d. 1959 bur Gladstone Cem Fredericton Jct Sunbury Co NB **single**.
6. MINNIE HERMAN ALEXAMDER b 19 May 1872 d 28 Jan 1889 of diptheria **dy.**
7. EDWIN ALEXANDER b 19 Jan 1876 d 11 Feb 1880 diptheria **dy.**

HARRIS

1.1.9.4.3.6.6.6.3 MARY ELIZABETH BOONE {m} 1.1.9.4.3.6.6.1.1 Thomas Odbur Harris
Children are with their father's underlined number Generation 9.

BOONE

1.1.9.4.3.6.6.7.1 REUBEN A BOONE m1 ?   McLaughlin; m2 Jenny ?
1. REUBEN BOONE
2. SPAFFORD BOONE
3. MELVIN BOONE
4. ARMINTA BOONE m Ezekiel Nason.
5. LAVINA ISALINA BOONE m1 ?   Mc Farlane; m2 Wesley Morgan.
6. FEMALE BOONE

PRIDE

1.1.9.4.3.6.6.9.5 VICTORIA NASON m Benedict Pride
1. CLIFFORD PRIDE **dy.**
2. LESSIE PRIDE b 07 Nov 1882 (d a young woman of TB) m Chester Mott d 1982/3, res Fredericton NB, dropped dead on the street. He m2 Charlotte Nason, alive in 1984. The Pride family operated a store at the head of navigation on the Oromocto River known as Pride's Landing. Later the family had a store further up the North Branch Oromocto River near the Highway Bridge (fr KLAD).

NASON

1.1.9.4.3.6.6.9.6 MANZER BOONE NASON m Josie Vail
1. ELSIE NASON b 1894 (d 1976 m Justus Nason who d before Elsie res Tracy (fr EAW).
2. ERNEST NASON b 1895 (d 1964) res Tracy NB **single.**
3. SARAH NASON b 02 Feb 1897 (d 11 Feb 1986) m Francis Pattullo who d 1975 Fredericton Jct NB (fr ACB). Sarah lived at Fredericton Jct NB (fr LN).
4. MABEL A NASON b 10 Sep 1898 m 28 Mar 1917 Clarence E Burnette (1.1.9.4.3.7.1.3.6.1) b 19 May 1895 d 20 Nov 1989, res Fredericton Jct NB. Obit: Clarence was survived by his wf, 1 son, 3 daus, 11 grchn, 9 Ggrchn (fr KLAD; LN). Clarence Burnett did a wonderful job of restoring the Pioneer Cemetery & received & retired a plaque from Fredericton Juction Village Council for outatanding Community Service. When he retired from the CPR in 1960 he began clearing growth, repairing and painting tombstones as a pastime. You can go anywhere in the graveyard with a lawnmower. The Tracey United Baptist Church now oversees the Cemetary.
5. LEMUEL NASON b 1901 m Ena Jobe d 1989, res Fredericton Jct NB **no chn.**

"Sarah Nason Patullo's son Ernest died in his sleep Tuesday p m 25 Sep 1984 at his mother's home at Fredericton Junction. She has two remaining children, David (school teacher) and Betty. Mabel's son Lloyd died about two weeks ago in St Andrews NB " (fr LN to KLAD).

NASON

1.1.9.4.3.6.6.9.8 EVERETT BOONE NASON m Annie Elizabeth Cowie
1. GEORGE ALMAN NASON b 1893 Cork Stn m1 Charlotte Phillips, m2 Sadie Blackmore "Stuart" d/o Kate & steppa Hiram Stuart.
2. JOHN NASON b 1903 Harwood Creek d 1976 Fredericton Jct NB **single.**
3. LILLIAN AUGUSTA NASON b 1897 (d 1965 bur Rural Cem Ext Fredericton) m1 Harry Phillips; m2 Donald Simmons b 1901 d 18 Mar 1986 ae 84 (sic) at Ferguson NB.
4. MARY NASON (d 1976) m Clarence Carr.
5. MYRTLE ABIGAIL D NASON 18 Mar 1987 **single.**
6. ANNIE ISABELLE NASON b 1901 d 1967 m Wilmot Burchill Nason b 1896 d 21 Oct 1987 m2 Mary Jane b 1902 d 1973

7 DELANEY NASON m Hale Nason b 1899 d 04 02 1987. Delaney, only living member of this family as of Feb 1990.
8 RUTH NASON b 1909 (d 1939 after childbirth) m Frank Nason. He is a 3rd cousin to bros Hale & Wilmot Nason.

NASON
1.1.9.4.3.6.6.9.10 PENNELL E NASON m Ellen A Grass
1 GEORGE IRVING NASON b 1901 McAdam NB (d 1962 Woodstock NB) at McAdam m 1923 Grace Marie Clifford b 1907 McAdam; she res Toronto ON.
2 ETHEL MAE NASON b 1903 (d 1967) m Hugh Rushton b 1901 d 1967.
3 CHESTER NASON b 1904 (d 1976 Chatham NB) **single.**
4 NELLIE MARGUERITE NASON b 1906 m 1928 Russell H Blair b 1899.
5 HELEN GERTRUDE NASON b 1908 (d 1971) m 1929 Bob Christie b 1905.
6 SPENCER ALBERT NASON b 1910 m 1930 Rhetta A Jollymore b 1907 d 1977.
7 RAYMOND HENRY NASON b 1912 McAdam NB (d 1981 St Stephen NB at McAdam) m 1949 Rhetta Enman d 1931.
8 RUSSELL EDWARD NASON b 1914 Milo ME (d 12 Jan 1973 McAdam NB) at McAdam, in 1942 m Eva Cleghorn of Tweedside b 1918.
9 WILLIAM ARTHUR NASON b 1918 McADam NB (d 1963) in 1941 m 1941 Edith Gardner b 1914. She m2 Luther Harley res Toronto ON.
10 ALFRED CLARENCE NASON b 1921 d 24 Jan 1989 **single.**
11 RUBY A NASON b 1923 m 1941 Milford Charters (fr ACB).

HAGERMAN
1.1.9.4.3.6.8.2.2 IDA MAY BOONE m Albert Hagerman
1 CORNELIUS HAGERMAN b 1888.
2 SHERMAN HAGERMAN b 1892.
3 ELLA HAGERMAN b 1899 (fr ACB)..

NASON
1.1.9.4.3.7.1.3.1 ADELINE NASON {m} <u>1.1.9.4.3.5.2.3</u> Jeremiah DeWitt
Children are listed with their father's underlined number Generation 8.

NASON
1.1.9.4.3.7.1.3.2 GEORGE FRANCIS NASON m1 1.1.9.4.3.6.5.2 Eunice C Nason. He m2 Mrs Annie Tracy Boone
1 WILLARD B NASON b 1867 d (1940) m Mary Lawless. Thomas & Margaret (below) were wits at Geo's marriage.

DeWITT
1.1.9.4.3.7.1.3.3 MARY JANE NASON m <u>1.1.9.4.3.5.2.2</u> Henry Leonard DeWitt
Children are listed with father's underlined number Generation 8.

NASON
1.1.9.4.3.7.1.3.4 THOMAS LEMUEL NASON m Margaret E Nason
1 ELLIE NASON m Larry Goodine.
2 EMILY JANE NASON b 1870 m 24 Sep 1889 Archie Charters.
3 ANNIE NASON m ? Dunlop.
m2 Mary Greer b 1850 (fr ACB).

BURNETT
1.1.9.4.3.7.1.3.6 MARTHA FINCH NASON m Henry Burnett
1 CLARENCE BURNETT m Mabel A Nason
He was named citizen of the year 1978 and was presented by the Fredericton Jct village council with a plaque for long and outstanding community service which was the restoration work he did on the Pioneer Cemetary. Clarence Burnett took us on a little tour the other day through the Pioneer Cemetry. What a wonderful job he had done and is doing!
He started looking after it in 1960 when he was pensioned from the C.P.R. where he had worked for a good many years.
He was telling us when he started after it in 1960 the graveyard was full of bushes, the tomestones were falling over and breaking apart. It was a sad sight if you go in to see it today the bushes are all cut down. You can go anywhere in the graveyard with a lawn mower.
He glued the tombstones together and cleaned all the moss off and painted them. They can be seen for miles away. He is doing this for a pastime. His grand parents were John Nason and Abigail Grass.
2 HARTLEY BURNETT & family lived the Back Tracy Road and had two daughters, Ruby & Leila.
3 HARRY BURNETT m Maud Lloyd lived Fredericton Jct.
4 ELVA BURNETT m Alfred DeWitt b 23 Apr 1878 (1.1.9.4.3.5.2.2.10).
5 MYRTLE BURNETT m Chester Harris (fr ACB).

NASON
1.1.9.4.3.7.1.8.1 FRANCIS GILBERT NASON m Sophia Bunker
1 ZAIDA/LIZZIE NASON b 1878 at Tracy NB.
2 CHESTER NASON b 1880 (d 1970) m1 1906 Ida May Golding; m2 Mrs Alma Nason Greer.

Leucas deWit

3	CARRIE NASON b 1887 d 1910.
4	SADIE NASON d from scarlet fever.
5	MILLIE ANNIE NASON b 1893 (d 1924) m 1911 Hugh Thomas.
6	AMY I NASON b 1896 d 1920.
7	ANNE M NASON b 1899 m 1926 Emerson Budd (ACB).

NASON
1.1.9.4.3.7.1.8.2 ZACHARIAH NASON m Nettie Marie Fleming
1. ZELMER NASON b ca 1891 Armourdale KS **dy.**
2. ROBERT B NASON 1893 (d 1976) m 24 11 1914 Eula Welsh.
3. LUCY HELEN NASON b 1985 (d 1971) m Joseph W Berg.
4. FRANCES ELOISE NASON b 1897 (d 1958) m1 1918 Frank Manning; m2 Roy Langdon.
5. ELIZABETH ISABEL NASON b 1899 m 05 Feb 1921 Clarence W Terry.
6. ZACARIAH MILES NASON b 1905 (d 1971) m 12 Apr 1926 Susan Robinson.

NASON
1.1.9.4.3.7.1.8.3 BENJAMIN JOHN NASON m Ada Nason
1. CLYDE NASON 23 May 1888 **single**.
2. BABY NASON b 27 Jan 1890? **dy.**
3. ROY A NASON b 08 Jun 1891 m1 Alma Greer; m2 Verla Kennedy.
4. GRACE NASON b 15 Sep 1895 m1 Arthur Rynax; m2 George Carl.
5. MAUD ELLA NASON b 26 Jul 1896 m Melvin Phillips.
6. MARY GLADYS NASON b 06 Feb 1898 d 28 03 1899 **dy.**
7. HAZEL NASON b 04 Mar 1903 m Murdo McLeod.
8. CORA NASON (d in Hospital) m Wilbur Rynax.
9. UNKNOWN NASON b 19 Mar 1905 d 22 Mar 1905 **dy.**
10. INA NASON b 28 Apr 1906 m James Jones (fr ACB).
11. FRANK NASON b 13 Jul 1907 (d 17 Mar 1978) m1 Ruth Nason. He m2 Faye Nason, a niece of Ruth's.

PHOEBE JANE (DeWITT) SMITH SAID 'IN NEW BRUNSWICK THEY HAD THREE CHOICES FOR MARRIAGE: HINJINS, HINGLISHMEN OR RELATIVES, SO THEY CHOSE RELATIVES', presumably reflecting the attitude of the day.

<u>READER'S DIGEST</u> DEC 1990 p 71/2 describes research being done on "THE METHUSELAH GENE". Many DeWitt families have routinely lived into their 80's, 90's and 100's. They must have inherited very good HDL (good cholesterol) genes with readings of four to five times higher protection than most people. "Isolating such a gene would raise long-term hopes of extending life expectancy". The longevity of many New Brunswick DeWitts is remarkable.

DeWITT
1.1.9.4.3.7.3.2.2 & <u>1.1.9.4.3.5.2.2.2</u> HENRY LEONARD DeWITT {m} Annabelle Harris (1.1.9.4.3.6.6.1.2.4)
Children are with their father's underlined number Generation 9.

DeWITT
1.1.9.4.3.7.3.2.4 & <u>1.1.9.4.3.5.2.2.4</u> NEHEMIAH DeWITT m Alice Drake
Children are with their father's underlined number Generation 9.

HARRIS
1.1.9.4.3.7.3.2.5 & <u>1.1.9.4.3.5.2.2.5</u> PHOEBE MARIA DeWITT m Albion Harris (1.1.9.4.3.6.6.1.2.4)
Children are with their mother's underlined number Generation 9.

HARRIS
1.1.9.4.3.7.3.2.11 & <u>1.1.9.4.3.5.2.2.11</u> MINNIE DeWITT m Sherman Harris (1.1.9.4.3.6.6.1.2.2)
Children are with their mother's underlined number Generation 9.

DeWITT
1.1.9.4.3.7.3.6.8 & <u>1.1.9.4.3.5.2.6.8</u> FREDERICK DeWITT m Elizabeth Gallison
Children are with their father's undelined number Generation 9.

NASON
1.1.9.4.3.7.3.6.9 & <u>1.1.9.4.3.5.2.6.9</u> BEATRICE THEODOSIA DeWITT m Burton Wilbur Nason
Children are with their mother's underlined number Generation 9.

DeWITT
1.1.9.4.3.7.3.6.11 & <u>1.1.9.4.3.5.2.6.11</u> GEORGE DeWITT m Regina Gallison
Children are with their father's underlined number Generation 9.

MUIR
1.1.9.4.3.7.4.1.1 MARY DeWITT m Henry Muir
1. FRANK MUIR m ? , div, a son Douglas res NF.

DeWITT
1.1.9.4.3.7.4.2.4 NORMAN WENTWORTH DeWITT m Katharine Ida Johnston
1. NORMAN JOHNSTON DeWITT b 01 Aug 1908 Lincoln IL (d 1966) m 1941 Lois Pfister. He was PROF. of CLASSICAL PHILOSOPHY. B.A Univ. of Toronto, 1930, M.A. 1933, Ph.D. John Hopkins Univ, 1938. Teaching fel, [Classical Philosophy] Victoria Coll, Univ. Toronto, 1933-34; instr. Classics, Adelbert College, West. Reserve Univ, 1938-41; Washington Univ, 1941-43, asst. Prof, 1943-45, Prof, 1946-49, head Latin dept, 1947-49; PROF. CLASSICS & CHEMN. DEPT, UNIV. MINN, 1949-Am. Counc. Learned Socs. Faculty fel, 1951-52. Am. Philol. Asn; Am. Class; Lea; Asn. Mid. W. & S. (secy-treas, 1942-45; pres, 1956; ed, 'Jour,' 1945-50) Philosophy of education; empirical humanism. "Urbanization and the Franchise of Roman Gaul", "College Latin." Add: Dept. of Classics, University of Minnesota, Minneapolis MN Directory of American Scholars, Volume III, 4th Edition. New York: R. R. Boeker Co., 1964. The fifth edition of D. A.s. indicates that Norman Johnson DeWitt died in 1966. (fr ICSP, LPD & Who's Who).

COLEMAN
1.1.9.4.3.7.4.2.5 SEMENA DeWITT m Alfred Brigham Coleman
1. MARGARET ELIZABETH COLEMAN b 26 Jul 1906 in Eng came to Can 1911 ae 5, at Burlington ON m 15 Oct 1933 Clement Algernon Baines s/o CA Baines & Ada Elizabeth Croydon (all fr MCB).
2. MARY ELECTRA COLEMAN b 1907 m 1934 Gordon Coburn.
3. ALFRED BRANT COLEMAN b 1909 m1 1928 Muriel Magee who d; m2 1949 Muriel Nugy.
4. KATHLEEN De WITT COLEMAN b 1913 m1 1936 Michael Phillips who d 1937. She m2 1940 F H Krenz.
5. ELIZABETH NASH COLEMAN b 1915 m1 1931 William Crop d 1940 (sic) m2 1939 K C McCauley d 1956.
6. SAMENA COLEMAN b 1918 (d 1967) m 1949 H J Sissons.
7. NORMAN COLEMAN b 1921 d 1926 **dy** (all fr MECB).

PETTIT
1.1.9.4.3.7.4.3.1 HIRAM PETTIT m Emma Jane Bryce
1. HONOR KATHLEEN PETTIT b 04 Feb 1898 (d Aug 1980) m1 Lewis L Saligman M.D. Lewis advised the boys to change their name. They chose DeWitt. Honor m2 William Beery Mikesell (fr RORP). Ruth Olive Pettit Ryder's letter in Oct 1980 to Dr I Carolyn Pellettier mentioned Honor's death.
2. IVA MARGARET PETTIT b 23 Feb 1900 m1 Walter Ramsay, 1 ch div; m2 William Ince **no chn**. Walter's son Ivan Ramsey had a son called Bob (fr HKPSM).

PETTIT
1.1.9.4.3.7.4.3.2 HERMAN PETTIT m Beatrice Bruce
1. MARION BRUCE PETTIT b 01 Mar 1891 had several chn, grchn.
2. ORA ROBERTSON PETTIT b 23 Dec 1893 m ? had several chn.
3. DORIS EVELYN PETTIT b 15 Nov 1895 m Seymour Ball, **no chn**.
4. WALTER MELVIN PETTIT b 13 Oct 1899; had several chn (info fr HKPSM).
5. ISABEL KATHLEEN PETTIT b 28 May 1901.

GRACEY
1.1.9.4.3.7.4.3.3 ALMEDA PETTIT m Alexander Gracey
1. DeWITT GRACEY b 01 Oct 1882 (d 1980) m Tina Lilburn div; a dau Ruth m Milan. In her letter 06 Feb 1978 Honor Petit Saligman Mikisell said she wrote Ruth (Gracey) Milan some years ago but got no reply. She was in Turlock CA (fr HKPSM, ROPR).

PETTIT
1.1.9.4.3.7.4.3.4 MELVIN PETTIT m Anna A Kenney
1. CAROLYN WALTON PETTIT b 27 Mar 1889 Romney Kent Co ON (d 13 Mar 1960) m 24 Jul 1912 Dr James F Nelson D.D. b 14 Dec 1886 d 03 Jun 1975.
2. LOIS EDNA PETTIT b 25 Jul 1890 d 17 May 1891 **dy**.
3. ANNA ALMEDA PETTIT b 14 Aug 1892 (d 08 May 1970) m 27 Jun 1916 Fred Aden b 23 Apr 1890 d 01 Jun 1965.
4. HERMAN DeWITT PETIT D.D. b 03 May 1894 m 22 May 1923 Marion St John b 03 Mar 1902, div.
5. RUTH OLIVE PETTIT b 09 Apr 1896 d aft 23 Jun 1979 m 26 Jan 1923 Milton Ryder b 18 Jan 1896 d 12 Jan 1976.
6. CLARE NEWCOMER PETTIT b 17 Nov 1898 m1 25 May 1921 Antionette Ramsay b 27 Nov 1975 d **no chn**. They adopted a boy in 1940 in CA. He m2 08 Jan 1977 Helen Bragg **no chn** (info fr ROPR).

HOLTERMANN
1.1.9.4.3.7.4.3.6 LOIS PETTIT m Richard Ferdinand Holtermann
1. WILLIAM IVAR HOLTERMANN b 23 Feb 1888 (d 21 Jun 1959) m 13 Nov 1913 Selena Minchall.
2. MARION LOUISE HOLTERMANN b 13 Oct 1899 m 15 Jul 1923 George Johnson Arnold.
3. SARAH ENID HOLTERMANN b 08 Sep 1891 (d 28 Jun 1945) m 23 Jul 1913 George Bates Rickard b. 17 Jun 1888 Nottingham\ Eng d.19 Jul 1937 Niagara Falls NY.
4. RICHARD SYLVESTER HOLTERMANN b 14 Aug 1893 d ? Jan 1899 **dy**.
5. DARBY GLEN HOLTERMANN b 20 Oct 1895 (d 23 Jun 1963) m 30 Oct 1916 Gladys Woltz (all fr ROPR).

MULHOLLAND
1.1.9.4.3.7.4.5.1 RUTH E ARMSTRONG m Thomas Wellington/Welly Mulholland
1. ANNIE MULHOLLAND b 1885 (d 1946 bur Mt Pleasant Cem Toronto ON) m 1906 William George Foxley.
2. JOSEPH MULHOLLAND b 1886 d 1897 bur Mt Pleasant **dy.**
3. SARAH MULHOLLAND b 1889 (d 1948 both bur Stoney Creek Cem Hamilton ON) m 1909 Arthur Jay Kenyon b 1877 d 1956 res Vinemount ON. Arthur was the s/o John Walsteholm Kenyon & Rachel McTwine.
4. ELSIE MULHOLLAND b 1891 res in 1977 in Central Park Lodge, Weston ON bur Mt Pleasant Cem, **single**.
5. NORMAN MULHOLLAND b 1894 d 1895 bur Mt Pleasant **dy.**
6. ALICE MULHOLLAND b 1896 Toronto m 1933 August Alfred Eklund; fr Elkhorn Co NE b 1892 d 1975 bur Mt Pleasant **no chn.**
7. RUTH MULHOLLAND b 1899 Toronto res there in 1978, m 1925 Joseph Henry Stephenson of Thornhill ON, b 1901 d 1975 both bur Mt Pleasant (fr GRAH).

ARMSTRONG
1.1.9.4.3.7.4.5.6 SAMUEL JOSEPH ARMSTRONG m Selena Maude Clarke
1. JOSEPH W ARMSTRONG b 28 Apr 1902 m 25 Sep 1925 Bernice.
2. GLADYS R ARMSTRONG b 25 Jul 1903 m 27 Jan 1920 Sheldon F Hyland b 24 Sep 1896 d 16 Nov 1952 bur Winona ON.
3. HUGH W ARMSTRONG b 14 Aug 1904 (d 04 Sep 1962) m 30 Jul 1930 Eleanor.
4. CLIFFORD R ARMSTRONG b 15 Oct 1906 **single**.
5. JOHN N ARMSTRONG b 15 Dec 1907 m Leona ? .
6. ELIJAH GRATTON ARMSTRONG b 10 Jul 1910 d 14 Nov 1945 m 15 Sep 1920 Evelyn ? .
7. JEAN G ARMSTRONG b 20 Oct 1912 m Herbert J Theriault.
8. SAMUEL GERALD ARMSTRONG b 06 Aug t 1915 m Kay.
9. GERTRUDE E ARMSTRONG b 26 Feb 1918 m 08 Jun 1943 Cyril Crossby (fr GRAH).

DeWITT
1.1.9.4.3.7.4.6.1 HIRAM SYLVESTER DeWITT m Eliza Jane Logan
1. JOHN WINFRED DeWITT b 02 Feb 1893 Napinka MB (d 19 Feb 1979 The Dalles OR) moved to CA in 1915, worked on a Long Beach Dairy Farm. There he m1 01 Apr 1917 Agnes Wood b 06 Apr 1890 Glasgow Scot d 31 Jul 1970 The Dalles. He m2 Frances Holverst.
2. CLARA ROSE DeWITT b 25 Jun 1894 Napinka MB, attended Brandon MB Normal School & taught at Medora, West Brenda, Tyvar & Yale (d ae 94). She m 07 Feb 1917 James Darcy Purvis b 24 Jan 1886 Wingham ON d ae 102 both bur Redvers. Chn b on farm 5 mi west of Redvers SK.
3. MYRTLE IRENE DeWITT b 29 Mar 1906 Napinka MB went to Winnipeg Normal School, has res in Regina SK since 1965 m 28 Oct 1931 Wilson Dean b 19 Sep 1903 Capron IL d 23 Jul 1965 Weyburn SK bur Rosewood Memorial Gardens, Brandon MB; chn b Fertile SK fr EJDL, MTD, BB: 618).

Ella Jane (DeWitt) Livesley provided information on the Napinka DeWitts for a Municipal History: <u>Bridging Brenda</u> Pub in October 1990. With permission her collected material is also available.

Sylvester DeWitt joined Mr Gaudin in his hardware business in Napinka. He and brothers Morgan and Harry bought and operated the business awhile also selling furniture, lumber and coal. Later they sold the lumber and coal business and just Sylvester continued with hardware and furniture and assisted Mr Dunbar and Mr Holden with the undertaking.

In December 1911 a fire destroyed the DeWitt hardware store which then operated out of a vacant building across the street until Sylvester erected a two storey building on the old site, the ground floor for furniture, the upstairs hall for movies, concerts, dances, fowl suppers etc. Later others used the lower level for a grocery store and the hall as a furniture store. Dismantled in 1978, the lumber was used in Melita for building houses. Sylvester owned the Massey Harris building across the street and a two-storey structure towards the east end of the railway avenue. After her husband's death Eliza Jane sold the house and moved to her daughter Clara Purvis' home.

DeWITT
1.1.9.4.3.7.4.6.2 MORGAN SAMUEL DeWITT m Emily Leigh
1. EMILY MAY DeWITT b 08 Feb 1899 Napinka MB (d 1984 in Regina bur by an only infant dau in Winnipeg MB) taught school, m 01 Jan 1941 Edward Frederick Parsons b 04 Dec ? Weyburn SK.
2. MABEL ANNIE IRENE DeWITT b 17 May 1901 Napinka (d 08 Nov 1973 Regina SK) a teacher at Napinka m 15 Oct 1934 William J McKenzie b Apr 1906 Howard SK d 20 Jun 1976 Weyburn SK both bur Howard. They had settled Porcupine Plains SK,
3. HOWARD LEIGH DeWITT b 20 Nov 1905 d 14 Mar 1907 **dy**, bur DeWitt plot Napinka Cem.

Morgan and Emily farmed then moved into the village. After dissolving the partnership with his brothers Morgan sold cars for the Ford dealer and did carpenter work, later was an Insurance Agent. Emily was known as an excellent cook and homemaker. The male Bank Clerks lived in rooms above the bank and had their meals at the DeWitts. Emily boarded the lady schoolteachers and myself (fr MTD in BB:619)

DeWITT
1.1.9.4.3.7.4.6.3 JOSEPH HARRISON/HARRY DeWITT m Katie Eleanor/Nellie Hall
1. NORMAN OSBORNE DeWITT b 12 Feb 1901 Purple Hill MB (d 04 Nov 1960 Vancouver BC) m ? Oct 1922 Beryl Green b ca 1900 Winnipeg MB. Norman served in the Ontario Provincial Police then the British Columbia Provincial Police, RCMP "E" Division 11 Aug-10 Sep 1950 in "Changes in Personnel list" A/Cpl DeWitt, N O Smithers Det, a 3/Cst DeWitt E H, University Detachment.
2. ALMA ALETHA ISABELL DeWITT b 04 Dec 1902 Purple Hill MB (d 17 Nov 1986) m 14 Dec 1925 Robert <u>Alexander</u> Rodgers b 13 Apr 1898 d 25 Nov 1955 Regina SK, chn b Regina. He who was a Detective on the Regina Police Force (fr EJB).

LIVESLEY
1.1.9.4.3.7.4.6.4 ELINOR JANE/ELLA DeWITT m Robert Livesley
1. MARY ELIZABETH EMMA LOUISE LIVESLEY b 04 Jul 1899 Napinka MN (d 30 Jan 1985) at Deloraine m 28 Sep 1929 Frederick Roy Steele b 02 Jun 1901 Deloraine MB d 14 Oct 1985, both bur Napinka; chn b Winnipeg MB.
2. MILDRED EUNICE JANE LIVESLEY b 11 Jul 1903 m 01 Jul 1961 Morgan Albert Snedden b 18 Dec 1899 Crystal City MB d 26 Nov 1963 Toronto ON bur Crystal City MB, **no chn**. Mrs Mildred E Snedden #514 1630 Henderson Hwy Wpg (fr MEJLS).
3. ROBERT <u>ARDEN</u> DeWITT LIVESLEY b 25 May 1916 Melita MB m1 14 Feb 1942 Gwendolyn Hibbert b 24 Aug 1920 Manchester Eng, d 25 Jun 1971 Winnipeg MB, bur Napinka MB. m2 19 Aug 1972 Margaret Kathleen Mountain b 04 May 1918 Sussex NB Can. (BB:620, fr EJDL, MTD).

SMITH
1.1.9.4.3.7.4.10.2 JOSHUA DeWITT SMITH m Sarah Jane Alway Smith
1. BEULAH SMITH b 22 Jul 1900 Winona ON (d 29 Apr 1973 Newmarket ON) m 1922 Erland Eckland. He worked for the C.B.C. and Time Magazine (fr HBD to ICSP).

SMITH
1.1.9.4.3.7.4.10.4 ARTHUR WESLEY SMITH m Adeline Ethelyn Martin
1. MARGARET JANE PENELOPE SMITH b 15 Aug 1914 Vineland Station, L1 C3 Clinton T Lincoln Co ON at United CH there m 18 Nov 1950 Ronald Claus Moyer s/o Ian Claus Moyer & Georgina Isabella MacLeod, b 25 Sep 1918 (Cherry Ave, Vineland Station) chn b Grimsby (fr MJPSM).
2. HAROLD WESLEY MARTIN SMITH b 01 Jul 1916 b L1 C3 m 18 Jan 1941 St Pauls United CH St Catharines ON Ida Alice Empringham d/o John Robert Empringham & Agnes Glenetta Muir, b 03 May 1917 Toronto ON, chn b St Catharines ON (fr ICSP).

SMITH
1.1.9.4.3.7.4.10.5 HOWARD BLAKE SMITH m Edythe Reid
1. JOHN <u>REID</u> SMITH b 06 Oct 1912 Winona m 21 Oct 1939 Gwen Ramsden b 13 May 1913.
2. HOWARD NAVARRE SMITH b 24 Jul 1914 d 18 Jul 1980 **single**. Howard is bur Dade Memorial Park, Miami FL; he was a hotel night clerk & was killed in a hold-up (fr HBS to ICSP).

SWEENEY
1.1.9.4.3.7.4.10.6 ELIZABETH ANN/BESS SMITH m Howard Malcolm Sweeney
1. GORDON AMBROSE SWEENEY b 05 Apr 1918 Hamilton ON; at St Andrews United CH, River Heights, Winnipeg MB m 10 Oct 1945 Vivienne Elaine /Bess Stone d/o G K Stone, res FL (fr HBD to ICSP).

DeWITT
1.1.9.4.3.7.4.13.2 NORMAN BRUNSWICK DeWITT m Alma Etta Pennington
1. ARTHUR NORMAN DeWITT b 05 Aug 1926 Douglas AZ m1 25 Jun 1950 Marjorie Washburn d/o Artemus Washburn & Minnie Louise Vogt, b 25 Nov 1925, div. He m2 Mrs Jean Pahl b 11 Apr 1933 (fr JDW).

SORENSON
1.1.9.4.3.7.4.13.5 LAURA BELLE DeWITT m Andrew Sorenson
1. HENRY JUDSON SORENSON b 23 Jul 1909 m 03 Apr 1947 Eloise Pumphrey d/o Walton H Pumphrey & Hettie W; **no chn**, res Alamagordo NW in 1979.
2. ANDREW SORENSON b 19 Jun 1912 m at Hillsboro NV 09 Aug 1937 Myra Mae Bays d/o Albert Bays Myrtle Lawrence, b 20 Jun 1920. Chn b Alamagordo NM.
3. CARROL ROBERT SORENSON b 14 Jan 1915 m Sep 1958 Ruth Strong of St Louis MO **no chn** (fr JDW).

WILKINS
1.1.9.4.3.7.4.13.7 JEAN DeWITT m Arthur Miller Wilkins
1. FAITH ALICE WILKINS b 11 Feb 1921 m1 03 May 1953 John Bergman Raeder s/o J B Raeder & Martha Mayme, b ? Apr 1918 Litchfield IL. They div 1959. He had a son by a former m, Jerry b ? Feb 1943. Faith m2 17 Apr 1960 Richard H Logan of IL.
2. ARTHUR NORMAN WILKINS b 24 Sep 1925 (fr JDW).

FOSTER
1.1.9.4.3.7.6.3.6 MARY ISOBEL/BELLE NEFF m Robert Foster
1. ELIZA O FOSTER b 29 Oct 1894 St Catharines ON m Allan Alexander Moyer. res 29 May Kitchener ON. Eliza had no middle name but added "O" from grandmother Ohmstead.
2. ROBERT NEFF FOSTER b 29 Oct 1894 St Catharines ON at Thorold Twp ON m 24 Feb 1927 Alix Beryl Turner of Thorold Twp ON d/o George A Turner & Lilliam M Brown, b 20 Jul 1895 Merriton ON d 1969. Robert was an accountant, res at 23 Welland St, S Thorold in 1971, then he res with his son (fr ICSP).

WILSON
1.1.9.4.3.7.10.1.3 MARY CECELIA ANN DeWITT m William George Wilson
1. MARY EDITH/MAE WILSON b 25 Aug 1896 Newdale MB (d 27 Aug 1966 Los Angeles CA) m 20 Dec 1924 Ralph Boyes b 11 Mar 1898 d 12 Jan 1965 CA.
2. MARGARET LILA WILSON b 05 May 1900.
3. MARTHA LILY WILSON b 05 May 1900.
4. OLIVE LUELLA WILSON b 05 May 1900, the triplets d from cholera Newdale MB.
5. FREDERICK GEORGE DeWITT WILSON b 25 Apr 1903 (d 12 May 1958 Dauphin MB) at Neepawa MB m 12 Jan 1936 Marguerite Isabelle Lowe of Rackham MB b 15 Oct 1915 Cobalt ON. Fred & brother Bill operated a sawmill with their father at Crawford Park MB from 1924 to 1938, then moved to Dauphin MB operating a mill along the north border of Riding Mountain National Park. Fred lost his arm while sawing logs 02 Mar 1927. His father held his thumbs in the arteries until a nurse in the area came. This happened at 4 P.M. He was taken by sleigh 18 miles to Erickson arriving 7 A.M. the following morning, then by train to Neepawa.
6. VIOLET WILSON b 28 Oct 1905 d 28 Nov 1905 Newdale **dy.**
7. CECIL McADFREN WILSON b 11 May 1908 (d 02 May 1972 Gladstone MB) m 09 Nov 1933 Sadie Elizabeth Galloway b 25 Aug 1910. Cecil was a buttermaker by trade. His 2nd name McAdfren was made up from the married names of his father's 3 sisters, Mc for McKenzie, Ad for Adair, & Fren for French.
8. CECELIA GEORGEANA WILSON b 24 Apr 1910 at Minnedosa MB m 07 Nov 1930 Hjalmar Christiansen b 29 Dec 1899 at Faxe, Denmark & came to Can in 1920. Hjalmar studied 4 yrs to become a butcher. [The author visited these relatives in June 1989 at Minnedosa MB].
9. WILLIAM/BILL FRANKLIN WILSON b 18 Nov 1911 (d 15 Jul 1960) at Minnedosa m 26 Jun 1935 Margaret Pasternack b 01 Sep 1914 Sandy Lake MB. After the family Sawmill closed in 1938 Bill worked for the Good Roads Department in Dauphin until his death (fr ACCH).

DeWITT
1.1.9.4.3.7.10.5.2 FREDERICK WILBERT DeWITT m Georgina Alma Dean Stewart
1. BEATRICE DeWITT b 1908 d 1920 at Fruitland ON **dy.**
2. MABEL DeWITT b 1910 d 1920 at Fruitland **dy.**
3. CHARLES CLIFFORD DeWITT b 29 Jan 1915 (d 19 Apr 1983) 69 yr Masonic service member of the T H Simpson Lodge #692) m 07 Aug 1937 Libby McBride b 15 Sep 1911 d 1985 (fr CCD1 & obit).

TRATO
1.1.9.4.3.7.10.6.1 CHRISTOPHER GEORGE TRATO m Edith Campaigne
1. VIOLET MAE TRATO b 1907 m O E/Mac Pearson, div.
2. ALBERT CAMPAIGNE TRATO b 1910 m 01 May 1940 Helen Ruth Burke b 1919.
3. JOHN HILLIARD TRATO b 1912 m Josephine Helen Thiede.
4. RUTH ELIZABETH TRATO b 1915.
5. MARION EDITH TRATO b 1918 m Donald A Mahr res Grand Rapids Mi (fr ICSP).

SWIFT
1.1.9.4.3.7.10.6.2 PANSY BLOSSOM TRATO m George Seth Swift
1. ELLEN SWIFT m Harold Murray.
2. PRUDENCE SWIFT
3. ELIZABETH SWIFT m ? Knight div (fr ICSD).

TRATO
1.1.9.4.3.7.10.6.3 ALBERT NELSON TRATO m Vera Seume
1. PANSY TRATO m Foye Pierce.
2. MAE TRATO m Norman Haddon.
3. IRMA TRATO m1 ? , div m2 ? (fr ICSP).

NORTON
1.1.9.4.3.7.10.8.1 MARY MARTIN m Hiram George Andrew Norton
1. CECIL HIRAM NORTON b 16 Sep 1900 Tapleytown ON m 04 Apr 1923 Gladys Agnes Robinson b 28 Jun 1903 d 24 Jun 1974 Burlington ON.
2. CLARA LOUISE NORTON b 17 Mar 1903 m 28 Feb 1925 William Earl Esury (fr ICSP).

DeWITT

1.1.9.4.3.7.10.10.1 IRA SMITH DeWITT m Edna Belle Barker

1. RHEA MARY ELVA DeWITT b 08 Apr 1907 Newdale (d 05 Nov 1988 Burlington ON) m 12 Jun 1930 William James Hugill s/o Jonathan Hugill & Ellen Kinnaird, b 24 Mar 1879 d 05 May 1954 of cancer at home in Beverly Twp Wentworth County ON. They farmed 125 acres Lot 29 Con 3 in Beverly Twp Wentworth Co ON, the Hugill home farm near Peter's Corners which was in the family for 150 yrs. The property ran from Hwy #8 to the 4th Con being two farms. William owned the back 50 acres and Alexander (a bachelor) owned the front 75 acres. Both farms were run by the two brothers and living with their sister Mary (spinster, missionary, schoolteacher) on the front farm. The house on the rear farm was allowed to run down. Other people helped themselves to parts of the house they needed until it completely fell down. The barn was used for hay storage for winter use feeding the dairy cattle. They did mixed farming, dairy Registered Ayrshire & Jersey cattle, grain, chickens & market gardening, selling milk to Bordens Dairy in Hamilton, grain to the Elevators in Dundas, potatoes and eggs to a meat store at the corner of King St & Locke St in Hamilton ON and to private homes. Edna DeWitt, Rhea's mother, along with Rhea's daughter Edna (stricken with Rheumatoid Arthritis) would clean, candle, grade & pack over 100 dozen eggs a week for market. Rhea worked on the farm along with any of the men and could milk cows faster than the milking machines, pitch wheat sheaves four times her height to store in the barn for thrashing later, stook a field of grain, pick potatoes, hoe turnips and feed the cows.

   RHEA DeWITT m WILLIAM HUGILL

   She would cook up dozens of pies, a 20 lb roast of beef, & get two meals each day for a thrashing gang of 17 people on a wood stove in the kitchen using old stump roots on hot late summer days. The children would anxiously wait until the thrashers were finished, to clean up the leftover pies. Only after William's death did Rhea have running water and central heat in the house. Prior to that there was no heat in the upper part (bedrooms) of the house. Rhea & son Murray (ae 17) farmed for another 3 years until Murray went to Ford Trade School in Windsor ON as an electrical apprentice, at which time they sold the dairy cattle and carried on with the grain and chickens. Rhea ploughed and worked the fields ready for son Murray to plant weekends when he came home from Trade School. Rhea, her mother & her daughter looked after the chickens and got the eggs ready for Murray & his sister Edna to deliver to market on Saturdays. In Jan 1963 Rhea, mother Edna, dau Edna & son Murray moved to 515 Bridgeman Ave Burlington ON. It was time for Rhea to relax and enjoy travelling. She made several trips out west to visit her brothers & sisters. On an early trip she took her mother Edna to meet, in Manitoba, a brother & sister and their families whom she had not seen for over 20 years. On another trip to B.C. she and her sister Elva toured down through California. This was a highlight, which she often talked about as to how much she enjoyed that holiday (fr MDH).

2. MAURICE WILBUR DeWITT b 07 Mar 1908 Newdale (d 05 Jan 1961 Brandon MB) at Brandon m 07 Jun 1942 Emily Mildred Surby d/o William Surby & Lillian Roscoe b 22 Jun 1912, d 05 Aug 1986 Brandon. Maurice worked in his dad's garage & later in the DeWitt's Sawmill. While employed at Kippen's Sawmill located in the Riding Mountain National Park he was testing the plainer mill equipment he had repaired when the cogs caught caught his sleeve and his left arm was crushed. To release his arm they had to run the equipment backwards. He was in Brandon & Winnipeg Hospitals for months. His arm was four inches shorter & his health damaged. He obtained a Stationary Engineers Certificate & was employed for several years by the Brandon Anglo Canadian Oil Cracking Plant. When unable to work because of failing health, two fellow workers worked an extra day each week with them assigning the pay to Maurice. The Company paid it at time and a half. At his funeral, despite distances and the weather, the church was crowded.

   MAURICE DeWITT m EMILY SURBY

3 LIONEL SMITH DeWITT b 28 Apr 1909 Newdale d 26 Oct 1930 ae 21 drowned while he was skating on Sandy Lake after breaking through an area of thin ice kept open by ducks. He was a happy person, a wellknown gifted athlete, swimmer, baseball player, with boundless energy, immensely strong & in demand by employers. He had almost drowned several times beginning at age two, but the last time he came up under solid ice & was stunned. He was a favourite in the family & District. He had returned the previous night from harvesting & stayed home to visit with his ma (Edna) & sis (Vona) rather than go to a dance with the others. Edna never really recovered her health from losing her twin sister (Elva at ae 28), Lionel's death, Maurice's accident & the worry of George overseas in WWII. Maurice & Lionel homesteaded 8 miles north of Sandy Lake in the Providence District (near a veteran uncle, primarily a WWI Soldiers's Settlement). The farms later were owned by brother George. Lionel was engaged to Mary Ankorn of Brandon

LIONEL SMITH DeWITT

4 SELENA ELVA DeWITT b 27 Dec 1910 Newdale MB at Ava & Bill Hamilton's Newdale MB farm (d 02 Jan 1977 Coquitlam BC, ashes scattered in the Fraser Canyon, a favourite place) at Brandon m 02 Sep 1928 Herbert Norman McFaddin s/o William Herbert McFaddin & m1 Belle McLennan, b 30 May 1904 Cardale MB d 17 Dec 1988 in Vancouver BC, trapped in a crosswalk & struck & run over by a truck loaded with telephone poles. Norman/Buster farmed, worked in the mines at Flin Flon MB, the shipyards in Vancouver during WWII, operated his own boat beachcombing business (retrieval & towing of logs) res Burnaby BC

SELENA ELVA DeWITT

5 IRA GEORGE DeWITT b 05 Mar 1913 Cardale MB (d 19 Nov 1994 at Sardis BC ae 81) res Chilliwack BC. He {m1} 31 Dec 1941 Joan Ann Funnel, b 1922 Brighton Eng div. at Stony Mountain MB. He m2 08 May 1948 Irene Elizabeth McGimpsey b 23 Mar 1920 Winnipeg d/o William McGimpsey & Elizabeth E Pearce. Irene served 3 yrs in the CWAC (Canadian Women's Army Corps) a Sergeant. George farmed in Providence District north of Sandy Lake. He bought Lionel's homestead at tax sale and later bought Maurice's making it a half section 350 acre. He cleared the land and sold the cordwood. He had 150 cords on hand when he enlisted Sept 1939 in the PPCLI (Princess Patricia Canadian Light Infantry) & was overseas by Jan 1940. He served 6 yrs as a Bren gun carrier driver, fought in Sicily & Italy. He returned home in 1945 on long service overseas leave. Demobilized, he worked in a factory a winter, operated heavy road building equipment for his dad, then was a Prison Peace Officer for 31 years & 3 months as a guard (C.X.4) at Manitoba Penitentiary in Stoney Mountain MB until retirement. In 1978 moved to Winnipeg. In 1986 moved to Chilliwack BC close to Agassiz where their son William was employed and near other relatives

IRENE McGIMPSEY m IRA GEORGE DeWITT

6 LILA BELLE DeWITT b 18 Aug 1914 Sandy Lake MB (d 23 Dec 1970 Brandon) graduated as an R.N. worked until fall of 1970. At Brandon she m 20 Aug 1942 Raymond Edward Bulstord Harpham s/o Walter John Harpham from Yorkshire Eng & Alke Jessie Matthews, b 20 Feb 1907 Tisdale SK d Sep 1979 Dauphin MB, both res & bur there. Raymond/Skelly was a CN Railway Construction Foreman.

LILA BELLE DeWITT m RAYMOND HARPHAM

6   VONA EDNA DeWITT b 12 Feb 1923 Sandy Lake, teacher, dressmaker, genealogist, at Brandon MB m 06 Jun 1942 Gilbert Doran Smith s/o Archibald Duncan Smith & Edith May Doran, b 11 Apr 1920 on the farm at Wassewa MB, d 14 May 1989 New Westminster BC. He was a farmer, bee-keeper, musician, then served 3 ½ yrs in the RCAF, Stevedore foreman, long-shoreman on grain, ships tie up & last as a railway car dumper operator loading coal or sulpher into ships at the Port Moody facility, res Coquitlam BC.

Our father, Ira Smith DeWitt, after his mother remarried and lived nearby, was raised by his maternal grandparents Ira Smith Horning & Dorothy Oliphant. After Grade 10 and some Business College education, he went west at about seventeen to help his Uncle Fred on his farm at Newdale MB. He was a farmer, grain buyer elevator operator, had an implement & garage business lost in the 1929 crash. He was a Councilor, then Reeve many years for Harrison Municipality MB & during his term built a small hospital in Sandy Lake. We have a 1922 Council picture. One funny story, when he was elected Reeve he received two votes from the Newdale area, claimed by several relatives & friends.

Ira rented a farm at Cardale MB after his uncle died. He had a threshing outfit with his brother-in-law William Hamilton. We have a picture of it and of his Manitoba Baseball Championship teams for 1906 an 1907. Dad played first base. One year they threshed Uncle Bill's crop first, then it snowed and snowed. Dad never did take off his crop. The man he rented from said he'd give him another chance. After spring planting was done he evicted him. They moved to a vacant log house in Sandy Lake. He herded cattle in Riding Mountain Park, then soon found employment as a Grain Elevator Operater. Dad and the two older boys had homesteads in the district.

Author
VONA EDNA DeWITT m GILBERT DORAN SMITH

By 1923 he again had a theshing outfit with his three sons. By 1930 he operated a sawmill at Providence District north of Sandy Lake first, then, depending on timber licences at, Lake Audy and last at Mafeking MB. As Reeve he oversaw road & bridge building. Later in private business he won the "Good Roads Award" for Manitoba. He served as a J.P. & school trustee.

In a mainly Ukranian District, Ira learned a little of the language & wrote endless business & personal letters free of charge, for any of his constituents asking his help. They called him "Hirry Dewet". As a child the author (Vona) thought everyone must have an "open" back door for people & their kids arriving anytime, always with "You take so & so outside to play". In later years she found it embarrassing to be greeted by people she did not recollect, who certainly knew her name. Ira was always active in politics attending the Liberal Provincial & Federal Conventions. Often a sitting Member or aspiring candidate came calling asking for help or advice on Riding business. Dad once said the total of all his concurrent unpaid public service jobs added up to 73 yrs. There is a recurring DeWitt family theme; the sawmill business & Mayor. Ira belonged to the Rossburn MB Masonic Lodge (fr VEDS and family members).

Gilbert Doran Smith's Parents

EDITH MAY DORAN
b 17 Oct 1880 in Meaford ON
d Aug 1975

married
29 Nov 1905 in Boissevain MB

ARCHIBALD DUNCAN SMITH
b 12 Oct 1875 in Woodville ON
d 24 Oct 1924

BOGARDUS

Leucas deWit

1.1.9.4.3.8.2.5.1 JAMES F BOGARDUS m Leona L Earl
1. EARL FRANCIS BOGARDUS b 28 Jan 1891 Gibson City IL.
2. LLOYD CLARE BOGARDUS b 20 Jul 1894 Milford IL (d 04 Jul 1957 Los Angeles) m Fern ? .
3. CLARENCE EDGAR BOGARDUS b 10 Sep 1896 Milford IL **dy.**
4. HAROLD EDWARD BOGARDUS b 28 Feb 1902 Chicago IL (d 07 May 1982) m1 Leah Newdeck, m2 17 May 1946 Jeanne Tice b 28 Sep 1923 (fr WBB).

BOGARDUS

1.1.9.4.3.8.2.5.2 EDWARD SHERMAN BOGARDUS m Hattie Hope Earl
1. ORVILLE EARL BOGARDUS b 16 Nov 1871 Clinton IL d 06 Aug 1963 (fr WBB).
2. ETHEL HOPE BOGARDUS b 29 Jun 1899 Piper City m 26 Jan 1918 Clyde Payne b 19 May 1894 d 27 Mar 1963.

BOGARDUS

1.1.9.4.3.8.2.5.4 HENRY ORVILLE BOGARDUS m Grace Myrtle Bowen
1. JULE WILLIAM BOGARDUS b 03 Apr 1902 Clinton IL (d 06 Dec 1975) m 06 Mar 1926 Margaret Kline b 06 Sep 1908.
2. HAROLD HENRY BOGARDUS b 16 Jul 1905 **single.**
3. MARGARET LOUISE BOGARDUS b 01 Aug 1914 d 23 Aug 1914 dy (fr WBB).

BOGARDUS

1.1.9.4.3.8.2.5.6 RUSSELL HERMAN BOGARDUS m Beaulah ? .
1. DELMAR BOGARDUS
   m2 Margaret A. McCullough
2. RUSSELL EUGENE BOGARDUS b 22 Sep 1922 Witchita KS m1 Beulah; m2 Betty Womack (fr WBB).

BOGARDUS

1.1.9.4.3.8.2.5.7 PHILLIP LEWIS BOGARDUS m Alberta May Barnett
1. MARGARET JANE BOGARDUS b 29 Jul 1927 Matoon IL m 19 Nov 1950 James W Williams b 11 Sep 1928.
2. LOUISE ALBERTA BOGARDUS b 14 Sep 1928 Clinton IL m 27 Jul 1948 Herman Chumbley b 27 Aug ? .
3. PHYLLIS ROSEMARY BOGARDUS b 25 Oct 1932 Clinton IL m 04 Sep 1954 Robert Williamson.
4. GRACE HARRIET BOGARDUS b 26 Sep 1939.
5. JACQUELINE ELLEN BOGARDUS b 27 Feb 1944 m 22 Aug 1965 Tommie McKibben b 05 Jan 1937.
6. JILL ANN MARIE BOGARDUS b 10 Oct 1945 Clinton IL m 17 May 1965 William Morgan b 25 Apr 1947.
7. LAURA KATHRYN BOGARDUS b 22 Jun 1947 m 24 Oct 1969 Marshall R Grover b 17 Nov 1936 (fr WBB).

BOGARDUS

1.1.9.4.3.8.2.6.2 ARTHUR PHIPPS BOGARDUS m Sarah Ann Wilson
1. FREDERICK WILSON BOGARDUS b 26 Jan 1913 m 24 Jun 1940 Mary Stanley Black b 15 Aug 1915 Vancouver BC. (fr WBB).
2. JEAN ISOBEL BOGARDUS b 05 Aug 1914 Vancouver BC m Howard D Cleveland b 06 Jan 1914 d 29 Sep 1965.

BOGARDUS

1.1.9.4.3.8.2.6.3 FREDERICK FRANCIS BOGARDUS m Maude Hill
1. ART BOGARDUS
2. BETTY BOGARDUS
3. DORIS BOGARDUS (fr WBB)

BOGARDUS

1.1.9.4.3.8.2.6.4 CHARLOTTE BOGARDUS m Harry Grafton Rowe Philip
1. GRAFTON BOGARDUS PHILIP b 20 Jun 1905 Los Angeles CA m 1933 Lois Scranton b 18 Jun 1912 Mendon MO.
2. STEWART PHILIP b 05 Jan 1909 Los Angeles m1 Jane McPhee More d 15 Jan 1972 m2 22 Feb 1973 Ruth A Bruck.
3. ELIZABETH MAE PHILIP b 24 Apr 1912 m1 ? , m2 30 Jun 1950 Robert Dietrich b Berlin 31 Jan 1912 (fr WBB).

CAIN

1.1.9.4.3.8.2.6.5 LENA GERTRUDE BOGARDUS m Charles Walter Cain
1. ELIZABETH CAIN b 24 Feb 1916 Vancouver BC m 20 Oct 1941 Michael A Pollard b 21 Dec 1909 Vancouver, div 20 Jan 1978 Reno NV (fr WBB).

ARNOLD

1.1.9.4.3.8.2.8.3 IDA BOGARDUS m Edward Arnold
1. IRENE AGNES ARNOLD (fr WBB).

MASON

1.1.9.4.3.8.2.8.8 JULIA BOGARDUS m Harry Mason
1. HELEN ELSIE MASON

BOGARDUS

1.1.9.4.3.8.2.8.9 ADORUM BOGARDUS m Thusnelda W Werner
1. THELMA IDA BOGARDUS b 29 Jun 1914 McKinley, Isle of Anes, Cuba m 1936 Maurice K Shepker.

Leucas deWit

2   LILLIAN BEATRICE BOGARDUS b 30 Aug 1916 McKinley d 06/08 Feb 1921.
3   GEORGE DORAM BOGARDUS b 19 Sep 1920 Queenston Heights ON m 03 Jan 1942 Gertrude Reynolds b 1920 Evans Center (?).
4   RUTH THURZA BOGARDUS b 26 Feb 1924 Eden NY m1 28 Sep 1946 Edward H Rice d 1960, m2 17 Feb 1979 Norman F Miller.
5   AMY CONSTANCE BOGARDUS b 08 Apr 1926 Lake View NY m ? Jun 1952 Frank H Wilson b 1923 d 08 Mar 1964 (fr WBB).

DeWITT
1.1.9.4.5.1.2.4.3 JOHN HENRY DeWITT m Ollie Mae Moon

1   OMAR LeROY DeWITT b 30 Dec 1905 Annawan IL, at Grand Rapids MI m1 09 Sep 1928 Hazel Phillips, div 20 Jan 1946. At Chicago IL he m2 07 Feb 1948 Dorothy (Kolanowski) Dunham b 04 Sep 1918. Dorothy had m1at Harlingten TX 13 Nov 1943 Playford W. Dunham b 10 Aug 1914, div. In retirement Omar's hobby was acting as a magician. He was an Engineer working in many overseas projects.
2   IRA ALLISON DeWITT b 20 Nov 1907 Annawan IL m 31 Dec 1941 Jane Schmiedeknecht, div. He m 2 at Anderson IN 25 Aug 1947 Mildred Cook.
3   MARGARET ELAINE DeWITT b 08 Nov 1909 Annawan IL, at Muskegan MI m 05 Mar 1928 Arthur Brown.
4   FLORA LOUISE DeWITT b 07 Aug 1911 Hancock MN, at Michigan City IN m 19 Feb 1937 Henry Baasch.
5   ALICE MILDRED DeWITT b 11 Oct 1913 Hancock MN, at Whitehall MI m Dale Brown.
6   EDITH MARY DeWITT b 06 Dec 1915 Whitehall MI, at Falmouth MA m 05 Oct 1942 Otto Anderson.
7   JAMES OSCAR DeWITT b 11 Jul 1920 Whitehall MI (d 04 Jul 1980 at Stevenville MI). At Elkhart IN he m 03 Oct 1948 Doris Holdeman (all fr OLD).
8   FRANCES RUTH DeWITT b 19 Sep 1922 Whitehall MI, at Waskegan IL m 17 Feb 1951 Herman Hendricks.

LOW/LOWE
1.1.9.4.8.8.6.1.1 CHARK ARMSTRONG/CHARLES A LOW/LOWE m Anne Lulu/Nellie Bland

1   HARRY DELBERT LOWE b 27 Jul 1893 Millcreek Twp Union Co OH (Taylor Twp res of parents) & (d 26 Jun 1970 Franklin Twp) m Marie Kramer.
2   MAUDE MARIE LOWE b 02 Aug 1898 Union Co (d 29 Jan 1966 Van Nuys, LA CA) m 23 Jun 1921 Lewis Lorain Miller s/o Samuel Albert Miller & Charlotte Belle Mitsch, b 07 Jan 1894 Goshen, Crampaign OH d 17 Mar 1939 both bur Ferncliff Cem Springfield (fr LBM research tbstns, Lewis' Will d cert, Maude's d.cert, m notice, b certs). Chn b Springfield Twp, Clark Co OH.
3   ETHEL MAE LOWE b 31 Oct 1900 Coffee (near Manchester) IN (d 29 Jan 1966 Springfield Twp Clark Co OH) m 22 Sep 1924 William Rheam Shroades (fr MLMB).

GENERATION 10

DEDRICK

1.1.9.4.1.2.5.2.1.1 FRANCIS VERNON DEDRICK m Phyllis Lucille Curtis
1. BARBARA DEDRICK m Orville Hindman.
2. LOIS DEDRICK m Eric Ridgen (fr FVD).

m2 Priscilla Spera

SMITHSON/STEPHENS

1.1.9.4.1.2.5.2.1.2 FLORENCE MAY DEDRICK m1 Charles Cecil Smithson
1. LENORE R SMITHSON m Gordon D Wallace.
2. JOHN SMITHSON m Marie Jewell, John's twin.
3. JOAN M SMITHSON m Edgar Woodger.
4. DONALD CECIL SMITHSON m1 Thelma Ferris. He m2 Mrs Wilma Teal.
5. GORDON DOUGLAS SMITHSON b 27 Apr 1933 m 15 Sep 1956 Elizabeth Jean Findlay.
6. YVONNE A SMITHSON m1 Don Joseph. She m2 Keith Davies.

m2 Calvin Stephens

7. KATHERINE STEPHENS m Robert Hogan (FVD).

PETTIT

1.1.9.4.2.1.2.3.4.1 ELSIE DeWITT NORTON m John Read Pettit
1. MARY DeWITT PETTIT b 01 Jan 1908 (P-DR:294).

HOLSMAN

1.1.9.4.2.1.2.3.4.3 KATHARINE DeWITT LEARNED NORTON m Gerald Holsman
1. MARY MARKOE HOLSMAN b 21 Jun 1912 (fr PDR).

PELTZ

1.1.9.4.2.1.2.5.3.1 WILLIAM L PELTZ m Katherine Hun
1. CAROLINE PELTZ m Edwin G Goodwin M.D. both of Albany, had three sons.
2. WILLIAM LEARNED PELTZ M.D. of Philadelphia PA, m Margaret Ruth Adams, had two sons.
3. MARY LEARNED PELTZ of NYC m Theodore B Russell M.D. of NYC, had 3 daus.
4. PHILIP PELTZ of Kenwood Mills near Albany NY m Elizabeth Davenport Hooper had 1 son. (P-DR:164)

PELTZ

1.1.9.4.2.1.2.5.3.2 JOHN DeWITT PELTZ m Mary Ellis Opdydke
1. JOHN DeWITT PELTZ Jr student at Yale in 1948.
2. HENRY STEVENSON PELTZ student at Harvard in 1848 & twin.
3. MARY ELLIS PELTZ graduated Vassar 1948 twin of Henry (all P-DR:164).

DUNN

1.1.9.4.2.1.2.7.1.1. ELIOT DeWITT DUNN m Rhoda Deas
1. ALLEINE DUNN grad of New Jersey Teacher's Coll m Roy E Jordan Jr. (P-DR:300)
2. SHIRLEY DUNN grad of Cedarcrest, Allenhurst PA; degree in Biological Chemistry, lived at her father's home (1948).

LENT

1.1.9.4.2.1.2.7.5.1 JOHN DeWITT LENT m Ruth Zubord
1. JOHN LENT Jr b 1916 attended Rose Polytechnic Inst d 1937 **single**.

m2 1920 Mildred Nadler

2. FREDERICK R LENT attended Dartmouth Coll; in 1948 Office Mgr of W J Holliday & CO Steel Manufacturers, Hammond IN, Lt US Naval Reserve WWII.
3. MARY R LENT, Wellsley Coll, m George V Butler.
4. MARJORIE R LENT, Wellsley Coll, m Sterling Garrard.
5. NANCY R LENT, Conneticut Coll for Women, kindergarten teacher.
6. JANE R LENT, Conneticut Coll for Women (P-DR:302).

LEWIS

1.1.9.4.2.1.2.7.5.2 ROSE DeWITT m Edmund V Lewis
1. KATHARINE DeWITT LEWIS grad Barnard Coll, M.A. Columbia U teacher of Music.
2. BARBARA LEWIS grad Barnard Coll also Music Dept Columbia U m Wesley Depp (all P-DR:302).

LEO

1.1.9.4.2.1.2.7.5.3 CHARLOTTE ELIOT LENT m Norton Blackstone Leo
1. CHARLOTTE ELIOT LEO b 02 Jan 1917 m David Henkel, Attorney-at-law & Junior Partner at Sullivan & Cromwell NYC in 1948.
2. NORTON BLACKSTONE LEO Jr grad from Princeton, single in 1948. He was in the 1st Light Infantry in the Philippines in WW11; then with Duane Jones Advertising. He lived with his mother (all P-DR:303).

Leucas deWit

STAHL/ADAMS
1.1.9.4.2.1.2.7.5.4 HARRIET DeWITT LENT m1 David Vinton Stahl
1. VIRGINIA LEE STAHL b 13 Jul 1916 m 1941 Robert Barry.
2. JANE VINTON STAHL b 08 Apr 1918 grad Brown U of 1938.
3. MARGERY DeWITT STAHL b 20 Mar 1920 grad Brown U of 1942 m David William Towler grad Brown U of 1942.
m2 1929 John Darrow Adams
4. JOHN DARROW ADAMS Jr b 16 Jul 1930 (all P-DR:303).

LENT
1.1.9.4.2.1.2.7.5.5 THEODORE DeWITT LENT m Lillian Rosine
1. THEODORE DeWITT LENT Jr b 06 Feb 1917 grad Perdue U 1939, Mechanical Engineer; Lt US Naval Reserve WWII, in 1948 Manager Omaha Branch Office of Armstrong Cork CO (P-DF:303).

DeWITT
1.1.9.4.2.1.2.7.7.2 JOHN DeWITT m1 Dorothy Courtney Lee
1. JOHN LEE DeWITT b 02 Nov 1919 NYC, at Brown U in 1938 then Columbia U; military service WWII.
2. THEODORE ABBOT DeWITT b 29 Oct 1921 NYC. He attended Lincoln High School NYC, Brown U 1940, Montana State Coll 1941 & Naval Air Service WWII.
- DOREE DeWITT stepdau of Dorothy Courtney Lee w/o Jefferson Hayes Davis, only grson/o President Jefferson Davis of the Confederate States of America.
m2 his cousin Dorothy Peck (all P-DR:304).

THOMIS
1.1.9.4.2.1.2.7.8.2 CHARLOTTE DeWITT m Wayne Thomis
1. WENDY THOMIS
2. HOLLY THOMIS
3. DAVID THOMIS
4. MARC THOMAS b 1948 (all P-DR:305).

DeWITT
1.1.9.4.2.1.2.7.8.3 JOHN DeWITT m Marjorie Boight
1. ABIGAIL DeWITT b 1941 (all P-DR:305).

DeWITT
1.1.9.4.2.1.2.7.8.4 THOMAS HOWLAND DeWITT m Ann Caroline Prior
1. RUTH ANN DeWITT b 1944.
2. THOMAS BURTON DeWITT b 1946 (P-DR:305).

BOOTEN
1.1.9.4.2.1.2.10.1.2 GERTRUDE VEDDER VERMULYE m Col John Booten
1. JOHN GRIFFIN BOOTEN Jr b 06 Jun 1913 NYC, U/o PA (Delta Phi) grad Massachusetts Institute of Technology 1937, m 1944 Catharine Anne Kage at Troy NY.
2. MARY VERMILYE BOOTEN b 23 Jul 1916 at West Point, at Fort Sam Huston TX m 02 Oct 1941 William Kent Titherington s/o Richard H Titherington (all P-DR:305).

HUTCHINGS
1.1.9.4.2.1.2.10.2.1 DeWITT VERMILYE HUTCHINGS m Allis Hardenburg Miller
1. FRANK MILLER HUTCHINGS b 29 Jun 1913 (C.W.O. in WW II).
2. ISABELLE VERMILYE HUTCHINGS b 09 Aug 1915 (AB U of Cal. at Los Angeles 1937).
3. HELEN HARDENBURGH HUTCHINGS b 13 Dec 1918 (AB U of Cal. At Berkley) m 14 Jun 1938 Charles H Watson b 28 Aug 1914, BA Georgetown U. 1938, Lt. US Naval Reserve WW II (all P-DR:310/11).

OVERBAGH
1.1.9.4.2.2.1.1.4.1 RICHARD BRINDLEY OVERBAGH m Isabel Freligh
1. GERTRUDE OVERBAGH b 04 Aug 1885 m Frank Emerson Fuller.
2. RICHARD FRELIGH OVERBAGH b 10 Sep 1887 m Catherine Mary Cantlin.
3. ISABEL OVERBAGH b 11 Nov 1889.
4. JOHN CALDWELL OVERBAGH b 24 Feb 1891 m Dorothy Adelaide Snyder.
5. WILLIAM HOYT OVERBAGH b 24 Feb 1891 Saugerties NY (d 1939) m 1916 Clarissa Agnes Pilgrim b 1892 d 1940 Saugerties d/o J G Pilgrim & Clara A Schmager (RDCFU).

PUTMAN
1.1.9.4.3.1.5.2.1.1 AMELIA E LAMBERT m J Seymour Putman
1. EVELYN PUTMAN b 1920 m ? Alkerton res Oshawa ON (fr the Museum, Picton ON).

DeWITT
1.1.9.4.3.1.5.3.2.2 WILLIAM JOHN DeWITT m1 Martha Whitehouse
1. CARROLL FLEMING DeWITT b 08 Feb 1913 Detroit, Wayne Co MI, at Metropolitan Meth CH, Detroit MI m 29 Jun 1935 Lillian Theresa Ferns d/o James Ferns Sr & Theresa McGlone, b 14 Nov 1915 bp 28 Nov 1915 St Leo's CH Detroit

d 24 Oct 1961 Brockhaven Memorial Hospital E Patchoque NY bur 27 Oct 1961 St Ann's Cem, Sayville NY. He was Manufacturing Engineer, Ford Motor Company at Detroit for 15 yrs, Wright Aeronautical Division of Curtis-Wright Corp, Woodbridge NJ for 10 yrs & at Grumman Aerospace Corp, Bethpage, LI NY for 20 yrs, Lived Oakdale LI, retired to Sarasota FL (all fr CFD, m2 16 Sep 1966 Mrs Mary Aurora (Scandaliato) Pararatto, Sayville NY; her chn Rosemary Pararatto b 19 Aug 1953 Rockville Center NY & Joseph Paparazzo b 04 Sep 1955 Queens NY (fr CFD)
m2 16 Mar 1920 Hulda Victoria Whitehouse
2   ALICE MAE DeWITT b 06 Jan 1926 Highland Park MI, m 07 Jun 1947 John Earl Conley b 07 Jan 1926, div 28 Mar 1980. Alice lived in Las Vegas NV worked at the Flamingo Hilton Hotel (LI is Long Island).

DeWITT
1.1.9.4.3.1.5.3.2.3 ROY DeWITT m Emma Jacobs
1   HILDA MAE DeWITT b 17 Sep 1909 Detroit, m 17 Nov 1928 Joseph Leonard Bourget res on Silver Lake Road in Fenron MI.
2   LAWRENCE IRA DeWITT b 18 Aug 1910 Gaines MI (d 18 May 1975 Redford Twp MI bur Oakwood Cem Gaines) m1 Olive Bell, no chn (Olive had a dau by a previous m, a Mrs Hybernia Jackson). Lawrence m2 Mary Carbone b 02 Jul 1911 Crabtree PA, 3 chn, div ? Feb 1966. He m3 Charlotte Marie Chaltron b 03 Aug 1926 Royal Oak MI who had 3 ch David, Claudia, Douglas Taylor. She & Lawrence had **no chn** (fr CFD).

MELLMAN
1.1.9.4.3.1.5.3.2.4 JEANETTE MAY/NETTIE DeWITT m Charles Philip Mellman
1   MARY KATHERINE MELLMAN b 21 Dec 1917 Detroit (d there 26 Mar 1949 bur Oakwood Cem) m1 Walter Siebert, div. He m2 Don Esterline. She had **no chn**.
2   ELEANOR MELLMAN b 25 Dec 1918 Detroit, MI m1 07 Aug 1938 Harry Ralpheimer Champion b 30 Oct 1911 d 09 Oct 1974 Blodgett Hospital East Grand Rapids MI, bur Oakwood Cem. Gaines MI. He m3 Alfred Ribone, div **no chn.**
3   MILICENT JEAN MELLMAN b 18 Feb 1928 Detroit (d 06 Jul 1978 North Detroit bur Oakwood Cem) m 04 Jun 1948 Robert Courtland Frank Learst called Lefty or Bob, b 26 Jun 1926 (CFD).

MacMICHAEL
1.1.9.4.3.3.1.8.1.1 ESTELLA MAUD BAILEY m John F R MacMichael
1   HELEN GLADYS MacMICHAEL b 16 Jan 1899 Harcourt NB res with sis, **single**.
2   FRANK ROBERTSON MacMICHAEL b 22 Nov 1903 Canan NB (d 05 Nov 1981 ae 77 Moncton NB) at Moncton. He m1 05 Oct 1925 Bernice Ruth McCowan d/o Robert H McCowan & Margaret Dempsey, b 09 Jul 1901 Sydney NS d 08 Jan 1963 Moncton ae 61 bur Elmwood Cem Moncton. He m2 Theora Getson b 12 Jul 1901 Dorchester NB.
3   RALPH BAILEY MacMICHAEL b 29 Oct 1907 Boistown NB, at Moncton m 22 Jun 1934 Marion Almira Goodwin, b 21 Dec 1906 d/o Henry K Goodwin & Melinda Taylor
4   MARY GERALDINE JUANITA MacMICHAEL b 16 Apr 1910 Rogersville NB m 14 Jun 1930 Ronald McDonald Currie, b 24 Jun 1910 d ? Feb 1972 div 1948 s/o Henry Currie & Maud Laughlin (fr MAH, SCBC).

BAILEY
1.1.9.4.3.3.1.8.1.3 BENJAMIN STUDLEY BAILEY m Florence Amelia Passmore
1   ETHEL FLORENCE BAILEY b 19 Jan 1907 Winnipeg MB (d 30 Apr 1969 Vancouver BC ae 62) m 15 Aug 1936 Rex Vivian Broughten, Doctor of Education UBC, d/o Henry Thomas Broughton & Annie Wilkinson, b 20 Aug 1906 Bletchley Eng d 15 Oct 1966 Vancouver BC bur Ocean View Cem Burnaby BC, **no chn**.
2   HAROLD BENJAMIN BAILEY b 21 Jul 1908 Gladstone MB (d 08 Nov 1962 Toronto ON ae 54 of TB) m ? , wf d one year later of TB (fr MAH, SCBC).

BAILEY
1.1.9.4.3.3.1.8.1.5 LESLIE OSBORNE BAILEY m Eva May Fisher
1   LESLIE ALEXANDER BAILEY b 28 Feb 1907 Winnipeg (d there 27 Mar 1972) m 20 Apr 1935 Jessie Lenore Reynolds b 11 Sep 1909 Rosetown SK (fr MAH; SCBG).
2   EVELYN MARY BAILEY b 25 Aug 1809 Winnipeg m 30 Jun 1932 Stanley George Thompson s/o Albert Martin James Thompson & Ada Grace Baker, b 02 Nov 1904 London Eng.
3   MABEL OSBORNE BAILEY b 11 Nov 1914 Winnipeg **single** (fr MAH,SCBG).

ECKMAN
1.1.9.4.3.3.1.8.1.7 DOROTHY INEZ BAILEY m Anthony Philip Eckman
1   LOUIS PHILIP ECKMAN b 09 Apr 1918 Winnipeg, Geologist, at Miami Beach (must be FL not Miami MB) m 26 Nov 1954 Marjorie Ann Briggs b 10 May 1930 Rockville Center NY (fr MAH, SCBG).

FAREWELL/McDOWELL
1.1.9.4.3.3.1.8.1.9 IDA PEARL BAILEY m Maurice Edmund Farewell
1   LORRAINE HANNAY FAREWELL b 31 Oct 1916 Winnipeg at The Pas MB m 14 Aug 1936 Leonard Stanley Fraser b 06 May 1911 The Pas MB s/o Albert Fraser & Lily Chambers
    m2 Fredrick Alexander McDowell
2   LESLIE THOMAS McDOWELL b 23 Dec 1921 Winnipeg m there 14 Jul 1942 Dorothy Stuart Jackson, b 30 Dec 1919 d/o William James Jackson & Cecile May Wood.

BAILEY

1.1.9.4.3.3.1.8.1.10 EWART GLADSTONE BAILEY m Augusta Daisy Olive Bennett
1. SHIRLEY CLAIRE BAILEY b 17 Aug 1923 Winnipeg m 14 May 1948 Robert Edward Goatcher, Systems Analyst, now retired res Naniamo BC, s/o Perry George Goatcher & Daisy Ellen Birch, b 11 Aug 1923 Winnipeg.
2. MARY CADENCE BAILEY b 30 Dec 1928 Brandon m 26 Jun 1954 William Garth Morris b 06 Jun 1930 Saskatoon SK.
3. KENNETH REX BAILEY b 19 Jan 1932 Winnipeg, at Toronto ON m 15 Sep 1962 Judith Rosemary Wood b 12 Mar 1940 div ? Oct 1972; m2 07 Jul 1972 Nadya Koshyishyn at Winnipeg MB (all SCBG).

RICHARDSON/CRAWFORD

1.1.9.4.3.3.3.2.1.1 EFFIE B SMART m1 Robert Richardson
1. ELSIE RICHARDSON
2. IRENE RICHARDSON

m2 Willis Crawford
3. AMY CRAWFORD (all fr BVEH, USA)

SMART

1.1.9.4.3.3.3.2.1.2 A T L SMART m1 Della McCutcheon
1. DONALD SMART
2. EMMA SMART

m2 Ida Bates Agrille (fr BBVH, USA)

STYLES

1.1.9.4.3.3.3.2.1.3 ESTELLE E SMART m Currie Styles
1. LAUREN STYLES m ? 2 chn.
2. RUTH STYLES (fr BBVH, USA)

HASKELL

1.1.9.4.3.3.3.2.1.6 PHOEBE MAE SMART m Herman Adelbert Haskell
1. EDYTHE FRANCES HASKELL b 03 Sep 1904 ME m1 Umberto Arias, m2 John Bast, m3 A Levesque.
2. HERMAN MERVIN HASKELL b 27 May 1906 Dexter ME (d 10 Aug 1970) m1 Estelle Gilbert; m2 Helen Clark.
3. UNA MAE HASKELL b 03 Jun 1908 Bath ME m Paul Nason.
4. EMMA BELLE HASKELL b 28 Mar 1912 Derby ME (d ? Apr 1986 Old Orchard Beach ME) at Portland ME m Payson Haley.
5. RALPH STILLMAN HASKELL b 26 Feb 1914 Milo Junction ME at Bath ME, m1 12 Apr 1936 Amos Burrell Ellis b 26 Oct 1915 Coplin Plantation ME d/o Everett Cornelius Ellis & Rena Burrell. At Wilton Town NY he m2 01 Jan 1978 Mrs Barbara (Brown) Vaughan b 18 Jun 1930 Boston MA d/o Chester & Mildred Skooj.
6. ELWYN LENORE HASKELL b 27 Oct 1916 Dexter ME m1Verna d; 2 step-chn. He m2 Audette Oudette
7. NEIL DOW SMART HASKELL b 16 Dec 1921 Dexter ME m1 07 Apr 1945 Mrs Arleen (Rockwood) Williams. <u>William Williams</u> stepson, Neil m2 Mar 1979 Mrs Arlene (Taggert) Cote. Elwyn & Neil were in the Services in WWII. (all fr BBVH)

STYLES

1.1.9.4.3.3.3.2.1.7 IDA FRANCES SMART m Lorenzo Stiles
1. EVELYN STILES
2. LLEWELLYN STILES
3. ELEANOR STILES
4. LORENZO STILES
5. EMMA STILES (fr BBVH).

SMITH

1.1.9.4.3.3.4.1.1.2 CLARISSA SCOTT {m} <u>1.1.9.4.3.3.5.3.3</u> Elgan Otis Smith
Children are with their father' underlined number Generation 9.

SMITH

1.1.9.4.3.3.4.1.1.3 DELILAH SCOTT {m} <u>1.1.9.4.3.3.5.3.2</u> David O Smith
Children are with their father's underlined number Generation 9.

SCOTT

1.1.9.4.3.3.4.1.1.7 WINSLOW SCOTT {m} <u>1.1.9.4.3.3.5.4.7</u> Alice Adelia Wooden
Childre are with their mother's underlined number Generation 9.

SCOTT

1.1.9.4.3.3.4.1.1.11 FRANK G SCOTT m Sadie Stephens
1. MYRTLE SCOTT b 1905 d 1928 **single**.

---

3. LYALL THOMAS McDOWELL b 14 Jun 1934 Winnipeg, at Burnaby m 29 Dec 1955 Shirley Ann Nyberg d/o Gunnar Nyberg & Effie Steeves, b 10 Jun 1936 Vancouver chn b Burnaby BC (fr MAH, SCBG).

McCRACKEN
1.1.9.4.3.3.4.1.1.12 ELIZABETH/BESS SCOTT m Stanley McCracken
1. ALLEN G McCRACKEN b 1906 (d 08 Jun 1980) Fredericton Jct NB, m 1933 H Arleen Segee d/o Charles Segee, Hattie Patchell (alive 2000) chn b Fredericton Jct (fr SDVSW).
2. HOWARD S McCRACKEN b 1907 (d 1962 of cancer) m Helen Smith of Central Blissville, **no chn**
3. BERTHA McCRACKEN b 1909 Fredericton Jct NB at St Paul's CH Fredericton NB, a schoolteacher, m Bortie/Bertie Neilsen b (d 1985) of Cardiff, Wales s/o a Danish Sea Captain. He came to Canada in the 1920s to New Denmark NB, then was employed as a chauffeur by the Fraser's Lumber Company in Plaster Rock NB. He was musician & the 4 chn took piano lessons also playing other instruments. They res Fredericton NB.
4. HARRY McCRACKEN b 1911 d 1969 of cancer, **single**.
5. ROY McCRACKEN b 1912 Fredericton Jct NB m Marion Price b French Lake NB in 1982 d 23 Jul 1999 dau of Hardy & Amy (Mersereau). Marion Price res White's Cove NB.
6. ALMA ELIZABETH McCRACKEN b 15 May 1914 d 1999 a schoolteacher, m Paul Wade b 20 Oct 1913 of Penniac NB. Paul d 26 Oct 1999 ae 83. He was a RCAF Veteran, then a NB Civil Servant until retirement (fr BMN).

DeWITT
1.1.9.4.3.3.4.1.4.1 COLEMAN/COLBY DeWITT m Clara Lindsay
1. ALVIN DeWITT b 1919 (d at Lower St. NB. In the Daily Gleaner 13 May 2002) m Evelyn N Smith, she predeased him.
2. CHARLIE DeWITT
3. MYRNA DeWITT m ? Waddington. Their chn were Holly, Bradley, Andrew, Heather.

DeWITT
1.1.9.4.3.3.4.1.7.1 PARKER DeWITT m Mazzie Harris
1. BURTON DeWITT b 16 Apr 1911 res Cartleton Co NB, m1 Inez Gertrude Ervine b 12 Jun 1918 d 1956 cancer of the liver. He m2 Pearl Giberson (info fr dau Sheila DeWitt Gillie, KLAD).
2. VERNON DeWITT b 21 Mar 1913 m Ella Belyea **no chn.**
3. JOSEPHINE/JOSIE DeWITT b 03 Jul 1915 m Arthur Johnson.
4. LEITHA/LETHA DeWITT b 10 Sep 1919 m1 Vincent Payne. He m2 Stewart MacLellan.
5. EUNICE DeWITT drowned **dy.**
6. IDELLA DeWITT b 08 May 1924 m Holland Taylor (info fr dau Sheila DeWitt Gillie to KLAD).

BURLOCK
1.1.9.4.3.3.4.1.7.3 JENNIE DeWITT m Carleton Burlock
1. HILMAN BURLOCK
2. LAURENCE BURLOCK
3. LLEWELLYN BURLOCK
4. HARMON BURLOCK (fr KLAD).

MERSEREAU
1.1.9.4.3.3.4.1.7.4 ANGELINE DeWITT m Arthur Mersereau
1. MILES MERSEREAU
2. MAY MERSEREAU
3. RUTH MERSEREAU
4. ROY MERSEEAU (fr KLAD).

KIRKPATRICK
1.1.9.4.3.3.4.1.7.5 DELILAH EUNICE DeWITT m David Kirkpatrick
1. MARGARET KIRKPATRICK m Ernest Kirkpatrick s/o Marshall Kirkpatrick; res Hoyt NB 2 dau.
2. MAY KIRKPATRICK m Lewis Clifford **no chn.**
3. EDNA KIRKPATRICK res Hoyt in 1982 still living 2000, m Parker Graham d before 1980.
4. RAYMOND KIRKPATRICK m Edna McCracken.
5. GRANT KIRKPATRICK b 1914 (d 1960 bur United CH Cem Hoyt NB) res Juvenile NB. He m Mildred Marie Graham res Juvenile NB. She m2 David MacGougan res in Hoyt
6. ALLISON KIRKPATRICK (d 1970's) m Florence Kirkpatrick d/o Silas Kirkpatrick & Mary Hoyt, b Wirral NB alive in 1982 res Hoyt.
7. VIDA EVELYN KIRKPATRICK b 1917 d 1926 ae 08-06-00 **dy.**
8. LIMAN KIRKPATRICK b 1912 **dy** (fr KLAD).

BRIGGS
1.1.9.4.3.3.4.1.8.1 PHOEBE DeWITT m Lewis Briggs
1. EVELYN BRIGGS m ? , son a druggist, dau a M.D. both in Halifax NS.
2. LEONA BRIGGS
3. EUGENE BRIGGS d 1981 in a farm accident.
4. FAY BRIGGS drowned **dy** (fr KLAD).

MALLORY

1.1.9.4.3.3.4.3.2.1 MAY DeWITT m Enrique Mallory

1. LESTER DeWITT MALLORY b 21 Apr 1904 Houlton ME (d June 1994 in Forest Lake CA.) m1 Nov 1930 Crystal Smith, of Vancouver BC, div 1937. He m2 21 Feb 1946 Eleanor Struck b 1913 d 11 Dec 1996 Forest Lake CA. The story of Lester's life and career as an Ambassador in the USA Foreign Service is after the last chapter of this book.
2. DONALD PLUMMER MALLORY b 23 Mar 1916 at Baker OR, m June McAllister Mallory.

Ambassador Lester DeWitt Mallory
1904 - 1994

CHRISTMAS LETTER WRITTEN BY ELEANOR MALLORY IN DECEMBER 1994
INCLUDING NEWS OF LESTER DeWITT MALLORY'S DEATH

Dear Friends of the Mallory family

This holiday letter brings with it our best wishes for the season. This year brought dramatic changes to our family. Soon after we moved, Les passed away. Now my vision is failing (lost an eye to a test procedure), so our son Les Jr. is 'picking up the pen' on my behalf.

Actually, we are relying on today's 'information highway', a computer. No matter how many times he explains it to me, I still do not understand how the computer works, and at my age why bother?

About this time last year, we left our lovely home in Leisure World for what I now call the 'last stop hotel'. The adjustment has not been an easy one. Nothing compares to the privacy and 'freedom' of your own home. We moved into a community called Freedom Village.

You know the type of place - three floors of apartments with halls wide enough for wheel chair races to the communal dining hall. We even have nurses to referee. By the time I get into a wheel chair I do not expect to have the energy to race. But, at least I do not have to worry about preparing meals. At the 'Chez Bland' dining hall, they cater to our every appetite. No spicy enchiladas, asada or stuffed grape leaves here. We are served only the best 'dormitory food' for my age group.

When we moved here last December, Les and I were relieved to be free of the responsibility of keeping up 'the old homestead'. After living all over the world, we knew how to settle into new surroundings with a minimum of fuss.

Then sadly, Les had to move on. In June he died of a heart attack. The first put him in the hospital and the second took him away. Fortunately Les Jr. came from Houston in time to be with him for several days. He suffered no pain and was very alert in the hospital.

Les put in a good strong 90 years. I have to admit that he was mentally stronger at 90 than a great many are at 65. He kept busy to the day he left for the hospital. In Intensive Care he would ask daily for an update on the world and domestic news. When for the third day in a row Les Jr. told him the only news coverage was that of the O.J. Simpson affair all he said was "Aah Nuts!"

Always an avid hobbyist, Les had again found a new interest. He was becoming a stock market Analyst and playing the small issues. Now that he is gone, I continue to receive piles of mail every week.

For those of you who heard about Les' death and wrote, we thank you. For those of you who are receiving the news for the first time, I apologize for not writing sooner.

Many of you in the Diplomatic Corps made contributions to the DACOR fund, and we thank you. Others wished to send something but at the time we did not know what to suggest. Now Les Jr. is setting up a scholarship fund for budding horticultural students at the University of British Columbia School of Agriculture. Those of you who knew Les before he became a Foreign Service officer may recall that he began his career in public service with the U.S. Department of Agriculture.

We certainly miss that New Englander turned internationalist. His subtle, dry wit always made us think twice before actually laughing. Come to think of it perhaps that quality made him a successful diplomat during some trying times.

Les was an excellent husband and father as well as friend. Those of you who enjoyed his friendship, also knew that special side of him. At his 90th birthday party Les Jr. made a toast which covered it all - "Thank you, for you have indeed made a contribution".

This Christmas Les Jr. will take time from his fledgling environmental company (Serengeti International) based in Houston to join me in California. Also joining us is my remaining sister Carmen, from Mexico City. To say the least, at this age we tend to lose a few every year. But one can never take away the memories. Oh yes, those were truly some very good times we lived through.

All the best to you, your families, your pets and your friends. May this be an enjoyable Christmas and a Happy New Year.

Hasta Luego,

ELEANOR MALLORY

OBITUARY OF ELEANOR M. MALLORY

Eleanor M. Mallory, 83 passed away December 11, 1996 at her home at Freedom Village in Lake Forest, CA.

Born in Mexico City, she grew up in Germany and Mexico, the daughter of Gustavo Struck and Maria Elena Bulnes. Her grandfather, Francisco Bulnes, married to Maria Teresa Irigoyen, was instrumental in setting policy for the Mexican government during the era of Porfirio Diaz.

In 1946 she married Lester D. Mallory, a U.S. Foreign Service officer who had been stationed in Mexico. After her marriage to the career diplomat, she accompanied him on his assignments to Cuba, Argentina, Jordan, Guatemala and Washington, D.C. Ambassador and Mrs. Mallory retired to Guadalajara, Mexico before returning to the United States to live in southern California.

Mrs. Mallory was an accomplished artist having exhibited her work in several countries. She is featured in the book "The Age of Grandeur and a Woman Who Lived It" by artist Evelyn Metzger.

Interment will be at the Rock Creek Cemetery, Foreign Service section, in Washington, District of Columbia.

Mrs. Mallory is survived by her son Lester D. Mallory, Jr. of Houston, Texas and her sister Carmen Struck de Ollivier of Mexico City.

OBITUARY OF JUNE LAVONA MALLORY

June Lavona Mallory, July 17, 1918 - January 1, 1997

Born to Ida and Walter McAllister of Buena, Washington, June came to Okanagan Falls with her family in 1925, where her father farmed the Matheson ranch.

June attended school in Okanagan Falls and formed many lasting friendships. She spoke fondly of her school days and the antics of her classmates.

In 1935 she married her husband of 53 years, Donald 'Buster' Mallory.

Moving to the United States in 1940 and after brief periods in Kelso and Yakima, Washington they moved to Ellisforde, Washington where they farmed, trained and raced thoroughbred horses for 15 years.

Okanagan Falls was always a special place for Bus and June and they returned in 1957.

The coffee pot was always full, ready for whoever dropped in. She was an avid reader with a keen interest in public affairs and she enjoyed camping, birds and animals.

Predeceased by her husband Buster in 1988. Ever to be remembered by her children, Lester (Margaret) of Summerland, Sharon (Tony) Thompson of Okanagan Falls, Donald 'Lucky' (Laura) of Okanagan Falls, twelve grandchildren and six great grandchildren, three siblings, Evelyn Keefe of Okanagan Falls, Norma Barrick of Olympia, Washington, four nephews and two nieces.

Goodbye Mum, find Daddy, put the coffee on, work on the ultimate crossword and enjoy your eternal rest.

No Service by her request.

SMITH

1.1.9.4.3.3.4.3.3.1 & 1.1.9.4.3.3.5.2.2.1 FRANK ELWOOD SMITH m Della Gartley
1   CLAYTON SMITH (fr LDM).

BAILEY

1.1.9.4.3.3.4.4.2.3 WILLIAM BAILEY m Alice Bell
1   JAMES BAILEY m Dorothy Keith (fr LDM).

HANSON

1.1.9.4.3.3.4.4.3.1 HAZEL DeWITT m John Hanson
1   STELLA HANSON b Carleton Co NB; m Lewis Cooper.
2   JOHN HANSON m Luella Glidden.
3   MARY HANSON b Carleton Co NB; m Nelson Beaulieu.
4   FRED HANSON m ? Shaw.
5   SHIRLEY HANSON m Thomas Lynch.
6   ROGER HANSON m Patsey ? .
7   GLADYS HANSON b Carleton Co NB; m Charles Hafford.
8   HAROLD HANSON b Carleton Co NB; m Rose Parks.
9   PAULENE HANSON b Carleton Co NB; m Elwood Glidden (fr LDM).

DeWITT

1.1.9.4.3.3.4.4.3.2 GEORGE DeWITT m1 ? Nason
1   ROY NASON DeWITT b 1905 m Eleanor DeWitt.
   m2 Ora O'Brien
2   JAMES DeWITT
3   FREDERICK DeWITT (fr LMD).

DeWITT

1.1.9.4.3.3.4.4.3.3 STANLEY DeWITT m1 Gertie Crane
1   MILDRED DeWITT
2   MADELINE DeWITT m ? Folkins.

Leucas deWit

3   LUKE DeWITT
     m2 Ella McKay
4   THOMAS DeWITT m Ella McKay.
5   EDWARD DeWITT
6   JOYCE DeWITT m ? Atherton (fr LDM).

SMITH

1.1.9.4.3.3.4.4.3.4 LAURA DeWITT m Perley Smith
1   HELEN SMITH m Murray Caddie.
2   ALICE SMITH m Wilfred Webb.
3   LEWIS SMITH m ? Melvin.
4   RONALD SMITH m Gwen Scribber (fr LDM).

CLUFF

1.1.9.4.3.3.4.4.3.5 MATILDA DeWITT m Roy Cluff
1   MARION CLUFF m Raymond Martin.
2   J EDWARD CLUFF m Lina Lowell.
3   LeROY FREDERICK CLUFF m Leila Miller.
4   JOYCE CLUFF m Everett Beals (fr LDM).

DeWITT

1.1.9.4.3.3.4.4.3.6 BENJAMIN DeWITT m Grace Boone
1   BESSIE HAZEL DeWITT m Arnold McDonald.
2   CARL DeWITT m Opal Harding.
3   DAVID DeWITT m Ruth Storer.
4   JAMES DeWITT m Ginger Johnson.
5   MARY IDA DeWITT m Joseph Kane.
6   LAURA FERNE DeWITT m Sydney Harrison.
7   FREDERICK DeWITT * m Loyola Culbane.
8   JAMES DeWITT
9   ALICE ANN DeWITT * m Kenneth Erickson.
10   GEORGE DeWITT (fr LDM).

DeWITT

1.1.9.4.3.3.4.4.3.7 JAMES LUKE DeWITT m Annie Lenentone
1   FREDERICK DeWITT
2   JAMES DeWITT
3   ALICE ANN DeWITT
4   GEORGE DeWITT
5   JOHN DeWITT (fr LDM).
    * There is confusion over which Frederick m Loyola Culbane and which Alice Ann m Kenneth Erickson in the two above families.

DeWITT

1.1.9.4.3.3.4.4.3.8 JUDSON HALE DeWITT m Freda Whitten
1   GENEVIEVE LEILA DeWITT
2   ROWENE GRAVES DeWITT m Albert Bauchard.
3   CARL RAYE DeWITT m Betty Lou Pryor (fr LDM).

RUSSELL

1.1.9.4.3.3.4.4.3.9 NELLIE RAY DeWITT m Lawrence Russel
1   ROBERT RUSSELL
2   RICHARD RUSSELL m Lillian Adams.
3   PATRICIA RUSSELL (fr LDM).

DeWITT

1.1.9.4.3.3.4.4.4.1 CLAUDE DeWITT m Mary Irvine
1   DOROTHY CATHERINE DeWITT
2   GWENDOLINE DeWITT
3   IRVING DeWITT (fr LDM).

DeWITT

1.1.9.4.3.3.4.4.7.1 J HENRY DeWITT m Lizzie Plummer
1   MERNA DeWITT
2   RUTH DeWITT
3   SHIRLEY DeWITT
4   ARTHUR DeWITT (fr LDM).

Leucas deWit

DeWITT

1.1.9.4.3.3.4.4.7.2 E RAY DeWITT m Lulu Carpenter
1. CATHERINE DeWITT
2. ELDON DeWITT m ? Logan.
3. EVELYN DeWITT (fr LDM).

GRAY

1.1.9.4.3.3.4.8.5.2 HALLIE GRAY m Edna Culbertson
1. ARNOLD GRAY
2. FRED GRAY
3. LORNE GRAY
4. GEORGE GRAY (fr LDM).

SMITH

1.1.9.4.3.3.5.3.3.1 & 1.1.9.4.3.3.4.1.1.2.1 EARL OTIS SMITH m Charlotte/Lottie Van Wart (1.1.9.4.3.3.5.5.1)
1. VIOLA SMITH b Wirrel NB, m Willard Kirkpatrick.
2. CLAYTON SMITH m Vera Ogden both b in Hoyt NB.
3. EVA SMITH m Robert Smith b Montreal QC lived Langeuil QC.
4. EILEEN SMITH b Hoyt NB d 1999/2000 m Walter Jeffrey b Young's Cove Rd res St John NB.
5. MURRAY SMITH m Grace Smith d/o Wallace Smith & Ada Dillon.
6. NEWTON SMITH b 1927 m Lydia Reader b 1934 both Hoyt NB (KLAD).

GOURLEY

1.1.9.4.3.3.5.3.3.4 & 1.1.9.4.3.3.4.1.1.2.4 ELLA SMITH m William Gourley
1. MARGARET GOURLEY m Walter Stewart.
2. MARY GOURELY m Donald Hetherington.
3. MURRAY GOURLEY (fr KLAD).

AMBERG

1.1.9.4.3.3.5.5.3.3 ALMA LILLIAN WHEPLEY m Irwin Amberg
1. LOEL AMBERG b 05 Mar 1928 m 03 Dec 1955 Cyril Baldwin Jr. They had a dau Loel Amberg (fr KLAD).

JORGENSEN

1.1.9.4.3.3.5.5.3.5 ETHEL WHEPLEY m Norman Jorgensen
1. CHARLOTTE JORGENSEN b 02 Mar 1932 m 03 May 1958 Walter W Patten Jr.
2. MURIEL JORGENSEN b 12 Mar 1935 m 12 Sep 1959 John Benish.
3. PRISCILLA JORGENSEN twin b 12 Mar 1935 m 24 Sep 1960 Jonathan Clark (fr MWD).

McCORKLE

1.1.9.4.3.3.5.5.5.5 DELLA VAN WART m Frank McCorkle
1. LOIS McCORKLE m William Greer res Fairvale NB.
2. CAROL McCORKLE m Frank Lawson res Wickham NB.
3. KENNETH McCORKLE had a dau Jeanette, res Hampton NB (fr MWD, DVSW:2).

KING

1.1.9.4.3.3.5.5.5.6 VERA BERNICE VAN WART m Charles King
1. RICHARD KING
2. ROBERT KING (fr MWD).

EMERSON

1.1.9.4.3.3.5.5.7.3 & 1.1.9.4.3.3.4.1.1.7.3 EDNA MARION SCOTT m Ernest Emerson
1. ELIZABETH EMERSON b 1934 m1 John L Welpley; m2 Robert Cormier.
2. CAROL EMERSON b 1944 m W D Parkhurst (fr MWD).

SCOTT

1.1.9.4.3.3.5.5.7.4 & 1.1.9.4.3.3.4.1.1.7.4 FRANK RAYMOND SCOTT {m} Ida Vivian Mersereau (1.1.9.4.3.6.5.3.2.1.6)
1. BEVERLY SCOTT b 1943 m1 William Waugh; m2 Philip Nason, res Fredericton Jct NB.
2. FRANK R SCOTT Jr b 1954.
3. LORI LEE SCOTT b 1961 m John Bigger, live Fredericton Jct NB (fr KLAD).

SCOTT

1.1.9.4.3.3.5.5.7.5 & 1.1.9.4.3.3.4.1.1.7.5 EARL W SCOTT m Mrs Marion (Richardson) Ferrin
1. EARLE L F SCOTT b 1950 Concord NH m Carol Wilcox b 1950.
2. JAMES M SCOTT b 1955. Stepdau Nancy Ferrin b 1935 m Daniel Isaacson b 1935 (fr MWD).

THOMAS

1.1.9.4.3.3.7.1.3.4. VERNON CHARLES THOMAS m Florence Elizabeth Corey
1. GRACE M THOMAS b 1904 (d 13 Feb 1983 ae 79 at Bangor ME, dau of Veroan Charles & Florence Eliz (Corey) Thomas. Obit Bangor Daily News 14 Feb 1983, funeral by Rev Rosemary Denman at the Howland Meth CH bur Howland Cem.

Leucas deWit

She is survived by dau Corrine Archer of Aurora ME, bro Benjamin, sis, Ida & Beverly, 4 grchn, neices & nephews. Siblings from the Obit.
2 BENJAMIN THOMAS of Freetown ME.
3 IDA THOMAS m ? Cole res Howland ME.
4 BEVERLY THOMAS m ? Batchelor of Wallingford CT (KLAD).

CROMBIE
1.1.9.4.3.3.7.3.2.1 CHARLES CROMBIE m Clara McFawn
1 KENNETH CROMBIE res Santa Barbara CA.
2 VAUGHN CROMBIE res Baton Rouge.
3 ALLAN CROMBIE res Boston (fr FCC).

CROMBIE
1.1.9.4.3.3.7.3.2.2 FORD CHIPMAN CROMBIE m Phyllis Wright
1 LESLIE CROMBIE (d 1978 Hoyt NB) m Bonita Cavanaugh b Wirral, Queens Co NB. Ford &Phyllis raised Leslie's one son Wade and the Cavanaugh's raised Wanda.
2 RICHARD CROMBIE m Dorothy Harnish of Wirral; lived Juvenile NB then Hoyt NB in 1990.
3 DIANNE CROMBIE m A C Brewin res Richmond BC.
4 DONNA CROMBIE m Richard Rice of Wirral res Brockville ON.
The Ford Crombie undated Obit mentions 7 grchn, 2 ggrchn, no names (info fr Ford Crombie's Obit).

CROMBIE
1.1.9.4.3.3.7.3.2.3 DONALD CROMBIE m Hazel Duplisea
1 WAYNE CROMBIE
2 ELLEN CROMBIE (all fr FCC).
3 CLAIRE CROMBIE b 1947 d 1953 drowned South Branch Oromocto River NB (fr FCC bur Blissville cem, Hoyt NB.

PARSONS
1.1.9.4.3.3.7.4.8.6 MARGARET PARSONS m Charles H Moore
1 MARJORIE PARSONS m Walter Webb res Ottawa.
2 DOROTHY PARSONS m Marvin Sines res Ottawa (fr KLAD).

PARSONS
1.1.9.4.3.3.7.4.8.10 THOMAS PARSONS m Addie Charlton
1 HELEN PARSONS m Allen Shirley d ? May 2002, res Hoyt NB (fr KLAD).

BUBAR
1.1.9.4.3.3.7.5.2.2 ZULA DeWITT m ? Bubar
1 HAROLD BUBAR
2 UNOWN NAME BUBAR. (fr KLAD).

DeWITT
1.1.9.4.3.3.7.5.4.1 RONALD WESLEY DeWITT m1 Kathleen M Smith
1 DIANE MAY DeWITT b 1946 m Douglas Alexander Mersereau. (1.1.9.4.3.3.7.6.2.4.5) s/o William Andrew Mersereau & Joyce Bell. Douglas is an Air Traffic Controller at Moncton NB, retiring in June 2002.
m2 1954 Katherine Lorena Alexander
2 ARTHUR/ART WESLEY DeWITT b 19 Jun 1956 m Tanya Harron b 11 Dec 1966 Hoyt NB d/o Douglas Harron & Rosiland Possy. Art worked for the Horticultural Nursery Department of Agriculture for 25 years, for a while at the same time as his father. When it closed Art was transferred to the NB Department of Transportation (fr KLAD).

COWIE
1.1.9.4.3.3.7.5.5.1 LENORA AGNES DeWITT m Robert Alexander Cowie
1 ROBERT COWIE Jr b 14 Aug 1933 NYC m 29 Apr 1960 Vanne Shelly res Toledo OH (fr RDB).

BUTCHER
1.1.9.4.3.3.7.5.5.2 RUBY LILLIAN DeWITT m John/Jack Samuel Butcher
1 HAZEL BUTCHER **single** (fr RDB) Res Saint John NB (RDB).

DeWITT
1.1.9.4.3.3.7.5.5.3 ARTHUR RAYMOND DeWITT m Viola May Burton
1 MADOLYN ROBERTA DeWITT b 19 Sep 1932 Saskatoon SK m 1953 Gordon Fleming res Richmond BC.
1 JOAN EVELYN DeWITT b 21 Dec 1936 Saskatoon SK m 1963 Peter Vale res Vancouver BC (fr RDB).

DeWITT
1.1.9.4.3.3.7.5.5.5 HAROLD DAVIS DeWITT m Kathleen Doris MacLean
1 LORNA JEAN DeWITT b 01 Dec 1944 Saint John NB m 1968 Joseph A Pickup (fr RDB).

DeWITT
1.1.9.4.3.3.7.5.5.6 ELLIS SCOULER DeWITT m Lily Edna Maltby
1 DAVID BURTON DeWITT b 21 Oct 1940 Halifax NS m 1963 NYC Judith Fox.
2 RUBY ROBERTA DeWITT b 05 Mar 1942 Halifax NS m 25 May 1964 Eugene Blois of Halifax.

3   ROBERT ELLIS DeWITT b 23 Jul 1944 Halifax NS m 1966 Vivian Whitman.
4   GAIL ISABELLA DeWITT b 11 Apr 1946 **single** (fr RDB).

COCHRANE
1.1.9.4.3.3.7.5.6.1 LILLIAN WEBB m Charles Cochrane
1   MURIEL COCHRANE m Edward Wheaton.
2   NORMA COCHRANE m 2nd wf/o Edward Wheaton.
3   HELEN COCHRANE m David Mason (fr RDB).

DUPLISEA
1.1.9.4.3.3.7.8.2.1 HATTIE BELL m Harley Duplisea
1   EDNA DUPLISEA b Blissville m Luther Slipp res Central Blissville NB chn b there.
2   ERWIN DUPLISEA b Blissville res Central Blissville d ? Dec 1982 **single**. (fr DMBN, KLAD).

BELL
1.1.9.4.3.3.7.8.2.2 ELDON BELL m Ruby Harron
1   VERNA E BELL m John Bertram/Bert Wood d 17 Nov 1989, res 321 City Line, Saint John West NB (Jan 28, 2000) survived by his wf, 2 sons, 1 dau, 1 bro, 4 sis & 6 grchn, funeral Patterson United CH, Wirral NB, bur Blissville Cem Hoyt. (Obit: Telelgraph Journal, Saint John [fr KLAD]). Eldon Bell d 03 Apr 1987 s/o George Melvin Bell & Lucinda (Charlton) Bell. Survivors: his only ch Mrs J Bertram Wood (Verna) of Saint John, a sis Mrs Andrew Mersereau (Joyce) of Saint John, 3 grchn Edwin, Dennis & Marilyn Wood, 5 Ggrchn (fr DMBN, KLAD).

MERSEREAU
1.1.9.4.3.3.7.8.2.3 JOYCE BELL m William Andrew Mersereau
1   IRMA MARION MERSEREAU b 1926 m 1944 Shirley Knorr res Fredericton Jct NB.
2   GEORGIANNA DARLENE MERSEREAU b 1929 m Grant Graham b Hoyt NB res Grand Bay NB.
3   MELVIN ANDREW MERSEREAU b 1935 m Jean Ogden b Hoyt NB res Grand Bay NB.
4   ELMER FRANKLIN MERSEREAU b 1937 m 1963 Joyce Russell res Grand Bay NB
5   DOUGLAS ALEXANDER MERSEREAU b 1946 m Diane May De Witt (1.1.9.4.3.3.7.5.4.1.1) d/o Ronald Wesley De Witt & m1 Kathleen Smith b 1946 res Riverview NB (fr DMBN, KLAD).

NASON
1.1.9.4.3.3.7.8.2.4 DOROTHY/DORA MINNIE BELL m Lee Gordon Nason
1   DONNA NASON b McAdom NB m T Richard Hart b Fredericton NB.
2   GLORIA JOYCE NASON b 1934 (d 26 Jan 1990 bur Blissville Cem) res McAdam NB **single**. Obit 27 Jan 1990 New Brunswick Telegraph Journal: survived by her father, sister, niece Mrs Danny Goulet (Tammy) Nephews Bruce Hartt of Ottawa & Tom Hartt of Guelph ON (fr DMBN, KLAD).

FOX
1.1.9.4.3.3.7.8.3.1 BEAUMONT BELL m Ernest William Fox
1   ALLISON FOX (d 1977) m ? res Dow Settlement, then Canterbury NB had 1 one son & 4 grchn.
2   MERLE FOX res Ottawa ON.
3   MARSHALL FOX of Jacksonville NB.
4   MARJORIE FOX m John Currie of Woodstock NB.
5   LOIS FOX m ClarkeWilson of Jacksonville.
6   NELMA FOX m Gerald Rosevear of Jacksonville. (fr DMBN via KLAD)

BELL
1.1.9.4.3.3.7.8.3.2 ELMER BELL m ?
1   THOMAS BELL res Farmington ME (fr DMBN, KLAD).

WARING
1.1.9.4.3.3.7.8.4.2 PAULINE BELL m Ed Waring
1   PATRICIA WARING
2   SUSAN WARING (fr DMBN, KLAD).

MERSEREAU
1.1.9.4.3.3.7.9.1.4 ELDON MERSEREAU m1 Vera Willis
1   BABY MERSEREAU
    m2 Ethel Bell
2   VINCENT MERSEREAU
3   PHYLLIS MERSEREAU m Glenn Whitaker (fr IMS via KLAD).
    m3 Stella Charlton

SMITH
1.1.9.4.3.3.7.9.1.5 ILA MERSEREAU m Alfred Smith
1   KATHLEEN MAY SMITH b 1921 (d 1947) as his 1st wf m Ronald W DeWitt (1.1.9.4.3.3.7.5.4.1).
2   WINNIFRED SMITH **dy**

Leucas deWit

3   REGINALD SMITH d WWII.
4   BARBARA SMITH m James Weston.
5   RUTH SMITH (d a young woman) m Charles MacMillan.
6   EVERETT SMITH m Eugenia Hoyt, div. He m2 Emily Cleghorn. Later she m2 John Boudreau.
7   DOUGLAS SMITH pensioned from the Canadian Armed Forces m Mary res Moncton NB.
8   CAROL SMITH m Randolph Carter of Central Blissville NB res Hoyt NB **no chn** (fr IMS via KLAD)

STACKHOUSE
1.1.9.4.3.3.7.9.5.1 ULA KINGSTON m George Stackhouse
1   WILLARD STACKHOUSE owns Stackhouse Photographic Services Saint John NB.

HARTIN
1.1.9.4.3.3.7.10.1.2 LOTTIE VIOLA DeWITT m Forrest Fenwick Hartin
1   STERLING HAZEN HARTIN b 08 Apr 1913 m 04 Jul 1933 Pearl Elizabeth Townsend.
2   ARLINGTOM MAYES HARTIN b 15 Feb 1915 (d 14 11 1979) m 22 May 1946 Geneva Marie Clukey.
3   RUTH ARLETTA HARTIN b 23 Nov 1916 (d 30 May 1986) at St Savior's Episc CH Bar Harbor ME, m 24 Oct 1946 George Melvin Cleaves.
4   GERALDINE MADONNA HARTIN b 02 Nov 1920, at Washington DC m 01 Jan 1944 Zina Blinn Corliss.
5   MADELINE VIRGINIA HARTIN b 22 Feb 1922 (d 08 May 1987) m 12 Jun 1945 Ralph Edward Hill.
6   MILFORD EUGENE HARTIN b 12 Apr 1924 m1 Florence Berry m2 24 Nov 1975 Betty Ann Nye.
7   THEODORE ARNOLD HARTIN b 03 Mar 1927 d 29 Jun 1948 **single**. He was found shot to death in his father's truck on Main St, near Webb's Garage, Island Falls ME.
8   RONALD EARL HARTIN b 08 Apr 1930 twin at Houlton ME m 16 Aug 1954 Patricia Ruth Nye.
9   DONALD BERYL HARTIN b 08 Apr 1930 twin m 25 Dec 1950 Elaine Ruth Whitney (all fr AML via KLAD).
10 CARROLL LaFORREST HARTIN b 04 May 1932 m 12 May 1956 Pauline Ann Bishop. All chn b Island Falls ME.

LANDERS
1.1.9.4.3.3.7.10.1.3 BESSE JEMIMAH DeWITT m1 Harry Landers
1. ERNEST LANDERS b 21 Mar 1920
2. LILLIAN LANDERS b 26 May 1922 Island Falls ME m Gordon Ellis of Bangor ME adopted son Ricky m had chn. **m2 Wallace Ireland** (fr IMS via KLAD).

BUNKER
1.1.9.4.3.3.7.10.4.1 BURTON BUNKER m Kate ? .
1   KATHIE MARIE BUNKER
2   GERALD BUNKER
3   BRIAN BUNKER
4   RALPH BUNKER
5   WILLIAM BUNKER
6   JAMES BUNKER
7   WESLEY BUNKER (fr KLAD).

THOMASON
1.1.9.4.3.3.7.10.4.2 RUBY BUNKER m William Thomason
   BASIL THOMASON m Patricia b 1951. They had 4 chn and live in Tracy NB. Basil was Mayor of Tracy, The Daily Gleaner Tuesday February 22, 2000 TRACY ELECTS NEW COUNCILLOR
   The village of Tracy had a new village councillor and for the first time in the tiny community's history a woman will fill the seat. Patricia Thomason was elected village councillor on Monday night during municpal byelections held in Tracy. The 49 year old grandmother was elated at the news she'd been voted into the position, left vacant when her husband, Basil retired from his council seat due to health problems. Thomason said she's excited to pick up where her husband left off and will rely on his almost 13 years experience as a former mayor and village councillor to guide her. The fact she's the first woman to serve as a councillor since the village was incorporated in 1966 is an added bonus.
2   VERNON THOMASON
3   AUDREY THOMASON m Douglas Coy.
4   ERNA THOMASON m ? separated, lives Westford NB (fr newspapers & KLAD).

DeWITT
1.1.9.4.3.3.8.1.6.5 JOHN HENRY DeWITT m Irene Brown
1   JANICE DeWITT m 01 Oct 1955 Neil Cruikshank res Ottawa ON.
2   ROBERT DeWITT b 1958 m Elizabeth Haig (no chn by 1979) res Saint John NB (fr MWD & RD).

DeWITT
1.1.9.4.3.3.8.1.6.6 HAZEN ARNOLD DeWITT m Grace M Tracy
1   ALBERT ERNEST DeWITT b 08 Jan 1930 m Barbara German res Moncton NB. Albert retired as Principal Riverview High School in Riverview NB (fr MWD).
2   GERALD ERWIN DeWITT b 20 Sep 1931 m Margaret Eugenie DeSaulniers res Sussex NB .

Leucas deWit

3   MARY ELIZABETH DeWITT b 18 Feb 1933 m John Douglas Hall res Fredericton NB.
4   ROBERT LEE DeWITT b 13 Feb 1939 m Katrina Anita Truffin. Robert is a practicing lawyer at Fredericton NB.
5   PATRICIA ANN DeWITT b 27 Oct 1940 d 18 Jan 1941 **dy** (fr MWD via KLAD).

BROWN

1.1.9.4.3.3.8.2.1.3 MINNIE WEBB m ? Brown
1   DOROTHY BROWN m ? Storme (fr Barbara Webb).

WEBB

1.1.9.4.3.3.8.2.1.4 ELWIN Z WEBB m Nellie Annabelle Nason
1   NELLIE ANNABELLE WEBB b 5 Dec 1922 d 7 d Dec 1922 **dy**
2   FRANK HERBERT WEBB b 3 Mar 1924 living in 2000 Licoln NB.
3   WILBUR LESIE WEBB b 15 Jul 1925 d 3 Nov 1962.
4   BARBARA WEBB b 14 Feb 1930 living in 2000 m ? Mitchell.
5   CAROL RAYETTA WEBB b 23 May 1934 d Mar (May) 1936 **dy** (fr Barbara Webb to KLAD).

HARRIS

1.1.9.4.3.5.2.2.1.1 ERNEST HARRIS m Elizabeth Phillips
1   HARLAND HARRIS b 1907 (d 1971) m Bessie McCleary.
2   RALPH HARRIS b 1912 d 1954 m Mildred Nason.
3   GRACE HARRIS b 1925 m Phillip Mills (fr IMWH, KALD).

DEWITT

1.1.9.4.3.5.2.2.2.1 FLORENCE MAY DeWITT m1 Ralph Webb. m2 George Moffit
1   IRMA MAVIS WEBB b 14 Jul 1920 m David Hartt.
2   GEORGE LEONARD WEBB b 5 May 1924 (d 20 Appr 1982) m Audrey Davidson (fr IMWH to KLAD).

TRACY

1.1.9.4.3.5.2.2.2.5 STELLA LILLIAN HARRIS m Erwin Abner Tracy
1   GAY WINNETTE TRACY b 19 Dec 1930 at Tracy NB. At Fredericton NB she m 15 Oct 1960 George McGuire.
2   BLISS LLOYD TRACY b 23 Nov 1932 was a Scientist at Hamilton ON m 12 Apr 1961 Mary Diane Oates b 06 Oct 1945 Toronto ON d/o Stephen Oates & Dorothy Eileen Mary Cook. Diane's cousin is Wildlife Painter Glen Oates. (fr IMWH, KLAD).

DeWITT

1.1.9.4.3.5.2.2.4.1 OTIS DeWITT m Florence Carr
1   BLANCHE DeWITT m Patrick Bennet.
2   GEORGE DeWITT m Violet Turnbull.
3   MARJORIE DeWITT m Leland Phillips.
4   MILDRED DeWITT (d 13 Jul 1992 bur Tracy NB Cem) m Ronald Golden s/o Lewis A Golden & Geneva I Phillips, d ae 69 (fr an undated clipping FREDERICTON GLEANER).
5   DOROTHY DeWITT m Howard Lyons.
6   BARBARA DeWITT m Leon Phillips (fr IMWH, KLAD).

MERSEREAU

1.1.9.4.3.5.2.2.4.2 ETHEL DeWITT {m} Winsell Mersereau (1.1.9.4.3.6.5.3.1.4)
1   ROBERT SHIRLEY MERSEREAU (d 13 May 1999 in Oromocto Pubic Hospital) m Jeannie Tracy Mersereau of Fredericton Jct NB. 3 sons, Stephan Derith, Gary Francine, Mark Wanda, 3 dau. Alice Clinch of St George, Marion Mosher of Saint John, Maxine Essensa (Don) of Toronto (Obit Gleaner).
2   ALICE MERSEREAU m Arthur Clinch of St George.
3   IDA MERSEREAU d 18 Apr 1999 m Major James Wattling of Toronto. Dau Carley McKee, res Weston, ON daughter-in-law Anne of Calgary, widow of late Jim Wattling Jr. 3 sisters, 1 brother interment Prospect Cem Toronto. Wattling Obit; Rural Editon June 1999.
4   MARION MERSEREAU m Stephen Mosher of Saint John NB.
5   MAXINE MERSEREAU m D Essensa of Toronto.
6   ARTELLE MERSEREAU d 12 Mar 1980 **Single**.
    Obituary: Fredericton Gleaner. Artelle Raymond Mersereau died 12 Mar 1980. He is survived by his mother Mrs. Ethel Mersereau of Fredericton Junction, brother Robert S Mersereau of Fredericton Junction, 4 sisters, Mrs Arthur Clinch (Alice) of St George NB, Mrs James Wattling (Ida) of Toronto, Mrs Marion Mosher of Saint John and Mrs Donald Essensa (Maxine) of Toronto. Funeral McAdam's Memorial Chapel, Fredericton, buried Gladstone Cemetery, Fredericton Junction. Pallbearers nephews Stephen Mosher, Brian Mosher, Stephen Mersereau, Gary Mersereau, Mark Mersereau, Mark Church (fr KLAD).

HARRIS

1.1.9.4.3.5.2.2.5.1 & 1.1.9.4.3.6.6.1.1 ALBION HARRIS m <u>1.1.9.4.3.5.2.2.5</u> Phoebe Maria DeWitt
Children are with their mother's underlined number Generation 9.

Leucas deWit

HARRIS
1.1.9.4.3.5.2.2.5.2 & 1.1.9.4.3.6.6.1.1.1.2 WALTER HARRIS m Edith Wood
1. LLOYD HARRIS m Dorothy Wood **no chn**.
2. RAY HARRIS m Helen Tracy **no chn** (fr LOH).

HARRIS
1.1.9.4.3.5.2.2.5.3 & 1.1.9.4.3.6.6.1.2.1.3 ALFRED/APPY HARRIS m Madeline ?
1. KENNETH HARRIS "d several years ago" 2 sons.
2. LESLIE HARRIS m Lois O'Leary, 4 sons (fr LOH).

RYDER/HOYT
1.1.9.4.3.5.2.2.11.1 & 1.1.9.4.3.6.6.1.2.1.12.1 RITA HARRIS m1 Gordon Ryder
1. SHIRLEY RYDER m Norman Artes d 09 Apr 2000. They lived in Fredericton Jct NB.
2. GLENNA RYDER (now deceased) m M Ogden.
   m2 John Hoyt
3. CAROL HOYT

HARRIS
1.1.9.4.3.5.2.2.11.2 & 1.1.9.4.3.6.6.1.2.1.11.2 TYLER HARRIS m Jennie Wood
1. GLENDON HARRIS {m} 1.1.9.4.3.4.5.5.2.4.3 Glenna Webb d/o Helen De Witt & Winfield Webb.
2. BETTY HARRIS m Tracy Blizzard res Tracy (fr KLAD).

NASON
1.1.9.4.3.5.2.6.9.1 & 1.1.9.4.3.7.3.6.9.1 FREDRICK ALBERT NASON m Rachel Lily Cook
1. BURTON COOK NASON b 1825 **single**.
2. RONALD DELBERT NASON b 12 Dec 1926 m 1948 Myrna Margaret Clarkson b 1929.
3. HERBERT RAY NASON b 1929 m1 Mary Tosh d 1955. He m2 1957 Marilyn Fowler b 1935.
4. ROBERT FREDRICK NASON b 1936 m 08 Dec 1956 at McAdam NB Karen M Moore b 1939.

NASON
1.1.9.4.3.5.2.6.9.2 WILLIAM EDGAR NASON m Amanda Evelyn Ross
1. GORDON EDGAR NASON b 25 Oct 1925 Saint John NB m 16 Aug 1948 Marjorie Stannix, res McAdam NB
2. EVELYN MABEL NASON b 31 Jan 1937 m Donald Taylor res Hamilton ON.
3. THELMA HAZEL NASON b 16 Mar 1928 m Willis Wilcox res Seal Cove, Grand Manan NB.
4. NORMAN ADELBERT NASON b 15 m 1929 at Hamilton ON m 20 Dec 1954 Helen Elaine Mighnan res McAdam NB.
5. STUART EARL NASON b 04 Apr 1931 m Norma Lillian Car d/o Gladstone Car and Norma.b 30 May 1937 Saint John NB, res Ocamse NB. (? Spelling error)
6. JOHN ROBERT NASON b 30 Sep 1933 **single**.
7. CECIL GERALD NASON b 09 Feb 1936 **single** res Saint John NB.
8. DAVID ARNOLD NASON b 14 Oct 1937 m 15 June 1957 Gloria Currie d/o Donald Currie & Helen Savidant b 09 Dec 1929 res Saint John NB.
9. EDNA ANN NASON b 04 Nov 1938 res Hamilton ON.
10. ROSS PAUL NASON b 11 May 1940 **single** res Saint John NB.
11. BARBARA JEAN NASON B 29 June 1942 **single** res Calgary AB.
12. EUGENE BRIAN NASON b 17 Sep 1943 (all fr RGD).

SULLIVAN
1.1.9.4.3.7.3.6.9.5 ALMA EVELYN NASON m John Sullivan
1. GERALD SULLIVAN B 15 Jan 1941 McAdam NB m 14 Sep 1962 Katherine Christie.
2. DONNA SULLIVAN b 08 Oct 1943 McAdam NB m 06 Jul 1863 Milton Currie.

MERSEREAU
1.1.9.4.3.6.5.3.1.1 ERNEST MERSEREAU m Margaret Moore
1. ELVA MERSEREAU **dy**.
2. AUDREY MERSEREAU m Jack Riordan.
3. PEARL INEZ MERSEREAU b 1910 d 5 Nov 1999 age 89 m Allen Peterson. Surviors 4 dau Audrey Nason (Walter) of Fredericton, Faye Nason (Harold) of New Maryland, Joan Thomas (Gary) of Dartmouth, Ellen Bagnell (Eric) of Beaverdam, 10 grandchildren, 11great grandchildren. Predeceased by her husband Allen (Bobby) Peterson her parents Margaret (Moore) and Erdest Mersereau two sisters Audery Riordan, Elva Messereau.
4. TRAVIS MERSEREAU m Melva of Fredericton Jct, **no chn**.

Dr Jack Riordan, s/o the late Audrey (Mersereau) Riordan was one of a team of three Scientists from Sick Children's Hospital in Toronto, who discovered the gene governing Cystic Fibrosis in 1989. Info fr Audrey's bro Travis Mersereau, in a news item in the <u>Rural Edition</u> issue 195, Nov 1989, p4 (fr GMW, KLAD).

Leucas deWit

MERSEREAU
1.1.9.4.3.6.5.3.1.4 WINSELL MERSEREAU {m} Ethel DeWitt 1.1.9.4.3.5.2.2.4.2 & 1.1.9.4.3.7.3.2.4.2
Children are with their mother's underlined number Generation 10.

HAWKES
1.1.9.4.3.6.5.3.1.5 EDNA MERSEREAU m George Hawks
1. THELMA HAWKES
2. IDA HAWKES (fr KLAD)

MERSEREAU
1.1.9.4.3.6.5.3.1.6 CLARENCE MERSEREAU {m} Gertrude Tracy 1.1.9.4.3.6.5.3.4.3.2
1. JOYCE MERSEREAU m1 ? Thompson, m2 William Gee, res High River AB.
2. RAYMOND MERSEREAU m Shirley Philips res at Nashwaaksis.
3. EMMA MERSEREAU m John Robins res High River AB.
4. ANNA MERSEREAU
5. MARIE MERSEREAU m William Davis (fr KLAD).

MOORE
1.1.9.4.3.6.5.3.1.7 HAZEL MERSEREAU m Harold Moore
1. UNA MOORE m Don Matthews, res London ON.
2. JOSEPHINE MOORE m Frank Palmer, res Saint John NB.
3. EDNA MOORE drowned in childhood **dy.**
4. ROBERT MOORE m ? res Oshawa ON. She m David Oshier (fr KLAD).

MERSEREAU
1.1.9.4.3.6.5.3.2.1 WINSLOW JAMES MERSEREAU m Freda May Noble
1. RAYMOND MURCHIE MERSEREAU d 11 Jan 2000 age 85 at Oromodo Public Hospital predeceased by his 2 brothers Vernon and Hilton; m Pearl Thompson res Tracy, 2 sons Rev Cyril Mersereau (Theresa) of Belmont NS & Rev Dana Mersereau (Bonnie) of Kemptville NS. 5 sisters, 1 Ruth Landfors (Robert) Newcastle Delaware. 2 Ida Scott fr Fredericton Jct, 3 Dorothy Philips (Noel) of Mazarolle Settlement, 4 Donna Hoyt (Scovil) of Hoyt, 5 Judy Beers of Fredericton Jct, (Rural Edition obit number 346 Feb 2000).
2. VERNON IVAN MERSEREAU d 06 Aug 1998 predeceased Raymond m Alice Palmer of 58 years chn Wayne, Cheryl, and husband Scott Gillespie and Irene (? Spencelayh) Mersereau. grnchn Keli, Jennifer, Renee Mersereau, Lisa (Dave) Mace, Rebecca (Gary)Richards, Josiah Gillespie, grgrnchn Kaleb and Kalie Mersereau, Megan, Gary, Ryan Richards, Chloe Mace. br Raymond (Pearl),Trevor, Glen (Joyce), sis Ida Scott, Donna (Scovil) Hoyt, Ruth (Bob) Lindfors, Dorthy (Noel) Phillips, Judy (Vern) Beers. Predeceased by parents, bother Hilton.
3. RUTH JOYCE MERSEREAU m Ralph Trader.
4. HILTON BENJAMIN MERSEREAU predeceased Raymond b 16 May 1922 d Mar 1997 m Eileen Gandy. Ashes at Gandy family plot Saint John NB 6 Aug 1998. Wife Eileen Gundy, son Peter m Claudette, Barry (son) m Debbie sons Micheal and Brian present. Daughter Marilyn not present but penned a tribute. (Rural Edition, Hoyt NB Sept 1998).
5. TREVOR EUGENE MERSEREAU m Lois Phillips res Traceyville NB.
6. IDA VIVIAN MERSEREAU m 1.1.9.4.3.3.5.4.7.4 Frank Raymond Scott res Fredericton Jct NB.
7. GLENWOOD BURTON MERSEREAU m Joyce Gallagher res Tracy.
8. DOROTHY ELIZABETH MERSEREAU m Noel Phillips.
9. DONNA MAY MERSEREAU m Scovil Hoyt res Hoyt NB.
10. JUDY ANN MERSEREAU m1 Gordon Artes (1.1.9.4.3.5.5.2.12.1.1.3) s/o Shirley Ryder & Norman Artes, div m2 Verne Beers res Fredericton Jct. Judy is Postmistress there (info fr KLAD).

MERSEREAU
1.1.9.4.3.6.5.3.2.2 CHARLES MERSEREAU m Lydia Phillips
1. EDWARD MERSEREAU
2. ROBERT MERSEREAU m Margaret ? dau Valerie res Windsor ON (fr KLAD).

MERSEREAU
1.1.9.4.3.6.5.3.2.3 JOHN MERSEREAU m Sadie Mullen
1. LENORE MERSEREAU m Payson Nason. Lenore & Payson died when their home was destroyed by fire Dec 1961. Their three children, Donald, Susan, & Kendall survived. Lenore escaped, on fire, but died that evening. Payson's body was found at the window, through which he had thrown the children, the youngest one, a mere infant (fr DBM, Doris w/o Treston Mersereau).
2. TRESTON MERSEREAU m Doris Byers.
3. JANET MERSEREAU m Douglas Duplisea (fr KLAD).

TRACY
1.1.9.4.3.6.5.3.4.1 LORNE TRACY m Eva Martin
1. NORMA TRACY m Russ Meeks.
2. INEZ TRACY m David McCamus, President of Xerox Canada (fr GMAW).

Leucas deWit

TRACY
1.1.9.4.3.6.5.3.4.2 YERXA TRACY m Evaline McDonald
1   JOHN TRACY (fr GMAW).

TRACY
1.1.9.4.3.6.5.3.4.3 GILBERT TRACY m Elizabeth Latcham
1   HERMAN TRACY m Enid Toner res Edmonton AB, 2 sons, 1 dau.
2   GERTRUDE TRACY {m} 1.1.9.4.3.6.5.3.1.6 Clarence Mersereau s/o Henry Mersereau & Emma Greensleeves.
3   KENNETH TRACY m1 Marjorie Tracy; m2 Mrs Beryl (Byers) Norrad, (fr GMAW).
4   GARNETT TRACY m possibly had 4 chn (fr KLAD).

ALEXANDER
1.1.9.4.3.6.5.3.4.4 STELLA AMELIA TRACY m Henry Humphrey Gordon Alexander
1   MARION ELIZABETH ALEXANDER b 1925 m 1954 Charles Seely res Ottawa.
2   GORDON TRACY ALEXANDER b 1927 m 1951 Hildegarde Meta Kiel. Gordon is V.P. at Montreal Engineering, Retired.
3   GLADYS MAY ALEXANDER b 1930 m 1955 Donald Bertram Webb, res Willowdale ON. Gladys is a twin of
4   DOUGLAS HAROLD ALEXANDER b 1930 m 1957 Evelyn Mary Leroyd, res Uxbridge ON (all info fr GMAW).

BOONE
1.1.9.4.3.6.5.4.3.1 ROY ANGUS BOONE m1 Lucy Phillips
1   EARL BOONE (had a dau Nancy).
   m2 Kathleen Jefferson
2   RALPH BOONE
3   RUTH BOONE
4   MARTHA BOONE
5   ROY BOONE (all info fr ACB).

BOONE
1.1.9.4.3.6.5.4.3.2 LOREN GILLEN BOONE m ?
1. BURTON BOONE
2. LOREEN BOONE
3. EARL BOONE
4. FRANCES BOONE (all info fr ACB).

BOONE
1.1.9.4.3.6.5.4.3.3 GEORGE WESLEY BOONE m Beatrice Webb
1. SHIRLEY BOONE m Leslie Brawn (fr ACB).

BOONE
1.1.9.4.3.6.5.4.8.1 MERLE BOONE m Rose Rhodes
1   BURTON BOONE b 1928 (fr ACB).

JONES
1.1.9.4.3.6.5.4.8.2 MONA BOONE m Clayton Jones
1   EDWARD JONES
2   MARILYN JONES (fr KLAD).

HARRIS
1.1.9.4.3.6.6.1.1.1 ALBION HARRIS m Phoebe Maria DeWitt 1.1.9.4.3.5.2.2.5 (& 1.1.9.4.3.7.3.2.5)
Children are with their mother's underlined number Generation 9.

DeWITT
1.1.9.4.3.6.6.1.2.4 ANNABELLE HARRIS m 1.1.9.4.3.2.2.2. Henry Leonard DeWitt
Children are with their father's underlined number Generation 8.

PRIDE
1.1.9.4.3.6.6.5.1.2 LILLIE AGNES ALEXANDER m Fenwick W Pride
1   IDA PRIDE b 1901 (d 1959) Fredericton Jct **single**.
2   DOROTHY PRIDE b 1904 Blissville NB schoolteacher of Barrie ON m William Frederick Pheasant at Fredericton Jct NB d 1984 s/o Frederick Pheasant & Elizabeth Duplisea, b Tracy NB res Coldwater ON. Dorothy has a dress that belonged to Minnie Alexander b 1872 & a hat that belonged to Edwin Alexander b 1876 (fr KLAD).

ALEXANDER
1.1.9.4.3.6.6.5.1.3 CHARLES FREDERICK ALEXANDER m Lena Davis
1   LORENA ALEXANDER b 1901 Lynn MA m 1924 Percy F Haley of Marblehead MA (fr KLAD).

STUART
1.1.9.4.3.6.6.5.1.4 BERTHA GENEVRA ALEXANDER m Henry Harvey Stuart
1   EULAH MARGARET STUART b 1901 Fredericton Jct NB (d 1977) at Sunny Brae NB m 29 Dec 1923 Wallace Nason b 04 Jul 1896 Tauten MA retired to Welsford NB d 21 May 1977 both bur United CH Cem Welsford,

Leucas deWit

s/o Parker Nason & Alida Steven. Wallace was a CPR Telegraph Operator, Veteran of WW1.

2. EDWIN ALEXANDER STUART b 1903 M.A. UBN 1930 MDCM McGill 1933 post graduate training took him to Royal Victoria Hospital Montreal, Royal Infirmary Edinburgh, Royal College of Surgery Edinburgh, Golden Square Hospital, London; m Katherine Winfield, **no chn.** He was a practitioner and educator in Orolaryngological medicine. Faculty McGill for 32 years and associated with Royal Victoria, Shriner's Hospital, Queen Elizabeth Hospital, Alexandra Hospital for infectious diseases and MacKay Institute for the deaf. Pres publicity when UNB granted him an honorary MSC.degree in 1978. Dr Stuart died in Halifax in 1998.
3. JOHN WALTER STUART b 1905 (d 21 Oct 1984) Harcourt NB, m 1939 Jean MacDougal b Sussex NB res Moncton NB d in the 1980's. John retired from the Math Dept Moncton High School.
4. EILEEN BERTHA STUART b 1907 Newcastle NB m 1935 E John Cram, **no chn.**
5. HENRY WILLIAM STUART b 1909 Newcastle m1 Armina Campbell; m2 Dora Palmer; m3 Ruth Kelly.
6. ALLAN PALMER STUART b 1909 (d 27 Jun 1974) m Mary Curry of Hortonville, NS. Allan Stuart received a Beaverbrook Scholarship at UNB BSc degree with honors in Mathematics and Cemestry UNB 1939 PhD McGill in 1942, 4 years with Canadian Army WWII Most of the time at Chalk River on secret chemical work. He returned to UNB on the faculty in Chemistry Dept in 1946, died January 27 1974 Royal Victoria Hospital Montreal. Surviors his wife Mary (Curry) son Allan W. Stuart, dau Susan, 3 bro Dr. E.A. Stuart, J. Walter Stuart, Henry W Stuart, 2 sis Eulah (Mrs. W.W. Nason) and Eileen (Mrs. E. J. Cram) (fr KLAD).

MOTT

1.1.9.4.3.6.6.9.5.2 LESSIE PRIDE m Chester Mott, he m2 Charlotte Nason.
1. GEORGE MOTT Blissville NB m1 ? Sherman; m2 ? ; res Kentville NS.
2. ELSIE MOTT b Blissville m James Nason, res Woodstock NB, 3 daus.
3. CHESTER MOTT b Blissville NB m Norma Nason, res Tracy NB, 7 sons.
Chester Jr m Norma, his stepma Charlotte's younger sis (fr KLAD).

NASON

1.1.9.4.3.6.6.9.6.1 ELSIE NASON m Justus Nason
1. PEARL NASON m Gordon Allen d 10 Oct 1973, res Fredericton Jct NB (fr EAW).
2. VERGIE NASON m Edward Wilson res Truro NS.
3. NELLIE NASON m Hazen Frederick Brawn res South Branch Lake NB d Saint John Regional Hospital 4 Jan 2000 ag 78 (fr EAW). Surviors wife Nellie (Nason) Brawn, 2 dau Darlene Carr of Westfield & Lorraine Hamilton (Dale) of South Branch Lake. Three sons Eric Frederick Brawn (Pearl), H. Avery Brawn (Lovann), Keith Brawn (Ann Marie) 7 grandchn and 1gr grandch. Predeceased by parents, three brothers and one son Raymond Avery.
4. EUGENE NASON (now deceased) m Vivian Nason. She m2 Matt Johnson.
5. RUSSELL NASON b ? Aug 1920 served overseas WWII, res Tracy, **single** (fr EAW).

PATTULLO

1.1.9.4.3.6.6.9.6.3 SARAH NASON m Francis Pattullo
1. ERNEST PATTULLO d mid 1980's survived by dau Debbie.
2. DAVID PATTULLO a schoolteacher, **single.**
3. BETTY PATTULLO (fr ACB, LN).

BURNETT

1.1.9.4.3.6.6.9.6.4 MABEL NASON m Clarence Burnette
1. RAYMOND BURNETT b 1918 d 5 Jan 1994 m1 Edith McLaughlin b 1917 d 1943, m2 Eva Smith d 1964. Sunbury Funeral Home in central Blissville was in charge of funeral arragments and I well remember attending the visitation at the Funeral Home the afternoon of Jan 7, 1994 while in the line waiting to speak with the family I was told by a friend, in place ahead of me, that Raymond's mother had just died at White Rapids Nuring Home Fredericton Jct. That was true so part of the family stayed at the visitation while necessary members left to make arrangements about their mother, whose funeral took place a few days later at Sunbury Funeral Home. (fr KALD)
2. DARYL BURNETT b 1919 d 1920 **dy.**
3. THEDA BURNETT b 1921 m James Saunders.
4. RETA BURNETT b 1923 m Gordon Taylor.
5. LLOYD BURNETT b 1925 (d ? Sep 1984 at St Andrews NB) m Corinne Sampson of that city.
6. HILDA BURNETT b 1929 m Gerald Mersereau (fr ACB, LN).

NASON

1.1.9.4.3.6.6.9.8.1 GEORGE ALMAN NASON m1 Charlotte Phillips.
1. PERLEY DAVID NASON b 1914 Harwood Creek, Saint John NB m 1940 Viola Evelyn Haywood b 1920.
2. BEULAH NASON b 1916 m Hazen Melbourne Mersereau **no chn.**
3. TRAVIS EDISON NASON b 1919 Little Lake NB, at Fredericton NB m 1955 Letha Phillips d/o Ora Philips of Tracy & Lula Nason.
4. CHESTER SMITH NASON b 1921 Little Lake, m 1944 Annie Nason b 1922 McAdam NB d/o William Edward Nason. Annie m2 1951 Arthur McCracken b 1912 d 1977.

Leucas deWit

m2 Sadie Blackmore Stuart. . . all chn but Stafford b at Tracy.

5   DORIS ODELLA NASON b 1930 m Harold Robinson b 1925.
6   MARGERY ALDANA NASON b 1932 m Edwin Alexander b 1927.
7   BYRON EDWARD NASON b 1934 at Tracy NB m Nora Woodworth b 1939 at Rusagonis NB d/o Foster Woodworth & Muriel Waugh.
8   STUART EVERETT NASON b 1936 at Tracy m Katherine Dawn Horne b at Tracy 1938 d/o Ronald Horne (storekeeper at Tracy) & Roberta Phillips.
9   VELMA LOVELLA NASON b 1939 m Odian/Dale Aubin.
10   STAFFORD NEIL NASON b 1941 **single**.
11   FRANCIS VINCENT NASON b 1943, a plumber, at Harvey Station NB m 06 Jul 1968 Margaret Harris d/o Arthur Harris & Alice Toner of Harvey NB.
12   ESTER ELAINE NASON b 1947 a twin, m Ronald Wood worth b 1944.
13   LESTER EUGENE NASON b 1947 m Murielle Aubin; res with prts.
14   RANDY LEE NASON b 1948 a twin, at Fredericton Jct m Dianne Aubin.
15   ROSE MARIE NASON b 1948 m Stephen Aubin b 1947.
16   ERROL GEORGE NASON b 1956 m Dorothy Guitard.

NASON

1.1.9.4.3.6.6.9.10.1 GEORGE IRVING NASON m Grace Marie Clifford

1   RUTH NASON b 1926 m1 Calvin Duplisea; m2 31 Dec 1981/2 Don Morrison d 29 Nov 1984. They had a son Don Duplisea b 03 Jul 1948.
2   WILFRED CLAUDE NASON b 1935 McAdam at Paris ON m ? Czeto.
3   ARTHUR ROY NASON
4   RONALD EUGENE NASON (info collected by KLAD).

NASON

1.1.9.4.3.6.6.9.10.6 SPENCER ALBERT NASON m Rhetta A Jollymore

1.   AUDREY NASON b 1931 McAdam NB (info fr KLAD).

NASON

1.1.9.4.3.6.6.9.10.7 RAYMOND HARRY NASON m Rhetta /Rhettie Enman

1   JEANIE FLORENCE NASON b 1949 m 1966 Brian McMullan b 1945.
2   SHIRLEY ELIZABETH NASON b, d 1950 **dy.**
3   ROBERT LLOYD NASON b 1952 m 1978 Lennie Stevenson b 1961.
4   LAUROE RAY NASON b 1956 (info collected by KLAD).

NASON

1.1.9.4.3.6.6.9.10.8 RUSSELL NASON m Eva Cleghorn

1   CECIL WILLIAM FREDERICK NASON b 1940 m 1962 Carolyn Hood b 1945.
2   MARLENE JOYCE NASON b 1953 m 1969 Eric Boone b 1953.
3   LEON RUSSELL NASON b 1956, at Harvey Station NB m Susan Joy McCullough b 1957 (fr KLAD).

NASON

1.1.9.4.3.6.6.9.10.9 WILLIAM ARTHUR NASON m Edith Gardner

1   BETTY I NASON b & d 1942 **dy.**
2   PAUL W NASON b 1943 d 1945 **dy.**
3   ROBERT T NASON b & d 1944 **dy.**
4   MILFORD NASON b 1948 m 1967 Linda Gail Harris b 1947.
5   ROY NASON b 1951 m 1972 Mary Ann Brown.

BURNETT

1.1.9.4.3.7.1.3.6.3 HARRY BURNETT m Maud Lloyd

1   BLOYCE BURNETT
2   DONALD BURNETT killed by enemy in WWII.
3   EDISON BURNETT a veteran of WWII.
4   BRIAN BURNETT known as Budd m Prue Huiltz. After Budd's death she married Vincent Boone & res Alberta. The four brothers are deceased (fr KALD).

NASON

1.1.9.4.3.7.1.7.1.2 CHESTER NASON m Ida May Golding m2 Alma Greer

1   ADELBERT NASON m Marion Day.
2   LOUIS M NASON m Audrey Ward.

TERRY

1.1.9.4.3.7.1.7.2.4 ELIZABETH ISABEL NASON m Clarence W Terry

1   NETTIE CLARICE TERRY b 22 Aug 1922 m 22 Sep 1949 Richard Wilson Brown.
2   JULIA ELIZABETH TERRY b 15 Sep 1924 m ? Andrews.

Leucas deWit

3 MARY KATHLEEN TERRY b 26 May 1930 m ? Dozier.

MERSEREAU
1.1.9.4.3.7.3.2.4.2 & 1.1.9.4.3.5.2.2.4.2 ETHEL De WITT m Winsell Mersereau (1.1.9.4.3.6.5.3.1.4)
Children are with their mother's underlined number Generatin 10.

ACKER
1.1.9.4.3.7.3.2.5.4 & 1.1.9.4.3.6.6.1.1.1.4 ELIZABETH HARRIS m Charles Acker
1 ELDA ACKER d 3 Feb 1998 at Oronocto Hospital age 85, m Harry Toole. Survived by one son Harold Toole Jr and wife Arlene, Fredericton Jct had 3 chn, 3 grdchn Pattie O'Donnell (Micheal), Joy Toole & husband Micheal Sullivan & Dwight Toole & wife Janet. 5 Great grchn Scott & Andrew O'Donnell Kevin Sullivan, Kyle and Asfton Toole. (Bur Gladstone Cem also Harry Toole at same) (fr KLAD).

HARRIS
1.1.9.4.3.7.3.2.5.5 & 1.1.9.4.3.6.6.1.1.1.5 CHESTER/BUD HARRIS m Myrtle Moon
1 FOSTER HARRIS d 20 Jun 1999 m Ursula Redstone retired to Fredericton Jct NB & had 1 dau Edna Harris who m Richard Mawhinney of Fredericton NB.
2 GUILFORD HARRIS res Harvey NB.
3 ARTHUR HARRIS res Harvey NB.
4 TRAVIS HARRIS res Harvey NB.
5 DONALD HARRIS res Cork?
6 HARRIET HARRIS res Hoyt NB.
7 KEITH HARRIS res Tracy NB.
8 IRWIN HARRIS res Tracy NB.
9 WALLACE HARRIS res Tracy NB.
10 ELDON HARRIS res Tracy NB predeceased bro Foster.
11 MARIE HARRIS m Lloyd Pollock res Harvey NB.
12 HILDA HARRIS m ? Wilkins.
13 ELOICE HARRIS m Harley Wilson res Fredericton Jct NB div predeceased Foster.
14 DEHLIA HARRIS m Stanley Bishop res Cork? Predeceased Foster.
15 EDITH HARRIS m Hazen Ball res Fredericton Jct NB (all fr LOH).

DeWITT
1.1.9.4.3.7.4.2.4.1 NORMAN JOHSTON DeWITT m Lois Pfister
1 LOUIS JOHN DeWITT b 1945 m 1973 Nancy Moravee.
2 KATHARINE DeWITT b 1946 m 1969 Edward H Connell.
3 MARGARET ANN DeWITT b 1948 m 1969 Michael Flemming.
4 NORMAN DeWITT b 1949 (fr LPD, Who's Who).

BAINES
1.1.9.4.3.7.4.2.5.1 MARGARET ELIZABETH COLEMAN m Clement Algernon Baines
1 ANDREW DeWitt BAINES b 17 Jul 1934 Toronto ON, M.D. Professor of Clinical Chemistry at the U/o Toronto Medical Services, m 28 Dec 1956 Cornelia Van Erk M.D.
2 LINDA BAINES b 1938 Toronto m 1956 H Neville Lyon.

COBORN
1.1.9.4.3.7.4.2.5.2 MARY ELECTRA COLEMAN m Gordon Coborn
1 JOHN COBORN b 1936 m 1961 Beverly Miller.
2 ADAM COBORN b 1938 d 1959 **dy**.
3 JANE COBORN b 1940 (all fr Mrs. CAB).
4 ELLEN COBORN b 1944 M.D. m 1975 Michael Jacobson. She works at Simon Fraser Medical Services Burnaby BC.

COLEMAN
1.1.9.4.3.7.4.2.5.3 ALFRED BRANT COLEMAN m1 Muriel Magee, m2 Muriel Nugy
1 ALLAN BRANT COLEMAN b 1929 m June ? (fr MCB).

CRIPPS/McCAULEY
1.1.9.4.3.7.4.2.5.5 ELIZABETH NASH COLEMAN m1 William Cripps
1 ANNE CRIPPS b 1932 m 1955 William Fullerton.
2 JOAN DOUGLAS CRIPPS b 1933.
m2 1939 K C McCauley
3 GARY McCAULEY b 1941 m 1970 Mary Kelly.
4 WALLACE GLEN COLEMAN McCAULEY b 1943 m 1975 ? Lyndell (fr Mrs CAB).

Leucas deWit

SISSONS

1.1.9.4.3.7.4.2.5.6 SAMENA COLEMAN m H J Sissons
1. BRENDA SISSONS b 1950 m 1973 R Hart.
2. MARY SISSONS b 1952 m 1973 T Mark.
3. DAVID SISSONS b 1954 m 1975 Heather McNaughton.
4. SAMENA SISSONS b 1956.

SALIGMAN/MIKESALL

1.1.9.4.3.7.4.3.1.1 HONOR KATHLEEN PETTIT m1 Lewis L Saligman
1. BRYCE (SALIGMAN) DeWITT b ?Feb 1922, PhD res Austin TX m 1951 Cecile Marette of Paris France, lived Austin TX.
2. LLOYD LEWIS (SALIGMAN) DeWITT b 1927 worked for the US State Department, m Betty Miller.
3. HUGH HAMILTON (SALIGMAN) DeWITT b 1934 Ph.D taught Ichthyology U of ME m Joanne Rice res near Dameriscota ME.
4. HIRAM PETTIT (SALIGMAN) DeWITT b 1936 m a Hungarian woman from Australia ? .
m2 William Beery/Mike Mikesall, no chn.

(in a letter fr HPSM)
"You will notice . . . that the boys changed their last name to DeWitt. Lewis (my husband) was partly Jewish and Saligman is one of the best. I liked it. But he was brought up by a Swiss Calvinist mother and partly German father in the Methodist Church! We have always liked the name Saligman and it means a lot to the family. But when the boys began going to Massachusetts to prep school and Harvard, they were automatically classified, even to letters in Hebrew from New York. This was a bit much. Actually the Jewish people, I find are terribly racist (We are the chosen people). They actually have ways of punishing anyone who has a Jewish name but is not of that religion or race. Anyway on advice from their father they changed the name to DeWitt legally preferring that to any number of others in their ancestry. I should have preferred Pettit as being obviously more consistent. I did not change mine until I married"

(letter 19 Oct 1980 fr Ruth (Pettit) Ryder)
"Bryce began getting anti-Jew flak as a budding young scientist in Europe. He talked it over with his father Lewis before he died suddenly in 1949. Later Honor and the boys considered `Pettit' but Bryce liked `DeWitt' and they legally changed. Their town and the surrounding farm people were furious. They loved Lewis. He grew up in Dinuba CA and came back to be their beloved family physician. Papa Saligman had a department store. They didn't know or care he was Jewish and knew little anti-Semitism. Mama Saligman was German. The boys were ¼ Jewish of course, charming, fine young men.

RAMSEY/INCE

1.1.9.4.3.7.4.3.1.2 IVA MARGARET PETTIT m1 Walter Ramsey
1. ROBERT RAMSEY had a son Ivan.
m2 William Ince, no chn (fr HKPSM).

NELSON

1.1.9.4.3.7.4.3.4.1 CAROLYN WALTON PETTIT m James F Nelson D.D
1. JAMES <u>MELVIN</u> NELSON b 12 Apr 1914.
2. HUGH De WITT NELSON b 21 Feb 1917 had a dau Marie.
3. RUTH <u>FRANCES</u> NELSON b 21 Feb 1921 m Ruth Francis McCay.
4. ANNE MARIE NELSON b 08 Feb 1923 m ? Holmes.
5. CAROLYN <u>JEANETTE</u> NELSON b 05 Jun 1927 m ? Thatcher (fr ROPR).

ARDEN

1.1.9.4.3.7.4.3.4.3 ALMEDA/MEDIA/MEDA PETTIT m Fred Arden
1. PHYLLIS RAE ARDEN b 27 Jun 1919 m ? Sanders.
2. FRED DOUGLAS ARDEN b 11 Nov 1922 m Mary Jo Mikesall d/o William/Mike Mikesall Mike m2 Honor (Pettit) Saligman who was Fred's mother's cousin. Fred was the third great grandson of Sylvester & Abigail (DeWitt) Pettit. He was alive in 1978. He had 2 sons. They res Calgary AB (fr HPSM).
3. RUTH OLIVE ARDEN b 01 Jul 1922 m ? Mahoney.
4. ALMEDA JEAN ARDEN b 24 Mar 1925 m ? Burtis.
5. MELVIN OLDHAM ARDEN b 26 Apr 1932 (& twin) **dy** (fr HKPSM, ROPR).
6. UNNAMED ARDEN (twin) **dy.**

Leucas deWit

PETTIT

1.1.9.4.3.7.4.3.4.4 HERMAN DeWITT PETTIT D.D. m Marion St John
1. FLOYD HERMAN PETTIT b 21 Mar 1924 Oakland, Alameda Co (d 30 Dec 1962 Happy Camp, Siskiyou Ca) m Lois Marie Magnuson b 21 Jan 1928 Two Harbors MN d 29 Apr 1964.
2. GERRY DeWITT PETTIT b 06 Sep 1926 Fowler CA. Dr Gherry Pettit has been a Prof at Washington State U at Pulman WA. Ruth Olive (Pettit) Ryder (ROPR) entrusted the Sylvester Pettit Bible to Gherry, oldest of the 3 grdsns. He had sons; he promised to pass it on to whichever of the 4 ggrdsns who would treasure it the most.

RYDER

1.1.9.4.3.7.4.3.4.5 RUTH OLIVE PETTIT m Milton P Ryder.
1. ARTHUR MILTON RYDER b 12 Nov 1923 Fowler CA engineer in a large company, in 1980 res 2 miles from his mother's home in Santa Clara Co CA.
2. DONALD GOWAN RYDER b 04 Apr 1925 Fowler CA.

PETTIT

1.1.9.4.3.7.4.3.4.6 CLARE NEWCOMER PETTIT m Antoinette Ramsey
1. CLARE MELBERT PETTIT b 04 Mar 1935 (adopted 1940 in CA).

RICKARD

1.1.9.4.3.7.4.3.6.3 SARAH ENID HOLTERMANN m George Bates Rickard
1. GEORGE PAUL RICKARD b 18 May 1915 Toronto ON d 29 Sep 1995 Seattle, WA m 27 Aug 1938 Barbara Ann Ray div.
2. GRACE ENID RICKARD b 28 May 1917 Brantford ON d 31 May 1995 Titusville FL, m 02 Mar 1939 John Marshall Bamfield III b2 Jan 1917 Niagara Falls ON Can d 28 Jan 1984 West Palm Beach FL.
3. JOHN W RICKARD b 1919 d Oct 1921 Montreal QC **dy.**
4. ROBERT PERCY RICKARD b 04 Aug 1921 Montreal QC with severe spinal deformities. There is more information on Robert & his father following the listing of his childen in Gen 11. Robert m1 08 Sep 1945 Westfield, NY Margaret Cameron Morgenstern b 19 Sept 1923 Westfield NY d.24 Apr 1964 Buffalo NY. Robert m2 24 Aug 1970 Marjorie Aline Hinds Warzeski b 13 Feb 1921 Baltimore MD d 28 Sep 1995 Zephyrhills FL.

FOXLEY

1.1.9.4.3.7.4.5.1.1 ANNIE MULHOLLAND m William George Foxley
1. JOHN WILLIAM FOXLEY b 1906 m1 1926 Virginia Morris, div, m2 Rosella Evers, m3 Jean Thacker.
2. WELLINGTON JOSEPH FOXLEY b 1909 m 1936 Doris Mary Meegan b 1908.
3. FRED HOWARD FOXLEY b 07 Jul 1913 Toronto ON m 1933 Helen Eva Randall b 18 Feb 1914 Detroit.
4. FRANK THOMAS FOXLEY b 1917 **single.**
5. BESSIE ROSE FOXLEY b 28 Jun 1917 m Lester Edwin Schultz b 25 May 1911.
6. CYRIL HAROLD FOXLEY b 1919 (d 1974 Detroit) m 23 Feb 1942 Gladys Edna Dowling b 30 Sep 1918 (fr MA, AMF and the Samuel Armstrong History).

KENYON

1.1.9.4.3.7.4.5.1.3 SARAH MULHOLLAND m Arthur Jay Kenyon
1. RUTH ELEANOR KENYON b 09 Oct 1911 Vinemount ON m 03 Dec 1938 Edgar Franklin Hysart b 12 Oct 1905.
2. LOUISE KATHERINE RAY KENYON b 12 Sept 1912 m 29 Oct 1929 Fred Isaac Stuart s/o James George Stuart b Grassie ON 08 Oct 1905 (fr EM, LK, RKS).

STEPHENSON

1.1.9.4.3.7.4.5.1.7 RUTH MULHOLLAND m John Stephenson
1. MARION RUTH STEPHENSON b 1929 m 1954 Malcolm Ralph Morrison b 1930.
2. JOHN WALLACE STEPHENSON b 1935 m 1960 Elizabeth Louise Hyde b 1936.
3. HENRY ALAN/HARRY STEPHENSON b 1938 m 1968 Norma Gail Smith b 1939 (**no chn** by 1977).
4. HOWARD WELLINGTON STEPHENSON b 1940 m 1972 Mary Jane Dick b 1944 (**no chn** by 1970) (fr EM, GRAH)

ARMSTRONG

1.1.9.4.3.7.4.5.6.1 JOSEPH W ARMSTRONG m Bernice
1. Elizabeth Ann Armstrong m Robert Straw.

HYLAND

1.1.9.4.3.7.4.5.6.2 GLADYS R ARMSTRONG m Sheldon F Hyland
1. GLENN E HYLAND B 06 Nov 1922 **single.**
2. OSBORNE HYLAND b 29 Mar 1924 m 01 Oct 1948 Vera S ? b 12 Dec 1921 (fr EM, GRAH reunion Winona ON).

ARMSTRONG

1.1.9.4.3.7.4.5.6.6 ELIJAH GRATTON ARMSTRONG m EVELYN ?
1. EVELYN GLADYS ARMSTRONG m Robert Anderson, 2 sons.
2. TONI ARMSTRONG, 1 son, 1 dau (fr EM).

THERIAULT
1.1.9.3.4.7.4.5.6.7 JEAN G ARMSTRONG m Herbert J Therialt
1. NORMAN THERIAULT m Karen ?   had a dau Lori.
2. MICHAEL THERIAULT m Jean.
3. ANDREA THERIAULT m Tom Jones (fr EM).

ARMSTRONG
1.1.9.4.3.7.4.5.6.8. SAMUEL GERALD ARMSTRONG m Kay   ?
1. CLIFFORD ARMSTRONG m Diane   ? .
2. JOHN ARMSTRONG m Marjory   ? .
3. WAYNE ARMSTRONG (fr EM)   ? .

DeWITT
1.1.9.4.3.7.4.6.1.1 JOHN WINFRED DeWITT m Agnes Wood
1. MARGUERITE IRENE DeWITT b ? Jul 1918 Long Beach CA, m Raymond/Ramon Egert. They had 4 daus.
2. GERTRUDE JEAN DeWITT b 11 Jul 1920 Long Beach, m John Manchas; 3 sons.
3. LOUISE DeWITT b 29 Mar 1922 The Dalles OR, m Fred Hibbeler; 2 sons, 1 dau.
m2 Frances Helverstat (fr EJDL).

PURVIS
1.1.9.4.3.7.4.6.1.2 CLARA ROSE DeWITT m James Darcy Purvis
1. RONALD JAMES PURVIS b Redvers SK 21 May 1918 m 12 Oct 1946 Joy Nixon b 19 Aug 1026 Wauchope SK, their chn b Redvers SK.
2. LAURA ROSE PURVIS b 28 Sep 1920 m 06 Mar 1948 Robert James of Calgary AB b 1918.
3. CLARENCE PURVIS b 27 Jun 1928 m 27 Mar 1965 Betty Ruth Symons.
4. WALTER MERTON PURVIS b Redvers 28 Mar 1934 m 18 Oct 1963 Dale Sauter. The siblings b Redvers (fr EJDL).

DEAN
1.1.9.4.3.7.4.6.1.3 MYRTLE IRENE DeWITT m Wilson Dean
All their chn b Fertile SK.
1. RALPH ERNEST DEAN b 14 Mar 1935 m ? Jun 1958 Alice Rutledge, Carievale; chn b Carnduff SK.
2. MURIEL IRMA DEAN b 30 Apr 1938 m 25 Feb 1961 Keith Hall b 06 June 1927 Clanwilliam MB.
3. PHYLLIS DEAN b 04 Jun 1943 m 17 Jun 1961 Clarence Funk b 27 Nov 1926 Winkler MB.
4. MELVIN DEAN b 05 Apr 1947 m 17 May 1969 Margaret Fargie b 16 Sept 1935 Nipawin SK (fr EJDL).

PARSONS
1.1.9.4.3.7.4.6.2.1 EMILY MAY DeWITT m Edward Frederick Parsons
1. EUNICE PARSONS b 14 Nov 1942 Winnipeg MB (fr EJDL).

McKENZIE
1.1.9.4.3.7.4.6.2.2 MABEL ANNIE IRENE DeWITT m William J McKenzie
1. WILLIAM De WITT McKENZIE b 15 Aug 1935 Tisdale SK.

DeWITT
1.1.9.4.3.7.4.6.3.1 NORMAN OSBORNE DeWITT m Beryl Green
1. KEITH NORMAN DeWITT b 20 Nov 1923 (d ? Oct 1966) m Barbara Hudson.
2. ERIC HARRISON/HARRY DeWITT b 05 Jul 1925 m Mary Pat Trick.
3. JOAN MAXINE DeWITT b 02 Jul 1929 (d 03 Dec 1979 Vancouver BC) m Eugene Ochetwa.
4. IAN MARTIN DeWITT b 26 Apr 1934 d ? Jan 1953.
5. GARTH DAVEY DeWITT b 21 Jul 1938 m Norma Wood (fr BGD).

RODGERS
1.1.9.4.3.7.4.6.3.2 ALMA ALETHA ISABELL DeWITT m Robert Alexander Rodgers
All chn b Regina SK (fr ICSP).
1. BRIAN ALEXANDER RODGERS b 10 Dec 1927 m 02 Feb 1952 Ruth Armstrong.
2. ROBERT FOSTER RODGERS b 09 Feb 1930 d 17 Aug 1937 Regina SK **dy**.
3. GEORGE HARRISON RODGERS b 21 Jul 1938 m 07 Jul 1973 Heather Flood 2 chn.
4. DONALD NOMAN RODGERS b 07 Aug 1940 m 10 Jul 1969 Sharon Brierly 3 chn (fr MEJLS).

STEELE
1.1.9.4.3.7.4.6.4.1 MARY ELIZABETH EMMA LOUISE LIVESLEY m Frederick Ray Steele
All chn b Winnipeg MB.
1. SHIRLEY ELEANOR STEELE b 25 Mar 1931 m 20 Jun 1952 John W Carleton b 30 July 1927 Swift Current SK.
2. MURRAY ROY STEELE b 23 Mar 1935 at Winnipeg m 07 Jun 1958 Lorraine Grant b 13 Mar 2937 Winnipeg MB; their chn b Winnipeg.
3. BABARA ANN STEELE b 10 Aug 1938 (all info fr MEJLS).

LIVESLEY
1.1.9.4.3.7.4.6.4.3 ROBERT ARDEN De WITT LIVESLEY m1 Gwendolyn Hibbert
1. ANN VALERIE LIVESLEY b 05 Jan 1946 Manchester Eng m 21 Feb 1970 Michael James Turner b 16 Jul 1946.
2. DAVID ROBERT LIVESLEY b 22 Jan 1948 Winnipeg MB m 09 Jan 1971 Lynn Arlene Blackburn b 28 Feb 1948 Winnipeg MB.
3. PHYLLIS DEAN LIVESLEY (fr EJDL, MEJLS).
m2 19 Aug 1972 Margaret Kathleen Mountain (Info fr EJDL, MEJLS).

ECKLIN
1.1.9.4.3.7.4.10.2.1 BEULAH DeWITT m Erland Ecklin
1. BEVERLY JOAN ECKLAND b 1926 m St Johns Anglican CH West Toronto by Rev Wm C Bothwell & Rev Clinton D Cross officiating Thursday 25 May 1950 in an evening ceremony, Richard Brenden Stapells of York Mills (a lawyer in Toronto ON) b 1925 Madrid, Spain s/o Herbert Gordon Stapells.
2. CLAIRE-ANN LOUISE ECKLAND b 1930 m 1953 Jose Santos-Perez b 1928 s/o Ambrosia Santos of Selamanca, Spain (Author in the Genealogical Helper that the ma's name often is appended to a ch's pa's name in Spanish countries) (research & wedding info fr ICSP).

MOYER
1.1.9.4.3.7.4.10.4.1 MARGARET JANE PENELOPE SMITH m Ronald Claus Moyer
1. ARTHUR WESLEY MOYER b 01 May 1952 at Virgil m 11 Feb 1984 Marlene Marie Reimer.
2. MARGARET JANE MOYER b 05 Jun 1953 m 14 Aug 1976 St Andrew's Anglican CH at Grimsby ON, Grant Sharp b Ponoka AB; res there.
3. CHARLES EDWARD MOYER b 25 June 1955 All siblings b Grimsby. Family res Ridge Rd Grimsby (fr MJPSM).

SMITH
1.1.9.4.3.7.4.10.4.2 HAROLD WESLEY MARTIN SMITH m Ida Alice Empringham
1. JOHN WESLEY SMITH b 18 Nov 1942 St Catherine ON, at Blachall Edinburgh Scotland St Columbia's CH m 24 Feb 1968 Gail Paterson Brewster b 10 Oct 1945 Edinburgh, Scotland d/o William Brewster & Mary Paterson. Div.
2. IDA CAROLYN SMITH b 19 Jul 1944 m 17 Aug 1968 John Ritchie Pellettier. Both earned M.D.'s at Queen's U Kingston ON 1969, res Guelph ON. John became a Psychiatrist.
3. PENELOPE JANE SMITH b 20 Sep 1947, at St Catherines ON m 18 May 1974 Werner Carl Stebler b 29 Jan 1946 Nunigen, Switzerland s/o Marcel Stebler b 23 Dec 1916 & Elisabeth Jeger.
4. ARTHUR WILLIAM SMITH b 01 Oct 1948 m St Catherines 05 May 1973 Constance Josephine Robinson b Montreal QC 24 Jul 1948 d/o Ben Robinson & June Davis.
5. HAROLD WESLEY MARTIN SMITH b 22 Dec 1952 m Bethel United CH, Trafalgar Rd, Oakville ON 01 May 1976 Mary Featherstone b 30 Aug 1952 d/o John David Elmer Walker Featherstone & wife Olga d/o Joseph Dorzinsky from Bobcaygeon ON (b 06 Nov 1916 Berlin ON). They res on a fruit farm. All siblings b St Catharine ON (fr ICSP).

SMITH
1.1.9.4.3.7.4.10.5.1 JOHN REID SMITH m Gwen Ramsden
1. RAMSDEN BLAKE SMITH b 24 Dec 1940 L 9 C 2 Saltfleet T, Winona ON m 19 Dec 1970 Shirley Nicklaus.
2. ROGER DeWITT SMITH b 25 Feb 1944 m 22 May 1964 Marilyn Ann Lang b 05 Apr 1942 (fr ICSP).

SWEENEY
1.1.9.4.3.7.4.10.6.1 GORDON AMBROSE SWEENEY m Vivienne Elaine Stone
1. ELIZABETH ANN/SIS SWEENEY b Orlando FL 23 Oct 1951 m 28 Feb 1976 Gregory Patrick Ganas b FL 10 Mar 1949 res 114 Magnolia Ave, Box 1855 Sanford FL.
2. MICHAEL GORDON SWEENEY b 05 May 1953.
3. JEFFREY STONE SWEENEY b 24 Apr 1956, all siblings b Orlando FL (fr ICSP).

DeWITT
1.1.9.4.3.7.4.13.2.1 ARTHUR NORMAN DeWITT m1 Marjorie Louise Washburn
1. GARY ARTHUR DeWITT b 14 Aug 1954 Los Angeles CA.
2. PAUL NORMAN DeWITT b 27 Nov 1956 Los Angeles CA (fr JDW).
m2 Mrs. Jeannie Pahl
Stepchn were Michael Pahl b 12 Nov 1953, Laurie Pahl b 27 Oct 1958, Julie Pahl b 02 May 1962.

SORENSON
1.1.9.4.3.7.4.13.5.2 ANDREW SORENSON m Myra Mae Bays
1. PATRICIA ANN SORENSON b 06 Oct 1939 Sweetwater TX m 1957 Henry Herschel Launspach Jr.
2. STEPHEN ERIC SORENSON b 24 Feb 1943 Palacios NM m 28 Dec 1973 Sue Ann Ryan V 06 Jun 1939 Sweetwater TX, res El Paso TX then Alamagordo NM in 1979 (fr JDW).

MOYER
1.1.9.4.3.7.6.3.6.1 ELIZA O FOSTER m Allan Alexander Moyer
1. ISOBEL MOYER b Kitchener ON, Lab Technician, **single**.
2. ARTHUR ANDREW MOYER b Kitchener, M.D. London ON m Jessie ? (fr ICSP).

Leucas deWit

FOSTER
1.1.9.4.3.7.6.3.6.2 ROBERT NEFF FOSTER m Alix Beryl Turner
1. DONALD TURNER FOSTER b 25 Aug 1929 Thorold, ON a Tool & Die Maker m 29 Sep 1951 Evelyn Marie Hamel d/o Eugene Hamlin & Mildred Simmons, b 05 May 1930 Thorold ON (ICSP).

WILSON
1.1.9.4.3.7.10.1.3.5 FREDERICK GEORGE DeWITT WILSON m Marguerite Isabelle Lowe
1. ARLEEN BERYLE WILSON b 25 Jul 1936 Winnipeg MB, at Dauphin MB m 12 Sep 1959 Frank Vegso b 29 Jan 1932 Wainwright MB (fr ACCH).
2. CECIL GEORGE EDMOND WILSON b 05 Jan 1937 Erickson MB.
3. JANICE WILSON (adopted) b 14 Nov 1951 m 06 Jun 1970 Robert E Preston b 26 Nov 1951 had 2 chn Marie Ann Preston b 08 Dec 1970 & Earl James Preston b 19 Dec 1973 (fr ACCH).

WILSON
1.1.9.4.3.7.10.1.3.7 CECIL McADFREN WILSON m Sadie Elizabeth Galloway
1. WILLA DIANE WILSON b 24 Oct 1934 Brandon MB m 14 Nov 1953 Gerald Richard Graham b 30 May 1933.
2. JOYCE CECELIA WILSON b 25 Apr 1938 Gladstone m 26 Aug 1961 John Ross Foster b 12 Jan 1937. Their two adopted chn Allen Foster b 30 Jan 1968 & Cecile Foster b 24 Jun 1969.
3. MYRNA MAY WILSON b 8 Jun 1939 Gladstone, MB (fr ACCH).

CHRISTIANSEN
1.1.9.4.3.7.10.1.3.8 CECELIA GEORGEANA WILSON m Hjalmar Christiansen
1. AVA CECELIA CHRISTIANSEN b 26 Mar 1932 Crawford Park MB, at Brandon MB m 28 Aug 1954 Kenneth Raymond Harris b 24 Jul 1927 Minnedosa MB.
2. OLE INER CHRISTIANSEN b ? Jan 1938 Erickson MB, at Regina SK m1 26 Dec 1958 Irene Dartmouth, div m2 14 Feb 1977 Kathy ? b Denver CO.
3. RAE GEORGE CHRISTIANSEN b 04 Mar 1945 Brandon MB (fr ACCH).

WILSON
1.1.9.4.3.7.10.1.3.9 WILLIAM FRANKLIN/BILL WILSON m Margaret Pasternack
1. RALPH WILLIAM WILSON b 05 Sep 1938 Crawford Park MB, at Dauphin m 10 Nov 1962 Verna Matychuck b 30 May 1944.
2. SHIRLEY ANN WILSON b 01 Apr 1940 Dauphin MB, at Halifax NS m 02 Nov 1962 Ronald Arthur Gates b 18 May 1940 (fr ACCH).

DeWITT
1.1.9.4.3.7.10.5.2.3 CHARLES CLIFFORD DeWITT m Libby McBride
1. FLORENCE LOUISE DeWITT b 23 Jul 1939 m 29 Sep 71 Geoffrey Tisch s/o Harvey Edward Tisch & Phyllis Evelyn Levi, b 05 Feb 1939 New Zealand (fr CCD).
2. THOMAS CHARLES DeWITT b 22 Oct 1941 d 25 Jan 1951 **dy.**
3. LORETTA DeWITT b/d 14 Aug 1943 **dy.**
4. ALMA DeWITT b & d 16 Aug 1948 **dy.**
5. NORMA LIBBY DeWITT b 07 Jul 1952 m 04 Sep 1976 Richard Leo teBockhorst b ? 1953 (fr CCD1).

PEARSON
1.1.9.4.3.7.10.6.1.1 VIOLET MAE TRATO m O.E. Pearson
1. SHIRLEY ELEAN PEARSON m Stanley Brown.
2. ELEANOR JOYCE PEARSON m Charles Jarslfer.
3. CAROL LYNN PEARSON m Daniel Hopler.
4. MARI LEE PEARSON m Robert Watt (fr ICSP).

TRATO
1.1.9.4.3.7.10.6.1.2 ALBERT CAMPAIGNE TRATO m Helen Ruth Burke
1. KATHIE JOYCE TRATO b 1946 d 1953 **dy.**
2. CONNIE DAWN TRATO b 1951 m 30 Sep 1973 Stephen Paul Carey b 1953 (fr ICSP).

TRATO
1.1.9.4.3.7.10.6.1.3 JOHN HILLARD TRATO m Josephine Helen Thielde
1. JUDITH HELEN TRATO m Arza/Pete Parrish, div.
2. JAMES HILLIARD TRATO m1 Carol Weinhorst, div; m2 Sally ? .
3. JOHN HERBERT TRATO m Theresa/Teri Mathews (fr ICSP).
4. JAQUELINE HOPE TRATO m David Edwards.

MAHR
1.1.9.4.3.7.10.6.1.5 MARIAN EDITH TRATO m Donald A Mahr
1. STEVEN ALAN MAHR b 1953.
2. DIANE LEE MAHR b 1958.
3. KENNETH GEORGE MAHR b 1962 (fr ICSP).

NORTON

1.1.9.4.3.7.10.8.1.1 CECIL HIRAM NORTON m Gladys Agnes Robinson
1. GRANT JOHN NORTON b 20 May 1924 Tansley, Halton Co ON m 06 Jul 1946 Doris Lillian McMillan b 25 Oct 1924.
2. BERNICE MARGARET MAY ROBERTA NORTON b 25 Oct 1926 Tansley ON m 03 Dec 1949 William Francis Stevenson b 17 Apr 1927 res Burlington (fr ICSP).

ESSERY

1.1.9.4.3.7.10.8.1.2 CLARA LOUISE NORTON m William Earl Essery
1. WILLIAM EARL ESSERY Jr. b 12 Sep 1925.
2. FRANCES MARY ESSERY b 21 Jul 1928.
3. GLADYS IRENE ESSERY b 26 Oct 1930 d 26 Oct 1938 **dy.**
4. BYRON NORTON ESSERY b 09 Apr 1933 (fr ICSP).

HUGILL

1.1.9.4.3.7.10.10.1.1 RHEA MARY ELVA DeWITT m William James Hugill
1. JONATHAN HUGILL b/d 22 Dec 1930 mother fell on icy path, **dy.**
2. ELVA HUGILL twin b 25 Dec 1931 premature d same day **dy.**
3. MARY EDNA NOREEN HUGILL twin b 25 Dec 1931 d 23 Mar 1976. Edna contracted Rheumatoid Arthritis at ae 12 & she slowly progressed to a wheel chair. She had one of the first hip replacements done in Hamilton. Many visits to the hospitals, the longest stay was over one year. She never lost hope and she was an inspiration to the other patients in the hospital. She had both hips replaced, one twice, and several other joints operated on; eventually she had no hip joint in one hip but still managed to walk. She did numerous types of needlework and at one time even taught a class. She never let her disability stop her from doing anything; she was a very determined person. Her brother Murray would take her on trips in the car and they had a weekly egg route and she always would go with him and keep the books. One trip he took Edna and his mother on a holiday to visit his brother Alex in Louisville, Kentucky.
4. RHEA GRACE ELEANOR HUGILL b 21 Jul 1933 Beverly Twp ON former Assistant Office Manager Emery Air Freight Toronto Airport, retired 01 Jan 1995. At West Flamboro Presbyterian CH m 21 Aug 1959 Ernest George Mayes b July 2 1927 an accountant at Carling O'Keefe, lived Bramalea. Retired now, they moved to Oakville and now res in Hamilton (in 2000) on the mountain. The newly built house keeps her happy building rooms in the basement using her fully equipped basement workshop
5. WILLIAM JAMES ALEXANDER HUGILL b 24 May 1934 Beverly Twp ON, at St Lukes Anglican CH Burlington m 14 Nov 1959 Shirley Diane Colvin d/o Ernie Colvin & Alice Morley, b 20 Aug 1939. Alex went through the Ford Trade School, Windsor ON moving back home on the farm, but continued to work in Process Engineering at Ford in Oakville for 13 years. He then worked for Parker Chemicals in sales and service for 13 years, moving to Richmond Hill ON, Louisville KT, Atlanta GA, now res in Clearwater FL & works for Coral Chemical as Southern District Manager. In 1994 he was diagnosed with Non Hodgkins Lymphoma. He took strong treatments at Clearwater which were good for 5 years. It then came back on him and he took different treatments which lasted another 2 years. In 2001 it came back and in 2002 he took more treatments which once again were successful in putting him into remission.
6. MURRAY DeWITT HUGILL b 30 Oct 1936 Hamilton ON m 12 Nov 1966 (at Kensingston Baptist CH) Marlene Leitha Ackles d/o Orville Vaughn Ackles & Leitha Dorothy Edna Fisher, b 09 Jul 1940 Hamilton ON worked as a legal secretary. Murray worked the farm with his mother for 3 years then took an Electrical Apprentice Training with Ford in Windsor ON a 4 years course. While at Ford Windsor he came home weekends and helped his mother work the farm and had an egg route in Hamilton. Mother would look after the chickens and his sister Edna and Grandmother would grade and candle about 100 dozen eggs each week. Rhea (mother) would also plough and work the fields making them ready for Murray to plant when he got home on the weekends. In 1962 his mother, sister Edna & Grandmother (Edna DeWitt) left the family farm at Peters Corners and moved to Burlington ON with Murray. At that time Stelco Steel Mill employed him for 9 months as an Electrician in the Cold Mill. He then worked at Ford Truck Plant in Oakville as Weld Engineer, Process Engineer and Dimensional Engineer, then Launch Co-Ordinator for Truck Body Shop until retirement from Ford in 1992. Since retirement they have taken at least two major trips each year and another to Vancouver, to help Aunt Vona with the DeWitt manuscript due for pubication early in 2004 (fr MDH).

MARLENE ACKLES m MURRAY HUGILL

DeWITT
1.1.9.4.3.7.10.10.1.2 MAURICE WILBUR DeWITT m Emily Mildred Surby (all fr VEDS)
1. LAUREL STANFORD DeWITT b 19 May 1943 Brandon MB at Hazelton BC m 03 Sep 1965 Linda Joy Rorick d/o Clifford Clinton Rorick & Hazel, b Sep 1946. Laurie joined the RCMP at age 19 serving in BC at Prince Rupert, Hazelton, Smithers, Cranbrook Golden, Kamloops, Trail and Kelowna retiring in 1996 after a very adventure filled career. They retired to Fruitvale BC.
2. MAURIETTE DAWN DeWITT b 05 Jun 1947 Brandon MB, at Victoria BC m 17 Jun 1972 Bruce Buck b 1946 Minnedosa MB; res Courtney BC. For many years Bruce was a hard rock miner. They res in Cumberland BC.

McFADDIN
1.1.9.4.3.7.10.10.1.4 SELENA ELVA DeWITT m Herbert Norman McFaddin
1. LORNE CIBBIT McFADDIN b 26 Nov 1929 Newdale MB, at Williams Lake BC m 12 Sep 1959 Muriel Eleanor Burke, b 09 Jan 1927 Kelowna BC. d/o Oswald Burke & Mary Catharine Saucier. Muriel is a retired nurse. They live at 150 Mile BC.
2. MARLENE ISABEL McFADDIN b 21 Oct 1935 Strathclair MB, at Vancouver m 07 Jul 1956 Douglas Charles Lindsay b 22 Jan 1933 SK, div. For many years Marlene had her own store called Cowichan Burls for which she manufactured beautiful assorted burl clocks, tables and curios. As an artist much of her work included Toll Painting scenes, or sea shells embedded in the designs. In retirement she has a dog kennel, raising Westies. The one enterpise was a K-9 Jacuzzi Pet Bather. Malene divided her 1.75 acres, built a new house on the .75 some years ago, moved into it recently and sold her other house (fr VEDS).

DeWITT
1.1.9.4.3.7.10.10.1.5 IRA GEORGE DeWITT m1 Joan Ann Funnel
1. SANDRA ANN DeWITT b 05 Oct 1942 Brighton m1 28 Mar 1964 John Floyd s/o Jim Floyd & Ethel, res Auxbridge, Middlesex Eng, div; m2 Lucas. Sandra had one son Kevin Floyd res Eng with one child.

He m2 Irene E McGimpsey
2. ALLAN LIONEL DeWITT b 21 Apr 1950 Winnipeg, computer programmer, res Stoney Mountain MB.
3. JAMES GEORGE DeWITT b 08 May 1953 Winnipeg, at Odeline RC CH Rothern SK m Karen Crowe, div; res Saskatoon SK.
4. WILLIAM SMITH DeWITT b 12 Mar 1954 Winnipeg, Peace Officer Kent Prison, Agassiz BC m 26 June 1999 Jeanette ? , transferred back to Stoney Mountain Penitentiary MB. George and Irene moved to Chilliwak BC after he retired. Since George's death Irene moved to Winnipeg and lives in a Seniors Complex (fr VEDS).

GEORGE DeWITT ---- >

HARPHAM
1.1.9.4.3.7.10.10.1.6 LILA BELLE DeWITT m Raymond Edward B Harpham
1. SHARON LYNNE HARPHAM b 18 Oct 1943 at Dauphin MB (d 26 Dec 2002) R.N. m ? Aug 1964 Rev Jack Nield b s/o Albertum Charles Russel Neild & Ida Mae Ebertson. Jack is a United CH minister served at Miniota MB, Peterborough ON, Pointe Claire QC and presently Ottawa ON. Sharon taught nursing at McGill U QC and was a Nursing Policy Consultant for Canadian Nurses Association. She did a great deal of traveling in Canada & overseas, an example to Denmark, Ethiopia etc.
2. DENNIS HARPHAM b & d ? Apr 1944 premature **dy**.
3. RAE FRANCES HARPHAM b 21 Nov 1947 Dauphin, m1 04 Sep 1965 Donald Gordon Johnson b ? 1944 Dauphin MB s/o R G Johnson & M Kydd; div. Rae m2 21 Aug 1999 Robert Benedict b 23 Dec 1949 s/o Joseph William Benedick & Jemmeha May Wright. They res in Surrey BC.
4. DAVID GLENN HARPHAM b 21 Aug 1956 d 28 Jul 1965. He suffered a brain tumor. Lila and Sharon, during his treatment, told him to pretend he was flying to the Moon with Neil Armstrong. The only time he felt sick was a day they couldn't be with him. He was such a sunny, delightful child. He succumbed to the second bout of cancer. **dy**.

Sharon (Harpham) Nield: The day after Christmas Sharon died as she wished, peacefully at home with her family and friends. She died as she lived, with grace and concern for others around her. Even living with cancer, Sharon felt very lucky to have four children of whom she was very proud, to have a successful career with important work to do, to: have wonderful loyal friends, to have a faith which gave her life depth and meaning. Her only regret was that she would not see her seven grandchildren grow up.

SMITH
1.1.9.4.3.7.10.10.1.7 VONA EDNA DeWITT m Gilbert Doran Smith
1. GAY SHARON SMITH b 28 Mar 1943 d 17 Apr 1943 Brandon MB; blue baby **dy**.
2. SHELLEY SMITH b 20 Feb 1944 d 21 Feb 1944 Gimli MB, premature **dy.**
3. CORINNE/CORI EDITH SMITH b 02 Oct 1949 m1 28 Feb 1969 David Reid, div; m2 07 Jul 1973 Herbert <u>Wayne</u> Stevens s/o Herbert Stevens & Vi, b 10 Oct 1949, div.
4. GILBERT IRA SMITH b 10 Jul 1952; served in the Coast Guard, Vancouver.
5. AIDA LOUISE SMITH b 19 May 1954 B New Westminster BC, employed by the Provincial Vehical Insurance Company (ICBC) posted to Victoria BC in 1903.
6. JULIA/<u>JULIE</u> EDNA SMITH b 02 Apr 1957 New Westminster BC, at Las Vegas NV m 24 Oct 1986 Howard Clement Webb b 19 Apr 1956 England s/o Derek Webb & Takako/Judy Innoe, res Harrison Hot Springs BC. Julie is Assistant Clerk & Treasurer there. Howie manages his mother's grocery supermarket in Agassi BC (fr VEDS).

BOGARDUS
1.1.9.4.3.8.2.5.1.4 HAROLD EDWARD BOGARDUS m1 Leah Newdeck
1. HAROLD EDWARD BOGARDUS Jr. b 30 Jun 1924 Los Angeles CA, m Hilda S Merill b Ajo AZ.

m2 Jeanne Tice
2. LINDA LOU BOGARDUS b 23 Mar 1947 d 28 Sep 1947 Pasadena CA.
3. DEBORAH JANE BOGARDUS b 25 Mar 1952 m1 Dana Morse; m2 Donald Gibson (fr WBB).

BOGARDUS
1.1.9.4.3.8.2.5.4.1 JULE WILLIAM DOGARDUS m Margaret Klien
1. RICHARD DEAN BOGARDUS b 03 Oct 1927 Centralia IL m 19 May 1949 Jacqueline R Clymer.
2. MARILYN JOYCE BOGARDUS b 30 May 1932 m 17 Feb 1951 Robert Earl Burton.
3. MARY GRACE BOGARDUS b 30 May 1932 m Leslie Schaefer.

BOGARDUS
1.1.9.4.3.8.2.5.6.2 RUSSELL EUGENE BOGARDUS m1 Beulah
1. RUSSELL EUGENE BOGARDUS Jr. b 21 Jun 1945 Chicago IL.
2. CAROL JEAN BOGARDUS b 06 May 1947 Haywood CA m Roger Soderberg.

m2 Betty Womack
3. DONALD EUGENE BOGARDUS b 09 Feb 1951 Witchita KS m 06 Oct 1973 Diane Ruth Winslow b 18 May 1953 San Mateo CA.
4. CYNTHIA JEAN BOGARDUS b 01 Aug 1954 NY (fr WBB).

WILLIAMS
1.1.9.4.3.8.2.5.7.1 MARGARET JANE BOGARDUS m James W Williams
1. PHILIP MICHAEL WILLIAMS b 14 Nov 1951 m 22 Jun 1974 Jane Ann Rous b 07 Jul 1952.
2. CHRISTINE MARIE WILLIAMS b 05 Nov 1954 m 13 Aug 1977 Mark Nordin b 26 Apr 1951 (fr WBB).

CHUMBLEY
1.1.9.4.3.8.2.5.7.2 LOUISE ALBERTA BOGARDUS m Herman Chumbley
1. ROBERT GENE CHUMBLEY b 03 Mar 1949 m1 05 Oct 1970 Margarette Elaine McIntyre; m2 13 Jun 1972 Phyllis Kay Grant b 19 Sep 1950; m3 04 Jul 1981 Carrie Louise Scott.
2. MARY ALICE CHUMBLEY b 20 Apr 1952 m 01 Nov 1970 Russel Madlem b 19 Dec 1949.
3. DEBORAH ANN CHUMBLEY b 04 Apr 1954.
4. NANCY ELLEN CHUMBLEY b 01 Dec 1955 m 18 Apr 1975 Dale Kncarem b 19 Oct 1957 (fr WBB).

WILLIAMSON
1.1.9.4.3.8.2.5.7.3 PHYLLIS ROSEMARY BOGARDUS m Robert Williamson
1. ROBERTA WILLIAMSON
2. PHYLLIS WILLIAMSON b 28 Jun 1967 (WBB).

MORGAN
1.1.9.4.3.8.2.5.7.6 JILL ANN MARIE BOGARDUS m William Morgan
1. PHILLIP DAVID MORGAN b 02 Jan 1980 (fr WBB).

GROVER
1.1.9.4.3.8.2.5.7.7 LAURA KATHRYN BOGARDUS m Marshall R Grover
1. JACQUELINE JOY GROVER b 02 Jan 1971 Morris IL.
2. JENNIFER ANN GROVER b 12 Mar 1974 Joliet IL (fr WBB).

BOGARDUS
1.1.9.4.3.8.2.6.2.1 FREDERICK WILSON BOGARDUS m Mary Stanley Black
1. PETER WILSON BOGARDUS b 02 Sep 1941 Halifax NS m Frances Lynn Campbell b 22 Feb 1940.
2. JOHN ARTHUR BOGARDUS b 20 Feb 1946 Vancouver BC.
3. LOUISE ANN BOGARDUS b 04 Oct 1951 Vancouver BC m 25 Aug 197? Tekeno Haeber (fr WBB).

CLEVELAND
1.1.9.4.3.8.2.6.2.2 JEAN ISOBEL BOGARDUS m Howard D Cleveland
1. CATHERINE CLEVELAND b 1943 Vancouver BC.
2. BONNIE JEAN CLEVELAND b ? Oct 1946 Vancouver BC.

PHILIP
1.1.9.4.3.8.2.6.4.1 GRAFTON BOGARDUS PHILIP m Lois Scranton
1. JOHN PHILP b 1935 m Sonya Sondergard (fr WBB).

PHILIP
1.1.9.4.3.8.2.6.4.2 STEWART PHILIP m1 Jane More McPhee More
1. JOAN GRAFTON PHILIP b 18 Apr 1938 m 1962 Arthur Jewel (fr WBB).
2. CHARLOTTE ANN PHILIP b 07 Sep 1942 m1 1964 Robert Lidstone; m2 1971 Jim Greig.
3. JAMES STEWART PHILIP b 28 Mar 1945 m 14 Jul 1973 Val Swaeeoff.
m2 Ruth A Bruck

POLLARD
1.1.9.4.3.8.2.6.5.1 ELIZABETH CAIN m Michael A Pollard
1. MICHAEL WALTER POLLARD b 20 Aug 1945 Corpus Christie TX m 15 Feb 1969 Catherine Ann Block b 15 Oct 1947 Reno NV.
2. MARY ALICE POLLARD b 16 Fekb 1947 Reno NV m John Walter Walkiewicez.
3. JAMES PATRICK POLLARD b 23 Oct 1947 Reno NV m 30 May 1970 Michele Ann De Marco.
4. SUSAN JOSEPHINE POLLARD b 22 Aug 1954 (fr WBB).

SHEPKER
1.1.9.4.3.8.2.8.9.1 THELMA IDA BOGARDUS m Maurice A Shepker
1. JEANNE MARJORIE SHEPKER b 22 Jan 1937 Buffalo NY m 22 Dec 1962 Rene Dorri.
2. PERK SHEPKER b 08 Oct 1939 d 17 Jan 1940 **dy.**
3. PAUL FRANCIS SHEPKER b 08 Oct 1939 m 25 Sep 1965 Shirley Favorite.
4. THOMAS OLIVER SHEPKER b 03 Apr 1945 Buffalo m 19 Aug 1967 Patricia Kirgt.
5. JUDITH RUTH SHEPKER b 26 Feb 1943 Buffalo d 11 Jan 1965 NY (fr WBB).

BOGARDUS
1.1.9.4.3.8.2.8.9.3 GEORGE DORAM BOGARDUS m Gertrude Reynolds
1. GEORGE DORUM BOGARDUS Jr. b 03 Jan 1943 Buffalo NY m 02 Oct 1971 Mary Muhs. chn b Buffalo (fr WBB).
2. DOUGLAS BOGARDUS b 28 Sep 1946 Buffalo NY m 11 Jan 1969 Lois Sterner; had a dau b Buffalo 09 Jul 1971.
3. GAY LINDA BOGARDUS b 30 May 1952 m 03 Mar 1973 Richard Preischel (fr WBB).

RICE/MILLER
1.1.9.4.3.8.2.8.9.4 RUTH THURZA BOGARDUS m1 Edward H Rice
1. GAIL ELIZABETH RICE b 22 Jan 1947 Buffalo NY.
2. KEITH EDWARD RICE b 30 Mar 1957. **She m2 Norman F Miller** (fr WBB).

DeWITT
1.1.9.4.5.1.2.4.3.1 OMAR LeROY DeWITT m1 Hazel Phillips
1. BABY DeWITT premature b & d 05 Jul 1929 **dy.**
2. MARILYN MAUDELL DeWITT b 18 Dec 1931 Muskegan MI d 14 Jun 1932 Shelby MI bur Mt Hope Cem Shelby; had Spina Biffida, **dy.**
3. OMAR LeROY DeWITT Jr b 03 Mar 1933 Muskegon MI, at Ann Arbor MI m 30 Aug 1959 Sue Tennant.
4. WAYNE FREDERICK DeWITT b 23 Jun 1935 Lakeview MI at Montague MI m 15 Jun 1957 Edythe M Hendrie. b 30 Jul 1938 Niagara Falls NY. Wayne graduated high school & Junior College at Grand Rapids MI; USA Airforce 1953-1956; night school 1957-1965 IL Institute of Technology, Chicago, Industrial Engineer, like his father (fr OLD).
m2 Mrs Dorothy Kolanowski (fr OLD).

MILLER
1.1.9.4.8.3.6.1.1.2 MAUDE MARIE LOWE m Lewis Lorin Miller
1. MARY LOUISE MILLER, b 16 Feb 1924 bp Fifth Luth CH Springfield Twp, Clark Co OH at Springfield m 07 Dec 1946 Jan Seeger Beery res Westlake Village CA s/o m1 Carl Dewey Snyder & Florence Bertha Seeger. She m2 1937 Robert Oliver Beery b 27 Jun 1923 bp St John's Luth CH Springfield; occupation Industrial Chemical Salesman (fr MLMB's m license, b & d certificates, legal adoption papers, name change).
2. CAROLYN ANN MILLER b 12 Jul 1925 m 17 Jan 1947 Thomas D Shepherd res Westlake Village CA.
3. ROBERT LEWIS MILLER b 14 Feb 1936 m 29 Dec 1958 Sandra Redford res Escondido CA (fr MLMB).

Leucas deWit

GENERATION 11

JORDAN
1.1.9.4.2.1.2.7.1.1.1 ALLEINE DUNN m Roy E Jordan Jr
1 PAMELA DeWITT JORDAN
2 NANCY LEE JORDAN
3 ROY E JORDAN Jr

BUTLER
1.1.9.4.2.1.2.7.5.1.3 MARY R LENT m George Vernon Butler
1 RICHARD VERNON BUTLER

GARRARD
1.1.9.4.2.1.2.7.5.1.4 MARJORIE R LENT m Sterling Garrard
1 GEOFFREY WAYNE GARRARD

HENKEL
1.1.9.4.2.1.2.7.5.3.1 CHARLOTTE ELIOT LEO m David Henkel
1 CHARLOTTE LEE HENKEL
2 DAVID HENKEL Jr

BARRY
1.1.9.4.2.1.2.7.5.4.1 VIRGINIA LEE STAHL m Robert Barry
1 SHEILA BARRY

BOOTON
1.1.9.4.2.1.2.10.1.2.1 JOHN GRIFFITH BOOTON m Catherine Ann Kage
1 SUSAN VERMILYE BOOTEN

TITHERINGTON
1.1.9.4.2.1.2.10.1.2.2 MARY VERMILYE BOOTEN m William Kent Titherington
1 WILLIAM K TITHERINGTON Jr b 1942.
2 ANN MARSELIS TITHERINGTON

OVERGAUGH
1.1.9.4.2.2.1.1.4.1.5 WILLIAM HOYT OVERBAUGH m Clarissa Agnes Pilgrim
1 GERALD HOYT OVERBAUGH b 04 Aug 1917 m Myrtle O'Brien Teetsel.
2 RODNEY PIGRIM OVERBAUGH b 15 Aug 1922.
3 WILLIAM WARREN OVERBAUGH b 16 Jan 1924 m Edna May Winnie.
4 THEODORE STUART OVERBAUGH b 02 Mar 1926 at Saugerties m Ann Lucille Mollet (RDCFU: 37).

DeWITT
1.1.9.4.3.1.5.3.2.2.1 CARROLL FLEMING DeWITT m1 Lillian Theresa Ferns
1 BARBARA CAROL DeWITT b 03 Jun 1937 Highland Park, Wayne Co MI, at Ridgewood NJ m 08 Mar 1957 William Ira Holmes b 07 Feb 1939 Tappan NY. The Orange & Rockland Lighting CO employed him. They live in Bauvelt NY. They have 2 chn, adopted 2 more & are prts of several foster chn (fr CFD).
2 LAWRENCE JOHN DeWITT b 21 Jul 1940 Highland Park MI, in the Marine Corps 4 yrs, was a Corporal as an Electronic Technician. After service he joined Grumman Corporation & later Fairchild Camera & Instrument Corporation as a technical representative. On 08 Apr 1966 Larry, a civilian, age 25, was attacked but escaped rioting mobs led by Buddhist monks in Saigon, Vietnam (see National newspaper coverage) m1 11 Mar 1967 Valerie Ann Bradshaw b 23 Apr 1945; moved from Oakdale IL to San Jose CA, div 1980, daus live with their ma in Hidden Hills Ca. Larry is owner & president of Commodity Refining Gold and Silver Exchange Corporation, Sherman Oaks CA; Lawrence, at Augora CA m2 21 Jul 1983 Laura Lambert.
3 JAMES WILLIAM DeWITT b 16 Dec 1947 Detroit, at Sayville NY m 08 Feb 1965 Donna Jean Fass b 11 Jul 1947 Jamaica NY. James is General Manager of Nutmeg Chrome Corporation, Hartford CT, lives in South Windsor CT.
4 WILLIAM THOMAS DeWITT b 07 Jul 1953 Detroit, m 07 Aug 1976 Theresa Hennesey d/o Edward Hennesey & Dorothy Ronkonkoma NY, b 23 May 1955 in the Bronx NY; William is employed by Grumman Data Systems Corporation, Bethpage NY.
m2 Mary Aurora (Scandaliato) Paparatto (fr CFD).

CONLEY
1.1.9.4.3.1.5.3.2.2.2 ALICE MAE DeWITT m John Earl Conley
1 RICHARD ALLEN CONLEY b 17 May 1948 Highland Park, at Las Vegas m ? Apr 1979 Sue. Richard is a self-employed painter, lived in Las Vegas.
2 CHERYL LYNN CONLEY b 26 Oct 1952 at Wyndotte MI, at Allen Park MI m 28 Sep 1972 Thomas Regnier, a building contractor, res Romulus MI.
3 ROBERT WILLIAM CONLEY b 17 Oct 1955 Dearborn MI res Las Vegas.
4 NANCY ANNE CONLEY b 30 Sep 1962 Dearborne MI m 10 Apr 1983 Mark Nelson (fr CFD).

BOURGET
1.1.9.4.3.1.5.3.2.3.1 HILDA MAE DeWITT m Leonard Joseph Bourget
1. JOHN CHARLES BOURGET b 10 Mar 1930 Detroit, at Manistee MI? m 24 Aug 1957 Katryn Ann Goodrich b 19 Nov 1933, res Rochester MI.
2. CATHERINE JEAN BOURGET b 13 Dec 1931 Detroit, eloped & m 17 Sep 1948 Richard Joseph Taubitz, remarried in church 10 Mar 1952 (fr CFD).

DeWITT
1.1.9.4.3.1.5.3.2.3.2 LAWRENCE IRA DeWITT m1 Olive Bell; m2 Mary Carbone
1. LINDA DeWITT b 28 Jul 1947.
2. JUDY DeWITT b 18 Nov 1948.
3. LARRY DeWITT Jr b 27 Nov 1950.
m3 Charlotte Marie Chaltron (fr CFD).

CHAMPION
1.1.9.4.3.2.5.3.2.4..2 ELEANOR MELLMAN m1 Harry Ralpheimer Champion
1. CHARLES PHILLIP CHAMPION b 28 Mar 1940 d 23 Sep 1963 bur Gaines Cem. He drowned in an Indiana Harbor ship canal while trying to assist a co-worker who also drowned. Charles was employed on a barge owned by the Capek Towing & Salvage CO of Whitehall MI.
2. PATRICIA ANN CHAMPION b 14 Jun 1942 MI, at Whitehall MI m 01 May 1965 Leo Joseph Scott b 29 Apr 1934 Oswego NY, div.
m2 Alfred Ribone div **no chn** (fr CFD).

MacMICHAEL
1.1.9.4.3.3.1.8.1.1.2 FRANK ROBERTSON MacMICHAEL m Bernice Ruth McCowan
1. FRANK ROBERT MacMICHAEL b 02 Feb 1931 Moncton m 27 Oct 1957 Valerie Stewart b 21 Jan 1933 Moncton.
2. LESLIE IAN MacMICHAEL b 05 Aug 1940 Moncton NB at St Stephens NB **m1** 15 Apr 1963 Barbara Clark b 15 Jun 1944 St Stephen NB; div 1972.
m2 Theora Getson. (fr MAH, SCBG)

MacMICHAEL
1.1.9.4.3.3.1.8.1.1.3 RALPH BAILEY MacMICHAEL m Marion Elmira Goodman
1. LINDA GRACE MacMICHAEL b 15 Nov 1936 Moncton, at the groom's pa's home in Burlington ON m 19 Aug 1961 Frank Stephen Raenden s/o Frank Raenden, b 10 Dec 1933 Staten Island NY.
2. JUDITH HELEN MacMICHEAL b 28 Feb 1940 Moncton m 08 Sep 1962 Montreal QC Harry Joseph Renaud s/o Harry J Renault, b 19 Mar 1939 bp St Augustines (fr MAH, SCBG).

CURRIE
1.1.9.4.3.3.1.8.1.1.4 MARY GERALDINE JUANITA MacMICHAEL m Ronald McDonald Currie
1. HENRY/HARRY ROBERTSON GEORGE CURRIE b 11 Apr 1931 Moncton m Phyllis Isabel McGowan b 06 May 1928 Hampton NB (fr MAH, SCBG).

BAILEY
1.1.9.4.3.3.1.8.1.5.1 LESLIE ALEXANDER BAILEY m Jessie L Reynolds
1. ELIZABETH LENORE BAILEY b 02 May 1947 Wadena SK, at Winnipeg m 10 Oct 1969 Donald Robertson Sutherland b 23 Jul 1941 Saskatoon SK (fr MAH; SCBG).

THOMPSON
1.1.9.4.3.3.1.8.1.5.2 EVELYN MARY BAILEY m Stanley George Thompson
1. MARION MABEL THOMPSON b 02 Feb 1935 Winnipeg MB, m Donald George McCartney s/o William McCartney & Marjorie Cornish, b 19 Feb 1935 Vancouver BC.
2. GRAHAM STANLEY THOMPSON b 11 Jun 1938 Winnipeg MB at Vancouver BC m 04 Aug 1960 Leilannie Mary Thomas d/o Charles Thomas & Euphemia Campbell, b 10 May 1940 Vancouver (fr MAH; SCBG).

ECKMAN
1.1.9.4.3.3.1.8.1.7.1 LOUIS PHILIP ECKMAN m Marjorie A Briggs
1. HEATHER ALLISON ECKMAN b 12 Nov 1964 Toronto ON.
2. CAMERON ANTHONY ECKMAN b 19 Apr 1966 Toronto (fr MAH; SCBG).

FRASER
1.1.9.4.3.3.1.8.1.9.1 LORRAINE HANNAY FARWELL m Leonard F Stanley Fraser.
1. LORNE DOUGLAS FRASER b 22 May 1937 Vancouver, at Merrit BC m 01 Dec 1962 Ethel Diane Koebl b 25 Jul 1943 Beaverlodge AB, div; she lives in Australia.
2. LARRY FREDERICK FRASER b 07 May 1945 m 02 Jul 1966 Verla Marie Bye d/o Marius Bye & Verna Inscho, b 17 Sep 1956 Edmonton AB.
3. LLOYD NORMAN FRASER b 18 Mar 1951 **single**, (when this was recorded).
4. LEONARD LYLE FRASER b 29 Jun 1952 Vancouver, at New Westminster BC m 25 Jun 1977 Diane Say VanLoo d/o Ernest VanLoo & Jean Degenhardt, b 16 Jul 1957 New Westminster (fr MAH; SCBG).

McDOWELL

1.1.9.4.3.3.1.8.1.9.2 LESLIE THOMAS McDOWELL m Dorothy Stuart Jackson
1. LAWRENCE WILLIAM McDOWELL b 15 Feb 1952 Montreal QC m ? (fr MAH: SCBG).

McDOWELL

1.1.9.4.3.3.1.8.1.9.3 LYALL THOMAS DOWELL m Shirley A Nyberg
1. LYALL BRADLEY McDOWELL b 19 May 1958 d 06 Mar 1966 Burnaby.
2. LORI EDITH McDOWELL b 08 Dec 1960.
3. ROBERT GUNNAR McDOWELL b 21 Mar 1964.
4. ALLAN FREDERICK McDOWELL b 06 Oct 1966 (fr MAH: SCBG).

GOATCHER

1.1.9.4.3.3.1.8.1.10.1 SHIRLEY CLAIRE BAILEY m Robert Edward Goatcher
1. MELODY LEE GOATCHER b 05 Mar 1953 Winnipeg.
2. SHIRLEY CAROLE GOATCHER b 30 Oct 1954 Winnipeg d 19 Feb 1962 **dy**.
3. LORI LYNN GOATCHER b 18 Jan 1962 Toronto ON.

MORRIS

1.1.9.4.3.3.1.8.1.10.2 MARY CADENCE BAILEY m William Garth Morris
1. STEVEN BRUCE MORRIS b 05 Mar 1961 Vancouver BC.
2. BARBARA KATHLEEN MORRIS b 30 Apr 1964 Vancouver BC (fr MAH; SCBG).

BAILEY

1.1.9.4.3.3.1.8.1.10.3 KENNETH REX BAILEY m Judith R Wood
1. KEVIN REX BAILEY b 17 Mar 1963 Toronto.
2. KARIN ROSEMARY BAILEY b 15 Jan 1965 Winnipeg.
m2 Nadya Koshtishyn.
3. THOMAS WILLIAM BAILEY b 19 Oct 1974.
4. TANYA KRISTINE BAILEY b 10 Feb 1977 (fr MAH; SCBG).

STYLES

1.1.9.4.3.3.3.2.1.3.1 LAUREN STYLES m ? .
1. KARL STYLES
2. SHIRLEY STYLES (fr BBVH).

ARIAS/BAST/LEVESQUE

1.1.9.4.3.3.3.2.1.6.1 EDYTHE FRANCES HASKELL m1 Umberto Arias, m2 John Bast; m3 A Levesque
1. LINDA LEVESQUE (fr BBVH).

HASKELL

1.1.9.4.3.3.3.2.1.6.2 HERMAN MERVIN HASKELL m1 Estelle Gilbert, m2 Helen Clark
1. BERNICE HASKELL b 27 Oct 1933 m John P Forrister.
2. SHIRLEY HASKELL all res NY State USA (fr BBVH).

NASON

1.1.9.4.3.3.3.2.1.6.3 UNA MAE HASKELL m Paul Nason
1. NANCY NASON (had 3 chn).
2. NEIL NASON (had 2 chn & 2 step-chn) all res NY State USA (fr BBVH).

HALEY

1.1.9.4.3.3.3.2.1.6.4 EMMA BELLE HASKELL m Payson Haley
1. JANET HALEY
2. JEAN HALEY
3. ROBERT HALEY
4. JUDITH HALEY m William Elkins (had 5 chn).
5. RALPH HALEY d ae 10 mo **dy**, all res NY State USA (fr BBVH).

HASKELL

1.1.9.4.3.3.3.2.1.6.5 RALPH STILLMAN HASKELL m1 Amo Burrell Ellis; m2 Mrs Barbara (Brown) Vaughan
1. PETER ELLIS HASKELL b 09 Nov 1936 Rangeley ME res Stratford CT in CT m Consuelo, div.
2. BRIAN STILLMAN HASKELL b 18 Sep 1938 Lewiston ME & served in US Navy in Japan m Mitsuko.
3. ERIC RICHARD HASKELL b 16 Sep 1943 Portland ME, at Westchester Co NY m 1967 Rosemary Martin, d/o Michael Martin & Bridgette Donohue, res Danbury CT.
4. BONITA LEE HASKELL b 14 Feb 1949 Portland ME, at New Milford CT m ? Feb 1969 David Ferris, res Luzerne NY all res NY State USA (all BBVH).

HASKELL

1.1.9.4.3.3.3.2.1.6.6 ELWYN LENORE HASKELL m1 Verna ? , m2 Oudette ? .
1. ANDREW DAVID HASKELL b 12 Jun 1967, all res NY State USA (fr BBVH).

HASKELL
1.1.9.4.3.3.3.2.1.6.7 NEIL DON SMART HASKELL m1 Mrs Arleen (Rockwood) Williams
1. SHEILA HASKELL b 25 Oct 1946 (son Brent)
2. SHERRY HASKELL b 25 Oct 1946 (son Raymond Miller) m ? Miller, div.
3. MARLENE HASKELL b 08 Mar 1954 **single** in 1990; Vice-President of Fleet Bank Bangor ME.

m2 Mrs Arlene (Taggert) Cote all res NY State USA (fr BBVH).

EMERSON
1.1.9.4.3.3.4.1.1.7.3 & 1.1.9.4.3.3.5.4.5.6 EDNA MARION SCOTT m Ernest Emerson

Children are with their mother's underlined number Generation 10.

McCRACKEN
1.1.9.4.3.3.4.1.1.12.1 ALLAN G McCRACKEN m H Arlene Segee
1. NORMA McCRACKEN b 11 Jun 1935, at Fredericton Jct NB m Robert Reid of Sussex, res there in 1982. Living Fredericton in Apr 2000 (all fr SDVSW)
2. GARDA McCRACKEN b 14 Nov 1938 m ? Minion; had 2 chn, div.
3. WAYNE McCRACKEN b 08 Apr 1944 at Fredericton Jct NB m Lynn Ramsey res High River AB in 1982 (fr BMN).

Obit Gleaner Allan G McCracken died 08 Jun 1980 s/o the late Stanley & Elizabeth (Scott) McCracken. Survivors: wife Arleen (Segee) son Wayne, daughters Norma E Reid of Fredericton, Garda Minion of Calgary, seven grandchildren, brother Roy of White's Cove NB, sister Mrs Bertie (Bertha) Nielson of Fredericton & Mrs Paul (Alma) Wade of Penniac; nieces & nephews.

NIELSEN
1.1.9.4.3.3.4.1.1.12.3 BERTHA McCRACKEN m Borties/Bertie Nielsen
1. PAUL NIELSEN b Harvey NB m Linda Ferguson d/o Arnold Ferguson also had a radio repair shop in Saint John, Linda had a beautiful light lyric voice, res Harvey, York Co NB.
2. PHILIP NIELSEN b Fredericton NB m Joycelyn LeGris. Philip died by drowning at Halifax some years ago; his body was not recovered; Joycelyn & family live in San Francisco CA.
3. DAVID NIELSEN m Carolyn Arnold res Keswick Ridge NB. He was a teacher & a well-known musician, played the violin, clarinet, saxophone, flute, piano and had his own band.
4. JOAN NIELSEN m ? Shaw div res Fredericton NB runs Shaw Pottery, has one ch (fr KLAD & BMN).

McCRACKEN
1.1.9.4.3.3.4.1.1.12.5 ROY McCRACKEN m Marion Prince
1. DAWN McCRACKEN b 06 Oct 1935 m ? Rattray, div. **no chn**. Lives White Cove NB.
2. PETER McCRACKEN **single** in 1982.
3. RICHARD McCRACKEN res Fredericton NB. m ? .
4. KENNETH McCRACKEN m ? res Fredericton July 1999.
5. STEPHEN McCRACKEN m ? lives Bayswater NB (fr BMN).

Dawn McCracken is quite well known artist, especially in the Fredericton area. From Nov 22 to Dec 6, 1989 she had an exhibition of 'Recent Paintings and Graphites' at Glerie West end Gallery, Westmont QC. She has exhibited in Montreal Museum Spring Shows, one-man show at the Walter Kickoff Gallery, Montreal. Currently she is employed as Graphic Artist by the New Brunswick Teacher's Association (fr KLAD in a brochure 1990).

WADE
1.1.9.4.3.3.4.1.1.12.6 ALMA ELIZABETH McCRACKEN m Paul Wade
1. NEIL HOWARD WADE m Jennifer Prosser, div. res Calgary, PhD in one of the Sciences employed by Montreal Engineering Co until his retirement.
2. RUTH WADE m Ralph Esau res Penniac NB. Ruth is a divorcee, now retired. She was head of the Emergency Department Oromocto Hospital.
3. CAROL ANN WADE m Robert Clowater res Penniac NB.
4. JUNE WADE m Dennis Allen res Penniac NB (fr KLAD).

DeWITT
1.1.9.4.3.3.4.1.4.1.1 ALVIN DeWITT m Elizabeth N Smith
1. CAROL DeWITT m David Williams.
2. ROBERT DeWITT m Jane ? .
3. PATRICIA DeWITT m Dale Nason.
4. MARY ANN DeWITT of Noonen BC.
5. BRENDA DeWITT deceased (fr The Daily Gleaner 13 May 2002).

Leucas deWit

DeWITT
1.1.9.4.3.3.4.1.7.1.1 BURTON DeWITT m1 Inez Gertrude Ervine, m2 Pearl Giberson
1. RAY DeWITT
2. WINSTON DeWITT
3. SHEILA DeWITT m W Gillie (fr SDG).
4. PAUL DeWITT b 1948 d 08 Dec 1963. Four boys were found in a car in a farmer's field dead from carbon monoxide.

JOHNSON
1.1.9.4.3.3.4.1.7.1.3 JOSPHINE/JOSIE DeWITT m Arthur Johnson
1. CHARLOTTE JOHNSON
2. EVELYN JOHNSON
3. NORA JOHNSON
4. JAMES JOHNSON (fr SDG as in Sheila DeWitt Gillie above).

MacLELLAN
1.1.9.4.3.3.4.1.7.1.4 LEITHA/LETHA DeWITT m1 Vincent Payne, m2 Stewart MacLellan
1. ERIC DeWITT MacLELLAN (fr SDG)

TAYLOR
1.1.9.4.3.3.4.1.7.1.6 IDELLA DeWITT m Holland Taylor
1. CONNIE TAYLOR
2. FREDDIE TAYLOR (fr SDG).

KIRKPATRICK
1.1.9.4.3.3.4.1.7.5.1 MARGARET KIRKPATRICK m Ernest Kirkpatrick
1. LEONA KIRKPATRICK m Kenneth Church res St John.
2. LORETTA KIRKPATRICK m Gary Goodine res Hoyt NB (fr KLAD).

GRAHAM
1.1.9.4.3.3.4.1.7.5.3 EDNA KIRKPATRICK m Parker Graham
1. EVELYN GRAHAM m Edward Kirkpatrick res Sand Brook NB.
2. MURRAY GRAHAM m Connie Ogden res Juvenile NB (fr KLAD).

KIRKPATRICK
1.1.9.4.3.3.4.1.7.5.5 GRANT KIRKPATRICK m Mildred Marie Graham
1. DERROLD KIRKPATRICK m ? He res Riverview NB & worked at the Meteorological Branch of the Department of Transport (KLAD).

KIRKPATRICK
1.1.9.4.3.3.4.1.7.5.6 ALLISON KIRKPATRICK m Florence Kirkpatrick
1. DONALDA KIRKPATRICK died in 1972 **single** (KLAD).
2. CAROL KIRKPATRICK m James Buttimer **no chn** res Hoyt NB.

MALLORY
1.1.9.4.3.3.4.3.2.1.1 LESTER DeWITT MALLORY m1 Crystal Smith
1. ENRIQUE/RICK DeWITT MALLORY b ? Sep 1932 d in Hawaii.
   m2 Eleanor Struck
2. LESTER 'Butch' DeWITT MALLORY Jr. b 03 Mar 1947 (fr LDM).

JEFFREY
1.1.9.4.3.3.4.3.3.1.4 & 1.1.9.4.3.3.5.4.5.1.4 EILEEN SMITH m Walter Jeffery
1. ARTHUR JEFFREY
2. EDWARD JEFFREY
3. BARBARA JEFFREY (fr LDM).

SMITH
1.1.9.4.3.3.4.3.3.1.5 & 1.1.9.4.3.3.5.4.5.1.5 MURRAY SMITH m Grace Smith
1. CALVIN SMITH b 1956 Optometrist in Fredericton.
2. ROWENA SMITH b 1959 m ? Boone who is employed Fredericton Works Dept.
3. DAVID SMITH
4. CHARLENE ADA SMITH b 1969 m lives in California (fr LDM).

COOPER
1.1.9.4.3.3.4.4.3.1.1 STELLA HANSON m Lewis Cooper
1. ALMA HANSON m Eugene Good & had a son named Eugene.
2. DAVID HANSON (fr LDM).

HANSON
1.1.9.4.3.3.4.4.3.1.2 JOHN HANSON m Luella Glidden
1. RUTH HANSON had dau Darlene last name unknown.
2. JACQUELINE HANSON, her chn were James & Johnny, last name unknown (fr LDM).

Leucas deWit

BEAULIEU
1.1.9.4.3.3.4.4.3.1.3 MARY HANSON m Nelson Beaulieu
1. MARLY BEAULIEU
2. SONYA BEAULIEU
3. DOUGLAS BEAULIEU (fr LDM).

HANSON
1.1.9.4.3.3.4.4.3.1.4 FRED HANSON m Shaw ? .
1. FRED HANSON Jr m Donna Carpenter.
2. GILBERT HANSON m ? Kelly.
3. CLARA HANSON (fr LDM).

LYNCH
1.1.9.4.3.3.4.4.3.1.5 SHIRLEY HANSON m Thomas Lynch
1. PATRICIA LYNCH
2. KAREN LYNCH (fr LDM).

HANSON
1.1.9.4.3.3.4.4.3.1.6 ROGER HANSON m Patsy ? .
1. HAROLD HANSON (fr LDM).

HAFFORD
1.1.9.4.3.3.4.4.3.1.7 GLADYS HANSON m Charles Hafford
1. CONNIE HAFFORD m Robert Gerry.
2. EVA HAFFORD m Vaughn McNally.
3. MICHAEL HAFFORD (fr LDM).

HANSON
1.1.9.4.3.3.4.4.3.1.8 HAROLD HANSON m Rose Parks
1. HELEN HANSON (fr LDM).

GLIDDEN
1.1.9.4.3.3.4.4.3.1.9 PAULINE HANSON m Elwood Glidden
1. JUDITH GLIDDEN (fr LDM).
2. HAROLD GLIDDEN
3. CAROLINE GLIDDEN

MARTIN
1.1.9.4.3.3.4.4.3.5.1 MARION CLUFF m Raymond Martin
1. EDWARD MARTIN (fr LDM).

CLUFF
1.1.9.4.3.3.4.4.3.5.2 J EDWARD CLUFF m Lina Lowell
1. JODY CLUFF
2. MARY ANN CLUFF (fr LDM).

CLUFF
1.1.9.4.3.3.4.4.3.5.3 LeROY FREDERICK CLUFF m Leila Miller
1. RICHARD CLUFF
2. KEITH CLUFF (fr LDM).

McDONALD
1.1.9.4.3.3.4.4.3.6.1 BESSIE HAZEL DeWITT m Arnold McDonald
1. PETER McDONALD
2. BENJAMIN McDONALD (fr LDM).

DeWITT
1.1.9.4.3.3.4.4.3.6.2 CARL DeWITT m Opal Harding
1. LAURA ALICE DeWITT
2. BENJAMIN FREDERICK DeWITT
3. MILES CARL DeWITT
4. LISA FLORENCE DeWITT (fr LDM).

DeWITT
1.1.9.4.3.3.4.4.3.6.3 DAVID DeWITT m Ruth Storer
1. WAYNE DAVID DeWITT (fr LDM).

DeWITT
1.1.9.4.3.3.4.4.3.6.4 JAMES DeWITT m Ginger Johnson
1. JEAN ANN DeWITT (fr LDM).
   (It's not clear whether it's Jean Ann or Jean & Ann).

KANE
1.1.9.4.3.3.4.4.3.6.5 MARY IDA DeWITT m Joseph Kane
1. JOEY KANE
2. JEAN KANE
3. ROBERT KANE
4. TERRANCE KANE
5. JAMES KANE
6. SHARON KANE (fr LDM).

HARRISON
1.1.9.4.3.3.4.4.3.6.6 LAURA DeWITT m Sydney Harrison
1. LYNDA HARRISON
2. GRACE HARRISON
3. PATRICIA HARRISON
4. SUSAN HARRISON
5. JAMES HARRISON
6. PAMELA HARRISON (fr LDM).

DeWITT
1.1.9.4.3.3.4.4.3.6.7 FREDERICK DeWITT m Loyala Culbane
1. JENNIFER ANN DeWITT (fr LDM).

ERICKSON
1.1.9.4.3.3.4.4.3.6.9 ALICE ANN DeWITT m Kenneth Erickson
1. ELIZABETH ERICKSON (fr LDM).

BOUCHARD
1.1.9.4.3.3.4.4.3.8.2 ROWENE GRAVES DeWITT m Albert Bouchard
1. SHERI LYNN BOUCHARD
2. BRYAN JUDSON BOUCHARD
3. LORI ANN BOUCHARD
4. WENDI BOUCHARD (fr LDM)

DeWITT
1.1.9.4.3.3.4.4.3.8.3 CARL RAYE DeWITT m Betty Lou Pryor
1. STEVEN CARL DeWITT
2. CYNTHIA ANN DeWITT (fr LDM).

KIRKPATRICK
1.1.9.4.3.3.5.3.3.1.1 & 1.1.9.4.3.3.5.4.5.1.1 VIOLA SMITH m Willard Kirkpatrick
1. VINCENT KIRKPATRICK
2. PAULINE KIRKPATRICK (fr KLAD).

SMITH
1.1.9.4.3.3.5.3.3.1.2 & 1.1.9.4.3.3.5.4.5.1.2 CLAYTON SMITH m Vera Ogden
1. NELSON SMITH
2. DWIGHT SMITH
3. LORRAINE SMITH
4. VALERIE SMITH
5. VIRGINIA SMITH (fr KLAD).

SMITH
1.1.9.4.3.3.5.3.3.1.3 & 1.1.9.4.3.3.5.4.5.1.3 EVA SMITH m Robert Smith
1. CURTIS SMITH
2. CATHERINE SMITH (fr KLAD).

SMITH
1.1.9.4.3.3.5.3.3.1.6 & 1.1.9.4.3.3.5.4.5.1.6 NEWTON SMITH m Lydia Reader
1. LYNWOOD SMITH b 1954 m Lynn Nason lives Hoyt NB, an electrician.
2. EDRIS SMITH b 1956 d 1963 **dy**.
3. ALDEN SMITH b 1960
4. TOBY SMITH b 1969 (fr KLAD).

STEWART
1.1.9.4.3.3.5.5.3.4.1 MARGARET GOURLEY m Walter Stewart
1. KENNETH STEWART
2. KATHY STEWART
3. LEONARD STEWART (fr KLAD).

Leucas deWit

BALDWIN
1.1.9.4.3.3.5.5.4.3.3.1 LOEL AMBERG m Cyril Baldwin Jr
1 SHELLEY AMBERG b 03 Oct 1956 m 03 Feb 1983 Hold McCord (fr KLAD).

BENISH
1.1.9.4.3.3.5.5.3.5.2 MURIEL JORGENSEN m John Benish
1 SUSAN BENISH b 09 Aug 1961.
2 LOEL BENISH b 05 Jul 1964.
3 DIANNE BENISH b 29 Aug 1965.
4 JOHN HENRY BENISH Jr b 01 Nov 1967 (fr KLAD).

CLARK
1.1.9.4.3.3.5.5.3.5.3 PRISCILLA JORGENSEN m Jonathan Clark
1 JONATHAN CLARK Jr b 29 Sep 1969.
2 CHRISTOPHER DeWITT CLARK b 12 Jun 1965 (fr KLAD).

WELPLEY/CORMIER
1.1.9.4.3.3.5.5.7.3.1 ELIZABETH EMERSON m John L Welpley
1 WILLIAM B WELPLEY b 1954.
2 JOHN WELPLEY b 1957.
3 MARY LOU WELPLEY b 1959.
4 CAROL ANN WELPLEY b 1961.
5 BARBARA JEAN WELPLEY b 1963 d 1971 **dy** (fr MWD).
   m2 Robert Cormier
6 ROBERT CORMIER Jr b 1967 **dy** (fr MWD).

WAUGH
1.1.9.4.3.3.5.5.7.4.1 & 1.1.9.4.3.6.5.3.2.1.6 BEVERLY SCOTT m1 William Waugh m2 Philip Nason
1 JEFFREY WAUGH b 1966 m   ?   res Fredericton Junction NB.
2 JANNIKE WAUGH b 1972 Graduate of UNB, BSc Chemical Enginering (fr KLAD).

SCOTT
1.1.9.4.3.3.5.5.7.5.2 EARLE L F SCOTT m Carol Wilcox
1 JANISE LYNN SCOTT b 1970 adopted.
2 DAVID JAMES M SCOTT b 1973 adopted.

CROMBIE
1.1.9.4.3.3.7.3.2.2.1 LESLIE CROMBIE m Bonita Cavanaugh
1 WADE CROMBIE
2 WANDA CROMBIE (fr FCC to KLAD).

SINE
1.1.9.4.3.3.7.4.8.6.1 DOROTHY MOORE m Marvin Sine
1 LYNDA SINE Ottawa ON.
2 PAUL SINE Langley BC chn Trina & Sabrina.
3 ALLAN SINE Vancouver BC (fr Sep 17/1990 Fredericton Gleaner via KLAD).

SHIRLEY
1.1.9.4.3.3.7.4.8.10.1 HELEN PARSONS m Allen Shirley
1 THOMAS SHIRLEY
2 SHARON SHIRLEY

MERSEREAU
1.1.9.4.3.3.7.5.4.1.1 DIANE MAY DeWITT m Douglas Alexander Mersereau (1.1.9.4.3.3.7.8.2.3.5)
1 ANGELIQUE DAWN MERSEREAU b 1969 St John NF m Michael Donahoe who has a flooring business in Moncton NB. Angelique is a Supervisor for a Tim Horton Franchise.
2 PATRICK DOUGLAS MERSEREAU b 27 Mar 1973 Grand Falls NF m Angela Smith of Salsbury NB. Patrick, like his father, is an Air Canada Traffic Controller at Winnipeg MB (fr KLAD).

DeWITT
1.1.9.4.3.3.7.5.4.1.2 ARTHUR WESLEY DeWITT m Tanya Harron
1 MISTY DAWN DeWITT b 14 Oct 1986
2 JESSICA ALEXANDRA DeWITT b 12 May 1991 (fr KLAD).

COWIE
1.1.9.4.3.3.7.5.5.1.1 ROBERT COWIE Jr m Vanne Shelley
1 ANNE COWIE b 18 Nov 1964 NYC employed Wellesey College.
2 ROBERT COWIE b 30 Dec 1968 Berwick PA, attending Cornell took a year off to concentrate on Music (1989-90).
3 RONALD COWIE b 05 Mar 1970 Berwick PA. Enrolled U of Cincinnati (fr RDB).

Leucas deWit

DeWITT
1.1.9.4.3.3.7.5.5.6.1 DAVID BURTON DeWITT m Judith Fox
1. LAURA LOUISE DeWITT b 25 May 1964.
2. ELIZABETH ELLEN DeWITT b ? Nov 1966.
3. ROBERT DOUGLAS DeWITT b 05 Oct 1969 (fr RDB).

BLOIS
1.1.9.4.3.3.7.5.5.6.2 RUBY ROBERTA DeWITT m Eugene Blois
1. JENNIFER LEE BLOIS b 22 Dec 1969 (fr RDB).

DeWITT
1.1.9.4.3.3.7.5.5.6.3 ROBERT ELLIS DeWITT m Vivian Ann Whitman
1. LISA ANN DeWITT b 29 Feb 1968.
2. ROBERT THOMAS DeWITT b 30 Jul 1974 (RDB).

SLIPP
1.1.9.4.3.3.7.8.2.1.1 EDNA DUPLISEA m Luther Slipp
1. RUTH EDNA SLIPP m George Burtt res Central Blissville NB.
2. RONALD SLIPP m 1977 Jane Thomas res Hoyt NB with their dau. Ronald & Duane operate hunting camps. Americans come mostly for bear, deer etc.
3. HAROLD SLIPP m Sharon Brawn res Fredericton Jct.
4. DONNA SLIPP **single**, res central Blissville NB.
5. DUANE SLIPP m Sherri Lorraine Hartt res Fredericton Jct.
6. WENDY SLIPP m Matthew Harris res Fredericton Jct (fr DMBN to KLAD).

WOOD
1.1.9.4.3.3.7.8.2.2.1 VERNA E BELL m John Bertram/Bert Wood
1. EDWIN WOOD
2. DENNIS WOOD
3. MARILYN WOOD m ? , family res 321 City Line, Saint John NB (fr DMBN to KLAD).

KNORR
1.1.9.4.3.3.7.8.2.4.1 IRMA MARION MERSEREAU m Shirley Knorr
1. REGINALD ARTHUR KNORR m ? Phillips.
2. HOWARD ALLISON KNORR m Evelyn Mailman.
3. LINDA DIANNE KNORR m Kevin Daley.
4. PAUL ANDREW KNORR m Debbie Phillips of Tracy NB.
5. DALE CHARLES KNORR b 1951 m Debbie Golden of Tracy NB (fr DMBN to KLAD).

GRAHAM
1.1.9.4.3.3.7.8.2.4..2 GEORGIANNA DARLEEN MERSEREAU m Grant Graham
1. WAYNE GRANT GRAHAM b 1952 m lives Grand Bay NB.
2. BRENDA JOYCE GRAHAM b 1956 (fr DMBN to KLAD).

MERSEREAU
1.1.9.4.3.3.7.8.2.4.3 MELVIN ANDREW MERSEREAU m Jean Ogden
1. MICHAEL MELVIN MERSEREAU b 1963.
2. STEPHEN EUGENE MERSEREAU b 1964.
3. JANICE LYNN MERSEREAU b 1969 (fr DMBN, KLAD).

MERSEREAU
1.1.9.4.3.3.7.8.2.4.4 ELMER FRANKLIN MERSEREAU m Joyce Russel
1. DENISE LEIGH MERSEREAU b 1964.
2. CAROL LYNN MERSEREAU b 1968 (fr DMBN, KLAD).

MERSEREAU
1.1.9.4.3.3.7.8.2.3.5 DOUGLAS ALEXANDER MERSEREAU {m} 1.1.9.4.3.3.7.5.4.1.1 Diane May DeWitt
Children are with their mother's underlined number Generation 11.

HARTT
1.1.9.4.3.3.7.8.2.4.1 DONNA NASON m T Richard Hartt
1. TAMMY HARTT m Danny Gaudet of Beaver Dam NB.
2. BRUCE HARTT of Ottawa NB.
3. THOMAS HARTT of Guelph ON (fr DMBN, KLAD).

WHITAKER
1.1.9.4.3.3.7.9.1. 4.3 PHYLLIS MERSEREAU m Glenn Whittaker
1. EDWARD WHITTAKER killed in a motor vehicle accident late 1970's.
2. NELSON WHITTAKER
3. SUSAN WHITTAKER lived Saint John NB (fr KLAD).

Leucas deWit

WESTON
1.1.9.4.3.3.7.9.1.5.4 BARBARA SMITH m James Weston
1. ALFRED WESTON
2. VALERIE WESTON
3. DONALD WESTON twin of
4. RONALD WESTON
5. LAVERNE WESTON (fr IMS to KLAD).

MacMILLAN
1.1.9.4.3.3.7.9.1.5.5 RUTH SMITH m1 Charles MacMillan
1. REGINALD MacMILLAN
2. DWIGHT MacMILLAN (fr IMS to KLAD).

SMITH
1.1.9.4.3.3.7.9.1.5.6 EVERETT SMITH m1 Eugenia Hoyt m2 Emily Cleghorn
1. BAYARD SMITH m Pam ? of Bathurst (?) res BC.
2. BRUCE SMITH m Carol Ogden of Hoyt NB, res BC.
3. DEBORAH SMITH m David Kelly res in Hoyt then went to AB.
4. ILA SMITH m Murray Parker, div; she res Hoyt NB.
5. MARTY SMITH joined the Armed Forces.

SMITH
1.1.9.4.3.3.7.9.1.5.7 DOUGLAS SMITH m Mary ? .
1. CHRISTOPHER SMITH
2. JEFFERSON SMITH
3. MATTHEW SMITH (fr IMS to KLAD).

CRUIKSHANK
1.1.9.4.3.3.8.1.6.5.1 JANICE SMITH m Neil Cruikshank res Ottawa ON
1. DEBBIE CRUIKSHANK b 1956.
2. DAVID CRUIKSHANK b 1958.
3. SANDRA CRUIKSHANK b 1959 m Larry Langdon res in Ottawa ON.
4. JOHN CRUIKSHANK b 1961 (fr IMS to KLAD).

DeWITT
1.1.9.4.3.3.8.1.6.6.1 ALBERT ERNEST DeWITT m Barbara Gorman
1. SUZANNE MARIE DeWITT b 05 Dec 1955 m Ian Gary Gaskin.
2. ALBERT OWEN DeWITT b 30 Oct 1957 (fr MWD).

DeWITT
1.1.9.4.3.3.8.1.6.6.2 GERALD ERWIN DeWITT m Margaret Eugenie Desaultniers
1. DONNA MAY DeWITT b ? Dec 1951 m Eric Munn.
2. GERALDINE LYNN DeWITT b 17 Oct 1952 m Francis Chambers.
3. KENNETH ERWIN DeWITT b 28 Jan 1961.
4. STEVEN ARNOLD DeWITT b 05 Jul 1967(fr MWD).

HALL
1.1.9.4.3.3.8.1.6.6.3 MARY ELIZABETH DeWITT m John Douglas Hall
1. DOUGLAS RICHARD HALL b 20 Apr 1952 m Brenda Graham.
2. JOANNE ELIZABETH HALL b 22 Jun 1960 (fr MWD).

DeWITT
1.1.9.4.3.3.8.1.6.6.4 ROBERT LEE DeWITT m Katrina Anita Truffin
1. MARK GREGORY DeWITT b 05 Jul 1963.
2. ROBERT LUKE DeWITT b 13 Oct 1969 (fr MWD).

HARTT
1.1.9.4.3.5.2.2.2.1.1 IRMA MAVIS WEBB m David Hartt
1. BRYON CARLISLE HARTT b 20 apr 1940 m1 Rosalea Philmon, m2 Guillemont Tanguay.
2. EDWARD RAY HARTT b 02 Sep 1942 m Coral Ann Skeldon.
3. DAVID WAYNE HARTT b03 Jul 1948 m Lyn Hare.
4. DEANNA MARIE HARTT b 23 May 1951 m Donald Duplisea.
5. SHERRI LORRAINE HARTT m 18 Mar 1959 m Duane Slipp (fr IMWH).

HARRIS
1.1.9.4.3.4.5.2.2.4.3 GLENNA WEBB m Glendon Harris (1.1.9.4.3.5.2.2.11.2.1)
1. MAUREEN HARRIS m Terrance Noble res Tracy NB (fr KLAD).

Leucas deWit

GOLDEN

1.1.9.4.3.5.2.2.4.1.4 MILDRED E DeWITT m Ronald Golden
1. SHARON GOLDEN m Cecil Luke.
2. CHARLENE GOLDEN m Gene McLaughlin.
3. DERITH GOLDEN m Stephen Mersereau of Fredericton Jct NB.
4. MILES GOLDEN res Tracy NB.
5. GREG GOLDEN res Tracy NB.
6. GALEN GOLDEN res Tracy NB.
7. MICHAEL GOLDEN res Tracy NB.
8. HOLLIS GOLDEN of Fredericton.

MERSEREAU

1.1.9.4.3.5.2.2.4.2.1 ROBERT SHIRLEY MERSEREAU m Jeannine Tracy
1. STEPHEN MERSEREAU m Derith   ? .
2. GARY MERSEREAU m Francine   ? .
3. MARK MERSWEREAU m Vanda   ? .
 (fr KLAD).

WATTLING

1.1.9.4.3.5.2.2.4.2.3 IDA MERSEREAU m Major James Wattling
1. CARLEY WATTLING m Bill McKee, Western ON.
2. JIM WATTLING m Anne   ?   of Calgary. Both parents were interred in Prospect Cem Toronto; Obit rural edition June 1999.

HARRIS

1.1.9.4.3.5.2.2.5.3.2 LESLIE HARRIS m Lois O'Leary
1. KEVIN HARRIS m Joyce Hanselpecker from Harvey NB. 2 chn Nicholas & Lucas.
2. MATTHEW HARRIS m Wendy Slipp from Central Blissville NB son Brandon dau b 1998.
3. MYLES HARRIS m Patty Hillman. 2 chn Jordon & Mike.
4. ROGER HARRIS m Ann Marie Long from Centreville NB, best man at Dale's wedding.
5. DALE WALTER HARRIS m1 29 Aug 1992 Shelly Marie Munro (fr DAILY GLEANER Fredericton NB). m2 10 Feb 2000 Stephanie Lynn Farrer (all fr LOH).

HARRIS

1.1.9.4.3.5.2.2.11.2.1 GLENDON HARRIS m 1.1.9.4.3.4.5.2.2.4.3 Glenna Webb
Child is with her Mother's underlined number Generation 11.

ARTES

1.1.9.4.3.5.2.2.12.1.1 SHIRLEY RYDER m Norman Artes
1. MARILYN ARTES m1 Eric Mersereau; m2 Edwin Nason.
2. CAROLYN ARTES m1 John Tapp m2 Lonnie Daley.
3. GORDON ARTES d 31 Dec 1999 a short time before his father {m} Judy Ann Mersereau (1.1.9.4.3.6.5.3.2.1.10) d/o Winslow Mersereau & Freda May Noble, a son Grant Artes [Grant & Kim (Currier) have a son Shane Currier]; div. Judy m Verne Beers & she is the Fredericton Jct postmistress (fr KLAD).

BLIZZARD

1.1.9.4.3.5.2.2.12.2.2 BETTY HARRIS m Tracy Blizzard
1. CLARK BLIZZARD
2. BRENT BLIZZARD
3. KRIS BLIZZARD (fr KLAD).

NASON

1.1.9.4.3.5.2.6.9.1.2 RONALD DELBERT NASON m Myrna Margaret Clarkson
1. LANCE R NASON m at Harvey NB 13 Mar 1949 ? Jun 1971 Beth Elaine Lister, div 1976.
2. WADE MacLEAN NASON b 14 Dec 1950 at Harvey **single**.
3. CURTIS NASON b 22 Mar 1953 at Harvey m 03 Dec 1977 Sharon R Tracy.
4. CRYSTAL JANE RAE NASON b 13 Mar 1936 at Stehens NB.

NASON

1.1.9.4.3.5.2.6.9.1.3 HERBERT RAY NASON m Marilyn Fowler
1. TIMOTHY NASON b 1955 at Toronto ON m   ?   div (fr MWD).

NASON

1.1.9.4.3.5.2.6.9.1.4 ROBERT FREDRICK NASON m Karen M Moore
1. SHERRY NASON b 1958 2 Montreal QC m 1978 Robert L Little.
2. TRACY NASON b 1963 Perth NB m Garnet McIntosh.
3. ZACKARY NASON b 1966 A McAdam NB ((fr MWD).

NASON
1.1.9.4.3.5.2.6.9.2..2 GORDON EDGAR NASON m Marjorie Louise Stannix
1. RANDALL ERIC NASON b 04 Jan 1949 McAdam NB m1 Lealey A Olmstead, div 1983. At the United CH Chipman NB he m2 02 Jun 1984 Pamela Nuttal d/o Daniel Nuttal & Marjorie Lillian Herring b 16 Sep 1944 of Crewe, Hasting Co, Manchster England. Pamela m2 Christopher Leonard Stevenson, div 1970.
2. AVERY RAYE NASON b 26 Aug 1950 at Harvey NB m 22 Mar 1974 Noreen Breau res Dalhousie NB.
3. JANIS MARIE NASON b 11 S2p 1952 A Harvey m 22 Mar 1975 Ronald Casavant res Vernon BC (fr MWD).

NASON
1.1.9.4.3.5.2.6.9.2..4 NORMAN ALBERT NASON m Helen Elaine Mighion
1. RANDAL EUGENE NASON b 14 Sep 1955 Hamilton ON m1 Carol Thurlow, div. He m2 06 Jan 1979 Nola Tipson, of Lincoln ME.
2. CINDY ANN NASON b 29 Dec 1956 Hamilton ON m Clement McGillicudy, div (fr MWD).

NASON
1.1.9.4.3.5.2.6.9.2.5 STUART EARL NASON m Norma Lillian Carr
1. STUART ALLEN NASON m 1953 Harvey NB at Saint John m ? Nov 1977 Ann Phillips
2. STEPHEN ROSS NASON b 1959 at Saint John m there 28 Aug 1892 Donna ? .
3. MARK GORDON NASON b 1963.
4. JOHN DOUGLAS NASON b & d 1963.
5. BARBARA AMANDA NASON b 1969(fr MWD).

NASON
1.1.9.4.3.5.2.6.9.2.8 DAVID ARNOLD NASON m Gloria Currie
1. MARTY DAVID NASON b 05 Sep 1958 Harvey NB, at Mcadam NB m 25 Feb 1984 Angela J Donnoyer b 18 Feb 1966 in PA d/o Lawrence Donnoyer & Marion Smith.
2. DEANNA DAWN NASON b 30 Aug 1960 Fredricton Jct NB.
3. SHAWN DALE NASON b 28 Nov 1968 McAdam NB (fr MWD).

SULLIVAN
1.1.9.4.3..5.2..6.9.5.1 GERALD SULLIVAN m Katherine Christie
1. TERRY SULLIVAN
2. TRACY SULLIVAN
3. CRYSTALL SULLIVAN (fr LPD).

CURRIE
1.1.9.4.3.5.2.6.9.5.2 DONNA SULLIVAN m Milton Currie
1. JEROME CURRIE (fr LPD).

SCOTT
1.1.9.4.3.6.5.3.2.1.6 IDA VIVIAN MERSEREAU {m} 1.1.9.4.3.3.5.5.7.4 Frank Raymond Scott
Children are with their Father's underlined number, Generation 10.

NASON
1.1.9.4.3.6.5.3.2.3.1 LENORE MERSEREAU m Payson Nason
1. DONALD NASON
2. SUSAN NASON
3. KENDALLS NASON

MERSEREAU
1.1.9.4.3.6.5.3.4.3.2 GERTRUDE TRACY m 1.1.9.4.3.6.5.3.1.6 Clarence Mersereau
Children are with their Father's underlined number, Generation 10.

TRACY
1.1.9.4.3.6.5.3.4.3.3 KENNETH TRACY m1 Marjorie Tracy
1. KATRINE TRACY
2. HARRIET TRACY
3. ROLAND TRACY
   m2 Mrs Beryl (Byers) Norrad (all fr GMAW)

TRACY
1.1.9.4.3.6.5.3.4.3.4 GARNETT TRACY m ? .
1. WYETH TRACY
2. KENSIL TRACY
3. GARNATT TRACY
4. UNKOWN NAME TRACY (info fr GMAW).

TRACY
1.1.9.4.3.6.6.1.2.4.5 & 1.1.9.4.3.7.3.2.2.5 STELLA LILLIAN DeWITT m Erwin Abner Tracy
1. GAY WINNETTE TRACY b 19 Dec 1930 Tracy, at Fredericton m 15 Oct 1960 George McGuire.
2. BLISS LLOYD TRACY b 23 Nov 1942 Milo ME, a Scientist, at Hamilton ON m 12 Apr 1961 Mary Diane Loates d/o Franklin Steven Loates & Dorothy Eileen Mary Crook, b 06 Oct 1945 Toronto ON. Dianne is a cousin of the painter of wildlife Glen Oates (fr KLAD.

PHEASANT
1.1.9.4.3.6.6.5.1.2.2 DOROTHY PRIDE m William Frederick Pheasant
1. EILEEN PATRICIA PHEASANT b 02 Dec 1931 Orillia ON, a teacher, at Coldwater ON m Stanley Snider s/o Stanley Damon Snider & Lauren Alexander White BA MED, b 24 Jun 1930 Shelburne ON bp at Odessa ON, a teacher.
2. DIANNE ELIZABETH PHEASANT b 05 Sep 1936 Orillia ON bp Coldwater ON m Robert Mercer res Coldwater On. All chn b Hanover ON (fr KLAD).

HALEY
1.1.9.4.3.6.6.5.1.3.1 LORENA ALEXANDER m Percy F Haley
1. RICHARD HALEY b 1925 m 1955 Elizabeth Drummer of Rowley MA. Richard was a Barrister (as of 1979) served overseas with the US Navy in WWII, res Marblehead MA.

NASON
1.1.9.4.3.6.6.5.1.4.1 EULAH MARGARET STUART m Wallace Nason
1. JOHN STUART NASON b 05 Nov 1925 Saint John NB, at St Stephens, South Bay NB d 09 Oct 1995 m 1949 Mary Louise Stewart b 1926 St George NB, res South Bay NB.
2. EILEEN SINCLAIR NASON b 22 Mar 1926 at Saint John NB became a M.D. m 1949 Kenneth Cambon M.D. & Surgeon, Quebec City QC. Both interned at Galveston TX. Eileen was a grad of UNB, Post Grad of Vassar, Eye Specialist at McGill, specializing in eye surgery in Vancouver BC. Ken wrote an account of his time in Japanese Prisoner Camp in WWII, Guest of Hirohito. Some of the present Japanese wish to tell it as it was and invited Ken and Eileen to visit Japan, which they have done on two occasions.
3. MARGARET KATHLEEN NASON b 11 Mar 1929 Upper Kent NB res Welsford **single**.
4. DAVID ALEXANDER NASON b 01 Mar 1931at Fredericton Jct res Harvey York Co NB m 1948 Shirley Wood of Harvey, York Co. David is employed by the CPR (fr KLAD).

STUART
1.1.9.4.3.6.6.5.1.4.3 JOHN WALTER STUART m Jean MacDougal
1. JOHN ALEXANDER STUART
2. JANET LOUISE STUART (fr KLAD).

STUART
1.1.9.4.3.6.6.5.1.4.6 ALLEN PALMER STUART m Mary Curry
1. ALLEN W STUART b Fredericton NB m Sue Hannon.
2. SUSAN STUART b Fredericton m Kevin Malone.

Allen Palmer Stuart graduated from the University of New Brunswick in 1938 with Honours in Mathamatics and Chemistry, PhD from McGill University 1942, four years service in the military WWII, Research Council of Canada on explosive gasses, etc. He returned to the University of New Brunswick, Department of Chemistry in 1946, there until his death 27 Jun 1974. He was granted an "Excellence in Teaching Award" there. The teaching award granted annually since his death is known as the "Allen Palmer Stuart Excellence in Teaching Award" (fr KLAD).

ALLEN
1.1.9.4.3.6.6.9.6.1.1 PEARL NASON m Gordon Allen
1. ELIZABETH ALLEN m Lloyd Whitaker res Hoyt NB.
3. EDITH ALLEN m Alden Thomas of Fredericton NB. He was on the City Ploice Force, now retired.
4. RAYMOND ALLEN **single**.
5. ELAINE ALLEN m William Humble res Hoyt NB (fr EAW).

WILSON
1.1.9.4.3.6.6.9.1.2 VERGIE NASON m Edward Wilson
1. MAXINE WILSON
2. KAREN WILSON deceased.
DEANNA WILSON
3. EDWARD WILSON
4. MARGARET ROSE WILSON
5. VALERIE WILSON (fr EAW).

Leucas deWit

BRAWN
1.1.9.4.3.6.6.9.6.1.3 NELLIE NASON m Hazen Frederick Brawn
1. ERIC FREDERICK BRAWN m Pearl ? .
2. DARLENE BRAWN m ? Carr of Westfield.
3. H. AVERY BRAWN m Lovann ? .
4. KEITH BRAWN m Ann Marie ? .
5. LORRAINE BRAWN m ? Dale Hamilton of South Branch Lake (fr EAW).

NASON
1.1.9.4.3.6.6.9.6.1.4 EUGENE NASON m Vivian Nason
1. ROLAND NASON
2. DOROTHIA NASON (fr EAW).

BURNETT
1.1.9.4.3.6.6.9.6.4.1 RAYMOND BURNETT m1 Edith McLaughlin
1. DARYL BURNETT m Susan Walker res Fredericton Jct NB.
  m2 Eva Smith d 1964 (fr EAW).

SAUNDERS
1.1.9.4.3.6.6.9.6.4.3 THEDA BURNETT m James Saunders
1. SUSAN SAUNDERS
2. NANCY SAUNDERS (fr EAW).

TAYLOR
1.1.9.4.3.6.6.9.6.4.4 RETA BURNETT m Gordon Taylor
1. JUDITH TAYLOR
2. KATHY TAYLOR (fr EAW).

BURNETT
1.1.9.4.3.6.6.9.6.4.5 LLOYD BURNETT m Corinne Sampson
1. WENDY BURNETT (fr EAW)

MERSEREAU
1.1.9.4.3.6.6.9.6.4.6 HILDA BURNETT m Gerald Mersereau
1. TERRANCE MERSEREAU
2. DEANNA MERSEREAU 1929 {m1} Randy Mersereau 1.1.9.4.3.6.5.3.2.3.2.? s/o Treston Mersereau & Doris Byers; div (m2) ? .
3. ALLAN MERSEREAU **single.**
4. BENTON MERSEREAU **single.**
5. COLIN MERSEREAU m   ? (fr EAW).

NASON
1.1.9.4.3.6.6.9.8.1.1 PERLEY DAVID NASON m Viola Evelyn Hayward
1. DOROTHY EVELYN NASON b 1941 Tracy NB m 1965 Joseph Savoy b 1937 res Saint John NB.
2. DONNA LEAH NASON b 1943 Tracy m 1967 Robert McGrath b 1934 res Darmouth NS.
3. LESLIE DAVID NASON, b 1945 Tracy NB, m 1968 Louann Carter d/o Claude Carter of Blissville & Geraldine Dupisea, b 1953 at Fredericton NB.
4. KAYE LUNN NASON b 1947 Tracy res BC.
5. PERRY A NASON b 1949 Fredericton Jct NB, at the Catholic CH there m Alvine Aubin d/o Frank Aubin & Yvonne Rosingnol, b 1952 Grand Falls NB. All chn b Fredericton Jct.
6. GEORGE BAYARD NASON b 1950 Fredericton Jct m 1973 Elizabeth Haslett b 1953.
7. MURIEL EILEEN NASON b 1953 Tracy m 1971 Eric Johnston b 1947.
8. JUNITA MARYLOU NASON b 1955 Fredericton Jct m Roger Lee Nason.
9. LEONARD PERLEY NASON b 1956 Fredericton Jct.

NASON
1.1.9.4.3.6.6.9.8.1.3 TRAVIS EDISON NASON m Letha Phillips
1. TEHWAUNA CHARLOTTE NASON b 1956 Tracy m 1973 Allen Harris.

NASON
1.1.9.4.3.6.6.9.8.1.4 CHESTER SMITH NASON m Annie Nason
1. GARY SMITH NASON b 1946 at St Stephen NB, m1 1969 Rita McBean, div m2 Mrs Brenda (de la Franir) Hartwell Chn b Fredericton NB.

NASON
1.1.9.4.3.6.6.9.8.1.7 BRYON EDWARD NASON m Nora Woodworth
1. KIMBERLEY ANN NASON b 1958.

Leucas deWit

2 DARLENE ELIZABETH NASON b 1959, Cpl, at Tracy m 20 Jun 1981 Luc Beauchesne fr Sherbrooke QC serving in the Armed Forces.
3 DAVID FOSTER NASON b 1960 d 1963 **dy**.
4 KEVIN BRYON NASON b 1962.
5 KELLY EDWARD NASON b 1962 d 21 Oct 1983 at Porcupine Creek, bur Tracy. He was killed racing an ATC bike down the railroad track & slid off the bridge down into the stream, hitting his head on a rock.
6 KELSEY TROY NASON b 19 Sep 1976 Victoria Public Hospital.

NASON

1.1.9.4.3.6.6.9.8.1.8 STUART EVERETT NASON m Katherine Dawn Horne
1 JAY STEWART NASON b 1960 Fredericton NB.
2 JODY DEAN NASON b 1961 Fredericton NB.
3 SHAWN MICHAEL NASON b 1967 Newcastle NB.

NASON

1.1.9.4.3.6.6.9.8.1.11 FRANCIS VINCENT NASON m Margaret Harris
1 PAMELA DAWN NASON b 1969 Fredericton Jct NB.
2 ANN MARGARET LYNN NASON b 1971 Fredericton NB.
3 SHARON ANN NASON b 1976 Oromotco NB.
4 PATTI NASON b Fredricton NB.

NASON

1.1.9.4.3.6.6.9.8.1.13 LESTER EUGENE NASON m Murielle Aubin
1 LINDA NASON b 1967.
2 JAMES LESTER NASON b 1972. twin of
3 JASON ALLAN NASON b 1972.

NASON

1.1.9.4.3.6.6.9.8.1.14 RANDY LEE NASON m Dianne Aubin
1 CHRISTOPHER NASON b 1970 Fredericton NB.
2 CURTIS NASON b 1975 Fredericton NB.

NASON

1.1.9.4.3.6.6.9.10.1.2 WILFRED CLAUDE NASON m ? Czeto
1 ROBERT ALLEN NASON b 1959 Barrie ON.
2 DAVID GEORGE NASON b 1961 Pembroke ON.
3 STEPHEN WAYNE NASON b 1963 Fredericton NB.
4 DENNIS ALFRED NASON b 1965 Kingston ON.

NASON

1.1.9.4.3.6.6.9.10.8.3 LEON RUSSELL NASON m Susan Joy McCullough
1 ADAM M NASON b 1981.

NASON

1.1.9.4.3.6.6.9.10.9.4 MILFORD NASON m Linda Gail Harris
1 WILLIAM ARNOLD NASON b 1968 St Stephens NB.
2 DARREN EDWARD NASON b 1970 Montreal QC.
3 CAROLINE FRANCES NASON b 1974 Fredericton NB.

NASON

1.1.9.4.3.6.6.9.10.9.5 ROY NASON m Mary Ann Brown
1 DALE EDWARD NASON b 1974.
2 SHERRI ANGELA NASON b 1977.
3 CARLA DAWN NASON b 1979.

BROWN

1.1.9.4.3.7.1.8.2.5.1 NETTIE CLARICE TERRY m Richard Wilson Brown
1 DOUGLAS NASON BROWN b 25 Nov 1948 m 15 Aug 1982 Sandra Silberstein.
2 CARTER WILSON BROWN b 02 Apr 1950.
3 MARK ALLISON BROWN b 25 Jul 1952.

WEBB

1.1.9.4.3.7.3.2.2.1.2 GEORGE LEONARD WEBB m Audrey Davidson
1 PETER MYRON WEBB m Lorraine Nason.
2 CANDACE MAE WEBB
3 STEPHANIE JOY WEBB m Brian Johnson.
4 TANYA WEBB
5 JERRY DAVIDSON WEBB (fr IMWH).

MOSHER

1.1.9.4.3.7.3.2.4.2.4 MARION MERSEREAU m Stephen Mosher
1. STEPHEN MOSHER Jr. res near Saint John NB.
2. BRIAN MOSHER a lawyer. Saint John (all fr LOH).
3. SANDRA MOSHER b 1945 m Glen Larson of St Andrews NB She d May 1976 in a car accident.

TOOLE

1.1.9.4.3.7.3.2.5.4.1 NELDA ACKER m Harry Toole
1. HAROLD TOOLE m Arlene ? (fr KLAD).

FLEMING

1.1.9.4.3.7.4.2.4.1.3 MARGARET ANNE DeWITT m Michael Fleming
1. WILLIAM JOHNSTON FLEMING b 05 May 1975 (fr LPD).

BAINES

1.1.9.4.3.7.4.2.5.1.1 ANDREW DeWITT BAINES M.D. m Cornelia Van Erk M.D.
1. NICOLE DeWITT BAINES b 05 Dec 1957 at Toronto ON.
2. NIGEL ERIC BAINES b 07 May 1963 at Toronto (fr MECB).

LYON

1.1.9.4.3.7.4.2.5.1.2 LINDA BAINES m H Neville Lyon
1. DIANE LYON b 1957.
2. DUNCAN LYON b 1959.
3. SAMENA LYON b 1966 (fr MECB).

COBORN

1.1.9.4.3.7.4.2.5.2.1 JOHN COBURN m BEVERLY MILLER
1. NANCY COBURN b 1966.
2. ANDREW COBURN b 1968 (fr MECB).

COLEMAN

1.1.9.4.3.7.4.2.5.3.1 ALLEN BRANT COLEMAN m June ? .
1. ALLAN BRANT COLEMAN Jr.
2. CANDY COLEMAN (fr MECB).

FULLERTON

1.1.9.4.3.7.4.2.5.5.1 ANNIE CRIPS McCAULEY m William Fullerton
1. TERRANCE FULLERTON b 1956 .
2. LESLIE FULLERTON b 1959.
3. DINAH FULLERTON b 1963 (fr MECB).

McCAULEY

1.1.9.4.3.7.4.2.5.5.3 BARRY McCAULEY m Mary Kelly
1. MORGAN McCAULEY.
2. GANNON McCAULEY (fr MECB).

DeWITT (formerly Saligman)

1.1.9.4.3.7.4.3.1.1.1 BRYCE DeWITT m Cecile Marette
1. NICOLETTE KIM DeWITT b in India, degree fr Harvard Law School, works in NY at Condert et Freres; Phi Betta Kappa U of Chicago, speaks French & Japanese.
2. JAN DeWITT studied Russian & Slavic Languages in Austin TX.
3. CHRISTINE HONOR DeWITT in 1979 working for an electronics firm & hadn't finished college.
4. ABIGAIL DeWITT 1978 freshman at Harvard, lives in the famous Yard; Majors in French Literature & dramatics. Family res Austin TX (fr HKPSM)

Letter 06 Feb 1978 fr HPSM.

Bryce is in <u>Who's Who.</u> He is a very good Theoretical Physicist with a degree from Harvard at age 20, Phi Beta Kappa at 19, crew-stoke, all around man inclined to be scholarly. He married Cecile Marette (French) whom he met at the Institute for Advanced Study at Princeton, when Dr Oppenheimer was there. I went to Paris to their wedding in 1951. Two or three years ago he was Visiting Fellow for a calendar year at All Saint's College, Oxford, England, there again the following summer. Next summer he will be in London. He will be collaborating with a British physicist on a book on quantum theory and relativity. He is head of the "Relativity Center" at the U of Texas at Austin. Cecile is also on the faculty there. They go all over the world to lecture and spend some time in France every year.

DeWITT (formerly Saligman)
1.1.9.4.3.7.4.3.1.1.2 LLOYD LEWIS DeWITT m Betty Miller
1   KATHLEEN DeWITT studied Engineering in CA.
2   ALEXANDER DeWITT res Washington DC (fr HKPSM).

Letter 06 Feb 1978 fr HKPSM

Lloyd Lewis DeWitt went to prep school where he won a scholarship prize then to Harvard where a low grade in math prevented him from getting more than a "magna" when he graduated. He went to Stanford (after a scarey concussion) where he almost finished a PhD in philology. But rather than teach English he suddenly joined the State Department as a Foreign Service Officer. He has been stationed in Germany, Afganistan, Iran, Chile, London and now (1978) in Washington DC.

DeWITT (formerly Saligman)
1.1.9.4.3.7.4.3.1.1.3 HUGH HAMILTON DeWITT m Joanne Rice
1   DIANE DeWITT studied Fine Arts at NH.
2   RACHEL DeWITT
3   PAMELA DeWITT (fr HKPSM).

DeWITT
1.1.9.4.3.7.4.3.1.1.4 HIRAM PETTIT DeWITT m "a Hungarian from Australia"
1   SOPHIA CATERINA DeWITT b 1974 in Italy.

Letter 06 Feb 1978 fr HKPSM.

Hiram is a teacher of ancient history and very scholarly. He was eight years in Rome and knows every corner; he has traveled all over the Eastern Mediterranean and Near East. He is a real classicist. When politics in Italy became difficult for the school in Rome he decided to resign and came home. But California schools are not very interested in Latin or Ancient History and he has not found yet where he really wants to be. He lives near me here. He is married to Hungarian girl brought up in Australia and they have a beautiful 3-year-old daughter Sophia Caterina born in Italy. There is a lot of red hair in the DeWitt-Pettit family. Sophia has beautiful red hair like mine <u>was</u> (all white now).

ARDEN
1.1.9.4.3.7.4.3.4.3.2 FRED DOUGLAS ARDEN m Mary Jo Micksall
1   MARILYN SUE ARDEN
2   FRED <u>THOMAS</u>/TOM ARDEN
3   CHARLES <u>MELVIN</u>/MEL ARDEN (fr ROPR).

RICKARD
1.1.9.4.3.7.4.3.6.3.4 ROBERT PERCY RICKARD m 1 Margaret Cameron Morganstern, m2 Marjorie Aline Hinds

Robert was born in Montreal QC 7 Aug 1921with severe spinal deformities, where his father George Bates Rickard was employed as a Mechanical Engineer but later accepted ordination as a Fundamentalist Minister and a post in New Bremen, OH. Resigning that post to better his family, moved to Woodhaven NY then moved family to Glen Rock NJ. The commencement of the "Great Depression" saw him employed selling insurance for Metropolitan Insurance Co. and garden tools on commission for Sears Roebuck later living in Ridgewood NJ, received financial assistance from family in England. In 1936 found employment through the Masonic Lodge as a Mechanical Engineer at the Carborundum Co Niagara Falls NYwhere he was killed in an industrial accident. Robert attended school in Ridgewood NJ but completed high school in Niagara Falls NY, drafted 1942 trained at Ft. Eustis VA, served in Artillery WWII in the Pacific, injured and discharged returned to Lewiston NY, worked as Expeditor and Contract Admin at The Coated Abrasives Div of Carborundum Co, attended U of Buffalo, trained as programmer & systems analyst on Univac I computer 1952, was Mgr Systems & Data Processing-Twin Industries, Buffalo NY. After death of wife Margaret in 1967 and collapse of AeroSpace industry, accepted position at Chicago Pneumatic Tool Co, Franklin PA, then as Manager, Mfg Systems at Talon, Inc, Meadville, PA married second to Marjorie Aline Hinds, ex-wife of Frank Stanley Warzeski MD, in 1979 Purchased motel in Salem VA, sold five yrs later at a profit, employed as Maintenance Mgr-large apart complexes in Roanoke VA to comply with Social Security requirements, retired 1984 to travel in a motor home but onset of rheumatoid arthritis in Aline forced sale of motor home and purchase of a home in Zephyrhills FL moved to Kingwood TX after Aline's death in 1995, then Meadville PA, currently resides Kingwood and does genealogy of his (and other) families in conjunction with LDS Family History Center.

1   JEFFREY CAMERON RICKARD b 15 Jun 1948 Niagara Falls NY m1 17 Jun 1948 Joan Marie Rifle b 17 Nov 1948 Smethport PA div, m2 Catharine Bemis div, with companion Pamela Ridge in Goshen NY.
2   PETER RICKARD b & d 1951 **dy** twin.
3   JOSEPH RICKARD b & d 1951 **dy** twin.
4   KURT ALAN RICKARD b 27 Oct 1952 Niagara Falls NY m 8 Dec 1972 Barbara Ann McGuire b 08 Jul 1954 Houghton MI (fr RPR).

FOXLEY
1.1.9.4.3.7.4.5.1.1.1 JOHN WILLIAM FOXLEY m1 Virginia Morris
1. JAQUELINE RUTH FOXLEY m Chalmer Rayner (fr EM).
2. BARBARA FOXLEY m John Wyke (fr EM).
m2 Rosella Evers div, now deceased.
m3 Jean Tacker (fr EA).

FOXLEY
1.1.9.4.3.7.4.5.1.1.3 FRED HOWARD FOXLEY m Helen Eva Randall
1. ROBERT ALLEN FOXLEY b 07 Nov 1945 m Merrilee Lane b 09 Sep 1946.
2. JOAN LOUISE FOXLEY b 12 Sep 1947. (fr MA)

FOXLEY
1.1.9.4.3.7.4.5.1.1.5 BESSIE ROSE FOXLEY m Lester Edwin Schultz
1. MARY FRANCES SCHULTZ b 12 Oct 1938 m Carville Mace Love, had one adopted son, Ty Eric b 25 Dec 1963
2. ARTHUR A SCHULTZ b 05 Dec 1939 m 28 Aug 1963 Linda Lee Engel, b 12 Feb 1945 div 1971 (fr MA,GRAH,EM)

FOXLEY
1.1.9.4.3.7.4.5.1.1.6 CYRIL HERALD FOXLEY m Gladys Edna Dowling
1. CINDY FOXLEY b 01 Jan 1955 (fr EM, LES).

HYSERT
1.1.9.4.3.7.4.5.1.3.1 RUTH ELEANOR KENYON m Edgar Franklin Hysert
1. PATRICIA RUTH HYSERT b 18 Sep 1939 m 31 Dec 1966 Bernard Stevenson b 18 Feb 1935.
2. PETER KENYON FRANKLIN HYSERT b 30 Nov 1940 d 26 Jul 1960 **dy**.
3. SHIRLEY ELSIE MAY HYSERT b 07 Dec 1944 m 05 Dec 1963 James Alexander Duffas b 05 Dec 1965.
4. EDGAR BRIAN HYSERT b 29 Jun 1947 m 23 Mar 1972 Elsie Joyce Baker b 04 Oct 1939.
5. SYLVIA DARLENE HYSERT b 26 Jan 1955 (fr MA).

STUART
1.1.9.4.3.7.4.5.1.3.2 LOUISE KATHERINE RAY KENYON m Frederic Isaac Stuart
1. GEORGE ARTHUR STUART b 04 May 1930 m ? May 1958 Shirley Ann Ecker b 02 May 1940.
2. NORMAN STANLEY STUART b 08 Jun 1933 m 05 Dec 1958 Lois Mabel Stuart b 08 Apr 1940.
3. FREDERIC EARLE STUART b 15 Jul 1935 m 20 Dec 1975 Gail Badgerow b 1942.
4. RAYMOND DOUGLAS STUART b 26 Jan 1940 m 10 Jun 1961 Sharleen Pearson b 05 Mar 1942.
5. JOHN DONALD STUART b 24 Feb 1944.
6. MARY KATHERINE RAY STUART b 19 Mar 1946 m 15 Jun 1968 Robert Charles Loose b 25 Aug 1939 Woodstock NB. All siblings b Wentworth Co ON (fr LKRKS).

MORRISON
1.1.9.4.3.7.4.5.1.7.1 MARION RUTH STEPHENSON m Malcolm Ralph Morrison
1. RALPH EDWARD MORRISON b 1961.
2. DOUGLAS ALLAN MORRISON b 1964 (fr EM).

STEPHENSON
1.1.9.4.3.7.4.5.1.7.2 JOHN WALLACE STEPHENSON m Elizabeth Hyde
1. KATHERINE RUTH STEPHENSON b 1963.
2. DAVID WALLACE STEPHENSON b 1965 (fr EM).

HYLAND
1.1.9.4.3.7.4.5.6.2.2 OSBORNE HYLAND m Vera S ? .
1. EDWARD HYLAND b 16 Sep 1949.
2. DIANE E HYLAND b 31 Mar 1951 m 13 Oct 1974 Edward M Hancock b 09 Aug 1933.
3. JANNIE E HYLAND b 26 Jun 1958.
4. SHELLEY E HYLAND b 20 Sep 1961(fr EM).

PURVIS
1.1.9.4.3.7.4.6.1.2.1 RONALD JAMES PURVIS m Joy Nixon
1. WENDY PURVIS b Sep 1948.
2. SHEILA PURVIS b Oct 1951.
3. JOCELYN PURVIS b Sep 1955.
4. KAREN PURVIS b Jan 1957.
5. MARGARET PURVIS b Feb 1959.
6. ERIC PURVIS b 26 Mar 1964.
7. AMY PURVIS b 31 Dec 1965 (All siblings b Redvers SK fr EJDL).

JAMES
1.1.9.4.3.7.4.6.1.2.2 LAURA ROSE PURVIS m Robert James
1. BRIAN ROBERT JAMES

Leucas deWit

2   DENNIS JAMES (fr EJDL).

PURVIS

1.1.9.4.3.7.4.6.1.2.3 CLARENCE PURVIS m Betty Ruth Symons
1   ANDREW PURVIS
2   WAYNE PURVIS
3   JOHN PURVIS
4   CHARLOTTE PURVIS
5   DONALD PURVIS
6   GORDON PURVIS (fr EJDL).

PURVIS

1.1.9.4.3.7.4.6.1.2.4 WALTER MERTON PURVIS m Dale Sauter
1   DAVID PURVIS
2   DARCY PURVIS
3   TIMOTHY PURVIS (fr EJDL).

DEAN

1.1.9.4.3.7.4.6.1.3.1 RALPH ERNEST DEAN m Alice Rutledge
1   CONSTANCE MAY DEAN b 06 Oct 1960.
2   MARVIN RALPH DEAN b 14 Mar 1962.
3   DENNA MARIE DEAN b 22 Jul 1963, all siblings b Carnduff MB (fr EJDL).

HALL

1.1.9.4.3.7.4.6.1.3.2 MURIEL IRMA DEAN m Keith Hall
1   HEATHER LOIUSE HALL b 05 May 1962 Steinbach MB.
2   DARRYL KEITH HALL b 27 Aug 1964.
3   CHERYL DAWN HALL b 21 Mar 1967.
4   ANDREA MARIE HALL b 21 Oct 1968.
5   CURTIS LEE HALL b 24 Jun 1971(#2-5 b Regina SK, fr EJDL).

FUNK

1.1.9.4.3.7.4.6.1.3.3 PHYLLIS ALMA DEAN m Clarence Funk
1   SHARON CELESTE FUNK b 12 Feb 1962.
2   MICHAEL CLARENCE FUNK b 05 Dec 1963.
3   RONDA MARIE FUNK b 07 Jan 1968 (all b Langenburgh SK, fr EJDL).

DEAN

1.1.9.4.3.7.4.6.1.3.4 MELVIN DEAN m Margaret Fargie
1   LORI JAN DEAN b 03 Oct 1971.
2   BRENT WILSON DEAN b 15 Nov 1972 (both chn b Noranda QC, fr EJDL).

DeWITT

1.1.9.4.3.7.4.6.3.1.1 KEITH NORMAN DeWITT m Barbara Hudson
1   WAYNE DeWITT resembles Irma DeWitt Roger's son Don; brown eyes.
2   IAN DeWITT moved to Prince Rupert, Cranbrook, Golden, Kamloops, Trail &Vancouver BC. The first five towns were places to which Laurie DeWitt (1.1.9.4.3.7.10.10.1.2.1) was posted.
3   WENDY DeWITT
4   DEBBIE DeWITT (fr BHD).

DeWITT

1.1.9.4.3.7.4.6.3.1.2 ERIC HARRISON DeWITT m Mary Pat Trick
1   PETER JOHN DeWITT
2   DAVID ERIC DeWITT
3   PATRICK NORMAN DeWITT (fr BHD).

OCHETWA

1.1.9.4.3.7.4.6.3.1.3 JOAN MAXINE DeWITT m Eugene Ochetwa
1   IAN OCHETWA
2   DEAN OCHETWA
3   LYNN OCHETWA
4   SUSAN OCHETWA (fr BHD).

DeWITT

1.1.9.4.3.7.4.6.3.1.5 GARTH DAVEY DeWITT m Norma Wood
1   KIM DeWITT
2   JAY DeWITT
3   MARK DeWITT (fr BHD).

RODGERS
1.1.9.4.3.7.4.6.3.2.1 BRIAN ALEXANDER RODGERS m Ruth Armstrong
1. ROBERT HARRISON GRANT RODGERS b 17 Apr 1954 m 22 Aug 1976 Elizabeth Short.
2. GREGORY ALEXANDER RODGERS b 18 Jan 1956.
3. BRIAN GARNET RODGERS b 23 Feb 1957.
4. KENNETH HILLYARD RODGERS b 14 Jul 1959 (All siblings b Regina SK).

CARLETON
1.1.9.4.3.7.4.6.4.1.1 SHIRLEY ELEANOR STEELE m John W Carleton
1. LYNDA ANN CARLETON b 08 Jun 1954.
2. GARY ROY CARLETON b 16 May 1956 (both chn b Montreal QC fr MEJLS).

STEELE
1.1.9.4.3.7.4.6.4.1.2 MURRAY ROY STEELE m Lorraine Grant
1. KELLEY ANN STEELE b 18 Sep 1960.
2. KATHLEEN DIANE STEELE b 05 Dec 1961.
3. GRANT MURRAY STEELE b 01 May 1965 (chn b Winnipeg MB fr MEJLS).

TURNER
1.1.9.4.3.7.4.6.4.3.1 VALERIE ANN LIVESLEY m Michael James Turner
1. MICHAEL JAMES TURNER Jr. b 16 Jul 1946 b Manchester Eng.
2. DAVID JOHN TURNER b 15 Jan 1978 b Winnipeg MB (fr MEJLS).

LIVESLEY
1.1.9.4.3.7.4.6.4.3.2 DAVID ROBERT LIVESLEY m Lynne Arlene Blackburn
1. KELLY JEAN LIVESLEY b 09 Jun 1973.
2. KEVIN DAVID LIVESLEY b 20 Mar 1978 (both b Winnipeg MB).

STAPELLS
1.1.9.4.3.7.4.10.2.1.1 BEVERLY JOAN ECKLIN m Richard Brenden Stapells
1. VICTORIA STAPELLS b 1954 m 1975 Richard A V Johnson s/o Charles Johnson of Mexico (Manager of Imperial Oil Chemical IN) b 10 Jun 1953.
2. ALEXANDRA STAPELLS b 1956.
3. ELIZABETH STAPELLS b 1959 all chn b Toronto where their father is a lawyer (fr ICSP).

SANTO-PEREZ
1.1.9.4.3.7.4.10.2.1.2 CLAIRE-ANN LOUISE ECKLIN m Jose Santos-Perez
1. KATHERINE SANTOS-PEREZ b 26 Jan 1955.
2. JOSEPH SANTOS-PEREZ b 27 Oct 1956.
3. PAUL SANTOS-PEREZ b 10 Jun 1960.
4. ERIC SANTOS-PEREZ b 07 May 1961.
5. MADELINE SANTOS-PEREZ b 19 Nov 1963.
6. MARGARET SANTOS-PEREZ B 19 Sept 1964.
7. ANN SANTOS-PEREZ, the family res in Madrid, Spain (fr ICSP).

SHARP
1.1.9.4.3.7.4.10.4.1.2 MARGRET JANE MOYER m Grant Sharp
1. NADENE LARA SHARP b 05 Mar 1979 (chn b Penoka AB).
2. SUZANNE ADELLE SHARP b 08 1981.

SMITH
1.1.9.4.3.7.4.10.4.2.1 JOHN WESLEY SMITH m Gail Paterson Brewster
1. JENIFER JANE SMITH b 03 Sep 1969 (chn b St Catharines ON).
2. PENELOPE JANE SMITH b 27 Feb 1976.
3. MARY SUSZANNE SMITH b 14 Dec 1979 (fr ICSP).

PELLETTIER
1.1.9.4.3.7.4.10.5.2.2 IDA CAROLYN SMITH M.D. m John Ritchie Pellettier M.D.
1. MALCOLM BROCK RITCHIE PELLETTIER b 06 Nov 1970 Guelph ON, graduate of Queens U. Kingston (fr ICSP).

STEBLER
1.1.9.4.3.7.4.10.4.2.3 PENELOPE JANE SMITH m Werner Carl Stebler
1. MARTIN ALEXANDER STEBLER b 01 Oct 1976 Berne Switzerland.
2. JAN BERNARD STEBLER b 27 Sep 1978 Solothurn Switzerland. Jan pronounced `Yawn'.
3. ANDREW CARL STEBLER b 11 Dec 1979 Solothurn bp 31 May 1981 Vineland Station ON (fr ICSP).

SMITH
1.1.9.4.3.7.4.10.4.2.4 ARTHUR WILLIAM SMITH m Constance Josephine Robinson
1. ARRON WINSTON RATE SMITH b 28 Apr 1974.
2. SAMANTHA SHAWN SMITH b 07 Nov 1977.

3 TRAVIS WESLEY JACOB SMITH b 13 May 1980.
4 NAOMI MERIAH SMITH b 05 Oct 1981. All chn b St Catharines ON (fr ICSP).

SMITH

1.1.9.4.3.7.4.10.4.2.5 HAROLD WESLEY MARTIN SMITH m Mary Featherstone
1 BENJAMIN BRODE SMITH b 19 Apr 1978.
2 SIMON DAIVD SMITH b 09 Jun 1980.(both b St Catharines ON fr ICSP).

SMITH

1.1.9.4.3.7.4.10.5.1.2 ROGER DeWITT SMITH m Marilyn Ann Lang
1. KATIE MICHELLE SMITH b 14 May 1972 adopted.
2. JEFFREY EDWARD SMITH b 26 Jun 1974 adopted (fr their mother – MALS).

LAUNSPACH

1.1.9.4.3.7.4.13.5.2.1 PATRICIA ANN SORENSON m Henry Herschel Launspach Jr.
1 SONJA LORENE LAUNSPACH b 19 Apr 1959.
2 KARL ERIC LAUNSPACH b 06 Apr 1961.
3 PAUL HERCHEL LAUNSPACH b 13 May 1966. All chn b El Paso NM res El Paso in 1979).

MOYER

1.1.9.4.3.7.6.3.6.1.2 ARTHUR ANDREW MOYER m Jessie ? .
1 PATRICIA MOYER
2 ANDREW ARTHUR MOYER (fr ICSP).

FOSTER

1.1.9.4.3.7.6.3.6.2.1 DONALD TURNER FOSTER m Evelyn M Hamlin
1 ROBERT FOSTER
2 EUGENE FOSTER
3 LEONARD BURTON FOSTER (fr ICSP).

VEGSO

1.1.9.4.3.7.10.1.3.5.1 ARLEEN BERYLE WILSON m Frank Vegso
1 GARY VEGSO b 20 Mar 1964 Brandon MB.
2 DEAN VEGSO b 15 Jan 1966 Brandon MB (fr ACCH).

GRAHAM

1.1.9.4.3.7.10.1.3.7.1 WILLA DIANE WILSON m Gerald Richard Graham (fr ACCH).
1 SHERRI GRAHAM b 01 Apr 1955.
2 WILLA JOAN GRAHAM b 03 Feb 1963.
3 SUSAN GRAHAM b 24 Sep 1966 (fr ACCH).

HARRIS

1.1.9.4.3.7.10.1.3.8.1 AVA CECLIA CHRISTIANSEN m Kenneth Harris
1 PAMELA CECELIA HARRIS b 15 Jun 1956.
2 GWENDOLINE CAROLE HARRIS b 10 Dec 1958.
3 CORINNE RAY HARRIS b 22 Dec 1961 (fr ACCH).

CHRISTIANSEN

1.1.9.4.3.7.10.1.3.8.2 OLE INER CHRISTRIANSEN m Irene Dormouth
1 WENDY LYNN CHRISTIANSEN b 04 Oct 1959 Regina SK.
2 LORI LEE CHRISTIANSEN b 1961.
   m2 1977 Kathy at Denver CO (fr ACCH).

WILSON

1.1.9.4.3.7.10.1.3.9.1 RALPH WILLIAM WILSON m Verna Matychuck
1 SHERRI RACHELLE WILSON b 21 Feb 1963 Dauphin MB.
2 DIANNE LYNN WILSON b 25 Dec 1963 Dauphin MB.
3 WILLIAM GARTH WILSON b 20 Apr 1965 (fr ACCH).

GATES

1.1.9.4.3.7.10.1.3.9.2 SHIRLEY ANN WILSON m Ronald Arthur Gates
1 KAREN RAE GATES b 10 Dec 1964
2 DEBRA ANN GATES b 08 July 1963
3 ALLEN WADE GATES b 17 Oct 1967.

TISCH

1.1.9.4.3.7.10.5.2.3.1 FLORENCE LOUISE DeWITT m Geoffrey Tisch
1 DANIEL TISCH b 13 Sep 1972
2 KATHERINE TISCH (CCD).

te BOCKHORST
1.1.9.4.3.7.10.5.2.3.5 NORMA LIBBY DeWITT m Richard te Bockhorst
1. RYAN te BOCKHORST
2. NINA te DOCKHORST
3. LORA te BOCKHORST
4. CARL te BOCKHORST (fr CCD).

BROWN
1.1.9.4.3.7.10.6.1.1.1 SHIRLEY ELEAN PEARSON m Stanley Brown
1. KENT SAVILLE BROWN (fr ICSP).

JARSTFER
1.1.9.4.3.7.10.6.1.1.2 ELEANOR JOYCE PEARSON m Charles Jarstfer
1. JOYCE LEAN JARSTFER
2. DOUGLAS CHARLES JARSTFER (fr ICSP).

WATT
1.1.9.4.3.7.10.6.1.1.4 MARI LEE PEARSON m Robert Watt
1. CAROL LYNN WATT & twin
2. MARI LEE WATT (fr ICSP).

PARRISH
1.1.9.4.3.7.10.6.1.3.1 JUDITH HELEN TRATO m Arza/Pete Parrish
1. DEBORAH LEE PARRISH
2. KRISTY LYNN PARRISH (fr ICSP).

TRATO
1.1.9.4.3.7.10.6.1.3.2 JAMES HILLIARD TRATO m1 Carol Weinhorst m2 Sally ? .
1. JILL HEATHER TRATO (which wf was her ma?) (fr ICSP).

TRATO
1.1.9.4.3.7.10.6.1.3.3 JOHN HERBERT TRATO m Theresa/Teri Mathews
1. JENNIFER TRATO
2. JULIE TRATO

EDWARDS
1.1.9.4.3.7.10.6.1.3.4 JACQUELINE HOPE TRATO m David Edwards
1. JONATHAN DAVID EDWARDS
2. DEBORAH RENEE EDWARDS
3. REBEKAH ANN EDWARDS (all fr ICSP).

NORTON
1.1.9.4.3.7.10.8.1.1.1 GRANT JOHN NORTON m Doris Lillie McMillan
1. ALAN CECIL NORTON b 13 Feb 1947 m 07 Oct 1972 Diane Irene Pawlak b 1950.
2. DAVID NORTON b 08 Jul 1949.
3. MICHAEL NORTON b 18 Jun 1955 (all fr GJN).

STEVENSON
1.1.9.4.3.7.10.8.1.1.2 BERNICE M R NORTON m William Francis Stevenson
1. BRIAN DOUGLAS STEVENSON b 23 Aug 1950.
2. BRUCE MURRAY STEVENSON b 17 Feb 1955 m 05 Jun 1970 Kimberley Ann Eady.
3. GLEN WILLIAM STEVENSON b 16 Feb 1957.

MAYES
1.1.9.4.3.7.10.10.1.1.4 RHEA GRACE ELEANOR HUGILL m Ernest George Mayes
1. WENDY MARILYN MAYES b 10 Apr 1961 Hamilton ON at Hamilton m 09 Aug 1986 Michael Milanetti b 09 Jun 1958 res Ajax ON. Wendy graduated from McMaster University Hamilton ON, Wendy in Chemistry, Mike in Computer Science (RGEHM).

HUGILL
1.1.9.4.3.7.10.10.1.1.5 WILLIAM JAMES ALEXANDER HUGILL m Shirley Diane Colvin
1. DENISE JOAN HUGILL b 05 May 1963 Burlington ON at Clearwater FL m 30 Dec 1995 Christopher Tod Heller b 02 Jul 1961 Ohio. Denise graduated from University of Florida in Gainesville Fl. Worked P/T for Continental Airlines, is a public school teacher in Education working in special Ed.
2. JEFFREY ALEXANDER HUGILL b 25 Apr 1965 Burlington d 07 Jan 1969 ae 3 yrs at Chicago IL bur Woodland Cem Burlington ON **dy.**
3. KATHARINE LYNNE HUGILL b 26 Jan 1970 Louisville KY, res Oklahoma City, OK 2002.
4. ELIZABETH ALLISON HUGILL b 19 Sep 1972 Atlanta GA. At Clearwater FL m 14 Nov 1998 Gary Harker b 18 Nov 1968 in England. Beth graduated from University of Florida in Gainsville FL in Business. Worked for 1 year for Nations

Leucas deWit

Bank. Quit and went to University of Edinburgh Scotland graduated with a degree in International Banking. Started working for Sutomoto Bank in New York City in 1998 (fr RGEHM).

HUGILL
1.1.9.4.3.7.10.10.1.1.6 MURRAY DeWITT HUGILL m Marlene Leitha Ackles
1. MARK WILLIAM HUGILL b 21 Mar 1970 Burlington ON has Downs Syndrome. Mark graduated Brock High School with Degree in Education 1997. Works at ARC Industries Burlington ON & at Lakeshore Music.
2. MARSHA JEANNE HUGILL b 07 Aug 1972 Burlington ON. Marsha graduated 1996 with Honours PHS Ed from Brock University, St Catharines ON. Works at Ford Parts Depot in Bramalea ON in the office, in Dealer Customer Service, now merchandizer
3. MICHELLE ANNE HUGILL b 08 Nov 1975 Burlington ON m McGill University Chapel QC 17 Jun 1999 Jeremy Tayor Bresnen b 04 Nov 1973 Montreal QC s/o of Kenneth Frank Bresnen and Ruth Marilyn Naylor. Michelle graduated 1999 with a BA in Music from McGill University in Montreal QC. Teaching flute & piano private students. Jeremy & Michelle opened a Skateboard store in Montreal on March 15, 2002
4. MELANIE EDNA HUGILL b 11 Jun 1977 Burlington ON. Melanie graduated 1999 with a BA in Music from Western University in London ON. Teaching music, privately in the home Burlington area and at Lakeshore music Burlington.. Moved to Montreal in summer of 2002 to teach voice and piano to private students.

DeWITT
1.1.9.4.3.7.10.10.1.2.1 LAUREL STANFORD/LAURIE DeWITT m Linda Joy Rorick
1. BRETT MAURICE DeWITT b 20 Apr 1968 Cranbrook BC, m 17 Sep 2000 Sylvia Sue Wong res Richmond BC.
2. TERRE LYNNE DeWITT b 09 Mar 1970 Cranbrook BC m   ?   . res Fruitvale BC.

BUCK
1.1.9.4.3.7.10.10.1.2.2 MAURIETTE DAWN DeWITT m Bruce Buck
1. KIMBERLY DAWN BUCK b 17 Mar 1976 Hinton AB.
2. JENNIFER DIANE BUCK b 24 Jan 1978 Victoria BC.
3. BRIAN BUCK b 05 May 1986. Family res Cumberland BC (fr KDMSC)..

McFADDIN
1.1.9.4.3.7.10.10.1.4.1 LORNE SIBBET McFADDIN m Muriel Eleanor Burke
1. KATHLEEN DONNA McFADDIN b 26 Feb 1961 Williams Lake,at Kelowana m1 25 Jul 1981 David St Amand res Sicamous BC; m2 Richard Crandlemire (fr KDMSC).

LINDSAY
1.1.9.4.3.7.10.10.1.4.2 MARLENE ISABEL McFADDIN m Douglas Charles Lindsay
1. JAMES ALLAN LINDSAY b. 20.May.1957 Vancouver BC, at Penticton BC m1 05 Jan 1971 Naomi Arajo d/o John Arujo & Maria, b 26 May 1959, res Duncan BC, div. Jim m2 24 Aug 2002 Mrs Susan Komo Rozenboom.
2. WADE CAMERON LINDSAY b 17 Jan 1960 New Westminster BC **single**.
3. MITCHELL GRAHAM LINDSAY b 26 Jul 1962 New Westminster BC & Charlene McDonald.
4. TRACEY DIANE LINDSAY b 03 Jul 1967 Duncan BC; m1 Vaughn Killan s/o Percy Killan & Louella, div; m2 29 Aug 1992 Michael Lundahl (all fr MIML).

FLOYD
1.1.9.4.3.7.10.10.1.5.1 SANDRA ANN DeWITT m1 John Floyd
1. KEVIN JAMES FLOYD b 10 Nov 1966 Hillingdon, Middlesex Eng m, one chn,div.
   m2 ? Lucas

DeWITT
1.1.9.4.3.7.10.10.1.5.3 JAMES GEORGE DeWITT m Karen Crowe
1. JEAN EDNA DeWITT b 14 Aug 1984
2. JONATHAN DeWITT b 1988 res SK (fr IGD).

NIELD
1.1.9.4.3.7.10.10.1.6.1 SHARON LYNN HARPHAM m Rev Jack Nield
1. LAURA JEAN NIELD twin b 07 Apr 1966 in Winnipeg MB. In Ottawa she m James William Earl Doris b 01 Apr 1962 Toronto ON s/o James Doris & Margaret Anne Casey.
2. JAMES ANDREW NIELD twin b 07 Apr 1966 in Winnipeg m 23 June 1993 Jennifer Vincent b 16 June 1968 in Montreal QC s/o Pierre (Peter) Vincent & Janet.
3. DONNA BETH NIELD b 26 Mar 1968 in Virden MB. In Charlevoix QC m 25 Aug 2000 Michael Joseph s/o David Joseph & Alice.
4. PETER JOHN NIELD b 06 Apr 1970 Peterborough ON m in Ste Anne de Bellevue QC 08 Jul 2000 Nancy Koluzs b 16 July 1970 d/o John Koluzs & Flore (fr RFHJB).

JOHNSON
1.1.9.4.3.7.10.10.1.6.3 RAE FRANCES HARPHAM m1 Donald George Johnson
1. RHONDA RAE JOHNSON b 20 Apr 1966 Dauphin MB, at Chilliwack BC m 24 Nov 1984 Ronald James Allan , b 01 Aug 1965 (all fr RFHJ).

2   MICHELLE DAWN JOHNSON b 20 Nov 1967 Churchill MB m Michael Nagy-Deak b 10 Dec 1957
3   MICHAEL JOHNSON b 22 Nov 1971 Chilliwack BC m Cindy Ann Smith Thomson. In Surrey BC (RFHJB).
m2 21 Aug 1999 Robert Benedict

SMITH
1.1.9.4.3.7.10.10.1.7.4 GILBERT IRA SMITH and Michelle Kotowski
1   KASIA ISABELLA KOTOWSKI-SMITH b 26 Jan 2002 Vancouver BC (fr VEDS)..

WEBB
1.1.9.4.3.7.10.10.1.7.6 JULIA EDNA/JULIE SMITH m Howard Webb
1   BRENNAN TOSHIAKI SMITH WEBB b 05 Feb 1988 Chilliwack BC.
2   JENNA V WEBB b 25 Aug 1989 b Chilliwack BC. Family res Harrison Hot Springs BC (fr VEDS).

BOGARDUS
1.1.9.4.3.8.2.5.1.4.1 HAROLD EDWARD BOGARDUS m Hilda S Merill
1   HAROLD JOHN BOGARDUS b 28 Mar 1950 Downer CA m 03 Jun 1978 Tisa Loman b 27 Mar 1954.
2   KRISS MARIE BOGARDUS b 28 Aug 1954 Lynwood CA m 08 Nov 1975 Paul Byron Rice b 28 Nov 1951 Augusta GA (fr WBB).

MORSE/GIBSON
1.1.9.4.3.8.2.5.1.4.3 DEBORAH JANE BOGARDUS m1 Dana Morse; m2 Donald Gibson
1   TAMRA MARIE MORSE b 19 Dec 1969 (fr WBB).

BOGARDUS
1.1.9.4.3.8.2.5.4.1.1 RICHARD DEAN BOGARDUS m Jacqueline R Clymer
1   THOMAS SCOTT BOGARDUS b 27 Jan 1962 adopted.
2   REBECCA LYNN BOGARDUS b 08 Mar 1965 adopted.
3   ROBERT KYLE BOGARDUS b 22 Nov 1967 adopted.

BOGARDUS
1.1.9.4.3.8.2.5.6.2.3 DONALD EUGENE BOGARDUS m Dianne Ruth Winslow
1   DONALD EUGENE BOGARDUS Jr. b 24 Aug 1974 Santa Clara CA.
2   DEAN BURTON BOGARDUS b 07 Jun 1976 Santa Clara.
3   JEFFREY PARK BOGARDUS b 28 Jan 1978 Payson UT.
4   CHAD LARKIN BOGARDUS b 10 Feb 1981 Payson UT (all fr WBB).

CHUMBLEY
1   **1.1.9.4.3.8.2.5.7.2.1 ROBERT GENE CHUMBLEY m Margarette Elaine McIntyre**
2   NATHAN GENE CHUMBLEY b & d 21 Dec 1971 **dy.**
m2 Phyllis Kay Grant
3   CHARLES EDWARD CHUMBLEY b 10 Feb 1975.
m3 Carrie Louise Scott (all fr WBB)

MADLEM
1.1.9.4.3.8.2.5.7.2.2 MARY ALICE CHUMBLEY m Russell Madlem
1   HEATHER MARIE MADLEM b 18 Aug 1973.
2   HOLLY ELIZABETH MADLEM b 19 Jun 1976.
3   HEATH WAYNE MADLEM b 18 Mar 1981 (all fr WBB).

KNCAREM
1.1.9.4.3.8.2.5.7.2.4 NANCY ELLEN CHUMBLEY m Dale Kncarem
1   JOHN HOWERS KNCAREM b 02 Apr (or Sep) 1975 (all fr WBB). ? spelling
2   JACQUELINE JOY KNCAREM b 22 Aug 1976.

BOGARDUS
1.1.9.4.3.8.2.6.2.1.1 PETER WILSON BOGARDUS m Frances Lynne Campbell
1   JOHN THOMAS FREDERICK BOGARDUS b 20 May 1969.
2   PETER JAMES BOGARDUS b 12 May 1971 (fr WBB).

HAEBER
1.1.9.4.3.8.2.6.2.1.3 LOUISE ANN BOGARDUS m Tekeno Haeber
1   SARA ANN HAEBER b 04 Oct 1951 (fr WBB).

PHILIP
1.1.9.4.3.8.2.6.4.1.1 JOHN PHILIP m Sonya Sondergard
1   STEVEN PHILIP b 1959 m Lori Brumleu b 14 May 1959.
2   SHEILA PHILIP b 1960.
3   DAVID PHILIP b 1962.
4   SCOTT PHILIP b 1963 (all fr WBB).

JEWELL

1.1.9.4.3.8.2.6.4.2.1 JOAN GRAFTON PHILIP m Arthur Jewell
1. WENDY JANE JEWELL b 16 Mar 1963.
2. CRAIG ARTHUR JEWELL b 29 Apr 1965.

LIDSTONE

1.1.9.4.3.8.2.6.4.2.2 CHARLOTTE ANN PHILIP m1 Robert Lidstone
1. LARA NAOMIE LIDSTONE b 23 May 1969.

m2 Jim Greig

2. JIM GREIG Jr b 09 Mar 1975 adopted (all fr WBB).

PHILIP

1.1.9.4.3.8.2.6.4.2.3 JAMES STEWART PHILIP m Val Swareoff
1. PAUL STEWART PHILIP b 01 Jul 1975.
2. JENNIFER NINA PHILIP b 06 Dec 1977.
3. LORA JANE PHILIP b 23 Jun 1980 (fr WBB).

POLLARD

1.1.9.4.3.8.2.6.5.1.1 MICHAEL WALTER POLLARD m Catherine Ann Block
1. ROBERT TRACY POLLARD b 02 Sep 1972.
2. PAMELA ANNE POLLARD b 20 Nov 1974.
3. THOMAS WALTER POLLARD b 22 Apr 1975 twin.
4. KERI ANN POLLARD b 22 Apr 1975 (fr WBB).

SHEPKER

1.1.9.4.3.8.2.8.9.1.3 PAUL FRANCIS SHEPKER m Shirley Favorite
1. ELIZABETH ANN SHEPKER b 08 Feb 1968 Buffalo NY

SHEPKER

1.1.9.4.3.8.2.8.9.1.4 THOMAS OLIVER SHEPKER m Patricia Kirgt
1. PETER WILLIAM SHEPKER b 31 Jan 1968 Cleveland OH.
2. JULIE ANN SHEPKER b 18 May 1974.

BOGARDUS

1.1.9.4.3.8.2.8.9.3.1 GEORGE DORAM BOGARDUS m Mary Muhs
1. TAMARA GAY BOGARDUS b 11 Nov 1972.
2. HEATHER MARY BOGARDUS b 25 Jan 1974 (fr OLD).

DeWITT

1.1.9.4.5.1.2.4.3.1.4 WAYNE FREDERICK DeWITT m Edythe Marion Hendrie
1. SHARON MARIE DeWITT b 05 May 1959 Oak Park IL, at Ft Madison IA m 19 Jul 1980.
2. BR IAN SCOTT DeWITT b 29 Sep 1960 Oak Park IL
3. CRAIG ALAN DeWITT b 08 Mar 1963 (OLD).

BEERY

1.1.9.4.8.3.6.1.1.2.1 MARY LOUISE MILLER m Jan Seeger Beery
1. CHRISTOPHER RANDALL BEERY b 27 Jul 1947 bp Advent Luth CH LA CA, at Encino CA Presby CH; m 21 Nov 1970 Marjorie Evans Hawley d/o James Evans Hawley & Mary Isobel Chisholm, b 27 Apr 1947 North Hollywood, LA CA (fr MLMB's Fam Rec; b cert). Christopher is with Global Dir-Mars Electronics.
2. CURTIS WAYNE BEERY b 08 Dec 1948 LA CA (d 01 Mar 1980 Birmingham AL) m 12 Dec 1970 Carol Wilkinson.
3. CYNTHIA JAN BEERY b 19 Aug 1952 Inglewood CA m 26 Mar 1988 William Lyle Lutz.

GENERATION 12

OVERBAUGH
1.1.9.4.2.2.1.1.4.1.5.4 THEODORE STUART OVERBAUGH m Ann Lucille Nollet
1. SUSAN ANN OVERBAUGH b 26 Aug 1953.
2. KATHEYN PILGRIM OVERBAUGH b 14 Aug 1954.
3. GARY CAMPION OVERBAUGH b 11 Mar 1958.

HOLMES
1.1.9.4.3.1.5.2.2.2.1.1 BARBARA CAROL DeWITT m William Ira Holmes
1. LAUREN JEANNE HOLMES b 08 Oct 1958 Nyack NY, m there 16 Jun 1979 Dennis Russell Menard b 10 Jul 1956 Plattsburg NY. He is a brokerage distributor, res Plattsburg NY.
2. DAVID SCOTT HOLMES b 09 Jun 1964 Nyack NY attended Clarion College PA majoring in Business Management.
3. TAMMY HOLMES adopted.
4. DANNY HOLMES adopted. The Holmes are the parents of several foster chn (all fr CFD).

DeWITT
1.1.9.4.3.1.5.2.2.2.1.2 LAWRENCE JOHN DeWITT m Valerie Anne Bradshaw
1. HOLLY BETH DeWITT b 03 Oct 1971 in San Jose CA.
2. LEE ANN DeWITT b 06 Oct 1977 Hidden Hills CA at Augora CA (fr CFD).

DeWITT
1.1.9.4.3.1.5.2.2.2.1.3 JAMES WILLIAM DeWITT m Donna Jean Fass
1. SCOTT WINSTON DeWITT b 17 Jul 1965 Bayshore LI NY.
2. RYAN JAY DeWITT b 30 Aug 1971 Rockville CT.
3. JOSHUA JAMES DeWITT b 08 Oct 1973 (fr CFD).

DeWITT
1.1.9.4.3.1.5.2.2.2.1.4 WILLIAM THOMAS DeWITT m Theresa Hennesey
1. KRISTIN HENNESEY DeWITT b 10 Mar 1980 Smithtown NY (fr CFD).

REGNIER
1.1.9.4.3.1.5.2.2.2.2.2 CHERYL LYNN CONLEY m Thomas Regnier
1. AMY REGNIER b ? Mar 1977.
2. ANGELA REGNIER b 27 Feb 1980 (fr CFD).

TAUBITZ
1.1.9.4.3.1.5.2.2.3.1.2 CATHERINE JEAN BOUGET m Richard Joseph Taubitz
1. SHELLEY ANN TAUBITZ b 05 Aug 1949 Detroit, m 1 12 Jan 1968 Bernard George LaClair b 23 Sep 1943 Detroit, div Apr 1972, **no chn**; m2 21 Jul 1972 Holger Junge b 29 Sep 1936. He m1 Christa Ellei in Germany, & div there Jan 1968, had chn Ute & Bridgette still living in Germany.
2. PAUL LEONARD TAUBITZ b 19 Jul 1950 Gaines MI m 12 Feb 1971 Rebecca Rae Nelson b 29 Jun 1953 Flint MI.
3. MARK DOUGLAS TAUBITZ b 20 Oct 1951 m1 10 Nov 1973 Jean Marie Stoddard b 24 Mar 1954 div m2 Mar 1980.
4. RICHARD JOSEPH TAUBITZ b 28 May 1957 Flint.
5. KATHLEEN DENISE TAUBITZ b 25 Jun 1959 Flint.
6. WILLIAM JOHN TAUBITZ b 04 Feb 1961 Flint.
7. JEANETTE MARIE TAUBITZ b 04 Mar 1966 Flint (fr CFD).

SUTCLIFFE
1.1.9.4.3.1.9.2.1.3.2.1 SHARON ELIZABETH TURNBULL m Ben Sutcliffe
1. LIZA ELLEN SUTCLIFFE
2. LAURIE ELIZABETH SUTCLIFFE
3. BRIAN EDWARD SUTCLIFFE (info fr MHKG).

SMITH
1.1.9.4.3.1.9.2.1.3.2.2 SUSAN ANN TURNBULL m David Smith
1. DAVID ROBERT SMITH
2. STEPHEN EDWARD SMITH
3. ANDREW MICHAEL SMITH (info fr MHKG).

SCOTT
1.1.9.4.3.2.5.2.2.4.2.2 PATRICIA ANN CHAMPION m Leo Joseph Scott
1. STEVEN SCOTT b 29 Jun 1966.
2. SHANE SCOTT b 16 Sep 1967
3. MICHELLE SCOTT
   m2 Alfred Ribone div **no chn** (fr KLAD).

Leucas deWit

MacMICHAEL
1.1.9.4.3.3.1.8.1.1.2.1 FRANK ROBERT MacMICHAEL m Valerie Stewart
1. RICHARD STUART MacMICHAEL b 27 Aug 1965 Moncton.
2. ROBERT PETER MacMICHAEL b 08 Feb 1968 Halifax NS.
3. GILLIAN RUTH MacMICHAEL b 05 Aug 1969 Halifax (fr MAH, SCBG).

MacMICHAEL
1.1.9.4.3.3.1.8.1.1.2.2 LESLIE IAN MacMICHAEL m Barbara Clark
1. JAN BRUCE MacMICHAEL b 06 May 1965 Moncton.
   m2 **Theora Getson** (fr MAH, SCBG).

RAENDEN
1.1.9.4.3.3.1.8.1.1.3.1 LINDA GRACE MacMICHAEL m Frank S Raenden
1. LESLIE ALISON RAENDEN b Staten Island NY.
2. ANDREW CRAIG RAENDEN b 15 Jan 1966 Staten Island NY (fr MAH, SCBG)

CURRIE
1.1.9.4.3.3.1.8.1.1.4.1 HENRY/HARRY ROBERTSON GEORGE CURRIE m Phillys Isabel McGowan
1. RONALD MALCOLM CURRIE b 12 Mar 1955 Halifax NS.
2. HENRY JOHN CURRIE b 14 Mar 1957 London Eng.
3. DONALD ANDREW CURRIE b 25 Apr 1961 St John NB.

SUTHERLAND
1.1.9.4.3.3.1.8.1.5.1.1 ELIZABETH LENORE BAILEY m Donald R Sutherland
1. LESLIE LENORE SUTHERLAND b 14 Jul 1971 (fr SCBG).

McCARTNEY
1.1.9.4.3.3.1.8.1.5.2.1 MARION MABEL THOMPSON m Donald G McCartney
1. JANET MICHELLE McCARTNEY b 07 Dec 1959 Vancouver.
2. CHERYL ANN McCARTNEY b 23 Sep 1963 Vancouver (fr SCBG).

THOMPSON
1.1.9.4.3.3.1.8.1.5.2.2 GRAHAM STANLEY THOMPSON m Leilannie Mary Thomas
1. BRUCE GRAHAM THOMPSON b 02 Jul 1963 London Eng.
2. HEATHER SHANNON THOMPSON b 17 Apr 1966 Calgary AB (fr SCBG).

FRASER
1.1.9.4.3.3.1.8.1.9.1.4 LEONARD LYLE FRASER m Diane Say VanLoo
1. JENNIFER DAWN FRASER b 23 May 1979 Surrey, BC.
2. JACQUELINE DIANE FRASER b 20 Jul 1980 Surrey (fr MAH).

FORRISTER
1.1.9.4.3.3.3.2.1.6.2.1 BERNICE HASKELL m John Phillip Forrister
1. STEPHEN LORE FORRISTER
2. LUNN MARIE FORRISTER
3. DIANE SUSAN FORRISTER
4. DANA ELIZABETH FORRISTER
5. TINA DENISE FORRISTER (fr BBVH)

HASKELL
1.1.9.4.3.3.3.2.1.6.5.1 PETER ELLIS HASKELL m Consuelo ? .
1. GREG HASKELL b 06 Aug 1961.
2. SHAWN HASKELL b 07 Aug 1962.
3. CHRISTOPHER MARK HASKELL b Oct 1969.
   m2 **Jan Baransky**
4. TERRA HASKELL (info fr BBVH).

HASKELL
1.1.9.4.3.3.3.2.1.6.5.2 BRIAN HASKELL m Mitsuko
1. MICHAEL STILLMAN HASKELL b 07 Jul 1978 (fr BBVH).

HASKELL
1.1.9.4.3.3.3.2.1.6.5.3 ERIC RICHARD HASKELL m Rosemary Martin
1. AMY HASKELL b 28 Feb 1968.
2. THERESA HASKELL b 08 Aug 1969.
3. BRIAN HASKELL unclear if this is Brian Everett or twins.
4. EVERETT HASKELL
5. HERMAN HASKELL b 05 May 1972.
6. MICHAEL HASKELL b 05 May 1972.
7. RALPH HASKELL b 05 May 1972 (info fr BBVH).

FERRISS
1.1.9.4.3.3.3.2.1.6.5.4 BONITA LEA HASKELL m David Ferriss
1　CHRISTOPHER FERRISS b 18 Aug 1969.
2　JENNIFER FERRISS b ? Nov 1972.
3　ERIN FERRISS b ? Apr 1974 (info fr BBVH).

REID
1.1.9.4.3.3.4.1.1.12.1.1 NORMA McCRACKEN m Robert Reid
1　PAMELA REID b 23 Apr 1957.
2　TIMOTHY ALLEN REID b 02 Aug 1958.
3　ELIZABETH ANN REID b 05 Jun 1953 (fr SDVSW).

McCRACKEN
1.1.9.4.3.3.4.1.1.12.1.3 WAYNE McCRACKEN m Lynn Ramsay
1　GREGORY ALLAN McCRACKEN b 04 Aug 1971.
2　ROBERT DEAN McCRACKEN b 11 Apr 1979 (fr SDVSW).

NIELSEN
1.1.9.4.3.3.4.1.1.12.3.1 PAUL NIELSEN m Linda Ferguson
1　WENDY NEILSEN b Fredericton NB. The family moved to Harvey Station NB, a town that had its own Music Festival. They also had a wonderful music teacher named Kate Jackson. Wendy m Ian Varty. They have a son Julian. After living in Toronto they moved to Cambridge Narrows NB (fr BMN). The several page newspaper stories include several beautiful pictures.
2　ERIC NIELSEN
3　TODD NIELSEN (info fr BMN to KLAD).

The New Brunswick Reader Nov 30,1996
　'Our Diva at the Met' - The story of Wendy Nielsen's journey from Harvey Station to New York City. A modest woman, devoted mother and extraordinary talent takes center stage next week at the Metropolitan Opera House. She has performed in Canada, the eastern United States and Europe. On Friday November 6, 1996 Wendy Nielsen will become the first New Brunswick born soprano to play a lead role on the stage of the Metropolitan. This woman with the "big voice" started her path to fame when she won her first singing trophy in Grade 2 at Harvey Station - and won them every year thereafter. Now she heads to New York with two busloads of New Brunswickers to cheer her on. The opera is Motzart's Cosi fan tutte. In fifty years the role has only fallen to a few super-sopranos like Maureen Forrester with the range to handle difficult areas.

NIELSEN
1.1.9.4.3.3.4.1.1.12.3.2 PHILIP NIELSEN m Joycelyn LeGris
1　RENE NIELSEN
2　OMAR NIELSEN (fr BMN to KLAD).

ESAU
1.1.9.4.3.3.4.1.1.12.6.2 RUTH WADE m Paul Esau
1　DEBORAH ESAU b 1964 m Derrick Peyton res Fredericton NB.
　She is a talented cartoonist. She has a large following in NB and was recently accepted into the prestigious national cartoonist society. She says she became really addicted to cartons when she see's people laughing at them. "Its more than a job. It's a way of life." She has procduced two books Day to Day and Surving Day to Day ($13..95 ea) being distributed by pubishers Tomas Allen and Son Ltd (The Daily Gleaner D1Wed 28 Feb 2001 fr KLAD).

KIRKPATRICK
1.1.9.4.3.3.4.1.7.5.3.1 EVELYN GRAHAM m Edward Kirkpatrick
1　DENISE KIRKPATRICK (fr KLAD).

GRAHAM
1.1.9.4.3.3.4.1.7.5.3.2 MURRAY GRAHAM m Connie Ogden
1　WANDA GRAHAM
2　PAUL GRAHAM
3　HEATHER GRAHAM (fr KLAD).

GOOD
1.1.9.4.3.3.4.4.3.1.1.1 ALMA COOPER m Eugene Good
1.　EUGENE GOOD Jr.

GERRY
1.1.9.4.3.3.4.4.3.1.7.1 CONNIE HAFFORD m Robert Gerry
1　CYNTHIA GERRY
2　SANDRA GERRY (fr KLAD).

Leucas deWit

McNALLY
1.1.9.4.3.3.4.4.3.1.7.2 EVE HAFFORD m Vaughn McNally
1 JANET McNALLY
2 ROSLENE McNALLY (fr KLAD).

SLIPP
1.1.9.4.3.3.8.6.2.1.1.3 HAROLD SLIPP m Sharon Brawn
1 ALISHA SLIPP
2 SETH SLIPP (fr KLAD).

SLIPP
1.1.9.4.3.3.8.6.2.1.1.5 DUANE SLIPP m Sherry Hart
1 SCOTT HARTT SLIPP (fr KLAD).

KNORR
1.1.9.4.3.3.7.8.2.4.1.2 HOWARD ALLISON KNORR m Evelyn Mailman
1 JEFFREY KNORR
2 KRISTA KNORR (fr KLAD).

DALEY
1.1.9.4.3.3.7.8.2.4.1.3 LINDA DIANE KNORR m Kevin Daley
1 KEVIN ANTHONY DALEY b 1965
2 CHRISTOPHER DALEY b 1967
3 HEATHER DALEY
4 SHAWN DALEY b 1973 (fr KLAD).

MUNN
1.1.9.4.3.3.8.1.6.6.2.1 DONNA MAY DeWITT m Eric Munn
1 SARA KATHERINE MUNN b 04 Dec 1976
2 KERRY VANESSA MUNN b 28 May 1978 (fr MWD).

CHAMBERS
1.1.9.4.3.3.8.1.6.6.2.2 GERALDINE LYNN DeWITT m Francis Chambers
1 TRACY LYNN CHAMBERS (fr MWD).

HARRIS
1.1.9.4.3.5.2.2.5.3.2.1 KEVIN HARRIS m Joyce Hanselpecker
1 NICHOLAS HARRIS
2 LUCAS HARRIS (fr LOH).

HARRIS
1.1.9.4.3.5.2.2.5.3.2.2 MATTHEW HARRIS m Wendy Slipp
1 BRANDON HARRIS (fr LOH).
2 Dau

HARRIS
1.1.9.4.3.5.2.2.5.3.2.3 MYLES HARRIS m Patty Hillman
1 JORDAN HARRIS
2 MARK HARRIS (fr LOH).

HARRIS
1.1.9.4.3.5.2.2.5.3.2.4 ROGER HARRIS m Ann Marie Long
1 ZACHARY HARRIS

NOBLE
1.1.9.4.3.5.2.2.11.2.1.1 MAUREEN HARRIS m Terrance Noble
1 KAREN NOBLE
2 SHAWNA NOBLE (KLAD).

At the Tracy Winter Carnival, Feb 1990 Karen Noble d/o Terrance & Maureen Noble was named "Miss Tracy 1990" & her sister Shawna was named "First Princess".

ARTES
1.1.9.4.3.5.2.2.12.1.1.3 & 1.1.9.4.3.6.5.2.1.10 GORDON ARTES m Judy Ann Mersereau
1 GRANT ARTES

TRACY
1.1.9.4.3.6.6.1.2.4.1.2 BLISS LLOYD TRACY m Mary Dianne Loates
1 MICHELLE CAROLYN TRACY b 13 Jul 1971 Paris, France.
2 JONATHAN EDWARD TRACY b 07 Nov 1975 Oromocto NB.

SNIDER
1.1.9.4.3.6.6.5.1.2.2.1 EILEEN PATRICIA PHEASANT m Stanley Snider
1. LEE PATRICIA SNIDER b 22 Jun 1957 Toronto ON.
2. WILLIAM ROBERTSON SNIDER b 21 Aug 1959 Sudbury ON.

MERCER
1.1.9.4.3.6.6.5.1.2.2.2 DIANNE ELIZABETH PHEASANT m Robert Mercer
1. WILLIAM FREDERICK MERCER b 09 Oct 1960.
2. ROBIN ELIZABETH MERCER b 21 Mar 1962.
3. PATRICIA DAWN MERCER b 10 Mar 1966.
4. SHEENA PRIDE MERCER b 17 Oct 1970.

NASON
1.1.9.4.3.6.6.5.1.4.1.1 JOHN STUART NASON m Mary Louise Stewart
1. WALLACE STUART NASON b 1952 m 1971 Karen Hopstein b 1953.
2. CHRISTOPHER NASON b 1955 m 1977 Paula Smith b 1957.

CAMBON
1.1.9.4.3.6.6.5.1.4.1.2 EILEEN SINCLAIR NASON m Kenneth Cambon M.D.
1. NOREEN CAMBON
2. MARIE CAMBON
3. UNKNOWN CAMBON

NASON
1.1.9.4.3.6.6.5.1.4.1.4 DAVID ALEXANDER NASON m Shirley Wood
1. DAVID <u>KENT</u> NASON b 1949 Harvey, York Co NB, now at Chester NS, m Marcia   ?   .
2. BRENDA LEIGH NASON b Harvey, York Co NB, at London Eng m ? Oct 1976 Joannes Vakarelis, res London.

STUART
1.1.9.4.3.6.6.5.1.4.6.1 ALLEN W STUART m Sue Shannon
1. SHANNON PATRICIA STUART b 1976 Fredericton NB.

MERSEREAU
1.1.9.4.3.6.6.7.6.4.6.2 DEANNA MERSEREAU (m) Randy Mersereau div.
1. JENNIFER MERSEREAU
2. RANDY GERALD/GERRY MERSEREAU b 02 Dec 1979.

NASON
1.1.9.4.3.6.6.9.8.1.1.3 LESLIE DAVID NASON m Louann Carter
1. CHARLOTTE NASON b 1971 Fredericton NB.
2. MICHAEL DAVID NASON b 1972 Fredericton NB.

NASON
1.1.9.4.3.6.6.9.8.1.1.5 PERRY ALLAN NASON m Alvine Aubin
1. JEFFERY ALLAN NASON b 1969.
2. MELVINA YVONNE NASON b 1970.
3. JEREMY LEE NASON b 1973.

NASON
1.1.9.4.3.6.6.9.8.1.1.6 GEORGE BAYARD NASON m Elizabeth Haslett
1. CHRISTINA NASON b 1975.

NASON
1.1.9.4.3.6.6.9.8.1.4.1 GARY SMITH NASON m1 Rita McBean div
   m2 Mrs Brenda de la Franier Hartwell
1. TODD MITCHELL NASON b 1971.
2. JAMIE SMITH NASON b 1973.

LARSON
1.1.9.4.3.7.3.2.4.2.4.3 SANDRA MOSHER m Glenn Larson
1. CHRISTIAN LARSON b 1967.
2. TODD LARSON b 1969.
3. JEFFREY LARSON b 1971.

TOOLE
1.1.9.4.3.7.3.2.5.4.1.1 HAROLD TOOLE m Arlene   ?   .
1. PATTI TOOLE m Micheal O'Donnell, 2 sons Scott and Andrew O'Donnell.
2. JOY TOOLE m Micheal Sullivan son Kevin Sullivan.
3. DWIGHT TOOLE m Janet McHatten, chn Kyle & Ashton Toole.

NASON
1.1.9.4.3.7.3.6.9.1.2.1 LANCE R NASON m Beth Elaine Lister
1 TERRI LYNN NASON b 27 Jan 1976 (fr MWD).

NASON
1.1.9.4.3.7.3.6.9.1.2.3 CURTIS NASON m Sharon A Tracey
1 APRIL LEIGH NASON b 31 Dec 1981.
2 DIRCK KIRK NASON b 13 Oct 1984 (fr MWD).

NASON
1.1.9.4.3.7.3.6.9.2.1.1 RANDALL ERIC NASON m1 Lesley A Olmstead m2 Pamela Nuttal
1 AMY LOUISE NASON b 12 Sep 1984 Fredericton NB.

NASON
1.1.9.4.3.7.3.6.9.2.4.1 RANDALL EUGENE NASON m1 Carol Thurlow div m2 Nola Tipson
1 TRACY LYNN NASON b 20 Jul 1975 (fr MWD).

McGILLICUDDY
1.1.9.4.3.7.3.6.9.2.4.2 CINDY ANN NASON m Clement McGillicuddy
1 CHYANNE McGILLICUDY (male) b 26 Aug 1979.
2 BILLY L. McGUILLICUDY b 30 Nov 1980 (fr MWD).

NASON
1.1.9.4.3.7.3.6.9.2.8.1 MARTY DAVID NASON m Angela J Donnoyer
1 DEVIN LEIGH NASON b 08 Jul 1984 Fredericton NB (fr MWD).

RICKARD
1.1.9.4.3.7.4.3.6.3.4.1 JEFFREY CAMERON RICKARD m1 Joan E Rifle div m2 Catherine Bemis div
1 DANA MARIE RICKARD b 22 Nov 1969 Oil City PA.
2 MARC CAMERON RICKARD b 29 Sep 1972 Oil City PA (fr RPR).

RICKARD
1.1.9.4.3.7.4.3.6.3.4.4 KURT ALAN RICKARD m Barbara Ann McGuire
1 CRAIG ALAN RICKARD b 28 Apr 1975 Hancock MI.
2 KELLY O'NEILL RICKARD b 28 Apr ? Lafayette IN.
3 KRISTIN MARGARET RICKARD b 28 May 1981 Lafayette IN.
4 COURTNEY ANN RICKARD b 19 Nov 1992 Kingwood TX (fr RPR).

FOXLEY
1.1.9.4.3.7.4.5.1.1.3.1 ROBERT ALLAN FOXLEY m Merilee Lane
1 ELISABETH CAROL FOXLEY b 16 Sep 1971.
2 JAMES RICHARD FOXLEY b 17 Oct 1972 (fr Grandma HERF, EM).

SCHULTZ
1.1.9.4.3.7.4.5.1.1.5.2 ARTHUR A SCHULTZ m Linda Lee Engel
1 ARTHUR ALFRED SCHULTZ b 24 June 1964.
2 MELODY ANN SCHULTZ b 01 Aug 1965.
3 DAWN MICHELE SCHULTZ b 12 Nov 1970 (fr EM, LES).

DUFFUS
1.1.9.4.3.7.4.5.1.3.1.3 SHIRLEY ELSIE MAY HYSERT m James Alexander Duffus
1 KATRINA MAY DUFFUS b 27 Sep 1967.
2 ROBERT JAMES DUFFUS b 20 Oct 1968.
3 PETER ALEXANDER DUFFUS b 31 Dec 1971.
4 JAMES JAY DUFFUS b 24 Oct 1974.

STUART
1.1.9.4.3.7.4.5.1.3.2.1 GEORGE ARTHUR STUART m Shirley Ann Ecker
1 BEVERLY ANN STUART b 16 Jun 1960.
2 DOUGLAS EARL STUART b 11 Jun 1961.
3 TIMOTHY GORDON STUART b 03 Oct 1962.
4 LORAINNE CAROL STUART b 08 Dec 1964 (fr LKRKS).

STUART
1.1.9.4.3.7.4.5.1.3.2.2 NORMAN STANLEY STUART m Lois Mabel Stuart
1 STEVEN WARD STUART b 05 Jan 1959.
2 CINDY LOU STUART b 03 Nov 1961.
3 PAMELA WENDY STUART b 29 Oct 1964.
4 GRANT PERRY STUART b 20 Dec 1969 (fr LKRKS).

STUART
1.1.9.4.3.7.4.5.1.3.2.4 RAYMOND DOUGLAS STUART m Sharleen Pearson
1 KRISTINE STUART b 29 Sep 1963.
2 SHEILA NOREEN STUART b 05 Dec 1964.
3 KENNETH RAYMOND STUART b 08 Jan 1973.
4 SHARON STUART b 13 Apr 1974 (fr LKRKS).

LOOSE
1.1.9.4.3.7.4.5.1.3.2.6 MARY KATHARINE RAY STUART m Robert Charles Loose
1 ROBERT JAMES LOOSE b 05 Jun 1973.
2 WILLIS FREDERIC ANDREW LOOSE b 18 Sep 1976 (fr LKRKS).

NORTON
1.1.9.4.3.7.10.8.1.1.1.1 ALAN CECIL NORTON m Diane Irene Pawlak
1 CAROL NORTON b 30 Oct 1973 Burlington ON.
2 HEATHER NORTON b 27 Aug 1976 Burlington ON (fr GJN).

MILANETTI
1.1.9.4.3.7.10.10.1.1.4.1 WENDY MARILYN MAYES m Michael Milanetti
1 ALEXANDRA NICOLE MILANETTI b 17 Jun 1990.
2 JEFFREY MICHAEL MILLANETTI b 26 Jun 1993. They res Ajax ON (fr RGHM).

HELLER
1.1.9.4.7.3.10.10.1.1.5.1 DENISE JOAN HUGILL m Christopher Tod Heller
1 ALLISON REIGH HELLER b 18 JUL 1997 Clearwater res Plam Harbor FL (MDH).

DeWITT
1.1.9.4.7.3.10.10.1.2.1.1 BRETT MAURICE DeWITT m Sylvia Sue Wong
1 BRANDON CALEB DeWITT b 14 Sep 2001 Richmond BC. His picture was in The Vancouver Sun baby contest.

ST AMAND/CRANDLEMIRE
1.1.9.4.3.7.10.10.1.4.1.1 KATHLEEN DONNA McFADDIN m1 David St Amand;
1 RYAN DAVID ST AMAND b 24 Nov 1981.
2 EMILY NICOLE ST AMAND b 14 Jun 1985.
3 SEAN LOUIS ST AMAND b 05 Oct 1990. Family res Sicamous BC.
   m2 27 Jan 1999 Richard Crandlemire
4 ANN-MARIE KATHLEEN CRANDLEMIRE b ? (fr MIML).

LINDSAY
1.1.9.4.3.7.10.10.1.4.2.1 JAMES ALLAN LINDSAY m1 Naomi Arujo
1 JENNIFER LOUISE LINDSAY b 20 Jul 1979 Duncan BC.
2 PATRICIA LINDSAY b 02 Oct 1984 Duncan BC (fr MIML).
   m2 Susan Komo Rozenboom

LINDSAY
1.1.9.4.3.7.10.10.1.4.2.3 MITCHELL GRAHAM LINDSAY and Charlene McDonald
1 CHANTEL RAEANNE McDONALD b 27 Oct 1990 (fr MIML).

KILLAN/LUNDAHL
1.1.9.4.3.7.10.10.1.4.2.4 TRACEY DIANE LINDSAY m1 Vaughn Killan
1 NICHOLAS MATTHEW KILLAN b 02 Nov 1985.
   m2 29 Aug 1992 Michael Lundahl s/o Vern Lundahl
2 LUCAS MICHAEL LUNDAHL b 04 Apr 1993.
3 BRADY PARKER LUNDAHL b 07 Jun 1994 (fr MIML).

ALLAN
1.1.9.4.3.7.10.10.1.6.3.1 RHONDA RAE JOHNSON m Ronald James Allan
1 JUSTEN DONALD JAMES ALLAN b 25 Apr 1985 b Abbotsford BC.
2 CHRISTOPHER REGINALD RAY ALLAN b 12 Jul 1986 b Fort Nelson BC.
3 NICHOLAS RONALD ALLAN b 12 Dec 1990 b Prince George BC family res Sardis BC (fr RFHJB).

NAGY-DEAK
1.1.9.4.3.7.10.10.1.6.3.2 MICHELLE DAWN JOHNSON m Michael ? Nagy-Deak
1 CAITLEN DAWN NAGY-DEAK b 19 Nov 1996 Prince George BC.
2 ANDREW MIKLOS NAGY-DEAK b 29 Aug 1998 Prince George BC.
3 DAVID ROBERT NAGY-DEAK b 06 Sep 1999 Prince George BC.
   Michael's other chn are Michael, Travis & Stacy (fr RFHJB).

RICE
1.1.9.4.3.8.2.8.1.4.1.2 KRISS MARIE BOGARDUS m Paul Byron Rice
1. KERIE MARIE RICE b 14 Oct 1976 Norwalk CA.
2. PAUL EDWARD RICE b 21 Sep 1979 La Mirada CA (info fr WBB).

BEERY
1.1.9.4.8.3.6.1.1.2.1.1 CHRISTOPHER RANDALL BEERY m Marjorie Evans Hawley
1. BENJAMIN EVANS BEERY b 26 Oct 1977 Poway, San Diego CA.
2. WILLIAM FRANKLIN BEERY b 20 Jun 1979 Poway, San Diego CA.

GENERATION 13

MENARD
1.1.9.4.3.1.5.2.2.2.1.1.1 LAUREN JEAN HOLMES m Dennis Russell Menard
1. LEAH MENARD b 20 May 1982 Plattsburg NY.
2. JAMIE LISA MENARD b 20 May 1982 Plattsburg NY.

LaCLAIR/JUNGE
1.1.9.4.3.1.5.2.2.3.1.2.1 SHELLEY ANN TAUBITZ m1 Bernard George LaClair m2 Holger Junge
1. HOLGER JUNGE Jr b 13 Dec 1973 Dearborn MI.
2. ANDREA SHELLEY JUNGE b 13 Nov 1975.

TAUBITZ
1.1.9.4.3.1.5.2.2.3.12.2 PAUL LEONARD TAUBITZ m Rebecca Rae Nelson
1. NATHAN TAUBITZ b 06 Dec 1976.

END

IMAGES OF MAY LIZZIE DeWITT MALLORY 1886 - 1976
by Grandson – Lester W. Mallory

Whenever I think of my Grandmother May, her mercurial temper comes to mind. It was explosive to say the least. Her view of the world was very basic, my way or the highway. She would have taken the devil himself on and not backed up an inch.

Many scenes of my childhood include strong language and someone leaving in a hurry with his tail between his legs. The most vivid one involved two trespassing hunters. We were farming acreage that was about 1.5 miles from home. It teemed with wild game birds. The place was posted liberally with no hunting and no trespassing signs. One of the signs was knocked down along side of their vehicle. Along came my grandparents, where she saw the pushed over sign, two men, and the dog in the field. Mount Etna would have not exploded any more spectacularly. She grabbed her shotgun and said git! They tried to argue, she cocked the shotgun and told them in no uncertain terms what she thought of them. They left very subdued. This particular incident stayed with her, and all you had to do was mention the man's name and she was mad again, even 30 years later. There were other occasions of a similar nature, though not as dramatic, nor memorable.

She had an awesome capacity for work. The only time she was not busy was when she was asleep. She would work like a man if the field with a hoe in her hands, drive the old mule on the cultivator or do the irrigation all on the same day. Then go to the house, cook a meal, do canning or housework. Relaxation for her was listening to the radio or watching T.V. while knitting socks for someone. Those hands were never still.

Her greatest strength was also her greatest fault. She was extremely protective of her own. This often caused unnecessary problems for her and her kin. People would give into her wishes rather than have a confrontation and many times it was extremely counterproductive for all concerned. With the world at large, she would take a like or dislike to someone. First impression was the governing one for her. If she liked someone they could do no wrong. If the shoe was on the other foot, God help you, she would not. The following are the most vivid of my childhood memories.

As she grew older, she of course, slowed down and her matriarchal position gradually eroded to the end years when she did not stir much from the house. Still even in the late years she could show the indomitable will that she had.
She showed if when my Uncle Lester was visiting. She was smoking a cigarette when he came on the scene. Rather than admit that she was smoking, she held the burning cigarette in the palm of her hand, burning herself, with never a peep out of her. She was an iron lady for sure.

As for her father, she never said very much. I got the feeling he was a stern, autocratic kind of person and another workaholic, who expected her to work the same way. The other thing she talked about was his interest in standard bred horses. I believe he was a shareholder in the W.M.Savage Racing Stables. There was a print of three stallions belonging to the Savage Stables that hung on the wall for many years. My sister may still have it. The other thing she mentioned, he died of a massive heart attack. She did tell me where and how, but I cannot remember for sure. I certainly got the feeling there was not a great deal of love, respect yes, for her father on her part.

Her mother she never spoke of that I can remember. Likely she did, but it was not memorable.

LESTER'S STORY ABOUT HIS GRANDMOTHER MAY DeWITT MALLORY

My grandmother May DeWitt lived with us and kept some 20 white Wyandotte hens. She did much of the cooking as mother went to the office with father. Mother was the bookkeeper and there were 3-5 agents selling insurance.

I will try to write something of my own background one of these days, which will fill in the years from 1905-1931. Mother's influence and activities will show there. In the meantime, just before June's account, which begins in 1931, a few lines may be added. She had an excellent memory of events and especially of people. At one time late in life she furnished such details of family antecedents. She was intelligent, and could relate events and probable causes and judge impending moves. She was a compulsive worker, never idle, and we all appear to have followed her example to a considerable degree. She was strong willed and determined and usually found means to get her way. On the whole she was a stronger character than father, although he often prevailed by taking an easier and perhaps roundabout route. She was not a gossip and inclined to keep her counsel, but was interested in all that went on about her.

In personal appearance she was attractive as shown by her photographs. She was neat in dress and well groomed. In later years she passed the time by knitting and crocheting, providing socks for grandsons and fine lace tablecloths of which I have one.

IMAGES OF MY UNCLE LESTER
by his nephew Lester W. Mallory

The first one that I remember, he and his first wife were visiting Okanagan Falls. I see them standing on the front door step.

The next one is a subsequent visit, when I got a lesson in table manners which has stayed with me to this day. He was an ultimate craftsman with a penchant for precision, which leads to the next image.

In the late 1930's Okanagan Falls did not have electric power. Somewhere someone had come up with a windmill driven electric generator. I remember him carving a propeller for this generator out of a fir 2 inch by 6 inch plank. It was installed outside the kitchen on a tall post. Low and behold, we had electric light even though it came from an old car headlamp.

Next was at Yakima in 1942. He and Crystal brought their son Enrique, her daughter Joan to my grandparents to stay for the winter. Nothing else comes to mind.

There is a considerable gap with only letters to my grandmother. There was a visit in the early fifties that comes to mind. I was turning a grindstone for him while he sharpened tools. I can also remember him sighting rifles, making tapered fly fishing leaders or any other hand intensive project that took his fancy.

There were other visits, but they do not hold memories for me until 1956. He was an avid fisherman and hunted, which leads to the next event. I took him and Butch into high country in the Cascades on a fishing trip. At this time Butch had never seen snow. Snow we found, Butch started to make snowballs, throwing them at his father. Uncle Lester took it in good humor, but when he said "stop" it stopped.

It was 1960 when I saw him exercise his position with an overbearing U.S. Customs agent. It was very low key and very effective. Needless to say the customs agent became very subdued and polite to say the least. No more intimidation of a very old man. This was the only time I ever saw this side of my uncle.

As the years passed, the images became less vivid and more on an adult level. Mostly conversation was about hunting and fishing or some new development of a technical nature. I was never very interested in his career and it was not discussed that I can remember.

My memories are mostly of his hobbies of working with his hands. I doubt there is little that he would not have been able to do. To what depth his knowledge went on any particular subject, I do not know. I suspect it was far from total, but much deeper than most people. He certainly taught me things that I would have taken much longer to learn otherwise.

He had a consuming interest in the world around him right up to his death. I often thought he would have made a great teaching engineer.

My own daughter is pursuing a career in archaeology, which he was extremely interested in. They had conversations about it. He said she was nuts, as there was no money in it. My retort was that it is better to do what you love than be miserable at something else.

I phoned him on his ninetieth birthday. After realizing I had got him out of bed, apologizing for that. We had a good visit, with him inquiring as to how my daughter was doing with her studies. His parting comment was she would never make any money at it. She had better marry money or she would starve otherwise.

It was only a matter of days after that, that death stilled his mind forever.

P.S. There are other instances that come to mind. They are not nearly as vivid or are third hand. I will attempt to set them down, but cannot vouch for their authenticity. With my grandmother, they are of her interaction with people. My uncle's hunting and fishing experiences have been related to me, by either him or my father. Another facet of his character, he was no snob. He was comfortable with anyone. Station in life had no meaning. If the person was liked, they were liked and respected.

JUNE MALLORY'S STORY

Bus and Harris Bazely rode over the mountains from Sardis to Okanagan Falls in the Fall of 1931. Dad and Mother followed in the Spring of 1932. The family rented the old McKinna house while building their own home on Lake Shore (about 10 years or so ago this house was moved half a mile or so up the road. Bus was sure it would not survive the move, but it did).

They brought the foxes, mink, marten, etc. with them. I can't remember mother having much to do with them, except during breeding and whelping season when she spent a lot of time in a little shack watching. Her hands were always busy knitting or crocheting. Guess the surveillance was to make sure foxes mated or something.

She had a little service station on Main Street, handling Shell products, candy, cigarettes, etc. I doubt it made any money. I think I probably ate up all the profits before Lester was born as I had a God awful craving for Jersey Milk Chocolate bars.

She joined the Women's Institute shortly after moving to the Falls, was elected secretary and retained that position until the moved to Yahima in 1942. She was also instrumental in getting a library for Okanagan Falls and for some time operated it from the house. Mother, was not much of a person to 'visit' anyone but she enjoyed card parties, concerts, meetings, etc. She and Bus used to go to some kind of dinner once a year and used to look handsome together all dressed up. I think it was something to do with Sportsmen's Club. Dad would never go anywhere. I can only remember him going 'out' twice, once to their 60th anniversary party and other time was to a dinner for pioneer families. I think you have a picture of this occasion, Dad, Bus, Lucky and Normie as a four generation family.

I know I wrote to you about Mother and Dad's anniversary party, but I can't remember if I ever told you that the Herald published a picture of Dad and Aunt Mary instead of Dad and Mother. I never did find out how it happened, but Mother was fit to be tied. She was even mad at Aunt Mary for sitting down beside Dad in the first place! She cancelled their subscription to the Herald (for awhile) and never forgave the woman who took the pictures and did the write up.

Mother had a hell of a temper and passed it on to Bus and Sharon. However, they all get over it quickly and I soon learned to accept it as 'full of sound and fury, signifying nothing'. I have never forgotten the first time I saw Mother mad. It is funny in retrospect but at the time I was really horrified, as I had never seen anything like that before.

Bus and I had just come down from the ranch one morning. Dad was contentedly turning the cream separator, while humming Clementine. Mother, at the sink washing dishes, suddenly yelled "for God's sake Rique, shut up". Dad said "Oh yow yow yow" and went on humming. Mother whirled, pushed the separator bowl full of milk on the floor, added a teakettle full of water and a pot of chocolate pudding to the mess. She stormed down the hall to the garage, jumped in the car, backed it out without bothering to open the garage doors and took off on two wheels. Dad just said "ho hum" and we began to clean up the mess. We had just finished when Mother came back. Not a word was said, it was as if nothing untoward had happened. Dad used to sing or hum a lot when he was puttering around. I don't ever recall Mother doing so. I heard her play the piano once. It sounded as if she was playing correctly, but there was no 'life' to it. She told me she had had lessons as a young girl but had never enjoyed them. She said her first piano was destroyed in a fire.

The 'ranch' was the tract of land up the lake across from Kalenden. Bus and Dad did a lot of work bringing water down from Derenzy Lake for this property and then Dad began to plant an orchard. Mother came up every day bringing Dad, who did not drive. She worked along with Dad, planting and irrigating the young trees. I used to wonder how she could do it – my own Mother did no outside work except tend her garden and chickens. Looking back, I realize Mother did not work as 'hard' as I thought. She made a lot of noise telling Dad 'how to'. (The water system for ranch was abandoned after Dad sold, and water was pumped from the lake. Last Fall, land up there somewhere was bought for housing development and they plan to reactivate it to supply the water. They got Bus to take them over the old trail into Derenzy Lake).

Bus and I moved to the States in 1940, very much against Mother's wishes. We went to Kelso, where Bus went to work for Weyehauser Pulp. However, Bus developed rheumatism in hips and doctor advised re climate so we moved to Yakima in the Spring of 1940 where Bus went to work for Murch De Grasse (he was a cousin or something of Mother's). That Fall, Mother and Dad having sold the property in Canada also moved to Yakima. They rented a house in Union Gaps. Mother put in a really bad time there; she had always had asthma attacks but they were constant there. She finally went to an allergist who found that among a lot of other things, she was very allergic to cedar and the house they were living in had all cedar closets.

The Winter of '42, Bus and Dad took a trip to Tonaska to look around. They found a 28 acre orchard which could be bought for $5,500 without a down payment, to be paid for on crop sharing basis and we all moved there in the Spring of 1943. It was an opportune time to buy. Dad had enough cash for us to live on and pay operating costs the first year. The first year's crop brought enough to pay for the place, gave Dad his money back and operated next year. In a couple of years he sold one block – about 18 acres for what he had paid for the entire place. The place made good money – about $17,000 yearly net profit until crop year '47 when prices dropped. In 1948 and '49 prices were poorer still and Bus and I went to work in a packing house to help make ends meet. It was good training for him when he went to work for the B.C. Tree Fruits. The winter of '49-50 was the year of the big freeze. There was almost 100% bud kill trees were severely damaged, many actually killed.

The first couple of years we all really worked hard. Spraying was a big item then. It seemed like about 4 days out of every 10 was put in spraying. We had a stationary spray machine, which would run 3 guns. Bus and Dad used one each, Mother and I split the other. One sprayed, the other operated the spray machine and vise versa. After DDT came along it was much easier, only a couple of applications were needed per year.

Mother did all of the bookwork and controlled the bank account. Until Bus signed the income tax forms each year, we actually did not know how much money we supposedly had made. Bus had always wanted to raise cattle. In '45 or '46 he found 60 acres for sale two miles south of home. After much persuasion he got Mother to agree to buy it. I think he paid $1,300. However, as at ranch at the Falls, as soon as he got a piece of ground cleaned for alfalfa, Dad had fruit trees planted. Theory was Bus could raise alfalfa between the rows, but as at the Falls, there was not enough water and the trees came first. Mother told Dad finally, he could not plant any more trees. Bus cleaned off final piece of arable land, planted it in alfalfa in the Fall and damned if the next Spring Dad didn't plant it in grapes. After that except for disking and that kind of work, Bus would have little to do with that project.

I don't want to give the impression Mother was stingy with the money, she was generous; maybe controlling the purse strings gave her a feeling of power. There was money for what we wanted, but she always went along to write the cheque. Of course, after Bus and I started working we had our own bank account. The orchard still paid its way, but could not support two families. About this time Mother was always complaining they were destitute. We did not take her too seriously as we knew the orchard had made much more than was spent and that Dad had made a lot (for those days) on the sale of his property in Canada. For instance, he paid $750 and two fox furs for the ranch, sold it at $15,000. Another 2-1/2 acre piece for which he paid $25 sold for $1,200. However, Mother said Dad had put it all into stocks and most of them were no good. I know he did buy stock, but how much he invested or lost, I had no idea. After his death Mother showed me a six inch pile of certificates, which were no good and she said they represented thousands of dollars down the drain. She had another pile, which she said would bring something (she turned them in and got $1,100). She kept half a dozen or so which she said might be worth something some day. I still have these, and don't think any of them are any good. Only one company still listed – New Privateer. 400 shares of that, but worth only few cents a share last time I noticed. After they moved to Canada, Mother always bought Alberta Premium Whiskey, as she said that was only investment on which Dad had made money. I am sure they were never as destitute as Mother would have one believe. Dad used to laugh when she would give him hell about it.

In the mid 40's Bus bought a couple of old thoroughbreds, which we raced around the bushes at the little weekend race meets. We won a lot of races, had a lot of fun and made a little money. In 1948, realizing we had one pretty good horse we went to Montana in July. We did well there, making over $2,000 in three weeks of racing, but also lost our good horse in a claiming race. That was probably the best we did racing, but Bus was hooked by that time. The next year we raced most of the Summer, worked in packing houses Fall and Winter and that became the pattern of our lives. Incidentally Dad invested in a race horse and that did turn out advantageously. In 1949 Dad bought a little mare for $1,000 which we raced for him. Shortly after he bought her, racing was taken into the Social Security system. We raced another mare, which we had bred and raised in his name also. Both mares could run a bit and while they did not make a great deal of money, they did well enough for Dad to qualify for his Social Security pension when he reached 65.

Neither Bus, nor I particularly liked the set up at Tonasket and in our travels kept looking for a place to buy. In 1953 or 1954 we found what we thought was a good buy for $2,000. Mother having told us there was no money left, we wrote to you asking to borrow it. We did not hear from you directly, but Mother wrote to us at Spokane and said you had written to her and said we could have the money, but only if she thought it was a good buy. She came to Spokane, we showed her the place; she did not approve and that was that.

In 1955 and '56 we trained a public stable as well as our own horses and did pretty well. We accumulated a little nest egg and in the Spring of '57 we moved to Canada. We knew Mother would really oppose it, so we said nothing about our plans. We bought the property at Okanagan Falls, cleaned the land, completed all the formalities of immigration before telling Mother and Dad. Dad accepted it okay but Mother hit the roof, about 10 times. There were quite a few noisy scenes before she finally gave in. All the property at Tonasket was in Bus and Dad's names. Bus wanted to divide home place and sell his share. This was finally agreed to, but Bus signed off his share of property, on the hill to Mother as part of deal.

We moved February 18, 1957. Mother wanted the kids to stay with her, but luckily they came with us. Sharon remained for several months, then she came too. We saw Mother and Dad often, they either drove up or we went down.

Mother bought some chinchillas and was breeding and raising them in the basement. They both spent a lot of time working around them. Mother seemed to like them more than she had the foxes. They were gentle little things. She treated them like pets and felt badly when it was time to pelt them.

After we had been up here for a couple of years, Lester decided to move up here too. Mother was very unhappy about it, but was unable to dissuade him and after he left, she decided she wanted to come back too. Dad did not want to leave Tonasket. He said he was too old to move again and there was a nice cemetery there.

Mother was not to be deterred and when the 2-1/2 acres below us was put on the market. She came up and bought it for $1,100. She finally got Dad to agree to sell the place on the hill at Tonasket. Dad told me he had to sell because Mother refused to drive him up there and it was too far to walk. When the place sold Mother began to build her house and make plans to move.

She bought a house plan and Bus and Manny McLean started to build. It was a hectic time. Mother would come up every few days to check on things and invariably would want something changed or added on. She'd raise hell. Manny would quit and Bus would get him to come back. The changes would be made and things were peaceful until she came up with some new idea. The original house plan was for two bedrooms and bath but kept growing. When she decided on three bedrooms, she asked Bus and I, to come live with them. We refused and when she realized we meant it, she asked Sharon and Tony if they would. When they agreed Mother decided they would need another bedroom as Sharon was pregnant with Wade at the time. However, the house was finally finished, home at Tonasket sold and the move made, as near as I can figure in July of '63.

Mother gave up driving when she moved back and did not think she could pass the driver's test. Her feet and legs had begun to bother her and she was pretty slow on the pedals. However, she became pretty active socially again, joining the W.I. and when it was formed, the Senior Citizens Club. Sharon and I or little June made sure she got where she wanted to go and home again. Dad seemed pretty contented. They had chinchillas in the basement and he puttered a lot with apple cuttings. He said he had always wanted to develop a new variety of apples.

Dad's health slowly began to deteriorate and they sold the chinchillas after about a year. He suffered frequently from what the Doctor called 'little strokes' periods of from a few minutes to several hours, when he wouldn't know who, or where he was. Sharon worried that he would wander away, but he always stayed on the place. He hallucinated that people were always trespassing and one of his tricks was to put up barricades to keep them out. There had at one time been a fence around the place; it was all taken down except the gate. I went barreling down over the hill one day and the gate was shut. I couldn't stop, so smashed right through it. Hit the bottom of a short steep pitch where there was another obstruction of apple boxes and two by fours. The jeep's brakes were almost non existent, so I plowed through that one too. Dad was there, and he was giving me the devil for trespassing. Mother and Sharon came out to see what the noise was about. Mother began giving Dad hell. Dad told Sharon to get the police to take 'those awful women to jail'. He didn't know us from Adam. Sharon led him into the house and got him to lie down. Mother didn't have much patience with him, but the kids thought it was sort of funny and we all learned to watch for barricades.

He finally had to be hospitalized because water works stopped up and he died peacefully on November 9th of 1965. Lester and Margaret were to be married on November 12th. Mother insisted they not change their plans. Dad was buried on Armistice Day and wedding went ahead as scheduled. Mother grieved for Dad but also felt relieved it was all over. The last month or so of his life were very painful for her. The only ones he recognized were Bus and Sharon, so she stopped going to see him. It was upsetting for her to see all the tubes and apparatus used to keep him functioning and she said she never wanted anything like that for herself.

At Dad's funeral she refused to leave the grave until the coffin was lowered and covering had begun. She asked Bus to stay until grave was filled which he did. She asked that same be done for her, so Tony remained at her grave. Darned if I know why?

After Dad's death, she continued to receive Social Security, although at a slightly smaller rate. Dad had not been gone too long when I read something or other that made me realize Mother was also eligible for Canada Old Age Pension. We applied, and not only did she get it, she also received a lump sum retro-active from July 1964, which was when she would have been eligible. I think she got about $1,700. Anyway, she went on a real spending spree. She was sure the government had made a mistake and just might want that money back, but if she didn't have it, they couldn't get it. I can't remember what all she got but know she bought a new fridge and range and a Persian Lamb coat. She was always a little annoyed that I had not found out about the pension earlier so Dad could have gotten it too.

Mother's health was generally good although had problems with one of her legs, which was numb and made her very unsteady. We were all afraid she would fall and break something. The last years of her life we did not leave her alone for any length of time. We would have her up here or go down there if Sharon and Tony were going to be away. We did it very casually as she resented being made to feel dependent.

She still went to all her meetings, teas, etc. and did a great deal of hand work. Sharon's kids are still wearing socks, caps and mittens she knitted. She made many articles, which she donated to her clubs to be raffled off. Just before her death, she had completed a beautiful lace tablecloth for the Women's Institute. It brought over $200 and she was really pleased.

Sharon always became alarmed if Mother became too amendable. She said if she became too meek and mild she was sick. Sharon called Tuesday morning and said she thought Granny was sick. I went down, she sounded a little 'wheezy', said she had a cold and was annoyed because she did not feel well enough to go to bingo that afternoon and to a pot luck supper that night. On Wednesday, Sharon wanted to call the doctor. Mother objected, but Sharon called him anyway. The doctor said Mother was in congestive heart failure and should be in hospital. She did not want to go, so Sharon said she'd look after her at home. Friday afternoon, Mother asked to be taken to hospital, so the doctor sent an ambulance for her. She was alert and cheerful Saturday; Sunday she seemed happy, but said she was too sleepy to talk. She slipped into unconsciousness Sunday night and died on Monday. I am sure she asked to be taken to hospital because she knew she was going and wanted to spare the kids the shock of her death occurring at home.

I have gone into a lot of detail, a lot of it unnecessary no doubt. One reason is when I start writing I don't know when to stop. The other reason is I thought Butch might be interested in knowing more of his Grandmother. Our kids and grandkids all loved her very much.

Mother could be pretty difficult at times, but there was something funny about the things she did. Mother always loved Christmas and liked a big fuss. We all spent Christmas day together, with either Sharon or I having the dinner. Mother always said she couldn't eat turkey so we had goose and turkey. She ate the goose meat, but preferred the turkey stuffing and gravy. One year Lester and Margaret raised ducks, so Margaret said shed like to cook and bring down a couple for dinner, so we did not get a goose. Christmas morning when Margaret brought the ducks in, Mother took one look and said, "I can't eat duck". We were pretty surprised, as she had eaten duck at other times. Sharon had some frozen chicken thighs in the freezer so she fried them up and the day was saved.

We used to get a kick out of Mother and her diet. If she didn't like something she 'couldn't eat it'. She liked to go 'shopping' and bought all sorts of 'goodies' – ice cream went into the freezer, but the other junk went into her bedroom. While we knew she shouldn't eat this kind of food, there wasn't much we could do about it. Dr. Sloan would give her the devil because her blood sugar was always high, but Mother would swear up and down, she had had nothing sweet for months.

I am sure you must have known Mother smoked, although I am sure she never smoked in front of you. On one of your visits here, Mother apparently thought you had gone out. She walked into the kitchen with a cigarette in her mouth and you were there. Sharon said Mother whirled around and practically galloped down to her bedroom, and a few seconds later strolled nonchalantly into the kitchen with a white pencil in her mouth. She did not smoke in front of Bus either, for a long time. We were in Penticton one day, Bus went to do something or other and Mother lit a cigarette. Bus came back unexpectedly and Mother crushed the cigarette out in the palm of her hand giving herself a nasty burn. I told Bus of it later, and he told Mother he knew she smoked and didn't mind at all. Thereafter she smoked around him.

Ruth Mallory told me she always got a laugh when Sharon and Mother came to the library. Sharon tried to censor what Mother should read. She told Ruth she didn't like for Granny to read any dirty books. Mother was just as determined to read what she wanted. She told Ruth that Sharon didn't think she knew anything. When Mother's eyesight began to fail, she could read only the large print books, which we could get through the library. Sharon was happy as they were pretty innocuous, but Mother said there was nothing to the damned things. Mother always said she couldn't eat pork because it would make her go blind. I don't know where she got the idea, but she ate ham. Actually she had cataracts, but they never reached the operable stage.

She bought a hearing aid when her hearing began to go. I have no idea what it cost, but she complained the rest of her life of how expensive it was. She would wear it, but would have it turned off a great deal of the time. When reminded to turn it on, she would say she was trying to save the batteries, as she couldn't afford new ones. I think a three month supply cost about $5.00 and after a plan called 'Pharmacare' came into effect, they cost her nothing. Pharamacare is a plan whereby people over 65 do not pay for prescription drugs, hearing aid batteries, etc. Mother thought it should pay for all drugs and would give the poor druggist hell when she had to pay for aspirin, vitamins and the like.

Mother did seem to have a real fear of being destitute. The days on which her pension cheques were due to arrive, she sat by the window and watched for the mailman. As soon as it came, she had to go down and deposit the cheques of 'they' might stop payment. If cheques did not arrive on the expected day, she was really upset.

She was quite upset at you once. On one of your visits you took some things up to the Penticton museum. I know this was done with Mother's consent, as the curator told me she had signed a release, or something of the sort. A few days after you had left she called and said she wanted to go to Penticton and get back the things she had 'loaned' to the museum. I didn't know anything about it, but said I'd take here in. I still don't know what the things in question were, but Mother was sure mad. The curator maintained she had given the articles, and she, that she had only loaned them. I got Mother to agree to 'loan' them a little longer, and we came home. Periodically she would demand them back, but finally forgot about them I guess.

One day Mother asked if I had any 'baby' pictures. I showed her the kids, grandkids, friends babies, my brother and sisters and mine. She chose mine and asked if she could have it for awhile. She brought it back in a couple of weeks, looking very smug and mysterious. I found out later that Women's Institute had a contest as to which member had been the cutest baby and Mother had won first prize. Elva Thomas told me about the contest, said the picture looked just like Mother, even to dimples in cheeks. I didn't tell her it was my picture. I must say, I felt flattered as it was the only beauty contest I've ever won. Mother told me later about the contest. She said all her baby pictures, if there were any, were destroyed in a fire.

Mother is gone now, but never forgotten. Memorial trees by W.I. and S.C. Clubs were planted in each of the parks downtown, and roses in her name are in the rose garden. An easy chair marked 'Grammy' was in the S.C. Club room for a long time after her death, but do not know if it is still there. I know it was especially for her to sit in.

Guadalajara 1984
AMBASSADOR LESTER DeWITT MALLORY
born April 21 1904 Houlton Maine, died June 1994.

This is undertaken in response to some urging although I entertain some misgiving about its utility. One admits in the beginning that there is a strong formative influence of what has been called the Protestant Ethic. The entire family background may well be called New England, despite the fact my forebears were United Empire Loyalists by origin and lived in New Brunswick, Canada from 1783 to 1900.

The Mallorys began in the New Haven Colony about 1640 and formed part of the history of the New World. The DeWitts, my mother's family, arrived also about the same time in New Amsterdam [New York] and settled in the Hudson River Valley. (See Some Descendants of Peter Mallory ob. 1691 also Some Descendants of Tjerck DeWitt in the Library of Congress]). Until 1914 there was virtually no border between Canada and the United States and ties were close. The family was Baptist, and in greatgrandfather's day, rather God fearing and primitive. Singing was enjoyed. Basically farming stock, accustomed to hard work, idleness was frowned upon. Education was a positive good and respected. The earlier generations had little schooling apart from the primary grades, general knowledge, and the Bible.

Family traditions and pride were fairly strong and at an early age I heard of the exploits of Sir Francis Drake. Oral history was common and probably promoted by proximity caused by the long cold winters. People knew each other. There was a general attitude that right was right and wrong was wrong, inculcated much by precept and example. Ones word was valued and a man known by it. Much of the so called New England influence I received from my grandmother who lived with us until she died in 1922 and I was 18 years old.

I don't know how my name was chosen. There were no Lesters in the family previously. My middle name, DeWitt, is that of my mother's family. My parents were married in Presque Isle, Maine and I was born in Houlton, but grew up in the west. There are more details in the family history under Enrique Mallory, my father and May DeWitt, my mother. Early years were rather lonely. My brother was born twelve years after me so there was no companionship until late in life. While living in Portland, Oregon, until I was about 10 there were no children around except a girl of the same age across the street named Dagmar Loy. We played together some. When slabwood arrived to be thrown in the basement of the Loy house we did so and were rewarded with magnificent dill pickles, as her father worked in a pickle factory and had a barrel handy.

At school age I walked several blocks to attend. Memories of this are nonexistent. A few events stand out. One was the street cries one night of the news boys selling the newspaper announcing the sinking of the Titanic. Another was the "silver thaw", cold rain, which froze to ice on hitting an object. The light wires trees and bushes were a fairyland of ice. A similar event apparently occurred in recent years. In that world of timber all houses were of wood. One night a house caught fire and I went with my parents to watch. It was a tremendous conflagration seen in the dark. The fire engine was horse drawn and the pump worked by steam. The picture is still vivid.

I was quite sickly as a child from asthma. A predisposition to allergies apparently runs in the family. Great grandfather Francis Drake suffered from asthma and mother had a number of allergies. In my case the attacks came in winter and I presume were caused by a combination of humidity and perhaps the feather- bed. I remember with distress a night of high fever with the doctor in attendance when I was being steamed and apparently given up.

This affliction I didn't have in summer, especially at the seacoast. Grandmother [Georgie Ann (Drake) Mallory] had two rental cottages at Bayocean overlooking the beach, and I spent the summer there with her. The beach was usually empty of people, the crabbing was great and clams abundant. It was a very pleasant time, but again rather lonesome. Ocean currents have since eroded [much or most of Bayoceaon.] I gradually outgrew that kind of asthma.

Discipline was never strong and I didn't receive much punishment. Once however when rather small I was fascinated by an evening bonfire about a block from home and didn't respond to repeated summons. Finally mother came for me, took me to the basement, peeled down my britches and gave it to me with a hefty piece of kindling. That memory remained.

There was considerable cooking from New Brunswick or Maine. Buckwheat pancakes with blackstrap molasses were great. Friday night white navy beans were put to soak and Saturday morning in a bean pot with a chunk of salt pork were put to bake all day to be served in the evening with steamed brown bread [done in a cylindrical can and called Boston Brown Bread]. One could add some molasses to one's beans if desired. In winter Sunday evening was oyster stew. When the smelts were spawning we enjoyed them in quantity. There was salmon fishing in the Willammette River near Oregon City. I remember poached fish with a white sauce, the ingredients of which I have never been able to learn. Surely it had flour, mustard and hard-boiled eggs.

Our home in Portland was comfortable. There was a large lot, many chestnut trees, a chicken house and run. There was a large living room, dining room, kitchen, two porches and upstairs three or four bedrooms. The house may well have been purchased as I remember, after we lived there some years, a fire place was installed, flanked by book cases, carpeting laid down and new furnishings.

While playing one afternoon I jumped from the rail of the front porch with my leg under me, which broke. I spent some time in a cast. This must have been about 1911 as not long after we made a trip "back east" and I believe I was seven years old. I don't remember much of the train trip except the berths on the Pullman and that I had a collapsible drinking cup and I saw a moose somewhere in Ontario.

Mallory Stories

On the return we came down to Boston and the harbor was a forest of masts of sailing vessels. From there I have no memory until some place such as Santa Fe, New Mexico where there was an Indian in full costume to have his picture taken for twenty-five cents.

In Woodstock, New Brunswick we stayed with Grandfather George Mallory and visited many relatives.

Religion was with my grandmother as my parents didn't attend church. A Christian Church was built near home, which was attended Sunday mornings. Baptism was by immersion so close enough to grandmother's background. I was in one of the boy's choirs. There must have been a hold over from eastern seaboard customs as I remember phrases from such Maritime hymns as "Throw Out The Life Line", as well as old favorites like "Shall We Gather at the River", the sonority and tone of which always induced solemnity and emotion during baptism.

It was after we moved to Dalles, Oregon in 1915 [See notes on Enrique Mallory] that I remember something of school. It was some distance away and I was usually taken by horse and buggy and later walked home. Perhaps it was the teacher as much as anything but new subjects such as hygiene stayed with me, whether the lesson was applicable or not, for example "don't drink anything too hot or one would crack the enamel of the teeth", and " don't locate the well too near the privy". Here again I didn't have any playmates as the farm was off by itself. The area was of interest as the field below the house yielded arrowheads and a mortar and pestle from days of Indian occupation. An abandoned Masonic Cemetery
was nearby and I often wandered there. I tried to make a clay bowl which cracked. I didn't know anything about slow drying or the addition of temper.

I recall efforts to dry fruit for winter, cherries and prunes. Christmas had a splurge of candy making. The best was a filling of bananas and confectioners sugar covered with chocolate. I shot my first quail. I had an Airedale dog.

We moved to Baker, where my brother was born but were not long there. Another school at which I apparently did all right was in 6th grade. I became aware there was such a thing as girls as one lived across the alley. I made models of a zeppelin and a plane to hang in my room. Trying to make a plane fly with rubber bands wasn't successful. I raised some pigeons to sell as squabs but there was no sale. Baseball beginning in a vacant lot. Memories of my first airgun. I probably caused some confusion in a man's irrigation system well out of town. He had used the canal of an old hydraulic placer mine. I went along diverting the water from irrigation until I got it to the monitor. However the stream wasn't great enough to sluice out any gold as the nozzle had been removed. Anyway one learned a lot of miscellaneous bits of knowledge. I remember very well that Ezra Meeker came to town [how many will remember his name?]. He had a cart drawn, as I recall, by one ox and was apparently seeking help on another transcontinental crossing. I got too close to his wheel and he ordered me away. He was a surviving remnant of the old west, worn felt hat, beard and all.

In the winter father bought furs. He sent out price lists to the area around about and gathered quantities together then shipped them to the fur houses in St. Louis. At that time St. Louis still was a center, carrying over from the very early days of the beaver catch by the Mountain Men.

From Baker, Oregon we moved to Calgary, Alberta, to a large house with a furnace, wood converted to gas, the first time I saw that fuel. The house was on an elevation and we could see across some distance to the Cemetery where literally hundreds were being carried for burial due to the influenza epidemic of the winter of 1916 [? (1918)]. The ground being frozen the bodies waited until spring for internment.

I went to school and suffered for lack of grammar. On entering I was given an examination required to parse a sentence. I didn't know what the word parse meant. Then they tried me on arithmetic, which was successful. The problem was in Oregon one didn't study grammar until about the eighth grade whereas in Alberta they had it in the sixth. I didn't know the parts of grammar until I encountered them in high school Latin. My grammar has been ever weak.

A feature of school in the euphoria of World War I was military training. We boys at age twelve and up drilled, marched and mounted arms. These were obsolete carbines, from where resurrected one didn't know. However they made a satisfactory rattle when the blocks were thrown open. All this didn't amount to much except to culminate in a church parade in uniform one Sunday morning.

Apparently financial resources were low, and father had no business or employment. In summer we went to a whistle stop on a railroad in southern Alberta called Manyberries. Father went shares with a farmer to grow potatoes but when they were dug the results were quite indifferent. During the summer we had gone to camp out and fish at Elkwater Lake, at what is today the Cypress Hills Provincial Park. Came the fall we went there to live in a small frame house unfinished inside, with only the studding and outside sheathing. There were a few acres of ground, a log barn, and complete isolation with the nearest neighbor miles away. Wood was there for the cutting, fish in the lake and no more. A farmer let us cut slough hay, which we stacked for the long winter months. We bought a cow, had a few chickens so there were eggs, milk and butter. Poplar poles were cut and peeled and mother made chairs and a setee. With cold weather coming on, tarpaper was put on outside to seal out winter winds. After some muskrats were caught mother and father tanned skins and made fur caps for each of us. I lived in moccasins during the snow period.

In the winter we fished through the ice on the lake and hung the fish to freeze in a tent. After the accumulation of a good many, father traded them for a quarter of beef with a rancher who lived on the plateau of the hills.

There was no school and no books to read. I found part of a book with stories of Scottish farmers, which was not at all exciting. There was one publication, which really added to my long-term education. It was a T. Eaton mail order catalogue, like those of Sears Roebuck and it was only a few years old. I poured over the pages time after time until I probably knew every item. There was a vast quantity of artifacts, a great many of which no longer exist. One learned a lot from the different shapes of snowshoes to the parts of harness and wagons. How many today would recognize a hamestrap or know what is the reach of a four-wheeled wagon?

I had previously acquired a shoemaker's last and did some minor repairs. I did learn, and haven't forgotten how to stitch with two threads. These were lines, and the tips tapered and stiffened with "heel ball". There was a trick to making up the thread by rolling on the thigh. I haven't seen it done in years, but it's a handy bit of knowledge. There were porcupines in the woods, which bothered no one until our mongrel dog attacked one. Getting the quills out of his mouth and face was a task.

Father proposed we trap muskrats, which had multiplied during the war years and were plentiful. He bought traps. At an abandoned farmhouse he found a quantity of iron stretchers which had apparently been used long before as they were rusted and many needed new hinge bolts which we provided with harness rivets.

The muskrats were in scattered ponds to the north of the hills in what were then cattle ranches with few inhabitants. The ponds were generally small. Beginning in the fall furs were prepared and shipped. I was allowed to trap on my own in the fall and received $.28 per skin. They were not then fully prime. By spring the skins were in prime condition and the market had gone up sharply, as I remember father received over two dollars each for one lot.

The procedure was to start out in the morning in the buggy drawn by two small horses, Mike and Pat, and spend the day going from pond to pond. The trapped rats were removed, the traps reset or changed to a new place. Bait was a piece of carrot with a dab of anise oil, set in a runway. Mother was an excellent shot and collected many with a small rifle. Returning toward dusk the skinning and stretching went on by lamplight. How many there were I'm not sure but memory indicates over 600.

This provided a turning point in family fortunes. By early summer a fruit farm had been bought at Naramata in British Columbia. Father drove us to Medicine Hat (thirty-five miles). He stayed behind and we went by train across the Rockies, arriving at Sicamous in the morning to change trains for Vernon, arriving early evening. We camped out until father arrived subsequently with household furnishings and a horse, Tony. Tony had been a cow pony, although large. He was equally good with the saddle, the buggy or plow. A house was rented in town, next to the Methodist Church and we were established. [This house has since burned down].

From this age onward memory is more complete, and here the problem is not what to include, but rather how much to leave out. World War I was at its height and one became conscious of it partly because we had news in Naramata, which we certainly didn't in the Cypress Hills. I recall a discussion of our grocer about the English landing at Zeebrugge. One realized that with so many men away in the army it wouldn't be long before one might join the colors.

The town school had two rooms, two teachers and eight grades. I had the seventh and eighth there and by then there were others ready for high school. This we had by doubling up in the room. British Columbia had three years of high school. I had the first two in Naramata and the third in Oak Bay High in Victoria. Organized sports we didn't have, but there were other activities. In the summer there was a daily swim in the lake. In the winter we had an occasional hunt in the hills, camping out in the snow. When there was enough snow near town we downhilled on sleds.

Published material other than schoolbooks was scarce and I wonder how we managed to be aware of things of interest. For example we built spark coils by winding primaries and secondaries using a vibrator and battery. We were aware of radio and I tried a receiver of a piece of galena and wire called a cat's whisker. It didn't work, as we had no transmitter within receiving distance. Fishing in the lake was poor but we went to a creek some miles away when there was a spawning run of Kokanees (salmon). During the winter my task was to split wood for the day and stack it beside the kitchen stove. That was several armloads. A couple of spring times, as the weather warmed, we hunted rattle snakes at what was a winter den. Caution was learned but one boy had to give up as he developed nightmares.

The climate of the Okanogan is well suited to fruit growing. The areas where developments, undertaken by some enterprising men who bought land, built dams in the mountains and sold plots to be irrigated. Naramata was developed by J. M. Robinson, who I believe had done similar things up the lake, for example at Peachland. The plots were small, five or ten acres, and really not economic units, but probably more affordable, and with mainly hand labor what one family could manage. Homes were usually built on the orchard plot. Apricots, peaches, pears, cherries, and apples were usual at the beginning. The climate is unusual in that it is north of the forty-ninth parallel, is semi-desert with about twelve inches of precipitation and hot summers. It lies east of the coast range of mountains and is altogether distinct from the maritime influence. A similar climate zone extends in the state of Washington south to Oregon, and has irrigated orchards and cattle production.

Father bought a second small orchard, which was resold afterwards to a British veteran. The government helped the former soldiers in resettlement. Further lands were acquired nearer the irrigation flume and vegetables grown. There hadn't been such commercial production around about and several acres were planted in tomatoes, eggplant, melons, cucumbers, etc. I remember hoeing tomatoes with the temperature at 110' degrees.

Father was an innovator and was often trying something new. He raised casaba melons, at a time, unheard of locally. He sold the lot of one ton to the Canadian Pacific Company for use on the transpacific run. I felt they were too green to ever ripen. Father also rehabilitated a green house near home and there raised the plants to be put in the field, as well as selling some in Penticton. There was a vacant lot in front of the house and this became a fruit tree nursery. Where Dad learned all the technique I don't know, as I don't remember him reading much. In any event I learned how to bud and graft.

A packinghouse was set up, fruit packed for shipment to the Prairie. We were pretty extended by then and when the bottom dropped out of the Market in 1923-24 we were badly hit.

In the meantime I had gone to the local school, and the fall of 1921 went to Victoria British Columbia. A house was rented, grandmother went along and later my parents spent the winter. The school, Oak Bay High, had a deserved good reputation. It was small and had good teachers. I did well in Chemistry and Physics, and pretty well in Botany, and not so well in French and English. The use of English I have always found difficult.

I engaged in no organized sports. However I had a bicycle and took fairly long rides from time to time. I attended Presbyterian Church, why chosen I don't know, but I sang in the choir and at Christmas we did the Hallelujah Chorus from the Messiah. The choirmaster was excellent. This paved the way to joining the glee club at university for two years.

Following school closing grandmother and I took the steamer to Vancouver and the night train to Penticton, arriving in the morning. Sitting in the kitchen about noon she fell over dead from a heart attack, perhaps brought on by the change in altitude during the journey. This was 1922.

Following the summer working at various tasks mother insisted I go to college. I wanted to stay and operate a fruit orchard but she prevailed. A house was rented in Vancouver and a friend, Raymond Manchester, who wished to study to be a Radio Operator and I lived in it and we did the cooking until parents arrived some months later. Our cooking was pretty rudimentary and the hot cakes we made for breakfast could serve for potholders by evening.

I registered in the faculty of Arts with the expectation of studying medicine. At the time there was a program of three years premed at the University of British Columbia to be followed by medicine at McGill University at Montreal. After a fairly short time I went to see the Dean of Agriculture and following a discussion switched to the faculty of Agriculture. Lucky it was I did so as it wasn't until seven years later I learned I had a red-green deficiency of vision. I would never have made a surgeon and might well have had some wasted years. However I have always felt with proper eyesight I would have made a good surgeon. The first mid-year I got a forty in English, which was below passing, and didn't do well in French. Biology, Chemistry, Horticulture and other subjects came more easily. The University was then in Fairview, next to the General Hospital. To take practical classes in Agriculture we had to take busses to Point Grey where the barns were and the campus was to be moved.

In the spring of 1923 we moved again to Sardis in the Fraser Valley. Again fruit buying, picking and shipping. The summer weather was pleasant in sharp contrast to the rainy, humid winters. Cyril Rayner was with us during this time. Came fall I went back to school and mother came down to keep a large house.

The second year of college was pretty heavy with fifteen hours of lectures and twenty-two laboratories as I had elected extra courses. I didn't distinguish myself but got by with my colleagues. Back in Sardis we had a very pretty home and orchard. The house was on a slight plateau, looking down to a spring fed creek lined with alder trees. Spawning salmon would migrate upstream up to our place which was only about one hundred yards from its origin. There was an apple orchard behind the house of about four acres of Thomkins Kings. There was a barn with a garage, a stall for a cow and a hayloft.

I tried to make a little money raising chinchilla rabbits to sell as breeding stock. They were nice animals, kept in the loft of the barn. I didn't sell many, perhaps enough to pay for feed. They were also good eating. The project was given up when we discovered they had coccidiosis.

There was a community hall of which various events took place. I played some basketball there. Carl Wilson and I undertook to do some winter trapping. As I recall our only success was a skunk. We skinned it, dried the hide and Carl mailed it to Vancouver via the British Columbia Electric Railway, which then ran through Sardis. Arriving on a Saturday morning it was kept in the small baggage room closed until Monday and the odor and complaints were many. It happened that Carl's father was station agent in Sardis and he was told of it promptly, "Send no more skunks!"

It was at Sardis that father got deeply in fur farming. He was especially interested in marten and mink, neither of which was successful. With foxes he had better success but it wasn't very rewarding financially. Looking back I realize that the effort was very well done with good cages and proper diet, as far as known in those days. The protein base was enhanced with such things as ground wheat for Vitamin E, etc. There was five horse power engine used to grind the feed, bones, etc.

The year 1925 was one of depression in Canada and I missed out the session of 1924-25, as there wasn't money to continue. I did what work around home as was needed but there wasn't any fruit activity in winter. Another young man and an older man and I undertook to cut cordwood in the hills for the hop dryers. This was non-resinous, mainly poplar. We were paid two dollars and fifty cents per cord. Since the winter days were short and it took time to walk to the hills we didn't accomplish much.

My earnings were from forty to fifty cents per day. In any event it was something to do.

Come spring there was the announcement of a building project. The Fraser Valley Milk Cooperative was to build a plant in Sardis. I got a job wielding pick and shovel and wheeling concrete; I got forty cents per hour. When the plant was finished it received milk from the area and shipped a part to Vancouver. The rest of the milk was separated and the cream went into butter, the skim milk into powder. Once operation began and by virtue of having taken a course in dairying, I became the first milk powder tester in Canada. I was able to go back to college in the fall.

The third year was better. I tend to be a slow starter but by then was integrated into the study system and did well. Besides there were only two of us in horticulture, which was the specialty chosen and we were close to our professor Dr. Barss. At the end of the year I received the British Columbia Fruit Growers Association scholarship of one hundred dollars which was a good deal at that time. Living was arranged in the Aggie House. Several students got together, rented a house, hired a cook and were able to survive on meager funds. The fourth year was much like the third. That year too we had an Aggie House.

I had a number of stimulating professors. Dr. Teddy Boggs in economics may not have been profound but he was an accomplished teacher and was soon recruited to Stanford.

J. C. Spencer in entomology likewise could teach, had a delightful personality and went out of his way to stimulate students. He got a biology club going of which I was the secretary. Dr. Sarrs I will mention later. Dr. Sadler in Dairying was a fine

Mallory Stories

professor and was a great loss when he apparently committed suicide. There were others whose memory is fresh, especially Dr. Paul Bovine in agronomy, Dean Clement in agricultural economics and Lloyd in poultry.

By the fourth year there was more activity among students with an annual dance, a graduation picnic, etc. When I began in 1922 there were six hundred students and upon graduation in 1927 there were 1200.

The fraternity movement only began to be felt at University of British Columbia about 1924-25. I was invited to join a small local which I did. It didn't amount to much as far as activities were concerned but there was a fine group of men associated together, Alpha Delta Phi which had a relatively few chapters in the United States and Canada was prepared to enter. There were some prominent alumni from Toronto living in Vancouver who were interested in forming a chapter. This would be near the active chapter at the University of Washington. Our local was accepted by Alpha Delta Phi and installation took place, as I remember in August 1926. The installation held in a Masonic temple was an impressive ceremony at which the choir from Seattle sang in the subdued light.

Came the end of classes and I received a job from the University to go on the Tree Fruits Survey [Dominion of Canada Survey now known as Stats Can]. This had been going on for a couple of years and I had worked on the records in preparing my Bachelor's Thesis. The survey was designed to find the factors, which made for success or failure in growing tree fruits, try to determine costs of production and related matters. Kenneth Caple, who had previously graduated in Horticulture was the other member of the team. We were furnished with an open Model T Ford Touring car, which wasn't in the best of shape but plugged along. I bought an eight by ten foot tent, two cots, borrowed a folding table, had an apple box of pots and pans and we were off.

At that time there was no road from Vancouver to the interior, except through the State of Washington. We made Bellingham the first night. The second day we drove over the Snoqualmie Pass, of which a picture still exists and we made Pateros by night. The third day we were in Penticton. Today it is a five-hour drive over a good road. I think thirty miles per hour was about our maximum and up hills we crept along.

It was quite an experience covering the Okanagan and the Creston area of the Kootenays. We had a special form, a sort of questionaire, which was used with the individual growers. There were well over one hundred. We urged them to keep records of production, costs, etc. Some were very precise and complete, others much less so and a variety of techniques grew up to seek results.

It was a pleasant summer and rich in experience. We camped out where there were campgrounds, and when not, along some creek or lakeshore. Things were safe in those days and we had no theft.

Came September and I went home; no job. I was rather lost. In mid winter I received word from Dr. Barss that there was an opportunity to act as Secretary of the British Columbia Fruit Growers Association. He had been Secretary for years. Just why he did this I never knew. It may have been partly that he had enough of the job, but I suspect he was being kind and thoughtful to me. As a student whose training wasn't being used, I accepted at sixty dollars per month, had space in the Agriculture building, took care of correspondence, edited a tiny journal, did odd jobs such as the unusual one of meeting with berry growers of the Lower Mainland about a problem. The meeting turned out to be seventeen Japanese in a Chinese restaurant.

I was able to attend some classes. In the summer I again went into the field on the survey, again with the Model T and again camping out. Back to the University of British Columbia in September, working over the records, being Secretary and again taking courses, I was able to graduate with a Master's Degree. Mother came down for the graduation. The third summer again the survey, but this time with a Model A.

At this point I wish to express a deep debt of gratitude to Dr. Alden F. Barss. He was the professor of Horticulture. I had listened to his lectures from my first year in 1922 through to 1927. In the last two years, it was virtually tutorial as there were two students and we were close to him. He was a good teacher. It was less this however than it was his human qualities which gradually I came to understand and appreciate. He was a Christian gentleman; I don't recall him speaking in criticism. He never used bad language. He was kind and thoughtful. He encouraged one. When I went back in mid winter of 1927-28, I'm sure it was his kindness that provided the job and the opportunity. From there as I will relate later, everything flowed. The eighteen months association with him after graduation was fairly close and I was strongly influenced by his precept and example. Such decency of criterion, patience and lack of hasty human judgements as I have, I owe to him. Much of this I did not realize until later in life and I am indeed thankful to him.

Another molding force was the Alpha Delta Phi. While we were raw and new, the traditions dating back to 1832 were somewhat felt. The ceremonies, the living together, the social life that took place became important to me. I was a country boy and while my lifestyle and manners were not beyond reproach, they were certainly improved in the fraternity house, where I lived for a year and a half. I am grateful for this too and I suspect some of it carried over to the protocol laden life when I became an ambassador. Dr. Barss was also an Alpha Delta from the Rochester Chapter.

A number of graduates in economics under Dr. Boggs had gained teaching fellowships at the University of California. In 1929 two friends were applying and for some reason I also applied for agricultural economics, I was accepted as a research assistant at seven hundred and twenty dollars per year. The depression being on, it was possible to live on sixty dollars per month, but with care. I took the bus to Berkeley, University of California, went to the Young men's Christian Association [YMCA] where I found a small room, together with Norman Gold of the University of British Columbia. We had a communal dining room for breakfast and dinner and got a noon sandwich where we could. The YMCA was in easy walking distance of school, had swimming pool etc. Our room was tiny but inexpensive. Norman moved to the International House after

Christmas. He had more money; his brother owned a clothing store in Vancouver. Howard Bakken, a Mathematics major joined me, and next term was a teacher in southern California. The second year my roommate was Tiny Castle, a former footballer, a major in zoology, which he then went to teach in the University of Montana. I lost track of him.

During the 1929-30 session, the Giannini Foundation was inaugurated for Agricultural Economics in the United States. To head it Dr. Howard Tolley, the Director for the then Division of Agricultural Economics of the United States Department of Agriculture was appointed. He was a relaxed, experienced administrator and gave a good deal of life to his association with the students. He brought with him the latest in statistics - Ezekiel's Book, which he had inspired. We all took multiple curvilinear correlation analysis with enthusiasm and it plus graphic correlation proved useful long after.

Dr. Toli conceived a study of the price of California table grapes and arranged for me to work on it for about two and a half months during the summer vacation. This extra money was most welcome. I was able to buy an inexpensive suit and a pair of shoes in San Francisco which otherwise would have been doubtful. The funding came from the Federal Farm Board and I was surprised years later to find the time had been credited toward Civil Service retirement. The Federal Government really has one well recorded. The study was published.

The second doctoral year was that of more courses. My assistantship didn't mean much work but I did grade papers for a couple of undergraduate courses including that of a still famous footballer, Wrong Way Riegels. He had scooped up the ball and headed for his own goal line when tackled by the also legendary Benny Lomm. At the close of the term approached we graduate students were apprehensive about jobs. Professional openings were few. Colleges were cutting back. The only possibilities appeared to be lectureships in the mid west at nine hundred dollars per year.

About that time I learned of a Civil Service examination for the post of Assistant Agricultural Commissioner at Marseille, France, an office of the Foreign Agricultural Service. I applied claiming I had a knowledge of French, which was stretching the truth a good deal, although I had had two years of agricultural French at the University of British Columbia. By great good fortune I was selected at twenty-six hundred dollars per year. I arranged to take my general examination with a board of five professors, which went all right and the future was brighter.

Again there was extreme kindness by one of the professors. He proposed to lend me a thousand dollars to permit my travel and expenses and that I should take out a thousand-dollar life insurance payable to him. This we did and I was all set for new horizons. I want home to visit my parents and in June left for Washington.

I should go back a bit for social like. My first year at Berkeley, I saw quite a bit of Vera Svaty. She was of Czechoslovakian parentage, born in Kansas and trained as a nurse in the Presbyterian Hospital in New York. Having worked some years she decided to have a year at college taking courses that might interest her. Unusually for those days she wore her hair short. She was rather short, not pretty but with a nice face. Her enthusiasm was catching and I think attracted me. We were never overly intimate and I believe she was older than I. At the end of the term she left for southern California apparently thinking that we would not make a good match. I saw her again fifteen years later at Nice, France in 1945 when I went into a government office and saw her at the counter in a Red Cross uniform. Returning to Paris we met again and she said she wished to marry me. I was obliged to tell her that it wasn't possible, as I was engaged. She was pretty upset. I asked why; she felt that then I was juvenile and now I was grown up. I have no word of her since. She was a sincere person.

There was a young couple from the University of British Columbia who had a house not far from the campus. I saw them from time to time. Next door lived a girl, Crystal Smith. We began to see each other during 1928-29. By the time school ended, and now having a job, we were engaged.

I went to Washington by train in June, got a room at the YMCA, and reported to the Department of Agriculture. I was there only a week when I was to leave for Marseille, France. I bought a white linen suit, which was then being worn and a few other things, went to New York and embarked. The trip was by an old vessel, which was certainly not one of romantic ocean travel. There was one other man on board, an Albanian student named, Albasan Albasani. He came from Albasan. The other passengers were a complete boatload of Gold Star Mothers. These were mothers of soldiers killed in World War I and for whom the government provided the trip. The crossing was about eight days.

Upon landing in France, I took a train to Paris and a night sleeper to Marseille. I checked my bag at the station and walked to the United States Consulate where the Agricultural Office was located. The Commissioner, Neil I. Nielsen, took me to a hotel just off the Place St. Ferreol and a block from work. It was far from luxurious, but convenient. I stayed there three months enduring the cooking.

A brief statement about the purpose of the work may be in order. At that time the United States exported wheat, especially Durham, fresh fruits, tobacco and cotton and imported many smaller items such as essentials oils, dates, figs, filberts, almonds, walnuts, etc. It was important to know what demand and competition could be expected. Our job was partly market reporting, but more importantly to forecast the expected crops. To accomplish this there was specialization by office. For example grain reporting was centralized in Berlin with contributions from London, Marseille and Belgrade. Washington received current weather reports from Argentina and an Attache in China reported by naval radio. This together with commercial intelligence from Australia and Canada gave a pretty complete appraisal of upcoming world supplies. I covered Belgium, France, Italy, Spain, Morocco, Algeria and Tunisia, making survey trips from time to time.

Similarly with other things, tobacco, fresh fruits, cotton and meat in London, dried fruits and nuts in Marseille etc. Some workers were specialists, for example in cotton and tobacco, others were from the crop Forecasting Service. In this respect my background in statistics served me well. At times there were some aberrations which left one asking. A case was Morocco where I had established series of yields and rainfall. The correlation looked quite good. However, when I came to use it in a forecast before harvest I was way off. I hadn't known that late April rains would bring a heavy attack of stem rust and sharply reduce yield. That year there was such. In any event I was able to start work rather promptly and as the years went by knew the area fairly well. During the days of the Facisti in Italy the estimate of wheat for Italy was easy, I learned to wait for Mussolini's announcement in June or July and subtract twenty percent.

There was travel involved, at first to North Africa and Italy, Switzerland and later to other areas. On the whole, it was interesting. I made an extensive study of date production and trade in the Algerian Sahara.

In the fall I rented a little furnished house out of town about two blocks in from the sea. My fiancee came by ship through the Panama Canal, as I remember in November. We were married and began to cope with foreign housekeeping. A son Enrique DeWitt was born in September 1932.

I managed quite well and repaid my debt to the kind professor in Berkeley. However in 1934 when President Roosevelt took the U.S. off the gold standard, there was an immediate cut of forty percent in terms of foreign currency. Then, with budgets slashed by the depression, cuts in personnel took place. I was informed to return to the United States and transport would be paid if travel began not later than June 30, 1933. Time was desperately short but by great good fortune an American vessel was leaving Marseille for New York on the thirtieth.

The prospects for return with no job caused no little worry. However we had a calm pleasant crossing. Arriving in Washington District of Columbia, good fortune, growing out of a chain of events begun in Vancouver, again occurred. The government had established the Agricultural Adjustment Administration to seek help for farmers. Within it there was a Special Crops Section and Dr. Howard Tolley came to Berkley, California to be in charge. The people in the Foreign Agricultural Service had been in contact with him and a job arranged for me. My previous study under him and the experience with the specialties abroad were very helpful. I went to work in the agricultural building with an increase in salary.

This was a time of intense activity. I worked as a so called economist preparing marketing agreements, working with the lawyer assigned to us who was Adelaide Stevenson, of future fame. On a couple of occasions we were a team sent to the Pacific Coast to hold hearings.

Frequently I had the task of pushing agreements through the pipeline. The legal division was headed by Jerome Frank who later became a Judge. His brother-in-law was there too, Lee Pressman, who subsequently was identified as a Communist, or with such leanings. Also present was Alger Hiss whose case is widely known.

Jerome Frank sat on the Canned Peach Agreement and would not clear it unless consumer grades were stamped on the can. This new idea was opposed by industry and by we "Agricultural" types who pointed out the grades for agricultural products had been widely developed and used and their use was brought about by education and not by pressure. The canning season was about underway when the agreement was finally cleared. There were several of these problems caused by "liberal minds in Legal".

By the summer of 1934 matters had calmed down in the United States Government and the Foreign Service was to be reinforced. I was asked to return to France which I was glad to do, at an increase in salary. The Office had been moved from Marseille to the United States Embassy because of tax problems with the Government. I received a title of Assistant Agricultural Attache'. The same man was in charge, N. I. Neilson.

Wheat was in surplus, with the United States seeking markets and France trying a variety of economic gagets with its own oversupply. There was much legislation, which I reported. This became so voluminous that I chose the subject for my Doctoral dissertation and had to grind it out as U. C. informed me that if it weren't presented I would lose out. Eventually it was done. I had to go to Berkeley for the examination, which was disappointing in that the Committee did not of course know the subject. We had a pleasant reunion, but the trip was expensive.

Being in the United States Embassy provided a wider horizon. We were invited to the weekly staff meetings, which were of interest but intelligence and high policy were not discussed.

During the first years one witnessed France going down hill pretty fast with the Popular Front government of Leon Blum. While we read the papers and were generally aware of broad movements, we never the less did not really get a feel of things. The rise of Hitler, the taking over of the Sudatenland should have brought greater concern personally than it did. One listened to Hitler's strident speeches, and I knew of Frenchmen in a Facist movement but wasn't too disturbed.

We did work fairly hard. It wasn't till long afterward upon reading <u>The Third Republic</u> by Shirer and Ambassador Bullitt's cables, to the President as found in his brother's book, <u>Personal And Secret For The President</u> that one learned what really went on around one.

The shocking conduct of Ambassador Joseph Kennedy, father of Jack, in London and the passage of code material to the Germans leaves one aghast.

When I first arrived in Paris, Jesse Isador Strauss of R. H. Macy was Ambassador and a fine man. He resigned for ill health; William Bullitt was transferred from a Moscow to replace him. One could write a book about Bill Bullitt, a perceptive, frank dynamic personality. The Embassy was more active, especially socially and the stories of events at the residence were legion. An example was the attendance of the Prime Minister at a dinner with his mistress when the wife walked in.

Bullitt's parties were famous and sought after. Later when I was alone I was usually asked, together with any other sturdy young men to dance the dowagers around. Many times my feet hurt.

I won't to try to assess the reasons, or speculate but merely record that my wife became enamored with a Frenchman who was a Nazi, went to Reno and divorced me in 1937. She returned to Paris unsure of herself but finally decided to marry him.

I moved to a small apartment with a helpful maid and carried on with a lot of work.

One of the Embassy staff had a well-worn Model A Coupe, which upon leaving, he gave to me. This was a great help in getting about. Subsequently I gave it to my assistant when I could buy another coupe from a departing officer. I very much enjoyed some winter weekends in the Solonge section of Loire Valley at a hunting preserve of Ben Gallager and "Mama." Ben had asthma; his brother ran a wholesale grocery business in Omaha. He could spend the summer on a lake in Minnesota, the winter in France. There I became well acquainted with Ernest Hemingway. I had time in the evenings to take in music and a high point was Wanda Landowska on the harpsichord. There was a Canadian couple in Paris and the wife played that instrument. I much enjoyed a few invitations to their apartment when she played.

On the Champs de Elysee there was a large cafe and restaurant with a gypsy girl orchestra. I enjoyed hearing them and went frequently. When his wife was away in the summer I went with Henri Cordier to the theatre, mainly light political reviews. I remember one with a scene of the French cabinet in heaven dressed as angels. St. Leon Blum was in red while the rest were in pink.

I had had a sort of chronic appendicitis, which was not serious. However I feared what might happen if I got a serious attack when I was in the far end of Sicily or somewhere in Africa. I decided to have it out as good insurance. The job was done at the American hospital, but unfortunately infection set in and I spent some time in bed, going down to a hundred and forty-four pounds.

Over the years one learned to appreciate French cooking and to have some discernment in wines. The latter I have lost. Memory is fresh of a few occasions. One lunch, with colleagues (fruit specialists) stands out. We had pheasant with sauerkraut and Mouton Rothschild 1924. We did non plus the restaurant staff with the collective knowledge of fruit. There was an informal get together of the few agricultural attaches extant with monthly luncheons at the Pied de Cochon, which would come up with some thing special, for example an entire rack of lamb. One went frequently to Tante Louse a couple of blocks from the Embassy. Their fillet of sole, Roquefort cheese, and Beaujolais was very satisfying.

One became pretty well acquainted with some of the American war press corps. The men in the Associated Press at that time, John Lloyd and Charles Foltz were close friends. I knew Ed Morgan of United Press fairly well. Some persons who seemed just ordinary types at the time went on to become famous. The representative of the Women's Home Companion for some time was Dora Miller and she invited small groups together. There I met Eric Severeid but paid little attention to him then and haven't seen him since.

The French do not entertain at home much except family or very intimate friends. One did not become integrated, partly because of that attitude and partly because there was adequate social contact among the Americans. I had two unusual friends, one the Baron Von Holstein and the other an Indian girl. Von Holstein had married an American and I met them on board ship going home in 1933. He was an accomplished pianist with terrific asthma. He couldn't go any place with his German background and Russian birth. He was divorced and pretty broke financially. The girl was studying violin. She was charming. I was invited to tea by her mother; any idea of close association would have been out of the question because she had been betrothed at something like the age of three years, although a Christian. She gave a sort of coming out concert at which Von Holstein was her pianist. I felt it was a shame that she played nothing but serious European music when she could have had a more appreciative audience by playing some Native Indian melodies. I can no longer remember her name (Philomina Tumbo Chetti?).

After two years in Marseille and five years in Paris, my French was adequate. True the theater left me in difficulty and some literary works. However, I could read Emile Zola with interest and follow the debates in the Chamber of Deputies. I have since lost it but again exposed to French for a couple of months I could get by.

A pleasant Sunday diversion, especially in summer, was to take the Metro to the outskirts of Paris where the flea market was located. I went there many times and occasionally found something I wished. I bargained from time to time during a year to buy a samovar, which we keep. There were various other items; two pairs of beaten up, Victorian low upholstered chairs. Rebuilt and reupholstered, they have served well ever since. There was a carved chest of walnut, which had apparently been cut down a bit, but the front is original and appears to be Renaissance. Some bric a bric was a normal purchase.

One day I went with a friend. He came out with an armload of African spears. When a dealer across the street saw this, he yelled in French, "Something for the mother-in-law". Although I didn't have a mother-in-law, I promptly bought the steel mace. I don't know it's provenance but it must be Turkish or Persian, finely decorated and of considerable antiquity. If ever used on an intruder, he would be hors de combat at once.

In the early summer of 1939, word was received of the opening of an office in Mexico and I was chosen to go as Attach. This was due directly to the interest of Henry Wallace, then Secretary of Agriculture in Latin America. He had felt the area was neglected. At the same time as my transfer, a man was pulled out of Berlin to go to Washington. I never learned whether Hitler and the possible eruption in Europe was being taken into account, although it was possible.

President Roosevelt, in response to repeated efforts of George Messersmith, then in Department of State, to combine the overseas services, issued Reorganization Order #2. This transferred the Foreign Commerce Service and the Foreign Agricultural Service field employees to the Department of State. There was some option for the employees whether to go to State or return to Agriculture in Washington I stayed with State.

The arrangements were a bit odd administratively. I was in State service but carried out a reporting job directed by Agriculture. It worked fairly well.

I left Paris in June on the fine ship with good food and good weather. Gordon Boals of the Berlin office and his German wife were already on board. It was a pleasant crossing.

Arrived in Washington and the necessary bureaucratic measures were taken care of. A week was spent in Agriculture. A second hand Nash car was bought for seven hundred and fifty dollars. I bought fishing rods, a Winchester Model 70 30/06 and took off for the West Coast and three months home leave. At that time at least, Agriculture allowed a large accumulation and gave one travel home once in three years.

I drove across via Ohio, the Dakotas, Montana, Idaho and swung north in Washington to the Okanagan Valley where my parents and brother lived. It was a fine late summer and fall. I went hunting several times, once for ten days on horseback to what is now Wells Grey Park with my brother Don and a guide and four horses. We wanted to get a grizzly bear but were unsuccessful. One afternoon, we were on a hill overlooking a valley when we saw a group of upland caribou coming over the opposite hill. When they went into the forest, we took off down the hill, across the valley and up the other side a bit to one side of where we thought the caribou would come down. It happened that we ended up above them; I was able to get a youngish bull. The meat was excellent and of very good flavour.

A grizzly was about, as he had visited the remains of a mule deer we had butchered. My brother saw him the next day but was not able to shoot. He said he looked like a three year old steer with short legs.

Returning, I ran the car off the road in the late afternoon. We slept on the road itself. My brother walked back a few miles where he saw a house and hired a man to bring a team of horses in the morning. He pulled us back on and we were able to get down to the highway. Today I'm sure we wouldn't dare to sleep on the road - we would be run over.

The fall weather was excellent with bright days and cool nights. Between my father's hunting license, that of my brother and myself we had deer from time to time. We pulled the meat high in a tree by ropes above the flies and it kept well. I learned that thin venison steaks and buckwheat pancakes made a superb breakfast.

When my holiday was over I drove back to Washington, was briefed in the Department of Agriculture and took off to Mexico. I had never seen a cotton gin and arranged to see one on the way, attending a visit made by Secretary Wallace at the Tuskegee Institute in Alabama. I visited Texas A and M College for discussions. And so on through Laredo to spend the night in Victoria. The road was then through Tamassunchale. Arriving, I put up at the Geneva Hotel for three months. Later I found a house in the Lomas de Chapultepec. The English landlady found me a cook whose young daughter served a bit as a maid, and a gardener who became the houseboy. They lived in and stayed with me for the five years I was there. They relieved me of most burdens in housekeeping. My effects arrived together with some things I bought in Washington but I did need bedroom furniture and had it made - a magnificent job of fine mahogany, which was given to me.

I started to take Spanish lessons but I did not continue long enough to do much good. I felt that office time so taken up was too much. My teacher was a Catalan Spaniard and I avoided some of the Mexican sing song accent. Over the years I became fluent but not always correct, as my foundation of grammar was inadequate.

The work began slowly. There was no background, no files, no information. Mexican production statistics were lacking, or out of date. There was no foreign trade data. Little by little things took shape. I became acquainted with the officials concerned, but in the beginning did not travel. The onset of World War II was to require a great deal of information, but that was still in the future as far as the United States was concerned. When work became heavier I hired a young man at $1200.00 per year as a clerk. He went on over the years to become an Agricultural Attache.

I was traveling in a car with the Official Mayor of the Ministry of Agriculture following an entomological meeting in Victoria when the news of Pearl Harbor came over the radio. It wasn't long before the demands on my office grew. Mexico was important for raw material especially the minerals. In agriculture the quantity of foodstuffs to be imported, or exported needed to be known. Medicinal plants, rubber and other items occupied us. Two more men were sent as part of the staff as we were four and two secretaries. Additionally I was made head of the local efforts of the Rubber Development Corporation. One doesn't need to go into details but I may say we were busy and succeeded in preparing many complete and basic reports.

An event, which was to have its sequel for Mexico and for me personally, was a visit of the Secretary of Agriculture, Henry A. Wallace. This was set up as a trip by car and Johnny Carrigan and I drove to Laredo to meet him. The Naval Attache and Military Attache were also detailed and went. There were a number of reporters and it made quite a cavalcade. His wife accompanied Henry. After some days in Mexico City where he met with officials a trip was set up to visit some of the countryside. I was assigned to go along with them. We took the then road to Patzcuaro over the Mil Cumbres. Frequent stops were made where Henry got out, looked around and especially examined the fields of corn. He had been a plant breeder, working on hybrid corn in the mid-west.

There was a very practical result of the trip. Upon return he was in touch with Dr. Emerson Fosdick of the Rockefeller Foundation, which had long provided funds and inspired research and control of tropical diseases. Henry convinced Dr. Fosdick that an effort should be made in nutrition--and specifically in agriculture. Later I received word of a commission of five scientists to come to Mexico to look over the possibilities of assistance. This was a high level group, Dr. Stakman of Minnesota who had long worked on stem rust of wheat problems in Mexico, Dr. Bradford of Cornell, Dr. Mangelsdorf, a botanist of Harvard with interest in corn, Dr. Bradford of Cornell, a soils man, and the other two whom I don't recall. They spent some time in Mexico and I tried to help. Later two other men came to do more work in the field. We were able to get them a pickup truck from the Ministry of Agriculture and they took off on an extended trip.

Eventually the Foundation approved the idea and negotiations were undertaken, and finalized to establish a joint research effort. The signal feature of the administrative arrangement was that it was independent of the government and thus the staff was not subject to the changes that occurred due to Mexican politics. First steps were breeding and selection of types of corn and the selecting of promising employees who were sent to the States for advanced training. Work went well and wheat was soon added to corn. This work continued for years with much success. An offshoot was a rice program for the Far East, which was carried out in the Philippines.

There has been much publicity about the "Green Revolution" of Mexico and success has been attributed to several people. In fact the credit should go to Henry Wallace who saw the need, perceived the solution, and arranged for its initiation.

When I arrived in Mexico the Ambassador was Josephus Daniels, editor of an influential southern newspaper. He had been Secretary of the Navy with President Wilson, and an Assistant Secretary then was Franklin Roosevelt. What prompted the appointment one doesn't know but it was surmised that Daniels, who was Head of the Navy in 1914 at the time of the attack on Vera Cruz, wanted somehow to make amends. The Administration of the Embassy was very relaxed, there were no problems, and Papa and Mrs. Daniels lived a fairly quiet life. When they entertained larger groups and the staff was present many slipped across the street for a quick drink as Daniels was a teetotaler and no liquor was served. Mrs. Daniels, who was in a wheelchair and a semi-invalid, was reputed to take a tonic, which had a great deal of spirits in it. Papa was rather ineffectual but pleasant, and gradually over a long period of incumbency became well liked by the Mexicans.

When Daniels left, his place was taken by a man of another character - George Messersmith, transferred from Cuba. He was a career officer, widely experienced, ran a rather tight shop and was one of the few who ever talked back to Hitler. With the war on the staff swelled until we were all told, about nine hundred and a separate building was rented to house the economic section, the present day Hotel Paris. I had the top floor.

Uncle George reviewed reports we wrote. I learned after a time to take things to him on Sunday mornings when he went across the garden to work by himself or to dictate his famous long letters. It was said he could express himself in a few well-chosen pages. One morning I had taken my quarterly report on sugar, which forecast a supply, which should have sufficed. He took it, glanced at the subject and put it in a drawer in his desk. I assumed it had been sent, but three months later, again on a Sunday morning, he pulled open the drawer, handed me the report and said I could send it. I imagine his action was due to the Mexican desire for more sugar from the United States and he wished to be sure of the facts; fortunately I was right. I developed much respect for Messersmith and as far as I know he had confidence in my work and judgement. Here again the association was to have later developments.

One time I was not able to help him, but I wasn't present to argue as I was in Washington in 1946. He had succumbed to pressure from the Mexicans to allow importation of a lot of Zebu bulls from Brazil. The Assistant Secretary for Latin America, Spuille Braden, called me to ask my opinion. He said Messersmith was all for importation etc. I advised against and had an ample experience in Europe of the danger. In any event it was approved on the grounds that the bulls had been vaccinated against foot and mouth disease and would quarantine on an island off Vera Cruz. They were, and later when imported, and the vaccine had worn off, or hadn't taken, there was an outbreak of foot and mouth in Mexico that cost the United States Government $300,000,000.00. Had it ever reached the States the damage would have been in the billions. It took strong measures and the Mexican Army to eradicate it.

Among the more or less strategic materials, which the United States searched for or tried to develop, were medicinal plants. To that end a Pharmacologist was assigned to the Economic Section of the Embassy and worked closely with us. He was Dr. Bonisteel, formerly Head of Pharmacology at Fordham University. A Systematic Botanist and a Plant Production man assisted him. The results of the efforts didn't amount to much but there was some production of essential oils. Bonisteel had a number of unusual expressions generally with a scientific terminology. For example a well developed girl he said had bilateral symmetry and one might be a prismatic bastard, meaning a bastard from all angles. I enjoyed field trips with him. Gilly, the botanist did a good deal of collecting and classifying. I was honored with the naming of a new species.

Among the developments of importance in which we played only a minor role was that of chemicals for use of night flyers. A basic substance, which could be elaborated, was found in a trillium lily in Louisiana. These were too small to be of use. It was desired to learn if relatives might be found in Mexico. A man came, cleared with us and took off for the tropics. He found a plant called a barbasco with a large underground bulb, which could be used. He obtained a truckload, which I arranged to be cleared at the border. From this a whole industry developed with synthetic hormones, which continues today. It proved sufficiently profitable for the Mexican government to move in and take it over on the grounds of giving more income to the Mexican gatherers. So far as I know this has depressed the operation.

Another product, this one of much importance, was rubber. In those days rubber was that grown naturally in the Far East from Hevea Braziliensis. First with the war on shipping was often destroyed to the extent that one could find balls of rubber along the Caribbean Coast from torpedoed ships. Later when the Far East was cut off entirely supplies became even tighter. Our efforts took two forms--production from extant wild plants, and planting of Hevea.

Here a bit of history to clarify the position. Early in the present century rubber was obtained from a shrub growing in the northern desert areas of Mexico. This was guayule. The rubber was in the form of small inclusions in the plant and obtained by grinding the woody plant and separating the rubber. Another source was a large tree in the Mexican tropics, called Castilloa Elastica. By cutting through the bark, a rubber containing sap or latex would flow out which was coagulated with smoke. The amount of production was relatively small but in the early 1900's was fairly well known. Although later it was of no importance commercially it was still employed by some persons in the tropics--and in 1940 I bought a poncho made of cotton which had been made waterproof with castilloa.

In Brazil, which was the most important source a wild forest tree was the Hevea. Rubber gatherers working the forest made it into balls by gradually adding layers of sap, smoking them. Such trees were scattered in the forest, and were subject to a fungus called the South American leaf disease. When plantations were attempted the concentration of trees provided proximity and leaf disease was severe. When the British smuggled Hevea seeds illegally out of Brazil and took them to South Asia the disease didn't go along. Plantations were developed, production grew rapidly and the rubber industry of Brazil collapsed.

To have plantations in the Americas meant some system of avoiding disease. The solution was found through a disease resistant strain, or clone. This did not produce much latex but by top grafting onto another good clone it worked. The grafting of rubber isn't too easy because of the latex and the fact that a large patch bud had to be used. Then came a further development when sports produced high yielding clones. A double top work was used, roots from ordinary Hevea seeds, a good clone used to from the tree trunk from which the latex could be extracted, and then when grown to some height a new top of resistant clones was added.

It was thought that we might get plantations started in Mexico. Accordingly a trip was set up with a tropical agriculturalist, the Official Mayor of the Ministry of Agriculture and I, to visit experimental areas. We flew to Tapachula, crossed the border into Guatemala and went by road to Guatemala City. We visited the banana plantations in Honduras and ended up on the tropical lowlands of eastern Costa Rica. There the Good Year Company was experimenting with top working of rubber trees. We spent several days in the heat and humidity. The end result was an experimental plantation in Southern Mexico. So far as I know latex is still produced, but not for cured rubber since synthetic does not permit price competition. At the same time guayule production was promoted and substantial areas planted in the north. These did not survive the end of the war.

One way or another I was pretty much involved and became the head in Mexico of the Rubber Development Corporation, a government entity. There were several men working and all sorts of schemes were used to try to get Indians in the tropics to produce more Castilloa, from sewing needles to shotguns as barter. The end result really wasn't worth the effort and expenditure.

Fairly early on a proposal came form the United States Department of Agriculture (U.S.D.A.) for a survey of the fruit industry. This was the brainchild of Fred (Doc) Motz who had been the pre-war fruit specialist in London of the Foreign Agricultural Service. We had cooperated closely for years when I was in Paris. He came to Mexico, I met him by car at Laredo and he ended up staying three months in my home. He was good company, we took several field trips, had a dark room made in the old Embassy basement and spent many an evening developing pictures for publication. Doc finished the manuscript in Washington and it was published in 1944 a volume of one hundred eighty-four pages, with me as co-author.

Another project, in fact my first in Mexico, was a study of the Vanilla industry. I went to Jalapa, Veracruz and Papantla, gathered information, took photos, etc. The resulting report was published in November 1941 and I believe is still a standard reference on the subject.

Not being subject to direction by the Embassy in my work, I had a good deal of freedom. One odd trip was on a beaten up boat along the shore of the Gulf of Mexico during the days when German submarines were so successfully active. There had been rumors of provisioning in Mexico. The Assistant Naval Attache set up an observation trip and I went along. We made a big show of going fishing, and did catch a few. We went from Vera Cruz north, putting into every river or inlet, getting some excuse to poke around and see if there were any drums of oil hidden away. We didn't find any. The end of the saga was an error by the Captain of the boat who misjudged the bar at Tuxpan and we ran aground, to be pulled off later by an oil company tugboat. A fellow American took us in his quarters where we had the luxury of a much-needed bath.

A pastime or hobby, which provided many pleasant hours, was shooting. There was a gun club a couple of miles up the hill my home and several of us from the Embassy became members. There was a skeet range, pistol targets, and a live turkey shoot across a valley, on a distance of four hundred ninety-five yards. We shot some skeet, and as ammunition was scarce I reloaded my shells. The turkey shoot was with high- powered rifles and I had my 30/06.

At one time, apparently sometime around the turn of the century, there must have been a special guard detail at the Embassy. We discovered 11 Krag Jorgeson rifles in the basement of which seven were complete and in working order. There was also considerable ammunition--220 gr. round point, mostly with the necks cracked. We obtained the rifles, had them converted to sporters and used them on the turkey shoot. The combination of the rifles and ammunition was wonderfully accurate in spite of the cracked cases. I once saw the assistant Military Attache get three turkeys with three consecutive shots. That cost him a good deal of beer as the custom was that a turkey hit meant a case of beer for those present. I disposed of the Krag when I left Mexico but rather wish I still had it. I never became a good wing shot, with twenty-two or twenty-three the most at skeet.

I managed a couple of trips home, travelling by car. The first was in my 1938 Nash. Time seemed short somehow and I drove hard, from Sanderson, Texas to Oakland, California in one jump and the roads were not then free ways. That was the trip when my brother and I went hunting for grizzly bears and ran off the road. On the way back I visited all the border consulates arranging for regular reports on agricultural conditions in each district.

Another time I came down to Los Angeles, spent the night with family friends and the next day about noon was in the desert near Blythe, California. I felt very shaky indeed, went to bed and couldn't move. Along towards evening the motel owner looked in and I asked him to bring my suitcases where I had medicine. I had a recurrence of malaria but next day the chills and fever were gone and I continued on. I had only one other recurrence and none since. Rather curiously I believe I got the malaria in Cuernavaca where it wasn't supposed to exist.

I have driven from Mexico to British Columbia a number of times, always with interest in seeing things along the way. More frequently I went in a rather straight line through New Mexico, Utah, Idaho, Washington right into British Columbia.

While the trips were rather intensive and sometimes tiring I enjoyed going through the country, seeing points of interest, and occasionally camping out. I am a Western by predilection and know more of the geography and history of the area than I do of the East. I like many of the odd names such as Medicine Hat, Okanagan, The Snake, Buffalo Hump, Moose Jaw, Damfino, Osoyoos, Coulee, Yellowhead, Boise, Muleshoe, White Bird, Nez Perce, Yakima and so on, many of Indian origin.

We had had close relations with officials of the Ministry of Agriculture, and the establishment of a joint Mexican American Agricultural Commission enhanced this. The Secretary of Agriculture and a group came form the United States and a series of meetings were held. Later the same took place in Washington of which the most interesting event was a visit to Beltsville where the latest experiments and findings of that Experimental Station were explained.

By the year 1944 one was integrated socially. There were parties by members of the Embassy staff, official functions of one kind or another, and our personnel lives. I had begun going with Eleanor Struck and we saw a good deal of each other. This was no sudden thing but had time to mature and be sure of ourselves. She had already some time previously undertaken to obtain American citizenship, as she did not feel really Mexican at heart, having been educated in Germany and was working at the Embassy in charge of Notarials. The matter of citizenship was to be of some importance since I would have been obliged to present my resignation from the Service if I married a foreigner. It so happened that Ambassador Messersmith undertook to promote our case and after I left Mexico he wrote a number of letters to the Department urging a favorable outcome. I believe there were three Assistant Secretaries of State prepared to help. Later when in Washington, and marriage, Eleanor had to wait less than a year for her final papers.

It was about November 1944 that word came to me of a transfer to Paris. This was less an order than a request. I accepted. Five years had passed since arriving in Mexico City. I had done a rather good job, knew the country, had acquired some Spanish and felt some satisfaction. Five years, some of them of pretty active work at an altitude of seven thousand four hundred feet, had left me feeling rather worn. It appeared a good time to change even to the War Zone. I also made a deal with Agriculture saying I would go, but wanted a transfer to Washington in about a year. This was for the purpose of marriage as I shall mention later. It was agreed to by Leslie Wheeler, head of the Foreign Agricultural Service.

My household effects were put in storage in Mexico City. Some how, I don't remember how, a trunk had been packed to go to Paris when and if possible. I flew to Washington to spend about ten days. There wasn't too much to get ready for. I was to have an assistant--Howard Cottam. We became acquainted and shopped around for some small necessary items. I was given, according to my level in the Foreign Service, a card showing the rank of a Brigadier General, in the event of capture by the enemy. We went by train to New York and thence to Fort Totten on Long Island. There was a military barracks where we waited for overseas flight. We were limited to one duffel bag (no suitcase). Every once in a while the loudspeaker would announce names and flight times. We would rush to open windows and listen.

Cottam got away a couple of days before me, as also had Marcelle, my Mexico City secretary. I hadn't expected the powers that be to follow my recommendation for her but they did, surprisingly. I was airborne in a DC4 carrying large fuel tanks inboard in bucket seats. It was a pretty long night when we were startled by great noise. The plane came down on a runway of metal treads in the Azores. By the afternoon we were in Orly. I made it to the Embassy to be informed of a billet in an Air Force mess down the street and opposite the Louvre. There by evening was Cottam and Marcelle. This was two days before Christmas 1944. The next night the last German air attack came, apparently aimed at a British communications vehicle in the Tuilerie garden. The bombs threw a chunk of tree on top of the Hotel and broke some windows, but no one hurt.

I took over our old offices in the Embassy on the Place de la Concorde. A number of prewar colleagues were back on duty. My great good fortune was to go to the basement and find all our files complete. This was a tremendous break. I knew generally about the agricultural situation but trying to develop reports completely new, with the French government in disarray would have been a monumental task. As it was we had basic data at hand to develop the food supply picture.

The French were pressing for shipments of foodstuffs but the Allied Military was more interested in ammunition and other hardware. The war was still intense and I had arrived right at the time of the Battle of the Bulge. With nothing to do at night in a blacked out city it was no great hardship to spend evenings at the office and we rather promptly got reports flowing.

There was one difficult period. The winter in Paris was cold, the unheated hotel room was damp and I contracted a severe chest cold that put me in bed for some time. The army doctor said he could dry me out at the hospital but suggested I wouldn't want to take up a bed needed for wounded men. I stayed in my room.

Come spring the weather improved and things looked up. The day of Armistice in May 8, 1945 was lovely and in the late afternoon the skies over Paris were filled with planes flying about - and shooting flares. I saw them from a roof top apartment of a friend on the Isle St. Louis.

Fortune was with me. On Agricultural Intelligence Combat Zone Headquarters had a Colonel in charge of Agriculture for the United States Army (part of the behind the lines security). He in turn had officers scattered about the country to report to him. The Colonel, Bruce McDaniel, was a long time friend from Redlands California, dating back to my agricultural adjustment days in 1933-34. We quickly collaborated. He needed some of our back data, and I needed current crop information. I was able to do one early field trip with him in a beat up old Buick loaded with gasoline cans. I guess I confused the people we visited as I had on Army clothes without insignia and wore a felt hat.

By summer I had received an office car and was able to get about some. By summer too, French agricultural officials were concerned about the approaching wheat harvest. They greatly needed binder twine. That twine in large part had come from the Philippines and was cut off. Mexican hennequen was being used not only for twine but also for ships hawsers. Come July I arranged a trip to Washington to go over a number of matters, especially with the supply people. I was also able to arrange in advance for Eleanor to visit Washington. It was at that time we went shopping for an engagement ring. We had a reunion.

Back to Paris, this time with the war over in Europe we made a daylight flight via Newfoundland, Iceland, and Scotland, again in a DC4. The rest of the year was fairly routine.

I made a long field trip with two companions from the economic section via Limoges (where we visited the Havilands) Bordeaux, Marseille, Nice, Lyon, etc. At that time I arranged for the production of a dinner service of Haviland China to be picked up later. I also made a trip to Belgium to see the Agricultural Attache' in Brussels and visited Bruges which I much liked, especially the Memling's paintings in the Hospice. I saw Henri Cordier from time to time. We had been good friends before the war. I went with him once on a hunting trip in the fall to a place in the Loire Valley owned by one of his relatives. As food was still scarce we each took our sandwiches but our host provided something special. He had a small cask of Eau de Vie of peaches from before the war. Each summer he put it in the upper story of a small barn and in the winter in the cellar. It received a special and rapid aging. It was most excellent.

Along in the fall our Air Force mess was closed down and I received a large room in the Crillon Hotel across the street from the Embassy. That was deluxe and something I shall never afford.

There were a number of good young officers in the army concerned with agriculture. Knowing we would need to recruit after the war, I arranged a trip to Germany to interview a number of them. This was Berlin, Frankfort, Heidelberg, Stuttgurt and overnight at Hitler's Eagles Nest. In Berlin one visited Hitler's office, it was still a shambles. It had had an enormous worktable of a red stone composition, now in bits. I have since regretted I didn't pick up a piece to be made into an ashtray. Come January 1946 I took off for Washington in a plane with good seats. The crew, because of time restrictions on flight, landed in Hamilton Bermuda for a stopover. I still have the cashmere sweater I bought there.

Back in the United States there was a terrible housing problem. Marriage was planned, but where to live was a problem. One had visions of a room someplace of indifferent attraction. Luck was with one again. One of the lady clerks in Agriculture whom I had known for years had a friend who was moving to the Middle West and had a small furnished house. I was able to rent it. It was in a convenient attractive area - Foxhall Village. Later when my effects arrived we moved the landlady's furniture to the large basement. It was a small but quite comfortable dwelling. We had pleasant neighbors.

Eleanor arrived in February and a lady Judge married us at City Hall on February 21. I had a wedding breakfast at the Carleton Hotel with the Leslie Wheelers, the Henry Wallaces (then Vice President) and the couple who were Eleanor hosts. We had, as I remember, guinea hen.

A son was born March 3, 1947 and subsequently named Lester DeWitt Mallory Jr. No name was agreed upon for the first three months and he was called Butch, to which he still is to us.

A very active and interesting period began. Agriculture assigned me as its liaison with State and I had a foot in both Departments. A complete over haul of reporting schedules for the field was undertaken and worked out. At the same time the Foreign Service of State needed expanding and a special entry was arranged with oral examinations. There were examining panels, usually with three State Department representatives, one from Commerce and one from Agriculture. It fell to me to represent Agriculture pretty steadily. The candidates and their performance were interesting. With such constant contact with the official in State on the administrative side I also got into the matter of the new Foreign
Service Act of 1946, usually to do some convincing in Agriculture. Jumping about as I did I was approached in May of 1947 with the news I had been selected to be one of the State Department Officers to attend the first session of the National War College. That would have been a superb experience. However on the same day I was approached with the news I had been selected as counselor in Havana. What to do. I told my two proposers that I couldn't choose and for them to work it out. The result was Havana.

This came about in a peculiar way. Harold Tewell was Assistant Chief of Personnel. He had told me about Havana to which he wished to return one day and to economic work. When this assignment arose he talked with me saying I was to be Deputy Chief of Mission and he was going as Economic Counselor. This didn't make sense as he was my Senior by grade, age and experience. He said we could get along. It was only later that we found out the probable reason. His wife was alcoholic. He didn't want the burden of the Protocol functions and public appearances with such a problem. We did get along and I consulted him frequently. That was another of those odd things which shape ones destiny.

I arrived in Havana, about the end of May. The Ambassador, Henry Norweb was on leave, and the Economic Counselor, Alfred Nufer in Charge. He had been nominated Ambassador to El Salvador and stayed on only a month. I was then a complete neophyte on such things, the man in charge. There wasn't time to worry as there was a proposed invasion of the Dominican Republic by the "Caribbean Legion." Men had been recruited among leftist groups from round about. A leading spirit was from Venezuela. Training was set up on a small island off the north east coast of Cuba. Fidel Castro was among those present. Our intelligence was good, and easy. Things leaked pretty easily in Havana. We had a daily flight from Guantanamo to Florida, which could observe any unusual development. We knew of the Schooner of arms sent by Arvealo of Guatemala. There were some perhaps unusual sources. Ernest Hemingway had a wide acquaintance and acceptance among the Cubans. He had done intelligence during the war and now provided us with timely bits. A cable to Washington became almost daily routine. I got some reputation in Washington as a political reporter but it was not deserved. The Ambassador returned after I had been in charge for sometime. How much to write of him I am uncertain. Perhaps Eleanor could do better in writing of his wife.

Henry Norweb might best be described as a patrician. He was born in England of American parents. He was tall, slender, good looking, well dressed, and had a curled mustache and all together of fine appearance. He had had a good education. His first post was Third Secretary in Paris, I believe, of least partly on Protocol. How he and his wife, Emery May got married I don't know but in those days Henry was a catch. She was also, for despite being something less than beauty she came from a family of Robber Barons of the coal country and was rich. They made quite a team, he was suave and almost genteel, she competent and forceful.

Fortunately we hit if off pretty well and I learned a good deal from him. One day he called on the Foreign Minister and upon his return I asked what had transpired of interest. He told me about Sherlock Holmes dog which wasn't there - that the important part of the conversation was what had not been mentioned. Functions at the Residence were beautifully done. Here again we were somewhat in the role of learners and we did so under masters of the art.

Unfortunately, or not, politics raised its ugly head and President Truman appointed Robert Butler as Ambassador, offering India to Norweb. He felt slighted and resigned. Butler came and perhaps the less said the better. He was gauche, crude, insensitive, and if one tried to keep him for a major mistake he feared one was trying to "get" him. I was told he barely escaped indictment for some monkey business on war profits. In short we didn't get along. My main effort was to hold the staff together as he was making life miserable for the administrative people with impossible and illegal demands.

One incident bears mention. There was a visit of four submarines to Havana. During the late evening a sailor was perched atop the statue of Jose Marti, the national hero. Whether he urinated there, as claimed, or some one threw a bottle of beer we don't know but all hell broke loose in the press. I was called about eight A.M. on Saturday and took off for the office. The Ambassador couldn't be located. At the office such preparations as possible were made. Our FBI liaison was in touch with the police. Finally toward noon the Ambassador showed up. The Foreign Minister was to walk with him to the statue and had had the great kindness to have a wreath ready. (The Minister Carlos Hevia was a graduate of Annapolis!).

The Havana correspondent of the Associated Press came upstairs to join us during the morning hours. A statement of "desagrave" was needed, that is sort of apology--or take-away-the-hurt. I simple couldn't think of words and Ben sat down at the typewriter and composed the necessary. This was given to Butler to deliver.

The whole matter calmed down in a few days but the Ambassador, I believe, never forgave me for not going with him. Perhaps I should have, but it wasn't necessary for one thing, and I considered it more important to be at the Command Post in touch with the Police. One way or another we didn't get a long and in 1949 I was transferred to Buenos Aires as Deputy Chief. I didn't know at the time that Butler had learned of the coming vacancy and had me kicked upstairs. That was a great favor.

Several times I was able to go fishing with Ernest Hemingway on the Pilar. We never caught a sailfish or a marlin but the trips were good fun. From Ernest I heard the story of the big marlin, which he wove into his book The Old Man And The Sea. There were other occasions when one got out to the country. A memorable one was a visit by a man and wife from Florida in a small amphibian. I went with them across the island to a lake where every cast brought a bass. When landing we had to avoid a log, but when we took off there wasn't any log - apparently a really large crocodile.

This is not the place to review political history and the things that took place during our two years in Havana. However mention may be made of the underlying influences; Cuba had a considerable history of grafting governments. The President at the time of my arrival was Grau San Martin. His mistress was his brother's wife. As an example she had eighty school teacher's salaries accredited to her and so it went. His successor, Prio Soccaras, was able rapidly to acquire property in Florida. The corruption was so great that the way was paved to a considerable extent for Fidel Castro - people were fed up, even the middle class.

Came the time to move again in June 1949 and we went via New York and the steamer to Buenos Aires. The ships were excellent, a couple of days out of New York we were in the Gulf Stream and thence south in balmy days. We stopped in Rio and there on the companion ship going north I saw my predecessor, Guy Ray. He was ill, transferred to Mexico where he died.

In Buenos Aires it was overcoat weather. We had a temporary cold apartment and had trouble finding a house. Fortunately an English man of one of the banks was transferred to Chile and we were able to get his Home. The rent was high and I was desperate. However a subsequent devaluation of the peso brought it down to moderate levels.

The Ambassador in charge was James Bruce of a prominent family. His brother David was better known and accomplished. He had been prominent in Democratic politics and was appointed by President Truman. He died in 1980. I don't think Jim Bruce worked very hard at his job, but he did get in a lot of bird hunting and fishing. He had not mastered Spanish. He was to leave within a month and about a week after arriving he took me to call on President Juan Peron. I was to be the translator. I told the President my Spanish wasn't very good, that I couldn't give a literal account but would faithfully transmit the sense of things. Everything went well and from then on I had his confidence. What I didn't know was that he understood a lot of English. I didn't really have my feet on the ground when Bruce left and I was again in charge, this time of quite a large operation. I called on all the Ministers of other Governments and the Ambassadors, beginning with the Dean, an Italian. He was helpful.

Social life swept us into the whirlpool rather promptly and was tiring, both because of the number of events and because of the late hours. There were one hundred and three Missions accredited which makes an average of about two national holidays a week, apart from all the other engagements including the American Colony. I was young enough to take it and after a time was able to get out on weekends to the country for some exercise.

I don't remember how long I was in charge, long enough to be well integrated with the Diplomatic Corps. After a time there came Staton Griffis, accompanied by Angie Duke and his wife Margaret. Angie had been given the title of Second Secretary and was a kind of shirt holder for the Ambassador. They lived in the very large Embassy, which we called "Grand Central Station." Anyone interested may read Griffis subsequent book entitled "Lying In State". Some persons thought the title should rather be "Laying in State". Our rather prim Argentine housekeeper was shocked when Griffis pursued the telephonist down the hall in his shorts. As far as I know he didn't catch her.

There was extensive entertaining at the Embassy. The ballroom accommodated eighty persons seated for dinner at tables for six. There were generally sixty or seventy with a waiter for each table. Dinner was followed by dancing. Eleanor was much occupied with these things being not only the ranking lady but also having a knowledge of the local milieu and speaking Spanish.

Social life, so called, was pretty intense, and pretty tiring. I insisted on getting to the office on time so sleep was often short. After the first year I tried to keep weekends free to get out in the country for some exercise. Fortunately I was younger and could take the pressure, which would not have been true in later years.

After Griffis left there was an interregnum of five months during which I was in charge. The Embassy presented no particular problems apart from a few personnel matters. We had no friction with the Argentine government since there were no things at stake or to be negotiated. When Eddie Miller the Assistant Secretary of State for Latin America was coming to visit, a trip was arranged to meet him in Montevideo for prior discussions. The Air Attache flew me over and there was a lunch by Chris Ravndal, the Ambassador and a review of the situation. I advised a do nothing policy, that we couldn't influence the Dictator and to just hold our fire. This was accepted and became known as the policy of "Masterful Inaction." Later this was attributed to Ambassador Burker, but it predated him.

There were two main activities to be followed, the current economic situation, and the activities of Peron and Evita. The economic situation was well covered by our Economic Staff and the Agricultural Attache'. The important sector was the agriculture and my background was of help in anticipating coming events.

Peron and Evita were something else again. He had been the child of an Argentine father and Scottish mother - perhaps illegitimate. In the Army he rose to Brigadier General, espoused the cause of labor against the "Oligarchs" and won election. He had drive and a certain subtlety but was not basically well informed and had little sense of how the economy worked. Evita, who had risen from a life of an entertainer of doubtful antecedents, had a sense of history, a faculty of declamation rivaling Hitler and championed the labor force. Her speeches were diatribes worthy of attention. Argentina was at that time close to being a Police State. There wasn't too much violence and most people were circumspect. We had one bombing of our library and there was a minor attack on our home one night but not serious.

Peron and Evita were the favorite victims of our liberal press and often sought some statement they could use. I didn't help them, as such attacks didn't accomplish anything, on the contrary.

One must admit that Peron was helped by a plentiful and rich food supply. Everyone ate very well indeed. Had food been short unrest very likely would have grown to an important level. I gained weight. A particularly enjoyable weekly lunch was held at the Jockey Club, an Oligarch Center. The counselors of England, France, Belgium, Uruguay, and one or two others met and had a round table. Griffis came by one day, saw us and said "God help the Ambassadors."

Eleanor was very active as Senior Lady in the Mission and was called on to translate for Evita whenever there was a visiting American delegation of which there were several. She became very well acquainted with her, to the extent of being invited to the Presidential Mansion and being shown her fabulous collection of jewelry. Eleanor should write her own impressions of this period.

Economically the country was going down hill. For national pride Peron bought the railway system from the British. Not only did this cost a good deal but feather bedding arose. It was said jokingly that the English had one track worker for eight kilometers of track and with Peron there were eight workers per kilometer.

At the end of the war Argentina had a considerable holding of gold and foreign exchange. This was dissipated. At the same time Argentina's traditional source of wealth was agricultural exports. Under Peron and his advisors there was a policy of setting up industry for consumer goods and manufactures. To pay for this an indirect tax was put on exports of grain and meat. Agriculture suffered, farm machinery became scarce, transport was short and the economy really strained. In short the economic policy while perhaps needing to help labor some, was going too far and the country is still suffering.

We were four years in Buenos Aires and during that time I enjoyed the really excellent hunting and fishing. Mostly it was for perdiz and ducks, only two hours away. One could go Saturdays. Then too at the Hacienda los Milagros with Laddy Buchanan there was, at the right time of the year, great shooting for doves. He had a patch of tall eucalyptus trees about four acres in size where doves came in during the late afternoon to roost. The birds were a virtual plague. We stood thirty or forty yards from the trees and took them as they came in. I am not a good shot but had so much practice that I could bring home a fair bag. That was where three servants became useful.

A German named Homan had established a large Hacienda in the hill country to the South. He brought over some of the European Red Deer or stags. They increased to the point that forage for cattle was getting short. I was welcomed to help out. A camp was set up. I flew down to San Martin de Los Andes and jeeped to the hunting area. It was rutting season and easy to locate game by the bulging. I took eleven head in three days with an Enfield 30/06 which I had converted.

Fishing was good too, but at some distance. Twice I went to the junction of the Parana and Plate rivers for Dorado--a splendid fish. Once I went to Villa Rica in Chile for a most pleasant ride down the river. Fishing was poor, as a volcano had spread ash the previous year killing off a lot of fish. We also could go to a fishing camp on Lake Melakina for trout and an occasional land locked salmon.

Twice I went to Tierra del Fuego. There one day I caught five land locks in the river and was able to release four unharmed. The days there with a chill wind but alone were great.

One sporting thing was European Hares at night. With Laddie at the wheel and me bundled up we could drive on a winter evening in one of the paddocks. When he saw a gray spot he tore after it. The hare would run, dodge and double. Laddy drove well and we usually got to shooting range. My best bag was eighteen. The hares were a plague to the livestock farmer. The Argentines wouldn't eat them, but I had several times a dish of civet de lievre.

The next Ambassador was Ellsworth Burker, a spare New Englander who had done well in the sugar refining business. He came by boat and Eleanor I went to Montevideo in the morning to meet them and returned on the ship that evening with them. He and his wife were very different from Griffis. They were refined and gentle people. He continued the policy we had initiated and there was a period of relative quiet in the Embassy.

The Bunkers also entertained a fair amount and were generally liked. We both were fond of them. Harriet Bunker was a fine person. He left Buenos Aires to be sent to Italy as Ambassador. Again we were left in charge. Evita was ill--cancer--although not admitted. She died and the public demonstration was something to behold. Eleanor went to the Lying in State and was singled out by Peron for special attention among the corps of Ambassador's wives.

Al Nufer, who had left me in Havana, had been serving as Ambassador in El Salvador and came to Buenos Aries. He was the first career chief in a long time. We got along all right.

I don't remember when but sometime, perhaps about 1951 or 1952 I was made a Career Minister.

President Eisenhower sent his brother Milton to Latin America for a sort of investigative tour. He was give special treatment and Peron took him to a football game. A reception of considerable size was given in the Embassy and during the evening I was handed a telegram saying the President proposed to appoint me Ambassador to the Hashemite Kingdom of Jordon. This was late 1953. We accepted, took the boat to New York, spent a short time in Washington and again by boat to Beirut where we arrived Thanksgiving Day. Following lunch we went by car to Amman on a cool black night with no signs of life during the five hour trip from Lebanon, a bit of Syria and into Jordan.

The place was a bit of shock after Buenos Aries. It was winter, barren, no trees, no grass and a small inconvenient house. Eleanor was pretty upset. In a very few days I had the ceremonial meeting with His Majesty King Hussein. He was a boy of eighteen. A bit of background may be in order here in view of the important role he has in the Middle East complex.

During World War I the Emir Abdullah, one of the sons of the Sherif Hussein of Mecca led a force of Arabs against the Turks, which at that time controlled the whole area of the Middle East. The British took Palestine, Syria, etc., and Abdullah moved into what is now Jordan and annexed the Jordan Valley up to what was the British Protectorate of Palestine. Abdullah was a great Sheik in the desert Arab tradition and was liked by his people. He was fond of the boy, Hussein, took him with him a good deal. When Abdullah was assassinated in Jerusalem at the Aksa Mosque in July 1951, Hussein was present. The Throne succeeded to Talal who was mentally disturbed. This lasted a short time when he was sent to a convalescent home in Turkey where he remained until death.

The young Hussein was sent to Harrow in England in 1952, aged sixteen and there was a Regency council on the death of his father. He was given six months at the Military School in Sandhurst in preparation for his duties. He was then brought back, made king of Jordan at the age of 17 but age 18 by the Moslem calendar in May 1953. The tutelage of his grandfather has served him well.

He received me in dress uniform. Thus began another interesting four years. At first things went a bit slowly, but the Jordanians, many of whom were from Palestine, were most hospitable and friendly. The first year or so was relatively easy for me. The British played the dominant role, pretty much Officered the Arab Legion, supplied arms and generally had strong ties. This was to change as the British found themselves withdrawing all over the world. The United States gradually took over by setting up a considerable aid program. We worked at everything from agricultural experiments to road building, providing some expertise and the money. I was in a way more concerned with the AID Program than with other things. At the end of four years I had become the Dean of the Diplomatic Corps - not so great an honor considering its size, and President of the Board of Governors of the Palestine Archeological Museum, something of real interest. We made a number of friends, some very close such as the Muhkars our neighbors.

Living was no great problem once we became accustomed to a bit different diet. Meat was in short supply except lamb or mutton which was from the fat tailed sheep and excellent. Lacking beef to a considerable extent we occasionally had camel. There was no fish. Rice was the standard starch. We had a Moslem cook and a house boy and Eleanor a room maid. The houseboy spoke English so there were no problems of communication.

Our residence, to use a glorified term was lacking in a lot of things. Before we left it had been enlarged with a fairly large sitting room and bedroom. I redid the garden entirely putting in flowers and grass. It was attractive.

Entertainment was usually in the form of dinners which were overly sumptuous with the Arab host pushing one to have more. From the time of arrival when social life was pretty much in the family and restrained, but the time we left there was a Social Club, something unthinkable a few years before - largely the Palestinian influence.

School for Butch was a problem. There were two possible - one run by the Dominican brothers and another one French. Both were tried with little success. Finally with the growth of the aid staff a small school was set up. His schooling left much to be desired.

I will get to some of the more serious side of life a bit later, and here will continue with personal matters. I didn't learn Arabic as I had been told it would take five years. Eleanor went to women's coffees in the morning and learned a good deal - including I suspect a lot of the intimate life of the Arab family. She took Arabic lessons.

We entertained moderately with dinners, cocktail parties and occasional dancing. Jack Dalgleish, head of the Air Force, started Scottish Dancing and invited the King together with the British Ambassador's wife, ourselves and a few others to make twelve. This was rotated by families. The King enjoyed dancing.

We did some travelling. Once to Petra, a fine experience. We slept in a tent, although a tomb would have been better as it didn't flap in the wind.

I went to Jerusalem once a month to attend meetings at the Museum. I spent a rainy night in a tent at Qumran and the next day a full exploration of the site of the Dead Sea Scrolls. Archeology was of interest as history lay all over the ground, quite apart from and before that of the Holy Land. We attended Christmas Service at Bethlehem and the washing of the feet by the Armenians at Easter.

The desert was an attraction and I liked to drive there - roads or not. I visited a small tribe several times and once took a show truck and movie at night - the men and women segregated.

Jericho was being excavated and was a place to stop and see progress on my way to Jerusalem.

The Director of Antiquities of Jordan became a good friend and I spent a little time in the local museum learning to make plaster casts.

Some of these things were possible because of our working hours, which began early and finished at two o'clock in the afternoon. Mostly I didn't return to the office in the afternoon.

There was some hunting for partridge. We got few, as there were not many, and it was hard hunting up and down hill. These Sundays gave me needed exercise. This was with my neighbor Nasri. By noon we were ready for a rest. A charcoal fir, a grill, lamb chops, arak and water with good Arab bread and we were content.

I went once to hunt gazelle and took Butch. It was some distance and we went in the afternoon, slept under the stars and got a couple the next day. They were good eating. On another occasion Nasri, Dr. Tesio of the Italian Hospital, and I drove to Bagdad and went a bit south to hunt wild boar. We brought back quite a load of meat and I served a special lunch with a complicated French sauce. So much for the lighter side of life! The rest isn't so easy to write about as some restraint is necessary.

Official contacts for me were usually the Prime Minister and head of Foreign Office. There was a succession of Prime Ministers but no language problem as they spoke either French or English. Things were agreeable until an election put in a strong leftist. I didn't see him often. Before too long he was removed.

As Nasser grew in power in Egypt and attempted to spread his influence, things became a bit difficult. Attempts were made on the life of the King. We had bombings.

One night about nine P.M. a junior officer arrived hurriedly saying the road to Aman had been sealed off by armored vehicles. I instructed him (he was well known to the King) to go to the Palace at once, find a way in and tell his Majesty. This he did. The King got in a car, took the Army Chief of Staff, who shook in his boots, and went to Mafrak, the Army Base. Hussien called the troops who were still a majority of Bedouins. Mounted on top of a tank, he told them there was a plot and to be loyal. They yelled to get at those responsible. The Chief of Staff, working for Nasser was in on the plot to overthrow the King. The plot fell through at once due to the King's courage and action.

At one time (also with ties to Nasser) Hussein and Dalgleish were flying from Beruit to Amman in a Dove, rather a small plane, when over Syria they were attacked by Mig fighters. Dalgleish took the controls and was able to out wit the attack and get over Jordanian territory.

It was a bit amusing that Dick Sanger, who had an apartment over that of the Egyptian Counsellor expressed concern over the Egyptian children because he learned there were bombs stored there. He was not a bit concerned for himself.

We had a pretty serious group of riots and destruction at one time, engendered by Nasser. There was damage to our machinery for the Aid Program. It was a bit hard to understand destruction of a pump by the very people who were to benefit from it etc. A couple of charitable religious groups were attacked, and they had been the most helpful in a direct way.

The refugees from the occupation of Isreal were numerous. They were many in Lebanon and Syria, but the largest group was in the Jordan Valley with a large camp at Jericho. Jordan had about 500,000 of them. The United Nations Relief and Rehabilitation set up, provided tents and food. The tents were cold in winter and in summer Jericho had temperatures of 120 degrees. The food supply came to 7 cents per day in my time. I don't know what it is today. The Palestine Refugee problem still continues with succeeding American Presidents not having the forth rightness or political courage to settle it. Perhaps the end will come in a general war, which is doubtful as Arabs don't get together, or in a cut off of petroleum supplies which will have more effect in the U.S. than the Jewish vote. If the Russians extend their influence enough in the area and the Red Sea then it may be too late; oil can be the deciding factor in geopolitics. This is written in 1980.

At one time there was a threat of invasion from Syria, which had Russian tanks. One day we were advised out of the blue that transport planes would arrive with arms. I arranged for the Prime Minister and Cabinet to be at the airfield and at the appointed hour some C 130s came in. Opening the hatches Arab Legion drivers brought out jeeps mounting 106 M M recoilless canon. Altogether it was quite a display and perhaps unnecessary for me to say in front of the Prime Minister and Press that they could stop any Russian tank.

As things became a bit tight politically we undertook definite plans for evacuation. In case of war we felt the Syrian border would be closed and the escape likely would be across the dessert to Baghdad but not by road. The critical shortage would be gasoline and water. For this we had vehicles such as water tank trucks in the AID program. The staff was informed of plans, a network of information provided for warnings. People were advised of the one suitcase permitted, etc. Our plans were in fact quite complete. When the time came the plan worked well, but it wasn't across the desert.

Nasser had been throwing his weight around about the Suez Canal. One Monday morning we had a cable ordering evacuation. Since there wasn't a war we could reach Beirut via Syria. I got as many men as possible to leave by car in the morning, including two Foreign Service Inspectors who had only arrived. I wouldn't permit women to go by road to Syria, but did arrange for two planes to come from Bruit, one in the early afternoon and one took off just at dusk. No problem.

The Suez war of Britain, France and Israel broke out. There was curfew and blackout.

The evacuees were lodged in Beirut and Italy. Eleanor decided to go to Mexico, so Butch could go to an American School, which was just as well because the whole thing lasted a long time.

In Amman we managed quite well. There was a skeleton staff but enough to carry on. Both code clerks stayed behind. They were good kids.

At home the store room that I had made into a sort of workshop was provided with blackout curtains and I spent a lot of evenings there making things.

I had a short wave radio and each evening listened for the news from the B.B.C. London. Very often the Turkish Ambassador, Kadri Rizan, who lived two blocks up the street would come down in the dark and join me. We would have a glass of sherry together and listen carefully.

Another episode but I was alone for nine months. I shouldn't leave Jordan without mentioning the junket of Ezra Benson. And junket is the only word for it. He was a prophet of the Church of the Latter Day Saints and the Secretary of Agriculture of the United States. I had word that he was on his way in a special flight of a DC4 accompanied by his wife and two daughters. From Hong Kong came a cable that he landing was proposed in Amman since Jerusalem airport would not accommodate the plane, and he would proceed at once to the Holy City. Began an exchange of cables across south Asia that I finally won saying he could not, in his position, land in Amman without making a courtesy call. That was arranged and I set up a morning appointment with His Majesty. So far so good!

We went to the Palace and after the usual exchanges Ezra presented two books to the King. He spoke of the Book of Mormon explaining their belief was descendants from a lost tribe of Isreal. This was a gaff of the first order but the King didn't turn a hair, keeping his composure.

After this the Secretary was all fired up to get to Jerusalem but I prevailed upon him, not without some difficulty, to attend a typical Arab lunch given by the Minister of Agriculture of Jordan. This was Hazza Majali, son of the paramount sheik of the Beni Sakr tribe. The Secretary said they didn't eat on Sunday giving their meal money to the church. I told him this didn't wash, lunch was free. We collected his family and drove south about twenty miles. There was a black goat hair tent, open on one side, where they sat. The lunch was brought in; an enormous tray carried by four men. It held a mountain of rice and a whole boiled sheep. Eleanor instructed the Bensons on how to eat with their right hands.

Once over we put them in a car, together with The Counselor, Dick Sanger, who had been working on a book on Jordanian History. Dick entertained them all the way pointing out prehistoric sites, events from the Bible and so on. They ended up happy. I wasn't because this junket cost the taxpayers a lot and served no useful purpose.

In 1958 I was appointed Ambassador to Guatemala. We had quite a departure at the airport and flew to Cairo. There we saw the usual pyramids, the market and museum and followed to Athens for a couple of days. A short stay in Washington and another chapter began.

It was back to Washington for a few days. I no longer remember how we traveled; perhaps Eleanor went on to Mexico and we went thence to Guatemala. I was able to order a new car for her; the Impala was just appearing. The two doors were attractive and served very well. Later they made it into a four door sedan and lost its lines. I called on the Charge' in Washington, Julio Ascencio.

I had some briefings, but very few really. There was an urge to get me on the spot as a new President was to be inaugurated and the Department desired I present my credentials before that event. This we did, having very few days from arrival to presentation.

Embassy residence was excellent. Built as a large family home, it opened up well. There was a terrace in the back over looking a very deep garden with a swimming pool, and high trees bordered a garden of lawn. I installed a system of lighting and at night the trees glowed in the light when we chose to turn them on.

There was a sitting room, a large living room, a large entry, a rather large dining room, a large loggia, four bedrooms, a sitting room upstairs and servant quarters. There was also a sort of plant room, which I used as a workshop. Altogether it was a very usable and pleasant place to live.

The new President was General and Engineer Miguel Ydigoras Fuentes. He was somewhat of a character. By and large he was a pretty good Chief of State as they go in Central America but his downfall was his family and good friends. There was just too much grafting and finally he was thrown out of office after we left. My relations with him were friendly and co-operative. I did go so far at one time to tell him that his son and son-in-law would cause him trouble. He promised reform but it did not take place. The Guatemalans we met were friendly and we made some close associations. For most countries Guatemala did not rank very high with the result the diplomatic corps was not of good caliber. The Mexican Ambassador and the British Ministers were exceptions. There was an American School, which Butch attended. Don't believe he distinguished himself but it was better than he had had before. There was also a Boy Scout Troop which he entered and apparently enjoyed. Both he and Eleanor made good use of the swimming pool.

Guatemala City is a bit over four thousand feet altitude. The weather is temperate without extremes and enjoyable. There is an extensive rainy season.

Guatemala is a country of strong Indian complexion. About one half of the population is Indian and the other half of some admixture, called Chapin. It has been a sort of back water for a long time with colonial aspects. The principal commerce was the export of highland coffee. A General Ubico, known as a dictator, ran the country with a strict hand for many years. It was said he was thrown out, which isn't true as he died in a hospital in New Orleans. His successor was a leftist named Arevelo. He gained prominence by a policy of liberality and was supposed to have been a good leader. This is doubtful as he could have done little without the store of gold which Ubico had built up over the years. He was helped by the communists. He came to my notice in 1947 when he sent a schooner load of Russian Arms to Cayo Comfies, which I have mentioned above.

Arevolos' successor, Arbenz, was overthrown by an invasion under Colonel Armas. Things were back to normal when Armas was assassinated in the Presidential Palace. Thenceforth Presidents were elected, usually military.

Out of these events there was a small facet which carried over to our times. The stongest support for a change from Arevelo was the "locatarias", the women who had stalls in the market. They played a part in the overthrow and were active politically. Eleanor paid some attention to them and in return received their gratitude, as they felt they were being slighted. We invited representatives to a Fourth of July reception which I mention elsewhere. Years later when Eleanor was in Guatemala they went to call on her with flowers.

Guatemala is a strongly Catholic country; and among Indians Christianity is an overlay on still remaining Pagan beliefs. The various holiday and feast days are well observed. Among them Easter of the town of Antigua is a notable occasion for its processions, when the images of the church are carried through the streets. This has become a well known tourist attraction.

The head of the church in my time was the Archbishop, a Chapin. He was a sweet and gentle man but one felt without much drive or influence. He took a special interest in the Indians and maintained a school for Indian boys. There were not enough priests throughout the country, and not enough local support for their maintenance. One group was effective as it had drive and support from the United States. These were the Mary Knoll Fathers who worked in the Indian Highland areas. I gathered the Papal Nuncio did not like this American effort, but then there wasn't much he did like. He was not the usual lighthearted Italian, but rather an introverted and seemingly discontented man. We didn't get along. He was replaced by another Italian of much broader understanding who had worked in the Vatican.

A Eucharistic Congress was announced for Guatemala. We were informed that the Papal representative would be Cardinal Spellman of New York. We offered to have him at the Residence but President Ydigoras wished that he use an unused Presidential Residence, unused since President Armas had been assassinated there. There was much coming and going for the Congress and the Cardinal got badly sunburned riding in an open car with the President.

Spellman had expressed a desire to go to the Indian center of Chichicastenango. I set it up. Then a day before his arrival, I learned it had been called off by the Papal Nuncio. I had to throw my weight around to get it back on schedule with a DC3 from the Guatemalan Air Force and one from Air Mission. Came the day we landed at at the only field a bit distant from Chichi. As we left the plane a deep song came to us from the nearby fence where kneeling men and women separately sang. The sound was striking. Spellman was visibly moved and I had tears in my eyes. He approached and blessed them. The village had hoped he would give a Mass but there wasn't time so he entered the Church and said a prayer to them. Then by car we drove over tortuous roads for a way. Near the village of Chichicastenango we were met by a delegation of Indian notables. We left the car and proceeded on foot; we were led by a "Confradia" in native costume with the staffs of office and preceded by one having the image of a white horse, Santiago or St. James.

The town was jammed with people in front of the church. This was the first Cardinal visit in history. Up the twenty or so steps Spellman accompanied by a couple of his Bishops, then into the Church where I feared trouble. The Indians there have a custom of lighting candles on the floor of the center isle. They would come there to pray in their mixture of Paganisim and Christianity, and often threatened the Saint if he didn't produce. There were hundreds of candles and Spellman, walking only a bit to one side swept up the aisle. I feared his crimson robe would catch fire it was so close to the flames.

The altar was flanked by several very colorful "Confradia" of several men. They were also the choir. The sung music was impressive, in part perhaps so felt by the emotion of the moment, but at the same time interesting.

A Papal Mass was given by the Cardinal in Latin and his accent from Boston could be cut with a knife. This didn't make any difference to the congregation for it was something very special. When it was over we went back to the planes, back to Guatemala City and a relief. I'm sure it only increased the Nuncio's dislike of things American and of me.

When the Congress drew to a close we held a major reception in the evening and as I recall, the President received along with the Cardinal. The Fourth of July is always a time of work for the Chief of Mission, and also for the staff and staff wives. Depending on the place and the size of the American Colony the arrangements vary a bit. In Jordon there was virtually no colony and the Fourth was pretty much an Embassy affair. We made it a picnic one year and I was able to get a special treat of hot dogs flown in.

In Argentina despite a restriction on invitations the receptions would run to fourteen hundred people. That meant a lot of liquor and snacks. We could always be sure that two little old Argentine ladies would sneak in, sit on a settee and pop snacks into their hand bags to take home. They were a fixture. Once it looked as though a current abuse of the United States would be a waiter's strike on the Fourth. This was prepared for by having First and Second Secretaries to man the bars. The strike didn't materialize. The Fourth meant a luncheon by the Society of the River Plate where a speech was required. I suffered through one of those.

In Guatemala the Fourth was a more fun occasion with a lot of people and a nice local response. There was the custom of sending huge floral tributes, which made for a colorful presentation. We, for the first time invited the representatives of the market women who were grateful; one got up on a wall and made a fighting speech in front of the President.

Eleanor organized things very well. Ordinarily we did not cater the hors d'oeuvres, rather she asked the staff to prepare various items, for which she reimbursed the cost. Thus we seldom had any tired food to serve. Liquor was no problem with import privileges and local supplies. We quickly learned to put away any silver ash trays or other bric-a-brac which might disappear.

Our Cultural Affairs people prepared a special showing in Quetzaltenango and I went to inaugurate it. There I saw the Opera House. It was a veritable little jewel, which was delightful. The story of its existence follows. A Guatemalan travelling in Italy became enamored of an opera singer. She agreed to marriage if she could sing and have an opera house. It was built in San Francisco, brought by boat in pieces to the coast and up the mountain to be assembled. I would have liked to hold a party in it.

Among cultural events was a visit by the National Symphony Orchestra from Washington. They gave a good concert to which the President was invited and then, even though late, we held a reception for the orchestra. The President and wife tagged along. The next day the orchestra gave a special session for children, with explanations of how it worked the various choirs of instruments and so on. However there was an unusual counter part. The Indian Boys School of the Archbishop had a Marimba Orchestra present, composed of small youngsters. When it came their turn they played and the members of the orchestra crowded down to watch.

There were a number of bombings, which mostly didn't make much sense. They apparently came from both the right and the left, mostly the latter. We had one at the Embassy which was in the early evening of July 1954. I was at home and rushed down. Damage was not extensive. A small crowd gathered and they quite evidently came in support for us and I was so moved that trying to thank them, I stuttered in Spanish. At the same time as our bomb there was one at the quarters of the Archbishop at the Cathedral. This was just too manufactured for belief and no attention was paid to it.

One evening there was a party at the home of the Chief of Air Mission. A visiting Colonel looking at his watch asked our host if he hadn't heard a bomb go off. Just then it did; apparently the military planted it but the timing was poor.

On another occasion one of the military told the Chief of Air Mission that it might be fun to put a small bomb at the Residence. He was told it might not be a good idea as he had been hunting with me.

Guatemala was a country of Mayan background. One of the great Mayan sites is at Tikal in the Peten. In 1959 work had only begun. I was approached for any needed help and was invited to see progress of the excavation. It was interesting indeed. Work continued for a number of years and is today a major tourist attraction. An important tomb had been opened shortly before my visit. They had a shoe box full of jadeite artifacts, mainly in the form of large beads. I subsequently learned the probable source of the jade and went hunting for it down the Motagua River and on a slope of the mountains to the north. I found a fair amount, including some chunks in a farmer's fence! This was what got me started on stones and lapidary that I was to pursue in Washington.

Fishing wasn't available locally. However there was some north on the Peten where the Pasion River came down. Mobile Oil had been prospecting the area for oil and had a camp at Sayaxche. I was invited to go with the geologist to fish. There was an aluminum boat, thirty-five horse power motor and a screened camp. In side streams we caught a smallish fish called "Blancos," good eating. In the Pasion one night I hooked a really large tarpon which I lost after an hour when he crossed the river and the line tangled in a fallen tree. Travelling on the Pasion was a delight and the scenery and vegetation most attractive.

I was to travel the Pasion later when the excavation of Altar de Sacrificios was started. Here was another site of major importance where the Pasion and Usumacinta Rivers joined. It was thought to be a crossing point from the Highlands to the tropical Peten.

Hunting wasn't much. We went a couple of times for dove with indifferent results. One night was different. Eleanor and I were invited to spend the weekend at a sugar mill near the south coast. At night at a small lake we went alligator hunting. They were small, about two feet long. One could shine their eyes and locate them. I got about eight and gained a reputation as a good shot. We put them on the floor of the jeep and drove back, when alligators began to crawl about. I hadn't hit a single gator but the rifle of rather good velocity had stunned them. My reputation suffered.

There is always some trouble between countries over fishing in their supposed territorial waters. The Mexicans came down for shrimp along the Guatemaln coast. The Air Force went out to either drive them off or bring them in, I don't remember which. The Mexicans talking back and forth in particularly nasty language about the Guatemalans, so enraged the pilots, who tuned in on their frequency, that they came down guns blazing and drove them to port. Big scandal; the Mexican Ambassador went to the Foreign Office and threw his weight around, and got rebutted. Relations apparently were broken. That evening I went to the Mexican Embassy and helped them burn files. Often one hears of it but seldom sees it.

The United States has an AID program covering many fields. To me it wasn't very successful, especially in agriculture. This latter was in part due to traditionalist ideas in the country, and partly the lack of competent leadership on the side of the Guatemalans. One program was a great success, that of self-help housing. There was a bright young man in charge. An area was selected. Teams of five were to build five homes together. They furnished the labor in off hours and we bought the materials. It worked out quite well. When houses were complete the President put on a show of giving out the titles. I visited the work several times. Later when I was in Washington the President invited me down for the inauguration of a small square, or as it was called Parque Mallory.

This was a small square with a simple monument holding a plaque with an inscription "To the Gringo" Ambassador Lester D. Mallory who reached the hearts of the Guatemalans. The President had asked us if we minded the use of the word "Gringo" instead of American since it would help in the use of the term as friendly rather than depreciation. He made a final fine gesture when we left, going with his wife to the airport to see us off. He put his private plane at our disposal to fly to the Highlands where we had sent our car with the chauffeur the previous day. This let us get well into Mexico by nightfall. It was thoughtful indeed.

After two years in Guatemala I was asked to go to the Department of State as Deputy Assistant Secretary for Latin America. Eleanor thought it would be a mistake and she may have been right. In any event we went in late 1959, bought a house in Foxhall Village almost across the street from where we started out in 1946. After a time Eleanor found a house in King Place which was more suitable. We sold and bought. The new house was attractive and comfortable. Butch started Military School in Maryland, subsequently to a boarding school, and finally to public school in our area.

I was in the Department for a year and things weren't working out too well. Someone said I might wish to join the Inter-American Development Bank which I did in November 1960. The Department offered me the Ambassadorship of Peru but I turned it down.

The IDB was a new experience. I stayed with it three years when I was sent as Representative to Panama. There we stayed four years before going to Guadalajara, as Project Engineer on a bank loan. We had visited Guadalajara before and liked it. The job there was really to learn whether we would wish to retire. No one had foreseen the rapid growth of the city which is now much less attractive.

The Bank paid a pretty fair salary plus tax. This was as good as it looked because the tax provision was for my salary alone. However, when salary and retirement were added together my bracket went up on income tax. However for the first time we saved some money. During Foreign Service we had not, and the eight years with the Bank gave us some backlog.

The year in the Department of State was pretty intense. I arrived early and worked late. On the whole it was fairly bureaucratic and I feel we suffered from lack of leadership. The problem of Cuba was present, but I didn't find much response to my ideas. On the whole there was somewhat an attitude of laissez faire regarding Latin America, which wasn't anything new as it happened before.

The Inter-American Bank was a change of work. I was on Technical Assistant where my background was of help. The assistance mostly was in the form of providing direct help, or small loans, to prepare projects for financing by the Bank. There was a wide range of subjects. After three years I was appointed Bank Representative to Panama to oversee loan projects. For the first year I was also in charge of Costa Rica until a Representative was appointed there. I went to San Jose about once a month for a three-day stay. This was interesting as far as the work was concerned, but also the vendors of artifacts who congregated around the Hotel in the evening. I bought some.

In Panama the climate is warm and humid. We were fortunate to get an apartment on a hill overlooking the city where there was some breeze. With three air conditioning units installed we got along quite well. Eleanor found a local maid to help. I had pleasant relations with the President and Ministers concerned with loans. We had friends in the Canal Zone where there was an active Lapidary Society with its own building and work shop. In the office I had an efficient secretary.

Following the introduction to jadeite in Guatemala I learned while in Washington of a course in lapidary work given in the evenings. I attended a couple of such courses and later one in gemology. This got me into lapidary work which I still follow as a hobby, every now and then cutting a stone, some good and some poorly. We cut a lot and I still have boxes of slabs which could be used. Now I do faceting. Since being in Guadalajara I have written a number of articles on related subjects which have been published in the Lapidary journal.

Butch attended High School in the Canal Zone. Eleanor did a good deal of painting and had a showing.

After four years in Panama, 1964-68 and with retirement age approaching it was time to think of the future. As mentioned above Guadalajara appeared attractive both for its good climate and the cost of living. It was arranged that I could go to Overseas Loan and thus was transferred with household effects from Panama and Washington. The climate still continues good, but in 1980 not the cost of living.

After a year I retired and was at loose end. On arrival we rented a house where we stayed two years and then bought our present home which is quite attractive.

I got started in going to the Archeology Laboratory of the Autonomous University of Guadalajara. This gradually absorbed my time. I was instrumental in having a School of Anthropology started which continues small. We have graduated a number of students, who fortunately have all found positions. I continue in this, now giving classes, first in Prehistory for which I wrote a short text and now in Classical Archeology of which I know little. Finally the world has come full cycle. I started out to be a professor but it took me some fifty years to get there. I have helped at the University for ten years without salary but it keeps one alive mentally and associated with young people. Now we are hoping to publish a journal and as of now I'm the editor.

The foregoing is pretty summary in nature and I suppose should be treated as a first draft. If and when the spirit moves me I'll elaborate but I don't expect that will be very soon. In the meantime I shall attach photographs to the originals for possible interest of descendants.

All this in a sense is a follow up to family history, which is incorporated, in prior notes on the Mallorys and DeWitts. Sufficient unto the day!

Please overlook errors. - The lady who typed this does not know English!

Clifford DeWitt

EXERPTS FROM THE STORY OF ONE FRUIT FARM
By Charles Clifford DeWitt 1915 - 1983

Our farm was located in the Niagara Peninsula and is part of Lot 17, Concession 3 of Saltfleet Township in the County of Wentworth. This farm had all the advantages of Ontario's finest weather plus the advantages of being located closely enough to Hamilton to afford a good market for the produce. It proved to be within the development area of Hamilton suburbs and was sold in 1972 for that purpose.

My grandfather, Charles W. DeWitt purchased the farm in 1900 and moved from his farm at Tapleytown to become a fruit grower. He sold Massey Harris Farm Implements and Mutual Fire Insurance. Indications are that he was a better salesman than farmer. A real gentleman and highly respected, he was noted for having never kept a record book of either business. No one will ever know how successful he actually was or how many people neglected to pay for value received. He was always proud to own a good horse, but had no respect whatsoever for an automobile. He never learned to drive properly and in his later years had utter disregard for signs, railways or traffic. He burned a complete set of bands out of the old Model "T" every time he went up the mountain. On several occasions he fell asleep at the wheel, crossed a ditch, a railway track and back on the road, without mishap. He never really had a serious accident in his life.

In 1902 he bought an 8 acre property right next to this farm, separated from it by DeWitt Road and gave it to my father Frederick W. DeWitt as a wedding present when he married my mother, Georgina Alma Dean Stewart.

Mother tells the story of the first car Dad brought home from Toronto. As he made the corner off # 8, Mother watched through the front window of the house. He was so excited and enthusiastic that he ran into the corner of the house instead of stopping in the back yard. I never heard about the damage. Whenever I meet older men and introduce myself, the first greeting I get is "I bought my first car from your Dad". I am proud to say that not one I have talked to has ever said he got a poor deal or was dissatisfied.

Grandmother Julia, Grandfather Charles and Dad Frederick all died within a year. Grandmother was 74 in 1926, Grandfather 77 in the Fall of 1927 and Dad 45 in the same year.

This left Mother with two farms and a big business and a 12 year old son – me. She sold the small farm and the businessand moved across the road to the big brick house. Unfortunately Dad had squandered most of the money, having died an alcoholic and with a liver disease. There were debts galore and a mortgage on this farm. Mother tried to operate the farm in 1928 with all the problems in the world. No money, no equipment, no farming ability and too soft hearted to be a good businesswoman. That fall she sold the farm to James Kay and Fred Graisley, who already owned the Ford Dealership in Dad's Garage. Mother retained the right to remain in the house and pay rent.

Let's go back a little to 1928 when the McBride family bought the small farm. I went to school until 1933, but was never a scholar. So every fruit season found all those who could find work, picking fruit. This included the McBride girl, Libby. The 5' 2" redheaded 98 pound doll I carted around and moved ladders for had hooked me real good. By 1935 we were real serious without a hope of matrimony. Her family was as bad off financially as mine was.

At 21 I had a job at Ford's Danforth Plant in Toronto. I was kept on until the middle of July in 1937 and was told to report back in the middle of August. With the prospects looking so much better, Lib and I decided to get married on the 7th of August, had a short honeymoon in the North Country – hauling a matchbox house trailer behind the Durant. When we came back the big house was full of boarders. The entire orchestra of "The Wright Brothers" who were playing at the dance hall on the west corner of the farm. I was too proud to move in with her folks, so we slept in the first garage in the back yard. We drove to Toronto and rented a six-room house on Rosevere Street and signed a year's lease. It took a week to clean the place and move all the second hand furniture down. Three trips with the old Model "A" truck. When we were leaving in the car the last time, everybody had a little cry, kissed good-bye and we promised to be back by Christmas.

When I reported for work the next Monday I was informed that there was no job for me. We packed up the old Durant and moved back home the same day. You should have seen the expressions on the faces at home.

Going back to my childhood, I would like to say it was filled with rich experiences. In public school at Fruitland Ralph Hill, Jim Douglas, Harris Askew and I formed a friendship that has lasted to the present time. We were seldom apart and shared many good times. I had the first bicycle so until the others got theirs; we rode double with the other two running beside. Dad was most generous in all respects and often went against mother's wishes to give me things in advance of my age – like a .22 rifle at 9 – the use of a secondhand car at 10, to drive all over the farm.. I took the head off the engine once and was not enough of a mechanic to put it back. Dad had one of the mechanics replace it and advised me to ask for help before trying something like that again.

After Dad died it was most difficult to adjust to poverty, especially for mother. The four of us went to Saltfleet High and in about the second year we dug a 1923 Model "T" Ford touring car out of a pile of junk in Mr. Hill's barn. It had not been used in several years and needed much repair work. We named it 'Susie' and drove it to school for the remainder of schooldays. That was on good weather days. We made one trip to 5 miles north of Huntsville in the summer of 1931. Our mothers loaded that car with groceries like you would never believe. My mother baked a fresh cherry pie, which was up side down by the time we got to Burlington. Every bit of juice trickled down through our clothes and whatever else was under it. We took pinion gear for the rear end and a connecting rod as spare parts and those were the only two parts required keeping us mobile. The first long hill outside Orillia gave us the first flat tire so we camped in the bush by a stream, not too far from the road.

That night a thunderstorm spoiled the milk and wet most of the groceries. In the morning we were all up except Askew, so we carried him to the stream and threw him in. He was an excellent swimmer so he hung on the bottom and played dead. We all went after him, clothes and all. It took us three days to forgive him. Later the rod went, so we parked where we were, drained the oil in a cooking pot, replaced the connecting rod and drove on. We did most of our driving at night to help protect the tires from the hot road. Our total assets for the trip were about $15.00 so by now they were a little short. On the return trip, we had 28 flat tires and a broken rear end. We used the three spare tires in every conceivable way, on top of each other, full of grass or just plain flat. At Brampton we stopped for the first time at a service station and pumped the tires up with an air hose and went the rest of the distance without mishap. We arrived home at about 4:30 a.m. and slept for two days.

We all acquired cars within the next year. We called them "Bugs" because they were only the bare chassis of Model "T" Fords. I paid $5.00 for mine and other friends were comparable. I built a racer body on mine and called it Ignuts and, with a license, drove it for several years.

Patriotism and the sincere wish to help the war effort were in everyone's minds. The Government instigated a program to enroll girls, 15 years and older, into a labour force to help agriculture. There were camps all through the Niagara Peninsula, all volunteers and supervised by qualified people. It was necessary to apply for your help requirements well in advance of the harvest season. I applied for 5 girls. Most of these girls had never seen fruit growing before or done a days work in their life.

The five I got were terrific. They came mostly from real good homes and were really full of enthusiasm. One little redhead from Kitchener fell in love with our old horse Dan and within a week completely took over all the duties of a teamster. She continued to call in here many years after the war was over just to say hello. When it was necessary to get some extra girls from another camp, it was most interesting to see how quick our girls found fault with new ones. They always worked twice as hard just to prove the extras were not needed.

Aunt Nell, by this time was crowding 80, was still by far the best fruit picker in the area. My opening speech to any of the new girls went something like this. "I realize you girls are from the city and have had no experience in the field. I will show you how to pick fruit properly and I do not expect you to pick it all today. It is not necessary to kill yourselves but I would like a reasonable day's work from each of you. For the first day if you keep up to that old lady over there, I will be satisfied." What appeared to be a real cinch turned out to be impossible? By noon Aunt Nell had as much as any two. After dinner, the spokesman of the five asked what they were doing wrong, or did they really have to keep up? It was real fun explaining the situation. It relieved all the tension of a new job and gave them a personal interest in the whole farm operation. They worked here from the middle of August to the first week in October for two seasons.

There was a happy situation between Ralph Hill, Jack Orr, myself and sometimes George Lounsbury. When it came to making contracts for fruit to go to the canneries, we all kept a close watch on each other and if it happened that one of us had more fruit than contract, we could usually get the surplus in on one of the other's contract. The cannery frowned on this action, but of course, could do nothing about it without definite proof. I was often asked at the inspection, "Well, whose are these Ralph's or Jack's?" It is quite evident that it was necessary to be especially attentive to qualify when filling the other fellow's contract in order not to jeopardize his reputation as a grower. Very rarely did any of us waste any fruit or fail to fill the contract we made, which was quite contrary to the average growers' ability to estimate his crop. Keep in mind that contracts were usually made very early in the growing season just after the fruit had been formed. If every year was exactly the same, estimating would be a cinch, but very often what appeared to be a bumper crop in June, when the contracts were made, could easily turn out to be a flop by harvest time. In fact, the whole operation was one big gamble from beginning to end. There were so many uncontrollable aspects of fruit growing such as weather, heat, wind, moisture and insect population variation. It was necessary to be in daily contact with changing situations in order to cope with events. To say the least it kept life interesting. Whatever else one could say about fruit growing, one would have to admit there were very few dull moments.

Spraying was a one-man operation - me, which left whatever help I had for other jobs. Very often Lib would drive that treacherous old 1923 Fordson, while I sprayed another part of the farm. I had put a new type belt-driven governor on the tractor, which I thought was the last word in efficiency. All at once the motor revved up to full speed and Lib started to yell (as only she could do). I made a record 100-yard dash, leaving the sprayer running and trusting the horses to stand, across the ditch towards her. I had no idea what had happened, but from the noise, it was evident the tractor was about to fly apart. By this time it had reached maximum speed and sounded like a B29. I was relieved to see her off the tractor and running toward me.

It seems that a small branch had flipped the belt off the governor and allowed the throttle to be wide open. I'll never know why she did not turn off the ignition. What she did do was put it out of gear, get off the tractor and run and yell. By the time I reached the tractor, it was boiling so hard it looked more like a steam engine rather than gasoline. I turned the switch and waited for about an hour while both the tractor and my wife cooled off.

That old tractor was really a gem. No self starter, just a crank on the front that usually required about a half hour of hard turning before a successful start. It would sometimes backfire and lift me right off the ground. It had no fenders and as the operator sat between the two rear wheels, each steel lug that passed you on either side dumped a cup full of dirt in your lap. The steering was direct drive, which meant if the front wheels hit a rut or stone, the steering wheel would turn right or left to the full extent, before you could stop the turn. You soon learned not to wrap your thumb around the steering wheel, after a few bangs with the spokes of the wheel. It had no brakes and three speeds forward, two working speeds and one travel speed which was entirely too fast. High gear wouldn't pull your hat off let alone pull any implement or wagon, but if you dared to give it the gas, top speed must have been over 20 M.P.H. and the roughest ride in Canada. The front wheels were cast iron and weighed about 500 lbs. apiece. They helped to keep the front end on the ground, but in no way made it easier to turn. On one of my trips home for dinner, having left the discs in the power-line, I put it in high and let her go down the lane by the apple orchard. I crossed the bridge over the ditch just dandy and turned the wheel to the right, to continue down the lane, which was at right angles to the first lane. It turned right just great, but when I tried to straighten out again, it had locked in a full right turn. I made a beautiful half circle and stopped when the front end was in the bottom of the ditch. The stop was rather sudden and left the front end about four feet lower than the back end. I'll never know why it didn't pitch me over the radiator. I was a little late for dinner that day.

During one of our conversations at the Loblaws Central Warehouse, Harry mentioned that his holidays were to start the next day. For lack of something better to say, I asked "why don't you and the wife drop in to our place and see how a good fruit farm is run?" The invitation was genuine, but it never entered my head that the big time operator would ever consider accepting. I knew him to be a top buyer for the whole Loblaws chain and assumed his holidays would be planned well in advance at one of the more exotic holiday places in Ontario. He said "We thought we might go to Niagara Falls, so we will drop in Monday sometime."

When I told the story at home, panic reigned supreme. You never saw a house cleaned so fast and well in your life. Sure enough, before 10:00 a.m. Monday, as the women were adding the last touches of dusting and polishing, Mr. and Mrs. Harry Mason step off the bus at our front door. It was not long after introductions that their easy, friendly manner convinced us they were our kind of people. This was the last week in September in 1943. Mother and Aunt Nell were here and Florence and Tom were pretty young, so we had a full house.

Harry and Barbara fitted in like one of the family and their original plan to visit Niagara Falls never happened, instead they stayed with us to make that week one of the most pleasant experiences in our life. I had no hired man so we were busy hauling apples and picking grapes for Loblaws and Kitchener.

Everything we did was a new experience for Harry and Barbara, although they had probably never worked harder in their lives, they seemed to enjoy it as much as we did. They practically took over the hauling in of the fruit with the horse (Dan) and the four-wheel wagon. Barb drove and Harry and I loaded on and off. The day started about 7:30 a.m. and lasted until the jobs for the day were done. Then it was dark outside and we had a few games of Bridge.

When Saturday came we made arrangements with Uncle Stan for Barb to ride with him to Kitchener and Harry came with us. Once there they both jumped in to do whatever job came up. At the peak of the day's business, one customer asked me to carry a bushel of apples to her car. Without hesitation Harry said, "You stay here, let the boy do it." So there goes one of Loblaws' top executives carrying a bushel of apples through the crowded market to a customer's car.

The ride home was something else. The girls decided they would ride in the back of the truck together while Harry and I drove. A Model "A" truck bounces in three directions at the same time, and being empty, the springs were as stiff as an oak plank. The road was rough and crooked and by the time we finally stopped to see how they were doing, they were ready to kill us both. They had been yelling and banging for ten miles, which we could not hear in the cab. Talk about being shook up. We changed places and Lib drove the rest of the way home and Harry and I soon found out what they were complaining about.

In the fall of 1944, in the early part of December, we had the biggest snowfall ever recorded. The good weather up to this point had allowed me to hire a large bulldozer, owned and operated by a Mr. Steinke or Hamilton. I had changed the course of the ditches on the farm from two north-south ditches, which were on high land at the foot of the escarpment, to one ditch, half way between the two, on lower land. The job took several days and it was too late in the day to take it home, he left the dozer in our back yard.

The snow started coming down just as we were parking the thing for the night. They were the biggest, heaviest flakes we had ever seen and it must have continued right through until morning, because when we looked out, there was over four feet of the stuff in our yard. I had hardly finished eating breakfast when Mr. Steinke phoned me. The whole city of Hamilton was completely snowbound and not a thing was moving. He was hired by the city to clear the streetcar tracks and because it was impossible to get here himself, he asked me to drive the dozer up #8 Highway until I met him coming the other way on the big snowplow from Hamilton.

The dozer was a large one and I had never driven even a small tractor, which had a hand operated clutch. He explained in great detail how to get it started, which was rather complicated and followed up with my first lesson in driving. When it finally started, I decided the only reasonable thing to do was to clear our own back yard before I lost the only machine that was capable of doing the job. The sense of great power was exhilarating and exiting and as I headed toward the barn, I promptly forgot about the hand clutch that would stop its forward motion. As I got closer and closer I pushed every foot pedal within reach to no avail. Just as the snow in front of the dozer was beginning to exert pressure on the side of the barn, I remembered the only lever that would stop it and pulled like heck. There is no doubt in my mind that the dozer was big enough to push the whole barn over, as this was the old frame building. That was plenty close enough because the wood was already beginning to creak.

I got a little more practiced at the job before I had, at least a path, out to the highway. It was only a guess where the pavement was located because I was the first on the road and everything looked the same between the rows of telephone poles on either side of the road. The six-inch control lever for the dozer blade was within easy reach and in a vertical position. Hand pressure forward forced the blade downward and pressure backward lifted the blade. If no pressure was exerted the blade would remain in that position. What Mr. Steinke neglected to tell me about it was the fourth position of the control handle that would allow the blade to float along the top of the ground.

So then I headed up #8 Highway. The first ten yards proved that with the blade down too far, it would dig into the blacktop and too high, it left a lot of snow. Six or seven inches was as close as I dared to go to the pavement, without risk of damage. Try as I would, I could not prevent the dozer from climbing on top of that few inches of snow and without realizing it, seven inches became fifteen, as I moved forward. Then when the snow became too deep to support the weight of the dozer, the front end tipped down and allowed the blade to dig within a few inches of the pavement again. The net result was a series of waves, spaced about fifty yards apart, thoroughly packed down, all the way from my home to Lake Avenue in Stoney Creek. It took the Department of Highways snowplows nearly two weeks to level it off again. Pa (my father-in-law) was with the department and was not too pleased.

The whole area was in a mess. All the side streets in Hamilton were completely blocked, which eliminated all deliveries for nearly a month. Main highways were somewhat better off when they brought one of the two biggest snowplows in Canada from Ottawa. It was the biggest Hotchkiss Diesel imaginable, a dump truck that carried ten tons of sand for ballast. The tires were seven feet high and two feet wide, four-wheel drive, single wheels all the way around and required no chains. The equipment included a 10-foot high nose plow on the front with an eighteen-foot long wing plow on the right hand side of the truck. Pa hired me to ride with the driver for a couple of night shifts and I'll tell you it was a real experience.

There were places on #20 Highway where the wind had made drifts that were nearly as high as the telephone poles. We cleared the whole road from Smithville to Ancaster without having to back up more than twice to take a run at it. We completely buried an abandoned car just west of Elfrida. I bet he was a few days getting that one out.

The winds are never as violent below the escarpment so #8 was plugged, but not drifted. When they finally got down to the pavement in front of our house the snow plows had pushed piles of snow so high that only the top six inches of the roof of each bus that passed was visible from our front window of the house.

Winter work on the farm really suffered and we managed to trim about half of the trees after the snow melted down far enough to walk through. We certainly could have done without that kind of storm.

It must have been in 1945 that we had the worst Spring I can remember. It was warm quite early and just as the blossoms were wide open the weather turned cold again. We had snowstorms to boot and it was a sad thing to see trees in full bloom covered with an inch of snow, which remained for over a week. Needless to say there was no fruit at all. Grapes and black currants, which always blossom three weeks later, produced the only fruit for that year.

I had a few pigs in the barn, certainly not enough to make a living from. So I took a job hauling live chickens, using my truck, for the Jewish people then operating in the old Terrace building. They bought chickens within a radius of 150 miles. So by starting early, we could make the return trip the same day. The pay was not great, but it beat trying to sell frozen blossoms. Jim Page helped too by hiring me to deliver potatoes from boxcars to the stores. Potatoes were imported from PEI and most cars purposely had 8 to 10 bags more than the shipping bill called for. Jim told me after, that I was the first trucker that actually delivered the extras to stores. Lucky I actually delivered the extras to the stores because finally I struck one that was short and I received no argument at all, not even from Billy Mitchell.

If anyone had told me I would some day be interested in nursing a bunch of old sows, I would have told them without hesitation that they were crazy, but such was the case. I had as many as 25 pigs at a time and found that in spite of looking so much alike, they were individuals in every respect. They were all clever and stubborn, but that is where the resemblance to each other stopped. Some were violent when provoked, some were docile and even tempered, but each had her own idea how to protect her family, where to build her nest for the young, or what kind of food she enjoyed most. Blended fish oil was one of the supplements to their diet to assure a good vitamin supply. It was expensive and in order to be sure that each got her share, I fed them from a tablespoon, one at a time. Most would line up and patiently wait her turn, but for some, it was necessary to disguise the oil in other food.

I kept the pregnant sows together in one or two pens, until they were close to the farrowing date and then moved them to their own pen. I miscalculated on one occasion and when I arrived in the barn in the morning, one sow already had two young pigs and was trying for more in a pen with five or so other sows. They had willingly given her complete rights to the only bed area and stood as far away as possible from the new mother. I moved them out until the litter was born and I had made arrangements for nursery accommodations.

For most hog raisers, the highest casualty rate was during the first two weeks of the young one's lives. The experimental farm at Guelph would suggest that out of the average litter of eight young pigs born in Ontario one would not dare to hope to have more than six left at the end of that period. Young pigs are off and running within two minutes of being born and their built in radar will lead them to the feeding station within five. If you gave a sow three full bales of straw, she would use every bit to make, what she thought was the ideal next for her young, well in advance of their actual birth. Regardless of how well or poorly she did the job it was impossible to change her plans for construction or location. Incidentally no two sows ever worked from the same blueprint or with the same amount of skill. Therefore, it was up to the farmer to build a sturdy rail, preferably round, around the perimeter of the pen 7 inches from the floor and 6 inches from the wall. This would give her a fair chance to lie down without crushing the one pound babies. It was most interesting to watch a four hundred pound sow, first drop cautiously to her knees, then on her belly and finally on one side or the other for the next feeding, while ten or twelve one pound weaklings jockeyed for an ideal feeding position. One loud squeal from any of the family and she is on her feet within a second, grunting loudly and trying to locate the problem. Only when she is satisfied the crisis is over will she try again. When you consider this happens 12 to 20 times a day, it is not hard to visualize the casualty list rising.

Kindness paid great dividends and most sows seemed to trust me to do what was to her advantage and they would allow me to handle the young, change her position etc. without becoming over-excited or angry. It is almost impossible to forcibly handle an angry sow – after all, what can one do with three or four hundred pounds of fighting fury, well equipped with a good set of teeth and only two feet high. The first litter a sow has must be quite a surprise to her because they would very often refuse to have anything to do with any of them. More than once it has taken me 8 or 10 hours to talk her into accepting her family. One sow, on seeing her first born, was absolutely terrified. I had to take the young one right out of the pen to prevent her killing it on the spot. It took half an hour to calm her down enough to convince her to lie down again to try for the rest of the litter. With every new birth, the procedure was repeated until we had eight healthy little pigs.

This was a well-mannered sow normally and she seemed to have confidence in me -but those little ones -no way. It was easy to get her to lie down by rubbing her belly and she had plenty of milk, but every time she got a look at the young one, she was on her feet and running. By this time the piglets are plenty hungry, so one at a time I held them while they got their belly full – out of the sight. I stooped beside her head, rubbed behind her ear with one hand and held the little fellow with the other. It must have been quite relief to get rid of some of the milk because it was evident the pressure was building. As I gradually brought more of the pigs to be fed she became more accustomed to the new experience. Several hours later she allowed all the pigs to be with her at the same time and when one walked past her nose without causing an explosion the battle was over. That sow went on to be as good as any I had and raised several litters of 10 to 12 healthy pigs. There was certainly a lot of work involved with plenty of problems to solve and the smell of the pens on a hot day was hard to live with, but no one could possibly say it was not interesting.

Having bought Uncle Stan's tractor in the fall of 1944 ideas for its use began to flow into my head. The nursery stock was now old enough to be planted in the orchard and 1600 holes looked like a big job, especially since 1400 were to be in the hard red clay. The hundred or so we had planted required work with a crowbar to loosen the clay past a foot deep, before it could be taken out with a shovel. With a hydraulic lift and a power-take-off shaft available, it looked like a faster and easier way to let the tractor do it. By Spring I had cobbled up a digger made from the rear end of a car, costing about $75.00, that would dig a 17" diameter hole about 18" deep in about 60 seconds. After proving it in the field, I wrote to Frank Butters in Windsor and found that he was interested in getting a patent to cover it. By July, we had drawn an agreement between him and I in which we were to share in any profits, the idea should bring included in the agreement was an idea only, of how to build a power driven Grape-hoe.

Frank hired Mr. Krassov, the Ford Motor Co. Patent Attorney, in his spare time, to make drawings and apply for patents in both Canada and U.S. It was a time of pleasant dreams of good fortune and high hopes. Several weeks passed as the potential agreement was drawn up. The meeting was scheduled for the first Monday – a matter of four days. During those four days, the money situation between the two countries completely changed and Ford of Canada was no longer interested in our million dollar ideas.

In the Fall of 1950, Lorne Lee made all the arrangements for us to hunt at Heridge Lake Lodge, a summer lodge located 5 miles south of Temagami or 65 miles north of North Bay on Highway #11. Lorne and Allen Lee, Lorne's son Lavern, Jim Corman, Elmer Wilson, Ralph Hill and I made a nice easy to manage party of seven. Our hunting area was about three miles away, which we traveled to by boat. We came out of a nice warm cabin after breakfast every morning, climbed into the boat and nearly froze to death before we arrived at our destination. After walking all day, working up a good sweat and a mild case of exhaustion, we again piled in the boat and froze all the way back to the camp. That system is for the birds.

Small cabins were built for summer use. Insulation was nil so until we lit the wood fire in the morning, the temperature inside and out were exactly the same. Jim, Ralph, Elmer and I shared one cabin and the remaining three shared a second cabin. They were only a short distance apart so we ate and played cards in our cabin and used the second one for sleeping only. We had a good hunt in spite of a few disadvantages like green firewood and a second rate cook-stove. We certainly had our fair share of laughs at minor instances that occurred during the season. Game was not plentiful, but we had all we really wanted to take home. I won the proverbial pot of a dollar apiece for the first deer shot and there were two other deer to add to the take. The last night in camp came and we settled everything between us financially, broke out the bottle and proceeded to celebrate the season. Allen, Lavern and I left the bottle to the rest and there was enough to get them flying high. Ralph supplied most of the entertainment trying to walk on top of the seven-foot high partitions in the cabin. About 2:30 a.m. we stoked the fire and climbed into bed.

It must have been nearly 4:00 a.m. when Ralph woke with a bang and asked, "What in hell's going on here?" He was loud and clear and this woke his bed-fellow Jim who answered just as loud "The place is on fire, Cliff, Elmer, wake up!!! I woke to see a little ball of fire in the peak of the roof about two feet in diameter. Excitement reigned supreme. We were all on our feet within seconds. Each had his own idea of a cure for the problem. Jim had noticed a fire extinguisher in the main lodge, which was about 40 yards away, a few days before. Ralph remembered he had parked his ½ ton Chevy truck within a foot of the west wall of the cabin. I figured with the help of the other three men in the other cabin, that we could easily extinguish the fire. Elmer decided to go back to the bedroom for his pants – a matter of 6 or 8 feet away from where we all stood dazedly watching the fireball getting bigger. Simultaneously, and only seconds after the first warning from Ralph, we all filed out the only door. Jim first, Ralph second and me in close pursuit and Elmer about 8 feet behind. It must have been when Jim opened the door; a gush of fresh air ignited nearly the entire cabin at once. When I looked back from ten feet in front of the cabin, the whole inside was fire and Elmer was falling out through the screen door, he just didn't have time to open it. It took six months to heal the blisters on the back of his ears and grow enough hair to look respectable.

There was an inch of snow on the ground and the temperature was well below freezing, so in bare feet, it didn't take me long to get to the other cabin. Lorne, Allen and Laverne pulled on boots grabbed a pail, and in less time than it takes to tell, we were all running toward the lake. There was an inch of ice on the water, which could not be broken by stomping close to shore. The bank was steep and by the time Lorne was far enough out to break the ice, he went in over his knees in ice cold water. In the meantime Ralph is sitting in his truck, trying desperately to get it started. It turned over rather slowly, in fact by the time it started both his feet were frozen to the pedals. The filler cap of the gas tank pointed directly toward the raging fire and there were a few anxious moments before the truck finally started.

By the time we reached the fire with the first pail of water, there was nothing standing more than a foot high. Shells were exploding, sparks were flying and there was absolutely nothing left. That building could not have burned faster even if it had been made of waxed paper. We all stood helplessly by watching all our belongings, except the pajamas we were wearing, turned to ashes. Lorne, Allen and Laverne had plenty of spare clothes, but unfortunately they were about half the size of those who had none. When we left for home we looked as though we were dressed for Halloween. My pants were donated to me by the man from whom we had rented the cabin, well worn and faded summer pants which I held up with a piece of rope. Allen loaned me rubber boots and a black turtle-necked sweater. Even though I stretched that sweater six times larger, the sleeves were above my wrists and it would not pull far enough down to cover my rope belt. The others were dressed comparably and it is too bad no one cared about taking a picture of us.

Daybreak came shortly after 8:00 a.m. and after an hour's search through the ashes, we found the keys to Jim's Studebaker. We loaded the truck with the other fellow's gear and the three deer and took off. I rode with Ralph and we bitterly lamented our many losses all the way to North Bay. Licenses, money, wallet, guns, clothing, blankets, etc. etc. were all gone. A doctor in North Bay patched Elmer up, well enough to take him home. Then as we gradually recovered from the shock and began to realize how lucky we were to be alive, the disappointment of our losses slowly faded to their proper proportions with every mile.

The spring of 1951 was beautiful and crops looked very promising. I had hired Bernd Vander Kolk, a new Canadian, emigrated from Holland. He and his wife Femi, were probably the nicest people we ever had living in the spare house. They came to Canada in 1948 and had worked for a Mr. Perin near Galt for a year, before coming to me in 1949. Bern was an honest, hardworking, ambitious and clever, a good living man, slow to anger and quick to respond to any kindness. When he started with me he knew little or no English and it was my extreme pleasure to teach as we worked together. As he advanced I attempted to pick out single words and explain their meaning. We trimmed two rows of grapes each while I got through all the different meanings of a simple word like "beat". We had many laughs and discussions and as time passed we became good friends, in fact Lib and I were Godparents to his first born.

Both the fruit business and the hogs were steadily increasing profits. In the fall of 1950 I spent over a thousand dollars repairing the barn. Most of the money was used up with a new aluminum roof and many steel stay-rods to pull the sides in at the top and thus take some of the sag out of the ridge. I also bought 20 full grown young sows, most of them already bred, at a cost of about $100.00 apiece, during the last part of April, in 1951.

It was shortly after dinner on the 24th of May, as I was returning to reload the sprayer, that I noticed a little bit of smoke coming out of the top of the west end of the barn. I put the tractor in high gear and lost little time coming to the house. Lib had already phoned for the fire department in Stoney Creek. It was a volunteer fire brigade and although there was no one at the station when the call came in. The fire truck arrived at the fire with a full crew in less than eight minutes. During those eight minutes I had filled the sprayer tank (160 gallons) from the 500-gallon tank on the truck, which was parked on the hill in McBride's back yard. The aluminum roof seemed to contain the fire until the heat melted a small hole, then seconds later, the roof is flames from end to end and about 75 feet high. I gave up trying to save the old garage, the closest building to the barn, when I saw the fire truck turning the corne. At this point I was certain the whole corner would burn to the ground. There were three houses and the two small garages plus a 500-gallon underground gasoline tank within 50 feet of the fire. Without the valiant efforts of the firemen they were gone. They placed a man with a fire-hose between the barn and Bern's house who kept the house, the garage and the gas pump alternately wet, as he directed it from one to the other. The heat became intense and the second hose was directed at the first fireman in order to keep him cool enough to remain at his post. In the meantime Bern is in the basement of the barn trying to get the pigs out of their pens. He stayed there far past the safety point and gained nothing. Every pen door was opened and the pigs driven out. Once they arrived at the open basement doors and heard the roar of the fire outside, they returned to the only safety they ever knew, their own pen. It was really disgusting to listen to the terrified squeals of about a hundred and twenty pigs as the first floor collapsed on top of them.

At the same time the fireman directed Femie to get out of the house while others helped carry most of the furniture and what few possessions they had to the safety of the front lawn. The heat was so intense it cooked the flowers to a dark brown that Femie had lined up in front of the window inside facing the barn, even though the storm window had not been removed. Then, when everything seemed hopeless, the wind shifted to blow from the north and took all that excess heat away from the buildings we were so sure were doomed.

Lib was just as busy as I was. Bill and Irvie Schwoob dropped in on their way to buy a bed in Hamilton and when Lib suggested there may be one stored in the barn that might be good enough; the three of them went out to look. Before they got halfway there they noticed the smoke about the same time as I had. She first phoned the fire department and then proceeded to warm Femie. Bern's sister and brother-in-law John and Johanna Lindeboom were living temporarily with them. They also had a small baby about the same age as Bern's. As things looked progressively worse, Irvie volunteered to take Flo and Tom down to their place, about a mile away and they moved the two babies to our front hall to make sure they could be easily carried to safety.

Lib had thought that it was utterly ridiculous that four grown men had walked empty handed from the fire at the hunt camp. To her it was unreasonable that we did not grab pants, shoes and coat as we passed them. After this fire she had no trouble changing her opinion. It happened at the peak of the excitement that one of the firemen came to the house to ask her for a pail and dipper to give those on duty a drink. Her mind was a total blank, she did not know where to look for one, nor did she ever think to give him our own pail and dipper sitting at the end of the kitchen counter.

By 4:00 p.m. the damage was done and the danger past. Every building on the corner, except our house, was on fire at one time or another, so undoubtedly they would have burned without the terrific work of the Stoney Creek volunteer firemen. The water was supplied by two tank trucks, my own and one owned by Ron Deuxberry. I don't know who drove mine, but between them, they hauled enough water from Stone Creek, to keep the pumper at full capacity. The crowds of people milled around to add to the confusion as firemen switched hoses from one place to another. It was hard to believe that there were those in that crowd, with such little respect for other people's problems or property that they stoop to stealing bunches of lilacs growing near the back of the house. Those who knew me, and there were many, offered their sympathy and assistance but out of the whole group Mr. Harry Biggar was the only one who donated $10.00.

The fireman remained on duty until nearly mid-night to be sure that a sudden breeze did not scatter sparks from the smoldering ruins. The next day the insurance adjuster appeared and helped me to remember the contents of the barn and when the list exceeded the value of the policy, we quit. The barn was insured for $1,800.00 and the contents for $5,000.00. There was no doubt that the building was a total loss but the adjuster required reasonable proof of its contents which was not quite so easy from a pile of ashes. He had to accept my word for quantities of such things as pigs, feed, straw baskets, ladders, tools, etc., and he was not satisfied until my figures reached $7000.00. After he was satisfied, it was necessary to agree to re-build the barn before the Farm Loan Board, who held the mortgage, would pass the insurance money onto me; in spite of the fact the money owing was less than the settlement.

Building a barn, feeding pigs and taking in the fruit harvest, all at the same time sure made for a busy summer. With no building available, we did most of the fruit packing on the front lawn and it was amazing how many people stopped to buy whatever we were working on at the time. This was the beginning of the retail business which grew steadily from year to year until it constituted nearly half of the profit realized from the sale of fruit. This selling bit was Lib's cup of tea and as soon as the season opened, she did that job very efficiently and rarely worked on the farm.

Normal operation of the farm had to continue and it seemed that every job we did, required that I buy something to replace that which was lost in the fire. My supplies of feed, such as ice cream cones and milk, were still available to me and with no place to store them; I decided to buy more pigs. The problem of where to put them was solved by George Lounsbury. He had an old barn on the plateau, directly behind the apple orchard, that he used to store out-dated implements. He very graciously allowed me to fence the side hill up to the barn and use it for storage and mixing of the feed. There was a well outside the barn that George believed to be strong enough to supply water for all the pigs I wanted to buy. I went to an Ancaster auction sale and bought over a hundred pigs of all sizes. The largest cost about $21.00 apiece and the smallest about $12.00. They varied in weight between 35 and 110 pounds.

We had never seen pigs grow as fast as that bunch. This was early in July so the weather was delightful, the days were long and the ground they were on was new. This eliminated the possibility of the pigs being infected with disease and they had lots of room for exercise. The trees on the side hill provided protection from the sun's warming rays. Conditions were ideal as they could dig in the dirt, run a quarter mile up and down, sun bathe or just laze in the shade.

The barn when completed was a thing of beauty. Sturdily built, serviceable and with plenty of windows, it was more than a barn. The cement floors and walls, plus the steel roof afforded the maximum fire protection and the layout proved to be just what I wanted. Even with the great amount of donated labour and the saving on the lumber, the cost was over $7,000.00, which resulted in a loss of about $12,000.00 because of the fire, a bitter pill to take.

Shortly after the middle of September, the weather turned abnormally cold, especially the nights. The pigs that had been growing so fast in the open air really slowed down. They ate the same amount, but it seemed to require all the feed they could eat to supply heat for their bodies. I bought a big load of baled straw and built a wall for a windbreak, inside the pen. Within 24 hours the wall was nothing more than a small pile of straw, scattered all over. As the barn was not yet completed, I was forced to sell all of them. That close enough to the weight, went to Gord R. Roberts, the butcher and the rest went to the auction sale.

To most city folks farming or fruit growing is at the bottom of the list as far as requirements for skill or ability is concerned. Some would believe that anyone who is willing to work long hours and dig in the soil could be the ideal farmer. May I suggest that these are only the first two requirements and here is a list of the rest, a good gambler, a businessman, a salesman, a planner, an entomologist, a biologist, a truck and tractor driver, a mechanic, a carpenter and sometimes a plumber. Of course, it always helps to be a welder and a good weather prophet. If you keep animals, and then you should understand animal husbandry, be a dietitian and a veterinarian. If you can keep books efficiently, it always helps to be able to meet people and handling labour problems is a must. It is lucky for me that good spelling is not too important.

Libby's father didn't have a clue about machinery and yet seemed to make pretty good buys. When they moved to the farmhouse, he was driving a 1925 Willys-Knight. It was the biggest, longest, and highest car on the road with enough windows to pass as a green house. They must have made very few because I do not recall seeing another one. That thing was fantastic.

The motor was a sleeve type, with no valves and only four cylinders. It had no pick up but could cruise forever at a pretty good speed without any maintenance care. It smoked like a diesel and I doubt if he ever changed the oil, just kept adding. He drove it as a car for many years, in fact until his job on the highway required him to supply a truck, for which he would be paid mileage. He then cut the back half off and made a small platform to take its place. This served until the highway department gave him a three-ton International snowplough and all. He had no use for a truck of his own so he had Del Peer strip it down and change it into a small tractor to be used on the farm. After several years he traded it for a Cleveland caterpillar orchard tractor.

That tractor came close to killing him several times because it would stand on its tail nearly every time he crossed a small ditch or tried to climb a sharp grade. The hand crank served two jobs, as a lever to shift gears and as the starting crank for the motor. He frequently parked the tractor in the basement of the barn facing the east stone wall. One time he removed the crank from the gearshift and inadvertently left the tractor in a forward gear. The first pull started the tractor forward with the motor running, just above idle speed. He had no time to get out of the way before it reached the stone wall. Luckily, the large flat drive pulley protruded far enough in front of the tractor to allow him to put one leg on each side of it and have enough room for his between the stone wall and the front of the tractor. It is a wonder he didn't have a heart attack while he waited for it to run out of gas or stall. As it happened, all Pa suffered was a few minor cuts and bruises on the inside of his leg and a deflated ego.

I built a giant mix-master, which held 200 gallons. It was a cylindrical, steel tank supported on four three-foot legs, with an opening in the top to receive and a flapper valve. It would allow me to drain it into a 40 gallon barrel, which was on two small wheels, with push handles on one end and spout on the other. The top of the mix-master was about two feet from the ceiling, placed under a hole through which all the dry feed could be shoveled from the feed storage upstairs. The 3,000-gallon storage tank for milk was connected to the mix-master by a 3-inch steel pipe, which had a valve for easy control of quantity and speed of delivery. The milk tank was also upstairs, placed just inside the big doors, so I could drain the 500-gallon tank mounted on my truck, into it. A small propeller mounted on a long shaft and driven by a ½ horsepower electric motor, when submerged to the bottom of the tank, kept the curds and whey well mixed to an even consistency.

The water supply came from a 200-gallon open top tank supported on four five foot legs and heated for winter feedings by a coal fired jacket heater. Another large valve controlled the amount of water required for each batch in the mix-master. The ice cream cones were stored on the third floor above the milk tank and put up there by means of a conveyor, on which they were dumped, a bag at a time, from my second truck. So when it is time to feed the pigs, this is the procedure. Turn on the one horsepower motor that drives the mix-master. Open both water and milk valves to the proper speed. Climb the ladder to the second floor and dump about 300 lbs. of finely chopped oats and barley into the mixture. Then 6 or 7 scoop shovels of dehydrated alfalfa pellets, 10 or 12 pounds of brewers yeast and finally enough ice cream cones or bread to end up with a mixture that will easily flow out of the four inch flapper valve on the bottom of the mix-master. The time it took was less than 15 minutes. By the time I got back downstairs and shut off both milk and water valves, I was ready to deliver the proper amount of mixture to each pen of pigs by means of the 40 gallon barrels. The flapper valve is easily activated by one quick motion, up to open or down to close, and the barrel is just as easily dumped into the desired trough so the time fir this job should not exceed another 15 minutes. This tank full will feed up to 250 hogs depending entirely on the proportion of large hogs in the barn at the time. It is not hard to understand how difficult it could be to maintain an overall total weight of hogs in the barn.

Monday was my usual shipping day and the number of hogs varied from 6 to 22, a full load for my truck. Wednesday was my buying day at Boston, Ontario, about 50 miles from home, and the number I bought varied from 20 to 50 depending on what size young pigs were available that day. The name of the game was to keep every pen loaded to capacity and an even flow of finished hogs to the butcher. It was hopeless to try to outguess the price trends of pork, even though you could be sure the price per pound could fluctuate as much as twelve cents. It could easily happen that the most expensive young pigs would bring the lowest price of the entire year when sold as pork, four months later.

It boils down this way. The pork price and the price of young pigs invariably rose and fell together, so if you replaced the pigs that were sold in the same week the chances of being hurt by price changes were minimized. This explains partially why those farmers who go in and out of the hog-raising business very often took a severe beating. Jack Orr bought about 100 young shoats one Fall because he figured he had a chance to use up some of his hired man's spare time, during the winter months. It turned out, by the time he paid for the pigs and feed, which I think was Purina, plus some straw for bedding all that was left was a big pile of manure and the experience. Nothing at all for the labour or anything else and keep in mind, Jack was an excellent bookkeeper.

With our system of feeding, we could cut the feed costs by at least 40%, which in turn boosted the normal $5.00 profit to as high as $15.00. My books, as poorly kept as they were, will prove that I never failed to show a profit in a year's operation and that some years were fantastic.

Our daughter Florence's 16th birthday present was her license to drive a car. She had no trouble passing the test for a chauffeur's license because I had given her permission to drive the car or trucks on the farm for more than a year before this. Incidentally, I found out later that she did not always stick to the farm but wandered as far as Binbrook on occasion. It was Flo's second year of driving experience when the dairy hired a new foreman in the yard. He was a young Danish lad full of vim and vigour, very bossy and a little drunk with his new found power. Flo drove to the proper place and loaded about half a tank of skim milk from the overhead tank, when this new man spotted her. He jumped on the running board of the truck and instructed her to drive over there to pick up some odd cans of returned milk. She was required to go ahead and back up several times to get to the right position to load these cans and she knew full well that a half tank of milk, was not a load to be rushed. He insisted on more speed, as he did not have all day for one simple job. That did it, as Flo put it in a forward gear and gave it the gas and when it was moving fairly well, she hit the brakes. The lid on the foot square filling hole at the front of the tank was not a tight fit by any means. The milk rushed to the front of the tank, hit the lid and completely drenched him from head to toe with half sour milk. Needless to say that was the last driving instructions Flo received from him.

In the summer of Flo's 17th year, we gave her a horse, a black and white pinto named Cricket. While unloading young pigs, one of the little devils managed to escape. It was no small chore to catch him as it could run fast and duck and dive better than a full grown one. I chased it back and forth across Highway #8 and up and down DeWitt Road. I was happy to see Flo riding Cricket toward home on DeWitt Road and yelled for help. To my surprise she stayed on the horse, I fully expected her to dismount and join the rest of us. In no time at all, she and Cricket were on the far side of the pig and from that point on there was no other direction he could go, except toward the barn. Fast or slow made no difference, quick stops, direction changes or just standing still Cricket was right beside him. Apparently she had been trained for this type of action because Flo had all she could do to hang on and duck the many tree limbs in the orchard. Instruction or guidance was not necessary, Cricket did it all herself. All we had to do was open the barn doors and watch the little pig walk in.

A few final words about raising pigs: As I gradually became better established with the dairy and the ice cream cone manufacturer my supplies increased in volume. This in turn prompted me to take advantage of the cheaper feed by using all the barn space to accommodate feeder hogs in place of sows. Undoubtedly sows returned greater profits per dollar invested, but as more dollars were available, it seemed logical to consider the yearly net profits. It was a reluctant step because I enjoyed dealing with the individual sow and the little pigs raised in our barn seemed to grow faster with less disease troubles. The day I sold "Rusty" the Tamworth boar, which I had raised from his birth, marked the beginning of the change of policy. I took him to the auction sale at Ancaster owned and operated by Gordon Shay. His appearance caused quite a commotion among those present, because he was the biggest hog that had hit the sale in many a day. Gord guessed his weight to be over 900 pounds and the betting began. Gord covered all bets at even money. To prove his weight was another thing because the only scales on the premises were in another building. Gord was understandably very reluctant to attempt to drive this monster through the ever increasing crowd of people and many parked cars and trucks in the open yard. He was as surprised as anyone was when I volunteered to guide Rusty to the scales with just a corn broom. Rusty behaved like a perfect gentleman. That 925-pound hog made more money for Gord in bets than in sales fees that day.

As soon as the sows were sold, I proceeded to buy young pigs in greater numbers. The art of feeding (our way) had already been mastered. Our biggest problem now was the added risk of getting more disease in the barn, as a result of the increased buying and the more crowded pens. Not long after the sows were gone and the barn was loaded to capacity, disease hit with a vengeance. I took one of the dead pigs to Guelph College for advice. Since I was not feeding the standard grain and concentrate, at which time all enthusiastic co-operative effort was completely dropped. The death rate was increasing and possibly there would be no pigs left to inoculate with a serum they were developing. We were now losing ten a day, including pigs that weighed 160 pounds. Roy, the Veterinarian, was here nearly every day. As a last resort he tried a drug called Sodium Arscinelate. Inside of three days the death dropped to half and by the end of week to nil.

It was most fortunate for me that the two businesses, hogs and fruit growing, worked so well together. Instead of running in competition, they actually complimented each other. When dollars were short, it was most convenient to be able to run bills at the feed companies while you waited for the fall payment of your total year's sales of fruit. By the same token, use that money to pay in advance, usually $1,000.00 to have dehydrated alfalfa hay pellets stored by Papel Bros. at Brantford for next year's food requirements. The great amount of straw purchased for bedding increased by ten fold by the time it was spread on the orchards in the form of manure. This was the best possible source of humus and soil nutrients.

Add to this the 40,000 gallons of liquid manure from the big cement tank that drained the hog pen floor and it is easy to understand why fruit production increased so rapidly.

Our normal procedure when loading pigs for weekly delivery was to first select those large enough from each pen, mark them with paint and proceed to get them all in the alley, before starting to load them on the truck. The loading ramp was about 10 feet long and 2-1/2 feet wide and a little less than a 45-degree incline. The one-inch high cleats on the ramp afforded good footing, but they were always reluctant to try anything the first time so it took a good amount of persuasion. The electric stock-prodder delivered a shock similar to that of a spark plug on a car, harmless but effective and certainly less brutal than hammering them with a board. It was about the size of a flashlight and the batteries were the same size. So by means of an old door, which was long enough to block off the alley, two men could start at the far end of the alley, move the door continually closer to the open door leading to the ramp and leave them no choice but to climb.

On Kent's first experience at this game, we had successfully loaded all but three of the 20 or more pigs. The leader, finding the truck rather crowded when he reached the top of the ramp, decided to turn and come back down. It was Kent's job to block its exit and when he saw it turn, he promptly squatted. Now may I say, there is not a heck of a lot anyone can do with a determined 200-pound pig, going downhill? The pig managed to get its head under Kent and once off the ground, he made a record trip the full length of the ramp, feet first and arms flying in every direction. He just had no time to either get his feet on the ground or grab the sides of the ramp. Van was pretty quick to take full advantage of a funny situation and as Kent was not hurt physically, he gave Kent a lot of criticism.

To make a good story even better, Van volunteered to show Kent how it should be done. You guessed it – either the same pig or another one put on a repeat performance with Van as the leading man. Kent didn't pull any punches and the second trip was not nearly so funny from Van's viewpoint. However, it did serve to put them on a more even footing.

This item followed a description of the collapse and rebuilding of their permanent hunting camp. The score for this season is a total blank in my mind, but you may be sure we all had plenty of laughs at a hundred small happenings. This was definitely the place to do all those things that are contrary to the rules of civilized living without fear of criticism or interruption. No radio, telephone or T.V., inquisitive neighbours or inhibiting laws to prevent you from doing what you please, cursing if you like, spitting when you want to or scratching where it itches.

In 1955 my financial position was such that I could afford to hire some expert help, instead of bungling through myself and Charlie Boden was elected. Charlie and Clara had no children and consequently his patience with children was rather short. Norma was just three years old, a going concern and anxious to be friendly. At first Charlie paid as little attention as possible to the little nuisance, locked all his tools securely as they were to be untouched. You have never seen a kid try harder to win a friend, she stood by and watched, at a respectable distance, for the best part of a day, chattering and smiling whenever the opportunity presented itself. By the third day she was offering Charlie an apple, and when he accepted the first one he must have known that he was hooked.

As days passed their friendship grew stronger and it was most interesting to see Charlie's smile get larger and larger when Norma met him at the door each morning. Before the job was finished, she was fetching him tools, handing pieces to him or just acting as general helper and it was evident Charlie enjoyed every minute.

The struggle to get enough water to feed pigs and spray trees ended in 1957. The drilled well in the center of the barn had a good flow of water, but the casing was only six inches in diameter, which limited the reserve supply. The pump was required to work a good part of every day and night, but the system was prone to mechanical failure and a real source of trouble. The next attempt was a pond at the foot of the escarpment. I used the pond as a water supply for spraying with the aid of a fast filler hose connected to the spray machine and the kids in the neighbourhood had a ball until I checked with my lawyer about responsibility. The law says that if I built a ten-foot fence that included a locked gate and anyone climbed that fence and was injured or drowned, it would be my responsibility. We decided to buy a $10,000.00 insurance policy, but the most effective protection was a large sign on the bank of the pond, which read – THIS WATER IS POLLUTED WITH POISONED SPRAY MATERIAL. It was untrue, but it kept the kids out. It was a shame to spoil their fun. Those were drought years and it was a pathetic sight to see a good crop of fruit begin to get smaller, instead of larger as it neared maturity.

In 1965 the Township put a water main up Homeside Avenue, a mere 500 feet west of the boundary of my farm, so I decided to go it on my own. The next spring, John Rogers dug the trench and I put in a 2-inch water line to my west boundary to a cement meter box. This part was cast iron pipe. From there it was almost 1,000 feet to the next cement box located on the lane about half way across the farm – a 2-inch plastic line. Both boxes were about 5 feet square and 4 feet deep with a one and a half foot square hole for access and a four inch round hole to allow a stand pipe from which to take the water. The top of the boxes was at ground level. From the second box we used a three-quarter inch plastic line to get to the barn and the house. Over a quarter of a mile of pipe, all underground – a rather ambitious program – but what an improvement.

In the year 1957 I bought 1,000 feet of aluminum irrigation pipe with 15 sprinklers, another step toward the elimination of nature's hazards on a fruit farm. The cost of the whole water system including irrigation pipes, etc. was right around the $1,000.00 mark and I found the second year of operation paid the bill, even considering the cost city water at 30 cents per thousand gallons. There is no accurate way to calculate the difference between irrigating and not irrigating an orchard because of the many unknown quantities of natural blessings such as rainfall, dew, or the capacity of the soil to retain moisture. But consider this – if you can increase the diameter of a 2-inch pear to 2-1/4 inches and all the pears in the orchard are the same size, then the number of bushels harvested will be doubled. The bonus received is those bushels of pears that have gained enough size to get over the minimum 2 inch diameter required by the factory's rules for No. 1 pears. Add to these advantages the increased vigor of each tree for next year's production. In any case, you may be sure that my small efforts were well rewarded because two out of every three years were dry enough to require irrigation.

There are great yearly hunting stories, but they are rather long to include in this condensed story. Both Gord and Charlie fitted into our hunt gang like a hand in a glove. We soon found out that Gord was not just a cook, but a qualified chef, having served as head cook at Manning Pool during his army days and as chef for Lady Eaton after the war. We had meals like you would never believe, since the first day Gord took over and we enjoyed his wit, humour and good fellowship. The highlight of nearly every hunt trip was the night Gord and Dick decided to 'tie one on'. It happened about once in every season that the lamest excuse to celebrate would start them off. Each had a bottle of rum and they proceeded to experiment with mixers. To follow up, everyone practically demanded western sandwiches just to see our chef at work. It took a lot of coaxing, which was really part of the fun, to get him started, but from there we would laugh until our sides and bellies were sore. It would seem that he could hardly make it to the skillet and then the stove and bending over to light the gas stove with a match, was no easy task either. All motion is less than half speed and it looks reasonable that the skillet will be burnt to a crisp long before he can prepare the eggs and bacon mixture to put in it. The next step – cut the bacon in small pieces – you would swear he could lose part of a few fingers with every whack of the razor-sharp butcher knife. Then the eggs, as he supported himself with one hand on the counter, he proceeded to break a dozen eggs, one at a time, with the other hand, holding each one about 2 feet above the bowl as the contents of the egg fell from the shell. He never missed the bowl, never broke a yolk or got shells in the bowl. He then picked up the bowl as he leaned against the counter and with a common table fork, beat the heck out of them. As he explains the procedure in great detail he is looking at his audience, whose eyes are fixed on the bowl, which is being tipped so that the egg whites hang over the edge by 2 inches. He never spilled a drop on the floor. With great gusto he poured the eggs into the skillet and then the chips of bacon from the second frying pan. The peak of the performance comes as he takes a firm grip of the skillet handle with both hands to flip the omelet. After a violent shaking of the pan and a few false attempts, he has never yet failed. Then he shot a little cheese in it and it was a western fit for a king. The above explanation does not come even close to describing the amount of fun and laughter; we derived as we watched what any T.V. program we have ever seen rarely tops. Charlie became headman of the improvement committee and never seemed to tire of fixing the camp to add to our comfort.

Of all the varieties of the fruit grown on this farm, it was pretty much of a toss up between apricots and apples when you tried to decide which derived the biggest benefit from our lawn sales. There were many farms in the Niagara Peninsula with perhaps one or two apricot trees, that served to supply the farmer himself and a few friends, but I knew of only two other orchards of apricots, that were large enough to be classed as commercial. One was between Grimsby and Beamsville and another east of St. Catharines. Both of these were at least twice as big as the 100 trees I called an orchard. It is little wonder then, that so few of the buying public ever knew about apricots grown in Ontario on the four or five acres out of a grand total of over 150,000 acres of fruit lands. For this reason only, they were just as hard to sell as they were to grow.

Apricots were the oddball extras on our farm, and I was glad to let Lib spend whatever she could make from their sale any way she pleased. Of course I had no idea in 1946 when I made this offer as I grafted the hundred plum trees to apricots, that their sale value would overpass the $1,500.00 mark per year. The arrangement became more important and funnier as sales increased and the years passed.

Out of the 5,000 seedlings I budded in 1937, only 110 of the 3,000 plum seedlings "took" and the rest were still wild trees. Now what the heck would I do with 110 healthy, useless trees? I certainly did not need any more plums on farms this size. On checking with the experimental farm in Vineland, I was told that they have several varieties of apricots, from which I can procure grafts. But they strongly advise me to forget the idea, for several reasons. Number one being, they blossom about 10 to 12 days ahead of any other fruit we grew, which should mean if they escape adverse weather during their wide open period, they will surely catch some frost after the blossoms are properly set. A fair prophecy would be one crop year in every four. Number two; I would be trying to grow a delicate fruit on the toughest, poorest soil in Ontario. Number three was the grafting union between plum and apricot is never too strong. Number four is they were very susceptible to tree borers, the same as peach trees (which I knew nothing about). Thus, contrary to all the best advice I could find, I did it anyway. I cut every limb off those trees and inserted grafts all in one year in the interest of saving time. I knew I should have done this over a period of 3 years. It seemed logical to me that I had little to lose because if it failed, I would pull all the trees out and plant again. Well, I must have done it right because I have never seen trees grow as fast, before or since. Some made 4 feet of new growth the first year and by the end of the second year, the trees were about the same size as before they were cut off. Quite naturally, the quantity of apricots was much slower to increase because the producing wood of the tree had to be more than one year old. The first crop came in 1948 and totaled no more than 10, 6-quart baskets and the increase over the following 23 years was slow and spasmodic. The all time high came in 1969, slightly under 600 6 quart baskets, which sold for about $2.50 each.

The prophecy of one crop year in four proved out for the first 10 to 12 years and was somewhat discouraging. If I could find a way to delay that early blossom season for just a few days' things might be different. The next year I picked the coldest week in February, to spread a mulch of loose straw a foot thick under each tree. The frost was deep in the ground and my hope was to keep it there a few extra days in the spring.

Bingo! That year was the first to yield a crop that could be termed even fair. A repeat of the same procedure the next year produced even a better crop. Two more years and I was convinced. I proudly announced my discovery to the experimental farm and was told in no uncertain terms that the air temperature was the determining factor in blossoming date, not the ground temperature. Assuming they knew the right answers, I deleted the straw program and had no crop that year. I will never know for certain whether their theory was correct, or if it was a matter of coincidence, but it seems odd that large crops followed the mulch program and there never was a good crop without it.

Lucky for me we did not get our big crops at the beginning of the apricot program because I would have never been able to sell them. They were totally unknown in the wholesale world as most storekeepers were unwilling to believe Ontario could produce apricots. Even the sale for imported apricots was limited seriously principally because they came to us from such distances as B.C., California, South Africa and Australia, which resulted in a high cost and fruit, which had to be picked before it matured. Ours could be allowed to ripen on the tree, which resulted in a great increase of flavour. So this is where the lawn sales came in. Each new customer had to be talked into buying their first basket and it took a good many years to convince enough people of their special qualities, so that we could sell the ever-increasing quantities in the three-week season of apricots.

Out of the 40 or more tons of Bartlett pears that went to the canning factory, we graded out the very choicest 200 bushels and put them, a few bushels at a time, with the apples and plums on the lawn. They sold for $2.00 over the factory price, which almost doubled the profit margin, and gave us a few more happy customers. The law states that any farmer is free to sell whatsoever he could produce, regardless of the quality or price, from his own property, if he does not advertise the same. We got in trouble when a government fruit inspector spotted our wagonload of green plums, which has a prominent sign, announcing 'Split Plums for $1.00 in a bag'. After heated words with the inspector, he did put a detention sign on the fruit. If I called the next day to their office in Vineland, they would send another man to remove the tag and allow me to dump the fruit in the garbage. As soon as the inspectors left, I made another pile of plums, as close to the wagon as possible and we sold additional 100 baskets by the end of the day.

The inspector demanded that each basket and bushel should be stamped with my name and address on it and the variety of fruit and the grade. I explained to their satisfaction, that about 90% of our customers preferred to take their fruit either in their own container or a paper bag plainly stamped with my name, address and phone number, in the interest of saving a little money. The chief inspector liked the idea so much that he took a few of our printed bags to the office hoping, to make this a legal procedure.

During the later years Turner Winery bought nearly all the grape crop except during the few over production years of the Niagara Peninsula. On one of these years I was forced to dump the last 4 tons into the pond because there were no buyers even on the lawn. The apples were by far the biggest volume sold on the lawn, both in fruit and dollars. We often had up to 400 bushels of apples, 50 bushels of pears, 30 bushels of grapes (red, white and blue) besides the 500 six quart baskets of the same varieties, all on the lawn at the same time. It was certainly a sight to behold and many stopped just to look, including tour buses with people from distant places.

The business grew from a 'once in a while' sale for one person to an 'all you could handle deal' for four people. The weekend sales grossed a thousand dollars during September and October, with some Sundays giving us $600.00. This represented a great many individual sales, something like 150 bushels of apples, plus 200 to 300 six quart baskets of apples, pears, plums and grapes per day. One would have to admit that the lawn made that difference between a meagre living to a comfortable income. Hours in the day meant nothing either, because once we we were selling by the bushel, we no longer moved the fruit off the law overnight, which resulted in serving customers well after dark on occasion. Our total losses to thieves did not exceed $50.00 and if you consider the time and effort involved moving that quantity of fruit twice a day – really nothing.

I was initiated into Thomas Hamilton Simpson Masonic Lodge in Stoney Creek as Numbered 692 on the register of the Grand Lodge of Canada, in the Province of Ontario. Immediately after I received my third degree, I was appointed organist for the lodge, which I enjoyed ever since. All efforts are voluntary, it is educational and you are bound to meet many outstanding men in every walk of life, who are just Masons once they enter the doors of the Temple.

We, of the Dun Wurkin Hunt Club, after much search and debate found a practically new Bren Gun Carrier, which had been in mothballs since the war. It was in a wrecker's yard on Front Street in Toronto. We bought it for less than $300.00. It was an army vehicle that had cost the government over $16,000.00 and it had less than 50 miles on the odometer. We cut off about 1,500 lbs. of armour plate with a cutting torch. We covered the driver with the roof and windshield of an old truck and made a few other minor modifications and it still weighed over 6,000 lbs. We had trouble going through deep water holes, as the wet brake linings wouldn't hold. The machine was built for the Sahara Desert, not beaver ponds and water holes.

The Ontario Hydro installed a new high voltage power line, at right angles to our road and about half way to our camp. They had no choice but to use our road to transport all the heavy equipment and whatever else is required to build a new power line. They made no attempt to keep the road passable because their equipment was big and powerful enough to get through anything. What was bad before soon became a disaster area. A letter to the Ontario Hydro gained nothing but a few promises. We used our two carriers every fall, beginning in 1962 to and including 1971.

Bill Cant, on Fruitland Sideroad, sold me the horse I wanted for $125.00. This bay coloured mare, 12 years or older, short legged, stocky and fat, with a kind disposition and lots of experience with Bill's children. So in an envelope, for Norma's 13th Birthday, a little poetry: We had to get you something
>And you are too young for a car
>So I found the only answer,
>In an old nag called STARR.

It was no trouble at all for Norma to rise early enough every morning to care for Starr before leaving for school and of course, again care for her when she arrived home. Bareback, Starr would allow as many kids as Norma could crowd on her. Two years later, we bought Norma a three-month-old appaloosa stallion colt for $35.00. She named it Shado. No colt ever received more attention and tender loving care than Shado did and I would suggest that very few colts have tried harder to return that kindness. He would follow Norma like a faithful dog and was quick to learn the meaning of whoa, walk, trot, turn, etc. while making circle after circle around Norma at the end of a 25 foot halter rope. He grew steadily in both stature and knowledge without losing any of the gentle kindness that was bred into him. It was real fun to see a full-grown horse grab Norma's coat zipper firmly between his teeth and playfully toss his head up and down the full length of her jacket. Jane Tudenham lived about half way to Barton Street on the west side of DeWitt Road. She was one of Norma's best friends and she too had her own horse. They decided to enter the horses in competition in some of the local county fairs, so a more serious training program was started.

The first was at Beamsville, about 20 miles away from home. Shado was not too enthusiastic about the ride in the horse trailer, but once there, he was absolutely enthralled with everything. He just couldn't believe there were that many horses in the world. The noise and clatter of the fair was not upsetting to him, but his curiosity insisted that he should look at and talk to every horse that passed him and the short legged ponies were a real mystery.

The girls entered the horses in the riding class, which required them to travel in a large circle inside a coral with 20 or more other horses and riders. They were judged on obedience as they were asked to change pace from walk, to trot, to canter and then reverse directions and then later for standing and leading. Everything went fine for the first few minutes as they were asked to walk slowly. Shado made the round at a slow trot with no difficulty and then for some crazy reason decided the horse behind him was getting too close and he would have none of that tail-gating. With the greatest of ease Shado turned around to face the horse behind him and traveled backwards at the same exact speed, with all the grace of a gazelle. Somehow Norma retained her equilibrium and after traveling quite some distance, Shado had gained a comfortable lead on the horse following him and was content to turn about and go the same direction all the rest were going. The judges were kind enough to overlook the first mistake, but the second repeat was just too much and Shado and Norma were among the first to be eliminated.

Sometime in 1969, Florence was working at Chedoke Hospital and found it impossible to look after Cricket. Norma volunteered for the job and Cricket was moved into the barn to make 3 horses to tend twice a day. When you remember all the baseball games Jane and Norma played, the training program for the horses, a couple of boy friends, 12th grade in high school plus a fair share of the farm work, Norma had to be one of the busiest 17 year old girls in Canada.

If you think about it seriously, a firm belief in God, good health and a good partner are the ONLY important things in life, the very things most of us take for granted.

[The unfinished manuscript is about 237 pages.]

BESCHRYVINGE
Der Stad
DORDRECHT,

Vervatende Haar Begin, Opkomst, Toeneming, en verdere Stant: Opgezocht, in 't Licht gebracht, en Vertoond, met vele Voorname Voor-Rechten, Hand-Vesten, Keuren, en Oude-Herkomen.

Als mede een Verzamelinge van eenige GESLACHT-BOOMEN, der Adelijke, Aal-Oude, en Aanzienlijke HEEREN-GE-SLACHTEN, van, en in, DORDRECHT, enz.

Zijnde de Voornoemde BESCHRYVINGE, Geçierd, en Verrijkt, met Verscheyde KOPRE KONST-PLATEN.

DOOR

MATTHYS BALEN, JANS ZOON.

TE DORDRECHT,

Gedrukt by *Symon Onder de Linde*, Boekverkooper, woonende aan de Vis In de Groote Gekroonde Druckerye. Anno M.D.C.LXXVI.

1677.

HISTORICAL BACKGROUND

To understand any Genealogy, it is necessary to understand the Geography of the family, its Economic basis, and the History of the family's time period. The DeWitt family (originally die Wit) came from the Low Countries in the late thirteenth century so far as we are able to prove. The Low Countries consisted of present day Nederlands (miscalled Holland), Belgium, parts of France, Germany, the Baltic countries and Poland. Today it is the seven Provinces, Groningen, Friesland, Drenthe, Overijessel, Utrecht, Gelderland, and Zeeland plus the Federal area which includes The Hague.

At the end of the sixteenth century, Europe was a mass of conflict with each city and state contending for supremacy or survival in contest with its neighbors. They were constantly forming and breaking alliances with other entities. Uppermost in this was religion, with not only Catholics against Protestant but Catholic sects against other Catholic sects and Protestant sects against other Protestant sects. Generally, religion was secondary to political power and its attendant wealth. At this point in time, 200 cities in Europe controlled more than fifty per cent of the commerce of the world.

The Royal family of Hapsburg's Empire stretched from the North Sea to and including the Mediterranean Sea and from the European Atlantic coast to the far reaches of present day Russia. The King Phillips (III, IV,V) of Spain were dominant in the family and oppressed and extracted wealth from all the peoples of Europe. Warfare and attendant slaughter was endemic as the population writhed under these Kings with their 'God given right to rule' with the blessings of the dissolute Popes at Rome who excommunicated all who rebelled against royalty.

The Thirty Years War 1618-1648 was not only a struggle between Emperor and Princes, but was fueled by the conflict between Catholics and Protestants with additional oil poured on the fire by schisms in each religion and the instigations of Rome as it jockeyed for positions to preserve its political aims. This war caused great decimation of the populations of North Europe and the destruction of many centers of learning. The dislocation of populations from Spain to the North Sea destroyed many sources of genealogical records as is well known to genealogists.

The teachings of Martin Luther took firm root among the northern countries of Europe and in particular with the Low Countries of present day Belgium, parts of France, Denmark, Sweden, Norway and parts of Germany and Poland and these areas saw the beginnings of rebellion and the desire for self rule increase against the Hapsburgs and their Princes. The Provinces of Holland engaged in active rebellion in 1568 and culminated in the Treaty signed with Spain in January 1648 when the Seven Provinces formed The United Provinces of Holland and escaped the politics and cruelties of Spanish rule.

The struggle was intensified and brought to fruition through the actions and courage of people like Jan DeWitt 1625-72 which prevented the Constitution from being weakened or abrogated by The Hague and ensured that freedom would continue for the Seven Provinces.

This long, hard and bloody struggle forged Holland into a world dominating sea power which colonized areas of the world from the Malaysian Archipelago to South America, Portugal, Africa and of course, to North America due to the explorations of Henry Hudson, who was employed by the Dutch to explore the river bearing his name. At least two DeWitts were with him and it is known that one served as Mate after the previous Mate was killed by Indians after raping an Indian maiden, which caused present day Cape May (Mei) to be named after him. Many of the DeWitts were instrumental in forming and operating the Dutch East India Company and the Dutch West India Company. A shift in power resulted in the increase of power of the English, although the Dutch did sail up the Thames River and threatened London, but withdrew without a shot being fired on either side. The three wars with England, 1651-4, 1665-7 and 1672-4 resulted in the withdrawal of Dutch influence from many possessions, including New Amsterdam which became New York in the honor of the Duke of York.

Compiled by Robert P. Rickard

University of British Columbia, Mercator, Gerardus. 1512 – 1594.
Atlas Minor . Special Collections: G1007/M42. 1610
Emden, Norden, Ooserbeus, Jever, Saderlant, GrootCelte

DORDRECNT de WITT CHARTS GENERATIONS 1 to 13
MATTY BALEN, JANS ZOON. BESCHRYVINGE Der Stad DORDRECHT, 1677

The de Witt family was prominent in Dordrecht and later in national politics, often Ambassadors, in business and other leadership roles for more than 300 years. A full translation of the 1625-72 is accounted one of the outstanding statesmen of his age. His tenure in office was marked by remarkable achievements in which he was ably supported by his brother Cornelius (1623-72). By 1652 [age 27!] Johan became Grand Pensionary of the Republic of the united Provinces, as the Netherlands was then called. In 1672 a mob literally tore them to pieces, said to be at the instigation of supporter of the Prince of Orange, William the III. Read about them in any encyclopedia.
Their line is from 1.4.1.2.7.4.4.6.3 Kornelis de Wit b 25 Jun 1623 (d 4 Aug 1672) m 21 Sep 1650 Maria van Berckel b 31 May 1632.

Jan die Witte died 1295 m ? p 1294
Gerard die Witte died 1314 m ? p 1294

Dordrecht

GENERATION 1
GODFCHALK

1 Godfchalk die Witte 1326 m ? van Houweningen p1294
1. Jan de Witte was Schepen [Councilar] six times 1367-82, Burgermeefter [Chief Magistrate] in Dordrecht, Holland.

GENERATION 2
die WITTE

1.1 Jan die Witte m van Ratingen
1. Adriaan die Witte 1402 d in flood from Artic storm.
2. Jooft die Witte, entered a Monastery & d there.
3. Maria die Witte
4. Witte die Witte buried in the Church of Saint Mifsael m Beatrix van Steene.

GENERATION 3
die WITTE

1.1.4 Witte die Witte m Beatrix van Steene
1. Jan die Witte s/o Wittenfz d 1450 m Maria Tak.

GENERATION 4
die WITTE

1.1.4.1 Jan die Witte m Maria Tak
1. Witte die Witte d 25 Mar 1507 'Raad 6 times between 1493-1504 'Veertig' 1496 m 1483 Maria Geom d 6 Sep 1504.
2. Maria die Witte
3. Judocus die Witte

GENERATION 5
die WITTE

1.1.4.1.1 Witte die Witte m 1483 Maria Goem
1. Joost de Wit d 25 Oct 1508
2. Jan de Witt (d 17 Jan 1565) 'Water-Schepen' m 14 Jan 1508 Kara van Beveren d 29 May 1556.
3. Roeloff de Wit b 1480 was Monk in 1516, a Convent Dordrcht d 1550.
4. Kornelis de Wit
5. Aletta de Wit she is Convent van S. Agniet in Dordrcht.
6. Maria de Wit m Dirk Kar Veertig 1508 Schepen 1509-10) d 1526 chn Dirk & Jakomina.

GENERATION 6
de WIT

1.1.4.1.1.2 Jan de Wit m Klara van Beveren
1. Witte de Wit **dy**. 2 Willem de Wit **dy**. 3 Maria de Wit **dy** 4 Jakob de Wit **dy** 5 Witte de Wit **dy** 6 Maria de Wit **dy**
7. Kornelis de Wit b 27 May 1519 d Aug 1550) m Beatrix van Slingeland d 23 Mar 1555.
8. Maria de Wit **dy**
9. Willem de Wit b 13 Apr 1516 (d 23 Aug 1596) m 29 Jan 1541 Maria van Wefel d 22 Jan 1593 He was Schepen six times 1573-82 'Borgermeefter' 1586-89-90 on Dordcht: 'Raad' for Prince William of Orange.
10. Witte de Wit b 21 Oct 1523 d 1609 m 25 Sept 1548 Alith van de Lee b 10 Aug 1529 their chn Maria & Margareta de Witt m each had 2 chn.
11. Jakob de Wit **dy**. 12 Dirk de Wit **dy**. 13 Maria de Wit **dy**
14. Willemina de Wit **dy**.

GENERATION 7
de WITT

1.1.4.1.1.2.7 Kornelis de Witt m Beatrix van Slingeland
1. Pieter de Witt b 1507 (d 29 Nov 1558) m Petronella Adriaans.
2. Witte de Witt m Agata Thymans **no chn**.
3. Johan de Witt buried in the Abby at Rijnsburg.
4. Frans de Witt b 1516 d 10 Nov 1557 m1 9 Feb 1539 Liduivi van Beveren b 1522, m2 29 Jul 1563 Katharina van Beverwyk b 1539 d 1608
5. Maria de Witt m Bartholomeus van Seginaert

de WIT

1.1.4.1.1.2.9 Willem de Wit m Maria van Wefel
1. Thomas de Wit **dy**. 2 Jan de Wit **dy**. 3 Godela de Wit b 1546 (d 13 Dec 1613) m Adriaan de Groene d 1603.
4. Thomas de Wit b 1548 (d Dec 1601) m Adriana van Scharlaken d 1625.
5. Kornelis de Wit b 22 Oct 1550 (d 21 Sep 1597) m 16 Dec 1578. Jacomina van Beveren b 14 Oct 1555 d 1639.
6. Nikloaas de Wit b 1553 'Atch 1600-03 Veertig Raad 1604-5, 1608-9 Schepen 1612-3, 1616-7, 1620-21 m Michaelia van Loon

7 Kriftina de Wit **dy**
8 Klara de Wit **single.**
9 Jan de Wit b 1567 (d 15 Sep 1625) m 18 Feb 1590 Jacomina van Barefleyn b 13 Jul 1572 d 11 Jan 1656 'Acht' 1604-10 'Schepen & Treforier' 1611-19 'Ontfanger Generaal van den Tolle van Geervlict' in 1613 -25 Dordrect.

GENERATION 8
de WITT

1.1.4.1.1.2.7.1 Pieter de Witt m Petronella Adriaans
1 Kornelis de Witt m Adranade Koning.
2 Beatrix de Witt m Jakob de Witte.

de WITT

1.1.4.1.1.2.7.4 Frans de Witt m Liduivi van Beveren
1 Alith de Witt b Dec 1539 (d 1584) m Kornelis van Beaumont d Jan 1587.
2 Kornelia de Witt b 12 Nov 1541 (d 20 Oct 1570) m Willem Stoop d 1598.
3 Katharina de Witt b 23 Oct 1543 (d 29 Oct 1605) m Jan van der Burch d 24 Apr 1601, 6 chn.
4 Kornelis de Witt b Apr 1545 (d 3 Apr 1622) m1 28 Sep 1568 Johanna Heymans b 12 Jan 1547 d 24 May 1602 m2 02 Sep 1603 Kornelia van Beverwyk b 11 Nov 1559 d 3 Apr 1622.
5 Jakob de Witt b 3 Jan 1548 (d 14 Dec 1621) m Elfa/Elifabeth Heymans d 1632.
6 Maria de Witt b 19 Feb 1551 m Dirk Stoop d Oct 1591, 4 chn.
7 Anna de Witt b 27 Oct 1552 m Johan Voffius.

de WIT

1.1.4.1.1.2.9.5 Kornelis de Wit m Jacomina van Beveren
1 Johan de Wit (d 22 Aug 1666) m 1611 Adriana van Hedickhuyzen d Dec 1655 He was 'Borgermeefter, en Secretaris van Woudrichem, Penningmeefter van den Land van Althena'.
2 Kornelis de Wit b 7 Jan 1587 (d 26 Aug 1624) m 15 Feb 1609 Elifabeth van Haarlem b 11 Oct 1587 d 8 Jan 1670.
3 Maria de Wit b 11 May 1589 (d 21 Jul 1616) m Apr 1614 Willem van Overftege. He married a second time.
4 Pieter de Wit b 20 Sep 1591 d 1636 m 20 Feb 1618 Judith van Gefel. He was 'Acht' 1625-29 in Dordreht
   Kornelis & Elifabeth **dy**.

de WIT

1.1.4.1.1.2.9.6 Nikloaas de Wit m Michaelia van Loon
1 Jooft de Witt d 1625 m 1617 Maria van Mewen 2 dau
2 Thomas de Witt d 18 Jan 1645 'Veertig 1627 Schepen 1629-30-1-7-8' [He was with East India Co. in Amfterdam 1637-45] m 12 May 1620 Jacomina Thibouts.
3 Helena de Witt **single.**
4 Maria de Witt d 19 Mar 1631 m1 Henrik Noey m2 9 Jul 1614 b 2 Jun 1591 d 17 Dec 1672 Pieter de Carpentier.
5 Willem de Witt (Acht 1626) in Dordrecht d **single.**

de WIT

1.1.4.1.1.2.9.9 Jan de Wit m Jacomina van Barefleyn
1 Johan de Wit b 15 Dec 1590 (d 18 Jun 1655) m 17 Oct 1619 Belia Stokmans d 22 Feb 1665.
2 Adriaan de Wit b 1592 d 11 Jul 1595 **dy**.
3 Willem de Wit b Jan 1595 **dy**.
4 Willem de Wit b 22 Apr 1596 (d 15 Sep 1629) m Katharina de Wilde.
5 Nickolaas de Wit b 8 Jul 1597 (d 1621) m Margareta.
6 Kornelis de Wit b 5 Oct 1599 (d 9 Jun 1643) m Maria van de Werken.
7 Maria de Wit b 30 Jun 1601 d 25 Mar 1673 **single.**
8 Jacomina de Wit b 8 Jul 1603 d 21 Oct 1639 **single.**
9 Thomas de Wit b May 1605 (d 23 Dec 1652) m 12 Oct 1632 Geertruyd de Koning d 2 Apr 1644 dau Maria m Johan Quirijn chn He was a Captain in ? Dordrecht.
10 Adriaan de Wit b 15 Feb 1607 d 4 Feb 1673 **single.**
11 Henrik de Wit b 15 Feb 1609 **dy**.
12 Klara de Wit b 2 Apr 1612 d July 11 years old.
13 Abraham de Wit b 27 Oct 1613 (d 9 Jan 1653) m 3 Feb 1638 Maria van Melifdyk.
14 Anmade de Wit b 13 Sep 1615 d 14 May 1642 **single.**

GENDERATION 9
de WITT

1.1.4.1.1.2.7.4.4 Kornelis de Witt m1 Johanna Heymans
1 Lidia de Witt b 15 Feb 1570 (d 1645) m1 21 Jun 1593 Johan van Wefel d 5 Jan 1595
   m2 4 Dec 1604 Anthoni de Hoog d 8 Sep 1646

Dordrecht

2 Andries de Witt b 16 Jun 1573 (d 26 Nov 1637) active in Government service m 23 May 1604 Elifabeth van den Honert d 1653.
3 Alith de Witt b 4 Jul 1575 m 12 Jan 1595 Pompejus de Roovere.
4 Kornelia de Witt b 9 Jan 1579 (d 23 Mar 1641) m 11 Oct 1605 Amelis van Hogeveen 11 Feb 1620, 3 chn.
5 Frans de Witt b 14 Nov 1586 d 29 Mar 1615 **single**.
6 Jakob de Witt b 7 Feb 1589 (d 10 Jan 1674) m 9 Oct 1616 Ann van den Corput b 24 Apr 1599 d 23 Jan 1645.

de WITT
1.1.4.1.1.2.7.4.5 Jakob de Witt m Elfa/Elifabeth Heymans
1 Frans de Witt (d 8 Nov 1610) m Margareta Rutgers d 31 Jun 1636.
2 Lidia de Witt m Kornelis Ruyfch, 3 chn.
3 Aletta de Witt m Oct 1597 Ifaak van den Corput.
4 Sara de Witt b 1591 m 5 Apr 1615 Jakob Focanus, 3chn.
5 Maria de Witt m Johan Nyffen, **no chn**.
6 Johanna de Witt m Daniel de la Vigne.
7 Adries de Witt **single**.
8 Kornelia de Witt m Thomas Baudicjius.

de WIT
1.1.4.1.1.2.9.5.1 Johan de Wit m Adriana van Hedickhuyzen
1 Gyfmar de Wit d 16 Feb 1670 m 1636 Petronella Bom van Kranenburg d 1673.
2 Kornelia de Wit m Matthys Drofte.
3 Maria de Wit m Henrik van Erp.
4 Adriana de Wit **single**.
5 Jacomina de Wit m Pieter van Nordingen.
6 Klara de Wit m 18 Sep 1646 Johan van Someren d 5 Feb 1647.

de Wit
1.1.4.1.1.2.9.5.2 Kornelis de Wit m Elifabeth van Haarlem
1 Kornelis de Wit d 5 Jun 1557 **single**.
2 Gysbert de Wit b 19 Jul 1611 (d 21 Dec 1674) m 14 May 1645 in Brazil to Donna Anna Pais d'Altro b 1612 He served as a Colonel, also in Brazil, in many important jobs, also in Afgozden, Portugal, Heeren, Staten, Generaal of Ber-igde Nederlanden.
3 Margareta de Wit b 17 Jul 1612 m Dirk van Emont d 6 Jun 1656.
4 Willem de Wit b 5 Jul 1614 (d 6 Sep 1652) m Anna Pufet.
5 Anthoni de Wit b 19 Nov 1615 d 27 Mar 1651 **single**.
6 Pieter de Wit d 20 Sep 1662 m 8 May 1644 Hafina Kofters, **no chn**.
7 Maria de Wit b 19 Aug 1623 **single**.

de WITT
1.1.4.1.1.2.9.6.1 Jooft de Witt m Maria van Mewen
1 Maria de Witt **single**.
2 Aletta de Witt m Herbert van der Mey.

de WITT
1.1.4.1.1.2.9.6.2 Thomas de Witt m Jacomina Thibouts
1 Een de Witt b 17 Mar 1621 **dy**.
2 Maria de Witt b 20 Nov 1622 m 14 Apt 1643 Goofwijn Houfflager d 22 Oct 1644.
3 Jofina de Witt b 22 Apr 1624 d 27 Jun ?
4 Een de Witt b 21 Jun 1625.

de Wit
1.1.4.1.1.2.9.9.1 Johan de Wit m Belia Strokmans
1 Johan de Wit b 15 Oct 1618 (d 27 Oct 1676) m1 5 Dec 1660 Petronella-Gysberta van Wouw b 1642 m2 9 Oct 1667 Katharina van Beaumont. He was 'Schepen' 1649-50-6-7 Veertig in Dordrecht and served important offices in Holland & Weft-Vriefland & Ambaffadeur-extraortinaris & Denemarken, Noorwegen, served in Republijcq in Polend 1670.
2 Nikolaas de Wit b 6 Dec 1621 d 1650 **single**.
3 Elisfabeth de Wit b 6 Dec 1624 **dy**.
4 Maria de Wit b 28 Oct 1627 m 20 Aug 1675 Arend Muys Holy.
5 Elifabeth de Wit b 28 Aug 1630 m 11 Nov 1633 Johan Talyarde b 4 Jul 1629 d 24 Jun 1657 3 chn.
6 Willem de Wit b 16 Oct 1633 **single**.
7 Adriaan de Wit b 18 Feb 1636 d 21 Mar 1650.
8 Anna de Wit b 27 Jan 1638 m 27 Oct 1671 Willem Brandivyk van Blokland 3 chn.

de WITT
1.1.4.1.1.2.9.9.4 Willem de Witt m Katharina de Wilde
1 Johan de Wit m Helena Roflil.
2 Johanna de Wit m Anthoni van Keppel.

de WIT
1.1.4.1.1.2.9.9.13 Abraham de Wit m Maria van Melifdy
1 Johan de Wit He had several important jobs **single**.
2 Hayman de Wit b 11 Nov 1641 d 22 Dec 1667 **single**.
3 Willem de Wit **single**.
4 Adriaan de Wit b 17 Apr 1645 d 25 Aug 1646 **dy**.
5 Adriaan de Wit 11 Feb 1647 (d 5 Jul 1676) m 30 Jul 1675 Elifabeth Rees chn Maria b 1676 & Adriaan b 1677.
6 Thomas de Wit b 19 Jan 1649 d 30 Jul 1673 **single** Lieutenant Army.
7 Sophia de Wit.
8 Michael de Wit **dy**.

GENERATION 10
de WITT
1.1.4.1.1.2.7.4.4.2 Andries de Witt m Elifabeth van den Honert
1 Johanna de Witt b 12 Aug 1608 (d 24 Apr 1662) m 13 Sep 1637 Marten van Perfijn d 1666, 3 chn.
2 Thomas de Witt b 7 Mar 1613 (d 24 Sep 1658) m 3 Feb 1636 Elifabeth de Grenn d 10 May 1642.

de WITT
1.1.4.1.1.2.7.4.4.6 Jakob de Witt m Anna van den Corput
1 Johanna de Witt b 30 Oct 1617 m 9 Jun 1637 Jakob van Beveren b 27 Jun 1612 she had 2 chn.
2 Maria de Witt b 22 Dec 1620 m Oct 1641 Deiderik Hoeuft had 3 chn.
3 Kornelis de Witt b 25 Jun 1623 m 21 Sep 1650 Maria van Berckel b 31 May 1632.
4 Johan de Witt b 24 Sep 1625 m 16 Feb 1655 Wendela Bickers b 1636.

DEWITT: Two Dutch Statesmen Cornelis (1623-72) and Jan or John (1625-72), brothers, born in Dort, and educated at Leiden. They were sons of Jacob DeWitt, burgomaster of Dort and the town's representative in the most powerful Dutch provincial assembly, called the States. The brother made distinguished contributions to their country's history.

Cornelis and Jan supported their father in his struggle to establish the supremacy of the States over the princely House of Orange. In 1650 the De Witt brothers achieved political prominence; Cornelis became burgomaster of Dort and a member of the States of Holland; Jan was appointed the leading functionary of the town of Dort with the title of Pensionary (q.v.) and the leader of the town's deputation in the States of Holland. Three years later, during the First Anglo-Ducth War (1652-54) in which Cornelis fought as a naval commander, Jan became the Grand Pensionary of the province of Holland and, thereby, the leader of the province's deputation in the State-General of the Republic of the United Provinces as the Netherlands was then called. Jan served in that capacity until shortly before his death.
Jan De Witt is accounted one of the out-standing statesmen of his age; his tenure of office was marked by remarkable achievements in which he was ably supported by his brother. Following the conclusion of the Treaty of Westminster (1654), terminating the First Anglo-Dutch War, De Witt negotiated with Oliver Cromwell, then Protector of England, a secret treaty, called the Seclusion Act. The Act provided that the office of stadholder of Holland be left vacant; members of the House of Orange were this barred from that office. In 1660 following the restoration of the Stuarts in England, the Act of Seclusion was abrogated. Jan De Witt never the less adamantly opposed the appointment of the Prince of Orange as stadholder. The resulting friction between the Dutch and English, and a sharpening commercial and colonial rivalry between them, led to the outbreak of the Second Anglo-Dutch War (1665-67). Cornelis and Jan fought in this war as naval commanders and Jan negotiated the Treaty of Breda, terminating the war.

In 1668 Jan DeWitt negotiated an alliance of Holland, England, and Sweden, against France, but in 1672, after France had succeeded in isolating Holland diplomatically, France and England made war on Holland. The Dutch turned for leadership to William III, Prince of Orange; the De Witt brothers were repudiated, and Cornelis, after fighting against the British and French at sea, was arrested on a charge of conspiracy and sentenced to banishment. Just before his release from prison, he was visited by his brother. A mob broke into the jail and lynched both men.

The Universal Encyclopedia Vol. 7 Unicorn Publishers of New York Author Wilfred Funk Inc.

de WITT
1.1.4.1.1.2.7.4.5.1 Frans de Witt m Margareta Rutgrs
1 Jakob de Witt b 1603 (d 1653) m Oct 1630 Sufanna Wateringe.
2 Maria de Witt b 1604 d 1628 **single**.
3 Wynand de Witt b 1606 **single**.
4 Aletha de Witt b 1608 m 28 Feb 1636 Haren Neve.
5 Francoyfe de Witt b Jan 1611 (d 8 May 1663) m 1633 Francifcus Strafelius d 8 Apr 1636.

Dordrecht

de WIT
1.1.4.1.1.2.9.5.1.1 Gyfmar de Wit m Petronella Bom van Kranenburg
1. Jan de Wit **single** 2 Sufanna de Wit **single** 3 Kornelis de Wit **single** 4 Anna de Wit **single**.
5. Willem de Wit **single**.
6. Adriana de Wit m Anna van Engelen one child Gyfmar.
7. Jakoba de Wit **single**.

de WIT
1.1.4.1.1.2.9.5.2.2 Gysbert de Wit m Donna Pais d'Altro
1. Kornelis de With b 30 Jan 1647 d Sep 1671 **single**.
2. Elifabeth de With b 23 Sep 1651 d 12 Apr 1675 **single**.

de WIT
1.1.4.1.1.2.9.9.1.1. Johan de Wit m1 Petronella-Gysberta van Wouw m2 Katharina van Beaumont
1. Johan de Wit b 06 Oct 1668.
2. Herbertina de Wit b 15 Oct 1670.

de WIT
1.1.4.1.1.2.9.9.13.5 Adriaan de Wit m Elifabeth Rees
1. Maria de Wit b 1676.
2. Adriaan de Wit b 1677.

GENERATION 11
de WITT
1.1.4.1.1.2.7.4.4.2.2 Thomas de Witt m Elifabeth de Grenn
1. Maria-Elifabeth de Witt b 1638 m 1656 Otto van Limborg in the army as Luytenant-Colonel.
2. Johanna de Witt b 1640 d 26 Oct 1676 m 1663 Thomas Claypoole 5 chn
3. Kornelis de Witt in army as Luytenant-Colonel b 1641 m 1666 Elifabeth-Maria Seys d 16 Mar 1671.
4. Thomalina de Witt b 1642 **single**.

De WITT
1.1.4.1.1.2.7.4.4.6.3 Kornelis de Witt m Maria van Berckel
1. Jakob de Witt b 29 Nov 1653.
2. Johan de Witt
3. Anna de Witt b Nov 1677.
4. Maria de Witt b 19 Oct 1669.
5. Wilhelmina de Witt b 3 Jul 1671.

de WITT
1.1.4.1.1.2.7.4.4.6.4 Johan de Witt m Wendela Bickers
1. Anna de Witt b 27 Dec 1655 m 30 Jul 1675.
2. Agneta de Witt b 16 Jun 1658.
3. Maria de Witt b 27 Sep 1660.
4. Johan de Witt b 27 May 1662.
5. Jakob de Witt d 10 Nov 1667.

de WITT
1.1.4.1.1.2.7.4.5.1.1 Jakob de Witt m Sufanna Wateringe
1. Frans de Witt b 25 Dec 1631 **dy**
2. Francoyfe de Witt b 8 Jan 1634 m Karel Reynierfz
3. Jakob de Witt b 8 Jan 1634 m ?
4. Maria de Witt b 25 Jul 1635.
5. Margareta de Witt b 4 Jan 1637 m ?
6. Wynand de Witt b 17 Jul 1638.
7. Frans de Witt b 8 Sep 1639.

GENERATION 12
de WITT
1.1.4.1.1.2.7.4.4.2.2.3 Kornelis de Witt m Elifabeth-Maria Seys
1. Maria de Witt b 1670.
2. Kornelis de Witt b 1671.

A BRIEF BIBLIOGRAPHY. Codes are used in text.

ALDFG	Ancestral Line of the DeWitt Family fr Garrett Co MD
AWGNY	"Abstracts of Wills Greene County 1800-1860"
AWUCK	"Abstract of Wills of Ulster County at Kingston NY Liber c,D"
BB	Bridging Brenda a Municipal History
BDRNA	Baptisms DRC New Amsterdam 1639-1730. "Trouw Boeck"
BDSD	Beschryvinge Der Stad Dordrecht. 1677 Witt pp 1295-1334
BG	Burhans Genealogy & as ODCKU
BMODC	Baptisms and Marriages Old Dutch Church of Kingston, Ulster Co NY 1660-1809
BMRC	Blue Mountain Reformed Church, 1852-1951
BR	Butler's Rangers
BRLC	Baptismal Record Linlithgo Reformed Church Livingston, NY
BRSRC	Baptismal Records of Shokan Reformed Church
CAG	Compendium of American Genealogy Vol 6
CBRUC	Commemorative Biographical Record, Ulster County NY
CDDGC	Greene County NY Catskill, RDC, Durham First Prebyterian Church, Durham, Second Presbyterian Church, Greenville Prebyterian Church
CDHM	Calendar of (Dutch) Historical Manuscripts
CHDSS	Calendar of Historical Documents in the office of Secretary of State
CLP	Confiscation of Loyalist Properties
CMABS	Court Minutes of Albany, Beverwyck and Schenectady
CMNA	Court Minutes of New Amsterdam
CMR	Court Minutes of Rensselaerswyck Vol 1668-1673 p926
CMRF	Country Marriage Registers in Ontario, Canada 1858-1869. Frontenac
CMRLA	County Marriage Registers of Ontario, Canada 1858-1869. Lennox & Addington County
CSNB	1851 Census of Sunbury County, New Brunswick, Canada
CSUC	The Centennial of the Settlement of Upper Canada by the United Empire Loyalists (Old Loyalist List)
CWNY	Calendar of Wills NY 1626-1836
DA	The Dutch in America Fact Book
DG	"DeWitt. Godwin" Handwritten book with original photos, Buffalo NY Public Library
DFT	"DeWitt Family of Tarrytown NY, Raritan NJ, Northumberland Co PA"
DFUC	The DeWitt Family of Ulster County from NYGBR Vols 17:251-259; 18:13-21; 22:3-6
DFUSC	"The DeWitt Family of the United States and Canada"
DHHV	Dutch House in the Hudson Valley before 1776
DHSNY	Documentary History of the State of New York
DRCA	The Record of the Dutch Reformed Church of Albany, NY 1683-1809
DRCAF	Dutch Reformed Church Austin Friars, London
DRCFU	'Births and Baptisms Dutch Reformed Church at Flatbush, Ulster NY"
DRCNP	Dutch Reform Church New Platz
DRCOH	"Records RDC Oak Hill, Town of Durham, Green County, NY
DRUC	Death Records Ulster County NY 1847/50
DSS	Dutch Settlers Society #39
EHS	The Early History of Saugerties 1660-1825
ELSJ	The Early Loyalists, St John; The Origin of New Brunswick Politics
ESKC	Early Settlers of King's County, Long Iskand
FFVS	Friends, Family Vital Stats, Family Units
FSUHL	Family Source Unidentified, Hurley NY Library
FT	"Family Tree" Columns in the Old Dutch Post Star
GCHSO	Garrett County Historical Society, Oakland MD
GCPR	"Green County Probate Records"
GHF	Genealogy of the Hoffman Family
GIUC	Gravestone Inscriptions of Ulster County NY
HGC	History of Green County NY with Biographical Sketches of its Prominent Citizens 1651-1800
HJSF	Henry Jockemsz Schoonmaker (1624-1683)
HNN	History of the New Netherlands
HPCM	History of Penobscot County, Maine (South Maxfield Cemetery, Augusta ME State Library)
HRC	History of Randolph Co WVA
IGI	International Genealogical Index done by the Latter Day Saints, Salt Lake Utah

Vona (DeWitt) Smith

IK&HD	Isreal Kinney & his Descendants
JFFGD	"James Fleming Family, Genealogy of Descendants"
K&S	Katsbaan and Saugerties Reformed Church, Ulster County
£	Indicates Money as the English Pound
L &A	Lennox and Addington County ON
LCMC	Lutheran Church Marriages, St John Church, St Thomas Ontario
LFGR	Loyalist Families of the Grand River Branch UEL
LONB	Loyalist of New Brunswick
LOO	Loyalist of Ontario
LNYNJ	Passenger Lists New York and New Jersey 1600-1825
LPS	Long Point Settlers
LSCRW	Loyalists Southern Campaign American Revolutionary War, #1,2,3
MACNB	Maurgersville Anglican Church, NB
MBO	Marriage Bonds of Ontario 1803-1834
MC	Munsell's Collection
MCDDC	Minutes of the Commissioners for Detecting & Defeating Conspiracies in State of NY
MCFOB	Minutes of the Court of Fort Orange, Beverwyck 1652-1656
MDVEB	"Mariah (DeWitt) Van Etten's (w/o Jonas Van Etten) Bible"
MGCG	Maryland's Garrett County Graves
MLNB	Marriage Licenses Issued by John Hazen, Justice of Quorum
MNMP	More Notices From Methodist Papers 1830-1857
MNNR	Marriages of Non-Norfolk Residents by Norfolk County Ministers
MNOO	More Notices of Ontario
MRAWC	Marriage Records Zion Lutheran Church of Athens. West Camp NY 1705-1899, Paul's Lutheran Church West Camp , NY
MRDNA	Marriage Records 1639-1801 Dutch Reform Church New Amsterdam [in Dutch]
MRRCC	Marriage Records of the 1st and 2nd Reformed Church of Coxsackie NY
MSDUC	"Martin Snyder Some of his Descendents 1698-1982
MSRUC	Marbletown RDC Ulster 1737-1944 bp 1746-1944, m 1796-1930; Stone Ridge Meth m 1858-1875, bp 1875-1884
NAP	New Amsterdam and It's People #1,2
NCMR	Norfolk County Marriage Records 1795-1870
NGSQ	National Genealogical Society Quarterly, #60, 61, 57
NP	Notar Papers 1 & 2
NYDCG	New York Detailed Census of 1855 Greene County
NYGBR	New York Genealogical & Biographical Record #5, 17, 18, 21, 26, 73, 82-92
NYHMD	New York Historical Manuscript: Dutch. Kingston Papers #1-3
NYHSC	New York Historical Society Collection 24-42 NY Wills to 1784
NYM	New York Marriages Previous to 1784
ODCKU	Old Dutch Church Kingston NY Baptisms and Marriages 1810-1909
ODNGG	Obituaries, Death Notices and Genealogical Gleanings from the Saugerties Telegraph
OFG	Oosterhout Family Genealogy
OGUC	Old Gravestones of Ulster County, NY
OHSC	Oakland Historical Society Collection MD
OMN	Ontario Marriage Notices
OPR	Ontario Papers and Records
OS	Osterhout Ulster County Genealogical Society Collection
OU	Olde Ulster #1-10
P-DR	Peltz-DeWitt Record; P-DS 1st Peltz-DeWitt Supplement; 2nd Supplement- Schoonmaker Record
RMMMW	Records Minisink-Mackeneck, Minisink, Wolpeth Church Records may also be MMW
PRDC	Plattekill Reformed Dutch Church 1835-1883
PSLPS	Pioneer Sketches of Long Point Settlement
QCNBM	Queens County New Brunswick [Canada] Marriages Volume A 1812-1861
RDCFH	First RDC Fishkill, Hopewell, Dutchess Co. 1731-1850
RDCFU	Births and Baptisms Dutch Reform Church at Flatbush, Ulster NY
RDCOH	Records RDC Oak Hill Town of Durham, Greene County, NY
RKAF	Rowley-King and Allied Families
RNA	Records of New Amsterdam #1, 2
RRCAU	The Rochester R(D)C 1736-1901 Accord, Ulster NY & Accord Meth

RRCR	Rhinebeck Reformed Church Records
SCCWC	Stoney Creek Cemetery, Wentworth County ON
SCMC	"Sunbury County, NB Canada Marriage Certificates
SCMR	"Sunbury County, NB Canada Marriage Register
SCNB	1851 Census Sunbury County New Brunswick
SDVSW	Smith-DeWitt-Vanwart-Scott-Wooden
SINY	Scandinavian Immigrants in New York 1630-74
SPLWC	St Pauls Lutheran Church, West Camp
SR	Settlers of Rensselaerswyck 1630-56
TCWW	The Catskills from Wilderness to Woodstock
TFFVS	The Friendly Family Vital Stats
UCPR	Ulster County New York Probate Records 1,2
UCRRR	United Church Records Roblin, Richmond ON 1823 – 17 May 1906
VSNBN	Vital Statistics from New Brunswick Newspapers
VTAL	Van Tassel and Allied Family Lines (1574-1974)
WHS	Publications of the Woodstock Historical Society 14/5
WLD	Wills of London District ON 1800-1839
WMBLA	Wesleyan Methodist Baptisms 1834-1898 Lennox and Addington Co ON

Abittir
　Gordon D 75
Acker
　Charles 164, 197
　Elda 197
　Nelda 222
Ackert
　Andrew 31
　Elizabeth 101, 122
　Issac D 31
　Maria 31
Ackles
　Marlene L 203, 229
Adams
　John D 148, 180
　Jr John D 180
　Lillian 186
　Margaret R 179
　Walter 48
Aden
　Fred 170
Agrille
　Ida Bates 182
Aiton
　David A 156
Albersen
　Hendrick 21
Alexander
　Bertha G 167, 194
　Charles 113, 137, 167
　Charles F 167, 194
　Douglas H 194
　Edwin 167, 196
　Esmond S C 167
　Gladys M 194
　Gordon T 194
　Harry H G 166, 194
　Ida S 167
　John 103
　Katherine L 161, 188
　Lillie A 167, 194
　Lorena 194, 219
　Marion E 194
　Mattie 139
　Minnie H 167
　Thomas W 137, 167
Allan
　Christopher R R 238
　Justen D J 238
　Nicholas R 238
　Ronald J 229, 238
　Dennis 210
　Edith 219
　Elaine 219
　Elizabeth 219
　Gordon 195, 219
　Raymond 219
Alysworth
　Sarah A 127
Amberg
　Erwin 159

　Irwin 187
　Loel 187, 214
　Shelley 214
Anderson
　Otto 178
　Robert 199
　Joshua 92
Andriessen
　Barbara 17, 21
　Christian 21
　Hendrick 21
　Jan 21
　Lucas 21
　Marritje 21
Andriessenborn
　Geertuy 21
Andrieszen
　Barbara 15
Anson
　Richard 40
Antinolli
　Henry V 52
　Henry 50, 52
　Lisa Marie 52
Arajo
　Naomi 229
Arbitter
　Bernice E 77, 78
　Gordon D 77
　Helen M 77, 78
Arden
　Almeda J 198
　C Melvin 223
　F Thomas 223
　Fred 198
　Fred D 198, 223
　Marilyn S 223
　Melfin O 198
　Phyllis R 198
　Ruth O 198
Arias
　Umberto 182, 209
Armstrong
　Annie 141
　Bruce 141
　Clifford 200
　Clifford R 171
　Elijah G 199
　Elizabeth A 199
　Eluah G 171
　Evelyn G 199
　Gertrude E 171
　Gladys R 171, 199
　Henry 62
　Hugh W 171
　Jean G 171, 200
　John 200
　John N 171
　Joseph W 171, 199
　Ruth 200, 226
　Ruth E 171

　Ruth L 141
　S Joseph 141
　S Joseph H 116
　Samena 141
　Samuel G 171, 200
　Samuel J 141, 171
　Toni 199
　Wayne 200
　Will D 141
Arnold
　Carolyn 210
　Edward 144, 177
　Frank 144
　George J 170
Artes
　Carolyn 217
　Gordon 193, 217, 235
　Grant 235
　Marilyn 217
　Norman 192, 217
Arujo
　Naomi 238
Ashby
　Emma V 75
　Marie 74
Ashley
　Emma V 72
　Jane C 90, 105
　Thomas 63
Aubin
　Alvine 220, 236
　Dianne 196, 221
　Murielle 196, 221
　Odian 196
　Stephen 196
Baasch
　Henry 178
Backer
　Nelly 100
　Petrus 100
Backert
　Elizabeth 35
Backhouse
　Adelaide 103
　Cornelius 103
　Edward 103
　Emma 103
　Hannah 103
　James R 102
　Jemima 102
　John 89
　John D 102, 103
　John Jr 103
　Lucretia 103
　Mary Ann 103
Backus
　Arthur 48
Badgerow
　Gail 224
Bailely
　Shirley C 209

Bailey
  Abraham W 108
  Annie 112, 128, 135
  Aramenta 127
  Benjamin S 108, 128, 150, 181
  Bliss B 128
  Catharine 155
  Charles A 127
  Charles J 108, 128
  Colinda 128
  Dorothy I 150, 181
  Elizabeth L 208, 233
  Ephriam M 108
  Estella M 150, 181
  Ethel F 181
  Ethel M 150
  Eva 155
  Evelyn M 181, 208
  Ewart G 150, 182
  George 128
  George R 150
  Gideon D 108
  Gideon D 128
  Harold B 181
  Hayward D 128
  Ida Pearl 150, 181
  James 185
  John 92, 108
  John T 108, 127
  Karin R 209
  Kenneth R 182, 209
  Kevin R 209
  Lelsie O 150
  Leona 128
  Leslie A 181, 208
  Leslie O 128, 150, 180
  Levina A 128
  Luke E 108
  Mabel C 150
  Mabel O 181
  Martha 128
  Mary A 128
  Mary C 182, 209
  Matilda 108
  Melissa H 128
  Murray 155
  Olive Y 128
  Otto A 128
  Phoebe E 108, 128
  Shirley C 182
  Sophia 128
  Tanya K 209
  Thomas W 209
  Verina 125
  William 155, 185
Baines
  Andrew D 197, 222
  Clement A 170, 197
  Linda 222
  Nicole D 222
  Nigel E 222
Baker
  Elizabeth 100
  Elsie J 224
  Jr Johannes 100
  Nancy 51, 52
  William 166
Bakker
  Abraham 100
  Annetje 100
Balbon
  Lowy 23
  Maria 25
Baldon
  Lowy 25
Baldwin
  Basil G 73, 76
  Dean D 76
  Jr Cyril 187, 214
Ball
  Hazen 197
  Seymour 170
Bamfield
  III John M 199
Baransky
  Jan 233
Barker
  Edna Belle 143, 174
Barnes
  Harrison 49, 51
  Harrison B 51
  Helen M 51
  Lillie 66, 70
Barnett
  Alberta M 144, 177
Barry
  Robert 180, 207
  Sheila 207
Bartholomew
  Abram 35
Bast
  John 182, 209
Batchelor
  Edward 136
Bauchard
  Albert 186
Baxter
  Anne 79
Bays
  Myra M 172, 201
Beals
  Everett 186
Beam
  Adam 120, 145
  Catherine A 145
  Edgar G 145
  James A 145
Beaman
  Martha 57
Beard
  Elizabeth 119

Beauchesne
  Luc 221
Beaulieu
  Douglas 212
  Marly 212
  Nelson 185, 212
  Sonya 212
Beck
  Elias 54, 59
  John 59
  Phoebe Jane 101, 121
  Polly 59
Becker
  Johannes 100
  Jr Johannes 88
Beery
  Benjamin E 239
  Christopher R 231, 239
  Curtis W 231
  Cynthia J 231
  Jan S 206, 231
Beesmer
  Arthur 48
  Eva 48
Bell
  Alice 155, 185
  Annie 162
  Ansley 161
  Beaumont 162, 189
  Ben 134, 162
  Charles A 134, 162
  Chester 45
  Dorothy M 162, 189
  Eldon 162, 189
  Elmer 189
  Elmer W 162
  Ethel 162, 189
  George 162
  George M 134, 162
  Hattie 162, 189
  Inez 162
  James 136
  John I 162
  Joyce 162, 189
  Marion 162
  Olive 181, 208
  Pauline 162, 189
  Simeon 162
  Thomas 112, 134, 136, 189
  Thomas D 134, 162
  Verna E 189, 215
  William 160
Belyea
  Annie 109, 131
  Ella 183
  Ruth 155
Bemis
  Catharine 223, 237
  Isreal H 128

Benedict
    Robert 204, 230
Benish
    Dianne 214
    John 187, 214
    Jr John H 214
    Loel 214
    Susan 214
Benjamin
    Francis C 36
Benn
    Charles H 43, 48
    Herman F 48
    Katie M 48
    Maggie 48
    Nettie 48
    Raymond 48
Bennet
    Patrick 191
Bennett
    Augusta D O 182
Bentham
    Mary 146
Benton
    Raymond 47
Berg
    Joseph B 169
    Louis 118
Berry
    Florence 190
    William F 239
Bigger
    John 187
Binkley
    II Rollin M 77, 78
    III Rollin M 78
    Rhonda Marie 78
    Tacon 78
Binner
    Elline D 52
    Fred 52
    Lynella A 52
    Mark F 52
Birch
    Frank 79
Birmingham
    Guy 131, 156
    Haddon P 129
    Hazel 156
    Mary 156
Bishop
    Pauline A 190
    Stanley 197
Bittner
    Alfred F 75
Black
    Mary S 177, 205
Blackburn
    Lynn A 201, 226
Blackmore
    Sadie 167
    Norton 148
Blackwell
    Mary A 27, 35
Blair
    Russell H 168
Bland
    Annie L 146, 178
Blizzard
    Brent 217
    Clark 217
    Kris 217
    Tracy 192, 217
Block
    Catherine A 206, 231
Blois
    Eugene 188, 215
    Jennifer Lee 215
Boardus
    Roberta 205
Boehen
    Henry 136
Bogardus
    Adorum 119, 144, 145, 177
    Albert 144
    Amy C 178
    Ann 144
    Anna V 145
    Art 177
    Arthur D 144
    Arthur P 144, 177
    Asa 144
    Benjamin 119, 145
    Betty 177
    Carol J 205
    Catharine 119
    Chad L 230
    Charlotte 144, 177
    Clarence E 177
    Cornelia 119, 144
    Cornelius 17, 119
    Cynthia 119, 144, 145
    Cynthia J 205
    Dean B 230
    Deborah J 205, 230
    Delmar 177
    Donald E 205, 230
    Dora 144
    Doris 177
    Douglas 206
    Earl F 177
    Edward S 144, 177
    Ethel H 177
    Francis 97, 119, 144, 145
    Frederick F 144, 177
    Frederick W 177, 205
    Gay L 206
    George D 178, 206, 231
    Grace H 177
    Gracie 145
    Harold E 177, 205, 230
    Harold H 177
    Harold J 230
    Heather M 231
    Helen A 144
    Helen E 177
    Henry 119, 144
    Henry O 144, 177
    Ida 144, 177
    Ira 144
    Irene A 177
    Jacqueline E 177
    James E 144
    James F 177
    Jean I 177, 206
    Jeffrey P 230
    Jill Ann M 177, 205
    John 144
    John A 205
    John T F 230
    Jr Benjamin 145
    Jr Donald E 230
    Jr George D 206
    Jr Harold E 205
    Jr Russell E 205
    Jule W 177, 205
    Julia 144, 177
    Kriss M 230, 238
    Laura 144
    Laura K 177, 205
    Lena G 144, 177
    Lewis B 145
    Lillian 144
    Lillian B 178
    Linda L 205
    Lloyd C 177
    Louise A 177, 205, 230
    Lucinda 145
    Mabel 144
    Margaret J 177, 205
    Margaret L 177
    Maria 119, 144
    Marilyn J 205
    Mary G 205
    Nora 145
    Orville E 177
    Peter 119, 144, 145
    Peter J 230
    Peter W 205, 230
    Phillip 119, 144
    Phillip L 144, 177
    Phyllis 205
    Phyllis R 177, 205
    Rebecca L 230
    Richard D 205, 230
    Robert K 230
    Russell E 177, 205
    Russell H 144, 177
    Ruth T 178, 206
    Tamara G 231
    Thelma I 177, 207
    Thomas S 230

Bogardus
  Verona 145
  Violet M 144
Boice
  Susan A 61, 65
Boight
  Marjorie 180
  Miriam 149
Bolinger
  Joseph 74
Bond
  Joseph 36
Boone
  Abigail 114, 138
  Abraham 94
  Absolom 13i7
  Ann 113, 136
  Annie 138
  Annie J 138
  Annie T 168
  Annis L 138
  Arminta 167
  Barletta A 138
  Burpee 138, 194
  Burton H 137, 166
  Catharine 109, 113, 129
  Charles 114
  Charles E 137
  Christina 134, 163
  Dayman 138
  Earl 194
  Ebenezer 94
  Edward A 137, 166
  Elizabeth 113
  Ella J 138
  Elzer 138
  Eric 196
  Everett 113
  Everett D 113
  Evert D 94
  Frances 194
  George 114
  George F 137
  George W 166, 194
  Gertrude 113, 137
  Grace 155, 186
  Hannah 113, 114, 136, 137, 138, 139
  Hannah A 136
  Hannah L 114
  Harvey 137
  Henry 94, 113, 137
  Herbert P 137
  Ida Mae 138, 168
  James 94, 114, 138
  James E 113, 137
  John 94, 113, 114, 137, 138
  John C 114
  John L 137
  Jr Everett 137
  Lavina I 167
  Lemuel 113
  Lillan 137
  Loreen 194
  Loren G 166, 194
  Martha 194
  Mary 113, 137
  Mary Ann 113, 114, 137
  Mary E 137, 138, 166, 167
  Mary M 137
  Melburn O 138
  Melvin 167
  Merle 166, 194
  Mona 166, 194
  Murray 94
  Olive O 138
  Rachel 114
  Ralph 194
  Reuben 167
  Reuben A 138, 167
  Richardson 114, 138
  Roy 194
  Roy A 194
  Roy Angus 166
  Ruth 113, 194
  Ruth A 114
  Ruth C 137
  Samuel 83, 94, 113, 114
  Sarah 113, 137
  Sarah A 138
  Sherman W 138
  Shirley 194
  Spafford 167
  Spafford B 138
  Susan 113
  Trietha 138
  Victoria A 137
  Violetta A 137
  W Murray 113,138
  William 94, 113, 114
  Catharine 136
Booten
  John 180
  John G 149, 180, 207
  Mary V 180, 207
  Susan V 207
Borhans
  Catharina 25, 29
  Jannetjen 25, 30
  Richard 23, 25
Bossard
  Aaron L 146
  Alexander 146
  Mary E 146
  William D 121, 146
  Wilson 146
Botts
  Lydia L 107, 127
Bouchard
  Albert 213
  J 213
  Lori Ann 213
  Sheri Lynn 213
  Wendi 213
Bouck
  Frederick 103
  Maria 25, 29
Bougt
  Catherine J 232
Bourget
  Catherine J 208
  John C 208
  Joseph L 181
  Leonard J 208
Bovee
  Franklin 41
  Frederick 41
  Nelson 41
  Pliny L 35, 41
Bowen
  Grace M 144, 177
Boyer
  Emma 66
  Emma L 70
  Sam 129
Boyes
  Ralph 173
Bradford
  Lulu 71
  Michael 51
Bradshaw
  Valerie A 207, 232
Brady
  Bessie 71
  Martha 119
Bragg
  Helen 170
Brando
  Abram 103
Branscombe
  Hannah 108, 128
  Rachel 108, 128
Brawn
  Darlene 220
  Eric F 220
  H Avery 220
  Hazen F 195, 220
  Keith 220
  Leslie 194
  Lorraine 220
  Sharon 215, 235
Breau
  Noreen 218
Breed
  Mary B 149
Breestede
  Jan 21
Breesteed
  Mary 82, 90
Brennaman
  George 70

Brennaman
　John 70
Bresnen
　Jeremy T 229
Brewin
　A C 188
Brewster
　Gail P 201, 226
Bridgen
　Anna M 90, 104
Brierly
　Sharon 200
Briggs
　Eugene 183
　Evelyn 183
　Fay 183
　George 129
　Hannah 108, 128
　Lewis 152, 183
　Marjorie A 181, 208
　Leona 183
Brigham
　Conna 78
Brink
　Margaret E 100, 121
　Peter 101
Brinner
　Fred 51
Britt
　Ira 38
Britton
　Lorne 156
Brobst
　Thomas 74
Broderick
　Joe 136
Brossen
　Charlotte 50, 51
Broughten
　Rex V 181
Brown
　Arthur 178
　Caroline 103
　Carter W 221
　Dale 178
　Dorothy 166, 191
　Douglas N 221
　Irene 163, 190
　Kent S 228
　Mark A 221
　Mary Ann 196, 221
　Nora 134
　Richard W 196, 221
　Stanley 202, 228
Browning
　Mary 63
　Thomas 63
　William 62
Bruce
　Beatrice 170
　Bertha 140

Bruck
　Ruth A 206
Bruhn
　Mary Ellen 51, 52
Brumleu
　Lori 230
Bryant
　Elizabeth 65
Bryce
　E Jane 170
　Emma J 140
Bryn
　John 32
Bubar
　Harold 188
Buck
　Brian 229
　Bruce 204, 229
　Jennifer D 229
　Kimberly D 229
Buckingham
　Obadiah 112
Bucklow
　J 63
Budd
　Emerson 169
Bunge
　Louise W 120, 146
Bunker
　Brian 190
　Burton 163, 190
　Frank 134, 163
　Gerald 190
　Gordon 163
　James 190
　Kathie M 190
　Oliver 163
　Ralph 190
　Ruby 163, 190
　Sophia 139, 168
　Wesley 190
　William 190
Burger
　Catherine 98
　Jones 31
Burgher
　Eliza 31
　Sally 31
Burham
　John 109
Burhans
　Annetje 35
　Augtustus H 36
　Catharina 28
　Catharine A 106
　Clara C 38
　Clinton 106
　Denslow 36
　Edgar W 32, 38
　Edward 91, 106
　Edwina 106

　Elizabeth 106
　Ephriam 44, 106, 126
　Frank W 38
　George 38
　Hendrick 36
　Hendrikus 29
　Hezekiah S 106
　Hiram 38
　Louisa 39, 44, 106, 126
　Marie 106
　Maritje 35
　Mary Jane 38
　Mary M 38
　Sara 34
　Sarah 27, 35, 41
　Sarah J 106
　Wilhelmus 28, 35
Burke
　Amos 44, 49
　Helen R 173, 202
　Muriel E 204, 229
Burlock
　Carleton 152, 183
　Harmon 183
　Hilman 183
　Laurence 183
　Llewllyn 183
Burnett
　Bloyce 196
　Brian 196
　Clarence 168
　Daryl 195, 220
　Donald 196
　Edison 196
　Elva 135, 168
　Harry 168, 196
　Hartley 168
　Henry 139, 168
　Hilda 195, 220
　Lloyd 195, 220
　Myrtle 168
　Raymond 195, 220
　Reta 195. 220
　Theda 195, 220
　Wendy 220
Burnette
　Clarence 195
　Clarence E 167
Burns
　Mary Ann P 67
　Mary Price 63
Burton
　Robert E 205
　Viola M 161, 188
Burtt
　George 215
Bush
　Aldert 58
　Anny 58
　Benjamin 54, 58
　Elizabeth 58

Bush
Eva 58, 61
Jacob 31
John 58
Jonathan W 58
Leslie 48
Magdalene 61, 65
Mary 58
Buswell
Bethia G 108, 129
Butcher
Hazel 188
John S 188
Samuel J 161
Butler
George V 179, 207
Richard V 207
Buttimer
James 211
Bye
Verla M 208
Byers
Doris 193
Caddie
Murray 186
Cain
Charles W 144, 177
Elizabeth 177, 206
Caldwell
Caroline G 125, 149
Jenny 156
Cale
Frederick 144
Cambon
Kenneth 219, 236
Marie 236
Noreen 236
Campaigne
Edith 173
Campbell
Armina 195
Frances L 205, 230
Ray 72
Cantlin
Catherine M 180
Carbone
Mary 181, 208
Carey
Stephen P 202
Carhart
Isaac 104
Carl
George 169
Carle
Andrew 34
Emma L 47
Lavina C 35, 41
Mary A 41, 46
Rufus 38
Silas 37

Carleton
Gary R 226
John W 200, 226
Lydna A 226
Carman
Peggy 54, 59
Carpenter
Donna 212
Lulu 155, 187
Carr
Abigail 137
Clarence 167
F Olive 137
Florence 164, 191
George O 137
James 137
L Thomas 137
Laura 137
Martha M 137
Mary Ann 137
Norma L 218
Otis 137
Sarah L 137
Victoria 137
William 137
William A 113, 137
Carter
Louann 220, 236
Randoloph 190
Casavant
Ronald 218
Case
Hugh 137
Jerusha 99, 121
Cassel
Peg 44
Casteel
Archibald 59
Elizabeth 59, 63, 69
Hamel 66, 70
Harland 70
Louisa 59, 62
Sarah 59, 63
Cato
Janet 79
Caton
Angeline 107
Angeline E 127
Cattle
Joseph 102
Cavanaugh
Bonita 188, 214
Chaffe
Jr Herbert G 49
Chaltron
Charlotte M 181, 208
Chambers
Francis 216, 235
Hannah E 63, 68
James A 116
Tracy L 235

Champion
Charles P 208
Harry R 181, 208
Patricia A 108, 232
Chapman
I M 120
Charlton
Addie 161, 188
Elena J 135, 163
Lucinda 134, 162
Stella 162, 189
Charnley
Marion 159
Charters
Archie 168
Milford 168
Chauncey
Francis A 51
Chauncy
Charles 52
Daniel 52
Francis A 52
Kimberly 52
Lia 52
Trina 52
Christiansen
Ava C 202, 227
Hjalmar 173, 202
Lori L 227
Ole I 202
Rae G 202
L 227
Christie
Bob 168
Katherine 192, 218
Christriansen
Ole I 227
Christy
Jenny J 71, 74
Chumbley
Charles E 230
Deborah A 205
Herman 177, 205
Marshall L 230
Mary A 205, 230
Nancy E 205, 230
Nathan G 230
Robert G 205, 230
Church
Kenneth 211
Churchill
Eunice 116, 141
Mary 130, 155
Clark
Alvery 74
Amy 136
Barbara 208, 233
Christopher D 214
Deborah 156
Edna N 156
Elise 72, 76

Clark
  Helen 182, 209
  Johnson W 156
  Jonathan 187, 214
  Jr Jonathan 214
  Mary Jane 114
  Wilmot 131, 156
Clarke
  Lillian 166
  S Maude 141, 171
Clarkson
  Myrna M 192, 217
Clay
  Harriet L 66
Cleaves
  George M 190
Cleghorn
  Emily 190, 216
  Eva 168, 196
Cleveland
  Bonnie J 206
  Catherine 206
  Howard D 177, 206
Clifford
  Grace M 168, 196
  John 138
  Lewis 183
Clinch
  Arthur 191
Clowater
  Robert 210
Cluff
  J Edward 186, 212
  Jody 212
  Joyce 186
  Keith 212
  LeRoy F 186, 212
  Marion 186, 212
  Mary Ann 212
  Richard 212
  Roy 155, 186
Clukey
  Geneva M 190
Clymer
  Jacqueline R 205, 230
Coates
  John A 103
Coborn
  Adam 197
  Andrew 222
  Ellen 197
  Jane 197
  John 197
  Andrew 222
  Gordon 170, 197
  John 222
  Nancy 222
Cochrane
  Charles 163, 189
  Helen 189
  Muriel 189
  Norma 189
Coenius
  Margaret 101
Cogswell
  Mary 94, 114
Cole
  Sarah 49
  Sarah E 45
Coleman
  Alfred B 140, 170, 197
  Allan B 197, 222
  Candy 222
  Dolores Y 76
  Emeline 64, 69
  Jr Allan B 222
  Kathleen D 170
  M Elizabeth 170, 197
  Mary E 170, 197
  Norman 170
  Samena 170, 198
  Wallace G 197
Coles
  Abraham 47
Collier
  Harriet 63, 66
Collins
  Eleanor 50
  Fred W 45, 50
  James R 51
  Robert 50, 51
  Mary 40
  Mae 133
Colter
  Mae 161
Colvin
  S Diane 203, 228
Colwell
  Hiram M 69
Compaigne
  Edith L 143
Conklin
  Isaac 121
Conley
  Cheryl L 207, 232
  John E 181, 207
  Nancy A 207
  Richard A 207
  Robert W 207
Conlon
  Margaret 116, 140
Connell
  Edward H 197
Connelly
  Anna 47
  Genevieve 73, 76
Conyes
  Anna E 101
  Carrie L 147
  Elizabeth 88, 100
  George 122
  Henry S 122, 147
  J Lemuel 126
  Jacob H 122
  James D 122
  Jason 122
  Mellisa C 122
  Rachel J 101
  Sarah Ann 122
  Sarah C 122
  William D 126
  William H 122
  Zacharias 88, 100, 101
Cook
  Albert 62
  Rachel L 165, 192
Cooper
  Alma 234
  Lewis 185, 211
Corey
  Caroline J 95, 117
  Florence E 187
  Mary C 95, 118
Corliss
  Zina B 190
Cormier
  Jr Robert 214
  Robert 187, 214
Cornelisz
  Tjaetje 15
Cornish
  George J 106
Costello
  Walter 135
Cote
  Arlene 182, 210
Countryman
  Abraham 89, 102, 103
  Fedella 103
  Valetta 103
Cowan
  Cathy 51, 52
  Harley G 149
Cowie
  Anne 214
  Annie E 138, 167
  Jr Robert 188, 214
  Robert 214
  Robert A 161, 188
  Ronald 214
Coy
  Douglas 190
Craft
  William 42
Cram
  John 195
Cramer
  Charles 41, 46
  Viola B 46
Crandlemire
  Ann-Marie 238
  Richard 229, 238

Crane
  Gertie 185
  Gertrude 155
Crawford
  Amy 182
  Willie 150, 182
Creekmore
  Betty 95, 115
Cripps
  Anne 197
  Joan D 197
  William 197
Crispell
  Sarah 91
Crispin
  Franklin G 146
Crombie
  Allan 188
  Annie 133
  Charles 160, 188
  Claire 188
  Dianne 188
  Donald 188
  Donald L G 160
  Donna 188
  Ellen 188
  Ford C 160, 188
  Henry 133
  Kenneth 188
  Leslie 188, 214
  Marcus 133, 160
  Richard 188
  Vaughn 188
  Wade 214
  Wanda 214
  Wayne 188
Cronk
  Samantha A 107, 127
Crop
  William 170
Cropley
  Isabella 97, 119
Crossby
  Cyril 171
Crowe
  Karen 204, 229
Cruickshanks
  James 104, 124
  John D 124
  Mary S 124
Cruikshank
  David 216
  Debbie 216
  John 216
  Neil 190, 216
  Sandra 216
Culbane
  Layola 186, 213
Culberson
  Annie 155
  Carle 156
  Ernest 156
  Faye 156
  Ferne 156
  Ronald 156
  William 156
  William E 131
Culbertson
  Annie 130
  Edna 187
Cunias
  Jacob H 101
  Sarah C 101
Cunyes
  Francis E 147
  Lemuel 105
  Rachel 126
Currie
  Donald A 233
  Gloria 192, 218
  Henry J 233
  Henry R G 208, 233
  Milton 192, 218
  Ronald M 181, 208, 233
  Jerome 218
  Mary 195, 219
Curtis
  Phyllis L 148, 179
  Polly 28, 36
Custer
  Alice 72
  Charles A 75
  Elma G 75, 77
  George R 75
  Homer D 72, 75
  Homer R 75
  III Emmanuel 68, 72
  Laura M 75
  Lulu Mae 75
  Virginia A 75
Cuthbertson
  Edna 156
Cutler
  Stanley 133
D Wiet
  Cornelis 56
d Wit
  Marytjen 80
Daily
  Julia 39
Daley
  Christopher 235
  Heather 235
  Kevin 215, 235
  Kevin A 235
  Lonnie 217
  Shawn 235
Dam
  Maritje 21
Dartmouth
  Irene 202

Davidson
  Audrey 191, 221
Davies
  John L 125
  Keith 179
Davis
  Ann 54, 57
  Bertha 137, 138, 146
  Charlotte 146
  Clark 121, 146
  Elizabeth 61, 65
  Ethiel 102
  Eugene H 146
  Lena 167, 194
  Lottie R 134, 161
  Maggie 129, 15
  Maud 146
  Minerva 146
  Rachel 54, 58
  Sanford 146
  William 193
Day
  Marion 196
de la Montange
  Peter 26, 31
Dean
  Brent W 225
  Constance M 225
  Denna M 225
  Lori J 225
  Marvin R 225
  Melvin 200, 225
  Muriel 200, 225
  Pearl M 76, 77
  Phyllis A 200, 225
  Ralph E 200, 225
  Wilson 171, 200
Deas
  Rhoda 148, 17
DeBolt
  Amanda B 72, 76
Decker
  Annatje 34
  Blandina 34
  Catharine 27, 33, 34, 40
  Cornelis S 34
  Cornelius L 34
  Elizabeth 41
  Elizabeth A 35
  Hannah M 34
  Harrietta 34
  Isaac 27, 34
  Isaac P 34
  Jane C 34
  Jane M 34
  Jeremiah R 34
  John I 27, 34
  Peter H 34
  Sophia 34
Dederick
  Catharine 90

Dedrich
  Joseph 123
Dedrick
  Abraham 102
  Abram S 123, 148
  Austin 102, 123
  Barbara 179
  Catharine 82, 89, 102, 103, 123
  Charles 102
  Christian 82, 90
  Cornelius 89, 102, 103
  Elias 90
  Elizabeth 103
  Emma 103
  Emma E 103
  Florence M 148, 179
  Francis V 148, 179
  George W 103
  Hannah 89, 102, 103
  Hannah C 102
  Harriet 102
  James 89, 103
  James W 102
  Jane 102, 103
  Jennie May 123
  Jerusha J 102
  John 89, 90, 102
  John W 103, 123
  Jr John 102
  Lois 179
  Louise J 102
  Lucas 89, 90, 103
  Lucy 123
  Luke 102, 103
  Mary 103
  N Lucretia 102
  Nancy A 103
  Rebecca 103
  Sally 102
  Salome 103
  Samuel 102
  Susan 102
  Theresa 102
  Warren S 123
  William 102
  William W 102
Delamater
  Anna 57
  Rachel 57
Delevan
  Aletha A M 48
Dell
  Charlotte 97, 119
  Jane 97
Dellamea
  Nicole B 78
  Victor 78
Delva
  Annatje 17, 22
DeMarco
  Michele A 206

DeMerchant
  Charles 151
Dench
  Melissa 102, 123
Depp
  Wesley 179
Depuy
  Sally 59, 62
DeSaulniers
  Margaret E 190, 216
Detlor
  Titus S 107
Dewid
  Jacob 91
D Wiet
  Cornelis 55
deWit
  Abraham 80, 82
DeWit
  Abraham P 92
deWit
  Aefje 17
Dewit
  Andrew 82
deWit
  Anna M 80, 82
  Annaatjen 80, 82
DeWit
  Annetie 55
  Ariaantje 55
  Ariantje 55
Dewit
  Arie 53
deWit
  Benjamin 53, 55
DeWit
  Catharina 94
  Charles 92
  Cornelis 53
  Deborah 99
deWit
  Evert 80, 83
DeWit
  Ezeckiel 53
  Geertrui 93, 92
  Hannah 56
  Henry 55, 93
  Issac 94
deWit
  Jacob 17, 53
  Jan 22, 53, 91
  Jan Lucas 80, 82
  Jannetjen 22, 80
DeWit
  Jean A 212
  Jeremias 56
  Joel 56
  Johannes 53, 56
  John 55, 82, 90
Dewit
  John I 90

  Joseph 82
deWit
  Leucas 17, 22, 80
DeWit
  Lewis V 55
deWit
  Lucas 80
DeWit
  Luke 92
deWit
  Luycas 22
DeWit
  M Agnes 134
  Maria 53, 54, 56
deWit
  Marritje 17
DeWit
  Mary 94
  Mary G 92
  Nancy 94
deWit
  Peek 17
DeWit
  Peter 55
  Petrus 53
  Phoebe 92, 94, 95
  Rachel 17, 82, 90
  Solomon 94
  Temperence 93
  Thomas D 92
deWit
  Tjerck 17
DeWit
  Wilhelm 53
  Willem 56
deWith
  Andries 17
  Geertruyed 17
  Jan 17
  Jannetjen 17
  Klaes 17
  Peter 84
  Taatje 17
  Tierck Claeszen 15
  Tierck Claszen 21
DeWitt
  A Eliza 126
  A Esther 116
  A Semore 127
  Aaron C 99
  Abel 68
  Abigail 95, 116, 129, 136, 140, 180, 222
  Abraham 59, 62, 83, 87, 90, 92, 93, 99, 106, 107
  Abraham A 126
  Abraham H 105, 126
  Abraham P 108
  Abraham T 112, 133
  Abraham V D 123, 148
  Abram 62

DeWitt
Ada 71
Ada B 125, 133
Ada T B 104
Adaline 67
Addie 145
Addie S 129
Adelia A 99, 121
Adeline 120
Adeline M 129
Albert 71, 74, 120, 127, 145
Albert E 190, 216
Albert J 126, 149
Albert O 216
Albert R 135, 163
Albert S 67
Alberta 67
Alberta M 75
Alenith 118
Aletha I 200
Alexander 66, 70, 99, 223
Alford O 135
Alfred 135, 168
Alice 65, 66, 71, 93, 126
Alice A 136, 157, 186, 213
Alice M 134, 178, 207
Alice Mae 181
Allan L 204
Alleyne 131
Alma 71, 136, 202
Alma A I 172
Alonzo D 155
Alvin 183, 210
Amanda 107
Amy 67
Amy E 77
Anastasia 165
Andrew 55, 104, 106
Andrew P 134
Andries 90, 91
Angeline 152, 183
Anita 74
Ann 107
Ann E 60, 62, 91, 105, 106, 141
Ann G 67
Ann S 135
Anna 71
Anna A 127
Anna G 129, 140
Anna J 109, 130
Anna M 104, 124
Anna V 136
Annatje 97
Anne F 135
Annetje 99
Annette 142
Annice 165
Annie 115, 126, 129, 130, 133, 149, 155, 159, 160
Annie J 135
Annie L 157

Annie R 132
Anninnett 142
Antinetta 117
Antoinett 120
Archibald 68
Archibald C 63, 66, 68
Archie S 150
Arlene 68, 70, 72, 74
Armenta 127
Arthur 64, 66, 71, 116, 186
Arthur L 126
Arthur M 124, 152
Arthur N 172, 201
Arthur R 161, 188
Arthur W 76, 188, 214
Asa S 163
Asa T 134
Ashael W 128
Aubry 71
Austin 130, 155
Azro 64
B Theodosia 164, 169
Baltus 66, 70
Barbara 191
deWitt
Barbara 22
DeWitt
Barbara C 207, 232
Barney 59
Beatrice 173
Beatrice L 73, 76
Beatrice T 136
Benedict 129
Benjamin 139, 155, 186
Benjamin F 212
Benjamin H 71, 74
Bernice E 74
Bertha C 125
Besse J 190
Bessie 149
Bessie H 186, 212
Bessie J 163
Betheul 129
Bethuel 109
Betty L 75, 77
Beulah 201
Blanche 191
Blandina 62
Bliss 71
Bordman 67
Boyd 71
Bradbury 150
Bradbury G 128
Brandon C 238
Brenda 210
Brett M 229, 238
Brian S 231
Bridget 67
Bridgett 79
Bryan G 69, 73
Bryce 198, 222

Brydon 72
Burton 183, 211
Burton M 131
C Clifford 173, 202
C Jessie 125
C Whitfield 66, 70, 74
Caleb 59, 62, 65
Carl 72, 186, 212
Carl E 77
Carl R 186, 213
Carol 76, 210
Caroline 118, 143
Caroline C 129
Caroline F 107
Carroll F 180, 207
Carson J 129
Catharina 56, 80
Catharine 74, 92, 99, 106, 108, 113, 125, 126,
Catharine A 104
Catharine E 127
Catharine S 136
Catherine 41, 63, 83, 97, 119, 155, 187
Cathrina 87
Celia 71
Chad R 78
Chambers 68, 72
Charles 62, 68, 72, 91, 98, 104, 112, 113, 146, 183
Charles A 129
Charles B 104, 163
Charles D 108, 129
Charles E 133
Charles H 74, 77, 120, 128
Charles R 72
Charles S 123
Charles T 90, 105
Charles W 118, 134, 143, 163
Charlotte 149, 164, 180
Charlotte A 135
Charlotte E 72, 75, 105, 130
Charlotte G 124, 148
Christiana S 109
Christina 62
Christine H 222
Clara 140
Clara J 112
Clara R 171, 200
Clarence 70, 71, 142
Claude 155, 186
Clayton A 142
Cleo B 74
Clifford 68, 72, 145
Clifford C 75
Clinton 65, 106, 123, 124,
Clinton J 133
Clowes S 129, 152
Clyde 71
Clyde C 73
Coleman 183

DeWitt
Coleman D 151
Cordelia 121, 125
Cornelius 60
Cornelius S 60, 64
Craig A 231
Curtis 72
Cynthia A 213
Cynthia J 62
Cyrus E 71
D Ludlow 129, 151
Daisey A 71
Daisy L 72, 76
Danie 121
Daniel 68, 72, 74, 99, 106, 109, 113, 129, 136
Daniel D 70, 76, 77, 79
Daniel W 112, 135
Danielle 78
Darrell W 77, 78
David 62, 129, 152, 186, 212
David A 72, 76
David B 188, 215
David E 225
David I 163
David O 66
David T 108, 128
David W 112, 135
Dayton 72
Debbie 225
Deborah 87
Delia 65
Delia S 120
Delilah 152
Delilah E 183
Della 74
Diane 223
Diane D 189
Diane M 188, 214, 215
Diantha 120
Dillon 78
Donald 72
Donald R 77, 78
Donna M 216, 235
Dora 71, 163
Doree 180
Dorothy 191
Dorothy C 186
Dorothy M 163
Dorr 105
E Darwin 76, 78
E Franklin 156
E May 171
E Millard M 149
E Ray 155, 187
E Verna 161
Earl 149
Edgar 120
Edith 69
Edith Mary 178
Edmund 68

Edna 72
Edna A 164
Edna L 73
Edward 120, 121, 146, 186
Edward F 68, 73
Edward H 120
Edward L 104
Edward M 157
Edward P 66
Edwards 98
Edwin 64, 117
Edwin G 128
Effie 71, 156
Eldon 187
Eleanor 165, 185
Eleanor R 165
Electra N 143
Elijah 68, 69
Elinor J 141, 172
Eliot Lee 124
Eliza 63, 99, 105, 107, 129,
Eliza J 98
Elizabeth 54, 63, 67, 91, 107, 112, 118, 126, 134, 143, 156,
Elizabeth A 115
Elizabeth C 131
Elizabeth E 215
Elizabeth M 125, 130
Elizabeth P 135, 161, 163
Ella 68, 128
Ella F 129
Ellen 68, 159
Ellen I 73
Ellis S 161, 188
Elmer 142
Elsie 71, 74
Elsie V D 148
Elsje 113
Emery J 133
Emily 120
Emily Jane 64
Emily M 200
Emily V 65
Emma 67, 68, 105, 128
Emma A 72
Emma F 163
Emma I 131, 156
Emma L 75, 77
deWitt
Emmerentjen C 15
DeWitt
Eppie E 131, 156
Eric H 200, 225
Ernest B 131, 156
Erville C 72, 76
Estella 133
Esther 71
Ethel 74, 142, 164, 165, 191, 193, 197
Etta 68
Etta R 127

Eugene 125
Eugene B 104, 125
Eugene C 69
Eugene N 73
Eunice 118, 129, 183
Evans 72
Evelyn 74, 187
Evelyn E 75
Evelyn R L 74
Evert 92, 97, 107
Ezekiel 55, 109, 130
deWitt
Faelde Claessen 15
DeWitt
Fannie 68
Faunelle 64
Flora L 178
Florence 118, 119, 143
Florence L 202, 227
Florence M 164, 191
Foster 67, 71
Frances 68, 74, 107, 127, 146
Frances C 125
Frances E 109
Frances R 178
Francis 68
Francis A 117
Frank 131, 145
Frank A 65
Frank H 125
Frank R 119
Franklin 64, 105, 123
Fraser 135
Frederick 71, 125, 127, 165, 169, 186, 213
Frederick A 69
Frederick E 136, 165
Frederick N 118, 143
Frederick S 129
Frederick W 143, 173
Fredia 70
Freeman 65
G Hamilton 112, 134
G Lyman 135
Gail I 189
Garret 123
Garth D 200, 225
Gary A 201
Geertrui 112
Gelina 135
Genevieve L 186
George 63, 64, 66, 70, 71, 72, 74, 95, 105, 118, 126, 127, 129, 133, 136, 143, 152, 165, 169, 185, 186, 191
George A 64, 69, 71, 130
George C 121, 143
George E 74, 157
George F 112, 115
George H 107, 117, 127, 131, 156

DeWitt
George Jr 118
George M 109, 131, 157
George S D133
George W 65, 72
Georgie 155
Gerald E 190, 216
Geraldine L 216, 235
Gerenia A 133, 161
Gerthrout 93
Gertroud 91
Gertrude 72, 95, 111
Gertrude J 200
Gilbert 71, 72, 76
Glen 156
Grace 41, 145
Grietje Classen 15
Guy 71
Gwendoline 186
H Clementine 134, 135, 161, 163
H Colfax 68, 73
H Leonard 135, 164, 166, 169, 194
H Sylvester 171
Hanford 134
Hannah 112, 115, 133, 134, 160
Hannah J 133
Hannah W 121
Harold D 161, 188
Harold E 75, 77, 78
Harold G 74
Harriet 91, 99, 106, 121
Harriet E 120, 145
Harris 67
Harry F 134
Hattie E 127, 149
Hattie Eudora 126
Hazel 155, 185
Hazel M 150
Hazen A 163, 190
Helen 74, 125, 148
Helen C 104
Helen G 106
Helen L 104, 124
Helen M 164
Helena R 150
Henrietta 117
Henry 59, 63, 67, 68, 83, 97, 99, 106, 108, 113, 116, 119, 120, 135, 138, 139
Henry L 129, 168
Herbert 136, 74
Herbert J 70
Hervey G 124
Hilda M 181, 208
Hiram 107, 116, 140
Hiram P (S) 198
Hiram S 141
Hiriam P 223
Holly B 232

Horace 66, 90, 104, 105, 165
Howard 72, 106
Howard L 171
Hugh H (S) 198
Hugh H 223
Hulda 63
I George 175, 204
I Robert 67
Ian 225
Ian M 200
Ida 68, 69

deWitt
Ida Claessen 15

DeWitt
Ida May 133, 160
Idella 183, 211
Ira 72, 98, 120, 127
Ira A 178
Ira C 150
Ira Clancy 127
Ira Smith 143, 174
Irene 74, 130
Irving 186
Isaac 94, 113, 115, 136, 137, 139
Isaac C 125
Isaac R 71
Isabella 64, 65, 119, 145
Isreal 99, 121
Isreal A 106
Isreal W 112, 150
J Austin 134, 161
J Catharine 105, 126
J Fred 130, 155
J Henry 143, 155, 186
J Mary 163
J Winfred 171
Jacob 68, 83, 95, 113, 115, 139
Jacob I 115
Jacob M 117
Jacob M N 142
Jacob T B 104, 125
Jacobus 87, 98, 99, 120
Jafferson 68
James 63, 68, 69, 104, 109, 117, 142, 145, 159, 186, 212
James A 130
James B 63
James G 204, 229
James H 67
James L 155, 186
James O 178
James R 75, 77
James V E 35, 41, 106, 126
James W 207, 232
Jamey D 78
Jan 222

deWitt
Jan Claetz 15

DeWitt
Jan Henry 83

Jane 63, 107, 108, 120
Jane Ann 105
Janet 157
Janette M 150
Janice 190
Jannetjen 23, 87
Japhet S 133
Jaspeth 136
Jay 225
Jean 142, 165, 172
Jean E 229
Jean F 74
Jeanette M 181
Jemima M 134
Jennett 60
Jennie 136, 152, 155, 183
Jennie J 125
Jennifer 79
Jennifer A 213
Jeremiah 60, 62, 113, 134, 136, 138, 168
Jeremiah W 112
Jeremy 136
Jeremy D 78
Jermiah 139
Jerome 68
Jessica A 214
Joan 76
Joan E 188
Joan M 200, 225
Johannes 54, 55, 91
Johathan 142
Johhanes 107
John 59, 62, 63, 66, 67, 68, 72, 87, 95, 97, 99, 104, 108, 112, 115, 116, 120, 121, 123, 124, 127, 128, 131, 134, 135, 148, 180, 186
John B 135
John C 104, 105, 123, 127, 129, 156,
John E 115
John G 107, 109, 127
John H 63, 67, 92, 109, 129, 146, 152, 163, 178, 190
John L 112, 133, 180
John T 70, 74
John V L 54, 59
John W 72, 75, 131, 156, 200
John/King 92, 109
Jon D 78
Jonathan 117, 119, 143, 229
Jonathan P 95, 117
Joseph 59, 62, 63, 65, 66, 67, 118
Joseph H 141, 172
Josephine 131, 183, 211
Joshua J 232
Joyce 186
Jr C Whitfield 70
Jr Harold E 77

DeWitt

Jr Jacob 95
Jr Jacobus 98
Jr John 104, 124, 141, 149
Jr Omar L 206
Jr Orlean 121, 146
Jr Peter 63
Jr Stanley W 78
Jr Thomas 118
Jr Warren 76
Jr William 68
Judson A 116, 142
Judson H 155, 186
Judy 208
Julia 118
Justin C 79
Justin D 78
Kate O 125
Katharine 123, 197
Kathleen 223
Katrine 123, 148
Kay 78
Keith N 200, 225
Kenneth E 216
Kevin 78
Kim 225
Kristin H 232
L Albert 127
Lafayette 67, 71
Larissa S 78
Larry 208
Laura 155, 186, 213
Laura A 212
Laura B 142, 172
Laura F 186
Laura J 136
Laura L 215
Laura R 77, 79
Laurel S 204, 229
Lavina 133, 160
Lawrence 71
Lawrence I 181, 208
Lawrence J 232
Lawrence J D 207
Lee A 232
Leitha 183, 211
Lelsey W 135
Lenora A 161, 188
Leo 71
Leona 74, 165
Lereigh J 118
Lester 71
Leucas 87
Levi 90, 105
Levy 117
Liddia 127
Lila B 175, 204
Lillian 64
Linda 208
Lionel S 175
Lisa A 215
Lisa F 212
Lloyd 71, 72
Lloyd L (S) 198
Lloyd L 223
Lodewick 135
Loretta 65, 202
Lorna J 188
Lorraine C 75
Lottie V 163, 190
Lou 72
Louis J 197
Louisa 62
Louise 66, 67, 200
Louise M 125
Lucas 99
Lucas E 83, 91
Lucinda 92
Lucretia 68
Luke 98, 107, 112, 127, 186
Luke A 127
Luke D 120
Luke E 109, 112, 130
Luke Emery 133
Lula 68
Lula E 70, 74
Lura 72
Lydia 108, 146
Lydia A 133, 161
Lyman G 131
M Cecelia A 143, 173
M Isabel 112
Mabel 131, 136, 159, 173
Mabel A I 164, 171, 200
Madeline 185
Madolyn R 188
Maggie (Davis) 152
Mahala 118
Manley 121
Margaret 62, 68, 72, 99, 136, 165
Margaret A 77, 79, 112, 119, 135, 197, 222
Margaret E 178
Margaret J 116, 142
Margareta 144
Marguerite I 200
Maria 54, 60, 82, 91, 120
Mariah 97
Marie 146
Marie E 75, 77
Marilyn M 206
Maritje 91, 105
Marjorie 191
Marjorie O 129
Mark 152, 225
Mark G 216
Marshall R 129
Martha 65, 71, 95, 107, 114
Martha F 115
Martha W 163
Martin L 116
Martin V B 104, 125
Marvell 159
Marvin 74
Mary 64, 66, 68, 74, 104, 105, 108, 112, 123, 124, 133, 139, 169
Mary A 67, 126
Mary Ann 119, 210
Mary C 117, 142
Mary E 62, 70, 72, 75, 108, 129, 136, 190, 216,
Mary G 105, 108
Mary I 186, 213
Mary J 112, 118, 128, 135
Mary Jane 104, 125
Mary Louise 123, 148
Mary M 125
Mary V 68, 72
Mary V B 121
Mathew 105
Matilda 155, 186
Matthew 67, 71
Mattie 68
Maude 70
Maurice W 174, 204
Mauriette D 204, 229
Mausell 67
May 155, 184
May L 152
Medora 64, 69
Melvin 130, 134, 136, 155
Merle 72
Merna 186
Michael 71
Michael A 77
Mike 67
Mildred 73, 185, 191
Mildred E 217
Miles 65
Miles C 212
Millard M 126
Milton 71
Minerva 64, 65
Minnie 66, 135, 161, 164, 166, 169,
Misty D 214
Morgan S 141, 171
Morrendy 115
Morris C 117
Moses F 105, 126
Mount 131
Myrna 183
Myrtle 71, 164
Myrtle E 164
Myrtle I 171, 200
Nancy 63, 66, 68, 108, 113
Nancy C 77, 78
Nathan 78
Nehmiah 135, 164, 169
Nellie 62, 71, 121
Nellie R 155, 186

DeWitt
Nelly E 64
Nicholaas 15
Nicole 78
Nicolette K 222
Norma L 202, 228
Norman 136, 197
Norman B 142, 172
Norman J 170, 197
Norman O 172, 200
Norman W 140, 170
Oakey 72
Odessa 67
Olive 70
Oliver B 75
Omar L 178, 206
Oram D 120
Orlean 99, 121
Orr 71
Orrin L 131, 159
Oscar 67, 146, 149
Otis 164, 191
P Jane 116
P Maria 135, 164, 169
P Marie 166
Pamela 223
Parker 152, 183
Patricia 210
Patricia A 77, 78, 191
Timothy 78
Patrick N 225
Paul 74, 211
Paul N 201
Pauline 72
Peggy D 62
Peggy L 75, 77
Peggy M 120
Permilly 120
Perry 66
Peter 59, 62, 63, 67, 87, 92, 94, 99, 106, 120, 126
Peter B 90, 104
Peter J 225
Peter R 119
Petrus 54, 81, 97
Phebe E 129
Phebe Jane 129
Philip 94
Phoebe 108, 113, 115, 130, 136, 152, 155, 156, 183
Phoebe A 112, 129, 134, 151
Phoebe D 130
Phoebe E 109, 131
Phoebe J 141
Phoebe M 191, 194
Phoebe S 109
Pieter 97
Platt 120, 146
Polly 62
Prudence 95, 116, 117, 118, 143,

Prudence E 143
Prudence S 118
R Luke 216
Rachel 54, 80, 88, 91, 223
Rainsford 136
Ralph 74
Randal P 133
Randall P 161
Ray 211
Raymond 67, 74
Rebecca 62, 63, 67
Rebecca J 63, 109
Rebecca S 77
Rena C 163
Renae 79, 79
Rhea M E 174, 203
Rheta E 161
Rhoda 116, 141
Richard 59, 63, 67, 69,
Richard C 59, 62
Richard J 77, 79
Rita 165
Robert 71, 78, 79, 190, 210
Robert A 77
Robert D 215
Robert E 157, 189, 215
Robert L 191, 216
Robert T 215
Robin 79
Ronald 77
Ronald W 161, 188, 189
Rosa 105, 179
Rowene G 186, 213
Roy 74, 181, 185
Roy C 150
Roy E 75
Ruby L 161, 188
Ruby R 188, 215
Rufus 67, 71, 109, 129
Russell 77
Ruth 72, 186
Ruth A 131, 180
Ruth Ann 156
Ruth H 149
Ryan J 232
S Elva 175, 204
Sadie 66, 70
Sally 62
Sally A 98
Salome 113
Samantha L 127, 149
Samena 140
Samuel 54, 59, 63, 66, 67, 116
Samuel L 128
Sandra A 204, 229
Sara 124, 148
Sarah 59, 62, 63, 65, 66, 67, 68, 69, 71, 75, 95, 104, 106, 115, 118, 119, 121, 124, 140,
Sarah Ann 62, 63, 117, 142
Sarah E 128

Sarah L 60
Sarah P 118
Saunders W 131
Scott W 232
Scouler B 134, 161
Sebe 120
Semena 170
Sharon M 231
Sheila 211
Sherman 73, 76
Shirley 186
Silas J 104, 123
Simon P 91, 99, 106, 121
Sophia C 223
Sophronia 67
Spafford 136
Stanely 155, 185
Stanley C 67
Stanley W 75, 77
Stella 68, 133
Stella L 164, 219
Stephen 62
Steven A 216
Steven C 213
Susan 59, 62, 63, 66, 67,
Susan E 77, 79
Suzanne M 216
Sybrant V 55
Sylvia I 74
Temperence 112
Terre L 78, 229
Theodore A 180
Theodore F 124, 148
Theodosia 142
Theron 120
Thomas 62, 63, 66, 68, 71, 72, 95, 109, 118, 133, 159, 186
Thomas B 180
Thomas C 202
Thomas D 109
Thomas H 130, 149, 180
Thomas O 109, 131
deWitt
Tialie Claessen 15
DeWitt
Tierck Claeszen 17
Troy 71
Truman 74
Truman A 71
Vada 68
Vaughn 128
Velma V 74
Verdo 72
Verna 72
Verna A 142
Vernon 183
Vespie 66
Victoria A 128
Violet 73
Virgie M 75
Vona E 176, 205

DeWitt
  Walter 71, 98, 120, 145, 146, 163
  Wanda C 75, 77
  Warren 73, 76
  Warren H 120
  Wayne 225
  Wayne D 212
  Wayne F 206, 231
  Webster 66
  Wendy 225
  Wilarlie 74
  Wiliam C 60
  Willard 74
  William 59, 60, 63, 64, 66, 68, 69, 72, 75, 118, 120, 126, 131, 133, 134, 136, 165
  William B 75
  William D 67, 71
  William H 64, 71, 74, 90, 104, 133
  William J 150, 180
  William L 68, 72, 107, 127
  William S 204
  William T 207, 232
  Winnifred 189
  Winston 211
  Xenophon 142
  Zara 142
  Zoriah 136
  Zuella 67
  Zula 68, 161, 188
Dick
  Mary Jane 199
Diederick
  Abraham 82
  Johannes 80, 82
Dietrich
  Robert 177
Dile
  Lea E 121
Dimmick
  Adaline 61, 65
Dolson
  Mary 59, 62
Donahoe
  Michael 214
Donaldson
  Beverly 52
  Kathleen 52
  LeRoy 50, 52
  Roger M 52
Donnoyer
  Angela J 218, 237
Doris
  James W E 229
Dormouth
  Irene 227
Dorri
  Rene 206

Dowling
  Gladys E 199, 224
Drake
  Alice 135, 164, 169
  Georgie A 129, 152
  Lula M 131
Drummer
  Elizabeth 219
Du Boys
  Annetje 25, 28
Du Casteel
  Dorcas 59, 63
  Mary 59
Dubois
  Caroline L 149
  Carrie O 149
  Elias 125
  Elijah 105, 149
  Franklin 48
  Leonard M 43, 48
  Lottie M 48
  Mabel 48
  Samuel V G 43
  Sarah A 31, 38
  Sarah Emma 43
Duff
  Robert 146
Duffas
  James A 224, 237
  James J 237
  Katrina M 237
  Peter A 237
  Robert J 237
Duffy
  Mary 50, 51
Dumon
  Catharina 57, 83
Dumond
  Abraham 57
  Anna 57
  Catharina 93
  Christian 57
  Cornelius 57
  Elisabeth 26
  Ellizabeth 31
  Harriet 57
  Ignatius 54, 57
  Igneas 57
  Jane A 37
  Jr Harmonus 57
  Petrus 57
  Sellie 57
Dumont
  Jacobus 57
  Jane A 31
  Maria 57
  Willem 57
Dunbar
  Cythia A 67, 71
Dunham
  Dorothy 178

Dunn
  Alleine 179, 207
  Eliot D 148, 179
  Shirley 179
  Theodore F 148
  Theophilus C 124, 148
  Waldo 160
Duplisea
  Calvin 196
  Donald 216
  Douglas 193
  Edna 189, 215
  Erwin 189
  Harley 162, 189
  Hazel 160, 188
Dupuy
  Maria 99
DuRose
  Phoebe 83, 92
Dutcher
  Josiah 29
Dyer
  George 135
Dykeman
  Lev 161
Eady
  Kimberley A 228
Eager
  Edward 103
Earl
  Hattie H 144, 177
  Leona L 144, 177
Eastlund
  Donald R 79
  Erik J D 79
Eastman
  Sarah 131
Eastwood
  Agatha 134
Eccert
  Peter 26
Echart
  Robert 72
Echlberger
  Winona 74
Ecker
  Shirley 237
  Shirley A 224, 237
Eckert
  John L 31
  Jr Isaac D 38
  Mary A 38
  Nehaniah S 32
  Peter 31
  Sarah J 32
Eckland
  Beverly J 201
  Claire-Ann L 201
  Erland 172
Ecklin
  Beverly J 226

Ecklin
    Claire-Ann L 226
    Erland 201
Eckman
    Anthony P 150 181
    Cameron A 208
    Heather A 208
    Louis P 181, 208
Edlefsen
    Dawn 51, 52
    Frederick 49, 51
    Frederick H 52
    Kirsten M 52
    Marin 51
    Martin 52
Edwards
    Catharine 98
    Catherine 87
    David 202, 228
    Deborah R 228
    Elizabeth 89, 103
    Jonathan D 228
    Rebekah A 228
Egbertsen
    Hannah 87, 99
    Jannetje 17
Egert
    Raymond 200
Eichelberger
    Winona 70
Eklund
    August A 171
Eligh
    Maria C 36
    Mary C 28
Elkins
    William 209
Elliott
    Clinton 160
Ellis
    Amo B 209
    Amos B 182
    Gordon 190
Elsworth
    John L 31
    Maria 31
    Peter 26, 31
Elwyn
    Arthur R 49
    Catherine 49
Emerson
    Carol 187
    Elizabeth 187, 214
    Ernest 160, 187, 210
Emery
    Lucretia D 112, 133
Emmerich
    John 28, 35
    Levi 35
    Marie 35
    Sally C 36

Emory
    William 27
Empringham
    Ida A 172, 201
Emrigh
    Maria 29
    Peter 25
    Petrus 29
Engel
    Linda L 224, 237
Enman
    Rhetta 168
Erickson
    Elizabeth 213
    Kenneth 186, 2113
    Ruth 48
Ervine
    Inez G 183, 211
Esau
    Deborah 234
    Paul 234
    Ralph 210
Essensa
    D 191
Essery
    Byron N 203
    Frances M 203
    Gladys I 203
    Jr William E 203
    William E 203
Estay
    Ernest 131
Esterline
    Don 181
Estes
    Maylord 132
Esury
    William E 173
Everett
    Louis 156
Evers
    Rosella 199, 224
Every
    Alice E 70
    Anna Mae 70
    Arthur 70
    Emerson 70
    George 70
    Joella 70
    Johnson 65, 70
    Otis 70
    Raymond 70
    William C 70
Fair
    Matilda 119, 144
Falkenburg
    Catharina 23, 24
Farewell
    Lorraine H 181
    Maurice E 181

Fargie
    Margaret 200, 225
Farrer
    Stephanie L 217
Farrow
    Seth 92
Farwell
    Lorraine H 208
    Maurice E 150
Fass
    Donna J 207, 232
Faust
    Amanda 52
    Elizabeth J 51
    George R 51, 52
    George W 50, 51
    Robert T 51
    Virginia A 51
Favorite
    Shirley 206, 231
Fear
    Joan E 50, 51
Featherstone
    Mary 201, 227
Feldman
    Evelyn L 46, 50
Feligh
    Moses 61
Fellows
    Blanche E 45
Felten
    Rachel A 122
    Zacharias 122
    Mary J 39, 44
    Helena 88, 101
    Laurens 88, 101
    Lucinda H 37, 43
    Polly 101
    Zacharias 101
Fennell
    Herbert 144
Ferguson
    Fanny 67, 71
    Linda 210, 234
Ferns
    Lillian T 180, 207
Ferrin
    Marion 187
Ferris
    David 209
    Thelma 179
Ferriss
    Christopher 234
    David 234
    Erin 234
    Jennifer 234
Ferron
    Marion 160
Fick
    Carolin 117, 142
    Cecelia 120

Fick
  Harriet 89, 102
  Libbie 142
Fiero
  Ann C 33, 39
Fiero
  Christian A 26, 33
  Mary E 33
  Sarah 33
Finch
  Willis 122
Findlay
  E Jean 179
Finney
  Elizabeth 104
Fisher
  Eva May 150, 181
Fleming
  Gordon 188
  Martha M 127, 150
  Michael 222
  Nettie M 139, 169
  William J 222
Flemming
  Michael 197
Flood
  Heather 200
Floyd
  John 204, 229
  Kevin J 228
Foland
  John P 32
Foley
  Trista A 78
Folkers
  Hendrick 15
Fonda
  Peter 34
Forbes
  John P 146
Forrister
  Dana E 233
  Diane S 233
  John P 209, 233
  Lunn M 233
  Stephen L 233
  Tina D 233
Foster
  Donald T 202, 227
  Eliza O 173, 201
  Eugene 227
  Isobel 201
  Jemima 127
  John R 202
  Leonard B 227
  Robert 143, 173, 227
  Robert N 173, 202
Fotler
  Maria 54, 58
Fowler
  Marilyn 192, 217
  Wellington 128
Fowles
  Allura S 129, 151
Fox
  Allison 189
  Ernest W 162, 189
  Judith 188, 215
  Lois 189
  Marjorie 189
  Marshall 189
  Merle 189
  Nelma 189
Foxley
  Barbara 224
  Bessie R 199, 224
  Cindy 224
  Cyril H 199, 224
  Elisabeth C 237
  Frank T 199
  Fred H 199, 224
  James R 237
  Jaqueline R 224
  Joan L 224
  John W 199, 224
  Robert A 224, 237
  Wellington J 199
  William G 199
France
  Alfred 38, 44
  Charles H 44
  Ella 41
  Jacob H 39
  Julia 35, 41
  Luella 44
Frankhauser
  Mabel 71, 74
Frantz
  Adele 49
Frare
  Sophia 36
Fraser
  Jacqueline D 233
  Jennifer D 233
  Larry F 208
  Leonard F S 208
  Leonard L 208, 233
  Leonard S 181
  Lloyd N 208
  Fraser Lorne D 208
  G J 70
  Audrey 75, 77
  Mattie 41, 45
Freel
  Annie 141
  James A 141
  John 141
  Magdalen 141
Freligh
  Ann E 61
  Isabel 149, 180
  Joel 57, 61
  Sarah 105
Friend
  Amy 68, 72
  Bertha 72
  Dacie 68, 72
  Frances L 77, 79
  Francis M 72, 75
  Gilbert 68, 72
  Letitia 66
  Louisa 63, 68
  Rehl 68
  Richard 70
  Sarah 55
  Stephen 68
  William 72
Fries
  Frank 68
Frye
  Christian 144
Fuller
  Frank E 180
  Marshall 128
  Weldon H 161
Fullerton
  Dinah 222
  Leslie 222
  Terrance 222
  William 197, 222
Funk
  Clarence 200, 225
  Michael C 225
  Ronda M 225
  Sharon C 225
Funnel
  Joan A 175, 204
Gaddis
  Clyde I 44, 49
  Harold I 49
  Helen E 49
  James 48
  Percy W 49
Gallagher
  Joyce 193
Gallison
  Alameda 136
  Elizabeth 136, 165, 169
  Regina I 136, 165, 169
Galloway
  Sadie E 173, 202
Gammage
  Susannah 118, 143
Ganas
  Gregory P 201
Gandy
  Eileen 193
Gardener
  Emma 130, 155
  Mary 133, 160
  Edith 168, 196
Garrard
  Geoffrey W 207

Garrard
    Sterling 179, 207
Garrison
    Esther 122
Gartley
    Della 155, 185
Gaskin
    Ian G 216
Gasper
    Tom 165
Gates
    Allen W 227
    Debra A 227
    Karen R 227
    Ronald A 202, 227
Gaudet
    Danny 215
Gaylord
    Lois 55
Gee
    William 193
Gehan
    George 136
Geig
    Jr Jim 231
George
    Winona 76
German
    Barbara 190
    Christianna 49
    Christine S 45
    Harry 49
    Harry G 45
    Lillian L 49
Gerry
    Cynthia 234
    Robert 212, 234
    Sandra 234
Getson
    Theora 181, 208, 233
Geyssens
    Randall 49
Giberson
    Pearl 211
Gibson
    Alfred 139
    Donald 205, 230
Gifford
    Bobby 79
    Daniel 79
    Tara 79
Gift
    Lisa 79
Gilberson
    Pearl 183
Gilbert
    D Smith 205
    Estelle 182, 209
Gillespie
    Harrison 32
    Job 26, 32
    John R 32
    Lemont 135
    Lydia C 32
    M Anita 70, 74
    Magdalena 32
    Margaret S 32
    Matilda J 32
    Wyntje C 32
Gillet
    Daniel 62
    Elizabeth 59, 62
    Charlotte L 104, 124
Gillie
    W 211
Glidden
    Caroline 212
    Elwood 185, 212
    Harold 212
    Judith 212
    Luella 185, 211
Goatcher
    Lori Lynn 209
    Melody L 209
    Robert E 182, 209
    Shirley C 209
Golden
    Charlene 217
    Debbie 215
    Derith 217
    Galen 217
    Greg 217
    Hollis 217
    Michael 217
    Miles 217
    Ronald 191, 217
    Sharon 217
Golding
    Ada 166
    Ida May 168, 196
    Madeline 164
    Martha 166
Good
    Eugene 211, 234
    Jr Eugene 234
Goodfellow
    Violet 141
Goodine
    Gary 211
Goodline
    Larry 168
Goodman
    Marion E 208
Goodrich
    Katryn A 208
Goodwin
    Edwin G 179
    James O 36
    Marion A 181
Gordon
    James 126
Gorman
    Barbara 216
Gotchalk
    Emma 127
Gourley
    Margaret 187, 213
    Mary 187
    Murray 187
    William 159, 187
Gracey
    Alexander 140, 170
    DeWitt 170
Graham
    A Grant 161
    Brenda 216
    Brenda J 215
    Charles A 126
    Evelyn 211, 234
    Gerald R 202, 227
    Grant 189, 215
    Heather 234
    James 126, 133
    James W 161
    Joanna 126
    John 107, 126, 127
    Jr John 126
    Leola 161
    Margaret 126
    Martha M 126
    Mildred M 183, 211
    Murray 211, 234
    Parker 183, 211
    Paul 234
    Sherri 227
    Susan 227
    Wanda 234
    Wayne G 215
    Willa J 227
Grant
    Lorraine 200, 226
    Phyllis K 205, 230
Grasekamp
    Harry 45
Grass
    Abigail 114, 138
    Ellen A 138, 168
    Henrietta 139
    Whitfield 136
    Verna 68, 73
Gray
    Arnold 187
    Charles 131, 156
    Fred 187
    George 187
    Hallie 156, 187
    Helen 156
    Kenneth 156
    Lorne 187
    Nina 156
    Otto 156
    Rhoda 156

Gray
  Sadie 156
Green
  Beryl 172, 200
  Elizabeth 115, 139
Greensfield
  Emma 136, 165
Greer
  Alma 169, 196
  Alma N 168
  Mary 139, 168
  William 187
Greig
  Jim 231
Grey
  Elizabeth S 114, 139
Grover
  Jacqueline J 205
  Jennifer A 205
  Marshall R 177, 205
Guitard
  Dorothy 196
Gulneck
  Maria 58, 61
Haddon
  Norman 173
Haeber
  Sara Ann 230
  Tekeno 205, 230
Hafford
  Charles 185, 212
  Connie 212, 234
  Eva 212, 235
  Michael 212
Hagerman
  Albert 138, 168
  Claribel 69
  Cornelius 168
  Ella 168
  Sherman 168
Haig
  Elizabeth 190
Haines
  Clara 36, 42
Haley
  George 130
  Janet 209
  Jean 209
  Judith 209
  Maggie 130
  Payson 182, 209
  Percy F 194, 219
  Ralph 209
  Richard 219
  Robert 209
Hall
  Andrea M 225
  Cheryl D 225
  Curtis L 225
  Darryl K 225
  Douglas R 216
  Heather L 225
  Joanne E 216
  John D 190, 216
  Katie E 141, 172
  Keith 200, 225
Halsey
  Harry 160
Hamel
  Evelyn M 202
Hamilton
  Dale 220
Hamlin
  Evelyn M 227
  Everlin B 104
  Minnie C 117, 142
Hancock
  Edward M 224
Hannah
  Boone 165
  Duncan 156
Hannay
  Mary E 128, 150
Hannon
  Sue 219
Hanselpecker
  Joyce 217, 235
Hanson
  Alma 211
  Clara 212
  David 211
  Fred 185, 212
  Gilbert 212
  Gladys 185, 212
  Harold 185, 212
  Helen 212
  Jacqueline 211
  John 155, 185, 211
  Jr Fred 212
  Mary 185, 212
  Paulene 185, 212
  Roger 185, 212
  Ruth 211
  Shirley 185, 212
  Stella 185, 211
Hardenbergh
  Allis 149
Harding
  Opal 186, 212
Hare
  Lyn 216
Harker
  Gary 228
Harnish
  Dorothy 188
Harper
  Basil 156
Harpham
  D Glenn 204
  Dennis 204
  Rae F 204, 229
  Raymond E B 175, 204
  Sharon L 204, 229
Harris
  Albion 135, 164, 166, 169, 191, 194
  Alfred 164, 192, 197
  Allen 220
  Alma 166
  Andrew 166
  Annabelle 135, 164, 166, 169, 194
  Arthur 164
  Benjamin 166
  Betty 192, 217
  Brandon 235
  Burpee 166
  Charles 166
  Chester 164, 168, 197
  Corinne R 227
  Dale W 217
  Dehila 197
  Donald 197
  Edith 197
  Eldon 197
  Elizabeth 164, 197
  Eloice 197
  Ernest 164, 191
  Foster 197
  Frank 166
  Frederick 135, 164
  George 166
  Glendon 192, 216, 217
  Grace 191
  Guilford 197
  Gwendoline C 227
  Hannah 137, 191
  Harriet 197
  Hayward 137, 166
  Hilda 197
  Howard 166
  Irwin 197
  Jaby 118
  James 166
  Jarvis 113, 137, 166
  Jennie 166
  Jordan 235
  Keith 197
  Kenneth 166, 192, 227
  Kenneth R 202
  Kevin 217, 235
  Lavina 164, 165
  Leslie 164, 192, 217
  Lillie 166
  Linda G 196, 221
  Lloyd 192
  Lucas 235
  Mabel 166
  Maizie 152
  Margaret 196, 221
  Marie 197
  Mark 235
  Mary 166

Harris
    Mary E 137
    Matthew 215, 217, 235
    Maureen 216, 235
    Mazzie 183
    Mina 166
    Myles 217, 235
    Myrtle 166
    Nicholas 235
    Pamela C 227
    Ralph 191
    Ray 192
    Rebecca 137
    Rita 164, 192
    Roger 217, 235
    Sherman 135, 164, 166, 169
    Stanley 166
    Stella L 191
    T Odbur 137, 138 166, 167
    Travid 197
    Tyler 164, 192
    Wallace 197
    Walter 164, 192
    William 166
    William C 137
    Zachary 235
Harrison
    Grace 213
    James 213
    Lynda 213
    Pamela 213
    Patricia 213
    Susan 213
    Sydney 186, 213
Harron
    Ruby 162, 189
    Tanya 214
Hart
    Lizzie H 121
    Marie L 45, 49
    R 198
    Sherry 235
    T Richard 189
Hartin
    Arlington M 190
    Carroll L 190
    Donald B 190
    Forrest F 163, 190
    Geraldine M 190
    Madeline V 190
    Milford E 190
    Ronald E 190
    Ruth A 190
    Sterling H 190
    Theodore A 190
Hartman
    Sarah 59, 62
Hartt
    Bruce 215
    Bryon C 216
    David 191, 216
    David W 216
    Deanna M 216
    Edward R 216
    Sherri L 215, 216
    T Richard 215
    Tammy 215
    Thomas 215
Hartwell
    Brenda 220, 236
Haskell
    Amy 233
    Andrew D 209
    Bernice 209, 233
    Bonita L 234, 209
    Brian 233
    Brian S 209
    Christopher M 233
    Edythe F 182, 209
    Elwyn L 182, 209
    Emma B 182, 209
    Eric R 209, 233
    Everett 233
    Greg 233
    Herman 233
    Herman A 150, 182
    Herman M 182, 209
    Marlene 210
    Michael 233
    Michael S 233
    Neil D S 182, 210
    Peter E 209, 233
    Ralph 233
    Ralph S 182, 209
    Shawn 233
    Sheila 210
    Shirley 209
    Terra 233
    Theresa 233
    Una Mae 182, 209
Haslett
    Elizabeth 220, 236
Hatch
    George O 127, 149
Hatfield
    Walter 156
Hathaway
    Wilmot H 156
Hauck
    Margaret 63, 68
Havens
    Samuel 113
Hawkes
    Ida 193
    Thelma 193
Hawks
    George 165, 193
Hawley
    Marjorie E 231, 239
Hay
    Mary M 112, 134
Hayden
    Annie 156
    Edith 156
    Evelyn 156
    Frank G 156
    Helen 156
    James 156
    Mary 156
    Ralph 156
    Samuel 156
    Samuel R 131, 156
    Sarah 156
Hayward
    Mary Ann 94
    Viola E 195, 220
Heller
    Allison R 238
    Christopher T 228, 238
Helverstat
    Frances 200
Hendricks
    Herman 178
    Phillip 32
Hendrie
    Edythe M 206, 231
Hendry
    Euphemia 109, 130
Henkel
    Charlotte L 207
    David 179, 207
    Jr David 207
Henline
    Nancy 78
    Nellie 71, 74
Hennesey
    Theresa 207, 232
Henry
    Adelaide 142
Herman
    Pettit 140
    Tracy 136
Hermans
    Lysbeth 15
Herring
    Anna 47
Hetherington
    Donald 187
Hewlett
    Harry 144
    Ilya 144
    Job 144
Hibbeler
    Fred 200
Hibbert
    Gwendolyn 172, 201
Hickey
    G N 156
    Richard S 125
Hicks
    Albert 127
    Benjamin 107, 127

Hicks
    James 127
    Thomas D 107
Higgins
    Annabel 75
    Betty 75
    Charles E 75
    Charles W 75
    George 75
    Linsey 75
    Robert W 75
Hill
    Aida Maude 144
    Helen 117, 142
    Marie S 50, 51
    Maude 144, 177
    Ralph E 190
Hillman
    Patty 217, 235
Hinchman
    Minnie 63, 67
Hindman
    Orville 179
Hinds
    M Aline 223
Hines
    Cinderella 122, 147
Ho
    Uphanie 109, 129
Hoagland
    Benjamin T 104, 125
    Charles T 125
    DeWitt 125
    George 125
    Helen C 125
    John W 125
    Mary E 125
Hoff
    Cornelis 87, 99
    Jan 100
    Pieter 99
    William 100
Hofman
    Marten 15
    Max 50, 52
Hogan
    Anna 27, 34
    Robert 179
Holbrook
    David 108
Hold
    Maria 36
Holdeman
    Doris 178
Hollenbach
    Theodore 125
Hollis
    Esther 74
Holmes
    Danny 232
    David S 232

    Lauren J 232, 239
    Tammy 232
    William I 207, 232
Holsman
    Gerald 148, 179
    Mary M 179
Holt
    Oscar 49, 51
Holtermann
    Darby G 170
    Marion L 170
    Richard F 140, 170
    Richard S 170
    S Enid 170, 199
    W Ivar 170
Holverst
    Frances 171
Hommel
    Abraham J 32, 38
    Charlotte 38
    David C 146
    Maria 81
    Sophia M 47
Hondorf
    Clara N 73
Hood
    Carolyn 196
Hooper
    Elizabeth D 179
Hopler
    Daniel 202
Hopstein
    Karen 236
Horne
    Katherine D 196, 221
Horning
    Catherine 92, 107
    John 117, 142
    Joseph 142
    Julia A 118, 143
    Selena 119, 143
Hostittler
    Ellen 75
Houghtaling
    Antoinette 124
Houlton
    Nettie L 129
House
    Mary J 63, 66
Houser
    John 74
Hover
    Charles H 104
    Jane C 104, 125
Howard
    Sarah 118, 142
Howey
    Cecilia P 144
    Frank 144
    John 144

Howland
    Gideon 99, 120
    Helen 120, 146
    Ruth A 124, 149
    Sarah M 137
Hoyt
    Alice A 130, 155
    Angeline 109, 131
    Anna 130
    Blanche M 130
    Carol 192
    Chloe C 112, 134
    Clemente 130
    Elsie 130
    Emerson 132, 159
    Eugenia 190, 216
    Frank 156, 159
    Irene 156
    John 156, 159, 164, 192
    Margaret A 112
    Marion 159
    Mount 156
    Myrtle 159
    Norman 129
    Phoebe 130
    Rebecca 130
    Roy 159
    Scovil 193
    Silas 130
    Thomas 130, 156
    Wellington 130
    William 156
    William E 109, 130
Hudler
    Maria G 58, 62
Hudson
    Barbara 200, 225
Huggins
    Charles W 71
Hugill
    Denise J 228, 238
    Elizabeth A 228
    Elva 203
    Jeffrey A 228
    Johatban 203
    Katharine L 228
    M Edna N 203
    Mark W 229
    Marsha J 220
    Melanie E 229
    Michelle A 229
    Murray D 203, 229
    R Grace E 203, 228
    W J Alexander 203, 228
    William J 174, 203
Huiltz
    Prue 196
Hulk
    Linda R 75
Humble
    William 219

Hun
  Katherine 148, 179
Hunt
  Richard F 47
Hurl
  Lester W 45
  Percy L 45
  William H 40, 45
Hutchings
  DeWitt V 149, 180
  Elsie L 149
  Frank M 180
  George L 124, 149
  Helen H 180
  Isabelle V 180
Hutchinson
  Helen M 102
Hutton
  George 44
Hyde
  Elizabeth 224
  Elizabeth L 199
Hyland
  Diane E 224
  Edward 224
  Glenn E 199
  Jannie E 224
  Osborne 199, 224
  Sheldon F 171, 199
  Shelley E 224
Hysert
  Edgar B 224
  Edgar F 224
  Patricia R 224
  Peter K F 224
  Shirley E M 224, 237
  Sylvia D 224
Ince
  William 170, 198
Ingraham
  Sarah A 33, 39
Ingram
  George 48
Ireland
  Wallace 190
Irvine
  Mary 155, 186
Jackson
  Dorothy S 181, 209
  Elizabeth 59, 63
  Mary 101
Jacobs
  Emma 181
Jacobson
  Michael 197
Jameison
  Margaret 118, 143
James
  Brian R 224
  Dennis 225
  Helen 106, 126
  Irene 74
  Rheta 135
  Robert 200, 224
Jarslfer
  Charles 202, 228
  Douglas C 228
  Joyce L 228
Jefferson
  Kathleen 166, 194
Jeffery
  Edward 211
  Arthur 211
  Barbara 211
  Walter 187, 211
Jewel
  Arthur 206
  Marie 179
Jewell
  Arthur 231
  Craig A 231
  Wendy J 231
Jobe
  Ena 167
Johnson
  Arthur 183
  Brian 221
  Charlotte 211
  Donald G 204, 229
  Eliza Ann 116, 142
  Elizabeth 112, 134
  Evelyn 211
  Ginger 186, 212
  James 211
  Matt 195
  Michael 230
  Michelle D 230, 238
  Nora 211
  R Rae 238
  Rhonda R 229
  Richard A V 226
Johnston
  Arthur 211
  Eric 220
  Katharine I 140, 170
Jollymore
  Rhetta A 168, 196
Jones
  Charles 132
  Clayton 166, 194
  Daniel 60
  Edward 194
  James 169
  Mabel 47
  Marilyn 194
  Mary 61, 65
  Mary E 34, 39, 44
  Tom 200
  William H 133, 161
Jong
  Peter 58
  Petrus 54
Jong/Young
  Christeintje 25
Jonnagh/Young
  Abraham 25
Jonngh
  Peter 29
Jordan
  Jr Roy E 179, 207
  Nancy L 207
  Pamela D 207
Jorgensen
  Charlotte 187
  Muriel 187, 214
  Norman 160, 187
  Priscilla 187, 214
Joseph
  Don 179
  Michael 229
  Nell 72
Junge
  Andrea S 239
  Holger 232, 239
  Jr Holger 239
Kage
  Catharine A 180 207
Kalter
  David 52
  M Richard 51, 52
Kamp
  Harold M 48
Kane
  James 213
  Jean 213
  Joey 213
  Joseph 186, 213
  Robert 213
  Sharon 213
  Terrance 213
Kay
  Mary 43, 49
Kear
  Arthur 50
Keater
  Angie 70
  Chauncey 65, 70
  Hurvey 70
Keigher
  Susan M 52
Keith
  Dorothy 185
Keller
  Maria 53, 55
Kelly
  Clara 134, 162
  David 216
  James 139
  Mary 197, 222
  Thomas H 108
Kelton
  Arthur 116, 142
  Frank C 142

Kemble
  Eliza C 42, 46
Kennedy
  Verla 169
Kenney
  Anna A 140, 170
Kenyon
  Arthur J 171, 199
  Louise K R 199, 224
  Ruth E 199, 224
Kerman
  Maria F 125
Kernyrk
  Maria 24, 26
Kerr
  Gertrude 36, 42
Kess
  Jannetje 100
  Silvanis 88, 100
Kidd
  Eleanor D 49
Kieber
  Margaret A 40
Kiefer
  John 106
  William 16
Kiel
  Hildegarde M 194
Kiernan
  William J 49
Kiersted
  Wyntie 17
Kilbaugh
  Michael 62
Killan
  Nicholas M 238
  Vaughn 229, 238
King
  Charles 160, 187
  Richard 187
  Robert 187
Kingston
  Ada 134, 162
  Ellen 163
  Fred 112, 134
  George 113, 137
  Hanford 134
  Ida 134, 162
  Joseph 137
  Malcolm 163
  Myrtle 163
  Orlo 134, 163
  Rachel 134
  Ula 163, 190
  William 134, 163
Kinney
  Abigail 83, 95
  Elizabeth 94, 113
Kintzel
  Harriet E 115, 139

Kirgt
  Patricia 206, 231
Kirkpatrick
  Allison 183, 211
  Burton 161
  Carol 211
  David 152, 183
  Denise 234
  Derrold 211
  Donalda 211
  Edna 183, 211
  Edward 211, 234
  Ernest 183, 211
  Florence 183, 211
  Grant 183, 211
  Leona 211
  Liman 183
  Loretta 211
  Margaret 183, 211
  Mary 134, 162
  May 183
  Pauline 213
  Rachel A 134, 163
  Raymond 183
  Vida E 183
  Vincent 213
  Willard 187, 213
Kleeman
  Barbara 52
Kline
  Margaret 177, 205
Kncarem
  Dale 205, 230
  Jacqueline J 230
  John H 230
Kneiffer
  John 44, 126
Knoll
  Aaron W 36
  Henry 29, 36
  Sally M 36
Knolle
  Henry 36
Knorr
  Ada 134, 163
  Dale C 215
  Howard A 215, 235
  Jeffrey 235
  Krista 235
  Linda D 215, 235
  Paul A 215
  Reginald A 215
  Shirley 189, 215
Knowles
  George B 136, 166
  Inez 166
  Russel 166
Koebl
  Ethel D 208
Kolanowski
  Dorothy 206

Koluzs
  Nancy 229
Kool
  Margaret 88, 101
Koons
  Catharina 59
  Mache 54, 59
Kortreght
  Hendrick 17
Koshtishyn
  Nadya 209
Kotowski
  Michelle 230
  Smith Kasia I 230
Kramer
  Marie 178
Krenz
  F H 170
Kriestler
  Catherina 93
LaClair
  Bernard G 232, 239
LaFortune
  Frederick 103
Laird
  Annis B 121, 146
Lambert
  Amelia E 149, 180
  E 127, 149
Lamphere
  Helen 49, 51
Landers
  Ernest 190
  Harry 163, 190
  Lillian 190
Lane
  Margaret E 76, 77
  Merrilee 224, 237
  Peter W 31
Lanendyke
  Almira 39
Lang
  John 167
  Marilyn A 201, 227
Langdon
  Larry 216
  Roy 169
Langedek
  Joel 26
Langendeck
  Peter 27
  Christina 26
  Petrus 27
Langendike
  Christopher 35
  Cornelius E 35
Langendyck
  Caty 31
  Christina M 31
  Cornelis 24
  Cornelius 31, 37

Langendyck
  Elizabeth O 31, 37
  Elizbeth C 35
  Henry 31
  Jan 31
  Jane E 31
  Joanna 31
  John 31
  John O 37
  Margaret A 31
  Melinda J 37
  Rachel A 37
  Sarah R 31
  Simeon P A 37
Langendyk
  Abraham S 40
  Adam 24
  Annaatje 25
  Annatje 26, 27
  Annetje 23, 31, 34
  C 24
  Catharina 24, 27
  Catharine 27
  Catrina 23, 25
  Christina 26, 31
  Christina C 34
  Cornelis 22, 23, 26
  Cornelis P 24, 27
  Cornelis S 27, 35
  Cornelius A 38
  Cornelius E 37
  Erwin 40
  Geertruy 23
  James 27, 34
  Jan 26
  Jannetje 23
  John 24, 26
  John O 43
  Jr. Lukas 27
  Lucas 23, 24, 33
  Lucas S 33
  Lukas 27
  Margaretta 27
  Margritje 27, 34
  Maria 23, 24, 25, 26, 27
  Mary 26
  Peter 35
  Petrus 23, 24, 27
  Petrus P 27, 33
  Salina A 33
  Sarah 26
  Zacharias 27, 34
Langendyke
  Abraham S 34
  Almira 33
  Carrie S 44
  Charles L 44
  Chris C 126
  Christina C 106
  Christine 37
  Christine C 41
  Elizabeth 44
  Elizabeth C 37
  Emma A 38
  Harriet 38
  Henry A 38
  Henry C 37
  Johannah M 37
  John 38, 51
  John A 38, 44
  John B 38
  Louisa 41
  Margarert A 38
  Margaret E 38
  Mary A 38
  Peter P 38, 44
  Robert 33
  Sylvester 34
Langenedyk
  Cornelius E 44
Lantz
  Karen 78
Larson
  Christian 236
  Glenn 236
  Jeffrey 236
  Todd 236
Lasher
  Barbara R 104, 125
  Betty 65, 70
  Cressie 47
  Emeline 36
  Inez 47
  Sarah 65
Latcham
  Elizabeth 166, 194
Lathrop
  Lorin W 125
Launspach
  Jr Henry H 201, 227
  Karl E 227
  Paul H 227
  Sonja L 227
Laurens
  Aefje 21
Lawless
  Mary 168
Lawrence
  Russell 155
Lawson
  Frank 187
Learned
  Grace H 123, 148
  Mary M 123, 148
  William L 123
Learst
  Albert 127
  Robert C F 181
Lee
  Bertha 71, 74
  Dorothy C 148, 180
  Earl 74
  Elizabeth 115, 139
Leg
  Julliette 36
Legg
  Abbie 42
  Abraham 42
  Alfred 42
  Alononzo O 36
  Carrie 42
  Charles 42
  Cora 42
  Cornelis W 30
  Cornelius H 36, 42
  Edwin 42
  Ira 42
  Jr William H 25
  Juliette 42
  Mary E 36
  Maude H 42
  Nellie 42
  Richard B 30, 36
  Silas W 36, 42
  William C 42
  William H 30
LeGris
  Joycelyn 210, 234
Leide
  Margaret A 45, 49
Leigh
  Emily 141, 171
Lenentone
  Annie 155, 186
Lent
  Charlotte E 148, 179
  Franklin T 148
  Frederick R 179
  Harriet D 180
  Jane R 179
  John D 148, 179
  Jr John 179
  Jr Theodore D 180
  Marjorie R 179, 207
  Mary R 179, 207
  R Nancy 179
  Rose D 148
  Theodore D 148, 180
Leo
  Charlotte E 179, 207
  Jr Norton B 179
  Norton B 179
Lepley
  Amy E 68, 73
Leroyd
  Evelyn M 194
Levesque
  A 182, 209
  Linda 209
Lewis
  Barbara 179
  Edmund V 148
  Elizabeth C 43, 47

Lewis
- Ida G 126, 149
- Katharine D 179
- V Edmund 179

Lidstone
- Lara N 231
- Robert 206, 231

Lilburn
- Tina 170

Liller
- Kacey D 78
- Robert D 78
- Robert T 77
- Tory D 78

Lillian
- Norma 192

Lincoln
- Susan 60, 64

Lindsay
- Clara 151, 183
- D Charles 204, 229
- James A 229, 238
- Jennifer L 238
- Mitchell G 229, 238
- Patricia 238
- Tracey D 229, 238
- Wade C 229

Lipsett
- Lizzie B 131, 156

Lister
- Beth E 217, 237

Little
- Robert L 217

Livesley
- Ann V 201
- David R 201, 226
- Kelly J 226
- Kevin D 226
- Mary E E L 172, 200
- Mildred E J 172
- Phyllis D 201
- R Arden D 172, 201
- Robert 141, 172
- Valerie A 226

Lloyd
- Maud 168

Loates
- M Dianne 219, 235

Lockhart
- Helen 156

Logan
- Eliza J 141, 171
- Henry 120
- Richard H 172

Loman
- Tisa 230

Lonedyke
- Celia J 39
- Jan S 33

Long
- Ann Marie 217, 235

Longedyke
- Sophia J 39

Longendike
- Amos 35

Longendike
- Christina 35
- Cornelius P 35
- Jane M 35
- Michael 35

Longendyck
- Elmer 43
- Emma J 43
- Fordyce 43
- Franklin D 43
- Ida A 43
- James E 43
- Jason 43
- Lelian A 43
- Lillian A 43
- Maggie 43
- Mary 32
- Mary E 43
- Rachel A 121, 146
- Sebastian D 43

Longendyk
- James 43
- Johana E 43
- Peter P 40

Longendyke
- Addison 41, 45
- Alice 41
- Alice L 47
- Allen 51
- Amy S 48
- Andrew A 40
- Arrietta 43
- Arthur 41, 45
- Arthur L 49
- Benjamin F 34, 39
- Blanche D 46
- Brian 51
- Caroline 37
- Carrie S 49
- Catharina 35
- Cecil K 47
- Charles 41, 44, 45
- Charles E 37, 40
- Charles M 40
- Charlotte D 40
- Christina 34
- Christina C 40
- Christopher 41
- Clarissa 40
- Claude S 47
- Clifford H 49, 51
- Cora 41, 46
- Cora A 43, 48
- Cora B 45
- Cornelia A 37, 40
- Cornelia M 37
- Cornelis P 41

Cornelius 34, 40
Cornelius C 34
Cornelius D 47
Cornelius E 41
Cornelius H 37
Cyrus M 41
Dennis 51
Dorothy 44
Dwight S 43, 48
Edward O 43
Edwin 41
Eileen 50, 52
Eleanor 51
Elizabeth C 41, 44
Ella 49, 51
Ella C 40
Elvina 41, 46
Elwood 50, 51
Emma J 48
Emma M 48
Erastus 40
Erle H 45, 49
Erle W 49, 51
Erwin 44
Ethel 45, 49
Fannie E 44, 49
Floyd 44
Frances E 40, 44
Franklin D 47, 48
Fred 49
George A 40
Gerras 40
Gladys M 49, 51
Grace 45
Gross 40
Gwen 51
Harmon 35
Harold J 51
Harold K 49, 51
Harold R 47
Hazel 45
Henry A 43
Henry M 40, 45
Hilda E 49
Hiram 33
Howard 50
Howard C 45
III Wm F 49, 51
James 34, 51
James D 37, 48
James H 45, 49
James M 49
Jane C 34, 38
Janet G 51, 52
Janice 51
Jason 41, 45
Jeanne A 51, 52
Jennie 46
Jennie E 47
Joanna M 44
Johanna E 37

Longendyke
John 33, 50
John B 34, 40
John Jr 51
John O 48
John V H 40
Joseph E 51
Jr. Cliff H 51
Katie 45
Kay R 51
Laura 50
Leeta W 48
Lillian A 48
Lotta D 45
Louella 45
Lydia E 33
Lynne 51
Mabel 45, 50
Mable R 48
Margaret J 40
Margaret L 48
Margaret M 45
Margaretta 31
Maria C 40
Marie E 40
Martha C 45, 49
Mary 33
Mary A 43, 44, 47
Mary C 37, 43
Mary E 35, 48
Mary Ellen 41
Mary F 38
Mary H 40, 47
Maud E 46
Melinda 44
Melissa 35, 41
Michael 41
Minnie A 40, 44
Miriam E 49, 51
Myrtle 46
Nathan 45
Nettie C 44
Nettie E 48
Nettie M 43
Nina B 45, 49
Norman 42, 46
Ornelia A 45
Paul 33
Pearl L 47
Peter 34
Peter H 34, 37, 40
Rachel 40
Rachel A 33, 44
Sara 34
Sara J 37
Sarah 31, 38
Sarah A 48
Sarah E 40
Sarah J 35
Sarah M 37
Simon P 43
Solomon 34, 43, 49
Sophia J 33
Stanley C 47
Stanley L 46, 50
Stuart A 49, 51
Theodore F 39, 44
Thomas 51
Titus 41
Tjerck 34, 40
Victor 41, 46
Victoria A 40
W Floyd 45
Watson L 47
Wilbur 41, 46
William A 41
William F 40, 41, 44, 45, 49
William S 35, 41
Zachariah 34
Longendytke
George O 40
Longyear
Angeline 61, 65
Anna 58, 61
Loose
Robert C 224, 238
Robert J 238
Willis F A 238
Lord
Frank 136
Louw
Abraham 101
Abraham D 88, 100
Annetje 100
Catharina 88, 100
Elisabeth 88
Eliza 101
Elizabeth 100
James 101, 122
Jannetje 88, 101
John 101
John A 88
Jr Abraham D 100
Lea 100
Levi 88, 101
Lucas 101
Margaret 101
Maria 100
Marytje 88, 100
Peggie 100
Petrus 88, 100
Polly 101
Rachel 88, 100, 101
Rachel A 101
Tjirck 101
Tobyas 101
Willem 100
Wyntje 88, 100, 121
Love
Carville M 224
Low
Abraham 80
Abraham A 100, 121
Alexander K 37, 44, 121, 146
Almena 122
Annatje 100
Catharine E 122
Chark 121
Chark A 146
Clara D 147
Eleanor J 146
Elisabeth 100
Elizabeth L 121, 146
Elmer Chark 122
Elmer E 146
Fannie A 146
Flora Bell 122
George A 146
Hattie G 146
James M 146
Jan A 101
John 122
John A 146
Jr Abraham 121
Levi 121, 146
Lucas E 100
Lucretia B 146
Margaret L 146
Martha Jane 122
Mary A 38, 44, 146
Mary E 146
Mary Jane 121
Rachel L 146
Rebecca M 121, 146
Rosa M 147
Samuel H 122
Sanford A 146
Sarah Eliza 122
Sarah M 146
Sylvester 121
Tine M 146
William E 146
William V S 121, 146
Wyntje 101
Lowe
Chark A A 178
Ethel Mae 178
George C 40, 45
Harry D 178
Marguerite I 173, 202
Maude M 178, 206
Lowell
Lina 186, 212
Lowther
Christopher S 106, 126
Helen 126
Lucas
Florence 143
Fred 143
Smith F 119, 143
Luhman
Mildred 47

Luke
  Cecil 217
Lundahl
  Brady 238
  Lucas M 238
  Michael 229, 238
Lutz
  William L 231
Luycaszen
  Andries 21
Lynch
  Joseph 72
  Karen 212
  Patricia 212
  Thomas 185, 212
Lyon
  Diane 222
  Duncan 222
  H Neville 197, 222
  Samena 222
  Vivian 164
Lyons
  Howard 191
  Thomas 150
MacCowan
  Carrie 135
MacDonald
  Robert B 49, 51
  Robert D 51, 52
MacDougal
  Jean 195, 219
Macklin
  Jan 17
MacLean
  Kathleen D 161, 188
MacLellan
  Eric D 211
  Stewart 183, 211
MacMichael
  Frank R 181, 208, 233
  Gillian R 233
  Helen G 181
  Jan B 233
  John F R 150, 181
  Judith H 208
  Leslie I 208, 233
  Linda G 208, 233
  Mary G J 181, 208
  Ralph B 181, 208
  Richard S 233
  Robert P 233
MacMillan
  Charles 190, 216
  Dwight 216
  Reginald 216
Madden
  Louise H 162
Madlem
  Heath W 230
  Heather M 230
  Holly E 230

Russel 205, 230
Magee
  Ephriam 37, 44
  Godfrey 44
  Muriel 170, 197
Magnuson
  Lois M 199
Mahr
  Diane L 202
  Donald A 173, 202
  Kenneth G 203
  Steven A 202
Mailman
  Evelyn 215, 235
Mallory
  Donald P 184
  Enrique 152, 184
  Enrique D 211
  Jr Lester D 211
  Lester D 184, 211
Malone
  Kevin 219
Malstein
  Neil 44
Maltby
  Lily E 161, 188
Manchas
  John 200
Manning
  Frank 169
Marette
  Cecile 198, 222
Mark
  T 198
Markel
  Hans 25
Marquiet
  Silvia 101, 122
Marrozziti
  Carolyn 49
Marsden
  Alice J 49
Martin
  Adeline E 172
  David K 77, 79
  Delano R 75, 77
  Edward 212
  Elisabet 57
  Elizabeth 54, 118, 143
  Eva 166, 193
  Franklin 38
  John H 118, 143
  Linda R 77
  Mary 143, 173
  Mary E 105, 126
  Phillip J 77
  Raymond 186, 212
  Rosemary 209, 233
  Ryan D 79
  Samuel 62

Martino
  H Elizabeth 45, 49
Mason
  David 189
  Fred 132
  Harry 177
  Henry 144
Massino
  Christina 38
Mathany
  Jane 66
Matheny
  Brooks 66
  Christina 66
  Elijah C 62, 66
  George 66
  George W 66
  Joanne 66
  Joseph M 66
  Mary A 66
  Rachel 66
  Rebecca 66
Mathews
  Theresa 202, 208
  Theresa 228
  Don 193
Matthiessen
  Harriet W 124, 148
Mattingly
  Anne 63, 68
Matychuck
  Verna 202, 227
Maulin
  Daniel 63
Mauterstock
  Laura E 47
Maxwell
  Oliver P 43
  Robert 52
May
  Juliet L 104
  Louise 125
Maybe
  Ernest 72
Mayes
  Ernest G 203, 228
  Wendy M 228, 238
McAdam
  A 217
McAffie
  Wallace T 156
McAllister
  June 184
McAuley
  Martha 137, 166
McBean
  Rita 220, 236
McBride
  Libby 173, 202
McCabe
  Beulah F 76

McCabe
  Darrell C 76
  Denver P 76
  W Marshall 76
  William M 72
McCamus
  David 193
McCartney
  Cheryl A 233
  Claude R 75, 77
  Donald G 208, 233
  Janet M 233
  John R 77
  Randi Sue 77
McCauley
  Annie C 222
  Barry 222
  Gannon 222
  Gary 197
  K C 170, 197
  Morgan 222
McClay
  Francis 198
McCleary
  Bessie 191
  Hazen 164
  James 137
  John 137
  Mary 137
McClung
  Charlotte 101, 121
McColley
  Laura 121, 146
McConnell
  James 162
McCorby
  Ina 71
McCord
  Hold 214
McCorkle
  Carol 187
  Frank 160, 187
  Kenneth 187
  Lois 187
McCowan
  B Ruth 181, 208
McCoy
  Patrick 32
McCracken
  Allan G 210 183
  Alma E 183, 210
  Arthur 195
  Bertha 183, 210
  Dawn 210
  Edna 183
  Garda 210
  Gregory A 234
  Harry 183
  Howard S 183
  Kenneth 210
  Norma 210, 234
  Peter 210
  Richard 210
  Robert D 234
  Roy 183, 210
  Stanley 151, 182
  Stephen 210
  Wayne 210, 234
McCroby
  Ina 67
McCullough
  Margaret A 119, 144, 177
  Susan J 196, 221
McCutcheon
  Della 150, 182
McDermand
  Sarah A 103
McDermott
  Germaine L 49, 51
McDonald
  Arnold 186, 212
  Benjamin 212
  Chantel R 238
  Charlene 238
  Christine D 52
  Evaline 166, 194
  Peter 212
  Sean E 52
McDowell
  Allan F 209
  Frederick A 150, 181
  Lawrence W 209
  Leslie T 181, 20
  Lori E 209
  Lyall B 209
  Lyall T 182, 209
  Robert G 209
McFaddin
  H Norman 175, 204
  I Marlene 229
  Kathleen D 229, 238
  Lorne G 204, 229
  Marlene I 204
McFawn
  Clara 160, 188
McGhee
  Donald 73
McGillicuddy
  Billy L 237
  Chyanne 237
  Clement 218, 237
McGimpsey
  Irene E 175, 204
McGowan
  Phyllis I 208, 233
McGrath
  Robert 220
McGuire
  Barbara A 223, 237
  George 191, 219
McHatten
  Janet 236
McIntosh
  Garnet 217
  Hazel 164
McIntyre
  Margarette E 205, 230
McKay
  Ella 186
McKee
  Bill 217
  Jane 59
McKenzie
  Harry 155
  Kenneth 155
  William D 200
  William J 171, 200
McKibben
  Tommie 177
McKinnon
  Margaret 136
McLaughlin
  Edith 195, 220
  Gene 217
McLean
  Janet 49, 51
McLeod
  James 130, 155
  Melvina 155
  Murdo 169
  Phoebe 155
  Sarah E 156
  William 155
McManus
  Ethel 45, 50
McMillan
  Doris L 203, 228
McMorris
  Robert B 79
McMullan
  Brian 196
McMurray
  Anna 40, 44
McMurrough
  John L 161
McNall
  James 69
McNally
  Janet 235
  Roslene 235
  Vaughn 212, 235
McNaughton
  Heather 198
Mea
  Victor Della 77
Meegan
  Doris M 199
Meeks
  Russ 193
Meff
  Ida 142
Meier
  Levi 26

Melbourne
  Hazen 195
Mellman
  Charles P 150, 181
  Eleanor 181, 208
  Mary K 181
  Milicent J 181
Menaard
  Leah 239
Menard
  Dennis R 232, 239
  Jamie L 239
Mercer
  Patricia D 236
  Robert 219, 236
  Robin E 236
  Sheena P 236
  William F 236
Merchant
  James 40, 45
  William T 45
Merill
  Hilda S 205, 230
Merkel
  Annatje 28
  Johannes 28
Merrill
  E Laura 68, 72
Merritt
  Ida P 42
  Ira DeWitt 42
  Peter 36, 42
  Sarah 106
  Sarah M 44, 126
Mersereau
  Albert 164, 165
  Alice 191
  Allan 220
  Alma 165
  Andrew 112
  Angelique D 214
  Anna 193
  Artelle 191
  Arthur 152, 183
  Audrey 192
  Benton 220
  Carol L 215
  Charles 165, 193
  Clarence 165, 193, 194, 218
  Colin 220
  Deanna 220, 236
  Denise L 215
  Donna M 193
  Dorothy E 193
  Douglas A 188, 189, 214, 215
  Edna 165, 193
  Edward 193
  Eldon 162, 189
  Elizabeth 136, 166
  Elmer F 189, 215
  Elva 192
  Emma 193
  Eric 217
  Ernest 165, 192
  Faye B 131, 156
  Fred 165
  G D 189
  Gary 217
  Georgianna 189, 215
  Georgie 136, 166
  Gerald 195, 220
  Gilman 151
  Glenwood B 193
  Harry 165
  Hazel 165, 193
  Hazen 165
  Henry 136, 165
  Hilton B 193
  Ida 191, 217
  Ida V 160, 187, 193, 218
  Ila 162, 189
  Irma M 189, 215
  James 134, 162
  Janet 193
  Janice L 215
  Jeannie T 191
  Jennie 165
  Jennifer 236
  John 113, 136, 165, 193
  Joyce 193
  Jr. Rainford 165
  Judy A 193, 217, 235
  Lenore 193, 218
  Louella 162
  Marie 193
  Marion 191, 222
  Mark 217
  Maxine 191
  May 183
  Melvin A 189, 215
  Michael M 215
  Miles 183
  Patrick D 214
  Pearl I 192
  Phyllis 189, 215
  Rachel E 112, 133
  Rainsford 136, 165
  Randy 220, 236
  Randy G 236
  Raymond 193
  Raymond M 193
  Robert 193
  Robert S 191, 217
  Roy 162, 183
  Ruth 183
  Ruth J 193
  Stella M 134, 161
  Stephen 217
  Stephen E 215
  Terrance 220
  Travis 192
  Treston 193
  Trevor E 193
  Vance 162
  Vernon I 193
  Victoria 137
  Vincent 189
  W Andrew 162, 189
  Winsell 164, 165, 191, 193, 197
  Winslow J 165, 193
Messick
  Granville 44, 49
  Margaret 49
Methany
  Darius E 70, 74
  John 66
  Susan 66
  William B 74
Meyer
  Abraham L 121
  Amelia 121
  Angeline 121
  Anna M 121
  Asa 121
  Christina 32
  Henry Clay 121
  Jonas 100, 121
  Jonathan C 41
  Levy 32
  Nelson 32
  Rachel M 32
  Ralph 121
  Sarah E 121
Meyndertzen
  Harriet 33
Middaugh
  Catharine A 34, 40
Mighion
  Helen E 218, 192
Mikesall
  Mary Jo 198, 223
  William B 170, 198
Milanetti
  Alexandra N 238
  Jeffrey M 238
  Michael 228, 238
Miles
  Fred 106
Miller
  Allis H 180
  Betty 198, 223
  Beverly 197, 22
  Carolyn A 206
  Charles L 40, 4
  Joan 156
  Leila 186, 21
  Lewis L 178, 206
  M Louise 206, 231
  Margaret E 44
  Norman F 178, 206
  Robert L 206
  Susan E 103, 123
  Victoria L 44, 49

Mills
   Phillip 191
Minchall
   Selena 170
Miner
   Sarah 41
Minot
   Maude 121
Mitchell
   Brenda M 137, 166
   Margaret 108
Mixter
   James H 38
Moffat
   Ann 130
   George 130
   John 130
   Margaret 130
   Robert 109, 130
   Rosynet 130
   Elizabeth 166
Moffit
   Alice E 165
   George 164, 191
Mollet
   Ann L 207
Moninger
   Kate 65
Montague
   M C 68
Montgomery
   Fred 143
Moon
   Myrtle 197
   Ollie May 146, 178
Moore
   Charles H 161, 188
   Dorothy 214
   Edna 193
   Harold 165, 193
   Harriet 95, 118
   Henrietta 115
   Josephine 193
   Karen M 192, 217
   Margaret 165, 192
   Robert 193
   Una 193
Moran
   Mary E 121, 146
Moravee
   Nancy 197
More
   Jane McPhee 177, 206
Morehouse
   Hinson 162
Morgan
   Phillip D 205
   Wesley 167
   William 177, 205
Morganstern
   Margaret C 223

Morris
   Barbara K 209
   Jane Ann 36
   Steven B 209
   Virginia 199, 224
   William G 182, 209
Morrison
   Don 196
   Douglas A 224
   Malcolm R 199, 224
   Ralph E 224
Morse
   Dana 205, 230
   Tamra M 230
Mosher
   Brian 222
   Jr Stephen 222
   Sandra 222, 236
   Stephen 191, 222
Mott
   Charles 137, 167
   Chester 195
   Elsie 195
   Emeline 114, 138
   George 115, 195
   Jr Chester 195
Moulton
   Amelia 34, 40
Mountain
   Margaret K 201
Mowat
   Ada 166
Mower
   Anna M 36, 42
   Susannah 56, 60
Moyer
   Allan A 173, 201
   Andrew A 227
   Arthur A 202, 227
   Arthur W 201
   Charles E 201
   Margaret J 201, 226
   Patricia 227
   Ronald C 172, 201
Muhs
   Mary 206, 231
Muir
   Frank 169
   Henry 139, 169
Mulholland
   Alice 171
   Annie 171, 199
   Elsie 171
   Joseph 171
   Norman 171
   Ruth 171, 199
   Sarah 171, 199
   Thomas W 141, 171
Mullen
   Sadie 165, 193

Munn
   Eric 216, 235
   Kerry V 235
   Sara K 235
Munro
   Shelly M 217
Murphy
   Harry J 135
   John 112, 135
   Martha 114
   William 135
Murray
   Harold 173
Myer
   Catharine 42, 35
   David L 33, 39
   Emma 39
   Harvey 39
   James H 39
   Lydia A 39
   Martha E 70
   Masom 75
   Rebecca 32
   Sally C 32
   Ten Eyck 39
   William H 39
   William M 32
Myers
   Argyle 75
   Martha E 65
   Rachel C 106
   Sarah C 38
Nadler
   Mildred 148, 179
Nagy-Deak
   Andrew M 238
   Caitlen D 238
   David R 238
   Michael 230, 238
Nash
   Cecelia 118
   F H 118
   George D 118
   James 95, 118
   James M 118
   Jane Ann 118
   Joseph P 118
   N J Christie 118
   Prudence 118
Nason
   Ada 139, 169
   Adam M 221
   Adelbert 196
   Adeline 113, 136, 138, 139, 168
   Alfred C 168
   Alma E 165, 192
   Amy I 169
   Angus 165
   Ann M L 221
   Anne M 169
   Annie 114, 139, 168, 195, 220

Nason
Annie A 139
Annie I 167
April L 237
Arthur R 196
Audrey 196
Avery R 218
Barbara A 218
Barbara J 192
Benjamin J 139, 169
Berton C 192
Betty I 196
Beulah 165, 195
Brenda L 236
Bryon E 196, 220
Burton W 136, 164, 169
C Smith 220
Carla D 221
Caroline F 221
Carrie 169
Cecil G 192
Cecil W F 196
Celestia 138
Charlotte 139, 167, 195, 236
Chester 168, 196
Chester S 195
Christina 236
Christopher 221, 236
Cindy A 218, 237
Clyde 169
Cora 169
Crystal J R 217
Curtis 217, 221, 237
D Kent 23
Dale 210
Dale E 221
Darlene E 221
Darren E 221
David 127
David A 139, 192, 218, 219, 236
David F 221
David G 221
Deanna D 218
Delaney 168
Dennis A 221
Devin L 237
Dirck K 237
Donald 218
Donna 189, 215
Donna L 220
Doris O 196
Dorothia 220
Dorothy E 220
Edna A 192
Edwin 217
Edwin E 139
Eileen S 219, 236
Elizabeth I 169, 196
Ella 139
Ellie 168
Elsie 167, 195

Emily J 168
Ephriam 114, 139
Ernest 167
Errol G 196
Ester E 196
Ethel M 168
Eugene 195, 220
Eugene B 192
Eunice C 138, 168
Evelyn M 192
Everett B 138, 167
Ezekiel 167
Faye 169
Frances E 169
Francis G 139, 168
Francis V 196, 221
Frank 168, 169
Frederick A 164, 192
Gary S 220, 236
George 113
George A 167, 195
George B 220, 236
George E 165
George F 136, 138, 168
George I 168, 196
Gerald 165
Gloria J 189
Gordon E 192, 218
Grace 169
H Ray 217
Hale 168
Hannah 92, 112, 113, 138
Hannah J 112, 134
Hardy 134
Harvey H 138
Hazel 169
Helen G 168
Herbert R 192
Ina 169
Isack 114
Isaih 114
Isreal 138
James 195
James L 221
Jamie S 236
Janis M 218
Jason A 221
Jay S 221
Jeanie F 196
Jeffery A 236
Jeremy L 236
Jody D 221
John 95, 114, 167
John D 218
John M 114, 138
John R 192
John S 219, 236
Junita M 220
Justus 167, 195
Kaye L 220
Kelly E 221

Kelsey T 221
Kendall 218
Kevin B 221
Kimberley A 220
Lance R 217, 237
Lauroe R 196
Lee Gordon 162, 189
Lemuel 114, 138, 167
Leon R 196, 221
Leonard P 220
Leslie D 220, 236
Lester E 196, 221
Lillian A 167
Linda 221
Lorriane 221
Louis M 196
Lucy H 169
Lynn 213
Mabel 195
Mabel A 167, 168
Manzer B 138, 167
Margaret E 139, 168
Margaret K 219
Margery A 196
Mark G 218
Marlene J 196
Martha F 139, 168
Martha I 139
Marty D 218, 237
Mary 114, 139, 167
Mary Ann 113, 135
Mary D 138
Mary G 169
Mary J 113, 135, 138, 139, 168
Maud E 169
Melvina Y 236
Merrit 139
Michael D 236
Mildred 191
Milford 196, 221
Millie A 169
Moses 138
Muriel E 220
Myrtle A D 167
N Annabelle 164
Nancy 114, 209
Neil 209
Nellie 195, 220
Nellie A 191
Nellie M 168
Norma 195
Norman A 192, 218
Pamela D 221
Patti 221
Paul 182, 209
Paul W 196
Payson 193, 218
Pearl 166, 195, 21
Pennell E 138, 16
Perley D 195, 220
Perry A 220, 236

Nason
  Philip 187, 214
  Randall E 218, 237
  Randy L 196, 221
  Raymond H 168, 196
  Robert A 221
  Robert B 169
  Robert F 192, 217
  Robert L 196, 200
  Robert T 196
  Roland 220
  Ronald D 192, 217
  Ronald E 196
  Rose Marie 196
  Ross P 192
  Roy 196, 221
  Roy A 169
  Ruby A 168
  Russell 195, 196
  Russell E 168
  Ruth 168, 169, 196
  Sadie 169
  Saphrona 137, 166
  Sarah 94, 113, 138, 167, 195
  Sharon A 221
  Shawn D 218
  Shawn M 221
  Sherri A 221
  Sherry 217
  Shirley E 196
  Spencer A 168, 196
  Stafford N 196
  Stephen R 218
  Stephen W 221
  Stuart A 218
  Stuart E 192, 196, 218, 221
  Susan 218
  T Earl 163
  Tehwauna C 220
  Terri L 237
  Thelma H 192
  Thomas L 139, 168
  Timothy 217
  Todd M 236
  Tracy 217
  Tracy L 237
  Travis E 195, 220
  Velma L 196
  Vergie 195, 219
  Victoria 138, 167
  Vivian 195, 220
  W Edgar 165
  Wade M 217
  Wallace 194, 219
  Wallace S 236
  Wilfred C 196, 221
  Willard B 136, 168
  William A 168, 196, 221
  William E 192
  Wilmot B 167
  Zachariah 139, 169
  Zachariah M 169
  Zackariah 114
  Zackary 217
  Zaida L 168
  Zelmer 169
Neal
  Barbara 130, 156
Neff
  Abraham 117, 142
  Alfred 142
  Alice 142
  Arthur 142
  Carlotte M 143
  Edgar 142
  Helen A 142
  J Edwin 143
  Jacob 95, 117
  James B 118, 142
  Jessie 143
  Mary I 143
  Mary Isobel 173
  Sarah A 117
  Susan 142
  Thomas D 118
Neilsen
  Bertie 183
  Wendy 234
Nelson
  Anne Marie 198
  C Jeanette 198
  Deborah 77, 78
  Hugh D 198
  J Melvin 198
  James F 170, 198
  Mark 207
  R Frances 198
  Rebecca R 232, 239
  Sarah A 120
Netherton
  Mildred J 45, 49
Nevers
  Phoebe 95, 115
Newbraugh
  Otto 72
Newdeck
  Leah 177, 205
Newkirk
  Charles 43, 47
  Christian P 47
  Edward J 47
  Ernest 47
  George A 47
  Issac N 47
  Jane E 47
  Peter E 47
  Ralph D 47
  Silas C 43, 47
Newton
  Alice 69, 73
Nickerson
  Mildred 49, 51
Nicklaus
  Shirley 201
Nield
  Donna B 229
  Jack 204, 229
  James A 229
  Laura J 229
  Peter J 229
Nielsen
  Bertie 210
  David 210
  Eric 234
  Joan 210
  Omar 234
  Paul 210, 234
  Philip 210, 234
  Rene 234
  Todd 234
Nine
  Luther 68
Nixon
  Joy 200, 224
Noble
  Ethel F 134, 162
  Freda M 165, 193
  Karen 235
  Shawna 235
  Terrance 216, 235
Nollet
  Ann L 232
Nordin
  Mark 205
Norrad
  Beryl 194, 218
North
  Katharine D L 148
Norton
  Alan C 228, 238
  Bernice M M 203, 228
  Carol 238
  Cecil H 173, 203
  Clara L 173, 20
  David 228
  Elsie D 148, 179
  Grant J 203, 228
  Heather 23
  Hiram G A 143, 173
  John T 123, 148
  Jr John T 148
  Katharine D L 179
  Michael 228
Nugy
  Muriel 170, 197
Nuttal
  Pamela 218, 237
Nyberg
  Shirley A 182, 209
Nye
  Betty Ann 190
  Patricia R 190

O'Brien
  Frederick 185
  James 185
  Ora 155, 185
O'Donnell
  Michael 236
O'Leary
  Lois 192, 217
O'Neal
  James W 61
Oakley
  Maria 54, 58
Oates
  Mary D 191
Ochetwa
  Dean 225
  Eugene 200, 225
  Ian 225
  Lynn 225
  Susan 225
Odterhoudt
  Sarah 39
Ogden
  Carol 216
  Connie 211, 234
  Jean 189, 215
  M 192
  Vera 187, 213
Ogger
  Marther 75
Olive
  Augusta D 150
Oliver
  Asa 108
  Melinda 108, 127
Olmstead
  Lealey A 218, 23
Omstead
  Charlotte 118, 143
Oosterhoudt
  Hendrikus 29
  James 29
  Peter 29
Oosterhout
  Ariaantje 22
Opdycke
  Mary E 148, 179
Oshier
  David 193
Osterhoud
  Annatje 29
  Jacobus 88
  Lucas 88, 100
Osterhoudt
  Alfred 125
  Amelia E 122
  Anna E 39
  Arietta 39
  Cornelia 101, 122
  Elias 101, 122
  John 122
  Louisa 126
  Martin S 39
  Mary A 39
  Mary E 126
  Nelson 39
  Peter C 122
  Tjerck L 39
  William 39
Osterhout
  Anna M 33
  Ariaantjen 53
  Catharina 87, 99
  Caty M 100
  Charity C 29
  Cornelis 29
  Cornelius 33
  Emma C 39
  Hendrick 29
  Hendrikus 25, 87
  Henry 99
  Jacobus 80, 87, 100
  Jane 29
  Joel F 33
  John O 39
  Maria 88, 100
  Marietje 53
  Martinus 88
  Peter 105
  Sarah 29
  Sarah E 33
  Sarah V K 39
  Silvan J 100
  Sophia 29
  Tine 29
  Tjerck 33
  Tjerck L 33
  Tjerk 26
Ostrander
  Mary L 125
  Stephen N 105, 125
  Titus 125
Ostrhoudt
  Peter P 125
Otis
  Cora E 105
  James 91
  Luzilla S 105
  Seth K 91, 105
Oudette
  Audette 182
Overbag
  Henry D 112
  Peter J 112
Overbagh
  Elena V 125, 149
  Gertrude 180
  Isabel 180
  James 112
  John C 180
  John V L 105, 125
  Kernlauck 125
  Louisa 105
  Maria V L 125
  Peter A 90, 105
  Peter J 93
  Peter T 125
  R Ann M 105, 125
  Richard B 149, 180
  Richard F 180
  Sarah M 105
  Solomon F 105, 125
  Titus 105
  William H 180
Overbaugh
  Catrina 53, 56
  Gary C 232
  Gerald H 207
  Katheyn P 232
  Peter T 149
  Rodney P 207
  Sarah M 125
  Susan A 232
  Theodore S 207, 232
  William H 207
  William W 207
Overgagh
  Peter T 125
Packard
  Rachel 119, 144
Page
  Mahala L 108, 128
Pahl
  Jean 172
  Jeannie 201
Palen
  Harley J 48
Paling
  Jan 17
Palmer
  Alice 193
  Dora 195
  Frank 193
Paparatto
  Mary A 207
Pare
  Susan 51, 52
Pak
  Maryann 102
Parker
  James 163
  Murray 216
Parkhurst
  W D 187
Parks
  Rose 185, 212
Parrish
  Arza 202, 228
  Deborah L 228
  Kristy L 228
Parson
  Thomas 161

Parsons
  Annie 161
  Benison 133, 160
  Blanche 161
  Charles A 161
  DeWitt 144
  Dorothy 188
  Edward F 171, 200
  Eunice 200
  Floyd 144
  George Erb 161
  Helen 188, 214
  Margaret 161, 188
  Marjorie 188
  Mary 161
  Percy H 161
  Prudence 144
  Rudman 161
  Stanley 161
  Steven 119, 144
  Thomas 188
Passmore
  Florence A 150, 181
Pasternack
  Margaret 173, 202
Patell
  Eva E 47
Patten
  Jr Walter W 187
Patterson
  Mary 112, 133
Pattullo
  Betty 195
  David 195
  Ernest 195
  Francis 167, 195
Paulsen
  John E 49
Pawlak
  Diane I 228, 238
Payne
  Clyde 177
  Vincent 183, 211
Peabody
  Doris 156
  Fred 156
Pearson
  Carol L 202
  Eleanor J 202, 228
  Mari L 228, 202
  O E 202, 173
  Sharleen 224, 238
  Shirley E 202, 228
Peck
  Dorothy 148, 180
Pellettier
  John R 201, 226
  Malcolm B R 226
Pels
  Anna 91

Peltz
  Caroline 179
  Catharine W 148
  Henry S 179
  John D 123, 179
  John P 148
  Jr John D 148, 179
  Mary Ellis 179
  Mary L 179
  Philip 104, 123, 148, 179
  Richard C 124
  Sarah 123
  William L 148, 179
Pennington
  Alma E 172
Perkins
  Edgar A 62
Persen
  Debra 80, 87
  Emily 38
  Geertruy 80, 83
  Lucretia 82, 89
Person
  Jane 99
  Jannetje 87
Peterson
  Allen 192
  Catharine 143, 118
Petit
  Hermon 170
Petrie
  Anna M 38
Pettinger
  George W 37
Pettit
  Almeda 140, 170, 198
  Carolyn W 170, 198
  Cecil C 141
  Clare M 199
  Clare N 170, 199
  Doris E 170
  Esther 140
  Floyd H 199
  Gherry D 199
  Herman D 170, 199
  Hiram 140, 170
  Honor K 170, 198
  Isabel K 170
  Iva M 170, 198
  Jane 140
  John R 148, 179
  Lois 140, 170
  Lois E 170
  Marion B 170
  Mary D 179
  Melvin 140, 170
  Morley 140
  Ora R 170
  Rachel B 140
  Ruth O 170, 199
  Sarah 140

  Sylvester T 140
  Walter M 170
Peyton
  Derrick 234
Pfister
  Lois 170, 197
Pheasant
  Dianne E 219, 236
  Eileen P 219, 236
  William F 194, 219
Philip
  Charlotte A 206, 231
  David 230
  Elizabeth M 177
  Grafton B 177, 206
  Harry G R 144, 177
  James S 206, 231
  Jennifer N 231
  Joan G 206, 231
  John 206, 230
  Lora J 231
  Paul S 231
  Scott 230
  Sheila 230
  Steven 230
  Stewart 177, 206
Philips
  Aaron 114, 139
  Bertha 136, 165
  Shirley 193
Phillips
  Ann 218
  Charlotte 167, 195
  Darius 138
  Debbie 215
  Elizabeth 139, 164, 191
  Fred 135
  Harry 167
  Hazel 178, 206
  Ida 139
  Jeremiah 136
  John 139
  Leamon 139
  Leland 191
  Leon 191
  Letha 195, 220
  Lois 193
  Lucy 166, 194
  Lydia 165, 193
  Manzer 166
  Martha 137, 139, 166
  Mary 139, 166
  Melvin 139, 169
  Michael 170
  Noel 193
  Phoebe 139
  Terine 139
  Wellington 136
Philmon
  Rosalea 216

Phipps
  Elizabeth 119, 144
Pickering
  Caroline B 160
Pickup
  Joseph A 188
Pierce
  Foye 173
Pike
  Catherine 99, 121
  James 151
Pilgrim
  Clarissa A 180, 207
Plass
  Harriet M 37, 43
  Maria 27, 35
Plummer
  Grace 156
  James 156
  Lizzie 155, 18
Polhemus
  Susan A 48
Pollard
  James P 206
  Keri A 231
  Mary A 206
  Michael A 177, 206
  Michael W 206, 231
  Pamela A 231
  Robert T 231
  Susan J 206
  Thomas W 231
Pollock
  Lloyd 197
Pomeroy
  Mary L 47
Post
  Cornelia 31
  Edith 161
  Elliot E 38
  Jane C 34
  John H 31, 38
  Peter L. 38
  Thomas 36
Powell
  George 38
Preischel
  Richard 206
Prescot
  Marie 139
Preston
  Robert E 202
Price
  Marion 183
Pride
  Benedict 138, 167
  Clifford 167
  Dorothy 194, 219
  Fenwick W 167, 194
  Ida 194
  Lessie 167, 195

Prince
  Marion 210
Prindle
  Leona 48
Prior
  Ann C 149, 180
Procunier
  Olive 123, 148
Prosser
  Jennifer 210
Provenzano
  Frank 48
Pryor
  Betty Lou 186, 213
Pumphrey
  Eloise 172
Purvis
  Amy 224
  Andrew 225
  Charlotte 225
  Clarence 200, 225
  David 225
  Donald 225
  Eric 224
  Gordon 225
  James D 171, 200
  Jocelyn 224
  John 225
  Karen 224
  Laura R 200, 224
  Margaret 224
  Ronald J 200, 224
  Sheila 224
  Timothy 225
  Walter M 200, 225
  Wendy 224
Putman
  Evelyn 180
  J Seymour 149, 1
Putnam
  Charles W 38
Quick
  Katharine 55
Quigley
  William H 47
Quinn
  John E 156
Raeder
  John B 172
Raenden
  Andrew C 233
  Frank S 208, 233
  Leslie A 233
Ramsay
  Antionette 170, 199
  Lynn 234
  Peter B 32
  Walter 170
Ramsden
  Gwen 172, 201

Ramsey
  Lynn 210
  Robert 198
  Walter 198
Ramson
  Ann E 32
  James 26
Randall
  Helen E 199, 224
Randsom
  Maria 32
Ransom
  Abijah 32
  Barzilla 32
  Catharina 26, 33
  Caty 32
  Charles A 39
  Charlotte 32
  Christina 26, 32
  Clarence 39
  David J 32
  Deborah 32
  Elizabeth 32
  Henry T 39
  James 24, 26, 32, 35
  James F 39
  Johah 32
  Joseph 26, 32
  Leah 32, 38
  Maria 26, 33
  Melvina 32, 38
  Rhoda 32
  Sally 32
  Sally S 38
  Samuel 39
  Sarah C 39
  Zacharia B 33, 39
Ransum
  Sary 26
Ray
  Barbara Ann 199
Raymond
  Roberta 79
Rayner
  Chalmer 224
Reader
  Lydia 187, 213
Redford
  Sandra 206
Redstone
  Ursula 197
Regnier
  Amy 232
  Angela 232
  Thomas 207, 232
Reid
  David 205
  Edythe 142, 172
  Elizabeth A 234
  Martha 127
  Pamela 234

Reid
    Robert 210, 234
    Timothy A 234
Reimer
    Marlene M 201
Relyea
    Andrew D 43, 47
    Benjamin D 43
    David H L 47
    Jane E 43, 47
    Johanna 43, 47
    Maggie 47
    Mary M 43
    Sarah Jane 43
Remsen
    Annatje 35
    James 28
    Lucas 35
Remsey
    Sary 32
Renaud
    Joseph 208
Rensem
    Polly 26
Rensen
    James 26
    Petrus 35
Reynolds
    Gertrude 178, 206
    Jessie L 181, 208
    Sally A 91
Rhoades
    Fordice 134
Rhodes
    Rose 166, 194
Ribone
    Alfred 208, 232
Rice
    Edward H 178, 206
    Gail E 206
    Joanne 198, 223
    Keith E 206
    Kerie M 239
    Paul B 230, 239
    Paul E 239
    Richard 188
Richardson
    Elsie 182
    Irene 182
    Robert 150, 182
Richmond
    David 32
    Helen V 125
    Hiland 32
Richtmyer
    Henry 38
Rickard
    Courtney A 237
    Craig A 237
    Dana M 237
    George B 170, 199

George P 199
Grace E 199
Jeffrey C 223, 237
John W 199
Joseph 223
Kelly O 237
Kristin M 237
Kurt A 223, 237
Marc C 237
Peter 223
Robert P 199, 223
Riddle
    Charles 70
Rider
    Lewis 36, 42
Ridgen
    Eric 179
Rifle
    Joan M 223, 237
Riley
    Angus 132
Rilyea
    Benjamin 37
    Priscilla C 43
Riordan
    Jack 192
Risdon
    Louise 140
Roberts
    Oscar 140
    Susan 109, 129
Robertson
    Floyd C 49
    Hamilton G 49
    Jr Robert L 49
    Robert L 45, 49
Robins
    John 193
Robinson
    C Josephine 226
    Constance J 201
    Gladys A 173, 203
    Harold 196
    Julia 62, 65
    Susan 169
    Wilmot 166
Rockwell
    Bartlett 155
Rodeheaver
    Betty L 75, 7
Rodgers
    Brian A 200, 226
    Brian G 226
    Donald N 200
    George H 200
    Gregory A 226
    Kenneth H 226
    R Alexander 172
    Robert A 200
    Robert F 200
    Robert H G 226

Rohrer
    Catherine 89, 103
Roland
    Tracy 218
Roosa
    Aldert T 54, 58
    Anne 58
    Catrina 22, 58, 80
    Elizabeth 58
    Lucas W 58
    Nancy H 58
    Natte 58
    Rachel 58
Roosekrans
    Dirrick 17
Rorick
    Linda J 204, 229
Rosa
    John 58
Rosevear
    Gerald 189
Rosine
    Lillian 180, 148
Ross
    Amanda E 165, 192
Rossi
    Myron 51
Rothersdorf
    Maria 53, 5
Rous
    Jane Ann 205
Rowe
    George 113
Rozenboom
    Susan K 229, 238
Ruehl
    Valetta L 74, 77
Rulk
    Linda R 77
Rumsey
    Edna 73, 76
Runsom
    Sally 32
Rushton
    Hugh 168
Russel
    Joyce 215
    Lawrence 186
    Robert 186
Russell
    Joyce 189
    Patricia 186
    Richard 186
    Theodore B 179
Rutledge
    Alice 200, 225
Ryan
    Sue Ann 201
Ryder
    Arthur M 199
    Donald G 199

Ryder
    Glenna 192
    Gordon 164, 192
    Milton 170
    Milton P 199
    Shirley 192, 217

Rynax
    Arthur 169
    Wilbur 169

Sagar
    Levi 101
    Margaret 101

Sage
    Catharine 36, 42

Sagendorf
    Emma 44, 106, 126
    George 44, 106, 126

Saligman
    Lewis L 170, 198

Sampson
    Corrine 195, 220

Sanders
    Catharine E 68, 72
    George 74
    Margaret 67, 71
    Mary J 66, 70

Sanderson
    Eleanor 49, 5

Sandford
    Malcolm A 161
    Ada DeWitt 161
    Alonzo 133, 161
    Edith 161
    Elliott 161

Santos-Perez
    Ann 226
    Eric 226
    Jose 201, 226
    Joseph 226
    Katherine 226
    Madeline 226
    Margaret 226
    Paul 226

Sargisson
    Flora E 129, 150

Saunders
    James 195, 220
    Nancy 220
    Susan 220

Sauter
    Dale 200, 225

Savage
    Arnold 75
    Aubrey 75
    Christina L 78
    Jennifer M 78
    Kenneth 78
    Kimberly A 78
    Mary 68, 72
    Teresa 71
    Theresa 67
    Tracy R 78
    Walter 71

Savoie
    Ida C 51, 52

Savoy
    Joseph 220

Sax
    Ann 46
    Anna 42
    Catharine 112
    Eliza Ann 31, 38

Schaart
    Sophia 24, 27

Schaefer
    Leslie 205

Schaeffer
    Fisher 74

Schmiedeknecht
    Jane 178

Schnider
    Catherine 49

Schobert
    Christian F 142

Schoonhmaker
    James C 124

Schoonmaker
    Abrah T 124
    Abraham 36, 101
    Alfred 33, 39
    Annatje 33, 2
    Catrina 83
    Charles A 122
    Charles W 147
    Christian 101, 122
    Eliz 147
    George P 122, 147
    Grace 147
    Henry W 39, 124, 149
    Jane 31, 37
    John B 101
    John D 124, 149
    Lenah 24, 27
    Lura C 147
    Martin D 122, 147
    Martin F 147
    Mary D 124
    Mary E 122
    Mary V 147
    Rachel 101
    Sally E 101
    Sarah 90, 104
    Sarah G 149
    Tjerck 88, 104, 124
    Tjerck E 101
    Walter 122, 147
    Walter W 147

Schop
    Jan L 29
    Lodewyck 25, 29
    Maria C 30
    Petrus 30
    Petrus P 36
    Ritchart 29

Schoub
    Charles 42
    Chauncey L 36, 42
    Chauncey U 42
    Ira H 36, 42
    Jesse 42
    Nellie C 36, 42
    Rosalia A 42

Schultz
    Arthur A 224, 237
    Dawn M 237
    Lester E 199, 224
    Mary F 224
    Melody A 237

Scott
    Adeline 132, 151, 159
    Bertha 166
    Beverly 187, 214
    Carrie L 205, 230
    Clarissa 132, 151, 159, 182
    David J M 214
    Delilah 132, 151, 159, 182,
    E Marion 160, 187, 210
    Earl W 160, 187
    Earle L F 187, 214
    Elizabeth 151, 183
    Florence E 151
    Frank G 151, 182
    Frank R 160, 187, 193, 218
    Fraser 151
    George 129, 151
    Georgiana 151
    Gladys L 160
    Harry 160
    Henrietta 151
    James M 187
    Janise L 214
    Leo J 208, 232
    Lori Lee 187
    Michelle 232
    Myrtle 182
    Roy W 160
    Shane 232
    Steven 232
    Walter 151
    William B 151
    Winslow 133, 151, 160, 182

Scranton
    Lois 177, 206

Scribber
    Gwen 186

Scribner
    Abigail 30, 36
    L Jane 108, 127

Sebyns
    Jannetje 21

Seeley
    Hannah 108, 128
    Hannah C 92

Seeley
  James 128
  Mary E 109, 129
  Rebecca 109
Seely
  Adeline 128
  Ann 128
  Asahel 135
  Charles 194
  George 128
  Hanna C 109
  James W 108
  Luke 128
  Perley 128
  Raymond 165
Segee
  H Arlene 183, 210
  Inez 165
Seitz
  Carrie M 126
Sereck
  Edward 75
Seume
  Vera 143, 173
Seyler
  George F 49
Seymour
  Lou 71, 74
Shank
  Belle 72
Shanks
  Samuel 137
Shannon
  Sue 236
Sharp
  Eunice 88, 100
  Grant 201, 226
  Nadene L 226
  Suzanne A 226
Shaw
  E M 129
  Frank 129
  Odber 130, 156
  Stella 160
  William 160
Shelley
  Vanne 214
Shepherd
  Mary 126, 149
  Thomas D 206
Shepker
  Elizabeth A 231
  Jeanne M 206
  Judith R 206
  Julie A 231
  Maurice A 206
  Maurice K 177
  Paul F 206, 231
  Perk 206
  Peter W 231
  Thomas O 206, 231

Sherman
  Eva 48
Sherwood
  Lulu M T 156
Shewell
  Edward T 107
Shirley
  Allen 188, 214
  Annis 114, 138
  Sharon 214
  Thomas 214
Shock
  Margaret 65
Shockey
  Lester B 76
Shoemaker
  John 39
  Nina L 39
  Tjerck 101
  William 39
  Hendrick 17
Short
  Chester R 48
  Claude L 48
  Elizabeth 88, 100, 226
  Ella 43, 47
  Ethel M 48
  Ezra 41
  Franklin W 48
  John 43
  Lettie E 39, 44
  Lewis M 48
  Margaret L 48
  Maria C 35
  Sarah K 48
  Warren H 48
  Watson J 43, 48
Shortt
  Dale R 51
  Dorothy E 50, 52
  Ethel B 50, 52
  Harold L 50, 51
  Kelli Ann 52
  Maria C 41
  Randy R 51, 52
  Richard G 46, 50
  Vivian J 50
Shroades
  William R 178
Shultis
  Susie 47
Siebert
  Walter 181
Silberstein
  Sandra 221
Simmons
  Donald 167
Simpson
  Margaretta K 61, 65
  Sarah J 61

Sinclair
  Dorothea 112, 134
Sine
  Allan 214
  Lynda 214
  Marvin 214
  Paul 214
Sines
  Diana R 77, 78
  Joe 68
  Keith L 77
  Loraine C 75, 77
  Marvin 188
Sisson
  Vera 165
Sissons
  Brenda 198
  David 198
  H J 170, 198
  Mary 198
  Samena 198
Skeldon
  Coral A 216
Skelton
  Frederick 140
Skidmore
  Bethanne 52
  Kenneth 52
  Kenneth R 52
  Kimberly A 52
  Sean A 52
  Stacey C 52
  Walter 52
Skipper
  Candace M 78
  Clester B 75, 77
  Kevin D 78
  Sherry L 77
  Stacey J 78
  William C 77, 78
Sleep
  Daisy E 161
Slipp
  Alisha 235
  Donna 215
  Duane 215, 216, 235
  Harold 215, 235
  Luther 189, 215
  Ronald 215
  Ruth E 215
  Scott H 235
  Seth 235
  Wendy 215, 217, 235
Slote
  Oliver 115
Smart
  A T L 150, 182
  Charles B 150
  Charles L 109, 129, 151
  Donald 182
  Effie B 150, 182

Smart
- Emma 182
- Estelle E 150, 182
- Ida F 150, 182
- Jr Charles L 129
- Lauren W 150
- Llewellyn B 129, 150
- Louisa 151
- Mary A 92, 109
- Moses G 108
- Olive 109, 12
- Phoebe M 150, 182
- Walter 151

Smith
- Aida L 205
- Alden 213
- Aleatha 132
- Alfred 162, 189
- Alice 186
- Andrew M 232
- Angela 214
- Arron W R 226
- Arthur 159
- Arthur W 142, 172, 201, 226
- Barbara 190, 216
- Bayard 216
- Benjamin B 227
- Beulah 172
- Bruce 216
- Calvin 132, 211
- Carol 190
- Catherine 213
- Charlene A 211
- Charlotte 111, 131
- Christopher 216
- Cindy 78
- Clapman 92, 111
- Clayton 185, 187, 213
- Corinne E 205
- Craig 79
- Crystal 184, 211
- Curtis 213
- Daniel 111, 131
- Daniel F 132
- Darrin 79
- David 211, 232
- David O 132, 151, 159, 182
- David R 232
- Deborah 216
- Douglas 190, 216
- Dwight 213
- Earl 159, 160
- Earl Otis 187
- Edris 213
- Effie G 155
- Eileen 187, 211
- Elgan F 159, 160
- Elgan O 132, 151, 159
- Elgan Otis 182
- Eliza Jane 62, 65
- Elizabeth A 142, 172
- Elizabeth N 210
- Ella 131, 132, 159, 187
- Ethel I 142
- Eunice 159
- Eva 213, 220
- Eve 187, 195
- Evelyn N 183
- Everett 190, 216
- Frank E 155, 185
- Fred 131
- Gertrude 132, 205
- Gertrude S 132
- Gilbert Doran 176
- Gilbert I 205, 230
- Grace 166, 187, 211
- Harold W M 172, 201, 227
- Helen 183, 186
- Howard B 142, 172
- Howard N 172
- I Carolyn 226
- Ida C 201
- Ila 216
- Irene S 109, 130
- Irving 159
- J Reid 172
- J Wesley 116
- Jane Carberry 122, 147
- Janice 216
- Jefferson 216
- Jeffrey E 227
- Jennifer J 226
- John R 201
- John W 141, 201, 226
- Joshua D 141, 172
- Julie E 205, 2
- Kathleen M 161, 188, 189
- Katie M 227
- Lewis 186
- Lorraine 213
- Lynwood 213
- Maide 132
- Margaret J P 172, 201
- Marshall 159
- Marty 216
- Mary A 111
- Mary Ann 131, 13
- Mary E 109, 129
- Mary S 111, 226
- Matthew 216
- May 132
- Melbourne 129, 132, 151, 155, 159
- Murray 187, 211
- Myrtle 159
- Nancy 111, 132
- Nancy S 92, 108
- Naomi M 227
- Nathan 131
- Nelson 213
- Newton 187, 213
- Ninor A 141
- Norma G 199
- Otto 156
- Paula 236
- Pearl M 155
- Penelope J 201, 226
- Perley 155, 186
- Peter 120
- Phoebe 111, 131
- R Blake 201
- Rainsford 131
- Randall 131
- Reginald 189
- Robert 187, 213
- Roger D 201, 227
- Ronald 186
- Rowena 211
- Ruth 190, 216
- Samantha S 226
- Sarah J A 141, 172
- Shelley 205
- Simon D 227
- Stephen E 232
- Thatcher 111, 131
- Thomas 103
- Thomas M 102
- Toby 213
- Travis W J 227
- Valerie 213
- Viola 187, 213
- Violet 159
- Virginia 213
- Warren 111, 132

Smithson
- Charles C 148, 179
- Donald C 179
- Gordon D 179
- Joan M 179
- John 179
- Lenore R 179
- Yvonne A 179

Snedden
- Morgan A 172

Snider
- Lee P 236
- Stanley 219, 236
- William R 236

Snyder
- Albert 126, 14
- Albert C 126
- Ann 53, 55
- Anna M 44
- Annetje 84, 97
- Annie 149
- Catharine A 44, 126
- Charles A 39, 106
- Christina 24, 2
- Clinton 44, 126
- Cornelia A 39, 124
- Dorothy A 180
- Edmund 32, 38
- Edwin C 39

Snyder
    Edwina 44, 126
    Elizabeth 26, 32, 44, 126
    Emma C 39
    George B 39
    Hezekiah 44, 126
    James S 32, 38
    Luella 44
    Margaret E 38
    Maria 44, 126
    Mary J 39
    Mary L 39
    Otis D 149
    Peter 33, 39
    Peter L 39
    Ransom 38
    Robert 68
    Rowena 149
    Sarah 39
    Sarah E 39
    Sarah J 44, 126
    Wesley R 39
    William 39, 44
Soderberg
    Roger 205
Sondergard
    Sonya 206, 230
Sorenson
    Andrew 142, 172, 201
    Carrol R 172
    Henry J 172
    Patricia A 201, 227
    Stephen E 201
Sparling
    Elizabeth 34, 40
Spencer
    Chester 87, 99
    Christine 119, 144
    James H 99
Spera
    Pricilla 148, 179
Spindler
    Ella 66, 70
Spoerline
    William 70
Sprague
    Elizabeth 57
Sprigs
    Stephen 29
Sproule
    James 127
Spurgeon
    Nancy 89, 102
St Amand
    David 229, 238
    Emily N 238
    Ryan D 238
    Sean L 238
St. John
    Marion 170, 199

Stackhouse
    George 163, 190
    Willard 190
Stahl
    David V 180
    Jane V 180
    Margery D 180
    Ruth 71, 74
    Virginia L 180, 207
Stall
    (Lown) Emma 40, 45
Stannix
    Marjorie 192
    Marjorie L 218
Stapells
    Alexandra 226
    Elizabeth 226
    Richard B 201, 226
    Victoria 226
Stark
    Alexander C 149
Staunegar
    Gloria L 76
Stearns
    Austin 89, 103
Stebler
    Andrew C 226
    Jan B 226
    Martin A 226
    Werner C 201, 226
Steele
    Barbara Ann 200
    Frederick R 172, 200
    Grant M 226
    Kathleen D 226
    Kelley A 226
    Murray R 200, 226
    Shirley E 200, 226
Steiding
    Emily M 79
    Jr Paul K 77
    Paul K 75, 77, 79
Stenson
    Bridget 52
    Dennis 52
    Francis X 50, 52
    Marie V 52
    Patricia A 52
    Patrick 52
Stephens
    Calvin 179
    Katherine 179
    Sadie 182
Stephenson
    David W 224
    Henry A 199
    Howard W 199
    J Wallace 224
    John 199
    John W 199
    Joseph H 171

    Katherine R 224
    Marion R 199, 224
Sterner
    Lois 206
Stevens
    Calvin 148
    H Wayne 205
    Sadie 151
Stevenson
    Bernard 22
    Brian D 228
    Bruce M 228
    Glen W 228
    Lennie 196
    William F 203, 228
Stewart
    Donald 136
    Georgina A D 143, 173
    Kathy 213
    Kenneth 213
    Leonard 213
    Mary L 219, 236
    Valerie 208, 233
    Walter 187, 213
Stiles
    Eleanor 182
    Emma 182
    Evelyn 182
    Llewellyn 182
    Lorenzo 182
Stoddard
    Jean M 232
Stol
    Jacob Jansen 21
Stone
    F Clark 69
    Vivienne E 172, 201
Storer
    Ruth 186, 212
Straw
    Robert 199
Strieder
    Carlton 45
Strong
    Jarrius B 120, 146
    Lois G 146
    Ruth 172
Struck
    Eleanor 184, 211
Stuart
    Allan P 195, 219
    Allen W 219, 236
    Anna W 44
    Arthur N 40, 44
    Beverly A 237
    Cindy L 237
    Douglas E 237
    Edwin A 195
    Eileen B 195
    Eulah M 194, 219
    Frederic I 199, 224

Stuart
   George A 224, 237
   Grant P 237
   Henry H 167, 194
   Henry W 195
   Janet L 219
   John A 219
   John D 224
   John W 195, 219
   Kenneth R 238
   Kristine 238
   Lois M 224, 237
   Lorainne C 237
   Mary K R 224, 238
   N Stanley 224, 237
   Pamela W 237
   Raymond D 224, 238
   Sadie B 196
   Shannon P 236
   Sharon 238
   Sheila N 238
   Steven W 237
   Susan 219
   Timothy G 237
   William A 44
Sturney
   Penelope 166
Styles
   Currie 150, 182
   Karl 209
   Lauren 182, 209
   Lorenzo 150
   Ruth 182
   Shirley 209
Sullivan
   Crystal 218
   Donna 192, 218
   Gerald 192, 218
   John 165, 19
   Michael 236
   Terry 218
   Tracy 218
Surby
   Emily M 174, 204
Sutcliffe
   Ben 232
   Brian E 232
   Laurie E 232
   Liza E 232
Sutherland
   Donald R 208, 233
   Leslie L 233
Sutton
   Elva 145
   Harry 145
   Nealy 145
Swareoff
   Val 231, 206
Swart
   George V 48
   William T 105, 125

Swartout
   Cornelius W 61
   Jacob 61
   John 57, 61
   Jr Thomas 57, 61
   William 61
Sweeney
   Elizabeth A 201
   Gordon A 172, 201
   Howard M 142, 172
   Jeffrey S 201
   Michael G 201
Sweet
   Charles F 131
   De Charles F 159
   Thomas 159
Swift
   Ellen 173
   Florence 173
   George S 143, 173
   Prudence 173
Swits
   Cornelis 17
Symons
   Betty R 200, 225
Tacker
   Jean 224
Tacon
   Albert 77, 78
   Andrea L 78
   Maralisa 78
Tanguay
   Guillemont 216
Tapp
   John 217
Tappen
   Richard 126, 44
   Richard W 106
Taubitz
   Jeanette M 232
   Kathleen D 232
   Mark D 232
   Nathan 239
   Paul L 232, 239
   Richard J 208, 232
   Shelley A 232, 239
   William J 232
Taylor
   Connie 211
   Donald 192
   Freddie 211
   Gordon 195, 220
   Holland 183, 211
   Judith 220
   Kathy 220
   Washington 101
Teal
   Wilma 179
teBockhorst
   Carl 228
   Lora 228

   Nina 228
   Richard 228
   Richard L 202
   Ryan 228
Teetsel
   Myrtle O 207
Ten Broeck
   Catharine 90
   Catherine M 104
Tennant
   Sue 206
Terry
   Clarence W 169, 196
   Julia E 196
   Mary K 197
   Nettie C 196, 221
Teunis
   Maria 17
Thacker
   Jean 199
Thayer
   M Jane 62, 65
   Thomas 66
Theriault
   Andrea 200
   Herbert J 171, 200
   Michael 200
   Norman 200
Thiede
   Josephine H 173, 202
Thomas
   Alden 219
   Angie 160
   Benjamin 188
   Beverly 188
   Charles E 133, 160
   Dedrick 103
   Edith 128
   Edith T 150
   Grace M 187
   Hugh 169
   Ida 188
   Jane 215
   Leilannie M 208, 233
   Marc 180
   Mary 113, 137
   Rebecca J 70, 74
   Sylvester 116
   Vernon C 160, 187
   Wayne 149
   William C 160
   Winifred I 160
Thomason
   Audrey 190
   Basil 190
   Erna 190
   Vernon 190
   Wm 163, 190
Thomis
   David 180
   Holly 180

Thomis
  Wayne 180
  Wendy 180
Thompson
  Bruce G 233
  Graham S 208, 233
  Heather S 233
  Marion M 208, 233
  Pearl 193
  Stanley G 181, 208
Thomson
  Cindy A S 230
Thorn
  Will 121
Thorne
  Elsie 99
  Elsie E 121
Thurlow
  Carol 218 237
Tice
  Jeanne 177, 205
Tiemann
  Gregory J 79
  Samantha E 79
Timmins
  Margaret 137, 167
Tipp
  Maria C 34, 40
Tipson
  Nola 218, 237
Tisch
  Daniel 227
  Geoffrey 202, 227
  Katherine 227
Titherington
  Ann M 207
  Jr Wm K 207
  William K 180, 207
Tolpa
  John 109
Toner
  Enid 194
Toole
  Dwight 236
  Harold 222, 236
  Harry 197, 222
  Joy 236
  Patti 236
Totliff
  Ansom 126
Towler
  David W 180
Townsend
  Ada M 142
  Caroline S 142
  Franklin 124
  Henry 117
  Henry G 142
  Pearl E 190
Tracey
  George 114
  Hannah 114
  Helen 197
  Sharon A 237
Tracy
  Alma 136, 165
  Basheba 139
  Bliss L 191, 219, 235
  Erwin A 164, 191, 219
  Fred 135
  Frederick H 139
  Garnett 194, 218
  Gay W 191, 219
  George 113, 136, 139
  George E 139
  Gertrude 165, 193, 194, 218
  Gilbert 166, 194
  Grace 163
  Grace M 190
  Hannah 94
  Harriet 218
  Helen 192
  Herman 138, 166, 194
  Inez 193
  Jeannine 217
  John 194
  Jonathan E 235
  Katrine 218
  Kenneth 194, 218
  Kensil 218
  Lillie 137, 166
  Lorne 166, 193
  Lydia 138
  Marjorie 194, 218
  Michelle C 235
  Norma 193
  Sarah 114
  Sharon R 217
  Stella A 166, 194
  Talmage 166
  Ula 166
  Wyeth 218
  Yerxa 166, 194
Trader
  Ralph 193
Trato
  Albert 118, 143
  Albert C 173, 202
  Albert N 143, 173
  C George 143
  Christopher G 173
  Connie D 202
  Irma 173
  James H 202, 228
  Jaqueline H 202, 228
  Jennifer 228
  Jill H 228
  John H 173, 202, 228
  Judith H 202, 228
  Julie 228
  Kathie J 202
  Mae 173
  Marian E 202, 173
  Pansy 173
  Pansy B 143, 173
  Ruth E 173
  Violet M 173, 202
Trick
  Mary Pat 200, 225
Trowbridge
  Issac 31, 37
  Mary J 37
Truffin
  Katrina A 191, 216
Tual
  Samuel 32
Tucker
  Caroline 83, 93
  George 115
  Oliver 115
  Salome 83, 95
  Wesley 136
Turk
  Violetta 126, 149
Turnbull
  Sharon E 232
  Susan A 232
  Violet 191
Turner
  A Beryl 173, 202
  David J 226
  Jr Michael J 226
  Michael J 201, 226
Vail
  Josie 138, 167
Vakarelis
  Joannes 236
Vala
  Raymon 47
Vale
  Peter 188
Valk
  Eudora 38, 44
  Susanna 30, 36
Valkenburg
  Leah 26, 32
Valkenburgh
  Eliza C 32
Van Aken
  Annie 46
  Edward O 44
  Elizabeth 37, 43
  Hattie 121
  Isaac J 37, 44
  Margaret 59, 62
  Mary E 44
  Matthew 62
  Rebecca C 106, 126
  Rufus C 44
  York Annie 41
  York Solomon 41
  York Sarah 41

Van Bramer
  William 45
Van Buerin
  Jennie 43
Van Bunschooten
  L 100
  P E 88, 100
  S 100
Van Buren
  Angeline 43
  Egbert 37, 4
  Katie 146
Van Doren
  Louise 104, 123
Van Dyck
  Abraham 123
  Elsie 104, 123
  Sarah 123
  Stephen 104, 123
Van Erk
  Cornelia 197, 222
Van Etten
  Catherine M 105, 126
  Jacobus 24, 27
  John A 106
  Jonas 91, 105
  Margaret E 105
  Maria 27
  Martha J 106
  Mary 91, 106
  Mildred 124
  Rachel C 106
  Sally A M 105
Van Gaasbeck
  Teunis 31
Van Hoesen
  William S 126
Van Hoorn
  Pieter Jansen 15
Van Hovenburg
  Titus 101
Van Keuren
  Andrew D 91
  Anna M 91
  Charles 91
  Gerretje N 91, 106
  Levi 82, 91
  Maria 91
  Mattys 17
  Peter H 91
Van Leuven
  Johannes 82
  John 90
  Marytie 90, 105
  Rachel 53, 54
Van Loon
  Elizabeth 83, 91
Van Orden
  Catharine C 112
  Henry 93, 112
  Henry D 112
  Jacob T B 112
  Samuel 112
Van Steenbergh
  Nellie 36
Van Steenwyck
  Jan A 15
Van Valkenburg
  Allen 44
Van Wagenen
  Eve 5, 57
Van Wart
  Alice L 160
  Charlotte 187
  Della 160, 187
  J Samuel 133, 160
  Lottie 159, 160
  Mabel A 160
  Rev 155
  Vera B 160
  Viola G 160
  Vera B 187
Vanaken
  Abraham 35
Vandeburgh
  James 34, 40
  Sarah I 40
Vandenburgh
  Marytje 17
Vanderbilt
  James 33
Vandermark
  Gilbert G 37
VanLoo
  Diane S 208, 233
Vanne
  Shelly 188
Varty
  Ian 234
Vaughan
  Barbara 182, 209
Vaughn
  Winifred 108, 128
Vedder
  Louisa E C 32
  Susan G 124, 149
  William A 32
Vegso
  Dean 227
  Frank 202, 227
  Gary 227
Veile
  Maria 53, 55
Vermilye
  Ashbel G 104, 124
  Elizabeth B 124
  Gertrude V 149
  Helen L 124, 149
  III Ashbel G 149
  Thomas E 124, 149
Vermulye
  Gertrude V 180
Verplanck
  Caroline 105, 125
Vincent
  Jennifer 229
Volkerts
  Divertje 15
Vredenburg
  Martha 41
Vrooman
  Mary A 125
Wade
  Carol Ann 210
  June 210
  Neil H 210
  Paul 183, 210
  Ruth 210, 234
Wales
  Alexander D 121
  Blake 121
  Jr Blake 99
Walker
  Eliza A 142
  Marcelia E 38
  Olelio 117, 142
  Susan 220
Walkiewicez
  John W 206
Wallace
  Cora E 124
  Gordon D 179
Walsh
  Betty 71
  Catharine B 123, 148
Ward
  Audrey 196
  William 103
Waring
  Ed 162, 189
  Patricia 189
  Susan 189
Warner
  Thusnelda 145
Warr
  Mari L 228
Warriner
  Ernest 156
Washburn
  Marjorie 172
  Marjorie L 201
Waterbuery
  Charles 121
  Henry T 121
Waters
  Robert 114
Wathen
  Leslie J 128
Watson
  Charles H 180
Watt
  Carol L 228
  Lucy 102

Watt
  Robert 202, 228
Wattling
  Carley 217
  James 191, 217
  Jim 217
Waugh
  Jannike 214
  Jeffrey 214
  William 187, 214
Weaver
  Charles 137
  Joe 72
Webb
  Annie 135
  Austin 134, 135, 161, 163
  Barbara 191
  Beatrice 166, 194
  Brennan T S 230
  Candace M 221
  Carol R 191
  Charles 138
  D Foster 164
  Donald B 194
  Elizabeth 135
  Elwin 164
  Elwin Z 191
  Emma A 112, 135
  Eva 164
  Frank H 191
  George 113
  George L 191, 221
  Glenna 192, 216, 217
  Gordon 164
  Howard 205, 230
  Irene 162
  Irma M 191, 21
  Jenna V 230
  Jerry D 221
  Joshua 112, 135
  Lillian 163, 189
  Lizzie 151
  Malcolm 164
  Manzer 134, 162
  Mary 163
  Maud 135
  Minnie 135, 164, 191
  Nellie A 191
  Peter M 221
  Rachel 108, 128
  Ralph 164, 191
  Sandford 164
  Stephanie J 221
  Tanya 221
  Walter 188
  Wilbur 135
  Wilbur L 191
  Wilfred 186
  Winfield 164
  Yerxa 164

Weeks
  Anna C 41, 45
  Florence 69
  Frances 32
  Henry 26, 32
  Henry J 32
  Jenne 32
  John J 32
  Priscilla J 32
  Rachel 122
  Rachel J 147
Wees
  Martha 63, 67
Weimer
  Alfred W 75
  Alma M 75
  Betty 75
  Evelyn 75
  Everett B 75
  Gilbert 72, 75
  Gladys I 75
  Mabel E 75
  Oliver E E 75
  Samuel C 75
Weinhorst
  Carol 202, 228
Welch
  Abraham 123
  Benjamin 102, 123
  Betty 67
  Cecil 75
  Harriet 123
  Jane 123
  Madison 123
  Mary 130, 150
  Susan 123
  Tobe 75
  William 123
Welpley
  Barbara J 214
  Carol A 214
  Frederick 132
  John 214
  John L 187, 214
  Mary Lou 214
  William B 214
Wels
  Jane 35
Welsh
  Eula 169
Wenne
  Annatien 29
  Christina 28
  Elisabet 57, 6
  Frederick 58
  Henri 58
  Jannetje 28
  Lucas 58
  Sarah 57, 61
Wennen
  Annatjen 28

Wennie
  Aanetjen 35
  Christian 57
  Cornelis 28
  Cornelis P 35
Wentworth
  Edward 166
  William 166
Werner
  Thusnelda W 177
Wespel
  Antje 58
  Conrad 54, 58
Wesple
  Johannes 58
West
  Catherine 99
  Elizabeth 99
  James 99
  Jane 99
  Peter 99
  Sally Ann 99
  Silence E 99
  William 87, 99
Weston
  Alfred 216
  Donald 216
  James 190, 216
  Laverne 216
  Ronald 216
  Valerie 216
Wheaton
  Edward 189
Whepley
  Alma L 159, 187
  Blanche L 159
  Ethel 160, 187
  Fred 159
  Gladys H 160
  Harold 159
Whetsell
  Mary Ellen 63, 67
  Rebecca 55, 59
Whipple
  Lucy M 123
Whitaker
  Glenn 189
  Jr William 100
  Lloyd 219
  Willem 88
  William 101
White
  Adele 70
  Marly L 39
Whitehouse
  Hulda V 150, 181
  Martha 150, 180
Whitenect
  Lottie 135
Whitman
  Basheba 11, 137

Whitman
  Vivian 189
  Vivian A 215
Whitney
  Austin P 126, 149
  Charles E 149
  Elaine R 190
  Frances 149
  Michael D 149
  Millard G 149
Whittaker
  Edward 215
  Glenn 215
  Nelson 215
  Susan 215
Whitten
  Freda 155, 186
Widdeker
  Elizabeth 100
  Jan 101
Wilcox
  Carol 187, 214
  Susan 78
  Willis 192
Wilkins
  Arthur M 142, 172
  Arthur N 172
  Faith A 172
Wilkinson
  Carol 231
Williams
  Arleen 182, 210
  Christine M 205
  David 210
  James W 177, 205
  Mary 98, 120
  Philip M 205
Williamson
  Amy 148
  Bessie 160
  George C 148
  George F 148
  Irene 148
  Mary L 148
  Robert 177, 205
  Thomas 133, 160
  William 160
Willis
  Vera 162, 189
Wilson
  Amos 166
  Amy 71
  Arleen B 202, 227
  C Georgeana 173, 202
  Cecil G E 202
  Cecil M 173, 202
  Clarke 189
  Deanna 219
  Dianne L 227
  Edward 195, 219
  Frank H 178
  Frederick G D 173, 202
  Harley 197
  Janice 202
  Joyce C 202
  Karen 219
  M May 202
  Margaret L 173
  Margaret R 219
  Martha L 173
  Mary 121
  Mary E 173
  Maxine 219
  Olive L 173
  Ralph W 202, 227
  Rena 72, 76
  Robert 144
  Sarah A 144, 177
  Sherri R 227
  Shirley A 202, 227
  Valerie 219
  Violet 173
  Willa D 202, 227
  William F 173, 202
  William G 143, 173, 22
Wilt
  Cecil 74
Windfield
  Elizabeth 43
Winfield
  Katherine 195
Winna
  Sarah 29
Winnan
  Cornelius 57
Winne
  Aaron 28, 36, 65
  Aida W 46
  Alfred 61, 65
  Alida 58
  Alonzo 65, 70
  Alvin 65
  Andrew A 65
  Angeline 35, 36
  Ann 65
  Ann M 82
  Anna 65
  Anna E 65
  Annatien 25
  Annatje 54, 58
  Arent 23, 25, 29
  Ariantje 57
  Arriantje 54
  Benjamin 58, 61, 93, 113
  Benjamin J 61
  Calvin 61
  Carharin 57, 61
  Catharina 26, 28, 35, 54
  Catharine 25, 42, 58
  Catherine C 46
  Charity 29, 87, 99
  Chauncey 70
  Christian 53, 54, 58, 61, 65
  Christian W 61
  Christine M 35
  Cornelia 57
  Cornelis 54, 57
  Cornelis L 25
  Cornelius 58, 61, 65
  Davis 70
  Elisabeth 65
  Eliza Ann 61
  Elizabeth 57
  Elizabeth D 46
  Ferris 65
  Francis 65
  Frederik 54
  George 35, 61, 65
  Gertjen 25
  Gideon B 65
  Hannah 29, 35, 36, 58, 61
  Harry 70
  Henry 58, 61, 62, 65
  Hezekiah 46
  I David 61, 65
  Ira 61
  Isaac 65, 70
  Isiah D 65
  Jacobus D 57
  James 61
  James A 36
  Jane 29
  Jannetje 25, 28, 35
  Jemima 61
  Johannes 28
  John 35, 58, 113
  John L 61
  John P 27, 35
  John V 42, 46
  Jonathan 54, 57
  Josephine 65, 70
  Jr Frederick 58
  Laney 61
  Lany J 36
  Lisabeth 54
  Loren 65
  Lucas 54, 58
  Margaret E 36
  Maria 25, 28, 29, 54, 58
  Mary C 36, 61, 65
  Mary J 36
  May 70
  Milton H 62
  Miriam 58
  Peter 58
  Peter A 35
  Peter C 42, 61
  Petrus 28, 35
  Petrus A 25, 28
  Polly 57, 58
  Rachel 54, 59
  Sally Ann 61
  Salomon 57

Winne
  Saphia 29
  Sara 54, 59
  Sarah 25, 28, 61
  Sefeya 29
  Silas 35
  Sophia 36
  Thomas 61
  William 28, 36, 61
Winner
  Annatje T 57
  Cornelius 61
  Frederick 57
  James 58
Winnie
  Edna M 207
  Theodore R 61
Winnow
  Lucas 58
  William H 36
Winslow
  Diane R 205
  Dianne R 230
Wippelar
  Coenradt 58
Wispel
  Sara 58
Wisper
  Abram 58
Wits
  Cornelis Claessen 16
Wittaker
  Levi 100
  Petrus 101
  Rachel 101
Wojciehowski
  John 48
Wolfersheim
  Albert 48
Woltz
  Gladys 170
Wolven
  Andrew D 126
  Elizabeth 126
  Jeremiah 106, 126
  Johanna 25
  Mary M 34
Womack
  Betty 177, 205
Wong
  Sylvia S 229, 238
Wood
  Agnes 171, 200
  Annie 92, 109
  B Lorraine 126
  Caleb R 127
  Chauncy 65
  Dennis 215
  Dorothy 192
  Edith 164, 192
  Edward 65
  Edwin 215
  J Bertram 189, 189
  Jennie 164, 192
  Judith R 182, 209
  Margaret 36
  Margaret M 42
  Marilyn 215
  Mary 92, 112
  Norma 200, 225
  Ronald 196
  Shirley 219, 236
  Trueman 164
  Willis 65
Wooden
  A Adelia 133, 151, 160
  Alexander 111, 132
  Alice A 182
  Annie M 133, 160
  Blanche 159, 160
  Charlotte M 132, 159
  Gertrude 160
  James N 132
  L Alma 159
  L Gertrude 132
  Lavina A 132
  Lillian 160
  Mahlon 160
  Robert 133, 160
Woodger
  Edgar 179
Woodworth
  Nora 196, 220
Woolven
  Anna M 126
  Christina 23, 24
  Samuel F 105, 126
Worden
  Ella M 133, 160
Wright
  Phyllis 160, 188
Wulfin
  Johanna 24
Wunderman
  S Z 40
Wyke
  John 224
Wynkoop
  Peter 26
Yaple
  Jane Ann 57
  Mary 57
York
  Carrie 40
  Charles T 41
  Clarence 47
  Edith M 47
  Emma 40
  Florence L 41
  George 41
  Georgianna 40
  Henry 47
  Jennie 40, 45
  John 40
  Jr Lewis 47
  Leah M 41, 45
  Levi 35, 40
  Lewis 43, 47
  Myrtle A 46, 50
  Sarah E 45
  Solomon V A 46
Young
  Abraham 29
  Christeintje 29
  Cornelius 29
  Hannah 29
  Hosea 29
  Jacomina 100
  Jacomntje 88
  Jeremiah 87, 99
  Jonas 29
  Maria 29
  Nancy 99
  Sally 99
Zeigler
  E Louise 45
  Jane 45
  William W 45
Ziegler
  Ann M 49
  Blanche E 45
  Elizabeth E 49
  Helen L 49
  Jane M 49
  Marjorie 45, 49
  William 40, 45
  William C 49
  William W 49
Zubrod
  Ruth 148, 179

ISBN 1412019567